Suicide
in the
Middle Ages

'If I go down to Hell, thou art there also.'
(Psalm 139: 8)

Suicide
in the
Middle Ages

by

Alexander Murray

VOLUME I

The Violent against Themselves

A Dio, a sé, al prossimo si pòne far forza
[Violence can be done to God, to oneself, and to one's neighbour]
(Dante Alighieri, *Inferno*, 11: 31–2)

Oxford   New York
OXFORD UNIVERSITY PRESS
1998

Oxford University Press, Great Clarendon Street, Oxford OX2 6DP

Oxford New York

Athens Auckland Bangkok Bogotá Buenos Aires Calcutta
Cape Town Chennai Dar es Salaam Delhi Florence Hong Kong Istanbul
Karachi Kuala Lumpur Madrid Melbourne Mexico City Mumbai
Nairobi Paris São Paulo Singapore Taipei Tokyo Toronto Warsaw
and associated companies in Berlin Ibadan

Oxford is a trade mark of Oxford University Press

Published in the United States by
Oxford University Press Inc., New York

British Library Cataloguing in Publication Data
Data available

Library of Congress Cataloging in Publication Data
Murray, Alexander, 1934–
Suicide in the Middle Ages / by Alexander Murray.
p. cm.
Includes bibliographical references (p.) and index.
Contents: v. 1. The violent against themselves—
1. Suicide—History. 2. Social history—Medieval, 500–1500.
3. Church and social problems. I. Title.
HV6544.M89 1997
362.28'094'0902—dc21 97-7806
ISBN 0–19–820539–2 (v. 1)

1 3 5 7 9 10 8 6 4 2

Typeset by Best-set Typesetter Ltd., Hong Kong
Printed in Great Britain
on acid free paper by
Bookcraft Ltd., Midsomer Norton
Nr. Bath, Somerset

ERRATUM

Two Notes on p. xix describe Plates 5(a) and (b), but only the first of these (numbered Plate 5) appears opposite p. 137. The publishers apologise for the omission.

Preface

On a clear night we can look up and be stunned by the stars, some of them galaxies as big as ours. When we are told their size and distance and age, the big numbers make us want to rush back indoors to the finite, familiar world of human beings. But have we not got things the wrong way round? In the few seconds it has taken to read this page so far, the number of electronic impulses passing through the reader's brain and nervous system is to be reckoned in billions, if not already trillions (10^{12}). Many are quite unpredictable, if only because some of *my* billions help affect some of *your* billions and vice versa. That is for two people, over a few seconds. But there are many of us, our lifetimes strung together over centuries. For numerical complexity, can the galaxies match that?

The result, anyway, we call history. Early Hindu arithmeticians are said to have created the sign for zero, 'o', on the model of the great 'space of heaven', resolving its infinities into a tiny circle.[1] In the same way we speak of history as a school 'subject', when 'subject' is the one thing it is not. It is far above our heads. But because the reality would be unbearable, we conspire to forget that the real human past cannot be comprehended, still less traced or written about, except in simplifications so crude as always to distort and often to falsify; the falsehoods of each generation, agreed by convention, being exultantly exposed in the next by 'research', itself overthrown in its turn. That battle of the generations no doubt lurches towards a quantum of truth. But behind the quantum is the unquantified, the living galaxies, one on another, of ricocheting trillions of impulses, further beyond reckoning than the stars are above anyone's head, and all of which, comprehended or not, happened with as much actuality as your reading of these words now.

These reflections could well preface any history book as a 'start-of-day' exercise, to be undertaken before picking it up. There is a special reason why they should preface this one. Unconventionally long, the book remains, to the author's certain knowledge, 'a mere introduction'. That has been said by authors of bigger books on bigger subjects. This one is about a single, recondite theme in a single period of history, a theme which has attracted academic attention so far mainly in articles, if at all. But the result is still a

---

[1] D. E. Smith and L. C. Karpinski, *The Hindu-Arabic Numerals* (Boston and London, 1911), 38.

mere introduction, for all that; and that fact, and the length, could not both be true at once unless history were infinite.

The tension between this infinity and the limits of a book have naturally left their mark on the latter, as to both form and content. The form of the book makes its transition to the finite by a means familiar for this purpose, that of one in three: it will be an *opus tripartitum*, each part distinct but related like the surfaces of a polyhedron. The division arises from the nature of the topic. Suicide in the Middle Ages seems at first glance only one subject, and has been treated as that by the few who have noticed it. But reflection shows it to be three. First there are the dead, the *suicidés*, a category on their own as they intended to be. But they could not be that unless the living who survived them were also a category on *their* own. The reactions of these survivors to suicide were of two kinds. On one hand, medieval law, religion, and convention normally looked on completed suicide with condemnation and horror, when at all; so the character and sources of that attitude will be the subject of Part II, *The Curse on Self-Murder*. But a more constructive attitude was possible, indeed necessary, since any human being might feel negative emotions which could, in principle, lead him or her to be a *suicidé* if the emotions went beyond a certain point. So the emotions needed exploring, and their exploration by medieval psychologists, poets, and pastors will form the subject of Part III, under the title *The Mapping of Mental Desolation*.

With the exception of their introductions and conclusions, each of the three parts will have its own argument, so it seemed appropriate to give each a volume of its own, with its own title. Each could even be read on its own, by a reader interested only in that aspect of the subject. I might have hesitated to adopt this structure but for an illustrious model. In mapping my own authorial doubts and difficulties, I have often turned instinctively—the instinct being both that of a child reaching for a mentor and that of a student knowing which mentor to choose—to a particular literary guide, the more boldly because he did the same to a classical model with an equal indifference in the matter of asking permission. The title-page of this volume will have revealed who this is, and he starts his services now, Dante's *Divine Comedy* being my apologia for the form of this *opus tripartitum*. Each of its parts, like these, has its own argument and can be read separately, yet the three form a whole, each member relating at all points to the others. This volume is therefore my *Inferno*; the next—on the principle that where there is life there is hope—my *Purgatorio*; the third, which ends on a note of hope positively heroic, my *Paradiso* and happy ending.

This is how the form of the book has sought to reduce the numberless to number. As to its content, the effect of its struggle with the infinite has been to leave it with massive limitations: for all its extent, my investigation will leave things out. One is sheer evidence. Despite the need to cast a wide net for evidence, for reasons to be explained in their place, I deliberately turned aside from potential areas of documentation in the knowledge that my labours would otherwise never be finished. Even the areas I searched kept producing, after the search, enough stragglers to discredit any idea that I had finally exhausted any major area. So more cases of suicide, and more documents showing attitudes to it, are likely to appear after those that follow.

Limitations of space and time have been more deliberate. My study is about medieval Europe. By Europe I have understood the four monarchies of England, France, Germany, and Italy; and by 'medieval', mainly the centuries from the millennium to 1500. That has to be 'mainly', because suicides have been taken from as early as the late ninth century, where any were known, and because the later end of the period is blurred by the belief, which I was taught young, that the Middle Ages ended in 1485. It certainly ends before 1500. After then there are far too many suicides, and books about them, to make my efforts necessary. So we 'die' definitively in 1500. This time-span still leaves uncovered the 'dark ages', that is, the centuries from the fifth to the early ninth. A small harvest would certainly be there to be studied: a suicide miraculously resuscitated by St Martin of Tours in Sulpicius Severus' *Life* of that saint;[2] half a dozen cases in Gregory of Tours' *Histories*;[3] and one or two other instances in biographies or chronicles.[4] In so far as stories of this period help explain later medieval analogues, or the prehistory of the suicide laws, they will play a part. But these early instances seemed too few, and the gap between them and the rest too long, to make their incorporation with the multitude after the millennium worth straining at.

A more difficult limitation to explain is that of subject-matter. I began writing with an idea of 'ordinary' suicide, and of ordinary people who committed it, in medieval Christian society. That left the alleged ritual suicide of the Cathar heretics, the *endura*, as an anomaly. The *endura*,

---

[2] *Vita sancti Martini*, ch. 8; ed. J. Fontaine (Sources Chrétiennes, 133) (Paris, 1967–9), vol. 1, p. 270.

[3] *Historiae*, bk 3, ch. 33; ed. B. Krusch and W. Levison, *Monumenta Germaniae Historica, Scriptores Rerum Merovingicarum*, vol. 1, pt 1, pp. 128–9; bk 4, ch. 26 (39), pp. 170–1; bk 5, ch. 34 (31), p. 230, lines 12–18; bk 10, ch. 18, pp. 510.3–4.

[4] *Vita Hludowici imperatoris*, § 30; ed. G. H. Pertz, *Mon. Germ. Hist., Scriptores*, vol. 2, pp. 623.27–9; and a doubtful case in *Annales regni Francorum*, a. 776; ed. G. H. Pertz and F. Kurze, *Mon. Germ. Hist., Scriptores* (octavo edition) (Hanover, 1895), pp. 46.6–10. Cf. A Bayet, *Le Suicide et la Morale* (Paris, 1922), 413, who attests his difficulty in finding reports of suicide in the period, 400–850.

suicide by starvation, affected to integrate its subject with a social grouping, not mark his isolation from it. So I touch on the *endura* only briefly, and at its more 'ordinary' edges, in Chapter 9 of this volume. On a comparable principle, while the occasional suicide by an individual Jew is included, I shall leave on one side group suicides by Jews in pogroms. These are relatively well-chronicled, and like the Cathars with their *endura*, sufficiently well-defined to beckon historians all of their own. A third omission, dictated now by chronology as well as subject-matter, is that of suicide in early Irish law and folk-tales. Like other exclusions, Irish material will occasionally be referred to in later parts of the book, in discussions of attitudes to suicide in literature. But it is far enough from the mainstream Christendom to avoid systematic exploitation in this book. The same goes for suicide in Islam.

In the matter of attitudes, several topics will be left uncovered or too slightly covered, but a list of them would read too like the contents of another book to be useful at this point. For instance, there will be too little said on the bearing of a suicide's previous life on the state of his soul, and on the allegory of despair specifically in church art. A look at my own 'Contents' page, and the indexes of the respective volumes, will indicate topics that *are* covered; and blanks can be calculated from there.

That this book is finite, about an infinite subject, therefore lays open a way to the historiographical future, so that interested scholars should find plenty of aspects to develop. Something comparable is true also of the past. The work of many scholars has already gone *into* the book. Because evidence on suicide is exceptionally elusive, heterogeneous, and scattered, I have relied on massive help from fellow-historians. The book may be short in relation to its subject, but it would have been too long for its author's capacities alone, and shorter without outside help. This help has been abundant. This chronicle of the friendless, that is to say, has relied on succour from many friends: it is a cooperative enterprise.

This fact was made plain to me at a stroke on the day Dr Henry Summerson, historian of medieval English criminal law, doubled my own cache of unpublished cases of suicide from English court rolls by a gift of his own findings, a gift he followed up with more transcripts, generous help in the verification of my own, and in the interpretation of all of them. In respect of other thirteenth-century English sources I had similar reinforcement from my Oxford colleague, Dr John Maddicott. His postcard tip-offs, arriving regularly through the Oxford inter-college mail, left me with only one anxiety: that the functionaries of the mail would be puzzled. Here is the kind of thing:

Exeter College. Tuesday.

Attempted suicide of King's escheator.

Cotton's Chronicle, 176.

Many other colleagues have been generous with expert advice on law and demography. They include Dr Roger Collins, who corrected me on the context of Visigothic Iberian councils; Dr Roy Hunnisett, to whom I turned for help in respect of coroners' rolls; and Professor Larry Poos, who advised on the population of Essex. My advisers on Italian suicide were numerous in proportion to the difficulty of finding any. They include Drs Philip Jones, Sarah Blanshei, Paul Kent, and John Henderson, and Professors Jean-Claude Maire-Vigueur, Attilio Baroli Langeli, Lauro Martinez, and Roberto Rusconi. Dr Robert Feenstra pointed me in the right direction on Roman law; and Mr Patrick Wormald gave me the privilege of reading in typescript parts of a book he is preparing on Old English law.

My dossier of evidence from miraculous and hagiographical sources has been equally enriched by help from friends. Dr Patricia Morison liberally gave me material from her own big dossier of *miracula*. Professor Henry Mayr-Harting, Dr Henrietta Leyser, and Fr. Simon Tugwell have given advice on single *miracula*. To Professor Christopher Houldsworth I owe the case which darkens the very beginning of the book; and to Professor Nigel Palmer, the Visions which will eventually, in the third volume, illuminate the end. Professor André Vauchez, besides years of encouragement, introduced me to miracles of Saints Nicholas of Tolentino and Margaret of Cortona; and Father Jeremias Schroeder, to that of Wolo of St Gallen. Dr Julia Smith advised me on a Breton case, and Dr Jenny Swanson on John of Wales. On matters palaeographical, I thank Dr Marco Doregatti for help in reading a text in sixteenth-century Venetian dialect, and Mr Peter Lewis for deciphering a French chancery hand that would otherwise have defeated me. Professors Michael McDonald and Simon Stevenson, experts on suicide *after* 1500, kindly allowed me to see work of theirs at a time when it was still unpublished. Before the Middle Ages, Drs Miriam Griffin and Margaret Atkins advised me on suicide in the ancient world (the latter especially in relation to Stoicism). On pictures, finally, Professor Julian Gardner has fulfilled his customary role as my chief adviser on art and sculpture, while nearer home I have also had valuable advice from Dr Martin Kauffmann. The extraction of Plate 4 from the Patrimonio Nacional in Madrid I owe to the skill and generosity of my former pupil, Carla Saint de Orleans Vertice.

I owe debts also to institutions. For a month the École des Hautes Études en Sciences Sociales in Paris allowed me to explore archives in Paris and discuss their contents with expert audiences. Before, during, and after that month I have had constant encouragement and advice from Professors Jacques Le Goff and Jean-Claude Schmitt, whose article on medieval suicide remains a seminal authority. From the same École, Mlle Cécile Quentel shared with me the results of her researches on female suicides in manuscript illustrations of Boccaccio.

Other learned medieval societies and university seminars have given valuable opportunities to test and augment ideas. It was between talks to the London Medieval Society and the London Wellcome Institute that the project of a book began. It was nourished in further seminars at the University of Reading, University College, Dublin, the University of Pennsylvania, the University of Perugia, and, at home in Oxford, in the Wellcome Unit for the Study of the History of Population, the Oxford University Medieval Society, and in many less formal seminars. Between these semnars I have had help from a less vocal institution, the Bodleian Library, to whose indefatigable reading-room staff I record an appreciation felt over years.

In my own College I have had counsel from a quasi-permanent advisory panel: Dr Christopher Pelling, on matters ancient and Greek; Dr Mark Smith, on those ancient and Egyptian; and Professor Helen Cooper, on all that is medieval and literary, English or European. Where I pretend acquaintance with neurology or psychology, sleuths would rightly trace the influence of Drs Kevan Martin and David Clark. So I hope governments will not abolish colleges, nor, let me hasten to add, graduate students. My own have reciprocated any engagement I have shown in their research more than amply, by reporting apposite items from their own sources. I mention with gratitude help I have had in this respect from Drs Thomas Mueller, Andrew Roach, Julian Roberts, James Gordon, Christopher Beiting, and Joseph Ziegler, and from Jessalynn Bird and Haidee Lorrey, the last of whom I also thank warmly for help as my research assistant during two busy terms. The task of preparing word-processed 'copy' fell to Diane Burton, whose good temper withstood not only the confrontation with footnotes in arcane languages but countless authorial revisions. I must be the best judge in the world of her patience. It is heroic.

A fruitful source of literary invention over the last century has been the axiom that medieval historians are intolerable to their families and close friends. (The axiom found tragic expression in Ibsen's *Hedda Gabler*, and its comic development need be sought no further than the late Kingsley Amis's *Lucky Jim*.) While I have always resented the axiom and secretly despise its devotees, there is an embarassing lack of counter-evidence in my own case. The victims know who they are, and I will not parade their names in public, with one exception which would otherwise cry out from the spaces between these lines. Throughout the years this book has been in the making, Claire Lamont has been not only its attentive adviser in matters pertaining to English language and literature, but an unfailing source of kindness, encouragement, and wisdom to its author, to a degree he cannot measure or repay.

Future scholars, then, are invited to supply this book's limitations. Present scholars and friends have already reduced them. I conclude with two brief remarks for potential readers, on the principle, 'you have been warned.' The first concerns grammar. In T. S. Eliot's *The Cocktail Party*, published in 1949, a woman recalls to a man an earlier love-affair between them which both had outgrown, and says to him:

> We had merely made use of each other
> Each for his purpose. That's horrible.[5]

The male personal pronoun is there borrowed for a phrase in which either or both sexes are envisaged. Any alternative would have made the sentence twice as long and reduced its impact. Because the present work inevitably concerns individuals, abstract and concrete, it very often requires a pronoun usable in such a phrase, so I have stuck with that bit of clean grammatical carpentry, not only because I was taught it at school, but because alternatives would both have aggravated the work's most obvious blemish and demonstrated an indifference to the well-tried mechanisms of grammar. If it is still thought that I offend against the democratic principle of gender equality, let me appeal to another democratic principle, majority. Medieval male suicides exceeded female by a ratio of two or three to one—a differential which has vanished, eerily, only in recent years, *pari passu* with the erosion of others.

My second brief warning concerns the unhappy character of the book's subject. Psychologists have shown that people of average temperament can become depressed by the mere reading of statements with depressing associations. That is, if a group of human 'guinea-pigs' is given a sheet of paper with such words on, even though the statements are isolated and not in paragraphs, and if they are told to meditate on them for an hour, the group will contract symptoms of depression not shared by a 'control' group equipped with similar word-lists randomly composed.[6] This work contains many depressing sentences. There is no reason why the reading of them should fail in a similar effect. I do not think a reader who feels a depressed mood

---

[5] (London, 1958), p. 137.
[6] Evaluation and literature: D. M. Clark, 'On the induction of depressed moods in the laboratory', *Advances in Behaviour and Response Therapy*, 5 (1983), 27–49.

coming on need appeal to a psychiatrist. The effect is normal, the cures traditional. One is to put the book down and read another. I shall refer in Chapter 2 to a medieval taboo on the mention of suicide. It was not groundless, and a historian would have no cause for self-congratulation if, in breaching the taboo at some centuries' distance, he frightened his own inexperienced contemporaries. This historian did not normally work on the subject after dinner. Let that be just one example of a score of common-sense prophylactics. We shall be walking through 'the valley of the shadow of death', but the walkers must do so with good heart. Its path does not ultimately lead downwards, or even go along on the level. The world this book is about is—notice I do not say 'was'—the real world. Only hard-boiled Manichaeans, if any have ever existed, believe this world was made by the Devil.

University College, Oxford
Hallbankgate, Cumbria
January, 1996

Acknowledgement

The lines by W. H. Auden quoted on p. 21 are reproduced by permission of Faber and Faber Ltd and Random House Inc.

Contents

Notes on Plates

Frontispiece: The Resurrection of the Dead
(Vatican, MS lat. 9820, *Resurrectio mortuorum*)

According to the Nicene Creed the resurrected Jesus immediately 'descended into Hell' to rescue the dead, before reappearing to his living disciples. This belief is alone among those attested by the creed which is not in the Gospel, but evidence for it is early and suggests influence from myths current in the milieu into which Christianity was born (like that of Orpheus's descent to the underworld). The early church fathers naturally accepted the tenet and concentrated discussion on what kind of underworld, who was rescued, and to what state they were brought.

It was not until the seventh century that pictorial art ventured on the problematic subject of the resurrection and on to this aspect of it in particular. It did so in a context of theological debate. The pictures, laden with symbolism, were designed to give force to an orthodox version of fundamental doctrines about the relation of Christ to God the Father and to Man.

The example here was made between 981 and 987, in southern Italy, to illustrate an *Exultet* roll. *Exultet* is the name and first word of a liturgical chant for the evening of Easter Saturday, still in use today in the form which became dominant in the ninth century. (It begins 'Let the angelic throng of Heaven exult!') The *Exultet* roll was a piece of parchment, sometimes over twenty feet long and anything between six and eighteen inches wide, on which the text of the chant was illustrated by pictures appropriate to each part of the chant. The picture was made upside-down so that as the deacon chanted the text he could flap the picture over the front of his lectern for the congregation to see. The rolls were written in Beneventan script (on which see pp. 280–1 below) because they were made in southern Italy, in the tenth and eleventh centuries the rich part of the peninsula, with extra cultural stimulus from frequent contact with Byzantium.

No element in the picture is without symbolic significance. For instance, the oval ring around Christ is a *mandorla*, symbol of the divine essence. The human figure of Jesus stands entirely within it except for extremities of his feet and robe, as he condescends to lift Adam and Eve from the flames. He bears the marks of the crucifixion on his hands and feet, and carries over his shoulder, like the resting lance of a warrior triumphant after a siege, a cross representing the sturdier counterpart on which Jesus was crucified.

That Jesus's posture proclaims will and energy is probably a hostile allusion to the Monotholete heresy, which held that the first and second persons of the Trinity shared a single will, and which was condemned by a council in Byzantium at the end of the seventh century. Antique models have been found in Heracles' dragging of Cerberus from the underworld, and in late Roman pictures of emperors, dragging captives or liberating provinces. The feebleness of Adam presents a contrast. He is old and bearded because he has waited hundreds of years for rescue. Eve is lucky to be there at all. Some versions leave her out and let her husband stand alone to represent the whole human race. She follows and consents as Jesus drags her husband to salvation by an arm already partly into the divine *mandorla*. The line of the latter appears through the human arm, to reflect the aetherial character of the dead Adam's body. The flames portray the underworld as peculiarly hellish. Below lies its broken gate, newly smashed by the cross. Above, from Heaven, David and Solomon and two prophets watch in approval, the former as a reminder of Christ's earthly descent, the latter in recognition of Old Testament prophecies of Christ's coming. (Literature: A. D. Kartsonis, *Anastasis* (Princeton, 1986)).

Photo: Biblioteca Vaticana. Reproduced by permission of the Vatican Librarian.

Plates

(between pages 136 and 137)

1. The first appearance of the word 'suicide'. (Paris, Arsenal, MS 379, fol. 73ʳ, lines 6–7.) The passage is from *Contra quatuor labyrinthos Franciae*, whose author, Walter of St Victor († *c*.1178), takes issue with Seneca's apologia for the self-killer and decries the latter as *suicida*. (See also p. 38.)

2. Henry of Hohenstaufen, king of the Romans, son of Frederick II Hohenstaufen. (London, British Library, MS Royal 14 E V, fol. 484ʳ.) An illustration to the *Cas des nobles hommes et femmes*, a French translation of Boccaccio's *De casibus virorum et mulierum illustrium* (*c*.1350), made for the duke of Berry in 1409 by Laurens de Premierfait. Henry's death occurred in February 1242 and gave rise to several traditions, of which one was suicidal: that under arrest, Henry had deliberately fallen from his horse while crossing a bridge, to avoid punishment by 'son pere l'emperor phedric'. Boccaccio offers the suicidal version as one of two alternatives. That it was this one the illuminator chose doubtless reflects a Renaissance taste for suicide as a 'strong ending'. (See pp. 53–5). The manuscript was made in 1470–1, probably for King Edward IV of England, then in exile in the Netherlands. (By permission of the Trustees of the British Library.)

3(a). The woman infanticide. (Oxford, Bodleian Library, MS Douce 374, fol. 63ʳ.) On the left a woman is killing her baby in the secrecy of a stable, while on the right the same woman has just stabbed herself and calls on the Virgin as her life expires. The elaboration of the story from thirteenth-century originals is described on pp. 265–71. The scene is one of many in *Les Miracles de Notre Dame*, a series of Marian miracles told in prose, *c*.1455, by Jean Miélot, a writer serving the dukes of Burgundy between 1448 and 1472. MS Douce 374 is the second volume of a manuscript of this work of which the first is in Paris, as Bibliothèque Nationale MS fr. 9198, dated 1456. The miracle of the woman infanticide is here represented in 'grisaille' by an illuminator probably to be identified as Jean le Tavernier, who worked at Oudenarde in the relevant years. The manuscript was in the Burgundian ducal library as late as the eighteenth century, but was bought by the collector Douce and bequeathed by him to the Bodleian in 1834. (By permission of the Bodleian Library, Oxford.)

3(b). The woman infanticide. (Paris, Bibliothèque Nationale, MS fr. 9199, fol. 65ʳ.) From volume 2 of a second manuscript of the same work, whose first volume is lost. The two manuscripts can be distinguished thus:

A. Vol. 1: Paris, Bibl. Nat., MS fr. 9198
   Vol. 2: Oxford, Bodleian, MS Douce 374

B. Vol. 1: Lost
  Vol. 2: Paris, Bibl. Nat., MS fr. 9199.

I thank Dr Martin Kauffmann for advice in identifying these manuscripts and their provenance. The illumination of this manuscript, too, can be assigned to Jean le Tavernier or his workshop. It begins its refinement of the picture in Plate 3(a) by reversing the image with the help of a mirror—a common technique when a scene was well known enough to be recognized.

4. The jealous wife of Rocamadour. (El Escorial, MS T-1-1, fo. 123, detail.) One of six panels illustrating a poetic version of a miracle of Our Lady of Rocamadour. Aware that her knightly husband pays private visits to a woman more beautiful than she, but unaware that her rival is the Virgin Mary and her husband's purpose prayer, a noble lady stabs herself. She is in due course resuscitated by the Virgin. (See pp. 272–4.) The miracle was included by King Alfonso X of Castile, the Wise (1253–84), in his *Cantigas de Santa Maria*, of which this richly illustrated manuscript, contemporary with the work's composition, is in the monastic library of El Escorial near Madrid. (Photograph supplied and authorized by the Patrimonio Nacional, Madrid.)

5(a). St James's pilgrim. (Paris, Bibliothèque Nationale, MS nouv. acq. fr. 24541, fo. 57^v), 'De Girart qui s'ocist par le decevement au deable comme il aloit a Saint Jacques'. A pilgrim *en route* for Santiago de Compostela stabbed himself to death on the suggestion of the Devil, disguised as St James (left) and was brought back to life. (See pp. 277–86.) The story originated in the eleventh century and won a place among the miracles not only of St James but of the Virgin. Here it illustrates the verse *Miracles de Nostre Dame* by Gautier de Coincy (c.1177–1236), a monk of Soissons. This ornate manuscript was made in Paris, probably by the well-known illustrator Jean Pucelle (†1334). As suggested by the fleur-de-lys pattern visible here in the background, its patron was probably a member of the French royal house, perhaps Jeanne de Bourgogne, wife of Philip VI. The pilgrim stabs himself in the throat rather than in the genitals, as in Gautier's text and its sources, an adjustment reflecting the sensibilities of a lofty patron.

5(b). St James' pilgrim. (Paris, Bibliothèque Nationale, MS fr. 9198, fo. 47^r.) This scene illustrates volume 1 of the manuscript whose second volume, in Oxford, was represented in Plate 3(a). On the left, a diabolic 'St James' tempts the pilgrim, while his two companions go on their way to Santiago. On the right, the true St James kneels before the Virgin and he pleads for the release of the pilgrim's soul from devils.

6 (p. 335). St Margaret of Cortona saves a professor. Margaret (or Margherita) of Cortona (†1297) saw in a vision that a man was about to hang himself. With two companions she rushed to prevent him, tearing the door from its hinges in her haste. The would-be suicide had already placed a rope round a spar. The two companions support the body's weight while the saint cuts the rope and the demon of despair vanishes top left. That the man is dressed in blue suggests he was a doctor of canon

law. The plate depicts a watercolour made *c*.1629 from a medieval mural, now destroyed, in the eastern bay of the south nave wall (second tier from the top) in the church of Sts Basil and Margaret in Cortona. See J. Cannon and A. Vauchez, *Art, Cult and Canonization: Margherita, Cortona, and the Lorenzetti* (London, forthcoming); and J. Cannon, 'Marguerite et les Cortonais: iconographie d'un "culte civique" au xive siècle', in A. Vauchez (ed.), *La religion civique à l'époque médiévale et moderne (Chrétienté et Islam)* (Rome, 1995), 403–13. I thank Dr Cannon for supplying me with a copy of her photograph and allowing me to reproduce it here.

Plates 1, 3(b), and 5(a) and (b) are reproduced by permission of the Bibliothèque Nationale, Paris.

List of Figures

List of Tables

Map

I

Introduction

Reform in the North

IN the late eleventh and twelfth centuries the churches of western Europe underwent successive waves of 'reform'. Pope Gregory VII and his allies reformed the papacy and bishoprics. Cistercians reformed the monasteries. Finally came the reform of regular canons, who lived by a rule like monks but one step less divorced from the rest of the world. It was the Premonstratensians, from Prémontré near Laon, who began this wave of reform, and it struck England around 1143–4. Half a dozen Premonstratensian houses were founded at once, especially in northern and eastern areas just then being settled, and the order went on expanding. It did so by taking on houses of the older Augustinian canons on request from their lay patrons, and canons in the older houses would then be told to obey the new discipline or depart, while a posse of new canons, complete with the new rule, would arrive to direct affairs. The result has gone down as one of the more successful monastic experiments. By the late thirteenth century the Premonstratensians had founded twenty-five houses in various parts of England, many to become famous and prosperous.

They had not always been. One of the earliest foundations was at Tupholme, ten miles east of Lincoln.[1] Around 1170, in the reign of Henry II, Tupholme got a message from a priest in Derbyshire to say that a local house of Augustinian canons was in straits, and needed reformers to take it over. The house in question was in wild country between Derby and Nottingham, its very name, Le Dale, suggesting recent colonization by Norsemen (or Normans). Long before, the story went, during Stephen's Anarchy, a hermit had lived at Le Dale in a cave. He was discovered on the brink of starvation by the local *seigneur* when out hunting. The lord gave the holy man income support from the rents of a local watermill. Inspired by that

---

[1] The following history is taken from the *Historia fundationis* of Le Dale in W. Dugdale, *Monasticon Anglicanum*, vol. 6 (London, 1830), 822–97, supplemented from *The Victoria County History: Derby*, vol. 2 (1907), 69–71, and local topography.

example, around 1160 the son of the same lord tried to establish a community of holy men in the same place, by importing Augustinian canons from ten miles to the south at Calke. But the site would not support so many, and in the end, because the land around was royal forest, the authorities stepped in and expelled the canons again.

This was the point at which the local priest got in touch with Tupholme. The priest was related to the lords, father and son, and shared their resolve to install a religious community. Tupholme's answer came in the form of six Premonstratension canons. They were to settle at Le Dale, with one as prior. The prior's office and his name, Henry, suggest knightly birth. He at once attacked the problems that had defeated his predecessors. One of his canons built a watermill. The community farmed what arable land they had, despite pilfering by lawless neighbours, and to get ready cash the canons cut off the tops of their oak trees to sell for timber. But food still ran short, and soon a request was sent to the mother-house for cash subventions to buy food in the villages round the forest edge. Then Prior Henry had a new idea. Living in the forest might have its drawbacks, but it also had an advantage, in that no one much outside knew what went on there. Legal ways of getting money, namely farming and forestry, had not sufficed, so Henry thought of an illegal way: making it. Unlicensed coiners elsewhere had been executed with the utmost gruesomeness. But that was if they were caught, and who would catch Henry in the penumbra of Sherwood, weeks from Westminster? Like his companion with the watermill, Henry was ingenious and soon became adept.[2]

The mother-house in Tupholme knew nothing of Henry's initiative. Nor did it have to. All it knew was that its subventions went on, if at a lower level than they would have without the secret industry, and that there was something wrong at Le Dale, even if no one knew what. After seven years' effort, Tupholme declared the experiment over and recalled the canons, all except Henry. Perhaps he had asked to be left there to keep an eye on the buildings, but really he had another motive. While coining, he had also been visiting a girl in the local village and, when left alone in his wilderness, he moved out of his skeleton of a monastery and went to live with the girl, the pair moving to a place at modest distance from both his monastery and her relations. The authorities in Tupholme still knew nothing. They were fifty miles away, news travelled slowly and, now that the community was no more, why should it travel at all?

The answer almost certainly lies with the local priest, involved as he had

---

[2] Dugdale, *Monasticon*, vol. 6, p. 894 for this and what follows.

long been in the founding of a viable religious house. He complained to the abbot of Tupholme. The abbot was indignant. With unanimous approval from the Tupholme canons, he sent an order to Henry to return to the mother-house at once. Henry did not reply. So a posse of men was sent, and Henry brought back by force to the abbey. Our account ends: 'Henry's heart was smitten by melancholy. Taking guidance from the Devil he got into a hot bath and opened veins in both arms; and in this way of his own free will—nay free folly—ended his life.'[3]

Soon after this episode the tireless priest got yet another set of Premonstratensian New Brooms, this time from Welbeck, a mere twenty-five miles away, to come and settle at Le Dale. They struggled like the rest to make a living from it and again gave up. Only around 1195 did the tide turn and the priest crown a lifetime's campaigning by persuading his rich relations to endow the house properly. They gave it the rents of a whole village, and offered the resulting 'package' to the mother-house of the English Premonstratensians, Newhouse, far away near Scunthorpe. These were tried experts and sent, not six, but nine, of their number; and at last, about 1200, omens began to multiply that the house would survive, fourth time round. Le Dale was re-ranked as an abbey, and flourished until the Dissolution of the Greater Religious Houses in 1539. One result was that, probably in the late 1230s or the 1240s, a canon called Thomas of Muskham wrote a history of the abbey's foundation.[4] To it we owe all we know of Prior Henry, and the manner of his life and death.

Thomas bestows on Henry's death seven contemptuous words: 'spontanea quin potius stulta morte vitam finivit' (literally: 'by a spontaneous or rather, foolish, death he put an end to his life'). These words were almost certainly the only epitaph Henry had in his own generation or any other. His body, found dead in the bath, would normally have been disposed of in an unmarked grave without ceremony or public prayer, outside any churchyard. The idea behind that custom was that the whole incident be forgotten as soon as possible. In Henry's case the goal might not have been achieved at once, since one person, at least, would have mourned the 'colloquy of passing sweetness' (to quote a contemporary love poem) of the gifted, unusual, delinquent man for whom she had been ready to brave her

---

[3] Ibid.: 'Quod audiens ejus abbas, sed et indigne ferens, cum fratribus ad ejus mandatum domum redire contempsit, misit, et per vim eum adduci fecit usque Tupholme; qui dolore cordis suscepto, adeo diabolico instigabatur consilio, quod in balneto calido, de utroque brachio sanguinem minuens, spontanea quin potius stulta morte vitam finivit.'

[4] The rarity of this account, as throwing light on the intimate life of the early Premonstratensians in England, is emphasized by D. Knowles, *The Monastic Order in England, 943–1216* (Cambridge, 1940), 361 n. 2.

family.[5] But rememberers of that kind are themselves usually forgotten. Henry's girl-friend got no epitaph at all, not even a snort from Thomas of Muskham.

But what of Thomas himself? Is he really any less 'forgotten', now, than the rest of them, a few modern specialist scholars of monasticism apart? He is certainly as dead; as dead, that is, as the 'foolish' Henry and his girl-friend, the family she left to go live with him, the priest and his rich relations, the pilfering villagers and the canons they pilfered from, all of them. Today, all are equally dead, and have been for seven centuries.

There was once a discipline, taught in books and assigned to professionals, whose aim was to conjure dead people to life and make them speak. It was called necromancy. Its function has long passed to historians, whose method is now the only one recognized. The method may seem by comparison mundane, but it is at bottom no less supernatural, indeed it is more so. For in hard, *natural* fact, Henry and his friends have long ago dissolved into their constituent molecules, and these have merged into the substances round us, animal, mineral, and vegetable; even *in* us, as we sit reading. No one would now suggest—and only a few bold spirits did so in the Middle Ages[6]—bringing all those particles back together again and raising people back to life *that* way; but there is another. When two living people talk to each other, each lets the other's thoughts and feelings echo in himself. There could be no language otherwise. It is the same mechanism, working in one direction, that lets us talk about dead people—like Julius Caesar, Shakespeare, or Gladstone (none of whom actually exists)—as if our words had any meaning. The mechanism must have been at work very early on in the history of mankind, at least since the first emergence of epic. It has grown more elaborate, and today we use a whole panoply of historical practices and disciplines, from popular songs, via heritage sites, to erudite history books. All of these are so much part of our culture we do not notice what it is they are doing. But the process is really the most mysterious in nature, for it is making a breach in the otherwise impregnable wall of time. Of course it is a small breach, and even that, to be any size at all, needs a mental effort. Ghosts, we are told, will not speak until they have tasted blood. They 'demand the blood of our hearts.'[7] But the smallness of the breach is not

---

[5] 'Praedulce colloquium': *Carmina Cantabrigiensia*, ed. K. Strecker (Berlin, 1926), 71, 16 (no. 27). The *Invitatio amicae* in which the expression appears (on the lips of a woman) was written probably in the tenth century and copied into the Cambridge manuscript in the eleventh; but would certainly have been known in the twelfth.

[6] e.g. the medical commentator Ursus of Salerno [† c.1225]: P. Morpurgo, *L'Idea di natura nell'Italia normannosveva* (Bologna, 1993), 13.

[7] Ulrich von Wilamowitz-Moellendorf, '*Greek Historical Writing*' and '*Apollo*'. *Two lectures delivered before the University of Oxford, June 3 and 4, 1908* (Oxford, 1908), 25: 'The

the issue. It is what is being breached. And just as, according to physics teachers, a mere matchboxful of the sun, placed on the earth's surface, would burn everything for hundreds of miles, so even the smallest glimpse into historical 'supertime' is enough to fill our little minds to satiety. More, and we would be overwhelmed.

This, anyway, is the kind of necromancy to which this book will aspire. Its aim is to lift Prior Henry from his unmarked grave, together with all who knew him and all like him and all like them, during the European Middle Ages. Once they are up and alive again there will be questions to ask, as there always are when strangers appear from far away. The suicides will be asked, 'How many were you?' and 'Why did you do it?' and other such questions; the survivors, 'What did you think, and do, about it, and why?' But our first and fundamental task is not the gleaning of information. It is the resuscitation of a particular people, one long extruded, by the manner of their death, into the deepest declivities of collective memory, below the rubbed, familiar surfaces of political and ecclesiastical history.

Surfaces imply depths. Depths explain surfaces. But they have different didactic functions, the former to acquaint us with identities, the latter to reveal essences. Their mutual relation will run invisibly through the structure of this book. Surface and depth, survivors and suicides, forgetters and the forgotten, were enemies. At the end of the Le Dale story, Henry ignored the summons from his mother-house and remained mentally 'absent' when he got there. The abbey repaid his memory with neglect and shame. That two-way antipathy was general. Since enemies must at first be interviewed separately, the antipathy is reflected in the division between the book's three volumes. As indicated in the Preface, Part I, occupying *volume* 1, will address the suicides, Parts II and III, occupying respectively volumes 2 and 3, the survivors and their attitudes. But the separation is tactical, and the human species remained one throughout, for all its different faces. By tracing how medieval minds began to appreciate this fact in respect of suicide, Part III will start bringing surfaces and depths together again, to reintegrate a species otherwise split in two.

As we take our first step towards the objects of this necromancy a word of advice is necessary: we must *dis*integrate ourselves from certain conventions of polite reading, and expect horrible sights. So did our guide, Dante,

---

tradition yields us only ruins . . . The tradition is dead; our task is to revivify life that has passed away. We know that ghosts cannot speak until they have drunk blood, and the spirits which we evoke demand the blood of our hearts. We give it to them gladly.'

when he first stepped into the *Inferno*; and his own guiding spirit, Virgil, issued this warning:

> Before us lies the region where, I said,
> Your eyes will dwell on people crushed by woe
> Where intellect to its own good is dead.[8]

Le genti dolorose. There will often be occasion here to remember that phrase, and the highly practical advice with which Virgil followed it. His pupil's emotional survival would depend, Virgil said, in the face of the sights of *Inferno*, on the deliberate suppression of natural human reactions:

> Now is the time to mortify your dread,
> To unpronounce the very name of fear.[9]

The advice will also apply here. Suicides and the damned, it is true, are not identical. My aim with the former is not to damn but to revive them. But even a revived suicide may be uncomely to look at, as will almost any category of person be that is defined by the manner of its death. That is a hazard of necromancy, and was so in classical times. In Lucan's history of the Roman civil war a man got a witch to raise a dead acquaintance to life and was aghast at the sight that struck him:

> The face was of a warrior as he dies,
> Not of one living. Pallor, cold and stern,
> Froze on the rigid cheeks. The staring eyes,
> Dumbfounded, flinched at the world's return.[10]

Here, the reader must steel himself for the same experience.

All these warnings prompt an obvious question. Why choose such a horrid subject? Why not write about the great and the good, on the time-honoured rule put by the Father of English History: 'if history relates good things of good men, the attentive reader is excited to imitate that which is good.'[11] By turning the rule upside-down, it may be asked, do I want to make my *readers* commit suicide? And if not, what reason can there be for making a hero of the apparently unheroic, an epitome (it might seem) of the small and bad? Put in a way more befitting the present necromantic business: why

---

[8] *Inferno* 3: 16–18: 'Noi siam venuti al luogo ov'io t'ho detto / Che tu vedrai le genti dolorose / C'hanno perduto il ben dello intelletto.' Partly from an *embarras de choix*, and partly from an occasional need to expose a particular feature, I have made my own translations from Dante.

[9] Ibid., 3: 14–15: 'Qui si convien lasciare ogni sospetto; / Ogni viltà convien che qui sia morta.'

[10] *Phars.* 6: 757–60: '. . . distento lumina rictu / nudantur. Nondum facies viventis in illo, / iam morientis erat: remanet pallor rigorque, / et stupet inlatus mundo.'

[11] Bede, *Historia ecclesiastica*, *praefatio*, in *Opera historica*, ed. C. Plummer (Oxford 1896), vol. 1, p. 5.

go off to rummage in a wilderness in twelfth-century Lincolnshire, and dig up someone who has been harmlessly let lie for so long? In a word, why this book?

Why This Book?

A writer does not have to be called Goethe or Gibbon to fall foul of the rule that he cannot be trusted to say how a book was conceived. Not that all writers are liars, quite. But once a book is brought to birth, the force of its creative idea can distort the memory of how that idea, among all the others, first distinguished itself as the one to write about; so I will avoid trying to go too deep. For a university lecturer, which I have been throughout the time this book has been in the making, there is an opposite danger, in that the story of how a subject is born can be too banal. It is often mere accident that gives rise to a project: a provocative remark in a book (in my case, one or two by well-known experts on medieval society, saying 'there was little suicide in the Middle Ages');[12] an invitation to lecture; and so on. When the point of decision comes, it is partly, too, decided by a scholar's assessment of his own pattern of academic experience as a qualification for tackling the requisite technicalities of 'subject X'. All these were part of the story here. But they are typical of the genre, so I shall avoid them and go straight, instead, to the two main ideas that respectively provoked and shaped this project.

The first idea was a mere hypothesis, one which must have occurred to many people. To anyone who has read any history there is no need to reiterate that earlier societies suffered innumerable physical ills: starvation, plague and disease, and a lot of killing and wounding, both by armies in war and by criminals or private enemies. Crimes in modern newspapers, appalling as they are, are outstripped in quantity and matched in atrocity by corresponding examples from most previous periods of European history. After centuries of effort—the hypothesis runs—many of these physical ills have been diminished in western society. They may come back. Some have been replaced by new forms of horror or redistributed to other parts of the globe. But in Europe and kindred societies, on the whole, it is hard to deny that some physical progress has been made.

Here lies the problem. The progress has not made everyone *happy*. The absence of physical challenge can sometimes even add to people's unhappi-

[12] Arno Borst, *Die Katharer*. Schriften der *Monumenta Germaniae Historica*, 12. (Stuttgart, 1953), p. 73: [of Leutard] 'einer der wenigen Selbstmörder des Mittelalters'; and G. G. Coulton, *Medieval Studies* (London, 1930), 78: 'suicide, the only crime of violence which was rarer then than now.' On other impressions of this kind, discovered in the course of these researches, see pp. 353–78 below.

ness. That may be why 'problems of the soul' (to borrow from the title of a famous book by the psychologist C. G. Jung),[13] have become more conspicuous in the twentieth century. If so, one more consequence follows. It means that suicide, and the melancholy of which it is the extreme expression, enters the human scene in the space occupied, long ago, by wolves, bears, tuberculosis, plague, fire, barbarians, and thumbscrews; and invites conquest in the same spirit.

This construction is not watertight. It presupposes, for one thing, more historical knowledge than is easy to come by: knowledge, for instance, as to whether medieval people really did care only about physical danger, and did not also have 'problems of the soul' like ours. But the main lines of it seemed to me plausible when I began this book, and still do. Indeed they seem more plausible now that I know more about suicide rates and social trends in their regard.[14] Why I mention it now is that it was that line of thinking, not any mere string of professional accidents, that launched this investigation. It concerned an important, real, human, modern problem, books or no books: one like cholera, or a prowling bear.[15]

That hypothesis set the work in motion. It explains its subject and genre. But the work would not have taken the form it has if these stimuli had not been matched by forces in the material itself. It was soon clear—by reflection, let alone any new discovery—that the subject concerned more than a handful of forgotten unfortunates. As a topic for study, suicide raised questions about a range of contiguous matters, in law, religion, and so on; then about matters contiguous to those, and more, each cluster of stars leading the eye to another behind it, to a point where, finally, the subject took on the appearance of an epitome of history itself, a single sign, a 'zero' to denote the entire heavens. This is always happening to historians. They come to see everything in terms of the stirrup, or liberty, or the salt trade. Nor is the result pure illusion, unless, like a medieval heretic, a historian thinks his own vision invalidates all others. But it can lead to confusion. So my own speculations in this broad

---

[13] *Seelenprobleme der Gegenwart* (Zürich, 1946).

[14] For the stimulus given to the suicide rate by the cessation of wars, and by the rise of unemployment and of one-person households, see S. Stack, 'Suicide: a decade review of the sociological literature', *Deviant Behaviour*, 4 (1982), 41–66; especially (respectively for each factor) 58, 48, and 54; cf. Chapters 15 and 16 below.

[15] I have been encouraged, since formulating this view, to find it well expressed by the ninth-century writer Hrabanus Maurus: *De ecclesiastica disciplina*, bk 3 [*Patrologia latina*, 112.1250C, 1250D–51A]: 'Est etiam genus tristitae pestiferum ac mortiferum, quod quasi passio per singulos cursus, ac varios casus obtinendi animam nostram habuerit facultatem, ab omni nos per momenta singula reparat divinae contemplationis intuitu, ipsamque mentem ab universo statu puritatis dejectam funditus labefactat et deprimit. . . . Velut amentem facit et ebrium. Sensum frangit, et obruit, desperatione penali, quamobrem non minori prospectu si spiritualis agonis certamina legitime curamus, desudare hic quoque nobis curandis est morbus . . . Est etiam illud detestabilius tristitae genus, quod non correctionem vitae, nec emendationum vitiorum, sed perniciosissima desperationem animae injicit delinquenti . . .'

field were given a job to do, to induce sobriety, the job of organizing the historical material, always much the hardest task (the mere telling of stories is easy). And that job, while it had the desired effect of curbing speculation on the highest levels, had also the unexpected result of positively generating speculation on a humbler one. This time the speculation was not hypothesis, it grew straight out of the historical material and could not be gainsaid. It concerned an innate characteristic of suicide, affecting everyone and everything concerned with it.

Suicide as an Extreme

Suicide, I take it, marks an extremity of human experience. I say 'I take it' because no one can be quite sure what anyone else is feeling; nor, if one could be sure, would there be any clear way of measuring the result comparatively. All generalizations about other people's inner thoughts rest on assumptions. Suicide is a more puzzling case than most. The last words of some suicides suggest they faced their end with calm or even nonchalance. A few—sometimes recorded as 'mad'—have leapt to death with gestures implying actual delight. (One or two will make an appearance in this volume.)[16] My assumption may be upside-down, but so may any assumption; and since we cannot dispense with them, that is mine. It turns those seeming contradictions—like the 'mad' suicide who enjoys it—into exceptions, explained by special circumstance, leaving the obvious truth all the less challenged. The truth is obvious because from a physical point of view the worst that can happen to anyone is to die. Other misfortunes take away part; death takes all. A wish to die can only result from the strongest negative impulses from life: loss, incapacity, failure, and pain. The mind of the suicide, while he still physically has one, is at the opposite pole of experience from rapture.

Suicide, then, marks an extremity. For those who do not commit suicide but consider its significance this has a number of consequences. From one point of view, that of everyday survival, most of the time and in the press of other business, the first consequence is that suicides do not matter. They can be ignored as too few. Extremes of human behaviour, as of human stature, follow what statisticians call a 'bell curve distribution'. The normal majority are represented by a hump in the middle of the 'bell', the midgets and giants by wedges at the side. Suicides are the tip of a wedge, a small minority. Even in modern countries with high rates of suicide those who commit it remain a small percentage of all deaths;[17] and the higher any

---

[16] For instance, in Ch. 12, p. 276 and Ch. 14, pp. 322–5.
[17] For some figures, see below, p. 355. Cf. p. 24.

group or profession rises above that low average, the more that group itself becomes a minority among other groups. No doubt it will be said they are still too many. One would be too many. But they remain in any numerical sense unrepresentative. To most men in the street, therefore, including the average social scientist or historian, to concentrate on suicides is to concentrate on a splinter, a social island, whose claim to his attention is less, in terms of pure numbers, than that of (say) people both of whose names begin with B.

Now this approach would be valid if suicides differed in kind from the rest of us. But they mark an extremity; that is, they differ only in degree, which means that their act, despite small numbers, has universal significance. This can be interpreted along two different routes. The first leads directly from the act of suicide, which can be read as a potential index of emotional peculiarities of the society in which the dead person lived. His miseries—loss, frustration, and others—are not generically unique to him; only unique in degree, or in their degree in combination, and in relation to his capacity to bear them. He is not an island. He may think so, but that is another of his representative miseries (a lot of people think they are islands). He is rather a promontory, leading back and forth from the mainland.

Of course many exceptional human categories are 'promontories' of this kind. But as an index of society the suicide has a special rank, for his act is normally extremely private,[18] and this gives its function as an index unique value where an index is most needed, in the realm of private and elusive emotions. It tells us of things people often do not wish to talk about or may not even know. This principle, together with the precision accessible to it, is illustrated throughout Émile Durkheim's classic study, *Suicide*,[19] and can be demonstrated by a single example from that book. Durkheim's statistics, based on various European countries in various years between 1850 and 1891, show that, while the ratio of male to female suicides was normally around 2 : 1, the male predominance among unmarried suicides was weakest in the 20+ age group and grew stronger after the age of 50.[20] Other things being equal, that is to say, unbearable misery struck women harder than men in the twenties, men harder than women as old age approached. We may speculate on this variation, and it may point our thoughts to the plight of unwanted young women, 'wallflowers' at an age in life when interests are social, and to that of old men who cannot look after themselves at an age

---

[18] On its privacy in the Middle Ages see below, pp. 22–7.

[19] (Paris, 1897); tr. J. A. Spaulding and G. Simpson (London, 1952). I shall quote from this translation.

[20] Ibid., p. 101. Cf. M. Halbwachs, *The Causes of Suicide* [Paris, 1930], tr. H. Goldblatt (London, 1978), 143.

when women, who no longer care about dances, can. If it does, so much the better. What is certain is that the statistic has given us a fact to speculate about, providing a searchlight into otherwise elusive areas of private emotion.

That is the first way an act of suicide can reflect things about other people than the one who dies: because it is an extreme, its teaching-power is both well in excess of the proportion of suicides to population, and peculiarly sensitive to the private. This principle, combined with another to be explained at the beginning of Chapter 3, will contribute the design of Part I, in this first volume. The quality of evidence will in general be threadbare in comparison with that of Durkheim and his successors, above all in the statistical field. But comparison with other surviving indices of medieval thought and feeling will, I hope, vindicate the narratives and deductions to be offered by my three categories of medieval source. They are meant to cast light on otherwise secretive layers of medieval hearts and minds.

But I said the universal significance of an act of suicide could be interpreted along two routes. That was only the first. The second route is similar but goes the other way, and touches the motives not, this time, of the suicide, but of those who react to his deed. For the results, like the causes, of suicide, are of a general kind, not limited to this or that human category. The heart-struck lover or bankrupt is victim to experiences everyone can recognize, in kind if not in degree; so the suicide of such a person touches a chord in those who hear of it. Here, too, his privacy is illusory. He may think he is performing the most private of private acts. He will never have to meet anyone again. But the fact is obvious to everyone else, if not to him (and whether he wishes it or not), that the act *does* have consequences for other people. The consequences can be serious, like many we shall see from the thirteenth and fourteenth centuries, where it is a question of an innocent man's being hanged for the murder of a person who in truth killed himself. There, suicide can amount to murder. Or the consequences can range right down to the barely perceptible feelings of regret, sympathy, or disapproval sparked off by news of the suicide by a person wholly unknown to us. It is still an effect. The results of suicide therefore teach the same lesson as its causes. The person who commits it, whatever his own thoughts on the matter, is not an island.

And this is what offers the historian his second way of reading suicide as an index. Because the act has effects on those who do not commit it, they react in ways which reveal things about them quite different from those taught by the plights of the dead persons, and these reactions, too, follow patterns deriving from the status of suicide as an extremity. They do so in three ways. First, suicide expresses the *nec plus ultra* of ordinary human unhappiness, and evokes pity or fear for this reason. This will be most obvious in the case of suicide themes in literature, to be reviewed in Part III. Second, the means of expression employed is an act of irreversible violence. It is an act of a kind—homicide—of perennial concern to law and ethics, but which in the case of suicide, where victim and perpetrator are the same, leaves law and ethics ambivalent, so that they oscillate. Third, because the outcome of suicide is the ultimate and most feared of mysteries, namely death, the impotence of reason, especially because there is no one to blame, gives a bigger role than usual to custom and intuition.

For these and other reasons I shall often in this book describe suicide as a 'maverick'. It is a maverick, that is, in the legal and ethical systems it impinges on, since it imparts its own paradoxical nature to all areas of thought it touches. But here too the appearance can mislead. Suicide in the abstract *appears* thus to be an island on its own. But it is really no more an island than the person who commits it, since, for all its maverick character, suicide again proves to lead back to the mainland of law, ethics, and religion, exposing peculiarities in their nature and structure. Once more I give a single illustration, from many we shall meet later. A study of suicide in Part II will show the extent to which medieval Christian ethics and law borrowed from pre-Christian Rome. That they did so borrow is well known, but suicide puts in relief the *extent* of their borrowing, since it was the most palpable exception. On this one, solitary point, pagan and Christian positions were antithetical.

The extreme character of suicide, then, colours social reactions in three ways. The three come together in its impact on religion. In the Middle Ages that means Christianity. Here there is a surprise, for the Christian God and the suicide have an important feature in common, one which draws them together, at the same time that it divides both from the majority of mankind, the 'hump' of the bell curve. It is that God, too, is an extreme. God is bigger than the biggest, smaller than the smallest, and accessible even to attempts at description only by the use of negative words like 'infinite'—which say he is beyond other extremes. God and the suicide may differ in other respects. But they are alike in their extreme character, so that their very relationship, whatever else it may be, has to partake of that character. The relationship can be seen from either end and is extreme either way. As a particular act of violence, suicide is the ultimate act of religious defiance, and hence renders the suicide God's worst enemy. Seen from the other end, however, the act expresses the ultimate in human suffering, which should render the suicide, in that respect, God's best friend. A priori, Christianity can pull both ways.

That a priori deduction leads me to complete saying why I wrote this book. Cardinal Newman said religion was a man's first concern. He had Christianity mainly in mind, and his remark gives historians of that religion a job that never ends. Christianity was meant to last for ever, and no unmistakable sign has appeared that it will not. One consequence is that each generation that adopts Christianity is a generation of heirs, receiving its doctrine and practice through a series of predecessors. Now it is well-known that heirlooms, whatever the intention of their original testators, commonly bear marks made by subsequent users—the burn on the George III dresser. Christianity is no exception. The question is bound to arise, which of its features, in any generation, belong to the enduring essence of the religion and which reflect only the priorities of an ephemeral milieu. Which is the burn, which the dresser? Put yet another way, which is its enduring core, which its disposable periphery? A lot hangs on the distinction.

Historians are therefore safe in their jobs, *ad infinitum*. But they face an equally enduring problem. It is cognitive. The generations do not merely succeed each other. They collectively evolve. In European history, evolution may be irregular but is undeniable: gaming gladiators have gone, science has burgeoned. This evolution has a consequence for historians. They will normally be looking at a society more barbarous than their own. To look back is to look down. That consequence, familiar to all practitioners, takes a particular form for the historian of Christianity, for he has the task of distinguishing core from periphery. Both will have passed through barbarous societies, the core unaltered, the periphery with adjustments to temporary needs. And here is the crux. The nature of the adjustments makes the task harder, for they will mostly be adjustments from spiritual to material. St Augustine, for instance, who knew all about spiritual war from his early days, was moved by contemporary emergencies to justify material war (with his doctrine of 'just war'). The same kind of pressure turns spiritual penance into material punishments, doctrinal purity into the physical extirpation of heretics, and so on. There are many examples. The church historian's problem is that material things are always easier to *see* than conceptual or spiritual ones. Looking back at the tradition, that is to say, as it passes through its barbarous societies, he will *see* the material first; that is, precisely the periphery, those features which contemporary guardians of the tradition developed to meet contemporary needs. Crusades, inquisition, taxes: these *are* the medieval church, seen from a distance.

This cognitive effect touches suicide like everything else. But suicide is an extreme, so it does so extremely. Thus the only thing the modern educated person is likely to know about medieval suicide is that 'the church' condemned it, cast out the suicide's body from the churchyard and declared his soul in Hell. That is easy to document, as will be clear in Part II. But was there nothing else? There should be, a priori, because suicide can be seen from the other end, as an outcome of extreme suffering. Yes, it is a negative outcome, whatever is said about its voluntary or involuntary character. What matters more is the zone of which it is an outcome, an extreme zone, that of the troubled mind. But did I not say God was an extremist? Should he not be at home here? The psalmist says he is, after all. 'The sacrifice of God is a troubled spirit,' runs Psalm 50/1 (v. 17). That puts the *un*troubled spirit, the hump of the curve, on the margin, and gives centrality to the wedge at the side. In this zone there will be failures, but are we to understand that 'the church' had nothing more to say than throw them out of the churchyard? In fact it *has* more to say, but what it has is of a kind hidden to the distant observer, looking back, behind a barricade of material paraphernalia, reflecting the doctrinal and legal conventions of a society more barbarous than his own. I plan to explore this territory and expose its mirages in the two later volumes, and the reader will then be able to judge what lies behind the apparent contradictions in the evidence.

The mapping of mental desolation, like other mapping, did not get far in the Middle Ages. But it got far enough to help define, by way of summary, the purpose these last few pages have been trying to identify. This *opus tripartitum* is an attempt to continue the mapping of desolation. The wilderness it maps is distant territory, on a margin; but it cannot safely be left there abandoned and forgotten, since it is at bottom everyone's territory, and it is dangerous territory, where accurate maps are needed. In a historical field where evidence is elusive, optical illusions countless, I have sought to wrestle with both in an attempt to improve the map; and, if only because I could find no way of getting into the heart of the territory but to see it in a Christian context, I have sought to re-examine, in particular, the relationship between Christianity, with its crucified God, and the epitomes of failure who are our subject. The book tries to rejoin extremes. The aim is not unthinkable. Look at the frontispiece.

A History of a History

Those, then, were the motives that created and shaped this book. Whether the same have played a part in previous writing on the subject is a question with its own interest, which can best be answered by a review of that writing. Since history is more safely written about the dead, I shall take the review as far as the Second World War and try to show that, like most historiography, that on medieval suicide has responded indirectly to wider political and cultural developments. After Napoleon, bureaucratic governments and social policies combined to breed a concern for what its pioneers called 'moral statistics'. That meant statistics about birth, marriage, death, crime, and similar incidents, as guides to otherwise invisible currents within a society. This concern began seriously in the 1830s, gathered momentum in the 1880s, and has been growing ever since. From around 1879, the focus began to sharpen especially on suicide, as an index of human strains and aspirations. This was the date of Enrico Morselli's book *Suicide*, published in Italian and translated into other European languages. This phase of the process culminated in 1897 with Émile Durkheim's *Le Suicide*—published in French and again widely translated—the book which, more than any other, established its subject as a specialization.

This chronology is distantly reflected in that of the historical study of suicide, with delays reflecting the character and accessibility of the data in different periods. For the Middle Ages the ground was broken by Louis Félix Bourquelot (1815–68), a French local historian and travel writer. He used time as a professor at Paris's famous École des Chartes to produce a 65-page article, published in three parts of the *Bibliothèque de l'École des Chartes* from 1842 to 1844. He called it 'Recherches sur les opinions et la législation en matière de mort volontaire pendant le moyen âge'.[21] As the title suggested, it concentrated on opinions and law, as also on France. But Bourquelot also marshalled relevant literary passages and cases of suicide from chronicles, which give his treatise lasting value. He remained nevertheless an isolated pioneer. A list of nineteenth-century works on suicide contains, apart from Bourquelot's essay, next to nothing historical before the 1850s. In 1847, for instance, a treatise on suicide by a Paris doctor who had become a Trappist monk (P. I. C. Debrayne), viewed its subject from 'philosophical, religious, moral and medical angles'.[22] 'Historical' is noticeably absent. Only after 1850 did such titles occasionally add the extra adjective. A sign of the times was the publication, in 1859, of Dabadie's *Les suicidés illustres. Biographies des personnages remarquables de tous les pays qui ont péri volontairement, depuis le commencement du monde jusqu'à nos jours.*[23] Its tiny duodecimo format, common to many books on this topic, suggests it may have been carried in ladies' and gentlemen's hand cases.

A growing awareness of the historical dimension of suicide was matched by developments in the study of law. Jurists have always been historians. In 1828 Jakob Grimm had published the first edition of his *Antiquities of Germanic Law* [*Deutsche Rechtsalterthümer*], a work destined to expand in

---

[21] Full titles and references will be found in the Bibliography on pp. 477–80.

[22] E. Motta, *Bibilografia del suicidio* (Bellinzona, 1890), no. 219.

[23] Ibid., no. 258.

three subsequent editions by 1899; and in 1840 the first volume of his German *Dicta* [*Weisthümer*], whose last volume was to be published posthumously in 1873.[24] Grimm's texts often documented ancient practice without explaining it, and although few of them had anything directly to say on suicide the approach was well adapted to this subject. The scholarly exploration of *Rechtsalterthümer* therefore fused with a general public interest in suicide to spur specialist scholars to action. In 1867 Victor Molinier, professor of law in the University of Toulouse, published a short treatise on the repression of suicide in that city during the Middle Ages. In 1868, a direct disciple of Grimm, Édouard Osenbruggen (1805–78), similarly a professor of law but in Zurich, published his *Studies on German and Swiss Legal History* [*Studien zur deutschen und schweizerischen Rechtsgeschichte*]. It contains new evidence of suicide cases and procedures from south-western Germany.

The last quarter of the nineteenth century saw literary interest in suicide reach an apogee. Between Morselli's book in 1879 and Durkheim's in 1897, serious studies, novels, poems, and articles on the subject multiplied, even to the point of breeding parody, so that titles could appear like *Suicide. A Comedy in Five Acts* (Milan, 1876).[25] The tidal wave at last floated historians off their bank of inertia. The last fifteen years of the nineteenth century and the first few of the twentieth saw no fewer than four historical doctoral theses on suicide, all with medieval material. Gaston Garrisson (1856–94), scion of a clan of lawyer-politicians of Montauban, and a minor poet, published his thesis on *Le suicide dans l'antiquité et dans les temps modernes* in 1885. It remained Garrisson's only history book, and once more focused mainly on France, but its legal material remains useful to scholars lucky enough to find a copy. The same can be said of the three other theses. A Bavarian Catholic priest, Mathias Inhofer, otherwise uncelebrated, published his prize-winning essay *Suicide: An historical-dogmatic treatise* [*Selbstmord, Eine historische-dogmatische Abhandlung*] in Augsburg in 1886, which includes still-valuable quotations from German conciliar legislation. Chronologically the last of the series was Ossip Bernstein's *The Punishment of Suicide and its Disappearance* [*Die Bestrafung des Selbstmords und ihr Ende*], prepared *c.*1900 and published in a Breslau legal series in 1907. Its author was a Russian émigré, who again ended as a professor of law, in Heidelberg. The book remained his only monograph, and still serves as a thesaurus of late fifteenth- and sixteenth-century legislation, especially from the Empire.

---

[24] For clarity's sake I give German titles first in English. Full original titles will be found with other details in the Bibliographies on pp. 473–4 and 477–80.

[25] Motta, *Bibliografia*, no. 354.

I have omitted the third of the four theses. This was by a Munich theology student, Karl August Geiger, and came out in 1888. Its subject was suicide in classical antiquity. Surprisingly, in view of the prevalence of suicide in ancient Greece and Rome, their historians were slower to treat it as a subject in its own right. They would only catch up twenty years after the appearance of Geiger's path-breaking thesis, with a full-length treatment of the subject, in a packed, 125-page article by the professor of Greek at Jena, Rudolf Hirzel. Hirzel's essay is still essential reading for classicists (and was recently republished as a separate volume). But classical suicide had aroused Geiger's interest in suicide, and the interest survived in a series of three articles of more direct medieval import. They were on suicide respectively in French, German, and canon law. All appeared in the *Archive for Catholic Ecclesiastical Law* [*Archiv für Katholisches Kirchenrecht*], in 1889, 1891, and 1899. Geiger was a Catholic priest and schoolteacher and became a well-known writer of pastoral handbooks and on questions of church–state politics. That his pastoral-political interests played a part in his suicide scholarship is confirmed by his author-ship of a polemical article on contemporary law, appearing in the same *Archive* under the title 'Critical Conclusions on the Laws Concerning Suicide'.

Since laws on suicide do not admit full explanation in terms of law alone, they invoke folklore and what is now called anthropology, so it was natural that the study of suicide law should extend also into these fields, on ground prepared by Grimm and his disciples. Perhaps the most important figure here was the Swiss pioneer of folklore study, Hanns Bächtold-Stäubli (1886–1941). In 1921 he founded the Association for the Study of Popular Culture (Verein für Volkskunde), and in the following year began publish-ing his massive, collaborative *Dictionary of Germanic Superstition* [*Hand-wörterbuch des deutschen Aberglaubens*]. Its ten volumes, the last of which would only appear in 1942, contain over forty distinct entries relating to suicide. The main one, under the word 'Selbstmord', was by the then current president of the same Verein für Volkskunde, Paul Geiger (Geiger is a common Swiss name: the two bearers of it here were apparently unrelated). Bächtold-Stäubli's contributors drew on a multitude of local studies, mostly written in the previous 200 years, and on secondary sources generally. They identify beliefs on suicide, nooses, ghosts, burial, and many related subjects, and cover most of central and northern Europe. The *Dictionary*'s approach is comparative rather than historical, and chronology is its weak feature, so the medieval credentials of most of its data have to be tracked down criti-cally. But on suicide, although most of the data can be traced only to the centuries after 1500, just enough of it is medieval to make it useful. It incidentally gathers together material taken from Grimm's *Recht-salterthümer* and from Osenbrüggen's *Studien*.

This recirculation of borrowed material draws attention to an important feature of the historiography of medieval suicide, newly discernible at that date. It was becoming cumulative. That is especially important in respect of evidence as elusive as that on suicide. It has to be gathered by many hands. While this applies to the discovery of legal provisions, and to evidence of folklore, it is above all true of single suicide cases, buried as they are in legal archives. The works I have mentioned so far, whether or not they deliberately clung to law and ethics, had to manage with relatively few such concrete cases. This lack could only be filled by a phalanx of local historians, each familiar with a particular collection of documents. The most productive of these (for reasons arising from the different developments of European legal institutions, to be explained in Chapter 6 below), were German urban historians. Thus a Frankfurt city archivist, Georg Ludwig Kriegk (1805–78), had in the same year as Osenbrüggen's *Studien*, 1868, published a richly documented survey of urban life in medieval Frankfurt, which included a score of suicides from the city's criminal registers. His example was followed in other medieval towns with similar results, notably in Hermann Knapp's two books on Nuremberg (1896) and Regensburg (1914). Although the independence of their jurisdictions made German towns especially fruitful in this respect, urban historians in other regions were producing comparable results. For instance, histories appeared of Abbeville in 1845, by Louandre, and 1906, by Prarond, both of which exploited the Abbeville 'Red Book', a criminal register which contains suicides. These are a mere handful of examples from a big genre. In England, where most towns did not have jurisdiction over suicide, these urban histories are only matched by regional or legal studies which include particular cases from royal judicial rolls, but in feebler concentration.[26]

One local historian became particularly interested in our subject. This was Emilio Motta (1855–1920), an Italian-speaking Swiss, who after training in Zurich as an engineer, decided to devote himself to the history of his people and founded the *Bullettino Storico della Svizzera Italiana*. Much of his work was done in archives in Milan. Motta discovered few suicides there but, perhaps because of contemporary public interest, found in them enough curiosity value to publish them in separate short articles in his periodical. These brought him the acquaintance of Enrico Morselli, the famous sociologist of suicide, and this combination—of antiquarian discipline with an awareness of a wider interest in the subject—impressed on Motta the need for a bibliography. His *Bibliografia del Suicidio* duly appeared in 1890.

---

[26] For more, see pp. 99–115 below.

Its 647 entries, which Motta deliberately confined to works written *after* the sixteenth century (classical works, he said, would have been too many and would have confused the list), remained a mere fragment of available writings. Motta acknowledged this, but his variegated list made an invaluable start. Despite his self-denying ordinance, it remains more useful to a historian than a much longer bibliography published in Augsburg, in 1927, by Hans Rost. The items in the latter total 3771 but include recent newspaper articles and omit even some of the titles I have mentioned here as of medieval interest (for instance, Osenbrüggen).

I have taken the outbreak of the Second World War as a convenient *terminus ad quem* for this 'history of a history'. There can be no doubt which book marked the latter's culmination. This was Albert Bayet's *Le suicide et la morale*, published in Paris in 1922 by Alcan, Durkheim's own publisher. Albert Bayet (1880–1961) was later to become one of France's best-known intellectuals and polemicists. His approach to suicide is best understood from his background. He was born a Catholic, attending Mass every day, but at the age of 19, soon after winning a place at the École Normale Supérieure, he fell in love (romantically, at a ball) with the daughter of Alphonse Aulard, the socialist historian of the French Revolution. Aulard was an anticlerical. His published works included a pamphlet called *Oui, nous voulons détruire l'église*. Bayet joined interests with the Aulard family and adopted an anti-Catholic, Aulardian view of the world. This double history appears to have been what fuelled Bayet's lifelong preoccupation with morality, the terms 'la morale' or 'moraux' appearing in at least four of his dozen or so major published titles.[27]

Le suicide et la morale was Bayet's first book, made from a thesis that had taken him over ten years of research. Inspired by Durkheim, if with a different set of moral suppositions, it took France as its field and chronicled the law and ethics of suicide from antiquity to his own day. Of the book's 800 plus pages, the medieval section occupies 200, or well over 300 if classical and early Christian antecedents are included. Although Bayet limited his focus expressly to one country, the same antecedents necessarily extended across the Mediterranean, while he gave his French sources, medieval and later, so thorough an examination as to make his book much the richest collection so far of medieval texts on the subject. If the book has one shortcoming it is one that reflects the author's moralistic starting-point. Interested above all in the jurisprudence of suicide, Bayet distinguishes two kinds of 'morale' on the subject: 'la morale absolue' and 'la morale nuancée'. The former condemns every suicide to damnation and the

---

[27] Bayet's life: F. Féraud and C. and M. Bayet, *La vraie légende d'Albert Bayet* (Paris, 1965). The writing of 'Suicide', 61–8; 'ethologie', or 'la science des faits moraux' as Bayet's chosen procedure, 51–9; marriage to Andrée Aulard, 187–9.

disgrace of earthly memory. The latter adds 'nuance', that is, qualifications and conditions. While strictly justified by his material, the distinction makes, in my view, a basis both too rigid and too slight for a study on this scale. As a consequence the book becomes a sort of binary catalogue. It allows author and reader little flexibility to reflect on the social aetiology of the various rules or, above all, how far they were applied.

Since the Second World War an explosion of medieval scholarship generally has extended all the categories of writing so far referred to, and I will leave to the footnotes and bibliographies the burden of indicating the landmarks of recent historiography.

At the beginning of this short 'history of a history' I raised the question what motives had inspired and shaped the historical investigation of medieval suicide. Enough of the history has been traced to permit suggestions. The works listed fall roughly into three categories. The first is the legal, folkloric, anthropological, or psychological dissertation, its starting-point an acknowledged curiosity of practice or belief (like the 'punishment' of the suicide's corpse). The study then proceeds outwards and chronologically backwards from that point. The second main category is that of the monograph by a local archivist or antiquary, whose intimacy with a single repository casts him as the discoverer of historical cases, otherwise irrecoverable. The third category is that of the publicist or polemicist, a writer demonstrably concerned with the life and aspirations of people of his own day, whose writings include some on public issues other than historical. Perhaps he owes his interest in suicide to a certain moral alertness, which renders unmistakable to him its maverick character in morals, religion, and law, and its capacity to shine light on dark areas in the system. The legal theses (like Bernstein) and folklore studies (like Paul Geiger) belong to the first category. The second covers the urban and local historians, like Kriegk. Garrisson and Bayet belong to the third; and Karl August Geiger appears to have grown into it, as Catholic polemicist. Postwar scholarship still distantly extends the same categories, though with a tendency to fusion, since some scholars combine the functions of diggers and processors. But the categories remain conceptually distinct, and have often been distinct in practice. That only underlines a lesson that emerges from the historiography as a whole: the need for a cooperative approach to the subject. A study of the *least* 'social' of acts, that is to say, is the one *most* social in the kind of demand it makes on its historical students. Once more—and it will happen often again—we are in the presence of extremes.

Will the categories be successfully combined in what follows? Setting out on his journey, an author can only hope.

2

The Secrecy of Suicide

About suffering they were never wrong
The Old Masters: how well they understood
Its human position . . .
In Brueghel's *Icarus* for instance: how everything turns away
Quite leisurely from the disaster; the ploughman may
Have heard the splash, the forsaken cry,
But for him it was not an important failure.

From W. H. Auden, 'Musée des Beaux Arts'[1]

Henry of Le Dale's suicide would have caused a momentary stir in his priory and village, a stir ending probably in an unmarked grave. I have addressed the question why anyone should wish to revive his memory, and that of others who died as he did. But another question follows, not why, but how, his memory can be revived. How can a historian set about rediscovering medieval people who killed themselves?

It is always wise to start any journey of discovery by assessing obstacles. The obstacles here have in the past derived from one circumstance, the intrinsically elusive character of the suicidal act. The person who commits it usually wishes to hide while he does it. Those who discover it usually wish not to publicize it afterwards, and the subject as a whole has commonly been tabu. There are perfectly good reasons for all these inhibitions.[2] But they make the historian's task harder, not least, in our case, that preliminary part of the task that consists in showing that the obstacle obtains in our particular field. How do you set about proving that something was there, but that there was a conspiracy of silence about it? All kinds of historical fantasy would be possible if that were not proved first. This chapter will therefore address that question in respect of medieval suicide. Its method will be to show that when suicide does get into the records there

---

[1] *Collected Shorter Poems, 1927–57* (London, 1966), 123–4.
[2] R. Hirzel, 'Der Selbstmord', pt 3, *Archiv für Religionswissenschaft*, 11 (1908), 417–76, on p. 458, n. 3, illustrates the essential solitude of the act of suicide in Greek antiquity and on p. 437, n. 1, refers to 'split traditions' on ancient suicides (cf. p. 48 below). Questions about the existence and extent of ancient tabus will be the subject of a later volume, but for a parallel to the following examples of hushed circumlocution, cf. Plato, *Phaedo*, § 62B.

are usually signs that, in some way, it is trying to escape them. The chapter will be a study of elusiveness, which will be shown in this case to have had three elements, related but distinct. These were the essential privacy of the suicidal act, as sought by those who did it; the obstacles put in the path of its general discovery by the few who knew of it; and the blanket of reticence with which tradition, as a whole, sought to cover the entire subject in both the abstract and the concrete. I start with the privacy.

The Privacy of the Act

Suicide does not always have to be private. Some classical suicides, like those of Lucretia or Cato the Elder, were endowed by those who recorded them with not merely a public but a histrionic quality. They were deliberate demonstrations of a moral. Other cultures, not excluding our own, have been acquainted with this type of suicide in both literature and fact. Jumping from a crowded bridge in broad daylight is one example. But this was not usually the case in the Middle Ages. While it is true that known medieval suicides do include a handful committed in the public gaze these are, with one exception, the suicides of persons under criminal suspicion, trying to escape arrest, not seeking publicity. As a general rule suicide was the most studiously private of acts.

This feature can be detected in the various categories of record that will serve this book. It can be detected first in records from law courts. In these, when a person is 'found dead' and identified as a suicide, it is made clear also that he died alone. This is not only generally the case and implicit in most records, but is expressly stated in the more circumstantial. The place of a suicide by itself commonly says as much. Thus one English suicide happened at 'a hermitage' near Seaford in Sussex in 1288.[3] Several more were committed by prisoners held in prison or the stocks, one of whom, at Faxton in Northamptonshire in 1285, is distinctly said to have stabbed himself in the stocks 'as he sat by himself at night'.[4] When the place and time alone are unrevealing on this matter we still often encounter phrases like 'no one else being present', as in two London coroners' verdicts of 1321 and 1322.[5] And it is sometimes emphasized that the suicide knew he was alone, and even took pains to ensure that he would be. An example of the first will be

---

[3] London, PRO, JUST 1/932 m 8. All references in this form are in the Public Record Office in London.

[4] JUST 1/623 m 11.

[5] *Calendar of Coroners' Rolls of the City of London, A.D. 1300–1378*, ed. R. R. Sharpe (London, 1913), pp. 37 and 60.

a homebound invalid we shall meet in Paris in 1423. He acted 'knowing that his wife and guardian were asleep'.[6] Examples of the second are numerous. If the trial witnesses were away from the suicide's home when the act took place, they will say 'he (or she) went home and . . .'; if they were in the house, their evidence will be 'he left his house and . . . [killed himself].' We shall see many illustrations of this deliberate quest for solitude, and it can come out in vivid detail. In the earlier of those two examples from the London coroners, in 1321, a woman had waited, before hanging herself, until her son went off 'to get food from the kitchen'. If that smacks of subterfuge, there is another case that smacks more, from Westgate hospital in Newcastle upon Tyne, in 1256, when the hospital chaplain pretended to be ill when his brethren went off to night office, only, when they had gone, to get up and hang himself.[7]

In offering such vivid detail juries could sin by excess. One such, in 1290, was at Whissendene in Rutland, near Melton Mowbray. The jury was prepared to swear that a man who had drowned himself in his own fishpond had not only picked a time for the act (at night) when his wife and household were asleep, inside the house, but that, once in the garden, the proposed suicide had 'looked everywhere, and when he saw that no one else was present' taken the fatal plunge. The jury could not have known this detail. The man had by chance, it is true, still been alive when fished out of his pond. But apparently he died straight afterwards, without recovering consciousness, so the jury imagined this detail. By doing so they illustrate two things: first, the lengths to which juries would go to emphasize that none of its members had any part in the alleged suicide (no one wished to be suspected of connivance, much less of murder); and second, it also shows—especially since the court did not challenge the story—that deliberate privacy was understood as a normal condition of the act. Why should anyone challenge it?[8]

A similar lesson is taught by religious literature, with its miracle stories. It might be thought that these, being imaginative, cannot rank as historical evidence. I shall say more on that. But the Whissendene jury has already shown how the boundary between judicial record and literary narrative was less than absolute. Miracles, for their part, even when they are not based on a manifestly factual incident, depended for their effect on being set in a probable context, so they at least tell us what people expected. This is especially relevant in respect of a suicide's quest for secrecy, since miraculous

[6] A. Longnon, ed., *Paris sous la domination anglaise, 1420–1436* (Paris, 1878), 111.

[7] W. Page, ed., 'Three early Assize rolls for the County of Northumberland', *Surtees Society*, 88 (1890), 83.

[8] London, PRO, E 368/61 m 21.

stories, by contrast with judicial evidence, normally concentrated on what came before the proposed act, rather than what followed it.

Miracle stories involving suicide repeatedly mention the perpetrator's quest for secrecy. Out of some eighty plus available stories on the subject only one tells of a deliberately public suicide. It is a leap from a public tower at Soest in Westphalia, placed around 1200 by the narrator, Caesarius of Heisterbach.[9] All Caesarius' other relevant stories—and these are, as it happens, on other grounds the more 'likely' ones—reflect the solitude of the act. An intending suicide will fall behind the party on an outing; climb into an attic; go outside 'with no one looking', or (in a monastery), rise while other monks are asleep, before attempting the deed.[10] Caesarius has been mentioned first because he is responsible for the only exception. It can be seen as an exception even from examples within his own collection. Outside it, the deliberate privacy of suicide is universal, and runs from one end to the other of the medieval period. In Gregory of Tours, already in the late sixth century, we read of a disgraced functionary who 'found a moment to escape' his family's suspicious vigilance and 'took advantage of being alone' to kill himself.[11] The motif burgeons in the twelfth century. A girl in a miracle by Thomas Becket waits until her mother has gone to church before attempting it.[12] Another girl, in a miracle of St Frideswide, will make her attempt *nocte . . . clanculo* (secretly and at night).[13] A third, this time a grown-up mother, in Rennes in Brittany, will fall back from the crowd before attempting to drown herself.[14] Examples could go on. The similarity of this trait to its equivalent in judicial records is unmistakable.

Both in diffusion and diversity the trait can indeed be said to be among the most general in this type of narrative. It is normal, for instance, in suicide miracles attributed to the Virgin Mary. In the most widely known of such Marian miracles, one known in many different versions, the secrecy of the act is part of the hardy core of all versions. In one the heroine makes her attempt 'when all the maids have left the house';[15] while in another version, the longest and most embellished of all (and in verse) the quest for privacy is described in hair-raising detail. I here attempt to reproduce the

---

[9] *Dialogus miraculorum*, distinctio 5, ch. 35; ed. J. Strange, 2 vols. (Cologne, Bonn, and Brussels, 1851), vol. 1, 318–19.

[10] The texts are set out below on pp. 336–9 and 344–5.

[11] *Historia Francorum*, bk 4, ch. 39[26]; *Monumenta Germaniae Historica, Scriptores rerum merovingicarum*, vol. 1 (Hanover, 1951), 171. 10–14.

[12] *Miracula s. Thomae Cantuarensis auctore Willelmo*, bk 3, ch. 3; *Materials for the History of Thomas Becket*, ed. J. C. Robertson. Rolls Series, vol. 1 (London, 1875), 258.

[13] *Miracula s. Frideswidae*, § 31; *Acta Sanctorum*, Oct. 8 (1853), 574 D.

[14] *Miraculum s. Melanii Redonensis*, § 2; *Acta sanctorum*, Jan. 1 (1643), 334, col. b A.

[15] J. Klapper 'Erzählungen des Mittelalters', *Wort und Brauch* (Breslau, 1914), no. 106.

verses in English. The heroine climbs down to a dark cellar before attempting her suicide:

> So long neglected had it been,
> The air was foul, rats fled unseen,
> Its walls all spiders, lice and smut,
> Its windows dark, its door now shut.[16]

This last quotation, it is true, is from a work of all but the purest imagination. But it only extended a trait common in any miracle story with a suicidal element. Most of these concern attempts, and because the 'hero' lives to tell the tale, he can give a convincing account of the subterfuges he has employed to win privacy. One such case is that of a Cistercian lay-brother who suffered from leprosy at the Belgian monastery of Villers, *c*.1300. The episode is reminiscent of that of the chaplain in Newcastle upon Tyne, quoted just now. The leprous lay-brother at Villers was worn out by disease, and by the very solitude it imposed on him. He resolved on suicide, and chose a night when neither his fellow-monks nor the abbey dogs, especially the latter, could be expected to interfere. So he selected Christmas Eve, when the dogs were chained and the monks in church. He was interrupted, and hence survived to tell someone all that.[17] Another such attempt, blocked by divine intervention, is from William of Canterbury's collection of Becket miracles. A girl, youngest of several sisters, stays awake all night planning her suicide. When the time comes, she goes into the inner room of the house on the pretence of tending her infant brother. But in fact, after shutting the door, she gets out of a window to reach the well where she proposes to drown herself. Again, as is usual with miracles, she was saved, so could reveal these preparations and how essential privacy was to them.[18]

Where the miracle story has usually its own mixture of fact and fiction, descriptions of suicide in what we usually call 'secular literature' are in one sense not a mixture at all. They are pure fiction. But for that very reason they too observe a kind of realism, for what function can fiction serve if it does not describe recognizable situations? So it is instructive that in medieval literary pictures of the suicidal condition a wish for solitude is normal. It enters as an elaboration of a theme found in some, if not all, classical

---

[16] Paris, Bibl. Nat., MS fr. 1546, fol. 137r: 'i leu en un destour estoit / ou assez de vermine avoit / Diraignes et de cloportes / Cele ot clos son huis et ces portes.'

[17] *Hist. monasterii Villariensis in Brabantia*, bk 3, ch. 8; E. Martène and U. Durand, *Thesaurus novus anecdotorum* (Paris, 1717), vol. 3, cols. 1368–9. Cf. F. Bourquelot, 'Recherches sur les opinions et la législation en matière de mort volontaire pendant le moyen âge', *Bibliothèque de L'École des Chartes*, 3 (1842–4) [= pt 1]; 4 (1844), 242–66 [= pt 2]; 456–75 [= pt 3]; pt 2, pp. 250–1; pt 2, pp. 250–1; J.-C. Schmitt, 'Le suicide au moyen âge', *Annales. Économies, Sociétes, Civilisations*, 31 (1976), 3–28; p. 26 n. 69; and below, pp. 320–2.

[18] As in n. 12 above.

models. An example is the twelfth-century French *Eneas*. Its author expands on nine pregnant words in his Virgilian model,[19] to describe, in almost as many lines, the dying Dido's insistence on solitude. Here is an attempt at the jingle, line by line:

> Leave me, O sister, Dido pleaded,
> Anxious not to be impeded
> Or observed, in the dread plan
> That in her fevered temples ran.
> Her sister left. She shut the door.
> The room was quieter than before
> With none to meddle, none to see
> The queen in her insanity.[20]

As French romance gained autonomy in the late twelfth century this feature strengthened its hold. Chrétien de Troyes' Yvain picks on a moment for his attempt because 'if I do it now no one will see me.'[21] The heartbroken Partenopeus of Blois—in a poem also dating from the last few decades of the twelfth century—resolves to die, and thinks he will be too closely watched in his native city.[22] In the early thirteenth-century French romance *Yder*, Queen Guenoïe sees to it that her retinue is dismissed before she goes off to stab herself in a lonely wood. There, her last act is to glance round to make sure no one sees: another scene of pure imagination, to be sure, and here a palpable literary device too—for in that last glance the queen sees the agent of her delivery, so that the story can end happily.[23] But still that does not change the underlying message. Secrecy was part of the act.

It might, of course, be said that this quest was a matter of mere mechanics. The suicide knew other people would obstruct him. That leper of Villers, solitary enough for most of the time, was concerned above all to make his attempt when the abbey dogs were tied up. The details attributed to other attempts may suggest the same practical motives, even in literature, as in the description just quoted from *Eneas*. Barring the occasional suicide

---

[19] *Aeneid*, bk 4, lines 452, 456.
[20] Lines 2020–7 (ed. J. J. Salverda de Grave (Paris, 1985), 62): 'la chambre bien delivrer / ne voloit pas que ele i fust, / qu'ele ne li contresteüst / et ne fust par li destorbé / ce qu avoit an volanté. / En la chanbre est tot solement, / n'i a qui li destort noiant / la desverie qu'el velt faire.'
[21] *Yvain*, line 3546 (ed. W. Förster (1912); reprint, ed. T. B. W. Reid (Manchester 1984), 98): 'tant con nus ne me voit.'
[22] *Partonopeus de Blois*, line 5495; ed. G. A. Crapelet, 2 vols. (Paris, 1834), vol. 2, p. 15: lines 5461–5: 'De soi ocire est li porpens, / mais ne li loe pas ses sens / Qu'il le commena à Blois à faire; / car il n'en poroit à cief traire, / Tant fort le gardent si ami.'
[23] *The Romance of Yder*, ed. A. Adams. Arthurian Studies, 8 (Cambridge, 1983), 110, 112. Cf. F. P. Knapp, *Der Selbstmord in der abendländischen Epik des Hochmittelalters* (Heidelberg, 1979), 185–6. Date: Adams, 11–13.

pact, family and bystanders would normally do all they could to prevent a suicide. They were, of course, never tired of telling this to courts. But there is no reason for the historian to disbelieve them.

A suicide's quest for privacy might, then, reflect no deeper motive than a tactical attempt to avoid interference. But it would be wrong to exclude a more radical reading. The quest was more instinctive. The suicide might go as far as to wish no one would *ever* know of his act, at the time or afterwards. Such a wish naturally forms one of the blackest of black holes in our evidence. So secret a deed, if successful, would retreat for ever from all human knowledge, the historian's included. But once more it is the edges of the black hole that show it is there. In several court cases the argument, back and forth, turns on whether a certain death was self-inflicted or not. The fallible court—and they often showed each other to be fallible by reversing each other's decisions—had only to make a wrong diagnosis once for there to be a 'case of the vanished suicide'. This probably suited what the dead man himself wanted. The manner of his death, if he had his way, would never, ever, be known.

This cannot of course be proved to the hilt from court records, but reason to take it seriously can be found once more in literature. The most painstaking of all medieval portraits of the suicidal mind, and by an author noted for realism, gives strong emphasis to this desire for suppression. Boccaccio's *Fiammetta* was written about 1343. Its heroine, an imaginary noblewoman, reviews in her mind the kinds of self-inflicted death open to her from the examples of the ancients. She settles finally on throwing herself from a height precisely because the death it would bring would be, not only certain and instant, but permanently unrecognizable as suicide: 'free from all infamy . . . people would never think my death had been caused by any cruelty or madness, but would impute it rather to an accidental fall, and blame fortune, and shed sympathetic tears on my behalf.'[24] Boccaccio's portrait was an attempt to depict, for sensitive contemporaries, a suicidal intention readers would have known how to criticize if the portrait had been wrong.

Its Concealment Afterwards

That a person about to kill himself looked for privacy is an obstacle to later historians. But long before that it was an obstacle also to judicial officers,

---

[24] *Fiammetta*, ch. 6, ed. C. Salinari and N. Sapegno. La Letteratura Italiana: Storia e Testi, 8, ed. E. Bianchi, C. Salinari and V. Sapegno (Milan and Naples, 1952), 1181.

These officers understood it as axiomatic that both suicides and their families sought to conceal this type of death. Part of their officers' duty was to uncover the subterfuge. Proof of this principle is to be found mainly in legal writings of a general character, like statutes and treatises, and especially—because of peculiarities in the legal growth of the areas concerned—in France and the Rhineland, rather than England. But what they say was in essence true anywhere. Two law-codes in particular make this clear. From Lille in the late thirteenth century there survives a code which expressly underlines the problems implicit in the identification of suicide. As the main reason, it sees the dying person's own quest for secrecy. Thus when a dead body is found, the code lays down, the authorities' suspicions should include suicide even if no one reports it: 'for he who attempts this desperate act never willingly does it openly'.[25] A comparable code of customs from Baden-in-Aargau in Switzerland, whose surviving text dates from 1384, prefaces its provisions on suicide with the condition that such-and-such is customarily done 'if someone commits suicide and if it becomes known',[26] as if the authors knew perfectly well that suicide often did not.

But it is a servant of the rising monarchy of thirteenth-century France who reveals this assumption most clearly. Philippe de Beaumanoir wrote his handbook for provincial royal justices, known usually as *baillis*, between 1280 and 1283. Beaumanoir wrote from experience, and inserted a long section on what in England would have been called coroner's duties: how to discover whether a death was natural or otherwise. When Beaumanoir comes to the subject of suicide the question he dwells on most is precisely how to tell it *is* suicide. A royal judge was often called on to decide these cases since the outcome determined, according to the law then and there, whether the dead man's goods went to his lord or to his family. So Beaumanoir gives detailed prescriptions. Sometimes his advice is straightforward 'for instance if the dead man is found hanged or if he has said "I shall drown myself" or "I shall kill myself, for this or that injury or misfortune I have suffered." '[27] But sometimes (and the space he gives it suggests this was common) 'the matter is so obscure that the truth cannot be known.'[28] Then, Beaumanoir says, it is of the utmost importance that the judge should investigate the circumstances and manner of death. The judge should discover,

---

[25] [F. de] Roisin, *Franchises, lois, et coutumes de la ville de Lille* (Lille, 1844), 121: 'car qui tel fait vuit faire et tel desperanche, ne se le fait-il mie volentiers en apiert.' Cf. Bourquelot, pt 2, p. 266.

[26] F. E. Welti and W. Merz, *Die Rechtsquellen des Kantons Argau*, pt 1: *Stadtrechte*, Vol. 2: *Die Stadtrechte von Baden und Brugg*. Sammlung schweizerischer Rechtsquellen, 16 (Arau, 1899), 46.17: 'und das kuntlich wäre'.

[27] *Coutumes de Beauvaisis*, § 1948; ed. A. Salmon (Paris, 1899–1900), vol. 2, p. 482.

[28] Ibid., § 1949; pp. 483–4.

for instance, whether the well in which the body was found was near to the home of the deceased, and was the well to which the deceased normally went to fetch water. He should discover whether the place was much-frequented or secluded. If the latter, it is more likely that the death was suicide: suicide here being discovered, be it noted, by its very quest for secrecy. After that he should enquire whether the deceased had enemies or had been threatened; whether he was drunk or mentally deranged; and so on.

Implicit in Beaumanoir's elaborate guidelines is a fundamental principle, and he ends by stating it: that suicide is often literally incapable of full proof. If a judge has to decide a case he must do so on the balance of presumptions, bearing in mind always that the presumptions must be 'open' before he can think of justifying forfeiture.[29] Beaumanoir cites a case to drive these points home. It was a case at whose hearing he had himself been present. A woman had died. Her lord alleged suicide on the grounds of a total of four *presompcions*, and took her property. Her heirs objected on the grounds that even if they granted these presumptions, which they did not, presumption was insufficient evidence to support the appropriation. The case was taken to a royal justice. The royal justice upheld the lord on a combination of two grounds: that the presumptions were strong (the decisive one being that the dead woman had previously threatened to 'do something to shame her friends'), and that in the context of this charge 'in all such obscure cases it is only by the force of presumptions that the truth can be known or proved.'[30] The uncertainty of suicide could not have been stated with more certainty.

Shame in Retrospect

The relations and close friends of a suicide, then, had reason to wish to hide or disguise the deed. In most places in medieval Europe legal consequences would threaten the next of kin, including loss of property. But here again it would be wrong, in assessing their motives for secrecy, to stop short at the most tangible. A suicide in the family was also a matter of shame.

To begin with, shame, not economic loss, was the issue on which families laid most emphasis when appealing to judges not to condemn their dead kinsmen for killing themselves. In some areas posthumous punishments for suicide were deliberately public. Here family disgrace gave the family as strong a motive for resisting, as the judges had for procuring, condemnation. Family honour is in these areas a regular element in appeals. In an

[29] Ibid., § 1952, p. 485.   [30] Ibid., § 1951; pp. 484–5.

appeal to the French Parlement in 1386–7, for instance, the widow of a man whose death looked *prima facie* like suicide pleaded for posthumous acquittal because 'she fears that the corpse of her husband may be judicially disgraced, which would be a perpetual reproach [*reprouche perpetuel*] to herself and her children.'[31] In a similar case in 1421 the appeal expresses the fear 'the supplicants and others, namely their relations and friends, who are notable people and of good descent, would suffer public insult [*vitupérez*] if the corpse had to be publicly executed.'[32] The notion that the punishment would strike especially hard at people of good social standing is also present in another French example of 1426. There the advocate for a widow and her family, in a case of suspected suicide, writes that public disgrace for the body 'could redound to the dishonour and prejudice of the said supplicants, who are well-established people of good reputation'.[33] Punishments in late medieval France were exceptionally degrading. That is one reason why testimony to this theme is available there. But the theme was not confined to one country. A notable case in Frankfurt, for instance, would be that of the city councillor Peter Becker, imprisoned for corruption in 1486. He committed suicide in prison and his sons, no doubt already overwhelmed by the measure of disgrace already incurred by their household, are found 'writing to beg that their father be not treated according to the city's tradition'— burial in the carrion-pit in broad daylight—'but to bury him by night'. A twilight compromise was reached 'so that the children do not suffer worse contumely [*nit ferner gesmehet werden*]'.[34] Similar cases from other towns in southern Germany emphasize the same feature.[35]

To have a suicide in the family was a matter of shame. Laws like those just referred to, which punished by publicizing the offence, drew their force from the shame that attached to suicide anyway. It is true that support went the other way too: shame and the laws fortified each other. But if any doubts remained about the independence of shame as a motive for concealment, they are settled by its presence even in societies free of repressive suicide laws. Late medieval Italian communes met this condition, yet the best authority on the matter still speaks of family disgrace. In Dante's suicide canto in *Inferno*, the poet ends by referring to a Florentine suicide whom Dante keeps studiously anonymous.[36] The anonymity puzzled commenta-

---

[31] Paris, Arch. nat., J.J. 130, fol. 152v. See below, p. 225.

[32] Longnon, *Paris sous la domination anglaise*, 19. Below, p. 222.

[33] Ibid., 208.

[34] G. L. Kriegk, *Deutsches Bürgerthum im Mittelalter mit besonderer Beziehung auf Frankfurt-am-Main* (Frankfurt-am-Main, 1868), 549, n.188.

[35] J. Dieselhorst, 'Die Bestrafung der Selbstmörder im Territorium der Stadt Nürnberg', *Mitteilungen des Vereins für Geschichte der Stadt Nürnberg*, 44 (1953), 64–5.

[36] *Inferno*, 13: 131–51.

tors, and Boccaccio, commenting on the passage in *c*.1370, suggests one reason why Dante kept the name quiet may have been 'through regard for surviving relations, who may perhaps be men of honour; and therefore Dante does not wish to stain them with the disgrace of such a shameful death.'[37] Benvenuto da Imola wrote a commentary on the same passage at about the same time. Perhaps considering various candidates for the suicide Dante may have had in mind, Benvenuto opts for the one of highest rank, 'because his offence would have been worse'.[38]

Law or no law, in other words, a suicide in the family was something the family would prefer to shroud in silence.

Discretion

While a family's shame attached to a particular suicide, a more general disposition of reticence attached to the subject of suicide in the abstract. Even to suggest it might ever be a right course of action was 'wicked'. By that I translate the Latin *nefas est dicere*, used by St Augustine of his opponents' position, in what is much the longest theological treatment of the subject available to medieval Christians, his chapters in Book I of *The City of God*.[39] One striking feature of theologians' writings after Augustine will be the sheer absence of mention of suicide as a subject; and it is likely that there, too, the concept that suicide was *nefas* played a part.[40] Our quarry now will be people, not an abstract subject, so all we need do is see how this wide inhibition applied also to narratives. It meant that when storytellers did mention suicide they did so with an anxious glance over their shoulders, as if the reader is being let into matters normally kept secret.

An example is at hand in a miracle attributed to Thomas Becket by his devotee, William of Canterbury. The martyr, William says, rescued a certain woman from suicide. 'Certain' there translates *quaedam*. In fact William

[37] *Esposizioni sopra la Comedia di Dante*, ed. G. Padovan, in V. Branca, ed., *Tutte le opera di Giovanni Boccaccio*, vol. 6 (Milan, 1965), 619: 'Nè è costui dall'autor nominato, credo per l'una delle due cagioni: o per i quali per avventura sono onorevoli uomini, e perciò non glivuole maculare della infamia di così disonesta morte.' For the alternative see p. 86 below.

[38] Benvenuto de Rambaldis de Imola, *Comentum super Dantis . . . Comoediam*, ed. J. P. Lacaita, vol. 1 (Florence, 1887), 460: 'Et crede, quod autor de industria sic fecerit, ut posset intelligi de unoquoque talium, licet forte possit intelligi potius de judice, quia erat maioris pretii, et gravius deliquit.' The Italian translation of Benvenuto's commentary by G. Tamburini (Imola, 1855), 340, mistranslates this passage and obscures its significance in the present respect.

[39] *De Civitate Dei*, bk 1, ch. 27; *Corpus Scriptorum Ecclesiasticorum Latinorum*, 40, section 5, part 1 (Turnholt, 1955) 28.38–41.

[40] The silence of early theologians will be discussed in *The Curse on Self-Murder* (ch. 6).

left her *un*certain, and had to battle with his own literary instincts to do so, for specific identification befitted a miracle collection of this sort, compiled to boost a saint. Most of William's stories meet this standard. But here, suddenly, like Dante later with his 'anonymous Florentine', and apparently for the same reason, William made a stark exception. He not only does not say who the 'certain woman' was. In this one, solitary story of his collection, he ensures the woman's anonymity so systematically as to produce a model of opacity. Let us read his whole story (or non-story).

A certain man [*vir aliquis*: the man, too, is uncertain] told me his wife had tried to take her life with a noose and showed me the halter she had put round her neck. But I do not wish to reveal her turpitude, since the man himself had kept the fact hidden from neighbours and relations, so that the miracle should not cause them confusion [*ne confundantur ex martyris visitatione*]. I speak of her deed in a general way [*de genere*]. What she did I leave shrouded for the sake of shame [*salvo pudore sub lodice relinquo*]. *Why* she did it I imagine to have been a suggestion of the Devil. *Where* she did it—lest I be charged with not saying [*ne nihil dicatur*]? In the world. *When* she did it? I have heard but have forgotten. She was saved from death by St Thomas and by her husband: the former by the means of his prayers; the latter by means of a knife.[41]

Later we shall reflect how few miracle stories, in relation to the vast number extant, refer to human rescues from suicide, that is, rescues other than by supernatural agency. So let the foregoing 'non-story' be remembered. To include an anecdote of this kind a good storyteller might have to accept literary humiliations which might prove a deterrent. His task was like that of a modern advertiser of cigarettes. He had to say it and not say it, all at once, so great was the dishonour attached to an individual suicide. The deterrent was such that a good narrator usually would not have told the story (or non-story) at all.

The miracle-writer who most conspicuously overcame this deterrent was Caesarius of Heisterbach, probably the best known of all medieval raconteurs of *miracula*. He was the exception that proves the rule. Caesarius' miracles drew heavily on his own experience and that of acquaintances, and were recorded in 1219–23 in his big Rhineland monastery near Bonn. While Caesarius' suicide stories constitute the richest single narrative treasury extant on the subject, it is again precisely here, in the most infor-

---

[41] *Miracula s. Thomae Cantuariensis*, bk 6, ch. 141 (ed. J. C. Robertson, 524). The tension under which the author is suffering, as he seeks simultaneously to give and withhold these details, was clearly accentuated by the requirement, foreshadowing that imposed by the *forma interrogatorii* applied to canonization miracles from the late thirteenth century, to give a particular set of data about the alleged miracle (Why? When? Where?). Cf. A. Vauchez, *La Sainteté en Occident* (Rome, 1981), 58–9.

mative of documents, that we learn why there were so few others. At the end of his first narrative in the group, on an attempted suicide, Caesarius writes:

I could tell you many recent examples of this sort of depression [*tristitia*], but I fear it would endanger weaker souls to read or hear such things [*quod infirmis non expediat talia legere vel audire*].[42]

At this point the storyteller and novice-master (which he was) wrestled within Caesarius' breast. The story-teller triumphed, for Caesarius goes brazenly on, the tabu once breached, to tell five more stories on the same subject. Perhaps in the few seconds in which Caesarius was expressing that fear the novice-master had changed sides, for the grim stories which he does relate are not presented without a moral. When the second opens, it is with concession to a different, and less inhibiting, principle:

When I speak or write of this sort of unspeakable [*nefandis*] tragedy I am not prepared to give the names of places or people, or the sort of religious order [*ordinis qualitatem*] involved, lest I seem to cover monks or nuns with some sort of shame [*ne aliquam religiosis inferre videar verecundiam*].[43]

In William of Canterbury's story the tension between the explicit and the obscure was so strong as to produce a literary curio. In Caesarius, the same immediacy, which earns most of Caesarius' stories historical attention, exposes his misgivings, augmented by the wish of a novice-master not to upset weaker minds. In opposite ways, the two writers reveal the same restraints.

These restraints, more tangible in some authors than others, are suffused throughout the miracle literature. Their presence is occasionally betrayed in a mere phrase. For instance, Andreas of Fleury-sur-Loire, who contributed to a collection of *Miracles of St Benedict* around 1050, told of an attempted suicide he had once witnessed as a child. Its very first words are: 'As the Apostle says "We cannot but speak of that which we have seen and heard."' We would be deaf not to hear that note of apology for raising the matter at all.[44]

The examples given so far have illustrated three express motives for silence on the subject of suicide: a feeling that the subject was *nefas*; a reluctance to shame relations; and a sense that bad examples could endanger the vulnerable. This sense of danger is implied by the very concept of things *nefas*, and could affect even a person who contemplated suicide. In the case

[42] *Dialogus miraculorum*, dist. 4, ch. 40; ed. J. Strange, vol. 1, 210.
[43] Ibid., ch. 41.
[44] *Miracula s. Benedicti*, bk 7, ch. 9 (ed. E. de Certain (Paris, 1858) 265). The reference is to Acts 4:20.

of completed suicides our witnesses have to be others, namely the survivors. In the case of mere attempts, testimony can come from the would-be suicide himself, or, if anyone has learned of it, his relations or acquaintances. In a third circumstance, that of mere temptation, evidence is much more likely to come exclusively from the victim himself, that is, if it comes at all, for such people did not easily speak of it. An example from Nuremberg will illustrate this. Around 1340 a Nuremberg citizen went to seek spiritual counsel from a holy nun who lived near the town, Adelaide Langmann. The citizen was deeply anxious, and kept speaking of a 'great temptation' that had weighed on him for nine years. He said he had never confessed it to his priest, nor revealed it to anybody else, and did not even wish to identify it to Sister Adelaide herself. She nevertheless divined it. It was the temptation to suicide, she said.[45] How, the modern reader may ask, had she divined it? The principal clue, surely, had been the very extreme of secrecy in which her visitor had wished to hide it. The lawyer Philippe de Beaumanoir identified suicide by the secrecy of the place of a death. Adelaide, the spiritual counsellor, knew enough of the soul to identify her visitor's private agony by the same reasoning.

Euphemism

The examples in this chapter will, I hope, combine to form an instrument helpful in the interpretation of all others. There were reasons—some have been seen and others are still to be seen—for thinking, speaking, and writing of suicide. But in their absence, and in the background even in their presence, the subject was not to be mentioned. The fragments of witness that do survive are better understood when we recognize the inhibition they had to overcome.

One last consideration will complete this preliminary lesson. There are few more sensitive indices to the suppressed areas of our thought, whether as individuals or as cultures, than euphemism. Euphemisms identify—and again it is by attempting to conceal it that they do so—what it is in our milieu we cannot easily digest. The indigestible things cannot be spirited away and may demand description. But we wish, usually on perfectly good grounds, that they were not so, so we refer to them with contrived imprecision. A study of these imprecisions is a guide to the psychology of those who use them. This is the case with medieval references to suicide, and an

---

[45] 'Die Offenbarungen der Adelheid Langmann, Klosterfrau zu Engelthal', ed. P. Strauch, in B. ten Brink and others, eds. *Quellen und Forschungen zur Sprach- und Kulturgeschichte der germanischen Völker*, 26 (Strasbourg, 1878), 44–5.

outline of medieval euphemisms on it will conclude this assessment of its innate secrecy.

Two recent studies of suicide in classical Rome have listed the wide variety of terms used for suicide in classical Latin, and drawn suggestive conclusions.[46] Among medieval authorities, especially the more classically minded, we shall often meet such classical terms: like *mortem sibi consciscere* (to inflict death on oneself), and *manus sibi inferre* (to raise a hand against oneself).[47] In medieval writings these terms have a different significance than in classical ones. This is not merely because the passage of each century adds a measure of archaism to the use of any classical term—even in Roman law where both those terms were common—but because of a radical difference in culture. Suicide was shameful in the medieval world as it was not in Rome, at least among the articulate classes. In medieval language these Roman terms therefore served as part of the vocabulary for expressing things people were reluctant to express. It will be shown later that Roman example gave twelfth-century writers both a stimulus and an opportunity to speak of the unspeakable. The same was true of Roman terms. Besides betraying the self-conscious erudition that such terms commonly evoke, the use of Roman expressions for suicide was, for medieval writers, already halfway to euphemism. That is commonly the case with terms borrowed from another language (as when we speak of a *ménage à trois* or an *inamorato*).

If doubt remained on this point it would be removed by the evidence of other euphemisms. Many medieval accounts of death leave a modern reader uncertain whether that author is referring to suicide or not. It is an unfortunate trait of writers of history books that they seek to extend their empires by interpreting terms with a bias that increases the importance of their subject. I am not immune to that temptation, but I am conscious of it and determined to resist. I hope the reader will judge when, and when not, among the examples in this book, we may be in the presence of a euphemism for suicide. The use of the expression 'to die of grief', for instance, will be shown in literature sometimes, but not always, to represent the deliberate softening of a suicidal incident in a model. The same expression in a chronicle or *exemplum* may, or again may not, envisage suicide. A storyteller as rich in contemporary detail as Caesarius of Heisterbach, and writing some forty years later, was the Dominican Thomas of Chantimpré.

---

[46] Y. Grisé, *Le suicide dans la Rome antique* (Montreal and Paris, 1982), 21–8, 291–7; A. J. L. Van Hoof, *From Autothanasia to Suicide* (London, 1990), 246–50.

[47] e.g. William of Malmesbury, *Gesta regum*, bk 2, § 139 in *Opera*, vol. 1, ed. W. Stubbs, Rolls Series (1887), 156; 'voluntarie in aquas praecipitio mortem conscivit'; Guido Vernani, in Venice, Bibl. Marciana, MS Lat. VI, cod. 94 (2492), fol. 14v: 'manus sibi iniciens'. These are typical of many similar borrowings of classical expressions for suicide.

He is an instructive example. On the boundary where Caesarius had hesitated, Thomas stopped dead. He never, ever, tells a story explicitly of a suicide. We hear a circumstantial story of a suicidal temptation, but no direct description of the completed act. On the other hand, several of Thomas's stories end with a hybrid reference to the subject's manner of death, a reference fuller than it needs to be, but less full than it has to be, if we are to understand exactly what the author has in mind. Thus an old woman who lost her long-maintained virginity 'through excessive remorse hastened her death in misery'.[48] A youth got into trouble and 'with the utmost impatience fell into despair and died'.[49] Among two or three other instances in Thomas's long collection are two references to gamblers, one of the proverbial stigmas of whose pastime was that it renders men, to use Thomas's words, *desperatissimi*.[50] It happens that one of Caesarius' suicides was a bankrupt gambler, and *exempla* from other sources can speak explicitly of such gamblers as committing suicide.[51] They help us judge Thomas's hybrid allusion. Once more he has said too little to certify that the death was suicide but too much to certify the opposite. It is as if he were deliberately looking for euphemistic expressions for suicide, for if he were, these would be precisely the sort of expressions he would use.

Thomas of Chantimpré is an especially instructive example of this trait, which one recent writer has felicitously termed, in the same connection, a 'rhetoric of confusion'.[52] But we shall see many more. One, for instance, will concern Wolo, a monk of St Gall. Wolo had a mysterious fall 'by the push, it is believed, of the Devil'. The episode is otherwise alluded to as Wolo's 'sin' when no actual sin is mentioned other than the 'fall', and the most elaborate liturgical measures are taken to help Wolo's soul, even though he made full confession of everything before he expired, and had absolution.[53] Other instances will include a twelfth-century classicizing tale whose Roman hero, begging permission from the Senate to commit suicide, cannot, when it comes to the point, even use a Latin euphemism for suicide

---

[48] *Bonum universale de apibus* [= *De apibus*], bk 2, ch. 30 § 47 [edn. of Douai, 1627, p. 353]: 'prae nimia amaritudine mortem acceleraret in planctu'. The expression *mortis acceleratio* is used less equivocally for suicide in, for instance, *Miracula s. Frideswidae, Acta Sanctorum*, Oct. 8 (1853), 576F; and in *Historia croylandensis, continuatio B*, in W. Fulman, ed., *Rerum Anglicarum Scriptores veteri* (Oxford, 1684), 519.

[49] *De apibus*, bk 2, ch. 51, § 9 [p. 476]. 'impatientissime desperatus mortus est'. A later chapter (pt 2, ch. 11) will examine meanings of the word *desperatus* and its cognates.

[50] Ibid., bk 2, ch. 49, § 8; (p. 448). cf. p. 310.

[51] See below, pp. 309–10.

[52] G. Signori, 'Aggression und Selbstzerstörung', in *Trauer, Verzweiflung und Anfechtung* (Tübingen, 1994), 123, with reference to elliptical references to suicide in early sixteenth-century German miracle books: 'eine Rhetorik dur Verwirrung'. She rightly, in my view, leaves open the question whether the 'rhetoric' was conscious or unconscious.

[53] See below, pp. 340–3.

but asks for, in the poet's words, 'the ambiguous gift with deliberate avoidance of the name [*ambiguum, sublato nomine, munus*]'.[54]

The significance of all these expressions can be judged in their place. But as illustrations of the variety of form such euphemisms could take, as well as their sometimes palpable character, one more especially deserves mention. It concerns 'misfortune'. The question is sometimes raised in connection with English coroners' records, of all periods, whether some verdicts of *infortunium*, or 'accident', may in reality have concealed suicides. That problem is among the most familiar in legal history. What is certain is that medieval professional lawyers were capable of using the word as a direct synonym *for* suicide, so customary had the euphemism become. That is, the word *infortunium* literally *means* suicide. The author of *Fleta*, a law treatise written probably under Edward I between 1290 and 1292, includes a chapter exclusively and expressly about suicide under the heading 'De infortuniis'.[55] The legerdemain could not be plainer. The same is to be heard in practical parlance. There, the tension it involved comes out in palpable self-contradictions. Thus a Yorkshire coroner's roll of 1355 tells of a man who was drowned *per infortunium* 'by the temptation of the Devil'.[56] Why 'by temptation of the Devil' if it was just bad luck? Another coroner's roll, from Shropshire in 1401, speaks likewise of a woman who 'per infortunium' drowned herself 'of her own free will'.[57] Further examples could be given.[58] As often happens in an area of factual uncertainty, consciousness of judicial error may have fed this particular verbal confusion. If a judge wishes to hide from himself that he has given an imperfect verdict, muddled language can help. But the two are not the same thing. The verbal confusion was conceptual; and, in the half-conscious way that euphemisms are, intentional.

Euphemism means reference to something by a term other than the proper one. A problem in medieval language in respect of suicide is that there *was* no proper term. The title of this book is in that important respect

---

[54] Bernard Silvestris, *Mathematicus*, Cantus 13, line 665; *Pat. Lat.* 171, 1377C.

[55] *Fleta*, bk 1, ch. 34, ed. H. G. Richardson and G. O. Sayles. Selden Society, 72 (London, 1955), 89.

[56] JUST 2/215 m 5: 'per temptacionem diaboli submersus fuit per inforunium'. Verdict: *Infortunium*. See R. F. Hunnisett, *The Medieval Coroner* (Cambridge, 1961), 21.

[57] JUST 2/148 m 4: 'seipsam per infortunium spontanee . . . demersit'. Verdict: 'Felo de se'.

[58] H. M. Chew and M. Weinbaum, eds., *The London Eyre of 1244*. London Record Society, 6 (1970), 55, no. 141: 'infortunium de se ipsa'. Two further instances show oscillation in the verdict. An Essex coroner's roll of 1389 [JUST 2/33a m 15 d no. 14] writes *infortunium* clearly in the margin when the corresponding entry says of a man that he 'Spontanea voluntate . . . Se suspendit cum corda'. A Wiltshire coroner's roll [JUST 2/202 m 2 d no. 3] similarly puts *infortunium* in the margin of an apparent suicide, while in a different ink *infortunium* was then deleted and replaced by *felo de se*.

anachronistic. But everything is evidence, even a vacuum. So let us try, finally, to read the meaning of this one.

The Word 'Suicide'

It is frequently stated in books on suicide that the word came into existence in English in the seventeenth century, appearing first in Sir Thomas Browne's *Religio Medici* in 1637 and subsequently gaining ground in the English language, and soon afterwards in French. The word has a Latin basis, *suicidium* putatively meaning 'killing of oneself' on analogy with genuinely Latin words like *homicidium* and *matricidium*. In view of this basis, the late origin may seem surprising, even to those familiar with the influence of classical Latin in English authors of Sir Thomas Browne's period. Significance has been read into it and no doubt rightly. But for medievalists the history of the word is more significant still. It had already been coined in the twelfth century.

The word *suicida* occurs, once each in two successive lines, in a work by the Paris Augustinian canon Walter of St Victor: *De quatuor labyrinthos Franciae*, 'The Four Labyrinths of France'. This work was a polemical attack on Peter Abelard and three other contemporaries thought by the author to share Abelard's errors.[59] The context in which it comes is a critique of Seneca. That is significant because of the pivotal status of suicide in the dialectic between Christian and Stoic moral systems.[60] Walter of St Victor is taking issue with Seneca's recommendation to kill oneself under some circumstances. At one point, punning with Latin terms, he compares the self-killer unfavourably with the *fratricida* (an established Latin word). Walter's phrase is 'he was a fratricide but worse, a suicide' (*iste quidem fratricida sed peior suicida*), and immediately he goes on to challenge any claim that pagans who killed themselves had any place in heaven: 'you do not imagine, do you, that he has a place in Heaven with the suicides Nero, Socrates and Cato?' (*putasne cum Nerone et Socrate et Catone suicidis receptus sit in celo?*)[61] A stark anachronism of this sort might suggest interpolation. But a look at the manuscript page (Plate 1) rules this out.

---

[59] P. Glorieux, ed,, 'Le "quatuor labyrinthos Franciae" de Gautier de S. Victor', *Archives d'histoire doctrinale et littéraire du m.â.*, 19 (1952), 187–335; p. 272, 13–16. The credit for discovering this important text is that of Knapp, who discusses it in *Selbstmord*, 56–8.

[60] Analysed by K. P. Nothdurft, *Studien zum Einfluss Senecas auf die Philosophie und Theologie des zwölften Jahrhunderts* (Leiden and Cologne, 1963), 78–80.

[61] Paris, Arsenal, MS 379, fol. 73r: [Seneca] 'in summa luxuria effeminatam animam ac si dormiendo evomuit. Miro scilicet ingenio, ipsam mortem mortisque dolorem vertit sibi in magnam voluptatem. Iste igitur non quidem fratricida, set peior suicida, Stoicus professione.

The word *suicida*, then, to denote the killer of himself (not the act), first appears in Latin in a work written around 1178, as an invention apparently of an Augustinian canon in Paris. The word does not appear again until Sir Thomas Browne. At least, no one has come up with an example of its use between Walter and Browne, and there is none in the evidence used for the present study.[62] And that raises a further question: why not? Twelfth-century Paris, after all, in which St Victor was a leading centre of moral theology, has some successful neologisms to its credit, like 'theology' and 'individual'. A book on the twelfth-century Renaissance, not to say any comprehensive dictionary of medieval Latin, will reveal many other new words devised in the period. Most of them took root and became naturalized. Why not *suicida*?

Three reasons can be suggested, in combination. One was the modest influence of Walter's book. It survives in one complete manuscript, which never left the library at St Victor, and one incomplete, which may have begun there but ended in the Vatican. Since Walter was librarian for St Victor, he may have been responsible for getting both copies to these destinations in the first place. Outside the book there is no sign of its having exerted influence, and inside, little to suggest it should have done, other than to have provoked the contemporary comment that the book was a 'bad act and a bad work'.[63]

But there was a subtler reason. Suicide is defined today as a deliberate act of self-homicide. Put another way, it is a result—one's own death—combined with an intention—in one's own mind—to secure it. But this moral syntax is relatively modern, and in medieval Europe, I hope to show in Part II of this book, it was only being seriously discovered in the twelfth century. Law, I shall try to show there, was still studded with testimonies to its original preoccupation with results, regardless of intention. In the case of suicide it was preoccupied with method, above all—the noose, the dagger, and so on. What that preoccupation signifies for the history of the word 'suicide'—otherwise than for, say, the word 'individual'—is that men's underlying moral conceptions were not at the stage of needing a word for

Epicureus morte. Putasne cum Nerone et Socrate et Catone suicidis receptus sit Celo? Crede mihi melius illi erat si natus non fuisset homo, malletque semper luxuriari in balneo.'

[62] The history is traced by A. J. L. Van Hoof, *From Autothanasia to Suicide*, 136–41, and that author's subsequent articles, 'A longer life for *suicide*', *Romanische Forschungen*, 102 (1990), 255–9, and 'Self-murder, a new concept in search of a Latin word', in *Eulogia, Mélanges offerts à Antoon A. R. Bastiaensen*. Instrumenta Patristica, 24 (Steenbrugge, 1991), 365–74.

[63] P. Glorieux, '"Mauvaise action et mauvais travail", Le "Contra quatuor labyrinthos Franciae"', *Recherches de théologie ancienne et médiévale*, 21 (1954), 179–93. Cf. 187: 'manque d'originalité', 'plagiat continuel'.

so specific a definition, a definition founded, that is, on a particular compound of intention and act.[64]

I said, they did not need the word. I should have said they did not need
it *enough*: enough, that is, to counteract an innate reluctance to think about
suicide at all. This is the third reason why the word was not used. After all,
some other names of dreadful crimes or sins did emerge in the twelfth
century, equally compounded of intention and act. Tracts on vices and
virtues abound in new names for them, or old names used in new ways.
Many of those new words acquired currency outside the theological circles
that devised them. But suicide was different. It was ostracized from this
great verbal colonization. This was another result of, and witness to, the
same tabu that engendered euphemism, a tabu that shied even, very often,
from the old Roman synonyms. Suicide was just too terrible to talk about.
So long as you were content with words that did not quite hit the nail on
the head, there were already too *many* words for it, approximate and archaic
though they might be. The very last thing people wanted was an accurate
term for the unmentionable thing itself. And it was the last thing they got,
for it was only in the 1630s and 1640s, nearly four centuries after Walter,
that the word 'suicide' was invented again. Its assumed, Latinate archaism
was still faintly euphemistic. But at last, by that time, it was destined to stay,
and to begin its triumphant colonization of European vocabularies.

[64] The background and parallels in Semitic and Indo-European languages are charted by
D. Daube, 'The Linguistics of Suicide', *Philosophy and Public Affairs*, 1 (1972), 387–437.

3

The Reticence of Chronicles

Behind them trod a line so long,
So long . . . I never could have thought
Death had undone that countless throng.

Dante, *Inferno*, 3: 55–7.[1]

The lessons of the last chapter have their intrinsic value. They also have an external, practical consequence in shaping the following investigation, in two ways. On one hand they determine how the documents are best approached, since, if suicide really was innately secret, its faint documentary appearances must be read with that in mind. On the other, if suicide really was so private, its privacy will tend to atomize the history that emerges, and challenges the historian to gather it into intelligible form. Each consideration is important enough, at the outset, to deserve a word more of explanation.

How to Find Out

SUICIDE AND DOCUMENTS

Let us start with the documents. Medieval historical sources are at the best of times spare and full of pitfalls, especially in the area of general morals and emotions. When it comes to suicide these difficulties are at their apogee. The relationship of suicide to the source can be described as positively hostile. That means that to find suicides the reader has to use the sources at the limit of their range, at the very point, in fact, where they are sparest and fullest of pitfalls. Because it is in the nature of a fugitive not to say where he is hiding the search must be wide. This has yet a further result. Taken over a wide range the sources will be heterogeneous, stretching from chronicles to financial accounts, miracles to theological treatises, poetry to private letters. Every scrap must be brought in. Since each of these

[1] 'E dietro le venía ì lunga tratta / di gente, ch'io non avrei mai creduto / che morte tanta n'avesse disfatta.'

heterogeneous sources will present its own peculiar kind of pitfall, their heterogeneity multiplies the danger presented by each, because each is different from the last. Not only must the search be exceptionally wide, in other words; it must be exceptionally cautious.

These reflections apply to the study of medieval suicide even as an abstract subject. They apply with special pertinence to that of the suicides themselves. The search for them will employ documents of several kinds, each kind distorting in its own way the truth it reveals. To minimize the distortion, and simultaneously extend the depth of the field of vision which the sources reveal, I shall divide the sources into three broad categories and obtain as complete a picture as possible from each separately, a picture adjusted by the special criteria appropriate to each. Then, at the end, when all has been done separately like the separate cooking of three constituents of a pie, the three pictures will be compounded. Each one, besides supplementing the two others, will both offer them and receive from them confirmation or correction in those particulars which reflect their several methods.

The form of this operation will be revealed by a glance over the chapter headings, which will also show what the broad categories are. They are 'chronicles' in Chapters 3–5, 'legal sources' in Chapters 6–11, and 'religious sources' in Chapters 12–14. Chapters 15 and 16 will then draw what common conclusions can be drawn from the three pictures together.

That strategy, devised expressly for its object of research, constitutes one practical result of the 'secrecy of suicide'. It concerns the documents. But there is a second practical result. This time it touches, not the documents, but the form of the history that emerges from them.

The integration of atoms

The history in question is one made up of isolated atoms. It must be. A suicide is by definition isolated, or thinks he is, from the rest of his race. At the moment of death he is in that sense the supreme individual. Quite apart from their physical elusiveness, that is one reason suicides have hitherto largely repelled the historian. The historian deals in groups, with their social structures and trends. A suicide *qua* suicide is a social anomaly. He cannot, as most historical characters can, be represented as part of a movement. He is not a pioneer, say, or consolidator, or theoretician, a king or a prophet. He may have been. But the student of suicide studies him at the moment he stops being. It is the moment caught by Lucan's necromancer:

nondum facies viventis in illo iam morientis erat.[2]

At that moment the suicide is to all appearances alone, out of history. There is plenty of medieval evidence to show that that is actually an illusion; showing it, among other ways, by way of certain fictional characters whose suicides appear as the last event in the continuum of whole lifetimes, making them whole people much like everyone else, but who merely died this way rather than another. But for the flesh-and-blood suicides of the Middle Ages that biographical dimension is usually denied. I shall recover it as far as the evidence allows, but that is not far.

The history that results will necessarily be a parade of separate individuals, one by one, individuals with no ostensible mutual connection, and often little resemblance, other than in the one peculiarity which cut each from everybody else. They are a convocation of loners. That comes near to being a contradiction in terms. The result will at first glance seem appallingly unhistorical, like a list, even a telephone directory. Surely, the reader will say, historical convention is right, that there can be no purpose in studying isolated points, each insignificant for anything else. The objection would be fair if the suicide's apparent isolation were real. But the message of this entire trilogy will be that it is not. After all, the most isolated soul, dead or alive, is reintegrated in the race in some measure by the mere fact of being known about by anyone living; and that measure grows in proportion as the isolated soul is seen as a special instance, an exemplar of things common to mankind. In my third volume I plan to argue that this was an approach taken already in the Middle Ages. It was one which, *inter alia*, helped them think rationally about suicide. It will perform the same function for us now, by allowing the isolated suicides to come together, despite their distinctly atomized appearance, and become the subject of a history book.

For all the inherent recommendations of this approach, I might not have dared take it if it did not enjoy the distinguished model I have already invoked, Dante's *Inferno*. Dante there rehearsed, one after the other, souls irretrievably damned, each with its own portfolio of sins and in eternal isolation. But they were brought back into an ensemble by a poet who, like a *pointilliste* painter, created an image from their multitude of points. Without the points there is no image. But it is the image that gives significance to the points, and this significance, in turn, draws back into human communion souls otherwise separate. Thus Dante's Farinata degli Uberti did not believe in an afterlife. He died, and there was an end of it as far as

---

[2] Cf. p. 6 above.

Farinata's beliefs were concerned. But that was not far. Through Dante and his generations of readers the unbelieving Ghibelline has had six centuries of afterlife, of a kind more orthodox beliefs, if he had had any, would never have earned. It is not Farinata's private faults as such, but their place in the scheme of things, that won him this involuntary immortality.

Like Dante the reader will therefore meet, in succession, individuals who in their lives had no connection with each other, and usually no resemblance. But they will be introduced, as in *The Divine Comedy*, in such a way as to reveal what principle binds them with the rest of mankind and makes them intelligible. Within each category of source that principle will be dictated by the circumstances in which the suicide died. By doing much the same with the cursed souls of Hell, Dante reversed their damnation and fused them back into the living thought of himself and his readers. The exercise here will be similar. It will weld the atomized suicides into a larger configuration, and in that sense bring them back to life.

That is the strategy. I said it involves the distinction of three categories of historical source, and it is time to start with the first. It is that of 'Chronicles'.

CHRONICLES

The word 'chronicle' is no sooner uttered than it demands qualifications, more, in fact, than it can have in the course of a short chapter. The categorizing of medieval documents is a task essentially endless. Any scheme will have anomalies. In the light of that sceptical consideration, and ruminating on the evidence as a whole, I settled for my trio of categories with no higher ambition than to serve the present single, parochial purpose. That practical function must justify the more obtrusive anomalies and explain, for instance, why some well-known medieval documents have been unceremoniously pushed across boundaries, and taken away from, or added to, otherwise familiar kinds of source.

Chronicles, the first category, will occupy this chapter and the next two. It will include most contemporary or near-contemporary narrative, written to be read, usually in prose, and conceived broadly as fact, in so far as that was distinguished from fiction.[3] This is the type of work modern students first approach when investigating the history of the period. Technical distinctions can be drawn between chronicles and annals, between both of these and history, and between all of them and biography, a few of the more secular examples of which last will be included. Some of the authors in these

---

[3] Orientation is provided by B. Guenée, *Histoire et culture historique dans l'Occident médiéval* (Paris, 1980), on genres, esp. 18–43.

genres, who carefully chose titles for their work to fit it into this or that sub-genre, might have protested at this confusion. But others did not care; and the truth remained, whether the authors cared or not, that a single genre could occasionally house, within itself, greater heterogeneity than any which split it from the others. The sources envisaged, therefore, consist mainly of those familiar, main narrative sources for political history which account for the bulk of the older printed collections of medieval *Scriptores*, from the various European countries. Additions and subtractions will be flagged as they arrive.

Now chronicles, thus defined, invite an opening generalization. They say little of suicide. This is a large, negative assertion, of a kind that would take as long to prove as it would do to comb through all those printed volumes, largely unindexed in this respect. But it is supported by considerations on various levels. On the most superficial, one is that today's medievalists have not found much suicide in their narrative sources, and that that is why even some of the best-read scholars have said, rightly or wrongly, that not many medieval people committed it. Another consideration is the rarity of suicide as an entry in indexes: if contemporary mention of it had been commoner, suicide would have impressed itself on editors as deserving an entry, their half-conscious reservations notwithstanding.

But there are deeper considerations to weigh in the same cause. This chapter and the next will look at the main ones. This one will enquire into the nature and reasons for chroniclers' silence; the next, into the special factors which urged chroniclers to mention suicide when they did. Between them, these enquiries will expose the mechanisms by which suicide did sometimes get into these mainline histories; and that will simultaneously explain why it usually did not. Acquaintance with these mechanisms will illustrate a hostility between suicide and this genre of writing.

I begin, therefore, with the nature and reasons for chroniclers' silence. This subject, in its turn, divides into two halves. One defines itself by reference to the chronicler; the other, to his subject. The chronicler, after all, was one who, in the main, wrote publicly about public figures. That meant that, writing publicly, he had to be sensitive to the tabus imposed by the mores of the great world he wrote for. So much for the chronicler. Secondly, the public figures he wrote about, being mainly nobility, lived a distinct kind of life, distinguished *inter alia* by its peculiar relation to violent death. Nobles mostly had other ways to die than suicide. Each of these considerations will now be illustrated, and we look first at the peculiar considerations which weighed on writers who wrote publicly, about public figures.

Whispers about the Great

Of the deaths of public figures the Franciscan historian, Brother Luke Wadding (†1657), made this observation:

Pythagoras and Empedocles, those gravest of philosophers died once each. But subsequent writers described each death in many different ways. This commonly happens with very famous men, since the greater a man's fame, the less certain its details tend to become. The reason is that persons unconcerned about the dead man's reputation are only too quick to believe what other people say, without bothering to research the truth.[4]

Wadding meant these remarks generally. But he had been provoked to them by the rumour of a suicide, and was commenting on an allegation that the friar-philosopher Duns Scotus (†1308) had died that way. The allegation, made by Wadding's senior contemporary Bzovius (and anticipating an early eighteenth-century vogue for grisly 'true stories' on the same lines), was that the famous Franciscan philosopher had been prematurely buried, had woken up inside his stone sarcophagus, and with loud groans and bellows had killed himself by bashing his head against the stone and biting his hands off like a madman.[5]

Wadding was incidentally Duns Scotus' editor, so he was also his loyal defender, and gave twelve big printed pages to the demolition of the suicide story. Two centuries, he pointed out, separate Duns Scotus' death and the story's first appearance. When it did appear, furthermore, it was already acknowledged as mere 'rumour'. Most conclusively of all, Wadding said, the story's details are rendered impossible by the customs of early fourteenth-century Franciscan burial as known from many reliable sources, in that the friars were then buried in earth, bound to a board, so that even a supposed corpse which revived could not have moved. What makes Bzovius' critical method all the more careless, his destroyer pointed out, is that Bzovius knew perfectly well, as everyone did, that much the same allegations had been made of Pope Boniface VIII's death in 1303. Indeed, had not Bzovius himself been present with 'the whole city of Rome' at the opening of Boniface's tomb in 1606? There it had been clearly shown that Boniface's body was in perfect condition, its head unbattered, its hands unbitten.[6]

---

[4] L. Wadding, *Annales minorum*, 3 (Lyons, 1636), 72.

[5] Ibid., 70–83. The vogue is chronicled by J. McManners, *Death and the Enlightenment* (Oxford, 1981), 48.

[6] Wadding, *Annales minorum*, 74. The notion that Boniface VIII had died in this way had begun at his rumour-laden trial and was current in Giovanni Villani's Florence (*Cronica*, bk 8, ch. 63; ed. A. Racheli (Trieste, 1857), 197). Cf. T. S. R. Boase, *Boniface VIII* (London, 1953), 350–1.

For all its length and strength, Wadding's exposure of the Duns Scotus legend bears no trace of *odium theologicum*. Among its lessons was that the suicide of a famous man could not be a bare fact. An attack had been made on the memory of the great philosopher, and Wadding had to defend him. The question of a great man's suicide was thus a 'live' subject. In this it was not unlike historical accounts of miracles and of heroic deeds— accounts also moulded by the partisanship of later ages—but in the opposite sense. 'Live' subjects like this are a familiar element in the critique of historical sources. Suicide is a special case, rendered so by the intrinsic tabu which covered it. This meant not only that the invention of suicide was one form of historical mischief-making. It meant also, conversely, that respectable chroniclers might suppress mention of a great man's suicide even if the story were true. In so far as they did so, great men's suicides must have vanished into an impenetrable darkness, a space, that is, where historical events can vanish irrecoverably.

Astronomers, aware that their means of cognition, light, is subject to the laws they are trying to deduce from what it tells them, have deduced that the cosmos itself contains such zones of impenetrable darkness. They call them black holes, and explain how, in them, gravitational force is too great, for light cannot escape, so that we can never see into them, only calculate their existence from the behaviour of light near their edge. History has its black holes. I do not mean the massive, natural ephemerality of most human thoughts and actions, in which those remembered or recorded form rare exceptions, stars in a black sky. I mean categories of thought and action innately antithetical to record, which hide from it as from an enemy. Among many examples of which historians have become aware is sacramental confession to a priest. If the penitent's words were recorded or remembered his sins would be put behind him less effectively. It is easy to think of other examples.

In the European Middle Ages, suicide is one. In searching for it, that is to say, we have to expect a historical black hole, and look for events in the act of vanishing into it. The first of the two sections of this chapter will consist of such an exercise, a review of historical events apparently caught as they run away from the observer. It will not be the suicide himself, now, that is pictured in the act of dying, *iam morientis*, but the record of it. The series will be called 'whispers about the great'. 'Whisper' means, there, a split or equivocal tradition about a famous person's suicide. Again and again when a suicidal act of disposition is attributed to a great and famous person we find the tradition divided. Many sources do not mention it. Perhaps only one does, among a dozen. This remains true whether we believe in the suicide version or not. Either a mischievous minority has invented it, as no doubt happened with Duns Scotus, or an appalled majority has concealed it. Whatever the facts behind the report, the latter comes as an equivocal whisper. The same feature, as it happens, has been noticed by classical scholarship in respect of many Greek and Roman suicides,[7] and it would leave its effect also in early Christian tradition.[8] So it cannot belong only to the European Middle Ages.[9] But this is the milieu in which it is our business to give it special attention. It has implications for our reading of chronicles as a genre, for it shows that objective reality occupied only one dimension even of the most reliable chronicler's narrative. The other was the affective magnetic field in which he wrote. What he wrote, that is to say, might well be 'true'. But since historical truth is infinite, chronicles could only write some of it. What they chose to write depended on a subtle geometry of forces, moral, political, and literary, guiding their pens, shaping their templates of memory and oblivion. This will be illustrated by six 'whispers' of this kind. They appear in two contexts, one male and one female. The former, with which I begin, is that of kings or high nobles suffering defeat, arrest, or other disgrace.

GREAT MEN, DEFEATED OR DISGRACED

The first case in the series is that of Edwin, half-brother of Athelstan, king of the English from 924 to 940. For the year 933 the Peterborough version of the Anglo-Saxon Chronicle records that: 'In this year prince (or Atheling) Edwin was drowned at sea.'[10] There is no reason to doubt that. But how did Edwin drown? A Worcester version of the Anglo-Saxon Chronicle, revised after 1042 and preserved only by an author calling himself Simeon of Durham, writing *c*.1129, goes a step further. For the same year it says: 'King Athelstan commanded that his brother Edwin be drowned at sea.'[11] By 1125 William of Malmesbury had put an even more circumstantial version in his *History of the Kings*. William says Athelstan's cupbearer had accused Edwin to the king of conspiracy, that the king was anyway under stress and reacted angrily, as follows:

The youth was in a plight pitiable even by those not related to him. But so greatly was the king influenced by the views of Edwin's accusers that, forgetful of family

---

[7] R. Hirzel, 'Der Selbstmord', *Archiv für Religionswissenschaft*, 11 (1908), 437 n. 1, identifying thirteen cases.

[8] Cf. *The Curse on Self-Murder*, ch. 8.

[9] Nor be dismissed as the effect of 'sensationalism', as by Signori, 'Rechtskonstruktionen', 39 n. 96, and 'Aggression und Selbstzerstörung', 117.

[10] Trans. G. N. Garmondsway (London, 1953), 107.

[11] Simeon of Durham, *Historia regum*, in Simeon's *Opera*, vol. 2, ed. E. Arnold. Rolls Series (1885), 93; cf. A. Gransden, *Historical Writing in England*, vol. 1 (London, 1974), 149.

bonds, he condemned his half-brother to exile, devising a method of unheard-of cruelty. This was that Edwin be put into a rudderless and oarless ship, crumbling with age, with no other company than that of his armour-bearer. The wind kept tending to bring the innocent victim back to the land. But all the time the gale in the open sea was thrashing the threadbare sail until the delicately-reared Edwin could bear his fate no longer. He sought death of his own will by throwing himself into the sea [*et vitae in talibus pertaesus, voluntario in aquas praecipitio mortem conscivit*]. The armour-bearer was of wiser counsel and did not follow him. Struggling now to escape the waves, now to propel the ship by swimming with his feet, he eventually got his master's body to land in the strait that divides Dover from Ushant.[12]

Afterwards, according to William of Malmesbury, Athelstan was sorry, put his cup-bearer to death and did seven years' penance. That repentance is confirmed by the cartulary of the abbey of St Bertin in Picardy a few miles from Ushant. An entry made within a generation of 933 records the favour Athelstan heaped on the monastery 'because the king's brother, King [*sic*] Edwin, had been buried in the monastery of St. Bertin'. The cartulary's version dates the incident to 932 and describes how 'the same King Edwin, when, because of some perturbation in his kingdom, got into a ship and tried to reach this part of the sea, but the ship foundered in the storms and he was lost in the waves. When his body was brought to the shore Count Adalolf received it with honour because he was a close kinsman and brought it to St. Bertin for burial.'[13]

Only the armour-bearer could have known what really happened. The Malmesbury version suggests ingenuity and perseverance in an armour-bearer who found and fished out his master's body and swam a ship to land. But it is not totally impossible. Nor, as I shall show in Part II,[14] would an abbey have been above the discreet burial of a suicide's corpse, least of all if his brother was a king. Athelstan was exceptionally grateful for something. An abbey which valued his gratitude would hardly have registered the suicidal version of his brother's death. All we know, and it is something the armour-bearer did not, is that the incident became subject to a divided tradition. The suicide story became a whisper.

My next whisper concerns the Emperor Henry IV of Germany. The famous dispute between Henry IV and Pope Gregory VII, which began in

[12] William of Malmesbury, *Gesta regum*, bk 2, § 139; in William's *Opera*, vol. 1, ed. W. Stubbs, Rolls Series (1887), p. 156.

[13] *Cartulaire de l'abbaye de S. Bertin*, ed. M. Guérard (Paris, 1840), 145: 'cum, cogente aliqua regni sui pertubatione, hac in maris parte, ascensa navi, vellet devenire, perturbatione ventorum facta navique collisa, mediis fluctibus absortus est.' My interpretation differs from that of Stenton, *Anglo-Saxon England*, 2nd edn (Oxford, 1947), 351.

[14] *The Curse on Self-Murder*, ch. 13.

1075, was reported by some dozen chroniclers, all of whom took sides more or less violently. One of those ranged against Henry was Bernold of Constance, and his report is to be read with this bias in mind. Henry had begun his reign as a minor in 1056, when potential hostility to his political plans was already formidable. But it was only in 1077 that his house began to fall about his head as he awoke, in his early thirties, to find the Empire ungovernable. For a decade he struggled and made some headway. But in the early 1090s he was baulked again, above all when his own now adult son, the future Henry V, joined the opposition. In 1093, aged about 50, Henry IV

betook himself to a castle and there remained without any regal trappings. He was in a state of extreme dejection and they say he tried to give himself over to death, but was prevented by his men and could not bring his wish to effect.[15]

Bernold's crucial words are: *seipsum, ut aiunt, morti traderi voluit, set a suis praeventus ad effectum pervenire non potuit.* The perfect tense of *voluit* and the men's intervention make 'tried to', not 'wanted to', the more likely translation. Henry IV did not in fact die until 1106, and in the end he wearied his enemies as much as they wearied him. But that was a lot. Henry's late letters breathe an impression of general world-weariness with life. Death, when it came, may not have been unwelcome.[16] Together with Henry's known hot temper, that gives Bernold's story credibility, for all that no other chronicler, on either side, says a word on it. It remained the essence of a 'whisper'.

The next three cases form a group on their own, not only chronologically but because the alleged suicide occurred in an immediate context of force. One is the death of Henry of Hohenstaufen, 'King of the Romans', eldest son of the Emperor Frederick II Hohenstaufen. Henry is known to have died on 12 February 1242,[17] at a moment when the current phase in the papal–imperial struggle was nearing its climax, and Frederick II his down-

---

[15] *Mon. Germ. Hist., Scriptores*, 5 (1844), 456.28–31. Cf. Knapp, *Selbstmord*, 78.

[16] Ed. C. Erdmann, *Die Briefe Heinrichs IV*, in *Mon. Germ. Hist., Briefe der deutschen Kaiserzeit* (Leipzig, 1937), esp. Letters 37–9 and 42 (pp. 49–58). I take this reference to Henry IV's letters as an occasion to say that the earliest expressly *suicidal* remarks I know of in a medieval ruler's letters is from 1461, in an unpublished letter by Federigo da Montefeltro, duke of Urbino, mentioned by W. Tommasoli, *La vita di Federigo da Montefeltro* (Urbino, 1978), 119, quoting Archivio di Stato di Firenze, Urbino, Div. G., Carteggi, filza civ, lettera 35. The duke felt defeated by gout, the Malatesta, and the death of his son, and confided his suicidal feelings to his doctor. An earlier and less explicitly suicidal example is the claim by Cardinal Pietro Colonna in 1311 that the persecution of his family by the late Pope Boniface VIII had gone 'adeo ut taederet me et ipsos frequenter vivere'; quoted from the posthumous trial proceedings printed in C. Höffler, 'Rückblick auf Papst Bonifaz VIII und die Literatur seiner Geschichte, nebst einer wichtigen urkundlichen Beilage aus dem vatikanischen Archiv in Rom', *Abhandlungen der bayerischen Akademie der Wissenschaften*, dritte (Historische) Classe, 3, pt 3 (Munich, 1841), 67.

[17] T. C. Van Cleve, *Frederick II* (Oxford, 1972), 379.

fall. In 1235 Henry Hohenstaufen, like his namesake the imperial heir in 1093 (mentioned in the previous example), had rebelled against his father. Captured and imprisoned, for the two years before his death Henry Hohenstaufen had been held at Nicastro, a castle whose ruins still stand in the mountains of Calabria, twenty miles south of Cosenza. Early in February 1242 Frederick sent soldiers to see his son in prison. Why he did so is a question on which the chroniclers, in agreement so far, begin to diverge. It was soon after this, anyway, that Henry died, either there at Nicastro or eight miles further north at Martirano, or perhaps somewhere in between.

The chroniclers in question give voice to three main traditions. Richard of San Germano, whose famous history of the Guelf–Ghibelline struggle was written at Monte Cassino, 200 miles to the north, offers what it is probably fair to call an official version. Richard proclaims firmly that Henry, imprisoned at Martirano, died 'a natural death [*naturali morte defungitur*]'.[18] In a chronicler generally biased towards the Hohenstaufen we may pause to notice the deliberate character of that assertion. Do we normally say of someone that he died 'a natural death'? It may be that Richard of San Germano knew of other rumours.

For other rumours there certainly were. A second tradition says Frederick had had Henry put to death. This was the version of Martinus Polonus (Martin the Pole), who wrote his famous and successful chronicle around 1270. As a Dominican friar and papal chaplain, Martin was normally biased against the Emperor, and his account of young Henry's death comes near to an allegation of murder. He writes that Frederick 'suffocated [Henry] in the filth of a prison [*carceris squalore suffocavit*]'.[19] A murder on these lines was alleged more directly in an account recorded by Thomas Tuscus, who wrote at Monte Cassino in the 1280s. According to Thomas Tuscus, Henry was 'strangled [*strangulari*] in prison on his father's orders'.[20] A similar tradition would be recorded by Benvenuto da Imola, Dante's famous commentator, whose commentary on *Inferno* XIII, where this passage appears, dates from 1370. Benvenuto says Frederick let Henry die 'in prison, through chains and ill-treatment' together with his (Henry's) two sons.[21]

That leaves a third tradition. It is that Henry, fearing his father's anger, had intentionally killed himself. Thomas Tuscus in fact gives the version of

---

[18] *Chronica*, ed. C. A. Garufi, *Rerum Italicarum Scriptores*, new series, 7, pt 2 (Bologna, 1937), 213.11–12.

[19] *Chronicon pontificum et imperatorum*, ed. L. Weiland, *Mon. Germ. Hist., Scriptores*, 22, 377–482; on pp. 471.37–8.

[20] *Gesta imperatorum et pontificum*, ed. E. Ehren Feuchter, *Mon. Germ. Hist., Scriptores*, 22, 483–528; on pp. 513.1–5.

[21] Benvenuto de Rambaldis, *Comentum super Dantis . . . Comoediam*, ed. J. P. Lacaita (Florence, 1885), vol. 1, p. 444. Cf. note 23.

Henry's death just quoted as an alternative to this: 'Seeing himself let down and betrayed by his father Henry threw himself, *as some say*, from the castle and thus killed himself by the fall, *while others say* he was strangled in prison on his father's orders.'[22]

The character of the whisper could not be more clearly declared. The character is confirmed by Benvenuto who also gives the 'murder' version as an alternative to suicide. Although Benvenuto puts the suicidal alternative second, it is the one which earns Henry any mention in Benvenuto's commentary at all, since *Inferno* XIII, where the passage comes, was the canto devoted to the fate of suicides. Thus, after giving the account of Henry's death in prison through ill-treatment, Benvenuto writes:

But others write that Frederick, through motives of regret for what he had done, sent for his son with a view to a reconciliation. But Henry, while he was *en route* under guard, fearing that his father was planning some cruelty additional to what he had already experienced, threw himself and his horse together from a certain bridge or rock, and thus died unhappily.[23]

'If this is true', Benvenuto concludes, then it is plain that Henry must suffer with other suicidal souls, whose plight occupies *Inferno* XIII.

Only one chronicle records the suicidal version of Henry's death without the other. It is anonymous, and has against its authority that it summarizes the last seven years of Henry's life in only a dozen lines. But for all its blemishes, this account remains the one closest to the event in both time and place. It is known by the title (probably a late addition) *Brief Chronicle of Sicilian Affairs*, and was written somewhere in the Sicilian Kingdom around 1272. According to the *Brief Chronicle* Henry fell, neither from a tower nor with his horse from a bridge or rock, but by falling, on his own, from his horse to the ground. It is describing Henry's journey from Nicastro to Martirano, a castle fifteen miles south of Cosenza and above the river Savuto, and tells how 'coming to the mountain which separates Nicastro and Martirano, Henry flung himself from his horse to the ground and lay as if dead. His escort got him as best they could to Martirano, and there he died, and was buried in the church at Cosenza.'[24]

---

[22] *Gesta imperatorum et pontificum, loc. cit.*: 'Qui deceptum et proditum a patre se videns, precipitem, ut aliqui ferunt, de castro se dedit ac precipitio se occidit, vel ut alii quidam ferunt, pater eum strangulari mandavit.'

[23] *Comentum*, 444: 'Alii tamen scribunt, quod Fredericus tandem poenitentia ductus misit pro filio, ut conciliaret ipsum sibi; sed Henricus, dum duceretur in via, timens, ne pater crudelius tractaret eum, cuius crudelitatem iam satis fuerat expertus, praecipitavit se simul cum equo de quodam ponte, sive saxo, et sic infeliciter expiravit. Quod si verum est . . .'

[24] *Breve chronicon de rebus siculis a Roberti Guiscardi temporibus inde ad annum 1250 . . . ab auctore anonymo, sed coaetano descriptum*, in J.-L.-A. Huillard-Bréholles, ed., *Hist. Diplomatica Friderici II* (Paris, 1852–9), vol. i, pt 2, Additamenta, pp. 887 ff. pp. 905–6: 'qui

Gardeners know that a change in atmospheric conditions brings some garden plants forward and suppresses others. The whispers about Henry of Hohenstaufen's death underwent this effect in the fourteenth century. The air became hospitable to a classical ethos, respectful of suicide. The suicidal version of Henry's death, as given by Benvenuto and the Sicilian *Brief Chronicle*, therefore throve. When Boccaccio wrote his *The Falls of Famous Men* in the late 1350s, he gave two versions: that the prince and his sons died in prison, and 'as others wish to have it' that Henry, when being led to his father bound and on horseback, deliberately plunged from his horse, from 'a bridge or a rock'.[25] When a fifteenth-century Italian scribe gave Boccaccio's book a *de luxe* edition, the picture of Henry's suicidal fall became the one illustration to Henry's life-story. It is a big one (Plate 2). By then the whisper had become a shout.

The 'history of the history' of Henry's alleged suicide forms a suitable preparation for a look at two comparable stories from the same Italian milieu. One is that of Ezzelino da Romano. Ezzelino was the Ghibelline ruler of Padua from 1237 to shortly before his death in 1259. He left a reputation for cruelty scarcely equalled in post-antique historiography. Ezzelino's defeat and death achieved the highest publicity in northern Italy and are recorded by well over a dozen chroniclers, contemporary or near contemporary.[26] The accounts vary across a smaller range than those concerning Henry of Hohenstaufen. The Milanese Dominican, Galvaneo della Flamma, says Ezzelino was defeated and killed in battle by the Milanese.[27] But Galvaneo's historiography has a reputation more for patriotism than for accuracy. All other chroniclers of Ezzelino's death agree on the main details. They say Ezzelino was battling for control of a bridge over the river Adda between Milan and Brescia. Surrounded by enemies, deserted by most of his own troops, Ezzelino was severely wounded and only rescued from the clutches of his exultant enemies by two knights from Cremona. They took Ezzelino to the nearby castle of Soncina and there, a few days later (the best accounts say five), exhausted by both his wounds and his 70 years,

---

veniens in montem qui est inter ipsum Nicastrum et Martoranum, dedit se in terram de equo et quasi mortuus fuit. Et ducentes eum custodes sui sicut melius poterant usque Martoranum, ibidem vitam finivit et in ecclesia Cusentina sepultus fuit.' The *Breve chronicon* is the only surviving document to which Benvenuto's 'alii . . . scribunt' (in the last note) could refer. But others may have perished.

[25] *De casibus virorum illustrium*, bk 9, ch. 16; ed. P. G. Ricci and V. Zaccaria, in V. Branca, *Tutte le opere di Boccaccio*, vol. 9 (Milan, 1981), 804–9. Cf. Benvenuto da Imola, *Comentum*, as in nn. 21 and 23.

[26] The indices of the old series of Muratori, *Rerum Italicarum Scriptores*, vols 8–11, alone identify fourteen accounts. I have based most of the following generalizations on these.

[27] Galvaneo della Flamma, *Manipulus Florum*, ch. 295, in *Rerum Ital. Script.*, old series, vol. 11, col. 689D.

Ezzelino died. That was on 27 September 1259. Most sources agree that he had consistently refused the church's sacraments and some add that, for this and numerous other offences, he went to Hell. (Dante adopted that view; cf. *Inferno* XII.) Most contemporary accounts which mention the matter have Ezzelino buried, Hell or no Hell, in an honourable tomb near the Palazzo Pubblico in Soncina.

The records of Ezzelino's capture and last days are up to this point unanimous, if differing in scale. But some say it was more than sacraments that Ezzelino refused. The knights of Cremona who had rescued him not unnaturally (to quote the fullest and most sympathetic contemporary biographer, Rolandino of Padua) brought to Ezzelino's bedside expert doctors, the most skilful that could be found.[28] Rolandino's Latin phrase *adhibitis sapientissimis medicis* could mean either that doctors just came and stood there, or that they were allowed to treat the patient; perhaps the honourable Rolandino blurs this point intentionally, as he does the next. For his chronicle goes off into a general disquisition on the limitations of medicine. Medicine cannot, as is well known, Rolandino protests, always heal a dying man. What Rolandino does *not* go on to say is that medicine never heals any man if the patient does not cooperate, which is what a small minority of other contemporaries say happened with Ezzelino. The Asti memoirist Guilelmo Ventura, in particular (also a strict contemporary), says Ezzelino 'did not permit' the doctors to cure him, and indeed that in the night after their visit, on what proved the last night of his life, Ezzelino 'tore at his wounds with his own hands', and was found dead in the morning like a rabid dog.[29]

Once more the suicidal account stayed in the soil and flourished as the air changed. A shift in the Italian cultural climate between 1259 and the early fourteenth century is caught up in the 'history of the history' of Ezzelino's death. Soon after 1311, a verse panegyrist of the Della Scalla lords of Verona, Ferreto de' Ferreti of Vicenza, wrote of Ezzelino:

> And after these extremities of care,
> They say, unwarmed by food, he yearned
> For the repose of death, and proudly spurned
> The doctor's art, the nurses' preferred fare.

---

[28] Rolandino, *Cronica Marchiae Trivixanae*, bk 12, ch. 9. *Rerum Ital. Script.*, new series, vol. 8 (pt 1), 166.27; cf. *Chronicon Marchiae Tarvisinae et Lombardiae,* ibid. (pt 3), 39. 6–9.

[29] *Memoriale*, ch. 2; *Rerum Ital. Script.*, old series, vol. 11, col. 156A: 'volentes eum curare facere a Medicis, non permisit; sed illa nocte propriis manibus sua vulnera laceravit. Mane vero facto, sicut canem rabidum, mortuum invenerunt.'

Ferreto adds, in good Renaissance idiom, that Ezzelino died 'cursing all gods'.[30] *The Tragedy of Ezzelino* by the Paduan humanist Albertino Mussato, Ferreto's contemporary, has the same tone. Its 'Messenger' tells of Ezzelino's death and of the now familiar gestures:

> ... copious meals refusing,
> And doctor's care and potions, life-infusing.[31]

For a true Roman soldier, model of the new-style Italian *signore*, the ostentatious contempt of death was a positive virtue and nothing to be hidden. So this heroically Roman version clung on, its suicidal tone partially softened as the Counter-Reformation succeeded the Renaissance. In the standard *Life* printed from the sixteenth century onwards, Ezzelino's refusal of help was put before the sojourn at Soncina and thus deprived of a directly lethal effect.[32] Lomonaco's *Lives of the Italian Captains*, meanwhile, in 1831, would revive the old suicidal whisper but briefly. According to Lomonaco, Ezzelino 'refused the help of medical skill because of his unspent and ill-concealed anger': nothing there about self-starving or the laceration of wounds.[33]

In comparison with that of Ezzelino, the next case, that of the Florentine hero Corso Donati, is both simpler and more puzzling. The sources are fewer and the suicidal element more doubtful. Corso was a Florentine Coriolanus, heroic in war but domineering at home. Corso was never a military dictator on the northern Italian model; but his critics feared he might become one, and Corso's death in 1308 bore this much resemblance to Ezzelino's. The contemporary who describes in most detail the civil commotion that killed Corso is Dino Compagni. Dino records Corso's death succinctly. Corso, Dino says, was trying to escape to the monastery of San Salvi, and was cut down and killed by Catalan mounted soldiers in Florentine service.[34] Writing at roughly the same time, Giovanni Villani is more circumstantial. Villani says Corso

---

[30] *Carmen de Scaligerorum origine*, *Rerum Ital. Script.*, old series, vol. 9, col. 1203A: 'Illic summa ferunt peragentem tristia, nullis / Incaluisse cibis, avidumque occumbere morti / Oblatas sprevisse dapes, Medicaeque opem, tumidumque oculis, et fronte superba, / Execrasse Deos omnes.'
[31] *Tragoedia Eccerinis*, *Rerum Ital. Script.*, old series, vol. 10, col. 798B: 'spernit oblatas dapes / Curas salutis, atque vitales cibos.'
[32] Pietro Gerardo, *Vita di Ezzellino terzo da Romano*, ch. 9 (Venice, 1560), fol. 103v–4r. Unlikely details, including the tyrant's burial in a Franciscan convent, combine to rob this version of the authority which A. Bonardi claimed for it, 'Della Vita et gesti di Ezzelino terzo da Romano' scritta da Pietro Gerardo, *Miscellanea di storia veneta*, serie secunda, vol. 2 (Venice, 1896), 1–149.
[33] Francesco Lomonaco, *Vite de' famosi capitani d'Italia*, vol. 1 (Lugano, 1831), 163.
[34] *Cronica*, in *Rerum Ital. Script.*, old series, vol. 11, col. 523B.

was making his escape alone when he was overtaken and captured by some mounted Catalans near the village of Rovezzano and led back towards Florence as a prisoner. As they were passing near San Salvi, Corso offered them a large sum of money if they would let him escape. But the Catalans insisted on sticking to their orders, which were to take him to Florence. Fearing to fall into the hands of his enemies and be subjected to popular justice, and having his hands and feet bound firmly, Corso let himself fall from his horse. When the Catalans saw him on the ground one of them thrust a lance into his throat, wounding him mortally, and they left him for dead.[35]

Up to this point Villani's sources told one story. Then they divide. According to some, the monks of San Salvi found Corso dead and buried him next day in their abbey 'with little honour . . . and few mourners, for fear of the commune'. But 'other people' said the monks found Corso still half-alive, carried him into the abbey, and received him, before he died, into a penitential relationship with the abbey.

Villani seems to prefer the latter version. It was more edifying, after all. In particular, it serves to expunge any nuance of a 'bad end' that might otherwise have attached to the foregoing story. What was the 'bad end'? Simply death without repentance? Or suicide? Corso's deliberate fall, though not over a ravine like Henry Hohenstaufen's, was at the very least desperate. He fell deliberately as if, knowing what he could expect from 'the justice of the people', he thought he might as well die now. For a consciously Christian writer like Villani that would have smacked of suicide. So he preferred the pious postscript.

The last example in this group comes from outside Italy and is still, partly for that reason, redolent of pre-Renaissance cultural conditions. It is that of John Beaufort, earl and then duke of Somerset, who died on 27 May 1444. Grandson of John of Gaunt and grandfather of Henry VII, Beaufort had spent his active life as an English captain in the later stages of the Hundred Years War. In the 1420s and 1430s he had fought in France with merit, or as much merit as the French military recovery allowed (the sixteenth-century publicist Bale would describe him as a 'full worthy werre-our'); and in 1443 Beaufort was duly rewarded with the post of captain-general of Guienne and raised to a dukedom. The new duke crossed to

---

[35] Bk 8, ch. 96 (ed. A. Racheli, 216, col. b): 'Compreso forte di gotte nelle mani e ne'piedi si lasciò cadere da cavallo. I detti Catalani veggendolo in terra, l'uno di loro gli diede d'una lancia per la gola d'uno colpo mortale, e lasciaronlo per morto: i monaci del detto monistero il ne portaro nella badia, e chi disse che innanzi che morisse si rimise nelle mani di loro in luogo di penitenzia, e chi disse che il trovar morto, e l'altra mattina fu soppellito in San Salvi con piccolo onore e poca gente, per tema del comune.' The phrase *compreso forte di gotte* is commonly read as meaning Corso was paralysed by gout, or possibly arthritis, in both hands and both feet. The detail does not affect the point of the story here.

France, but after inconsequential raids in Normandy and Brittany withdrew to Rouen, wintered there, and in the spring, without ever entering Guienne, returned to England and died.[36]

How? The 'official' version, recorded in Beaufort circles within a year or two of the duke's death, said the latter was due to 'an unexpected infirmity [*ex inopinata infirmitate*]'. But the exact nature of the infirmity never became public and other stories circulated. Towards 1450 one would be told by Yorkist opponents of William de la Pole, the duke of Suffolk later executed by Edward IV, to the effect that Beaufort's death had been the result of de la Pole's plotting. Another, nearer in time to the event but in a poetic source with no special claim to authority, said Beaufort had been killed by a bull. But there were two more circumstantial accounts. Thomas Basin's *Histoire de Charles VII*, written in Lisieux in the 1460s, is the fullest chronicle of the Norman battles in which Beaufort had been involved. Basin treats Beaufort's *inopinata infirmitas* as a result of his moral delinquency, namely an unwillingness to bear disgrace bravely. The duke was 'a man of inordinately proud and presumptious spirit,' alleged Basin, 'but he was vain and inefficient in his deeds.' Basin goes on to say how Beaufort went home after the campaign, fell ill and died within a few days, 'his petulance and pride being unwilling to bear patiently any sort of disgrace or injury.'[37]

Sudden infirmity; murder at the instigation of William de la Pole; a bull; a fit of anger. This inconsistency is itself a historical document. If people do not know something why should they pretend they do? Suicide begat euphemism. Euphemism can in turn beget inconsistency. Spades and shovels become confused. So the diversity in four of the accounts of John Beaufort's death should prepare us, with a sense of expectation fulfilled, to read a fifth. It comes in a continuation to the abbey chronicle of Crowland near Peterborough, a continuation added in or soon after 1470, by the abbey's prior. The prior pays close, if disapproving, attention to both the French war and the activities in it of the high nobility. Since he wrote from his own knowledge and that of 'reliable informants' his authority is substantial.[38] Under the year 1437, the year in which John Beaufort was released from a long captivity in France, the Crowland prior sketches the ex-prisoner's career

[36] The accounts of John Beaufort's career, including the various versions of his death, are calendared in *The Complete Peerage*, new edition, ed. G. H. White, vol. 12, pt 1 (London, 1953), 48, n. (b). The authority of the Crowland chronicler is assessed by A. Gransden, *Historical Writing in England*, vol. 2 (London, 1984) 408–10.

[37] Thomas Basin, *Histoire de Charles VII* bk 3, ch. 17; ed. C. Samarin. Classiques de l'histoire de France au moyen âge, 2 vols. (Paris, 1964–5), vol. 1, p. 284: 'tantam proinde animi mesticiam accepit, non valente ipsius petulentia atque superbia probra quecumque vel injurias ferre pacienter, quod infra paucos dies morto inde contracto, ex hac instabili luce est subtractus.'

[38] Gransden, *Historical Writing*, vol. 2, 408–11.

and pauses especially to describe its end. After inconsequent campaigning in 1443–4, in northern France, the Crowland prior says that Beaufort, accused of treason there, was forbidden to appear in the king's presence, and that

the noble heart of a man of such high rank upon his hearing this most unhappy news, was moved to extreme indignation; and being unable to bear the stain of so great a disgrace, he accelerated his death by putting an end to his existence, it is generally said, preferring thus to cut short his sorrow, rather than pass a life of misery, labouring under so disgraceful a charge.[39]

This chronicler does not beat about the bush. Rather he beats *in* the bush, saying three times, in differing ways, that Beaufort killed himself; and twice as many times that his noble heart, of *such* high rank, was under intolerable strain: at *such* disgrace, at *so* serious a charge. The uneasy repetitions reveal their author's revulsion. He does not like the fact he is reporting. It is the same revulsion which, if the fact were true, would have made less scrupulous chroniclers conceal it. Both the diversity of the accounts as an ensemble and this particular feature of the last combine to make the Crowland version a credible candidate, as another classic whisper about the suicide of a great man.

Six examples have been examined. That is not to say that more could not be found.[40] But the feature in question is one revealed better by the depth than the quantity of examples examined. The six male examples are more suggestive still when augmented by two female. Medieval suicide statistics, such as they are, point to a male:female ratio of about three to one. So two female cases to six male is appropriate. What great women were 'whispered' to have killed themselves?

GREAT WOMEN, MISSING THEIR HUSBANDS

With kings and high nobles it is a military or political trauma that occasions suicide. With women, it is loss of a husband. At least, that is the

---

[39] *Historia croylandensis Continuatio B*; ed. J. Fell and W. Fulman, *Rerum Anglicarum Scriptores* (Oxford, 1684), 519 (I quote the translation of H. T. Riley, *Ingulph's Chronicle of the Abbey of Croyland*. Bohn's Library (London, 1854), 399): 'Infausti igitur rumoris nuncium indignantissime tulit tam inclyti viri cor egregium, imo tanti dedecoris ferre non valens maculam, propriam procurando, ut ferunt, acceleravit mortem, praesentem potius eligens brevi sub compendio terminare tristitiam, quam infelicem sub opprobrio diutius transfigere vitam.'

[40] The criteria for inclusion remaining a matter of judgement, I have excluded, for instance, the death of Charles VII of France despite Bourquelot's belief that 'suivant toute apparence' it was brought about by self-starvation (pt 3, p. 461 and n. 4). The unfriendly Pius II's *Commentaria*, bk 6 [ed. Jean Gobelin (Frankfurt, 1614), 164.36–8] says Charles 'patris dementiam imitatus, veneno se periturum existimans ab omni cibo abstinuit', but too many eye-witness accounts of Charles's last illness survive to put in doubt that it was his infection that prevented his eating; M. G. A. Vale, *Charles VII* (London, 1974), 188–9.

message of this little assemblage of samples. But the two female examples add a message of their own: that a chronicler, especially when writing at the limit of his normal range of interests, can repeat even a true story as if it were imaginative literature. Whatever they say is then a 'whisper', and the historian has no means of knowing whether to believe it.

The first of this pair is Blanche of Castile, mother of Louis IX of France. As regent for her young son, Blanche of Castile would leave a reputation for political toughness, but an incident of 1226 suggests another side to her character. Her husband, Louis VIII, had died in that year, on 8 November, at Montpensier in the Auvergne, almost certainly of dysentery caught in the Midi in the aftermath of the Albigensian crusade, having reigned for only three years and at barely 40 years old. Blanche had married him in 1200 when she was 12. She had shared his vicissitudes for a quarter of a century, including his aborted attempt to conquer England. His death was a blow.

So big a blow, by one account, that Blanche attempted suicide. The account is in a rhyming chronicle of the years 1213 to 1244 by Philippe Mousket, a Tournai patrician who had taken part in some of the events he describes and wrote poetry in his leisure moments.[41] Mousket's description of the death and mourning for Louis VIII contains details appropriate to an eyewitness and he describes Blanche's reaction to the rumour that her husband had died by poison, thus: 'She would have killed herself for grief had men not held her, against her will.'[42] Mousket says the queen's sorrow is wholly exceptional for one in her position, and proves her intense love for her husband, a love she had evinced long before and which was mutual: 'for they loved each other so strongly that both acted in one accord. Queen never, ever, loved her lord so much.'[43] After the mere rumour of Louis's death grows into a certainty the poet expands on the grief of Blanche and others in the royal household. She 'was crimson with anger and sorrow. Nor was that a wonder, for he had always been an excellent husband from the beginning until his death. But to what end? Envy and death pursued and savaged him. Philip [the late king's brother] too was crushed by grief, and so were the other brothers, the counsellors and ushers. For the queen wept such that all wept with her.' The poem's style remains near enough to that of a *chanson de geste* to leave doubt whether the story is to be taken literally. Was it a 'topos'? Although no other chronicler denies or confirms the scene the doubt is enough to make the story another whisper.

[41] *Chronique rimeé de Philippe Mouskes*, in M. Bouquet, *Recueil des historiens de la Gaule* (Paris, 1738–1904), vol. 22, p. 39. Cf. Knapp, *Selbstmord*, 83, who uses the edition of Baron de Reiffenberg, 2 vols (Brussels, 1836–8), vol. 1, p. 553.

[42] Bouquet, p. 29, lines 27303–4: 'Ki se fust ocise de duel, / S'on nel tenist outre son voel.'

[43] Bouquet, p. 29, lines 27145–8: 'Quar il s'entramoient si fort / Que tout ierent à i acort / N'onques mais roïne n'ama / Son signor tant.'

Similar doubt attaches to a second unique account of a woman's suicidal act. It concerns Donna Maria Coronel, wife of one of the most powerful noblemen in Andalusia in the time of King Pedro the Cruel of Castille (†1369). In 1352, in rebellion against the king, Maria's husband don Alonso Fernandez Coronel went to solicit allies among the Moors of Africa and later in Portugal, thus abandoning his wife for a year. During the year she died. A tradition about her death was recorded by Juan de Mariana, the first twenty books of whose enormous *General History of Spain* appeared in Latin in 1592.[44] It said Maria Coronel had committed suicide through *ennui* at the long absence of her husband and, more particularly, through incapacity to resist her own 'dishonest desires [*deshonestos desseos*]'. To borrow from a slightly abbreviated English translation of 1699, Donna Maria was 'not able to endure the absence of her Husband, or resist her unchaste desires,' and 'rather than yield to them, is said to have put burning coals into that Part which molested her.'

The literary reminiscence this time is not that of a *chanson de geste* but of a Renaissance *histoire scandaleuse*, a character which would be heightened by the English translator's amendments and abbreviations, and by his addition of an 'it is said' to Mariana's much earlier more assertive account. Mariana's is the only surviving history to say anything of the death of this lady. But he used big libraries and had access to fourteenth-century works now destroyed, and when a contemporary scholar, who also had access to works now lost, challenged the reliability of the *General History* as a whole, his long list of its errors did not include the story of Maria Coronel's suicide. That does not mean the critic knew it was true. But it does leave the story in the limbo where, the examples so far have suggested, many such imputations about royal and high noble persons ended.

I have tried to explain and demonstrate the rarity of suicide in writers who 'wrote publicly about public people'. That they also wrote for respectable people fortified their inhibitions against the mention of suicide. That was one reason for reticence. But there was another. The public people they wrote about were mainly nobles; and nobles, as a general rule, did not commit suicide. That, in turn, was largely because they did not have to.

---

[44] Book 16, ch. 17. I have used the Castilian translation published in Madrid in 1616–17 as *Historia general de España*, p. 45: 'Su muger doña Maria Coronel, por no poder sufrir la ausencia del marido, quiso mas perder la vida, que dexarse vencer de malos y deshonestos desseos: assi fatigada una vez de una torpe codicia, la apagó cō un tizon ardiendo, que metio con enojo, por aquella mesma parte donde era molestada, muger digna de mejor siglo, y digna de loa, no por el hecho, sino por el desseo invincible de castidad.' Cf. Capt. John Stevens, trans., *The General History of Spain*, 1 vol. (London, 1699), Bk 16, ch. 8, p. 269; Bourquelot, pt 3, p. 460; and Knapp, 125.

Nobles and War

One hazard in the study of history through books, the only way to it, is that bookish habits can cloud the reader's appreciation of what was actually the most important of noble 'privileges' (the word means 'private laws', or rules attaching to a person's status). This was the obligation to fight whenever there was fighting to do. The fighting in question meant savage, bloody, man-to-man fighting (archery was ignoble), usually on horseback and with swords, daggers, and lances. This kind of fighting was mortally dangerous if you were skilled, and lethal at once if you were not. The 'Wars of the Roses' may not have destroyed the English medieval nobility, as was once believed, but they still destroyed a lot of nobles, whose young heirs carried on the line. In this the wars were typical, wars probably being more destructive of nobles the earlier in the Middle Ages we look. Most English kings mentioned in Bede's *History* died in battle. Even in the twelfth century, with its 'renaissance', and far from Europe's two crusading frontiers, a close-up look at the lives of noble French youths shows they were very often killed in their twenties. Their well-publicized access to rich heiresses was largely a function of wars and tournaments, factories of widows. But it is debatable if, without the class that pursued this martial way of life, Christian Europe and its chronicles would have escaped destruction by one of the even more military regimes which repeatedly threatened it, from the Huns onwards.[45]

This consideration prefaces the second half of an answer to our question, why there is so little suicide in medieval chronicles. Their subjects were mainly noblemen, either as that or as upper clergy. The involvement of nobles in fighting and military games almost certainly lowered their suicide rate. 'Almost', only, because we are talking largely of psychology, and the psychology of military suicide is a delicate matter. On one hand, danger stimulates instincts of self-preservation: if someone is trying to kill you, you will be less likely to wish to kill yourself. That is one reason why suicide rates in modern periods, when rates can be measured, go down during wars.[46] On the other hand it has been observed that some modern armies have had high suicide rates, both because soldiers possessed the means, and because—on Durkheim's reading—soldiers have a black-and-white code of honour and dishonour, success and failure.[47] The same may have been true

---

[45] K. B. McFarlane, *The Nobility of Later Medieval England* (Oxford, 1973), esp. 268–78; J. C. Campbell, *Bede's Reges and Principes*, Jarrow Lecture (Jarrow, 1979), 5–9; G. Duby, 'Les "jeunes" dans la société aristocratique dans la France du Nord-Ouest au xiiᵉ s.', in the same author's collected essays, *Hommes et structures du moyen âge* (Paris, 1973), 213–25.

[46] M. Halbwachs, *The Causes of Suicide* (London, 1978), 208–14.

[47] Durkheim, *Suicide*, 228–39.

in some areas of the Roman world.[48] In the next chapter we shall see medieval cases, too, of suicide committed by persons in disgrace who may have been answering the same impulse of black-and-white honour. I have not found this principle extended in any marked degree to the medieval field of battle in the form of overt suicide, Roman fashion, by soldiers faced with certain defeat. Rare exceptions throw into relief the general absence of this feature: still-pagan Norsemen, falling on their spears on the Norman coast in 925 when surrounded by Hugh the Great's Franks; sacrilegious Englishmen, who have crossed a river to rob a Welsh monastery in 1245 and, overtaken on their way home, prefer to drown in a mountain torrent than face grim retribution by the enemy.[49] What we do sometimes find, on the other hand, is Christian knights tempted to kill themselves *after* the battle, when enemies have only wounded them, and left them without hope of further battle or other stimulus to live.[50]

That debate need not be concluded now. That is because the question at issue depends less on medieval soldiers' motivation than on their opportunity. Hand-to-hand fighting was dangerous. It exalted, among those expected to engage in it, the virtue of physical courage; exalted it as high above the level of other virtues, in noble circles, as many people in all circles sunk the sin of suicide below other vices. Yet, extremes though these were, it could be hard to distinguish them in practice or even, indeed, in principle. The distinction between selfless courage, on one hand, and culpable rashness, on the other, might pose questions too awkward to attract regular treatment by moral theologians. But in war the questions came up. They might have to be judged in a split second. The soldier-theologian had to weigh up his *sic et non* in the heart of battle.

It is in the nature of things unlikely that the soldier's mental debate would ever find its way on to scholastic parchment. But unlikely is not impossible. By chance a real-life debate on this area or question of this kind did find its way from the battlefield to the schools. We find it discussed at length, in an 'Any Questions' session in Paris University in 1291, apropos of a certain

---

[48] How true is assessed, with reference especially to Roman *devotio*, by M. Griffin, 'Philosophy, Cato and Roman Suicide', pt 2, *Greece and Rome*, 33 (1986), 193.

[49] Flodoard, *Annales*, year 925 (*Pat. lat.*, 135, 435C): 'Quod videntes Normanni, qui armis vitam pro posse tutabantur, postquam spem vitae amisissent, quidam, ut enatarunt, jugulati sunt. Et alii quidem Francorum necabuntur gladiis, alii propriis oppetebant telis.' Matthew Paris, *Chronica majora*, year 1245; ed. H. R. Luard (Rolls Series), vol. 4, p. 482: 'Quidam autem ex nostris, malentes fluctibus involvi et mori submersi quam arbitrio inimicorum interfici, se ultro marinis undis perituri commiserunt.'

[50] Below, pp. 318–19. The point expounded in this paragraph is rightly noticed by H. Kühnel, '"... da erstach sich selber" Zum Selbstmord im Spätmittelalter und in der frühen Neuzeit', in K. Hauck and others, eds., *Sprache und Recht* (Berlin and New York, 1986), vol. i, p. 482.

knight at the siege of Acre in 1291.[51] Turks, the questioner reported, had hopelessly outnumbered Christians. One of the Christians had charged fearlessly at the Turks on his own and been killed at once. If all had done the same, some people said, the crusading state might have been saved. But all had not. So did the act not constitute a reckless and wrongful act of self-homicide?

The Master of the debate, Henry of Ghent, began it by saying 'yes':

Suppose [he said] our soldier had no reason to expect the support of the others, or that they were prepared for battle, but dashed off at the enemy on his own, all the same. He would be exposing himself to death without reasonable cause. For he ought to have realized that his private efforts could achieve nothing, and in such circumstances his act would be one of folly, not of courage.[52]

But Master Henry knew perfectly well that a battlefield and a classroom were two different places, and that the moral issues of the former could not always be well judged in the latter:

but the mere fact [he went on] that the man dashed out ahead *solo* to the attack, exposing his life, is not by itself sufficient basis to judge that this was not an act of courage.[53]

Did not Aristotle say in the *Nicomachean Ethics* that courage is shown *par excellence* in speedy reactions to emergencies? The soldier's lone dash at Acre, Henry thought, seemed to fit that definition.

Our soldier—and I have heard people say he should by rights have been made a commander of others—therefore dashed out with the utmost dispatch. Perhaps having lain in armed watch like the others and ready for battle, so that the moment he heard the sound of movement from the Saracens in the Acre suburbs, he leapt up and, in the belief that others would follow, charged the enemy on his own.[54]

Despite his initial show of impartiality Henry warms to the soldier as he goes along. The man was a hero.

[51] Henricus de Gandavo, *Quodlibeta*, no. 15, question 16; ed of Venice, 1613, fol. 394v–98v: 'Utrum miles irruens praevolando consortes suos in hostium exercitium faciat opus magnanimitatis.'
[52] Ibid., fol. 395rb: 'Si ergo miles noster non confidens de commilitonum adiutorio, nec putans eos paratos, ut semel ad bellum procedant, solus in hostes praevolando insiliit, ipse abque omni rationabili causa morti se obtulit, debens scire, quod nihil per se solum proficere potuit, et sic opus non magnanimi, sed stulti egit.'
[53] Ibid., 'Sed nec ex hoc, quod iste praevolans solus in hostes irruit, et in periculo mortis se exposuit, iudicari potest certitudinaliter, quod opus magnanimi non egit.'
[54] Ibid., fol. 395va: 'Miles ergo noster, qui ut audivi dici, dux aliorum in bello esse debuit, quam citius occurrisset, forte iacens in excubiis armatus cum aliis, et paratus ad bellum, statim audito tumultu et discurrentibus Sarracenis per vicos exiliit, et putans commilitones suos se consecuturos in hostes solus irrupit.'

For the emergency there and then called for hand-to-hand fighting, and demanded that those engaged in it should prefer death to servitude and dishonour, and resist evil. And because I believe that this was how things actually were I also believe, firmly, that what our soldier did was indeed an act of courage, and that it was because he was courageous by character that, when the emergency struck, he reacted as he did, performing an act of the utmost fortitude, namely to die bravely for the faith and for the city, rather than run away and live in disgrace, or even, since flight might have proved impossible, be enslaved by the Saracens.[55]

Henry knew everything depended on the defence of Christian frontiers. He had decided the question with his heart more than with his head.

If scholastics found difficulty in that question, thrown to them by the doubts of onlookers, was it any easier for a chronicler? Presented with an account of behaviour which could be interpreted either way, and granted the ambience in which chroniclers wrote, the latter must be excused for having plumped for their own interpretation. A nobleman who died through bravery in battle, even reckless bravery, was morally par for the course. A nobleman who wished to die, in other words, had no need to kill himself because it was only too easy to *be* killed. In the moral world in which most noblemen lived, and whatever theologians might say, this fact was well-known enough to be all but a truism. In the Italian prototype for Chaucer's *Troylus and Criseyde*, Pandarus restrains young Troilus from suicide for this reason: it would be so easy, he says, to achieve the same effect in war. Temerity, even mere inertia, would be enough.[56]

Earlier, I reviewed six examples of chroniclers' equivocation, about whether or not to report the suicidal version of a great person's death. Here, it is a question of an ambivalence in the act itself. Four examples will illustrate it, all from well-known sources. In each episode, elements of two dispositions are discernible, the courageous and the suicidal. The relative strength of the two will differ as they proceed, progressively from example to example, so that the four together represent a scale from the purely 'courageous' to the purely 'suicidal'. The object of the ensemble is to show how hard it would be, in both practice and theory, for a nobleman at war

[55] Henricus de Gandavo, ibid., fol. 395[va]: 'Quia si ita fuit, quia tunc tempus, necessitasque postulabant decertandum esse manu, et mortem servituti turpitudinique esse anteponendam, et malum fugiendum, quod re vera ita puto contigisse, idcirco dico credens firmiter, quod opus militis nostri erat opus magnanimitatis, ex cuius habitu repente elegit opus summe arduum, honeste scilicent mori pro fide, et civitate, quam fugiendo inhoneste vivere et forte fuga incerta non subveniente iugum servitutis Sarracenorum subire.'
[56] Boccaccio, *Filostrato*, pt 7, stanzas 44 and 45 (ed. L. Surdich, E. D'Anzieri and F. Ferro (Milan, 1990), 355–6): 'E se pure a morire i pensier gravi / ti sospignean per sentir minor doglia, / non era da pigliar ciò che pigliavi, / ch'altra via c'era a fornir cotal voglia; / e ben te la doveano i pensier pravi / mostrar, per ciò che davanti alla soglia / della porta di Troia i Greci sono, / che t'uccidran sanza chieder perdono. / [Stanza 45] Andremo dunque contra i Greci armati, / Quando morir vorrai, insiememente.'

to distinguish between these dispositions, for all the moral gulf theologians drew between them.

JOHN, KING OF BOHEMIA

John of Luxemburg, king of Bohemia, died fighting for the French at the battle of Crécy in 1346. Five or six years before this he had gone blind. The manner of his death is narrated by Froissart. Froissart was not above inventing picturesque details, but even if he invented this one, he told it as true and for the admiration of fellow knights: it was their ethical world he illustrated. Froissart's admiration for the chivalric virtue of its hero is untouched by even the faintest misgiving that the act might have been immoral. He tells how King John was told by his men that the battle had begun.[57] The king was in full armour and armed, 'but could see nothing because he was blind'. John asked his knights how the battle was going, and they described the incipient confusion of their own side. 'Ha,' replied the King of Bohemia. 'that is the signal for us.' The account goes on:

Then the King said a very brave thing to his knights: 'My lords, you are my men, my friends and my companions-in-arms. Today I have a special request to make of you. Take me far enough forward for me to strike a blow with my sword.'

The knights consented, and so as not to lose the king in the press of battle they tied their horses together by the bridles, set the king in front so that he could strike the enemy, and rode forward. The king's wish was fulfilled.

He came so close to the enemy that he was able to use his sword several times and fought most bravely, as did the knights with him. They advanced so far forward that they all remained on the field, not one escaping alive. They were found the next day lying round their leader, their horses still fastened together.

The significance of the episode lies in John's blindness. He could not by any stretch of the imagination have fought effectively. The case is in that respect unique. But it would not be too hard to make a collection of comparable episodes from chronicle accounts of battles, in which a knight goes into battle with a near-certainty of dying there.

JACQUES DE CASTEL

A promising field for the search would be the crusade, where the moral paradox involved was at its most acute. A belief coeval with the crusading

---

[57] *Chroniques*, bk 1, ch. 60, § 279; ed. S. Luce, *Chroniques de J. Froissart*, vol. 3 [1342–1346]. Societé de l'Histoire de France (Paris, 1872), 177–9. I quote the translation by G. Brereton (Harmondsworth, 1978), 89–90.

movement was that death incurred while crusading was a form of martyrdom. That meant, since the early martyrs were the very prototype of Christian saint, that the crusader who gave his life in battle would certainly go
to heaven. An objection might be raised that such a military 'martyr'
inflicted death as well as suffering it, and some writers raised that objection. But they did not do so strongly enough to shift, among those who
fought on crusades, a belief so nourishing to the courage of their armies.

Martyrdom, of whatever sort, excluded prodigality with one's own life.
Catholic theologians had made that quite clear at the time of the persecu-
tions of the early church. But a demarcation which knights could hardly
draw in secular battles had even less chance in religious ones. It should not
have surprised us that it was in a crusading context that the occasion had
arisen for that Paris debate, of 1291, about the reckless knight at Acre. We
know nothing more of that knight in particular. But we do know a little
more about the similar case of Jacques de Castel, who died on Louis IX's
crusade at Damietta in 1250. Joinville, whose *Life of Saint Louis* leaves
no doubt that the Damietta campaign involved fights as bloody as any
in the crusading movement, explains that Jacques de Castel died after
the other crusaders had decided that the Turks were too strong for them,
and the crusade should return to Damietta and thence to France. Then he
says:

There was in the army a most valliant man called Lord Jacques de Castel, bishop
of Soissons. When he saw that our soldiers were departing for Damietta he, who
had a strong desire to go to God, did not wish to return to the country where he
had been born, but rather hastened to go to be with God. So he spurred his horse
and rushed at the Turks all alone, and they killed him with their swords and put
him in the company of God, numbered with the martyrs.[58]

Although I know of no crusading account that states a knight's self-destructive intention as directly as Joinville, others tell of 'martyrdoms' almost as
reckless.

It is not my aim here to confuse or distinguish suicide and such martyrdom, only to mention that such deaths in battle quite often occurred, and
were close to whatever moral boundary there may be. Meanwhile yet other
deaths in battle came closer to suicide. This was when their motive lay elsewhere than in the practice of sheer courage. For instance, a man's whole
fortune might hang on a battle. If he was fighting in it and saw no future
worth living for if he lost, there was a quick way to finish it all.

---

[58] Ch. 77 (§ 393); ed. N. de Wailly (Paris, 1906), 164. The editor challenges Joinville's identification and names the bishop as Gui de Château-Porcien. That does not affect the present
argument.

MANFRED OF HOHENSTAUFEN

This appears to have been the case with Manfred of Hohenstaufen, half-brother to the Henry Hohenstaufen whose death was investigated a moment ago. It is the Florentine historian Giovanni Villani, whose accounts of recent Italian politics generally rested on well-known traditions, who describes Manfred's death in this way. After the death of his father, Frederick II, in 1250, Manfred laid claim to the principal Hohenstaufen legacy in Italy, namely the Kingdom of Sicily and Southern Italy. This defied the Papacy, which by 1265 had procured an ally strong enough to act. On 25 February 1266 Charles of Anjou and his French army confronted Manfred near Benevento, and after a day of fighting it was clear to Manfred that his kingdom was lost. Villani writes:

Being left with only a handful of followers Manfred behaved as a brave lord should, preferring to die in battle as king, than flee in disgrace. . . . As he put his helmet on, a silver eagle on its crest fell down in front. He was dumbstruck by this and said to the war-leaders next to him in Latin *hoc est signum Dei* ['This is a sign from God'], because I put my helmet on with my own hands in such a way that it should not fall. But he kept to his purpose and, taking heart, plunged into the battle incognito, striking like any other noble into the thickest of the fray. But his followers, lacking his courage and endurance, were soon routed, and Manfred was killed, beset on all sides by enemies.[59]

A king's fortunes, then, might depend on a battle whose inherent danger offered escape if things went wrong. Courage and despair could look so alike that there is no saying how much medieval military courage may have hidden sentiments like those attributed here to Manfred. It is not too difficult to find deaths *à la* Manfred scattered through chronicles of war, deaths of soldiers, that is, whose apprehension of defeat lowers the threshold at which a soldier is ready to risk his life, to the point of throwing it deliberately away.[60]

---

[59] *Cronica*, bk 7, ch. 9 (ed. Racheli, p. 114, col. b).

[60] e.g. Doukas, *Historia Turco-Byzantina*, bk. 39 § 11, has the defenders of the walls of Constantinople in 1453 as having hurled themselves to death from the wall; in H. J. Magoulias, trans., *Doukas' The Decline and Fall of Byzantium* (Detroit, 1975), 223. Raoul de Nesle, constable of France, died *à la* Manfred at the battle of Courtrai in 1302; *Extraits d'une chronique anonyme intitulée Anciennes Chroniques de Flandre*, ed. N. de Wailly and L. Delisle, in Bouquet, *Recueil*, vol. 22, p. 379B–D: 'le gentil connestable de France, qui estoit nommé Raoul de Neelle, s'estoit embatus sur cent de Gand, où il se combatoit par fière vertu; lesquelz Gantois eussent voulentiers sauvé ledit connestable. Mais onques, pour chere qu'ilz lui sceussent dire, ne se vault rendre; ains dist qu'il ne vouloit plus vivre quant il véoit toute la fleur de crestienneté morte. Puis se férit en eulz, si les abatit par deux, par trois; et quant ilz veirent que ainsi les mettoit à mort, ilz l'abatirent de son cheval, el illec le tuèrent.' (Cf. Schmitt, 'Le suicide au moyen âge', 22, n. 26.) Since such medieval accounts of battles run to thousands of pages I forbear to attempt a list of examples. Galbert of Bruges, *De mulctro*,

I should say it *seems* to have lowered the threshold. For how could a chronicler know what the soldier's thoughts were, except by appearances? How can we? I shall come back to this question in the unique case of a medieval soldier who survived the crisis, and whose conscience in the matter was intimately investigated. But the very fineness of the discussion reviewed there will underline the principle at issue here, namely that usually the matter could never be settled, even to the soldier himself as he fought in the heat of the moment.

Lano da Siena

But none of this means there were not actual, recognized desperados, who volunteered for battle because they had finished with life, who, later romantic language would say, had 'joined the foreign legion'. Battle offered ample dangers to anyone capable of bearing arms. My last example in this group was such a man. At least, he was according to one arm of another split tradition. Lano da Siena, whose full name was probably Arcolano Maconi, is known to have died in 1287 at the battle of Toppo, in Tuscany, fought between the armies of Siena and Arezzo. Siena was beaten and Lano was among its many dead. Thirteen years later Dante met Lano in *Inferno* (13: 115–22), in the gallery of Hell adjacent to the suicides'. But Lano's presence there does not mean he physically killed himself. He and his fellow-sufferers had committed economic 'suicide' by prodigality, since Lano had been a rich young nobleman but a spendthrift, and had got through his enormous inherited fortune and become a beggar. An exclamation put on the lips of Lano's spirit may nevertheless reflect, if it did not originate, a more literally suicidal tradition. Dante has Lano in Hell pursued by dogs, and crying 'Come quickly, come quickly, death!' (V. 118) Dante's own use of the line is far from explicit and it has divided critics ever since. But already in the 1340s Dante's son Pietro, commenting on the *Comedy*, said Lano thus 'begged' for death in Hell because he had intentionally sought it on earth to escape the misery of bankruptcy. 'Lano had been rich and became poor,' Pietro explains, 'and as a desperate man threw himself to die among his

---

traditione et occisione gloriosi Karoli comitis Flandriarum, ch. 75; ed. J. Rider, *Corpus Christianorum, continuatio medievalis*, 131 (Turnholt, 1994), 128. 18–26: 'inficiebant illos et desperatae vitae horror et incertae mortis futurae turpitudo. Maxime eis fuisset pietatis quidem donum indultum si mori licuisset quomodo fures aut latrones suspendio perierant. Igitur cum in turri sese praepararent exituros, unus juvenum per fenestram altiorem turris, gladio projecto, prosilire praesumpserat et sese raptim in carsu animaverat. Quem quidem conscientiae reatus condemnaverat, fortis animi sui liberatatem corpore exequi paratus erat. In ipso ergo raptu alii eum retinuerunt et simul cum ipsis in carcerem ire compulsus est.'

enemies.'[61] Boccaccio and Benvenuto da Imola repeat the tradition in the 1370s. 'Reflecting on his miserable state,' wrote Boccaccio, 'and thinking it would be intolerable to live in poverty when one had been accustomed to great riches, he flung himself among his enemies, in whose midst, by a chance that he had deliberately wished, he was killed.'[62] Benvenuto is quite as sure. Lano 'deliberately rushed into the thick of the fight and was killed, fighting fiercely', he wrote, adding for precision that Lano 'rendered destitute . . . sought to escape his suffering by death'.[63]

Chivalric courage, then; a crusader's 'martyrdom'; the desperate bravado of a king in defeat, or of a hopeless volunteer: to the naked eye this band of dispositions was seamless. It provided, at the bottom end, an opportunity for self-destruction indistinguishable from fortitude, so indistinguishable, even no doubt to the desperado himself, that the nobility had no need of others. If acts, being signals, can also be euphemisms, the death of Boccaccio's Lano da Siena was another. It was a 'perfect murder' whose essence is that it does not look like one. As a type, I hope, it completes one explanation for the rarity of palpable suicide in the medieval nobility, and therefore, for a large part, in the common history told by chronicles.

Those four examples were all described from the outside. That was commonly how war was described, and with these four it could not be otherwise since the soldiers were dead. Presently we shall have the opportunity, given by a unique configuration of events in early fifteenth-century France, of glimpsing the internal, moral position of a soldier in desperate military straits. Then, the same near-confusion will be visible from within. Meanwhile these brave or desperate knights have a postscript. It will set their ambivalence in relief by showing what pure, indisputable military suicide could be; and simultaneously that they too, whatever the moral subtleties arising from battle, still saw suicide *per se* as deeply shocking.

[61] *Petri Allegherii super . . . Comoediam Commentarium* (Florence, 1845), 161: 'Lano qui de divite factus est pauper, et ut desperatus se moriturum inter inimicos praecipitavit.'

[62] Boccaccio, *Esposizioni sopra la Comedia di Dante*, ed. G. Padoan, in V. Branca, ed., *Tutte le opere di G. B.*, vol. 6 (Milan, 1965), ch. 89, p. 624: 'ricordandosi del suo misero stato e parendogli gravissima cosa a sostener la povertà, sè come a colui che era uso d'esser ricchissimo, si mise infra' nemici, fra' quali, come esso per avventura disiderava, fu ucciso.'

[63] Benvenuto de Rambaldis, *Comentum* (as in n. 21), vol. 1, p. 455: 'qui ditissimus magnum patrimonium suum brevi tempore consumpserat, ingessit se sponte in praeliantium globum, et ibi fortiter pugnans occisus est. . . . quia depauperatus timens canes sequentes eum, quaerebat evadere a stento per beneficium mortis.' The other arm of the split tradition: R. Piattoli in *Enciclopedia Dantesca*, 2nd edn (Rome, 1984), vol. 3, 569, with other references and doctrinal background.

THE ASSASSINS

The case is from a crusader's account of a visit to the extremist Muslim sect of the Assassins. In 1194 Henry of Champagne, titular Christian King of Jerusalem, went to visit the Old Man of the Mountains, head of the 'Hashish-ins' or Assassins, at the Old Man's invitation and with a view to alliance against the Turks. The main contemporary chronicle of Henry's reign, the *Estoire d'Eracles*, describes the count's arrival:

The lord of the Assassins came to meet him and received him with honour, took him to his territory and showed him his castles. As they came to the strongest, Rast, he said to the count:

'Sir, your retainers would never render you the strict obedience mine render me.'
'That could well be', replied the count.

Then the Old Man shouted to two of his retainers who were on the tower. The two of them threw themselves down into the moat, breaking their necks. The count was astonished and said to the Old Man, truly he did not have a man who would do that for him.[64]

The story circulated widely in crusading circles, mostly in longer versions. In some the Old Man wants to go on with the display and the count begs him to stop. In one, further assassins kill themselves with swords. In any version the story is barely credible. That was why it was told. Its shocking character served its audiences to emphasize the gulf between any courage they might display in battle and pure, abhorrent, non-Christian suicide.

Having thus tried to answer the question why chronicles contain relatively few suicides, we turn next to look at occasions when chroniclers *did* mention the matter, and to ask, in the light of the lesson just learned, what special factors urged them to do so.

[64] *L'Estoire de Eracles Empereur*, bk 26, ch. 23; in Bouquet, *Recueil*, vol. 2 (Paris, 1859), pp. 216 [version 1]; 210, 230–1. Comment: S. Runciman, *History of the Crusades*, vol. 2 (Cambridge, 1954), 89.

4

The Probing of Disgrace

Most chronicles wrote 'publicly about public figures', and we have seen two reasons, one in the authors and one in the people they wrote about, why suicide should figure so little in their products. But other areas of historical writing were freer of these restraints. In some, the focus of a writer's interest was close enough to the life of the lowly to record their images, and to do so in a quantity sufficient to raise the chances that their narrative would capture suicides from social levels below that of kings and dukes, levels, that is, where reputations were less protected by tabu. In others, a quasi-historical record is moved by its very rationale to examine real-life cases of suicide. In both areas of record, in one through an accident and in the other through its essence, the suicidal incidents are broadly of one kind: they attach to a man (all examples are male) who has risen to fame or consequence and is suddenly brought low by disgrace and punishment, immanent or actual.

For the same reason as before, because they are few, each illustrative example will be presented with enough background to allow judgement of its nature and likelihood. We turn first to certain chronicles with a close-up focus on contemporary society and learn about their suicidal 'type'. I have loosely called the type that of 'the fallen *arriviste*'.

A Rare Exception: The Fallen Arriviste

Luke de La Barre

Few chroniclers had a finer focus on contemporary society than Orderic Vitalis, whose enormous *Ecclesiastical History* was written between 1114 and 1141. In Book 12, probably written in the 1130s, Orderic includes the following episode:

After Easter the king held judgement on the culprits who had been captured in Rouen. . . . One of the men sentenced to be deprived of his eyes was Luke de La

Barre, on account of the mocking songs he had composed about the king and for various effronteries . . . The executioners acted on these orders. But when Luke realized that he had been condemned to spend the rest of his life in shadows he decided it would be better to die than to live in darkness, and as the guards grabbed him he struggled against them for all he was worth in the hope of injuring himself. Finally, even as they held him, he managed to smash his head against the walls and stones like a madman, and so ended his own life miserably, to the sorrow of the many who had recognized his courage and wit.[1]

Orderic dates the episode shortly after Easter 1124. The king in the story was Henry I of England. Luke de la Barre was a *miles* or knight, holding land from the Count of Flanders. Shortly before this episode he had been among a group of Picard knights who had fought against Henry at Pont-Audemer (near the mouth of the Seine), where Henry had an interest as duke of Normandy. Henry had won, captured them, and let them go free again complete with their horses and weapons. But soon afterwards Luke's suzerain the Count of Flanders had called on his vassals to fight against Henry. Luke answered the call and was again captured. This time he was denied the clemency owed to a knight who fought for his suzerain. The reason, experts in the relevant law agree, was that by letting Luke depart with his weapons on the previous occasion Henry had imposed on Luke an obligation not to fight him again, even for his suzerain. Luke's 'indecent songs' about Henry were an added offence. Although Henry sat in Rouen as duke of Normandy, he judged Luke on this point by an English law which protected the king from *lèse-majesté*. During Henry's judgement on the rebels at Rouen the Count of Flanders, Luke's suzerain, loyally protested that Henry was flouting custom by mutilating knights captured in war in the service of their lord. Henry gave the above explanation of his sentence and, according to Orderic, the count acquiesced. Luke did not, and killed himself rather than accept it. Perhaps the sentence fell more heavily on this intelligent rebel because, like his count, he had not expected such severity.[2]

THOMAS FITZSTEPHEN

The wrath of Henry I was the occasion for a second suicide mentioned in Orderic's *History*. It was that of Thomas Fitzstephen.[3] Thomas Fitzstephen was one of those who, by a single act, changed the course of history, unsung.

---

[1] Book 12, ch. 39; ed. M. Chibnall, vol. 6, (Oxford, 1978), p. 354. I have slightly altered the order of words in Dr Chibnall's translation to suit the present purpose.

[2] Cf. M. Chibnall, *The World of Orderic Vitalis* (Oxford, 1984), 126, 190.

[3] Bk 12, ch. 26; ed. Chibnall, vol. 6, pp. 294–301. For a list of other accounts, see p. 298 n. 1.

A reason he is unsung is that he was anxious not to be. He had changed history for the worse, at least in the eyes of the contemporaries from whom he had most to fear. Death offered him the oblivion he nearly got. Thomas was a shipowner and skipper, son of the skipper whose ship had carried Duke William of Normandy to Pevensey Bay in 1066 and who had been the duke's chief skipper ever since. In November 1120 William's son, Henry I, had gathered a fleet at Barfleur on the north-eastern point of the Cherbourg peninsular, to return to England with his army. Orderic says that Thomas approached King Henry to offer his ship for the royal service as usual, parading his family's past service and offering a gold piece. But the king had chosen another ship and would not alter his choice. He entrusted Thomas instead with the transport of his son William and of some nobles, hundreds of them. The skipper's procurement of these important patrons delighted Thomas's oarsmen. The nobles had fought successfully in Normandy and were rich and carefree. When the sailors asked for wine it was dispensed, so freely, in a ship now overloaded, that a few cautious passengers disembarked. But towards evening the rest put to sea and, once under way, saw the king's fleet in front of them across the calm water. Competitiveness ran strong in Norman royal veins and young William ordered his skipper to urge his oarsmen to overtake the king's ships. As they all strained to do so the helmsman's attention wandered, the ship struck a rock, awash at low tide, and sank.

The notorious 'White Ship' disaster, which this was, involved the immediate loss of all on board except for two. Orderic identifies them as a Rouen butcher called Berold and a young Norman nobleman. He says these two clung to a spar through the night, waiting for rescue. The young nobleman was overcome by the cold and drowned. But Berold 'the poorest of all' was eventually rescued, and was clearly the authority for all these details. Orderic's account tallies with those of four or five briefer contemporaries, and, despite small inconsistencies, it would be unduly sceptical to deny that his story was basically factual. It includes this:

The skipper Thomas gathered his strength after sinking for the first time and, recollecting himself [*suique memor*], raised his head above the waves, and seeing the heads of those who were trying to cling to the spar he asked: 'What has happened to the king's son?' When the shipwrecked men answered that he had perished with the others, Thomas said: 'For me to live any more is misery.' So saying, with wrongful despair [*male desperans*], he chose to sink there and then, rather than be destroyed by the anger of a king maddened by the loss of his son, or drag out years of punishment in irons.[4]

---

[4] Ibid., p. 298 (second paragraph).

Orderic is alone in describing the precise manner of Thomas's death. Even a skipper's suicide could be in that measure whispered; and, no doubt, variously judged. For we are surely back here with the desperation of a Manfred, of one in the thick of violent events who sees all he has to live for as lost, and death so close and so anonymous—as this would certainly have been but for the memory of the one survivor.

HENRY DE BRAY

Comparable to both of these accounts from Orderic is the story of an attempted suicide in the *Historia anglicana* of Bartholomew Cotton, a Benedictine monk of Norwich who wrote between about 1292 and his death in 1298. Like Orderic, Bartholomew Cotton enjoys the highest reputation as a chronicler. He wrote close in time to the events he described and with a lively sense of narrative, supported where possible with documents. His political narrative of Edward I's reign includes instances of the king's vigour in punishing corrupt judges. One such was Henry de Bray.[5] Promoted as a clerk in the royal service, Henry de Bray reached high office in 1278 as a member of the king's first judicial commission for south Wales. Later he became Escheator, the functionary who supervised succession to tenants-in-chief. Cotton describes Henry's decline and fall in 1290 as one among many contemporary instances of what can happen to those who 'muddy themselves with the dirt of landed possessions', and who by personal disgrace become 'an opprobrium to their neighbours and a warning to their acquaintances'. Such men, Bartholomew says, can fall into deserved oblivion 'without even one of their dear ones to comfort them'. This harsh assessment was shared by its victim, if Cotton's account of Henry's fall is to be believed. It runs:

Soon after Trinity Sunday [28 May] in the same year, [1290] Master Henry de Bray, the king's principal Escheator, was sentenced by the king to life imprisonment and to lose his 33 virgates of land and other possessions, for raping virgins and other crimes. So overwhelmed was his spirit by this sentence that as the king's guards were taking him by boat along the river to the Tower of London he got up in the boat and tried to throw himself in and drown [*prae nimio animi dolore sursum in scapha resiluit, et se in aqua submergere voluit*]. The guards prevented him and held him firmly until he reached the Tower. But once there he tried to kill himself by running head-first against a wall, so that by the damage it did to his brain, at least, he would

---

[5] Ed. H. R. Luard, Rolls Series (London, 1859), 176. On Cotton, see A. Gransden, *Historical Writing*, vol. I (1974), 439–49. On Henry's earlier career, see F. M. Powicke, *The Thirteenth Century*, 2nd edn (Oxford, 1962), 415; and (on Escheators), 63–4.

be as someone throwing himself from a height [*ut saltem cerebro laeso praecipitem se fecisset*].[6]

Cotton does not say whether this final attempt succeeded. Was the chronicler 'whispering', unlike Orderic in an analogous case? He all but confesses as much. For all such miscreants, Cotton says at the end of the episode, *oblivioni dati sunt*. No more is ever heard of Henry de Bray. It is unlikely that anyone will ever know why.

BÉRENGAR COTAREL

My fourth example is that of Bérengar Cotarel, Marshal of the fourteenth-century papal court at Avignon. The suicide of this fallen *arriviste*, in 1340, is related by two anonymous *Lives* of the Avignon pope Benedict XII, and confirmed in all essentials but the act of suicide (on which the tradition is yet again split) by papal letters and accounts. Benedict, formerly Jacques Fournier, Cistercian bishop, and inquisitor of Montaillou, was pope from 1334 to 1342. The tensions between the French and English kings were in those years fast turning into what we now call the 'Hundred Years War'. A critical moment came in spring, 1340. A Genoese nobleman, Nicholas Fieschi, was returning home from England with an English royal commission to visit Avignon. There, on the night of 14 April Fieschi, his son, and their servant had been woken by armed men who had smashed a way into their hostel and kidnapped them, letting the Fieschi party carry nothing away but their shirts. The Fieschis were then led by a devious nocturnal route onto French territory.

The papal court heard the news next morning. This was Good Friday, which made the offence worse. Benedict XII's letter on the subject says the curia must be safe for all comers, and be seen to be. The pope's first target was the king of France, who quickly disclaimed responsibility and got the prisoners brought back safe and sound to Avignon. But some of the attackers, it transpired, had been members of the papal police itself. Worst of all, they had acted with the connivance of their chief, the Marshal, the very man whose responsibility it was to protect law and order. The pope 'incensed by the spirit of fury', in the words of the 'Second Life of Benedict XII', 'fulminated terrible sentences of the utmost severity' against all concerned regardless of rank. What this meant in practice was that the attackers were hanged on a beam stuck through the window of the house where the attack had been made.

---

[6] Ed. Luard, 175–6.

The Marshal, suspected of being the secret ringleader, was meanwhile sent to prison pending enquiry. No doubt he expected a similar fate.

Aware of his guilt [the 'Second Life' goes on] the Marshal refused the quantities of food and drink offered to him, however trusty the men who brought it. Bitten by his evil conscience he did not hang himself with a noose like Judas, but had poison brought to him by his own henchmen, and took it, killing himself of his own free will [*sponte*]. He had already been put under various sentences of excommunication and was now condemned as a traitor to the pope, to the curia and to all employed there—and as one who did not recognize his Redeemer at the end. Dressed in the headgear of his office [*mitratus*] he [meaning 'his body'] was dragged from prison and carried publicly round Avignon on the shoulders of sergeants who had stayed loyal [to the pope] and then to the bank of the Rhône, where his body was exposed to the birds and reptiles rather than given proper burial. And with that last sound his memory perished, his name a disgrace for ever.[7]

The 'First *Life* of Benedict XII' tells the same incident more briefly, saying only of the suicide that in prison 'he died untimously through an excessive grief, killing himself.' It adds to the posthumous details that the place where the corpse was disposed of was 'where malefactors are put', and that it was put in a wooden chest between two carts 'as a terror to others'.[8]

The main anomaly in these accounts concerns the Marshal's identity. While the 'First Life' does not name him, the 'Second Life', whose account of the incident is the most circumstantial (it takes up nearly a quarter of the *Life*) identifies him as a Toulouse lawyer (*jurisperitus*) called John, and says Benedict called him to the curia as a reformer and thence made him Marshal. But papal registers and accounts say nothing of this John. Rather they name as Marshal, at several dates just before the incident, one Bérengar Cotarel. Cotarel was a minor squire or *demoiseau* of Agde and Châtelain of Camon in the county of Foix, Benedict XII's own county of origin. So that identification is perfectly likely; and early in 1343 payment would be made to an officer 'for the expenses of the trial relating to Bérengar Cotarel, formerly Marshal of the curia'. We are almost certainly, therefore, not dealing with an intellectual who wandered from safe paths, but rather with a tough Languedoc soldier of fortune, guilty of misreading political signals at a dangerous moment.[9]

---

[7] E. Baluze, ed., *Vitae paparum avenoniensium*, new edn by G. Mollat, vol. 1 (Paris, 1914), 213–14 (*Vita secunda*).

[8] Ibid., 205–6. The expression used for the suicide is 'pre nimio dolore premortuus est, se ipsum interimendo' (p. 206).

[9] And who may possibly have had his own quarrel with the Fieschi, cf. *Vitae paparum avenonensium*, vol. 2 (Paris, 1928), 330. K. H. Schäfer, *Die Ausgaben der apostolischen Kammer unter Benedikt XII [etc.]* (Paderborn, 1914), 225, cf. 112. For the story of the *attentat*, see G. Daumet, ed., *Benoît XII. Lettres closes [etc.]* Bibl. des Écoles Françaises d'Athènes et de Rome,

ANDREAS ZAMONETIČ

The last of this group of examples comes from the very end of the Middle Ages, but its character lies near enough to the others to confirm and colour their message. It concerns Andreas Zamonetič, a Dominican friar of Slovenian birth, who rose rapidly in his order, became a cardinal and archbishop under Pope Sixtus IV (1471–84), and fell sharply from favour to die in 1482. To make Zamonetič an *arriviste* is to side with his enemies. If he had been born in Saxony, called Luther, and become an Augustinian, he might have been remembered as another of history's great men, at least by some; and by others, for other reasons if, like Pope Sixtus IV, he had been born in Italy, joined the Franciscans, and been called della Rovere. There was not much in it, and enough of a dissentient 'whisper' survives, in fact, about the alleged suicide of Zamonetič to qualify him as a great man who deserved it. But that was not the view of those who wrote the history. For them, Zamonetič was an *arriviste* shooting star, who disgraced himself and died ignominiously in well-earned defeat.

Early in his career Zamonetič had taught in Padua alongside Francesco della Rovere. When the latter became pope as Sixtus IV he promoted Zamonetič to a Slovenian archbishopric and made him cardinal, and in 1478 the Emperor Frederick III crowned it all by appointing the cardinal archbishop as his own imperial representative at the curia. In the 1430s the curia had fought off alleged reforms proposed by the council of Basle. But now Zamonetič took up the council's torch and found fault with the curia. Tension between him and Sixtus grew to a point where, in 1481, Sixtus imprisoned the critical Slovene. Released, Zamonetič staged a canonistic *coup d'état*. Relying on his status as cardinal and imperial envoy, and on the revolutionary constitution bequeathed by the council of Basle, he summoned a new council to Basle and called on pope and emperor to attend. The stake was high, and Zamonetič lost. A mere handful of European churchmen responded, and Sixtus easily persuaded Frederick III to arraign his rebellious protégé. A special tribunal met in Basle. Zamonetič protested that it was he, not his accusers, who stood for the true Christian church, and that he was ready to die for it. He was not called to. He was made to sit in prison in leg-irons, listening to pleas that he recant. This lasted a year, during which the cardinal stuck to his views.

At the very end of 1483, and no one knows under what pressure, Zamonetič changed his mind and did recant. His retraction, made in the presence

3rd series (Paris, 1899 and 1920), 447–52 and pp. xxxviii–xlii. For identity and milieu, see B. Guillemain, *La cour pontificale d'Avignon, 1309–1376* (Paris, 1966), 436, though neither of the *Vitae* quite say, as Guillemain does, that the body was 'exposé au gibet des condamnés à mort', still less that it was 'jeté dans le Rhône'.

of a notary and of high-ranking witnesses, is dated 2 January 1484, and can be read in the chronicle of Nicholas Glassberger, a member of Sixtus' order (the Franciscans) hostile to the presumptious Dominican. Glassberger says the latter's motive in retracting was to buy freedom from prison. If so it failed, since all it bought was release from the leg-irons. Zamonetič was kept under house arrest while envoys were sent to Rome to ask the pope what to do next. They departed on their journey, which normally took about a fortnight there and back, and returned with good news. The pope said the cardinal could go free, and they went straight to his prison to tell him.[10]

Their shock had been sharpened by the cardinal's custodians, who apparently gave no warning of what they might see. Shown into the prisoner's lodging, all the envoys saw was the prisoner's body, hanging from the ceiling by a twisted towel. Zamonetič had hanged himself a few days earlier, on 12 November. Glassberger has no doubt about the motive. The cardinal's patience had given way, he says,

because he was not allowed to go free. Rushing into despair, he took a towel, and in custody though he was, and before the return of the envoys from Rome, turned cruel hands on himself to become an associate of Judas and strangle himself by hanging.[11]

Only when the envoys had surveyed the scene with their own eyes were officers sent for from the city police to take down the body and dispose of it. As the case was one of suicide, the body was put in a barrel and thrown into the Rhine from a bridge, with the effect that the barrel split as it hit the water and spilled the corpse into the torrent, bound for the North Sea.[12]

So, at least, says Glassberger. But the alleged suicide of an imprisoned radical is always suspect. This one is no exception. The custodians' delay in the removal of the body could be read in two ways. They may have waited to let the returning envoys see for themselves that the prisoner had hanged himself. Or that may have been a pretext, for a delay whose real purpose was to allow evidence to decay. Official assassination may be mere hypothesis. But it is possible; after the failed *putsch*, Zamonetič may have been a dangerous embarrassment to emperor and city. More significant, the hypothesis was contemporary, for six months later a Basle citizen was arrested for having, informers said,

---

[10] *Chronica fratris Nicolai Glassberger*, in *Analecta Franciscana*, vol. 2 (Quaracchi, 1887), 486. I read the pope's favourable reply in the envoys' exclamation: 'Nesciebas, quod misericordem dominum habebas?'

[11] Glassberger, ibid.

[12] Glassberger, ibid. My account of the end of the cardinal's career is mainly based on Glassberger, ibid., 481–6.

cast serious aspersions on the Burgermeister and Council of Basle by secretly spreading fictional, untrue allegations that the archbishop of Krain, who despaired of God's mercy and killed himself in prison, was victim of an assassination procured by these authorities.[13]

The rash conspiratorial theorist had to retract and give a monetary guarantee that he would never open his mouth on the subject again.

A free city able to enforce this condition is not the historian's friend, so doubt will always remain about the Slovene cardinal's suicide. But the Basle archive backs Glassberger's version, and recent historians of the city, as of the late fifteenth-century church, have accepted it as probable. In this they preserve, necessarily, the priorities of the contemporary establishment who wrote the sources. It was an establishment which thought it had dispatched the Hussites, and did not know, as we do, that more was to come a bare generation later, or that the religious strains the Reformation put on some of its leading *dramatis personae* would make the ruined, isolated Slovene a precursor. In their lack of suspicion that a major historical change was round the corner, and Zamonetič a herald of it, Glassberger and the others were thoroughly 'medieval'. So, appropriately, they wrote the suicide down as that of a shooting star, who shot too far and got his deserts.[14]

OTHERS

As a corpus of material to work from, a handful of examples may be a second-best. A complete inventory would be better. But to make one would be impracticable for more reasons than the very large quantity of the texts in question. The main reason is a problem of definition. Chronicles record innumerable deaths and near-deaths, of which some could doubtless claim

---

[13] *Urkundenbuch der Stadt Basel*, vol. 9, ed. R. Thommen (Basle, 1905), 10, no. 16 [21 June 1485]: '*Matthias Bratteler von Volkensberg, der sich gegen Bürgermeister und Rat von Basel mergklich verschuldet und sy mit erdichten unwarhafftigen wortten hinderwert zů rugk geschuldiget habe, den erzbischoff Craynenn, als der an der barmherzikeit gottes verzwwyf- felt im selbs in ir gefengknúsze den tod angetan hatt, verschafft haben sollen vom leben zum* [tode] *ze pringen, ouch min eydtpflict gegen Anthenyen Scherman, irem burger, ubersehen und der deshalb einige Zeit gefangen gehalten worden war, schwört, freigelassen, Urfehde und stellt Bürgen.*' The italicized words are a modern editor's summary.

[14] R. Wackernagel, *Geschichte der Stadt Basel* (Basel, 1916), vol. 2, pt 2, 885 is the most attentive of Basle or ecclesiastical historians to the sources on subject, contrasting in this particular with A. Stoecklin, *Der Basler Konzilsversuch des Andreas Zamonetič vom Jahre 1482* (Basle, 1938), 200, 209–11, and J. Schlecht, *Andrea Zamonetič und der Basler Konzilsversuch vom Jahre 1482* (Paderborn, 1903), vol. 1, who omits the matter altogether. The same A. Stoecklin in *Lexikon für Theologie und Kirche*, vol. 10, cols 1307–8, nevertheless allows the suicide as probable, as does K. A. Fink in J. Jedin, ed., *Handbook of Church History*, vol. 4 (Freiburg, 1969), 546. Kühnel, 488–9, treats the suicide as certain.

the status of 'suicidal incidents'. But the considerations reviewed in respect of military desperadoes are only a few of those which obstruct clear definition. Without it, a search in the chronicles would be to search a haystack not for needles, but for anything which might in some lights look like a needle. On the same grounds there can be no question of relying on indexes, whose compilers have to rely on definitions already established—as well as, like chroniclers, usually averting their eyes from the very object we are on the hunt for.

So there cannot be an inventory, only a selection. What the selection suggests is that in chronicles, the suicide *à la* Luke de La Barre, of a person suddenly disgraced and arrested, was not so rare as to be unheard-of or even unmentioned in writing. A chance will occur later of assessing the frequency of the same kind of suicide in legal sources, and it will then be easier to measure the degree of chroniclers' reticence. But the samples just given show it was modified: that suicide could, on occasion, be described for what it was, with the less hesitation the more a chronicler's sympathies lay with the punishing authority. Even the shortest allusions harmonize with this rule. One such is that story of Leutard, the heretic of Champagne *c.*1000, in Radulf Glaber's *Histories*. Discredited by his bishop and shorn of his popular clientele, the unsympathetic Radulf says, without a trace of euphemism, that Leutard 'plunged into a well to his death [*semet puteo periturus immersit*]'.[15] Around the middle of the twelfth century, according to an only moderately probable-sounding story by the English satirist Walter Map, a shamelessly rapacious abbot met a nemesis which made him 'turn his teeth upon himself and die with his hands all bitten to pieces'.[16] A similar but more credible brief notice, softened to a 'whisper' perhaps because its subject was a high noble, comes in the chronicle of Alberic of Trois Fontaines. It concerns the death of Regnauld, count of Boulogne, in 1226. Regnauld had fought on the wrong side at Bouvines in 1214, was captured and imprisoned by Philip Augustus of France, and left in prison through that and the next reign. On the death of Louis VIII, Regnauld hoped the regent—none other than that suicidally heartbroken widow, Blanche of Castile—would let him out. Like Luke de la Barre, Regnauld had raised his hope too high. Disappointed, in the Capetian historian's brief, marginally qualified words, Regnauld 'put his life to an end, they say, by a voluntary death'.[17] A series of less equivocal suicides by the mighty fallen

---

[15] Book 3, ch. 11; ed. J. France (Oxford, 1989), 90–1.

[16] *De nugis curialium*, dist. 1, ch. 10; ed. M. R. James, rev. C. N. L. Brooke and R. A. B. Mynors (Oxford, 1983), 14: 'obvians ulcio dentes proprios in se fecit immittere corrosisque perire manibus.'

[17] *Mon. Germ. Hist., Scriptores*, 23, pp. 631–950, on p. 91. 12–14: 'Pro socio eius Renaldo

were those ascribed to many Knights Templar after their arrest and accusation. 'Some,' said the king's orator in 1308, noting the fact among the
'joyous and admirable' features of this *cause célèbre*, 'hanged themselves,
others killed themselves [with swords], while yet others threw themselves
from a height.'[18] Equally frank is the report of the suicide of Jacques de
Lors, a satellite of the grand vizier of Philip IV, Enguerrand de Marigny. On
Philip's death in 1314 Enguerrand had fallen victim to an intrigue, and the
circle who had risen with him now fell. Jacques de Lors was accused of
sorcery and imprisoned, and Jacques, no doubt anticipating a cruel death
(his wife was to be burned alive) 'through desperation hanged himself with
a noose'.[19] A similar message, finally, can probably be read in the account
of the suppression of a Paris rising in 1381–2, when ringleaders were
beheaded, and the pregnant wife of one of them leapt to her death from a
high window in her house.[20]

This handful of cases suggests a rule. In the ordinary, mainstream historical chronicle, they suggest, the only suicide likely to be mentioned
directly and unmistakably is that of the fallen favourite or functionary. This
impression is confirmed by a look at two genres which, though strictly inter-
lopers in the world of chronicles, share the same set of influences in this
particular. One is a particular kind of poetry—so particular as almost to
constitute a genre in itself—and its commentary; the other, the 'show' trial.
Let us examine them in that order.

Dante, Pier della Vigna, and the Anonymous Florentine

The more nearly a chronicle approached in character to an 'official history',
the more exclusive its attention to the great and famous. In the same
measure, the shyer it was of suicide. This pair of factors, taken together,
explain tensions we have found in reports of those few cases at a high social
level where suicide can be conjectured. But of major historical writings, and

Boloniensi comite quidam laboraverunt, sed in vanum. Qui interim circa sequens pascha vol-
untaria, ut dicitur, morte vitam finivit.' Cf. Bourquelot, pt 2, p. 245.

[18] *Willelmi de Plasiano orationes*, no. 1, in G. Lizérand, ed., *Le Dossier de l'affaire des Templiers* (Paris, 1964), 116: 'V°, quia in captione eorundem aliqui ex eis metu criminum sibi
impositorum, desperati de Christi misericordia, laqueo se suspenderunt, alii se occiderunt,
alii se precipitaverunt', cf. 114: 'Jocunda et mirabilis'.

[19] *Continuatio chronici Guillelmi de Nangiaco*, in Bouquet's *Recueil*, vol. 20 (Paris, 1840),
613A: 'in carcere [vinctus] ex desperatione laqueo se suspendit, et postmodum uxor ejus con-
crematur.' Cf. Bourquelot, pt 3, p. 461, n. 3.

[20] Jean Juvenal des Ursins, *Histoire du roy Charles VI* (Paris, 1653), 33: 'La femme d'un
d'eux, qui estoit grosse d'enfant, comme desesperée se precipita des fenestres de son hostel,
et se tua.' Cf. Bourquelot, pt. 3, p. 461 n. 1; Schmitt, 24 n. 36.

outside show trials, there was one exception to these rules, the *Divine Comedy*. To call this work history is not to limit it, since it combines at least three personalities—poetry and philosophy being the two other main ones. But one remains history. Our guide chose to populate his allegorical-philosophical poem with real historical figures. They were mostly from Italy in the century before he wrote, and whom he knew of from wide reading and experience. Their very inclusion, even where Dante says no more about them, is a historical statement. It says 'so-and-so had such-and-such a vice or virtue', and it was this vice or virtue that fixed his particular place in the other world. This is of course biased history. It is constrained, not least, by the obligation of Dante's characters to play the allegorical part assigned to them without too much fuss or psychological nuance. But Dante was too good an observer to eliminate the nuance altogether, even at the cost of consistency. That is one more proof that he is talking about real people whose reputations he knew. Like the chroniclers, he preferred the famous. In Dante's case this was because the famous alone could serve his didactic purpose (cf. *Paradiso*, XVII, 136–42). In so far as history is an ensemble of biographies, then the *Divine Comedy* is, from one angle, a chronicle. With due adjustment for its peculiarities, historians have used it as that ever since it was written. They have done so with all the more profit because, being more than history, it gave rise to a mass of contemporary written comment on its historical aspects.

While these qualities recommend the *Divine Comedy* to all historians, one quality in particular recommends it in a study of suicide. Of deliberate intent the *Comedy* mentions the otherwise unmentionable. It can do so because the tabu subject is set in a prophylactic context, that of its punishment in *Inferno*. So it is no strain on the writer's purpose, as it would be to a chronicler's, to give space to the least mentionable sin of all.

Pier della Vigna

All this explains why Pier della Vigna should have become the most widely-known of all medieval suicides, being the main representative of eponyms of this volume, 'the violent against themselves' who occupy the second ring of the seventh circle of Hell and are described in *Inferno* XIII. The 'violent against themselves' have been turned into trees, and when Dante, in ignorance, pulls a bough from one of the trees, a voice protests. After a brief intervention by Dante's guide Virgil, the spirit within the tree speaks. It proves to be that of Pier, and says:

I am he who held both keys of the heart of Frederick [II]. I turned them, opening and closing the locks so deftly as to exclude almost everyone from his secrets. I was loyal to that high office, and indeed sacrificed to it both sleep and daily strength. But the harlot [envy] whose lustful eyes never turn from Caesar's house—fate and vice of courts—enflamed all minds against me. These, once enflamed, passed on the flame to the Emperor, and thus my honourable happiness changed to trouble and contention. My soul was proud, and I believed I could escape the disdain of others by death. A guiltless man—I swear my innocence to you by the fresh roots of this tree—I became guilty against myself.[21]

The nucleus of Pier's confession reads thus in Dante's Italian:

> *credendo col morir fuggir disdegno,*   71
> *ingiusto fece me contra me giusto.*
>
> [Believing I could flee disdain by dying,
> I made myself unjust against myself, though just.]

While this passage still, strictly, stops short of mentioning the unmentionable, its reticence can be attributed to Dante's general partiality for ellipsis (a form of oblique reference that leaves readers to supply the key). The context of this passage, and incidentally an echo of St Augustine's famous passage on suicide in line 72 (the same paradox concerning the crime of killing an innocent comes in the suicide chapters of *The City of God*),[22] put beyond doubt that Dante's Pier is referring to suicide.

We know something of Pier della Vigna's career from other sources, and can evaluate Dante's allusion. Born in Capua around 1190 of relatively humble parents, Pier had distinguished himself in the University of Bologna both as a student of law and as a writer of Latin prose and verse. Recommended to Frederick II's service in 1221, he swiftly rose to be the chief counsellor of the Emperor's Sicilian court. At the Council of Lyons in 1245, which affected to depose Frederick, Pier was the Emperor's principal defender. But in 1249, for reasons neither contemporaries nor today's historians can agree on—though Dante and his commentators say it was all empty calumny—Pier was suddenly arrested, and probably blinded. Tradition then characteristically splits. All contemporary authorities except one—from Pisa, around 1260—say Pier's death was by suicide. One tradition, recorded but not believed by the commentator Benvenuto da Imola, was that Pier threw himself from a high window of his palace in Capua, just as the Emperor was passing below. Another, reminiscent of the suicide story about Frederick's son Henry of Hohenstaufen, says he deliberately fell to his death from the mule on which he was being transported. But most say Pier died by hitting his head against the wall of his place of

---

[21] *Inferno*, 13: 58–75.
[22] *De civitate Dei*, bk 1, chs 17 and 19; *Corpus Christianorum, series latina*, 47 (Turnhout, 1959), 18. 5–10 and 20, 25–40.

confinement, disagreeing only about where this was: the castle of San Miniato near Pisa or, less probably, in one or other of the city's churches. The debate here stems less from the usual split tradition about suicide than from the secrecy commonly attaching to the deaths of victims of absolute monarchy. The debate went on then—the well-informed Benvenuto da Imola did not know the answer—and still generates scholarly literature. Perhaps the most credible of the accounts is that of Matthew Paris, normally in the know on Italian politics. Matthew says that Pier, having been handed over by Frederick to the Pisans, Pier's mortal enemies, for execution, knocked his head against the column to which he had been chained on the grounds, in Seneca's words, that 'to die at an enemy's hands is to die twice.'[23]

THE ANONYMOUS FLORENTINE: RUCO DE' MOZZI; LAPO DEGLI AGLI

In *Inferno* XIII the tree which encloses the soul of Pier della Vigna is part of a small forest. Other identified characters appear in the canto, though it is not absolutely clear that the poet meant all to be understood as suicides. One is that prodigal Lano da Siena, whom we heard accused of having flung himself suicidally into battle at Toppo (though it was not Dante, let us recall, who said so). But the suicide of the last spirit mentioned in the canto is not subject to doubt. He confesses plainly:

> *Io fei giubbetto a me delle mie case.*   151
> (I made myself a gibbet out of my own dwelling.)

What is in doubt is the identity of the speaker. The lines are more elliptical than usual and do not identify this alleged suicide, beyond making clear he was a Florentine.

Since the fourteenth-century commentators, too, were puzzled by the passage, and feverishly curious about scandals in their city, they wrote a lot on *Inferno* XIII, 151. The result is that we learn of not one, but at least two possible Florentines who probably killed themselves in the 1290s. According to one local tradition, first recorded in the *Ottimo Commento* of Andrea Lancia and repeated throughout the fourteenth century, Dante's anonymous suicide was the banker Rucco de' Mozzi who 'having ruined his business,

---

[23] Matthew Paris, *Chronica majora*, year 1249 (ed. H. R. Luard, 7 vols., Rolls Series (London, 1872–83), vol. 5, p. 69). The Seneca quotation is in Luard's note, ibid., vol. 3, p. 27 n. 5. For Matthew's access to news, see R. Vaughan, *Matthew Paris* (Cambridge, 1958), 11–18. In general on Pier, see T. C. Van Cleve, *Frederick II* (Oxford, 1972), 520–3: E. Bigi, in *Enciclopedia Dantesca*, 2nd edn (Rome, 1984), vol. 4, pp. 511–16 ('Pietro'); and vol. 5, pp. 477–8 ('Suicidi'). The former article includes a substantial modern bibliography specifically on the manner and place of Pier's death.

through misery and desperation hanged himself by the neck in his house'.[24] Commercial and civic records help identify this Rucco, giving the elements of his career: born in or shortly before 1233, son of the founder of the Mozzi bank, Rucco was named in Florentine civic registers in one capacity or another between 1267 and 1285. Active in England and France between 1253 and 1262, he was dead by 1292, though the records do not say by what means. On the basis of the Dante commentators alone, Rucco was once thought to have been a victim of a Florentine banking crash in 1300. But if he was dead by 1292, and by suicide induced by ruin, his death would have rather to be linked with political attacks on the Mozzi and other Italian bankers, in England in 1290 or in France in 1291. In that case *delle case mie* of line 151 must be understood to mean Rucco's house in England or France unless, that is, he went home to Florence before hanging himself. One of these hypotheses, but no other, would reconcile the commentators' tradition with the documents.[25]

Another, larger group of fourteenth-century Dante scholars favoured another identification: Lotto degli Agli, 'who [in the words of the same Francesco da Buti] was a judge, and because he gave a wrong sentence hanged himself by the neck with his silver belt'.[26] Documentary sources again fit with the story, showing that Lotto degli Agli was a famous Florentine judge, active in many cities of northern Italy between 1261 and 1291, and occasionally serving the Guelf city government in some high diplomatic capacity.[27]

OTHER ANONYMOUS FLORENTINES

But some of the Dante commentaries go further, and say, in ways various enough to suggest a core of common tradition on the matter, that suicide

[24] The quotation is from the late fourteenth-century Francesco da Buti, *Commento sopra la Divina Comedia*, at verse 151 (ed. C. Giannini, vol. 1 (Pisa, 1858), 367): 'e però dice che s'impiccò per la gola in casa sua, e questi si conta che fosse messer Rucco de' Mozzi, il quale poi ch'ebbe destrutta la sua facoltà, per dolore er per disperazione s'appicò per la gola in casa sua; e però finge l'autore che le cagne lo stracciassono.' The 'dogs who tear at him' are the creditors. Cf. *Ottimo Commento della Divina Comedia* (Pisa, 1827–9), vol. 1, p. 254, where the identification is made more briefly.

[25] The records are examined by E. Chiarini in *Enciclopedia Dantesca*, vol. 3, p. 1052 ('Mozzi'), with arguments for Florence as the place of Rucco's death, against the preference of R. Kay, 'Rucco di Cambio de' Mozzi in France and England', in *Studi Dantesci*, 47 (1970), 49–57, who prefers France, on grounds which include the French origin of the word *giubbetto*. For other suicides occasioned by late Capetian crackdowns see pp. 80–1 above.

[26] Da Buti, *Commento*, verse 151: 'E chi dice che fu messer Lotto degli Agli, il quale era giudice, e perchè diede una falsa sentenzia s'appicò per la gola con la sua cintola dell' ariento'. Cf. *Ottimo Commento*, vol 1, p. 254.

[27] A. D'Addario in *Enciclopedia Dantesca*, vol. 1, p. 78.

is, or was in the years just before 1300, endemic to their city. Around 1340 Dante's son Pietro Alighieri, rather than identify the anonymous suicide, commented on the passage only that 'men hanging themselves is a common occurence in that city.'[28] (Pietro wrote in Verona, having shared his father's exile: hence the audible note of contempt.) Benvenuto da Imola, commenting in Florence in the early 1370s on the same passage, assigns Florence's *penchant* for suicide firmly to the past: 'It cannot easily be conjectured who the author is speaking of here, since there were at that time many Florentines who hanged themselves.' To Benvenuto, Rucco and Lotto come in merely as examples of a class, introduced after this general statement with a 'such as'. And Benvenuto ends his brief search for names with a sweeping 'and many others whose names I do not remember'.[29]

These remarks are suggestive enough of a suicide epidemic in Dante's time. They are given a degree more force by a particular theory embraced by some commentators. Dante, they said, had deliberately left the name of this suicide out. This was because there were so many suicides in Florence at that time that each citizen was free to attach Dante's allusion to someone he knew or to a kinsman who had died in this way. Boccaccio, whose lectures on Dante were about contemporary with Benvenuto's, was one who held this view. After suggesting that the man may, as one alternative, have been left anonymous for fear of shaming the family of the man he had in mind, Boccaccio goes on:

but another reason may have been that at that period, as if it was a curse sent from God, many in our city hanged themselves, so that each reader could apply the lines to whomsoever he wished from that large number.[30]

---

[28] *Petri Allegherii super . . . Comoediam Commentarium*, ed. V. Nannucci (Florence, 1845), 162: 'Faciendo loqui illum spiritum in cespite laceratum, dicendo quod est Florentinis: loquendo auctor hic a communiter accidentibus. Nam saepe accidit in illa civitate homines se ipsos suspendentes.' This and other references to Rucco and Lotto are given and discussed by G. Masi, 'Fra savi e mercanti suicidi del tempo di Dante'. *Giornale Dantesco*, 39 [= new series, 9] (Florence, 1838); and from a less historical, more literary angle by K. Maurer, 'Die Selbstmörder in Dantes "Divina Comedia" ', *Zeitschrift für romanische Philologie*, 75 (1959), 306–20.

[29] Benvenuto de Rambaldis, *Comentum*, vol. 1, p. 460: 'Ad quod sciendum, quod non potest bene coniecturari, de quo autor loquatur hic, quia multi fuerunt Florentini, qui suspenderunt se laqueo eodem tempore, sicut quidam de Modiis nomine Ruchus, et quidam dominus Lothus de Aglis jurista, qui data una sententia falsa ivit domum, et statim se suspendit; et multi alii, quorum nomina non memini. Et crede quod autor de industria sic fecerit, ut posset intelligi de unoqueque talium, licet forte possit intelligi potius de judice, quia erat maioris pretii, et gravius deliquit.'

[30] *Esposizioni sopra la comedia di Dante*, ed. G. Padovan, in V. Branca, ed., *Tutte le opere di Giovanni Boccaccio*, vol. 6 (Milan, 1965), 629–30: 'per ciò che in que' tempi, quasi come una maledizione mandata da Dio, nella città nostra più ne se ne impiccarono, acciò che ciascun possa aporlo a qual più gli piace di que' molti.'

While Francesco Buti would echo the same general opinion, one early commentator was more specific. Jacopo della Lana, whose commentary on the *Inferno* dates from before 1328, used Dante's lines as occasion to attribute not just suicide as such, but particular methods of suicide, to Florence and to its subject neighbour Arezzo. Jacopo comments:

the vice peculiar to Florentines is to hang themselves just as that of Aretines is to throw themselves in wells. In this passage Dante is speaking of all the Florentines who behave thus, so that each reader can apply it to an appropriate kinsman of his own.[31]

If suicide really had, finally, as these commentators suggest, become either endemic or epidemic in early fourteenth-century Florence, we might expect suicide to have left a mark in contemporary folklore. It did. It is again the commentators who confirm this, and two in particular. One was the exiled Pietro Alighieri. After saying men often hang themselves in 'that city', Pietro goes on, shadowing elliptical words Dante has put in the mouth of his anonymous Florentine suicide, to explain why:

The reason is that Florence was founded with Mars in the ascendant. Mars is a bringer of war and death, leading people to the extremity of such desperate acts. In pagan times the Florentines venerated Mars, but now they do not, but rather [venerate] Saint John the Baptist. That is why Mars acts in this way. His statue used to stand on one of the Arno bridges in the said territory, his anger against the Florentines being modified by this fact. Let this be enough.[32]

Haec sufficiant. These two words betray here, as often elsewhere, an author's unconscious embarrassment at incipient confusion, confusion made worse in Pietro's case by the exile's ignorance of Florentine toponymy. For every Florentine knew it was the Ponte Vecchio, not just any bridge, which had had the celebrated equestrian statue at the end, a statue whose wear and tear had reflected its long and mysterious history, and which had finally been finished off by the flood of 1335; many superstitions were attached to it. If Piero was too ignorant or reticent to explain this, others went further. Before

---

[31] I quote from L. Rocca, *Di alcuni commenti della Divina Comedia* (Florence, 1891), 32: 'Però che de' Fiorentini è proprio vizio d'appiccare se medesimi, come degli Aretini di gettarsi ne' pozzi qui di tutti quei di Firenze che ciò fanno si ragiona acciò chè ciascuno legendo, del suo parente si creda.' Cf. Masi, 200, n. 5.

[32] *Petri Allegherii . . . Commentarium*, p. 162: 'et ratio, quia sub ascendente Martis constituta est Florentia, qui est planeta bellicosus et mortifer, conducens etiam ad tales desperationes. Modo qui tempore Paganesmi Florentiae adorabatur Mars, modo non, sed sanctus / [p. 163] Joannes Baptista, ideo sic ibi facit: de cujus statua tunc erat adhuc super quodam ponte Arni in dicta terra. Ex quo in totum non est iratus dictus Mars contra eos. Et haec sufficiant.'

1333 Boccaccio had heard old men talk of the Mars superstitions. Those which concerned suicide he repeated to Benvenuto da Imola; and Benvenuto, who lived and worked in Florence, and knew the same story about Mars and Florence as Pietro, but from closer to, gives details. 'If a boy threw a stone or mud at the statue [of Mars], grown-ups would tell him "you will come to a bad end."' And what sort of bad end? Boccaccio had seen with his own eyes. 'One such [he had told Benvenuto] was drowned in the Arno, another hanged from a noose.'[33] Benvenuto, acting here as reporter of the superstitions, does not say outright, as Pietro does, that the vindictive Mars was the cause specifically of suicides in Florence. He only makes Mars cause the city's *tristitia*, mediated by the city's substitution of slothful avarice for its earlier virtues—that is, of the florin (which bore the Baptist's emblem) for martial valour. But the two examples he has just given of *tristitia* do bear a suicidal interpretation, and the whole passage comments, after all, on a speech by a suicide in the *Inferno*. So it looks as if Mars' anger with Florence did, according to even the best Florentino authorities, help establish the fourteenth-century city as the Promised Land of suicide.

Two contemporaries of Dante give independent confirmation of these Florentine memories, and help explain his and his commentators' dark allusions. One is the Sienese lyrical poet Cecco Angiolieri, who died in or around 1312. Cecco, in a poem written probably around the last decade of the thirteenth century, says disappointment in love has driven him to think of suicide. What puts him in mind of it is the examples of others who have killed themselves for this reason. But he does not find those examples in his native Siena, but rather in Florence, thirty miles away:

> When I used to hear that a Florentine
> had become so distracted with grief
> that he had hanged himself.

---

[33] Benvenuto, *Comentum*, vol. 1, p. 461: [after a history of the statue, ending with its destruction by the flood] 'Unde narrabat mihi Boccacius de Certaldo se saepe audisse a senioribus, quando aliquis puer proiiciebat lapidem vel lutum in statuam: Tu facies malum finem; quia ego vidi talem, qui hoc fecit, qui suffocatus est in Arno, et alium qui suspensus est laqueo. Et subiungit autor unum valde mirabile, quod videtur consonare isti antiquo errori florentinorum; quia videtur expresse dicere, quod Mars, iratus propter iniu- / [p. 462] riam sibi factam in mutatione ista, semper faciet Florentiam tristem.' Benvenuto ends by spelling out as specifically suicidal an allusion Dante has left in ellipsis [p. 464]: 'Et ultimo iste spiritus florentinus tangit formam suae miserandae mortis, dicens: "Io fei gibeth a me delle mie case". Idest ego suspendi me in domibus meis. Nam gibeth in lingua gallica idem est quod furca, sive locus ubi fures suspenduntur.' On Florentine superstitions about Mars generally, and the probability that the statue had actually represented Theoderic the Great, see R. Davidsohn, *Geschiche von Florenz*, vol. 1 (Berlin, 1896), 559–60 and esp. 748–52, cf. C. T. Davis, '"Il buon tempo antico"', in N. Rubinstein, ed., *Florentine Studies* (London, 1968), 45–69, on p. 49 and n. 1.

It seemed to me a godly miracle.
But now . . .[34]

Florence clearly had a reputation, at least in one of its rival Tuscan cities.

Actually, at least in two. To the north-west was Pistoia. Cino of Pistoia, too, had been a poet, but from 1314 he became a lawyer and died, probably around 1330, as one of the most distinguished jurists of his age. In one of his commentaries on Roman law Cino is distinguishing between different motives for suicide. The crucial distinction is between the criminal guilt of an accused and all other motives. Under 'other' motives Cino lists:

because of impatience at the discomfort of some illness, perhaps toothache, or because of raging madness, or shame arising from debt, as the Florentines do [*ut faciunt Florentini*].[35]

Later in the commentary he returns to the subject in similar terms:

Those who kill themselves through boredom with life, or from fury, or shame, or if it is provoked by some other cause, as very many Florentines do [*sicut faciunt plerunque Florentini*].[36]

There is ambiguity in the Latin of each of those two passages taken separately. It relates to whether the *sicut* relates to the clause just before (about debt) or to all the variety of motives Cino has listed: that is, whether Florentines were noted for suicide for debt only, or for any suicide. But doubt is dispelled by the juxtaposition of the two passages. Suicide from *all* these worldly motives, apparently, was a vice peculiar to Florentines. Cino, who had lived for a time in Florence, not only says so; he says so *en passant*, as illustrative of a legal principle, and as if the fact itself were one commonly accepted in the world of northern Italian lawyers for whom such jurists wrote. Indeed, to judge from echoes of Cino's remarks in later commentary, it was accepted far outside that world, and long after.[37]

None of these writers was a 'chronicler'. But Dante and his Florentine elucidators, though they wrote in genres of their own, used the historical writings of their time and shared the same sources and perspective. Their one difference, in respect of the historical records that tell us of medieval

[34] Quand' i' solev' udir che un fiorentino, in Cecco Angiolieri, *Canzoniere*, ed. C. Steiner (Turin, 1925), 22–3: 'Quand' i' solev' udir che un fiorentino / si fosse per dolor sè disperato / ched elli stesso si fosse 'mpiccato/si mi parev' un miracol divino; / ed or . . .'

[35] Cinus de Pistoia, *Commentarium super codicem*, bk 6, rubric 22, no. 2 (edition of Frankfurt, 1578, fol. 364r): 'propter impatientiam doloris alicuius infirmitatis, forte ob dolorem dentium, seu propter rabiem furoris, vel pudorem aeris alieni, ut faciunt Florentini.'

[36] Ibid., bk 9, rubric 50 [fol. 569v]: 'qui se taedio vitae interimunt, vel furore vel pudore, vel alio instigatur, sicut faciunt plerunque Florentini.' Cf. Masi, 'Fra savi e mercanti', 199.

[37] e.g. Johannes Igneus, *Commentarii*, § 78 (Lyons and Orleans, 1539), fol. 99v: 'Et in eo medio Florentini morbi in damnum creditorum curantur' [*c.*1500].

suicide, was that they had a positive stimulus to mention it. Dante was obliged to do so by the systematic character of his moral scheme. (That this was the source of his obligation is confirmed by comparison with contemporary theologians, who were moved by the same compulsion.) But Dante remains a 'chronicler' in this respect, that in reaching for a living example he makes a chronicler's choice, that is, a fallen functionary, Pier della Vigna. Dante could not have helped knowing of other suicides in his time, like those lovelorn suicides of whom Cecco wrote. But he availed himself of his customary ellipsis to protect the tabus. It was only because the ellipsis created an 'itch' in the next generation of readers, reared in the gossip of the Tuscan metropolis, that Dante's commentators racked their own and others' memories for flesh-and-blood examples. Here, for once, was a positive stimulus to hunt for cases and to speak about the shameful epidemic.

The stimulus lost none of its force in the fifteenth century. I quoted just now a poem by Cecco Angiolieri, where the poet plays with the thought of suicide. By the beginning of the fifteenth century this kind of poem had become a genre with a name of its own, the *disperata*. The normal message of a *disperata* was a threat of suicide if a woman, commonly the addressee, maintained her scorn for the poet. No doubt women in all centuries have been unsure how to read lovers' rhetoric of this kind. But the historian is in no better position. Once a poetic form like this has been accepted the reader cannot tell how ingenuous it is, whether (in this case) the author really *was* on the point of suicide. So the genre cannot concern us further now. By chance, however, poetry does come to our aid in respect of one author of *disperata*, who *is* said to have killed himself—the only doubt being whether this was for the same reasons as those expressed in his melancholy poems. That remains a matter of judgement.

The poet in question was Saviozzo of Siena. His proper name was Simone da Serdini, and if he did kill himself he did so in 1419, after a sixty-year lifetime, sufficiently productive to give his poetry a high contemporary reputation, and fill nearly 300 pages in its modern edition.[38] Now soon after Saviozzo's death yet another Tuscan poet, Gambino of Arezzo, wrote a close imitation of Dante's *Inferno*, and in it he pictured an encounter between himself, Gambino, and the damned spirit of Saviozzo. In the poem Saviozzo tells his visitor why is there. He explains how he had taken employment with the tyrant Tartaglia da Lavel, and how Tartaglia

---

[38] By E. Pasquini, *Simone Serdini da Siena, detto il Saviozzo, Rime.* Collezione di opere inedite o rare, pubblicata dalla Commissione per i Testi di Lingua, vol. 27 (Bologna, 1965).

Had me imprisoned in Toscanella,
And through fear that he might put me to death
I deprived myself of this lovely life.[39]

The visitor protests his shock that the more famous earlier poet should have come to 'woeful Dis' by 'having chosen the bad path', and Saviozzo, correspondingly, asks his visitor to excuse his 'folly', on returning to the world of the living.[40] So there is no mistaking Gambino's meaning.

Gambino had been a boy of seven at the time of Saviozzo's death. Toscanella is a place near Imola, on the Via Emilia, where the trouble-prone Saviozzo may well have been imprisoned. An anonymous note to what was allegedly Saviozzo's last poem says he killed himself with a knife,[41] and that, again, is not implausible. But there is inconsistency in the traditions, namely about the date of Saviozzo's death and about which tyrant imprisoned him. And that has led one scholar, at least, to treat this tradition as another 'split' one. If scholarship as a whole has been swayed the other way, an important factor has been that some of Saviozzo's poems express embitterment with life, and even a resolve to end it. They are a kind of *disperata*, though an unusual kind. How they are to be interpreted is a question I hope to address in another context, being content now with the likelihood, even a strong one, that the sixty-year-old Saviozzo did kill himself in prison, if from no more poetic a motive than the well-founded apprehension of an imminent grim death at a tyrant's hand;[42] adding one more name, thereby, to those of suicides known to Tuscan poetic circles in and after Dante's time.

The men who formed these circles were unusual writers in an unusual society. They may not teach us direct lessons about suicide in medieval historiography generally. But their work grew out of the side of that historiography, partly like it, partly unlike. Indirectly, by way of both these resemblances and these differences, Dante and his elucidators together, as

---

[39] 'I' fui senese e chiamato Saviozzo. /Innamorato uscii di fuor tapino! / Cancellier fui d'un franco sulla sella / Tartaglia da Lavel fier paladino. / Fecemi incarcerare in Toscanella / Per tima el non mi fesse dar la morte / Mi priva' io di questa vita bella.' Printed in G. Volpi, 'La vita e le rime di Simone Serdini detto il Saviozzo', *Giornale storico della letteratura italiana*, vol. 15 (Turin, 1890), 1–78, on p. 16. Literature and discussion: E. Pasquini, 'Saviozzo', in V. Branca (ed.), *Dizionario critico della letteratura italiana* (2nd edn, Turin, 1986), vol. 4, pp. 102–8.

[40] Ibid., 17: '"Ancor par che mi doglia tue ferite / Pigliasti 'l mal cammin per le vie torte / Che t'han menato alla dolente Dite. / Le rime tue nel mondo ancor su suona / E spezialmente le tue *Infastidite*, /. . . degna canzona . . ." Ripose: "Lasso, quando tornerai / Scusami su della mia gran follia / Che mal si può scusar come tu sai."'

[41] *Rime*, ed. Pasquini, 68: 'Canzon di Simone di ser Dino da Siena, cancelliero del conte d'Urbino, la qual composta essendo in presone, con uno coltello miseramente si uccise.'

[42] I hope to return to Saviozzo's 'suicidal' poetry in Part III.

a group, themselves constitute a commentary on the more ordinary, prosaic historians' treatment of the same subject.

The same can be said of a second category of documentary source related to, while different from, the common chronicle: the show trial.

The Show Trial: The Risks of a Soldier

Dante mentioned an example of suicide because he was systematic. His commentators went further because it is the business of commentators to be explicit. Another set of motives, but with the same effect, touched a second type of record which, like the first, had reason to sweep over recent history. I have called it the show trial. A show trial is a trial whose purpose is less to procure a sentence than to give it public justification. Two such trials, each with appropriately drawn-out proceedings, illustrate the exceptional character of their records in the present respect. Both were presented as trials for heresy by courts constituted as inquisitions. This type of court, a late medieval invention fed by the revival of Roman law, was promising soil for the trials of this character. Its authoritarian procedure offered, to any prince who could lay hands on it by way of a politically 'tame' churchman, the sharpest legal instrument available for the destruction of political enemies. Where a Renaissance prince might have used poison, a late medieval king could use the inquisition. Trials by the heresy inquisition were naturally frightening for contemporaries. They were meant to be. And for two reasons such trials are valuable to the historian of suicide. A peculiarity of inquisitorial procedure was that every word was recorded, almost as by a tape-recorder, by notaries and professional clerks whose accuracy was their professional *raison d'être* and can often be verified. Secondly, far from being a hostile environment for the mention of suicide, like most history, such proceedings actually welcomed it, for a simple reason: an allegation of attempted suicide could add to the stigma loaded deliberately on to a defendant already doomed.

Among inquisitorial show trials of individuals both the most notorious examples illustrate this mechanism. The first case need not detain us long. It is from a trial which had no other purpose than to blacken the memory and annul certain sentences of a dead pope, on the only charge, heresy, for which a pope could be condemned. The case was that of Boniface VIII. It will be recalled from the last chapter that the Counter-Reformation Franciscan historian Luke Wadding, while disposing of the rumour that Duns Scotus had killed himself by knocking his head against a wall, did the same, more effectively still, for a similar rumour about Boniface VIII, by referring to the proven integrity of the corpse when Boniface's tomb was opened in 1605.[43] The only addition called for by Wadding's report is that the legend about Boniface had had a longer and more substantial genesis than its equivalent about Scotus, for it had begun in the context of Boniface's posthumous trial, soon after the pope's death. One of the numerous allegations made then, to disgrace Boniface's memory, was that he had died, when he died (on 11 October 1303), by hitting his head against a wall. The rare susceptibility of that charge to disproof is an added accessory, where appropriate, in the assessment of some other 'whispers' of this character, as it is in respect of Duns Scotus.

But let us turn to the second of the two show trials in question, which deserves more attention. Not only do its proceedings, long and professionally reported like the others, offer a rare chance of hearing a voice from a social level normally inaudible, that of a peasant. In respect of suicide, the accused was to elaborate, in response to probing questions from theologians, the inner and psychological aspect of a kind of military daring which was surveyed in the last chapter from the outside. It gives us a rare insight into a military mind in the face of death. The soldier in question *nearly* died in a way that must have been common in the profession: that is, in a dangerous and almost desperate attempt to escape enemies, a little like that of Corso Donati (if less desperate). The soldier I refer to so obliquely was Joan of Arc, and the event, her leap from the tower of Beaurevoir, between Cambrai and St Quentin, in 1430. Any confirmation needed for the quality of Joan's trial as 'show' is provided by her English captors' remark when they gave her to the French court: if you find her not guilty, they said, give her back to us.[44]

As for Boniface, so for Joan, the prosecution fortified its case then, and weakens it now, by the promiscuous character of its allegations. The most constant—instance of a genuine dilemma bothering the church in those years—was that Joan had obeyed what she called her 'voices', understanding them as those of two saints, Michael and Catherine. But army gossip had been combed for other possible accusations, and one was that Joan had attempted suicide.

The charge ran that on 24 May 1430 Joan, dressed as a man, had led an unsuccessful sortie against the Anglo-Burgundian besiegers of Compiègne. She had been taken prisoner by the Burgundians and locked in the tower of Beaurevoir some forty-five miles to the north. The Burgundians were less obnoxious to Joan than the English, whose expulsion from France she saw

---

[43] See p. 46 above.
[44] P. Champion, *Procès de condamnation de Jeanne d'Arc*, 2 vols (Paris, 1920). The English captors' remark is in vol. 1, p. 15.

as her mission. When, therefore, after four months in the tower of Beaurevoir, she heard that her captors were to hand her over to their English allies
she became 'irate', as she put it at her pre-trial examination on 9 January
1431.[45] When first challenged about the incident at Beaurevoir the following was her account. (I have translated it literally from the Latin in which
it was recorded in court, mostly *oratione obliqua*, from Joan's own original
vocal account in French.)

When she knew the English were coming to get her she was much angered; yet the
voices often told her she should not jump from the tower; and finally, for fear of the
English, she jumped, and commended herself to God and the Blessed Mary, and
was injured in the jump. And after she had jumped the voice of St Catherine told
her to be cheerful, and that Compiègne would be relieved. And [Joan] said that
she was constantly praying for the garrison at Compiègne, on St Catherine's advice.
(110)

As an instinctive theologian Joan was a model. The above account of her
jump surrendered nothing to her enemies, because it makes her intention
mere escape, with divine sanction. But Joan had apparently lost consciousness after the jump, and on recovering she had used compromising words.
The prosecution would not let this go. What had she said? Having been
unconscious at the time Joan could sidestep this one and answered:

that some people had said she was dead; and as soon as the Burgundians found that
she was alive they told her she had jumped. (110)

The baulked prosecutor now put a leading question and got part of the
answer he was looking for:

Asked whether she had said [after her jump] that she would prefer to die than fall
into the hands of the English, she replied that she had said that she would sooner
give her soul to God than be in the hands of the English. (110)

This was all said at Joan's preliminary hearing. More would be made of
that last point in the trial itself. But in the pre-trial examination, before
turning from the subject, the prosecutor asked Joan if she had 'been angry
and blasphemed the name of God' after her fall. Joan again gave a solid
reply: she never cursed the saints or swore.[46]

---

[45] J. Quicherat, *Procès de réhabilitation et de condamnation de Jeanne d'Arc*, 5 vols (Paris,
1841), vol. 1, 109–11. The 'micro-politics' behind this incident are described by J. Prévost-
Bouré, *Jean de Luxemburg et Jeanne d'Arc* (Paris, 1981). The fall: ibid., 95–6. A picture of
the ruins of the outer tower of the castle Beaurevoir faces ibid., 96, but since the original
tower from which Joan jumped was destroyed, the height of her cell therefore remains guesswork. Since all further references in this chapter are to volume 1 of Quicherat's edition, I
simply give its page numbers in the text.

[46] Quicherat, vol. 1, 111: 'nunquam maledixit Sanctum vel Sanctam, et quod ipsa nunquam
consuevit jurare.'

Had Joan's intention really been suicidal? Having got thus far at the preliminary hearing the prosecution returned to the matter when Joan was re-examined in prison in early March, and came straight to the point:

First, for what reason [*causa*] had she jumped from the tower of Beaurevoir? (150)

Joan had been captive for the best part of a year and now met her prosecutors' demand by coming as near as she ever did to a confession of attempted suicide:

She said she had heard it said that all the inhabitants of Compiègne over the age of seven years were to be put to fire and sword, and that she would sooner die than live after such a massacre of innocent people; and this was one reason for her jump. The other was that she knew she had been sold to the English, and that she would prefer to die than be in the hands of the English, her enemies. (150)

This sounded like mortal sin. It posed the question how Joan's 'voice', St Catherine, had reacted. Corroborative evidence for the suicidal intention now tumbled out as Joan repeated an exchange she had had in the tower with the voice of St Catherine. She admitted to the court that the saint had urged her almost daily *not* to jump, encouraging her to believe that God would soon come to the aid of both her and the besieged inhabitants of Compiègne. Hearing this, Joan said, she hoped she, Joan, could be at Compiègne when the help came. The saint had replied that Joan should accept gratefully what God gave her and prophesied that Joan would not be released before she had seen the king of England. Joan's retort to the saint, as she recalled it to the court, was again what the prosecution was looking for:

On my word, I would like not to see the king of England and would prefer to die than be put into the hands of the English. (151)

When pressed further about allegedly 'blasphemous' language attributed to Joan after her jump (the words turned out to be: 'How can God let the innocent people of Compiègne die, who have been so faithful to their Lord?') (151), Joan told the court about her virtual unconsciousness in the aftermath of the fall. For two or three days after it she had been too injured to eat or drink and had no appetite to do so. Meanwhile, nevertheless, St Catherine had taken any guilt there was in Joan's leap out of the court's hands. For comforting the semi-conscious Joan, the saint had told her to make confession and ask pardon for her jump. With this encouragement, and further prophecy of divine aid for Compiègne, Joan at last ate some food and recovered (152).

No one has ever doubted that Joan's prosecutors were ingenious politicians. But for all their university degrees they were imperfect theologians.

They had wrung from her a partial confession of suicidal intention. It was partial only, because it was clear that Joan had not known for sure she would die by jumping from the tower even if, in taking that risk, she had still thought death preferable to capture. The prosecutor returned constantly to this question. Had she believed she would kill herself by the jump? Joan said no. She had 'commended herself to God', and had jumped in the hope of escaping the English (152). And again:

'I did this not out of despair [*pro desperando*] but in the hope of saving myself physically, and going to the help of a lot of people in need.' (160)

But even if the suicidal intention had been proved, as Joan saw with more clarity than her accusers, the theological anomaly remained that any mortal sin she had incurred was not a matter for the inquisitorial court but for confession. She raised this point more than once (152–3; 159) and returned to it on the last occasion the matter was discussed:

'After the jump [Joan said] I confessed and sought pardon from God.' And she obtained God's pardon. And she believes that the jump was not a good act but a bad one. And she said she knows she had been pardoned by a revelation St Catherine made to her after her confession; and it was on St Catherine's advice that she confessed. (160–1)

Had a big penance been awarded for this sin? Joan replied that she had already done a 'large part' of the penance by the injury she had sustained in falling. Finally—this was where 'heresy' might, in principle, have been detected—did Joan believe that the sin she had committed by jumping from the tower had been a mortal sin? 'She did not know, and left the matter to God' (161). That was not good enough for Bishop Cauchon's court. As we all know, Joan was finally 'released to the Secular Arm', that is, burned. But it was on the basis mainly of the same proceedings that her name was cleared twenty-five years later, and, 477 years later, prefixed by 'saint'. So some authority, somewhere along the line, must have thought her answers on the question of attempted suicide, in that tight military corner at Beaurevoir, were appropriate to a citizen of Heaven.

5

The Reticence Broken
The Preoccupations of Local and House Chronicles

THE people this book is about did not mean us to know about them. They did not even want contemporaries to know. When the latter found out, as they usually had to, those who did so were naturally reluctant to think of what they knew, still more so to discuss and remember it, let alone write it down for us to read. So the suicides, or suicidally minded, or allegedly suicidally minded, people we have discovered have been caught 'fleeing the camera'.

The investigation has nevertheless gone far enough to identify a strategy for their recovery. By deliberately placing each case of the few whose record has survived these 600 years in the context of the document which reveals it, the modern student can judge its relation to the larger reality in the background, a reality for the most part irrecoverable. No arithmetic is implied there. Arithmetical problems about medieval suicide rates will be addressed later. All that *is* implied is that an incident which enters a record does so for a special set of reasons, and that it is only in full consciousness of these that the historian's necromancy can have its effect, and bring back the dead to life. Precisely because suicides are only caught 'fleeing the camera', that is to say, it matters, case by case, to know the make and position of the camera they are fleeing from.

In the broad category of historical writings I have grouped as 'chronicles', general confirmation has been found for the principle we learned by quite other means: that suicide, if it occurred and if a writer knew about it, was not usually a fact to record as part of mainstream history. Silence was one testimony to that. Another was split traditions about high-ranking persons suspected of suicide. Yet another was the specific character of the main exception to the rule: that, political history being largely about rises and falls, it was when a man fell, and his fall ended in suicide, that the momentum of his narrative most regularly carried a historian into the otherwise untrodden territory.

But in chronicle literature as a whole there are two further kinds of exception. The way they 'prove the rule' is that they belong in zones of historical writing where that genre borders on two others, with different origins and preoccupations. These are legal documents on one hand, and on the other, writings like miracle stories with a specifically religious purpose. The precise definitions of these, and the motives for which they recorded suicidal events, will be analysed in the sections devoted to them. But the considerations that shaped them are anticipated in some chronicles. It is the aim of this chapter, last of the three to look at the most directly 'historical' genre of source, to rehearse suicide cases which did get into the genre, but on its frontier zones. These frontier zones are occupied by what I shall call 'local and house chronicles'.

The most notable of early medieval historians, for whom Orosius and Prudentius had been models and Bede a pioneer, found a focus for their narrative in the fortunes of one big idea, Christianity. There was room for difference about what sort of Christianity was involved. Different parties found their own ways of shaping the common inheritance. But the idea, however reshaped, kept its grandeur of scale. Whatever the story was, it was related to the long-term scheme of history from Genesis, via the Incarnation, to the establishment of the church, sketched out by the fourth-century Christian historians. But the scale admitted degree, and even historians of the widest sweep could stoop to particularism. The narrower ones stooped very low, and within the huge genre of historiography there grew up a type of history notable for just this, particularism. Its history was an apologia for one place, one institution, one community, even for one person. This did not necessarily make it less 'Christian'. But a chronicle's particularism made a difference to its use for our own present particular need, because the focus of the chronicle, being more confined, rendered its author less subject to the canons imposed by fame. He became correspondingly more subject to impulses not only permissive, but positively favourable, to the mention of the unmentionable.

The impulses in question are the two I have called 'legal' and 'religious'. By a legal impulse I mean one that moved a particularist chronicler to set down, in case the matter should ever be challenged, any fact which confirmed the jurisdiction of his house. By a religious impulse, I mean one in its own way also defensive, but defensive of a set of values and beliefs, in which a narrative suicide could serve as the negative pole, a cause or result of evil.

The essence of these two effects will be clear from examples. I shall review these in two groups, respectively of urban and monastic origin. Since there are two 'impulses' in each, one legal and one religious, the structure of this chapter will be like a square split in four quarters. The first two quarters will deal with urban chronicles, in turn with 'legal' and 'religious' impulses in them, the second two, the same in monastic chronicles. Perhaps I should add that I did not conceive this geometry before reading the sources. It arose from long perusal of them. This, it gradually transpired, was how suicides got recorded; these, the types of 'camera' from which the suicides were trying—but here failing—to run away.

Suicides in Town Chronicles

THE GOSSIP OF LAW-COURTS

We turn first, then, to late medieval town chronicles. While we shall meet suicides in the town chronicles of several northern areas, one stands out as their special home. Germany's priority is dictated by the state of written evidence, and ultimately by the conditions that produced this entire body of writing. What these conditions were, and why more or less peculiar to the Empire, I shall explain later in the context of legal records.[1] The reader of chronicles need only know, at this stage, that in the Empire there were literally hundreds of small curias, in contrast with the single English one; that each was a writing-centre, administering government in the local vernacular; and that the historiography that emerged was accordingly decentralized. German town chronicles, dating from the middle of the fourteenth century onwards, are correspondingly voluminous, already filling over 38 volumes in their standard printed edition. (Begun in 1862, it is still far from complete.) These chronicles are both like and unlike their monastic equivalents. They are like, in that they give an insider's account of one community from a viewpoint of natural loyalty. They are unlike, in that the urban chronicles are in every sense vernacular. That is true of language but also of perspective. Because *Stadtchronike* were born of decentralized conditions peculiar to their milieu they bequeath to us, rather as the Icelandic sagas do and for the same reason, a written sounding from cultural levels normally seen as out of bounds by other historians of their time.

The result is that *Stadtchronike*, in stark contrast to most other kinds of chronicle, are positively generous in reporting suicides. Besides the gossipy disposition natural to a local chronicle there are two particular reasons for this. One was legal. Many German town chroniclers show steady interest in

[1] In Ch. 11.

the day-to-day workings of the law. This is easy to understand when we learn that nearly all of them were administrators of some sort and some had legal qualifications. Even those without such qualification worked close to the mighty Town Council, enjoyed access to its archives and, more important in respect of suicide, the gossip of its law-courts. As well as being first to get news of what went on in the town prison, or place of execution, town chroniclers shared the Town Council's interest in the rights, jurisdictions, and legal custom that gave the town its self-respect.[2]

So a town chronicler would relate local history as one conversant with legal affairs. Suicide was likely to come to their attention on this ground. This fact is most obvious when suicide was committed in prison. Thus the Augsburg chronicle of Hector Mülich records for 1437 that:

Bartholomew Sultzer stabbed himself to death in prison. He had raped a virgin, so was handed over to her brothers with permission to imprison him. He tried to get out by burning a hole in the wall and, failing, stabbed himself.[3]

The clipped account does not say if it was the city prison from which this man had tried to burn himself out. But in any case we must owe knowledge of the case indirectly, at least, to the gossip of legal officers. It is the same with a case from Regensburg in 1411. Whether indeed the source that tells of it counts as a chronicle is a moot point. It reads like one, and the early nineteenth-century Regensburg antiquarian Gemeiner quotes it verbatim in his own 'Regensburg Chronicle'. But the 'Yellow Town Book' it began in had at least partly the character of a legal register. This is how it reports the case, from June 1411:

A convicted man had been duly hanged on the gallows. Now there was a poor invalid who had been reduced to misery and destitution by debts to the pig dealers. The day after the hanging, this man went out early, took a big, heavy ladder—it would normally have taken three or four men to carry—put it up against the gallows and hanged himself with a rope right next to the convict. He did it as skilfully as if it had been the work of a professional hangman. He was cut down and thrown into the Danube.[4]

---

[2] The association of the chronicles with town government is emphasized with other peculiarities by F. R. H. Du Boulay, 'The German town chroniclers', in R. H. C. Davis and J. M. Wallace-Hadrill, eds. *The Writing of History in the Middle Ages. Essays presented to Richard William Southern* (Oxford, 1981), 445–69, especially 446 f., 456. The chroniclers' undemonstrative interest in legal practice and precedent does not earn it inclusion among the 'seven distinct motives' which Prof. Du Boulay ascribes to them on pp. 448–9. But is it not an eighth?

[3] C. Hegel, ed., *Die Chroniken der deutschen Städte*, vol. 22 (Leipzig, 1892) [= Augsburg, vol. 3], 77: '[1437] erstackt sic Bartholome Sultzer selb in der väncknus, er hett ain junckfrölin notgezogt, darum ward er seinen prüdern gegeben, in zuo vermaueren. also wolt er ain loch in die wand prennen und ersticket.'

[4] C. T. Gemeiner, *Die Regensburgische Chronik*, 4 vols (Regensburg, 1800–24), vol. 2, 400:

Behind these factual sentences we almost hear the exchanges of the city henchmen, as three of them huffed and puffed to remove the big ladder, wondering aloud how the sick, skinny man on the gallows could have lifted it all by himself. Whatever his other shortcomings, a writer like this one was close to the event he described.

And that last detail, the throwing of the body into the Danube, is typical. The occasion for a chronicler's mentioning suicide was very often the sanctions which followed it. The nature and rationale of the sanctions cannot be our concern now.[5] But their demonstrative character deserves attention now because one thing the sanctions proved was jurisdiction, so that it is actually to the posthumous 'punishment' that we here owe our knowledge of the case in the first place. This is attested by the regularity with which the punishment is included in the report. One anonymous Nuremberg chronicler, for instance, mentions a total of three suicides. For all three, however reticent of other detail otherwise, he mentions the posthumous sanction or a reason for its absence. Here they are:

On the following Saturday [4 March 1469] the wife of the sacristan at the new hospital, a notable flagellant, hanged herself. People said she had lent Nicholas Muffel 200 gilders and that sorrow at the loss of them may have been her motive. She was burned.

During the year 1477 a goose thief hanged himself in the Nuremberg prison. He was burned in the ditch.

During the year [1478] a Nuremberg schoolmaster deliberately stabbed himself to death on the Bamberger Weg. He was not burned. It was said that he had given the bishop four gilders to be buried at St Martin's in Bamberg.

A hint of the character and motive of the *Küsterin*, or sacristan's wife, in the first example, is the only luxury this writer allows himself beyond the bare fact of the suicide. That is all typical of a legal record.[6]

'Man hatte einen Mann um sein verschulde Sache an den Galgen gehangen. Den andern Tag danach war ein armer Kranker Mann Martel der Schweintreiber, von Geldschulden wegen in grosser Armuth und Elend, frühe hinausgegangen, hatte eine grosse schwere Leiter, mit der sonst drey bis vier Mann wohl zu schaffen gehabt, an den Galgen gehoben und sich mit einem strang dem des Tages zuvor Gehangenen so nah und maisterleich an die seitegehangen, alz ob ez ein henkcher mit allem vleizz getan hiet. also slug man in ab und slaipfte in dy Tunaw.' I have perforce followed Gemeiner's amended spelling, except for the last three lines, quoted from the original by H. Knapp, *Alt-Regensburgs Gerichtsverfassung, Strafverfahren und Strafrecht biz zur Karolina* (Berlin, 1914), 219.

[5] See *The Curse on Self-Murder*, ch. 1.

[6] *Die Chroniken der deutschen Städte*, as above, vol. 10 (Leipzig, 1872) [= Nürnberg, vol. 4], 310: '[1469] 4 Mar. Item darnach am nehsten sambstag frücke da erhing sich die Küsterin zum Newen spital, was eine grosse gaisterin, und man sprach, sie het dem Niclas Muffel zwai hundert gulden gelihen, het sich villeicht vor laid erhangen. Man verprennt sie.' Ibid., 350: '[1477] Item in dem 1477 jar da erhieng sich ain gensdieb in der gefenknuss zu Nürmberg, im

The same reasoning helps to explain a striking concentration of suicides in a single year of the town chronicle in Metz. This section of the chronicle, which is anonymous, records four successful suicides, together with two attempts and some less specific references. The author himself thought these were years of disaster. The suicides were one aspect of the disasters, though more as a portent than as a result. He chose to mention some half a dozen suicidal incidents and two-thirds of them, whatever the brevity of his other details, with some allusion to their legal consequences.[7] The first case records a mysterious rumour from Strasbourg. We know, from Strasbourg sources, that the suicide in question has been wrongly identified as that of 'a bishop'. But the rumour may have referred to a high church official whose manner of death is otherwise unknown. The Metz account says:

In January [1484] news was brought to Metz that a bishop of Strasbourg had hanged and strangled himself, and that the judicial authorities of Strasbourg had [and then the sanction] . . .[8]

The second example, being native to Metz, is richer in detail:

On Thursday, December 2 [1484] a former town messenger of Metz hanged and strangled himself in his granary in the house he lived in. He was more than sixty-five years old, called Jean Robert, and was a rich man, hotelier of the Hotel à la Croix in the rue des Gournais. And no one could ever find out the why or wherefore. On the same day the judicial authorities were informed and [executed sanctions].[9]

In useful historical detail the third example falls between the first two:

In the same period there was a dragoon [*compaignon*] in Metz who, while dining, stuck a knife right into his throat and killed himself, and, like the other [the sanction follows] . . .[10]

Of the four suicides in the Metz chronicle—all in this section—the odd man out was significantly a monk. The monk's clerical status would rob the city authorities both of jurisdiction over, and direct knowledge of, how his remains were disposed of. The entry runs:

loch man verprent in.' Ibid., 352: '[1478] 17 Feb: In dem jar da erstach sich mit willen selber ot sulmaister von Nurmberg auf Pabenberger weg. man verprent in nicht. man sprach, er het dem pischof 4 gld. geben, daz man in grub zu sant Mertein zu Pabenperg. und het im hie ain opfer und kain sibent, und darnach starb sie rechtz tods an Petri Pauli.' A *sibent* was a Mass for the soul on the seventh day after burial.

[7] J. F. Huguenin, ed., *Les chroniques de la ville de Metz (900–1552)* (Metz, 1838), Cf. Schmitt, at nn. 21–2, 27, and 38.

[8] *Chroniques de . . . Metz*, 472.

[9] Ibid., 471.

[10] Ibid.

In the same month in the abbey of St Pierremont [a Premonstratensian house, twenty-five miles north of Metz] there was a monk who hanged and strangled himself.[11]

No punishment is mentioned. This silence may even conceal the chronicler's indignation that a monk, unlike a citizen, could escape without any.

The Metz chronicler also records two attempted suicides. The first concerns a notary and is strangely circumstantial.

It happened at the same time in Metz that a man called Godair, the notary, went off along a little alley called Vaizelle, near the palace, and by temptation of the Devil tried to cut his own throat. But he was rescued and talked out of it by Collin Menal who, deeply shocked, remonstrated with him and said it was a bad thing to have done [*c'estoit mal fait*]. Godair was taken away and arrested, and questioned about what he thought he was doing in thus trying to murder himself. And he answered that he had met six big personages, dressed in black, who made him do it. Collin had not seen them. But they cannot have been other than devils.[12]

The chronicler's next entry tells of the burning of three witches and reminds us that the golden age of devils was at hand.

The notary Godair was arrested but not, apparently, punished. Punishment for an attempt was anyway an uncertain area,[13] and the authorities may also have been embarrassed that this offence had been committed by someone so close to the administrative circle, as 'le notaire' must have been. Before describing the other attempt in the Metz chronicle I would like to corroborate this reasoning by reference to another *Stadtchronik*, of Nuremberg. Nuremberg was ahead of Metz in the definition of its law on attempted suicide. Johann Müllner's *Annals of Nuremberg* record, among official acts of 1393, a decision by the city council that any citizen who tried to stab himself to death in the Council Rooms should be excluded from them for three years.[14] It is not hard to guess that an incident must have lain behind that decree. For the punishment to make its point, the incident must have involved a man commonly present in the council rooms. Müllner was perhaps still too much of a traditional chronicler to mention the case, but he was also too fastidious to ignore the legislative result. And all this implies, for the historian, and ápropos of the Metz notary, that it was only in a mature city government that anyone knew what to do if a colleague attempted suicide. Metz in 1484, in other words, was still in this respect immature, hence no mention of any punishment for the notary.

The other attempted suicide in the Metz chronicle did incur punishment.

---

[11] Ibid., 472.   [12] Ibid., 474.
[13] Cf. *The Curse on Self-Murder*, ch. 12.
[14] Quoted by H. Knapp, *Das alte Nürnberger Kriminalrecht* (Berlin, 1896), 118 n. 7.

This one concerned, not an administrative colleague, but an intemperate young soldier. The entry runs:

On Wednesday after Candlemas in the same year [Wednesday, 3 February 1485: this was the 'same year' by the chronicler's reckoning] another dragoon hanged himself in Metz. He was called Jean Ruxay, and the cause of his deed is said to have been the intemperate love he had for a young woman he had living with him. Some fellow-dragoons had ventured to invite her out. He was caught in the act, given help at once, and cut down unstrangled. And as soon as the judicial authorities were told, they had him arrested and whipped.[15]

It is here, where inhibition was at its lowest and a writer's interest combined with his access to information, that a chronicle at last approaches a portrait.

The character of all these anecdotes, then, whether from Nuremberg, Augsburg, or Metz, suggests that they came from the purlieus of a court-room, and that it is thanks to the author's status, and to the loose structure of his chronicle, that memory of them survives. In this category the chronicle of Donaueschingen in Bavaria remains an odd man out. Because this town remained within the jurisdiction of its traditional counts, the counts of Zimmern, not only is the chronicle called after them, rather than the town (though it belongs by character in the 'town' category); it was much less sure of its jurisdiction. The truth is harder to come by for that reason.

Why so, will appear from a look at its report of a suicide. It should be explained that the date of the case, 1455, coincided with a specific crisis in German legal development: the apogee of the power of the Westphalian court of the *Veme*. The secret proceedings and secret membership of the *Veme* affected most of western Germany at this date. Not only did sentences of the *Veme* evoke terror. They struck across a web of older jurisdictions, causing confusion all the greater because no one knew about the sentences until after their execution. It was the impact of this confusion on another law-minded chronicler that brought the following case into his record:

In the year 1455 after Christ's birth a well-to-do, successful peasant called Ulrich Huen was living in Winzlaw in the free lordship of Zimmern. All his life he had been a miser, such that he thought of nothing and desired nothing but temporal possessions. On Easter Sunday, 1455, he went to the fields to see how well his harvest

---

[15] *Chroniques de . . . Metz*, pp. 471–2: 'Le mercredi apres la chandelleur, audit an, se pendit encore à Metz un autre compaignon, nommé Jehan Ruxay. Et disoit on qu'il avoit ce fait pour l'amour desordonnée qu'il avoit à une jonne garse qu'il entretenoit et que aulcuns com-paignons vouloient festoier; lequel fut trouvé au fait et subitement secouru et despendu et ne fut point estranglé. Et incontinent que la justice en fut advertie, / [p. 472] ilz le firent appre-hendeir et, à force de verges, tout nud tres bien chaistoyer.'

was growing, thinking to get a good price for it. While doing so he was overcome by despair, so great that he hanged himself, on a tree in a forest not far from Winzlaw.[16]

So far the story may be judged psychologically unsophisticated. It relies on moralization without observed detail. But it is not intrinsically incredible, so matters are only complicated by what comes next. The writer goes on:

It was a herdsman from the village who raised the alarm. Many people of all ages went out from the village to the forest to see the shocking sight. They thronged round. But no one could be found with either will or authority to remove the body from the tree. For it was the view of many people that this was the work of the Westphalians [i.e. the *Veme*], and that [the peasant] had been sentenced to execution by their secret court. For such commonly happened in Germany at that time. But there was a girl from Winzlaw present. By female standards she held many privileges, including freedom from the Westphalian jurors. So that the unfortunate man could be buried she climbed the tree and cut the noose, and the man was buried.[17]

That is the end of the suicidal part of the story. On its own it sounds plausible.

But the clock then strikes thirteen; that is, the sequel to the tale casts doubt on what has gone before. For the rest of the account is about a 'private war', declared against the commune of Wenzlau by the aforementioned girl's powerful uncle. He accused the village of having forced the girl to commit her contempt of the dreaded *Veme* court by cutting down the corpse. The village, he contested, had thus put his niece in mortal danger from the vengeful *Veme*. That quarrel may not directly concern the suicide. But it did directly concern the neighbouring communes, who laboriously reconciled the parties. It consequently concerned the chronicler who wrote it all down. So, as often happens with our suicides, the motive for its being recorded is simultaneously a reason why it may be untrue, for there were clearly two views in Donaueschingen about whether the death was a suicide. The chronicler opted all the more firmly for the suicidal one because he disliked the girl's uncle, and wished his readers to believe an account that rendered the baron's revenge more capricious. Although what he leaves us affects to be a 'portrait' of a suicide, therefore, it is possibly, for all these reasons, a false one.

One motive, then, these German examples show, why some town chroniclers broke with the general reticence and mentioned suicides, was that such

---

[16] H. Decker-Hauff, *Die Chronik der Grafen von Zimmern* (Donaueschingen and Stuttgart, 1964), vol. 1, pp. 227.7–14.
[17] Ibid., 227.14–25.

a historian might have within himself, half-hidden in the vernacular man of letters, a lawyer with an ear cocked for incidents touching the judicial rights and doings of his town. I said the conditions for such chronicles obtained especially in the Empire, but that does not mean their kind of rapportage was unknown elsewhere, only that it was rarer and more varied in character. In fifteenth-century France the self-confidence of towns was too precarious to breed an equivalent genre. But records that approach it confirm that, if town chronicles had existed, they would not have lacked suicides. One example illustrates this well. It is the vernacular *Journal of a Paris Burgher* kept by a university graduate who survived civil turmoil and the English occupation of Paris, and kept a journal from 1405 to 1449. It reads as if the author felt and wished to fill the lack of any other ground-level city chronicle for the stirring events he covers, indeed as if his *Journal* was, unofficially, such a chronicle but kept on behalf of the University, whose interests the writer rarely misses a chance to extol. Like the other records this one was a mélange of crimes, horrors, grain-prices, natural disasters, and political explosions as seen from his own street; and here, duly, we do find our suicide.

On 10 June 1413, St Landry's day, the eve of Pentecost, messire Jacques de la Rivière, knight, and Simon de Mesnil, esquire, were brought out of the King's Palais and dragged from there to the Halles, at least Jacques de la Rivère was, for he was dead. He had killed himself by hitting himself hard on the head with a full quart of wine. He had struck so hard as to break his head and brain right open.

So he was easy to drag. The living prisoner was put on a cart and made to hold a cross, then both had their heads cut off, and 'people said at the execution that the arrest of these two was the best thing that had happened for the kingdom for twenty years past.' Thus the anonymous graduate diarist. A German town chronicler would have said what happened to the bodies. The Paris diarist lacked that particular interest in jurisdiction, but was in closer touch with the people's satisfaction, as also, perhaps, their inaccuracy, since another account, in the more formal chronicle of Jean Jouvenal des Ursins, gives the marginally more credible explanation that Jacques's head had been split by an irate captain of the guard, who had attacked the prisoner with an axe. So it was not just a head that was split. Tradition, too, suffered its familiar fate.[18]

A bigger exception to the German monopoly was England, where a new genre of vernacular town chronicle emerged in late fifteenth-century

[18] J. Shirley, *A Parisian Journal, 1405–1449* (Oxford, 1968), 72–3, a translation made straight from Vatican, Reg. Lat. 1923, of a text otherwise only available in an edition by A. Tuetey, *Journal d'un Bourgeois de Paris*, Société de l'Histoire de Paris et de l'Ile de France (Paris, 1881).

London. It had begun as a record of mayors, and although the chronicles are usually anonymous we know that sometime mayors, and other city officers, were among their authors. The lists are duly filled out by history, rather on the model of the monastic Easter tables, centuries before. Some of the history is political. The first chronicles of the genre were written out in 1461, the year of the Yorkist victory in the civil war, giving London merchants the government they longed for, so Yorkist expeditions get honourable space. But the bulk of history, together with earlier sections translated from older Latin chronicles, is made up by a citizen's casual ephemera. One sixteenth-century critic of the genre dismissed the authors as simpletons: 'poor Latin-less authors . . . lay chronographers that write of nothing but the mayors and sheriffs and the dear year, and the great frost.'[19]

But he reckoned without social historians, for the vernacular chronicles' net dragged lower than any Latin equivalent and concentrated especially, as in Germany, on the day-to-day workings of the law. Again, suicides come into the picture for this reason. I know of two. One is in 'Gregory's Chronicle', the relevant part of which is usually attributed to William Gregory, a skinner who died in 1467 after having served his years respectively as sheriff and mayor. Gregory records for the year 1441 that

there was pynner [a maker of pins] hyngge hym sylfe on a Palme Sonday. And he was alle nakyd save hys breche' and then he was caryd in a carte owte of the cytte.[20]

Even this bald report, it will be noticed, shows the legally-minded writer knows and cares what happened to the body. The suicide duly comes in a context, on neighbouring pages, of burnings of witches, heretics, and pederasts, and of hangings, drawings and quarterings; all the fruit of a scaffold's-eye view quite a match for anything in Germany.

The second example betrays a more commercial preoccupation, as seen by a draper and an ex-sheriff. It comes in *The Great Chronicle of London*, written very early in the sixteenth century, almost certainly by Robert Fabyan, a draper and member of the Draper's Company. Fabyan had been sheriff in 1493 and long remained an alderman.[21] His interests correspond with this background, and he accordingly notices a draper's suicide which occasioned disappointment to the then sheriff. It happened in the mayoralty of William White, in 1490.

---

[19] Thomas Nashe [†1601], quoted by A. Gransden, *Historical Writing in England*, vol. 2 (London, 1982), 241; ibid., 220–48 for the London chronicles in general. For William Gregory and his Chronicle, ibid., 230.

[20] J. Gairdner, ed. 'The Chronicle of William Gregory, Skinner', in *The Historical Recollections of a Citizen of London in the Fifteenth century*. Camden Society, 123, new series, 17 (1876), 55–264, on p. 184.

[21] Gransden, *Historical Writing*, vol. 2, 231–2.

In thys mayers tyme a Taylour named Roger Shavelock Dwelling w'yn ludgate and holdyng there a Shopp well storid wyth drapery, kut his awne throte.[22]

That is all on the suicide: name, place, method, date. But it is more than all, for the drapery has nothing to do with it. The writer has already betrayed preoccupations which run riot in the sequel. For the suicide-tailor's stock, he goes on, was worth no less than a thousand marks 'or nere abowth'. There was duly a scramble. The then sheriff's men searched every gutter and cranny of the store for the dead man's effects, only to be challenged for its possession, its value once known, by the king's almoner. The king was Henry VII. His almoner was unlikely to be left in the lurch in such a tug of war. Nor was he. The almoner promptly regranted the suicide's property to the widow on condition she marry a named servant of his own, a condition which she met.[23] It is the same lure, then, as in Germany, that brings suicide to the urban chronicler's pages: the everyday workings of law.

France, then, and England; each, at least in its capital city, offered a partial exception to the German monopoly of the kind of *Stadtchronik* that had space for suicides. The third exceptional area was Burgundy. The economic heartland of Burgundy fell in what are now the Benelux countries and were a mass of cities, self-conscious enough—both despite ducal government and because of it—to breed a mentality comparable to that of the German town scribes, agog for local news. Georges Chastellain (1415–75) was more than a town chronicler. Some contemporaries called him the greatest writer of their age. But his historical works, filling some ten thousand pages, have some of those *Stadtchronik* qualities. By birth a thorough Fleming, Chastellain spent his literary life in Valenciennes, one of the duchy's main seats of government, and in an official residence where he recieved a government salary to 'put in writing the latest matters of interest'. Chastellain was thus well placed to hear news from both court and city, and we cannot be surprised that his chronicle reads at times like those of Frankfurt and Metz.

Nor, therefore, that it can mention suicide. Chastellain accordingly tells of a suicide which occurred in Valenciennes in 1461. He dates it to 1 November, All Saints' Day, when a 'big, stout clog-maker' of the town, aged sixty or more, and 'fairly rich according to his status', got up early from the conjugal bed, leaving his wife asleep, and 'hanged himself in his chamber, with a rope he had prepared in secret the night before.' Chastellain goes on: 'He hung so low that his legs dragged on the ground, and no one ever saw so

---

[22] A. H. Thomas and I. D. Thornley, eds., *The Great Chronicle of London* [*Guildhall MS 3313*] (G. W. Jones, London, 1938), 243.
[23] *Great Chronicle*, 244.

horrible a sight or so deformed a creature as this villein, found hanging.'
Had Chastellain gone to look? More probably he had heard an account from
an eyewitness, who may have added the following psychological detail, that
people said the clogmaker had gone to confession the evening before on the
Vigil of All Saints. It was this confession, they said, that had allowed the
'Enemy' to deceive his victim, giving him the false hope that his soul would
be saved even though he might destroy his body by 'despair'.[24]

Chastellain had noticed that low-class man's suicide only because it had
happened under his nose, in Valenciennes. Elsewhere, notoriety alone could
bring a deed of this kind to his notice. Enough notoriety attached to one
attempted suicide to win it, rare for an attempt, a place in a chronicle. Since
it happened shortly before the clog-maker's suicide and Chastellain records
it just before, it may indeed have been this notorious attempt that prompted
Chastellain to turn to the subject at all, and bring the clog-maker in. At all
events, at some date near the end of October, at Chateau-Porcien, seventy
miles south of Valenciennes, a high nobleman had tried to stab himself to
death with a knife. What made the act notorious was that the duke, Philip
the Good, had made an official visit to the Chateau-Porcien a few days
before, and that the nobleman was a principal functionary of the town. A
ducal visit was no ordinary event. The contrast between its attendant fes-
tivities and the nobleman's rash act sent a shock through the population.
The culprit was Anthoine de la Barre, master of the household of the lords
of Croy, and hence a leading figure in the town. Chastellain attributes his
act to 'some frenzy which took hold of the man for three or four days in
succession'. But he simultaneously hints at a more particular motive. Shortly
before the attempt, Anthoine had asked his wife—'une belle gentil femme',
daughter of a celebrated squire in Ponthieu—whether, in the event of his
death, she would undertake not to remarry. His wife, 'not knowing what
sort of answer to give to such a question, asked what he meant and what
had prompted such a pointless enquiry'. That is all. All we know other than
that is that, one morning very soon after the duke's departure, Anthoine
rose early from his bed, went off alone to get a knife, and tried to stab
himself in the stomach. According to his own later account, the knife was
blunt and he had to place its point on his stomach and run against the side
of a table before could do himself serious injury. But that nearly killed him,
and when a servant arrived Anthoine was 'as if dead'. The servant's shriek
alerted the household, who arrived on the scene and were duly horror-
struck, none more so than the wife. So the half-dead magnate was carried

---

[24] Georges Chastellain, *Chronique*, bk 6, ch. 50; in *Oeuvres*, ed. K. de Lettenhove, 8 vols.
(Brussels, 1963–4), vol. 4, 170–1. On Chastellain: J. Calmette, *The Golden Age of Burgundy*
(London, 1962), 193–5; R. Vaughan, *Valois Burgundy* (London, 1975), 32–3.

away and nursed, in the hope, Chastellain says, that his life might return, 'even though, had it not been for the man's soul, death might have been the better outcome.' Anthoine did not die. But the moment that fact became clear, the once-great man was banished from his town and residence, and disgraced for ever.[25] As attraction to a chronicler, to the quality of public scandal the episode no doubt joined that of the fall of an official.

The everyday gossip of city government, then, could act as a lure, to attract suicide into a historian's record. There was a second lure. It derived this time from supernatural beliefs, shared to a greater or lesser degree between the chronicler and his compatriots, and bearing on their common interests. The belief was that which linked natural calamity with human wrongdoing. It gave all concerned, not a taboo but its opposite: a positive, curious, scandal hunting prurience for things otherwise taboo.

SUICIDES AND BAD WEATHER

The main calamity that touched everyone in this way was bad weather. An interest in unusual weather was older even than the mature chronicle form, and is found in the early chronological tables from which chronicles grew. A bad harvest or very cold winter could characterize a year and help lend structure to a series of years in the memory. So weather belonged among subjects of chronicles from the beginning, and a keen interest in it survived long after other ways had been found for fixing dates. The survival of this interest was ensured by a second factor: an association of good and bad weather with good and bad human acts. Throughout the Middle Ages we know some people believed that saints' relics, at least if they were in the right place and properly treated, procured *good* weather.[26] Suicide conversely had a bad effect, unless, again, the effect was neutralized by appropriate ritual. This last condition could mean anything from prayers and penance, down to ritualistic maltreatment of the body. We only have to remember that weather affected crops, and hence food supply, to appreciate the supreme importance of this association, for which perfectly good scientific reasons were then thought to obtain.[27]

[25] Chastellain, *Chronique*, ibid., 171–2. I am unable to date this incident nearer than to a few days *before* the suicide of the clog-maker, and can offer no explanation of Chastellain's treating 'Saint-Martin' (normally 11 November) as earlier than All Saints' Day (1 November), other than the unlikely suggestion that it is St Martin of Vertou (†c.601) who is in issue. His feast-day was on 24 October.

[26] A. Vauchez, *La sainteté en Occident* (Rome, 1981), 542–4; E. W. Kemp, *Canonization in the Western Church* (Oxford, 1948), 169–70.

[27] Because demons lived in disturbed air. See, for instance, Herrad of Hohenbourg, *Hortus*

Thus a writer will say 'this year, on such-and-such a day, winds destroyed crops, and people said it was due to such-and-such a suicide.' These entries are again to be found predominantly in German chronicles. In an anonymous one from Augsburg, for instance, we read how in 1300, on St Mark's day (Monday, 25 April):

a wretch called the Straussmair died by hanging himself, and the same day came a thunderstorm and struck three women in a goatstall, vegetables rotted in the fields, and the same day a man drowned in the lake. So St Mark's day was appointed as a day of fasting so that God should protect us from suicide by hanging [*gechentod*].[28]

A second case with the same message is one from Zurich in 1417. A priest who had killed himself (*hat sich entleibt*) is mentioned for that year in one of the town chronicles because of a dispute about the bad weather, the town council having complained to the church authorities that

Our confederates and the whole land are complaining because, they believe, the dreadful weather we have had for so long is the result of the burial in consecrated ground of a man of this kind who had killed himself.[29]

In Basle, in 1439, we read the same. The chronicle of the city's resident diplomat-lawyer, Henry of Bernstein, includes this entry:

On 4 June [1439] a respectable Basle woman called Mrs Beringer went off her head, around midnight, got up [from bed], got on to the roof and jumped off to her death. She was buried at St Leonard's. And it rained continuously for nearly a week, and people said it was because her body was in consecrated ground. So the Basle city council decided that she be dug up and thrown into the Rhine. This decision taken, on the 9 June the rain let up a little. Then it began again and continued for another day and a night.[30]

Deliciarum. Studies of the Warburg Institute, 36 (London and Leiden, 1979), vol. 1, p. 245 (ch. 490): 'Itaque [Judas] in aere strangulatus elevatur, demonibus in aere commorantibus associatur. Aer vero pro demonibus eum abhorrens a se repulit.' Most of the same idea is found in William of Nottingham's commentary on Mt. 27, in Oxford, Bodleian, MS Laud Misc. 165, fol. 531v: 'elevatus [Judas] in aere, socium demonibus se ostenderet in hoc aere caliginoso habitantibus.'

[28] *Anonymous chronicle*, 991–1483, in *Die deutsche Chroniken*, vol. 22 [*Augsburg*, 3] (Leipzig, 1892), p. 462: 'da man zalt 1300 jar an sant Marx tag da starb ain erber man, hiess der Straussmair, ains gechentods, und desselben tags kam ain wetter und erschluog drei frawen bei dem ziegelstadel, die kraut dörten in den äckern, auch desselben tags erdranck ain man in dem loch; da ward sant Marx tag aufgesetzt ze fasten, das uns got behüet von ainem gachen tod & c.'

[29] Quoted by E. Osenbrüggen, *Studien zur deutschen und schweizerischen Rechtsgeschichte* (Schaffhausen, 1868), 339: 'hat sich entleibt'. Ibid., 441: 'unser eidgenossen und gemein land dar uf schryen und meinen, daz sy daz gross unwetter, so yetz lang zit gewesen ist, da von haben, daz man einen sölichen menschen, der sich selber ertödet had, in dem gewichten ertrich liegen lasse.'

[30] A. Bernoulli, ed., *Basler Chroniken*, vol. 5 (Leipzig, 1895), 479.23–430.3: 'Am 4. tag des

Again, that same chronicle of Metz, which records five consecutive suicides in the year 1484, adds that they were followed by heavy rain, a late grape harvest, and conditions too bad for sowing.[31] Meanwhile in the Lüders chronicle of Nuremberg, for 1497, a possible reference to suicide—possible because of this very association, together with the ellipsis—can be read in an account of how

This year the Devil took away a monk of Heilbrunn, body and soul . . . and there came the biggest tempest that anyone had ever seen, and people thought the city would be destroyed. It happened at four o'clock in the morning.[32]

It would grow even easier to illustrate this feature from chronicles after 1500. But it is already clear, before that date, that a common community interest in bad weather served a suicide, often of an otherwise obscure person, as passport into a town record.

Among this group of chronicle entries, too, there remains one odd man out. This time it is odd mainly on account of place but also, for that reason, of time. It is from Italy, where town chronicles of this kind developed early. Two Venetian chronicles record a severe tempest and flood of 1342, together with a belief that they had been caused by a suicide. Both are written by members of Venice's patrician class, and tell an identical story in different words. The earlier, a work of uncertain authorship called *Chronicle of Venice from the beginning to 1478*, describes the event first in a circumlocution now familiar to us, but straight afterwards spells out what is meant.

It appears that there was, here in Venice, a schoolmaster, who through poverty or despair gave himself, body and soul, to the Enemy, in that he was found to have hanged himself by the throat.

The writer goes on:

For this reason there came a dreadful tempest here in Venice such that none greater was ever seen. The water rose so high that ships were floated on to the land and the

brochmonats was eyn eersamme frow ze Basel, mit nammen die Beringerin, kam umb mitternacht von sinnen, und stůnd uff und gieng uff das tach, und sprang ûber das tach ab ze tod; ward zu sant Leonhardt vergraben. Und regnet fast umb die seb. zyt; meint man, es wer dorumb, das sy in gewychten leg. Do beschlosz dez rodt von Basel, man solt sy uszgraben und inn Ryn werffen. Do sollichs beschach, uff den 9. tag des monats, hort es ein wenig uff regnen; und fieng dornoch wider an, und triebs ein tag und ein nacht.' Henry of Bernstein: ibid., 329–49. Cf. H. R. Hagemann, *Basler Rechtsquellen im Mittelalter* (Basle, 1981), 286 n. 970.

[31] *Chroniques de . . . Metz*, as above (p. 102), 472. Cf. Schmitt, p. 21 n. 22.

[32] Quoted by J. Dieselhorst, 'Die Bestrafung der Selbstmörder im Territorium der Stadt Nürnberg', *Mitteilungen des Vereins für Geschichte der Stadt Nürnberg*, 44 (1953), pp. 62 and 173, n. 23 [from Nürnberg, Stadtbibl. MS 447, p. 581]: 'Dis iahr führte der teuffel einen heilsprunner münch mit leib und seel hinweg, geschahe . . . mit dem allergrössten sturmbwindt, das man vermaindt, es werde die ganze statt einfallen, geschehen umb vier uhr in der Nacht.'

bridges were under water. It rose hour by hour, against the expectation of the citizens, who thought at each hour that it could rise no further.[33]

The calamity was accompanied by the sight of a galley full of devils.

In a later Venetian chronicle, but one consistent with the same tradition, the cause of the same tempest is revealed to an old fisherman by St Mark, the city's protector. As a guide to the nature of the belief in question its story is worth hearing. According to the chronicle, St Mark tells the fisherman about the suicide of the schoolmaster and instructs him to tell the authorities, presenting him with a ring from his finger as proof of the vision. The fisherman duly tells some city officials, who recognize the ring, repurchase it for St Mark's at a price fixed by the saint during the vision (5 ducats) and take the old man to the Doge and Council to re-tell his story there; and the fisherman repeats, as St Mark had instructed him, how 'the schoolmaster who was at San Felice had been found hung by the neck.' At this the Doge and Council ordain a procession and a Mass at St Mark's, in gratitude to the saint for abating the storm, and to make amends for the suicide.[34]

Suicides in the Chronicles of Religious Orders

We have crossed one side of the square, then, and covered both its legal and its religious quarters. The process is now to be repeated on the other side. I said just now that the town chronicler, especially in decentralized Germany, was moved by two impulses, legal and supernatural, to bring suicides into his narrative. These writers were mostly laymen and wrote only in the vernacular, but clerical, Latin writers were subject to analogous motives. Although they worked in appropriately different ways, the same two factors, legal and

[33] Venice, Bibl. Marc., MS Ital. VII, 53 [7419], cart. fol. 162v: 'el par che el fose qui in uenetia uno maistro de schuola el qual o per povertade o per desperation el se dava in anima et in corpo al inimicho et questo perche el dito maistro fo trouato che luj medesmo se avevasse apichado per la gola et per questo el uene una grandissima fortuna qui in uenetia di modo che mai fo uisto la major. et l'aqua cresete tanto che nave le fondamenta et pontj de uenetia erano soto acqua . . .' [At the foot of fol. 163r two patrons saints make an appearance to the stupefied city and confirm]: 'che questo causaua uno el qual se a inpichado luj mede[s]mo per la gola'.

[34] Venice, Bibl. Marc. MS Ital. VII. Cod. 321 [8838], cart. fol. 73r: [St Mark tells the *vecchietto*] 'manifestali [= the *procuratori*] tutto quello che hai uisto, che questo è stato un Maistro de scuola, el qual è morto disperado, che per sua mala vita fase questo, ma la gracia de Dio per le preghiere l'ha guarita. Quo dicto, Beatus Marcus disparuit, et la fortuna cessò. . . . il uecchietto tolse l'annello datoli per s. Marco et mostrollo a quelli dicendo, che da S. Marco lo haueua habudo et che li hauea ordinado lo douesse mostrar, et che per premio suo li douessano dar ducati cinque et non più. Li Procuratori uisto l'annello, assai se maravegliano, conosiendo quello denar di S. Marco, perche andati al Santuario . . . [the *vecchietto*] facendo relation, come il Maistro de Scuola che stava a S. Felise, era stà trouato appiccado per la gola ad una coluna.'

supernatural, are to be seen at work here too, and with the same result. By 'here' I mean history written in religious orders. I start with a monastic chronicle which illustrates the former of the two effects.

A MONASTERY AND ITS RIGHTS

The first part of the chronicle of Dunstable priory, in Buckinghamshire, is normally called the Dunstable 'Annals'. It was written by various members of the priory over the course of the thirteenth century, and concerns itself mainly with the priory's domestic affairs, especially finance. 'Of all thirteenth-century chronicles,' writes Dr Gransden, historian of medieval English chroniclers, 'it gives the most vivid picture of a predominantly agricultural economy of a religious house.'[35] This preoccupation implied, in its turn, a constant interest in law. The reader learns of the priory's disputes with neighbours about rights and boundaries, about its dealings with the town of Dunstable, and with its bishop, the bishop of Lincoln. The writers support these accounts with documents from the priory's own archive as well as from Crown records.

In English law, suicide had enough consequences to render it of direct interest to a chronicle of this kind. In particular, a suicide's act put his inheritance in jeopardy and, because a suicide was supposed not to receive church burial, it robbed the local church of its burial right. Both effects concerned a property-minded monastic writer, so it should not surprise us to find that it is precisely in a chronicle of this proven character that there appear some of the few suicides to feature in this kind of history. The Dunstable Annals mention three, without shame or circumlocution.

One is of a rich and famous man holding high public office. The case is in fact another 'whisper about the great' since, while we know about the man and his career, no other source mentions the suicide, and we are bound to notice that the source which does mention it is the one most emphatically *un*interested in the rest of the man's career. The man in question was Walter de la Haye. He pursued his career in Ireland, became deputy governor for Edward I, got involved in a family quarrel, killed his own nephew and then himself. To the Dunstable annalist most of these great matters are peripheral. All he says is:

[1295] In this same year Walter de la Haye committed felony in Ireland by killing his nephew, his brother's son, and afterwards himself.[36]

[35] A. Gransden, *Historical Writing in England*, vol. 1 (London, 1974), 424; and more generally 424–9. The chronicle, under the title of the first part, *Annales de Dunstaplia*, is edited by H. R. Luard, *Annales monastici*, vol. 3, Rolls Series (1866), 15–420.

[36] *Ann. de Dunstaplia*, 401.

The writer's motive for mentioning the suicide was not that Walter was a great man. His interest was in property. Walter had married a local heiress. His death raised issues of succession to estates within a few miles of the community. At the time of writing, these had been occupied by the wife's relations who had acted, the chronicle says, on seeing that Walter's sons failed to stake a claim. By recording these details the writer was defending the interests of the possessors, his neighbours, and hence the stability of property in the region. From records relating to Ireland, it appears likely that he had even lengthened the family's title by antedating Walter's death by two or more years.[37]

We hear of Walter's suicide, then, because the story was not so much about him as about rights affecting the monastery. A similar rule admitted to the same Annals two other suicides from the opposite end of the social scale. They were apparently recorded because the Dunstable priory had failed to get its way in refusing them burial, being overruled by the Knights Hospitaller 'whose privileges we fear'.[38] But the bare facts are again there.

[1274] In this same year the wife of Benedict Young spontaneously threw herself into a well and died.[39]

[1283] In this same year a serf of John Durant the younger of Dunstable [the Durants were rich wool-merchants and creditors of the priory] threw himself into John's well and died.[40]

Two entries in the 1287 Bedfordshire Eyre roll probably record the same suicides, offering a precious overlap between our types of source. The monk's clipped style is similar to that of the King's clerk. Nor were his motives so different: a monastery beset by thrusting powers like towns and wool-merchants, had need to register its rights. This need, echoed in the chronicle, was what opened its pages to suicide. We shall see the same forces at work in northern France, but in records with almost no pretence, this time, to be more than criminal registers.[41]

SAINTS AND THEIR ENEMIES

Besides institutional rights, there was a second reason for a monastic historian to mention suicide. Like the urban chronicler, but on a higher plane

---

[37] Cf. *Handbook of British Chronology*, ed. F. M. Powicke and E. B. Fryde (London, 1961²), 149–50.
[38] *Ann. de Dunstaplia*, 260.
[39] Ibid.
[40] Ibid., 297–8. Cf. London, PRO JUST 1/12 m 35 and 35 d (*infra*, p. 434).
[41] See below, pp. 180–2.

of religious sophistication, his monastic counterpart could allude to suicide as a negative pole in a story designed to affirm religious beliefs. The chronicle is here contiguous to the saint's *Life*. The same motif will appear often, in the chapters below which deal with saints' *Lives*, as the 'Judas'-type suicide.

The saint's *Life* was a very old and persistent literary form. This antiquity and persistance is reflected, in chronicles, in the wider chronological spread of our examples. The earliest in my dossier is from the early eleventh century, in a history of what is now southern Holland between the years 997 and 1018. It is the *De diversitate temporum*, by Alpert of Metz. Alpert had been born in Utrecht, but was a monk in Metz when, *c.*1021, he wrote what remains one of the best-informed historical sources for that period. Its title can be translated *How Times Change*. At one point the author exalts the saintly merits of a former bishop of Utrecht, Ansfrid. But where many contemporaries would have done this by listing the bishop's posthumous miracles, Alpert takes another approach. He admits that *few* miracles were recorded for Ansfrid. But that, Alpert insists, was only because he had shunned the publicity that miracles entailed, and preferred to place his hopes of Heaven on a pure conscience. That he *had* a pure conscience is confirmed by the fate of someone who tried to challenge it. Alpert tells the incident from his own experience. Its protagonist is a 'demoniac' who had slandered the saintly Ansfrid. Alpert writes:

I once heard a demoniac itemize the crimes he himself had committed and he included among them that he had bombarded the bishop with slander, without grounds. While Ansfrid was still a monk the man had said scandalous things about him. Despite all this, the demoniac's confession insisted, he had in fact known nothing whatever reprehensible about Ansfrid and was moved by nothing but envy, born of his own malice.[42]

Alpert explains why he has included this reminiscence:

I have briefly repeated this incident so that no one should think that Jesus Christ forbore to grant Ansfrid the power of miracles because of any shortcoming in the bishop's holy life. The truth is that Jesus granted him more, much more, namely eternal life in his own heavenly kingdom.[43]

That purpose may or may not have been achieved by the demoniac's testimonial. But it is not the end of the story, which is that the demoniac, despite his opportune confession, killed himself:

[42] Alpert of Metz, *De diversitate temporum*, ch. 15 (ed. A. Hulshof (Amsterdam, 1916), 22–3).
[43] Ibid. (p. 23).

A few days later [after the confession], while everyone else was asleep, the wretch went and hanged himself.[44]

The reader may think it unfair that after so generous a confession the demoniac should still be punished. Yes, it is unfair. In that measure this is a bad story, and historically more convincing for that. Alpert's motive for including it is anyway clear enough. *That*, he shows, is what happens to someone who slanders so holy a man. The bishop was not, after all, so short on divine miracles. His accuser had been punished, as the traitor Judas was, and as a warning to imitators.

A second example of this motif is in the *History of the Church of Durham*, written soon after 1104 and formerly attributed, with only partial justice, to the Durham monk Simeon. Early in the *History*, in a section mostly copied from earlier historians, the writer is discussing the Anglo-Saxons' veneration for St Cuthbert, buried at Durham, and finds occasion to mention the belief that women should not enter cemeteries. This 'belief' had probably grown up only in the previous decade or two.[45] But the writer, ascribing it to ninth-century Northumbrians, describes the rule as 'still strictly observed' in his own day, and gives examples from recent memory to show what sanctions protected it. One woman, for instance, died on the very night of her trespass. In another incident, 'not dissimilar', the writer says:

A rich citizen—he afterwards become a monk in this community—had a wife. She was always hearing from people about the various beautiful ornaments the church possessed, and these accounts fired her feminine avidity. She had to see these attractions. She was unable to control the enthusiasm she had thus conceived and her husband's position set her above [the control of] other women. So she took a path through the cemetery. Punishment followed, for not long afterwards she lost her wits. She bit her tongue off, and parted from her madness and her life at the same instant, for she slit her own throat. [How it happened was that] since she could not be held at home she would wander in various places, no one knew where. One day she was found lying dead under a tree, her throat covered in blood, and in her hand the knife with which she had killed herself.[46]

The Durham writer ends here, refusing further detail on this or on any comparable incident.

---

[44] Ibid.: 'Qui tamen miser paucis diebus post, ceteris dormientibus, suspendio mortem sibi conscivit.'

[45] According to a paper by the late Rosalind Hill, 'St Cuthbert, the women and the weasel', given to the Ecclesiastical History Society in March, 1970, and still unpublished. Professor Hill generously allowed me to refresh my memory by the loan of her text.

[46] Simeon of Durham, *Historia dunelmensis ecclesiae*, bk 2, ch. 9; ed. T. Arnold in Simeon's *Opera*, vol. 1, Rolls Series (London, 1882), 60–1.

Plenty of other divine manifestations against the audacity of women could be recounted. But since we have to pass to other matters let this, for brevity's sake, be enough.[47]

Plura . . . divinitus ostensa: this time there is no ambiguity because the woman's suicide is sufficiently explained. It was *divine* punishment.

Let me borrow the Durham chronicler's words: 'since we have to pass to other matters let this, for brevity's sake, be enough.' The other matter we pass to is a third example of the same kind of story. This one is exceptional in a number of ways, not least in that it comes in the Chronicle of Fra Salimbene of Parma: an indiscreet, vivid, disorganized mine of report and gossip, written in the early 1280s, and fed with the author's reminiscences of his own early days in the Franciscan order around 1240. One of these reminiscences concerned a certain unnamed Franciscan lay-brother, with whom the author had once gone begging in the manner of early mendicant friars.

I was a young man [writes Salimbene] when I lived in Pisa, and one day I was taken begging by a certain lay-brother, an imposter, full of vanity. He was Pisan and had at some stage, while living in the [Florentine] suburb of Fucecchio, been pulled by the brethren out of a well into which he had thrown himself—through what folly or despair enticed I know not. Later, a few days after we had gone begging together, he vanished. No one could find him anywhere. So the suspicion gained ground among the brethren that the Devil had carried him off. [We do not know.] The man himself will [certainly] know.[48]

This Franciscan story differs from the others in two ways. First, Salimbene does not say that the lay-brother committed suicide or even attempted it. The man had fallen down the well *nescio qua stulticia vel desperatione temptatus*. While allowing the possibility of a suicidal intention the expression is deliberately vague, both in starting *nescio qua* and in its offer of an innocent alternative. Reason has been seen for regarding such equivocation not only as consistent with a suicidal meaning but, in some circumstances, as a mark of it. A weaker application of the same principle can be made to the lay-brother's final disappearance. *Suspicati sunt* is vague. The allegation that *diabolus asportasset* is vague. The final *Ipse viderit* is essentially an inverted repetition of *nescio qua*. The narrator, that is, deliberately refuses to be drawn on how the man died.

A second peculiarity helps explain the first. It is that Salimbene is not writing about any dead saint or saints, but about himself. This 'vain' man had nearly exercised a decisive influence on Salimbene's life. This is shown by an incident told just before this passage in the chronicle. On their shared

---

[47] Simeon of Durham, 61.   [48] *Cronica, ad an.* 1229; ed. G. Scalia (Bari, 1966), 60–1.

begging trip the man had introduced Salimbene to dazzling sights but had left the novice discouraged. During the journey a stranger had approached the pair and, recognizing the nobly born Salimbene, had begun to upbraid him for wasting his promise on the religious life. Salimbene, the man argued, was his parents' only son and heir, and should return to his home in Parma. A begging life did not become him. That evening, the combination of the stranger's tirade and the lay-brother's 'vanity' nearly proved too much for Salimbene's Franciscan vocation. In the event he was reassured by a vision that very night. But he remembered the crisis long afterwards.[49] The biography in which the lay-brother had played the villain was thus the writer's own. The lay-brother was hence almost a 'Judas', a type for whom suicide was a fitting end.

Here, then, are three suicide stories, all from chronicles written by members of religious orders. What they have in common, beyond that origin, is their literary character. None had anything to do with legal rights or property. Rather all cases shared, as their *entrée* into the chronicle, the quality as illustrations of nemesis. A story has good and bad characters, and the latter come to a bad end. We reach here the second boundary of chronicles as a narrative category. In the suicide stories told earlier, from both urban and monastic writers, chronicle shared a frontier with law, recording rights, precedents, and the daily incidents of justice. Suicide, forbidden in more lofty narrative, came onto the historical page for this reason. In the last three cases history has accommodated suicides for a second motive, distantly analogous to the weather superstitions that put suicide in town chronicles. It was a dreadful fate reserved for 'bad' people, with a position in the story antithetical to that of its saintly hero.

In recording matters of law, and in contrasting good and evil, it hardly needs saying that these historical works performed indispensable social functions. They were so indispensable that they were not left to history alone. Specialized forms of writing developed to serve them. In looking for cases of suicide in chronicles, the vehicles of public history about public people, we found the genre as a whole reticent on the subject, and exceptions explained by reasons peculiar to themselves. The strongest exceptions lay on two opposite frontiers of the genre, legal and religious. These have shown us where to look next. It is time to cross the first of these frontiers and look at a kind of record where suicide was not a stranger, intruded by exceptional circumstance, but at home.

---

[49] Ibid. Salimbene's own references to his family can be found through the index to Scalia's edition, p. 1214.

6

Suicide and Judicial Records

In searching the past no student can be blamed for looking first at contemporary chroniclers. They wrote for him. But in the matter of suicide their reticence has been emphasized by its very exceptions, thrust into the narrative by considerations special to themselves. Reticence is itself a form of communication; and that of the chroniclers has revealed, among other things, the directions the search must now take. Those special areas, law and religion, whose peculiar conditions caused chroniclers to utter on suicide, had their own documentation, beyond any chronicles. They are therefore the areas, among medieval writings generally, where suicides were most likely to be recorded. That is a hair-thin logical deduction, but a moment's reflection will give it more substance.

Legal and Religious Sources

SIMILARITIES AND DIFFERENCES

Suicide was an extreme, a death supremely dreadful. This fact, the same which put an antipathy between suicide and most narrative history, had the opposite effect in many legal and religious documents. Take the legal first. Law represents public authority, an authority which claims a monopoly in violent death and tries to stamp out unauthorized kinds. Its efforts to do so normally start with a sign of failure, that is, a corpse. Since the corpses that result from suicide and from murder look much the same, suicide cannot avoid being caught up in any legal machinery designed to prevent murder; and if in the machinery, then also in any documents the machinery leaves behind.[1]

---

[1] Together with the sources named in the bibliography, with their editors' introductions, and books named in particular footnotes, the main secondary authorities underlying these and related reflections have been: A. Esmein, *A History of Continental Criminal Procedure, with special reference to France*, translated from the French edition of 1882; ed. W. E. Mikell

It was the same extreme character of suicide which meanwhile guaranteed its presence in some kinds of religious writing, those whose aim was to teach morals and spiritual values through miraculous narrative. *Miracula*—to use a convenient general term—were aimed directly not, like their judicial counterpart, at law and discipline, but at private hopes and fears. The target was the 'internal court', *forum internum*, or conscience, not the external, or *forum externum*. Far from starting with a corpse, *miracula* therefore lost all interest in a body once the soul had gone, unless, that is (by a miracle) the soul was to come back. Their function was to show a living soul what wonders God could do for it in its need, at a saint's behest. So a writer in the genre who ignored the most dreadful of deaths would have abused his art. Suicide marked a supreme crisis. Nothing could show a saint's saving power to better advantage. The same logic, it is true, could work upside-down to ensure that a few stubborn enemies of saints, the Judases, *did* die this dreadful death on the principle 'serve them right.' But the main passport of suicide to miracle stories, and the reason our search must go to them, was the occasion it gave to saints to prevent it.[2]

Judicial records, then, and miraculous narrative, are genres distinguished as a pair in this context above the genres we grouped together as 'chronicles'. The truer the chronicle was to its historical function the more suicide-shy it was; the nearer these judicial records and *miracula* were to theirs, the more 'suicide-prone'. Distinguished thus, as a pair, above other genres, judicial and miraculous records are also distinguished from each other. Again, let us take law first. A judicial record derives from a legal process. The process related to a historical incident, and was set in motion by its physical outcome. The outcome (in a homicide) was a corpse; as in a detective story, that corpse dominated the process, and the pattern of revelations and silences in the records can be traced to this origin. Thus corpses do not speak: so the records reveal next to nothing about any mental agonies preceding an act of suicide except, and this occasionally, by inference and where there is serious doubt, backed by living witnesses, about the suicide's mental responsibility. Nor will judicial reports normally record attempts at suicide, much less mere temptations, whatever their moral content, for these left no corpse. From a historian's viewpoint these are limitations. But they are offset by corresponding advantages. A corpse, because it belongs to a particular

---

(Boston, 1913); Sir F. Pollock and F. W. Maitland, *The History of English Law before the time of Edward I*, 2nd edn (Cambridge, 1898; reprint with introd. by S. F. C. Milsom, 1968); F. Lot and R. Fawtier, *Histoire des institutions françaises au moyen âge*, vol. 2: *Les institutions royales* (Paris, 1958), Bk 4: 'La justice'; and S. F. C. Milsom, *Historical Foundations of the Common Law*, 2nd edn (London, 1981).

[2] Guides to hagiography as a genre are listed on p. 252 n. 2 below.

person, place, and time, has a positive, fixed, unique character, and this too leaves its imprint on the sources. A judicial record nearly always gives the name of the person, usually the method of death and the place, and often the time even, occasionally, to the hour. Again, because a corpse could not speak it posed the question how it came to be there. That meant historical research, and therefore expense. The courts' way of meeting the expense (since a corpse cannot defend its own property, and where the dead man could be proved to have been some sort of criminal) was by distraint on the dead man's effects. The effects were therefore valued, giving judicial records of suicide a financial flavour. The flavour is so strong that some are little more than accounts, itemizing a suicide's possessions with corresponding pedantry. Thus while we may be told nothing whatever of a suicide's mental state, his chattels can be listed down to the last bucket and broom, their value to a halfpenny.

This positive, fixed quality is the dominant characteristic of judicial records. As often, a dominant characteristic hides its recessive opposite, and here the opposite is the same records' capacity for latent fiction. Bodies, after all, can be cosmetically disguised. So too can records concerning them, and these are more likely to be so, the more coercive the system of authority in which they are made. Frightened functionaries like their records to look good. Besides, medieval courts were not like efficient lawnmowers, simply mowing flat everything against the law. They pretended to be. But all that the pretence earned them was a place as one player in the complicated games that kept such justice as there was. One modern specialist warns that the disjunction between the demands made of documents respectively by legal and by historical correctness renders at least one set of judicial records, those of late medieval English assizes, 'factually worthless'.[3] That not only goes too far (all past data teach something) but it brushes past the only consideration that can unlock the records, namely the micro-politics that made them. In England, for instance, before the rise of the modern jury in the Tudor period—the jury, that is, that stands on the same footing with the judge in hearing the evidence—a judge relied on local jurors and coroners for the facts.[4] The grim power of Plantagenet royal

---

[3] J. S. Cockburn, 'Early modern assize records as historical evidence', *Journal of the Society of Archivists*, 5 (1975), 224. Quoted, with further comment on the varying historical reliability of different records and to the coroner's credit, by S. J. Stevenson, 'Suicide in south-east England, 1530–90; the legal process', *Continuity and Change*, 2 (i) (1987), 60 [the page-reference '244' is a mistake for '224']. The sceptical case is put with authority and moderation by E. Powell, 'Social research and the use of medieval criminal records', *Michigan Law Review*, 79 (1981), 967–78.

[4] For this and the following, see T. A. Green, 'The Jury and the English Law of Homicide, 1200–1600', *Michigan Law Review*, 74 (1976), 414–99. For coroners see pp. 132–3 below.

justice was in this measure illusory in that its application lay largely in the hands of jurors from the local community, locals who had their own ideas of justice and soon got wise to their capacity, so long as they did not disagree, to tell stories likely to procure it. This was especially true with homicide, whose degrees and kinds have always exceeded the subtlety of laws aimed to prevent them, laws which in the Middle Ages had hardly any subtlety at all. So it was especially true also of suicide. We shall see records of 'suicide' clearly deriving from the jurors' agreement to rob the gallows of a man they believe innocent of the kind of murder *they* thought he should be hanged for, for instance, of a notorious local bully. So they say the bully committed suicide.[5] That will be even more obvious in France in the Court of Requests,[6] where micro-politics were *sui generis*[7] but where the storyteller's rhetoric was as much, or more, in demand, if the substratum of alleged fact were to produce the required result. Neither in England nor in France does any of this show the stories were fiction. They were not pure fantasy. The art of leading dangerous courts by the nose is too subtle for that. What it does show is that, without context, the records' ostensible factuality will mislead. Proposed as bare truth they have a fictional side, and fantasy can lurk there.

The opposite is true of our second main category of source, *miracula*. Just how much historical incident may lie behind this or that medieval 'miracle' is a question endemic to the genre, and best tackled only in particular instances. But there only has to be some incident behind it, however little, to show how the relation of incident to document differs from that in a court record. The miracle lays weight on different aspects of the incident and is at risk from different distorting factors. Thus in *miracula* places are seldom defined, dates hardly at all. The naming of characters, even where credible, usually stops short at a 'John' or a 'Margaret'. Where the function of courts was to convict the right person for the right offence, miraculous narrative, free of that duty, devoted the same quantum of care to the moral aspects of a case. This is largely why it says a lot on motives for suicide, on psychological states which could produce it, and on the thoughts, and internal conversations, of people tempted by a suicidal impulse. The genre was better able to describe these thoughts and states for another reason. A miracle, for all that it relished the dire danger of suicide, ultimately aimed at salvation, so the suicidal person in a miracle had usually survived. Survivors tell tales, including tales about their thoughts and actions before an expected death. It is true that the minority, the punishment suicides—the

[5] Below, pp. 155, 171–4.   [6] Below, pp. 212–17.
[7] This and the following consequence are described by N. Z. Davis, *Fiction in the Archives* (Stanford, Calif., 1987).

'Judas' suicide, here the recessive opposite—said quite as little about motive as do judicial records. But the proper suicide miracle was not like that. It was a miracle precisely because its subject lived to tell the tale. So while *miracula* tell more of projected than of actual suicide, they tell of it, for that reason, from within.

Thus the two types of source promise different patterns of information, each dictated by its origin. This difference prescribes the way we must study them. To read a single account from either a 'judicial' or 'miraculous' source, at face value, would no doubt teach us a little about medieval suicide. To read it in the context of its origin would teach more. To compare this lesson with that from all other stories from the same category of document, more still. In the following chapters we shall do all of this, but then go one step further. Because the judicial and miraculous patterns of information are different they are also complementary, giving generically different perspectives on the same phenomenon. So when each has been studied on its own, and a picture drawn from it, the results will be collated, both to provide a further control on the method followed in each, and to allow general conclusions about the suicides who occupy the book. Suicides from judicial sources will be examined in the next five chapters, those from religious in the following three; while Chapters 15 and 16 will attempt, from all three categories of source, to construct a composite and general portrait of the suicides.

We stand, then, at a fork in the road. Having taken our bearings we proceed down the first road to begin the search for suicides among judicial records.

How to approach the judicial records

Bearing in mind the innate secrecy of suicide, it was resolved at the outset of our investigation to take a wide sweep. That means, here, the gathering of judicial records from as many medieval jurisdictions as will easily yield them. The search whose results follow has included England, France, Germany, the Low Countries, and Italy. 'Suicide-prone' judicial records in these places have yielded a total of over 500 cases. All of them, a handful of 'fantasies' apart, are witnesses to actual suicides committed by people before 1500.

Most of the records are very brief, a few of them long and circumstantial. All are historical 'cameras', which it will be my aim in these chapters to focus as nearly as possible on the individual suicides. But the resulting portraits will lack depth if they are taken in ignorance of the apparatus through which they have come. Those 500 cases, after all, remain an infini-

tesimal speck in the populations from which they are drawn, varying estimates of which run at all medieval periods confidently into millions. Each
case, besides reflecting the suicide of an actual individual, is potentially representative of the broader, less visible reality behind all of them. It is this
broader reality we are after. And that means we must not be content with
a pile of snapshots, but aim to interpret the snapshots as more or less representative of the suicides who never got photographed, and *that* means we
must examine the cameras through which the pictures came. Translated into
practical procedure, this dictates a *modus operandi* analogous, in this particular field, to that adopted for the ensemble of all sources. Put another
way, it means the distinguishing, within the judicial sources, of their own
sub-categories, so that each of the latter can provide its own picture. These
miniature pictures will then be compared and interpreted to provide a more
general judicial picture, and it is this last which will go forward, when
the time arrives, to the final comparison with data from chronicles and
miracula.

Let me illustrate all this geographically. Figure 1 depicts the chronological and national distribution of the 500 suicides from judicial sources. Prima
facie the distribution suggests many strange things: that no one committed
suicide before 1170 and that suicide began in England; that England retained
a national propensity throughout the thirteenth century for this mode of
death while in Germany, for reasons known to itself, it was the advent of
the Habsburgs that introduced suicidal conditions absent under the Hohenstaufen. If the chart had been able to distinguish different types of records,
furthermore, it would have suggested on the same basis that life under an
ecclesiastical jurisdiction was less tolerable in France than elsewhere, since
a substantial minority of those French cases come, in fact, from the eccle-
siastial records. All of these impressions can be proved to have no direct
relation to the historical realities of which the records are a distant reflection. The proof involves looking at the conditions under which the various
kinds of judicial source came into existence, and that is what the rest of this
chapter will attempt.

Corpses and Kings

Corpses have been a subject of enduring human interest, if only, today,
mainly in detective thrillers. Materially useless, a corpse announces a death
and hence, by way of sympathy or mere prudence, stirs in the living their
own love of life. This interest, naturally, has had legal expression, focusing
mainly on bodies which may have been killed—unauthorized

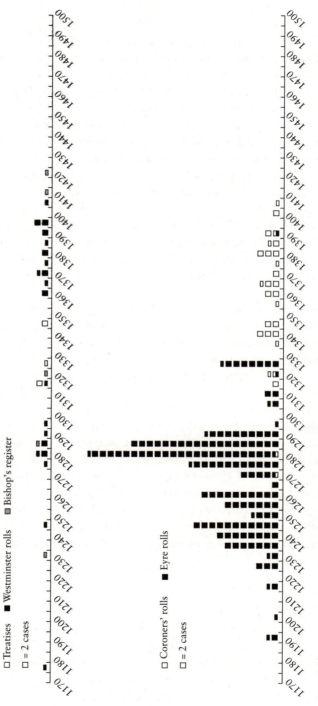

1 Chronological distribution of cases: English judicial records

□ Treatises　■ Bishop's register

□ = 2 cases

■ Westminster rolls

□ Coroners' rolls　■ Eyre rolls

□ = 2 cases

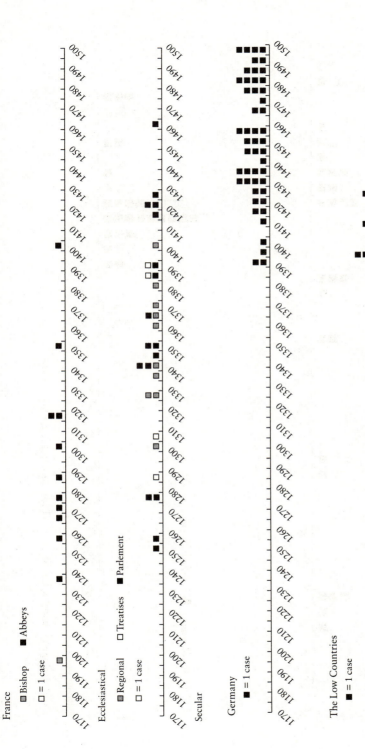

France

■ Bishop   ■ Abbeys

□ = 1 case

Ecclesiastical

■ Regional   ■ Parlement

□ Treatises

□ = 1 case

Secular

Germany

■ = 1 case

The Low Countries

■ = 1 case

2 Chronological distribution of cases: French legal records
3 Chronological distribution of cases: legal records from Germany and the Low Countries

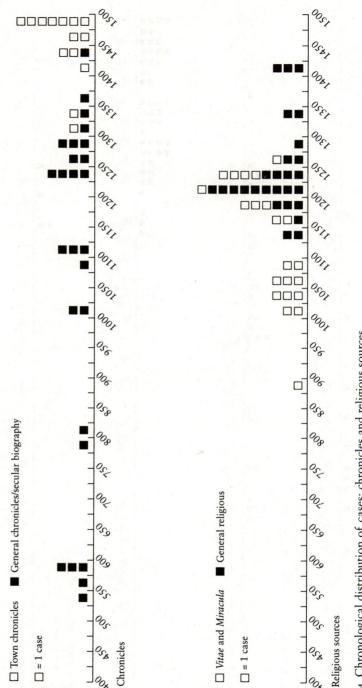

□ Town chronicles ■ General chronicles/secular biography

□ = 1 case

Chronicles

□ *Vitae* and *Miracula* ■ General religious

□ = 1 case

Religious sources

4 Chronological distribution of cases: chronicles and religious sources

manslaughter (Latin: *homicidium*) having been the prime enemy of the criminal law and consequently the main stimulus to its growth.

In European history, the concern of law for homicide has been set in motion by two principles. One can be called the horizontal principle, the other, the vertical. By the horizontal, it is the dead man's relations and friends, or his kinship group, that settles scores. If someone walking along finds a corpse on a lonely road and it is not that of his kinsman, it is not his business. This principle of justice, though widespread and old, is strictly not *our* business either. For it depended on speech and memory—perhaps angry speech and many, long memories—but not on written record. So it has left, at best, only the barest vestiges of itself or of the corpses which set its procedures in motion. The actualities of kinship justice remain for that reason the biggest black hole of legal history. They must have been there, but are nearly all invisible.

When the horizontal principle does become visible, furthermore, it is always alloyed with the other principle, the vertical. The Germanic *wergeld* system, for instance, whereby the kin-group of a killer paid a set tariff to that of his victim, is witness to the horizontal principle but also to an attempt by king or community to regulate it. It is witness also, that is, to the vertical principle. This latter is a central theme in the history of criminal law, so central, indeed, as from some angles to be identical with it. By the vertical principle, the duty of prosecuting homicide belongs to an abstract social entity over and above an individual or kin-group. Post-medieval idiom has called this entity the 'state'. *Status* is indeed an old Latin word, appearing quite early with a hint of the modern sense.[8] More important, the idea of an abstract social entity was represented by various *aliases* including the classical abstraction *res publica*, 'public thing', but employing more often, for practical purposes, one of the analogues for 'kingdom' (the word 'king' is cognate with 'kin'), or in Latin, *regnum*.

As an enemy of homicide, and hence an investigator of corpses, a *regnum* had two advantages over a kinship group. Its justice was more abstract, so it was less likely to perpetuate violence; and it was comprehensive. A king was a 'kinsman and protector to all . . . strangers, poor people, and those who have been cast out, if they have no-one else at all to take care of them', in the words of a twelfth-century English law-book.[9] Kill a total stranger, on a road never so lonely, and you had injured at least two people: not just

---

[8] As 'Status regni', *Ordinatio imperii* [AD 817], ed. A. Boretius, *Mon. Germ. Hist., Capitula Regum Francorum*, vol. 1 (1883), p. 270, 36. cf. *The Cambridge History of Medieval Political Thought. c.350–c.1450*, ed. J. H. Burns (Cambridge, 1988), 174–5; also 350, 479.
[9] *Leges Henrici primi, c.10 § 3; ed. L. J. Downer (Oxford, 1972), 108–9.

your victim, or his kin if he had any, but the king who ruled over you both. So any violent death became the king's concern.

This fact has an importance all of its own in relation to medieval suicide. The rise of the vertical principle of justice distinguished crime, as a wrong against the Crown, from tort, as a wrong against another citizen. In theory it was all crime that was thus distinguished. But careful study of the law's workings has shown how stubbornly the old horizontal principle endured under the cloak of the new. Thus even in the fifteenth century, in England, it transpires again and again to have been the injured group that activated royal justice.[10] Just as, in the period of *wergeld*, the horizontal principle is found in alloy with the vertical, so the latter is never, in practice, found without an alloy of the former. This is what makes the rise of a specifically criminal law of special importance for suicide. For it makes suicide a maverick: suicide was the only crime *incapable* of initiating an action by kindred. Even parricide (another early maverick: what kinsman can avenge Abel, killed by his brother? Only God can avenge it) stood a better chance. So suicide was on its own. Either the king avenged it *qua* public justiciar, be this at the expense of the very family which would have avenged any other kind of homicide; or no one did. Suicide, where a crime at all, was thus a public crime *par excellence*. In England, where the gravest public crimes were distinguished as felony, the rule holds in a special way, since the status of suicide *as felony* can be shown to have been correspondingly unique.[11]

So it is with kings, and public investigators of unnatural death, that the following group of chapters will mainly be concerned. The explanation for that choice as just given also starts explaining the anomalies of Figure 1. The sort of kingship that prosecuted homicide did not strike root in Germany and Italy. It is this fact, not any national immunity from low spirits, that robs Germany and Italy of early judicial suicide records. Records from England and France conversely reflect their earlier experience of the king *qua* investigator of corpses: in England, as keeper of the 'King's Peace'; in France, when its time came, as a hybrid between a 'seigneur of seigneurs' and a revived Roman emperor.

English and French judicial records on suicide are therefore distinguished as a pair above other kinds. Our process of differentiation is on course. For they were also, like the larger categories of record, distinguished from each other.

---

[10] E. Powell, *Kingship, Law and Society* (Oxford, 1989), esp. 66, 86.
[11] I hope to demonstrate this in *The Curse on Self-Murder*, ch. 2.

IN ENGLAND AND FRANCE

The question 'how?' invokes the entire political history of both monarchies. The history can be summarized as a comment on one event, the famous one of 1066, when a vassal of the king of France successfully took over the precocious, wealthy, temporarily disjointed, Anglo-Saxon monarchy. That Conquest has often been scored up as a victory of France over England. In legal and administrative terms it was the opposite. In England, the king's possession of precarious overseas possessions made him maximize potential English revenue to defend them, and through machinery that would function in his absence. So he had to centralize Anglo-Saxon institutions of public justice on the Crown, in a manner which underlined their revenue-raising aspect. The raising of revenue, in its turn, meant accounts, returnable to the Exchequer, and that, at the end of this long causal chain, meant written records. This lies behind the abundance and early date of the English judicial records of suicide in Figure 1 (see p. 126).

In France the effect of 1066 worked the other way. It hindered the formation of a centralized king-justiciar. Not only did the French king lack the specific legacies and stimuli which his English equivalent was using to his profit. More important, the fact that one of the French king's vassals was himself a king (namely of England) meant that all his vassals were that, each seigneur being a petty 'king' in his own jurisdiction. Every time the real king of France tried to realize his royal power at the expense of any one seigneur, the seigneurs *en bloc* could turn to a leader of the opposition effectively unbeatable. The efforts and failures of the Capetian kings to erode this obstacle lasted from just after 1066 to the end of the medieval period. In fact they define the medieval period—crusading, chivalry, ducal patronage, and other hallmarks of specifically medieval France being direct results of its decentralized structure. But effort usually has its rewards. Medieval France was not entirely deprived of its suicide records, for French royal efforts to centralize authority took a step, in the thirteenth and early fourteenth centuries, which had the effect of leaving behind a set of real-life suicide 'portraits' unequalled by any other medieval source, in a way I shall explain in a moment.

It is these large-scale political circumstances, not any local peculiarities in the incidence of suicide, that account for the national assymetries in the spread of judicial evidence on suicide depicted in Figure 1. Having assured ourselves of that, let us turn first to England, and see how judicial suicide records came into existence there.

The English Rolls

The first medieval record of suicide from any judicial process, anywhere, comes in an English treasury account, *alias* Exchequer pipe-roll (so called because rolled like a pipe) for Henry II's nineteenth regnal year (19 December 1171 to 18 December 1172). However, all this pipe-roll relates is that there was 'a woman who hanged herself', her chattels being worth 7 shillings and a penny.[12] Even multiplied, such data would hardly count as bringing a dead person back to life. The records nevertheless expand quickly in number and detail. That they do so was due to the creation of two judicial offices. Together these two supply the great bulk of cases used in this book. They are the coroner and the justices in eyre.

THE CORONER AND THE JUSTICES IN EYRE

In the reigns of Henry I and II the task of inspecting corpses, as a preliminary to court proceedings, had belonged to sheriffs and the watchdogs sent to overlook them, the local justiciars. In practice the corpses would first have been inspected by the sheriff's officers or servants (in Norman French, *baillifs* and *sergeants*). There is no reason to believe the system was watertight even under the two Henries. The crown, at least, judged that many homicides were slipping away, especially after 1189 when Henry II was dead and his son Richard I away on a crusade. As or more important, the confiscations or 'fruits of justice' associated with homicides were also slipping away. The last straw came with Richard's capture in 1194. The regent, Hubert Walter, had to find a king's ransom. This meant exploiting financial resources to the full, and he improvised.[13]

One result was the creation, almost certainly in that year, of the oldest surviving English legal office, that of *custos placitum corone*, guardian of pleas of the Crown. The title indicates how his office was originally conceived though in fact it never quite amounted to that: there were 'Crown

[12] *Pipe Roll Society*, vol. 18 (London, 1894), 108, § 8. These and other cases referred to are listed in the appropriate place in the Register on pp. 433–56 below.

[13] R. F. Hunnisett, *The Mediaeval Coroner* (Cambridge, 1961); with the same author's articles: 'The Origins of the Office of Coroner', *Transactions of the Royal Historical Society*, 5th series, 8 (1958), 85–104; 'The Medieval Coroners' Rolls', *American Journal of Legal History*, § 3 (1959), 95–124 and 324–59; 'The Reliability of Inquisitions as Historical Evidence', in *The Study of Medieval Records: Essays in Honour of Kathleen Major*, ed. D. A. Bullough and R. L. Storey (Oxford, 1971), 206–23. For earlier officers, see Hunnisett, 'Origins', and *Medieval Coroner*, 1–3. The events of 1194: Hunnisett, 'Origins' 103–4. Four coroners to a shire: Hunnisett, *Medieval Coroner*, 1 and 116. Property qualification: Hunnisett, 'Reliability', 210. No actual monopoly of Crown pleas: Hunnisett, 'Rolls' 101. Early titles: Hunnisett, *Medieval Coroner*, 1. Delays and neglect after 1500: Stevenson (1987), as in n. 3 above, 49; the writing of own rolls, ibid., 61.

pleas' that coroners never handled, and by far the biggest part of his duties was, in fact, to watch out just for homicides. This meant the coroner must investigate, ideally within twenty-four hours though actually up to three weeks or more, any death which might be suspected as other than natural. He had then to adjudge whether it was caused by misadventure (*infortunium*), homicide, or suicide. The investigation consisted in his inspecting the body and, if there was any doubt, the empanelling and questioning of local witnesses. These normally numbered twelve, and had to state on oath what they knew of the matter.

To do all this properly the coroner must have two qualities, both of which bear on the way we read his reports. He must live reasonably near. The tenth-century Anglo-Saxon shires (*comtés* in Norman French) were still divided into 'hundreds', of which there were usually four to a shire and each of which grouped together several villages. The number of coroners to a shire was originally to be four, and at some time after the creation of the office each came to be expected to work ideally in one 'hundred', though in practice most had more. (In boroughs, coroners acted in groups of two or more, and this may represent the original intention in the counties too, rendered impracticable by distance.) The coroner's second quality was that he must enjoy social standing. Originally three of the four were to be knights and one a clerk; apparently they had been meant at first to act in concert and the clerk to do the writing. But once each coroner had his own hundred it is likely that, besides probably being literate himself, a coroner would also have his own clerk. Both requirements would have amounted to a property qualification, because literacy costs money. By the early thirteenth century the coroner was appropriately a well-known official, usually well-respected. His title was shortened at first to *coronarius* and later to the familiar *coronator*.

If the coroner did establish a 'Crown plea' of homicide or suicide his duty, according to the time-honoured system of justice, would in theory have been to report it to the sheriff for judgement at the county court. But the Crown's trust in the sheriff and his county court was not absolute, or the coroner would never have been invented. The coroner had in fact been conceived as accessory not to the sheriff, but to an officer only slightly older than himself, the travelling royal justices, or justices in eyre.[14]

[14] Origin of the eyres: D. Crook, *Records of the General Eyre*. Public Record Office Handbooks, 20 (London 1982), 1–8; and the same author's 'The later eyres', *English Historical Review*, 97 (1982), 241–68. The 'superior eyre': Powell, *Kingship, Law and Society*, 55. 10–20 minutes per trial: ibid., 78. Other successors to the eyre: ibid., 51–64. Coroners' attendance at gaol delivery: ibid., 60. The system as a whole: ibid., 47–85. The degree, manner, and timing of the royal assumption of jurisdiction involving the death penalty are explored by J. B. Post, 'Local jurisdictions and judgment of death in later medieval England', *Criminal Justice History*, 4 (1983), 1–21.

These judges *in itinere* (naturalized into Norman French as 'in eyre') were another of the creations of Henry I's reign to be elaborated by his grandson, the Plantagenet Henry II. A pair or more of experienced lawyers would be dispatched periodically—ideally the period was seven years but it could stretch out longer—to a named county to check how the county court had handled such 'Crown pleas' as had arisen since the last visit. If necessary they were to re-hear the cases. Eyres had many other duties besides these—so many that in the late thirteenth century they became known, superfluously, as 'general' eyres. But the use of top-level judges as maids of all work in the shires broke down, not least because their old-style exactions made them unpopular. So in the 1290s the eyre was gradually withdrawn and replaced, through the redeploying and invention of more particular judicial commissions.

Created by the eyre, meanwhile, the office of coroner survived it. By the middle of the fourteenth century coroners were reporting to a variety of judges but increasingly to the quarterly sessions of the Justices of the Peace. The Justices of the Peace, in their turn, would report to the biennial assizes, descendants of those thirteenth-century judges of 'gaol delivery' whose task was to hold fifteen-minute trials of everyone in this or that gaol. Above them all, meanwhile, occasionally *en route* itself on a 'superior eyre', stood the main criminal court in London, the King's Bench.

How the rolls were made

The whole achievement of the system, crude as it was under the twelfth-century sheriffs, finer under the thirteenth-century Eyre, and recognizable, with the fourteenth-century Justices of the Peace, as one of centralized criminal justice, lay in its capacity to coordinate functionaries over space and time. So writing was necessary. This fact was understood only gradually. The growth of records, like that of courts, was therefore in unceasing evolution as new practices were invented. The main elements alone were stable enough, and that by a small margin, to allow an attempt at reconstruction.

The case began, I say yet again, with a corpse. The person who 'first found' [*primus invenit*] the corpse was by old English tradition obliged to 'raise the hue'. This could mean as little as telling the sheriff's bailiff. But if a first finder failed to do that little he might be suspected of unlawful homicide and would be lucky to get off with an amercement. ('Amercement', by the way, was another Norman French term and meant the buying of the king's 'mercy', that is, a monetary fine.) The coroner would then be called to see the body. If it had been buried without a *visum coronatoris* ('an inspection by the coroner') the village or those directly responsible would again be amerced. When the coroner did see the body he had to judge if the death was natural. If this were in doubt he would have to find twelve jurors from the four nearest villages to swear to a credible explanation. These, in their turn, would be amerced if they were later found to have lied, as quite often happened.[15]

The writing down of these procedures may already have begun by this stage. Anomalies in a coroner's roll of 1387 suggest that, at that date at least, a total of four kinds of preliminary note-taking would accompany the inquest: a list of potential jurors; notes taken during the hearing; a list of actual jurors; and a draft for the final report.[16] Whether or not such elaborate notes were taken in the early thirteenth century, none survive. All we know for sure is that the coroner would end by dictating to his clerk—or (by the late fifteenth century, at least) writing for himself—a final account of the proceedings, assigning the death either to natural causes or to misfortune, homicide, or suicide. The formats in which coroners presented this information varied almost to infinity.[17] Some accounts are in the first person, some more formal; some long, some short. The essentials can be presented in different orders. Whatever the length or format, the report was 'enrolled': that is, written in Latin (from the late fourteenth century it could be in French) on a prepared sheepskin. The skins bore several entries each, would be sewn together either end-to-end like a flat chain or, more often, by the tops like a modern wall-calendar. It thus became a 'roll' for presentation to the justices in eyre. A few coroners' rolls survive in the Public Record Office. They have supplied forty-three suicide cases to the present dossier.

The justices in Eyre, for their part, were supposed to scrutinize the coroners' rolls and see if they accepted all the verdicts. If they were unsure they could put questions about them to the Eyre jury.[18] This was, in theory at least, another group of twelve respected local persons, specially chosen for the eyre and bound by oath to give answers to a set of questions known as the 'Articles of the Eyre'. (At first there were nineteen such articles but by 1329 the list had grown to nearly 150. Their form broadly resembled that of a modern questionnaire.) On a doubtful case of homicide, the Eyre jury would be presented with a new set of questions and answer them with a formal statement in writing called the *veredictum*—a term not to be confused with the 'verdict' or final decision of a court (the *veredictum* was more

---

[15] Examples will be seen in Chs. 7 and 8.

[16] Hunnisett, 'Reliability', 221–2.

[17] Hunnisett, 'Coroners' rolls', 98, 100, 106, 109, 111.

[18] C. A. F. Meekings, *Crown Pleas of the Wiltshire Eyre, 1249*, 33–7; and Crook, *Records of the General Eyre*, 34–5. Articles of the eyre: Crook, *Records of the General Eyre*, 34; 'Later eyres', 242. Making of Eyre rolls: Crook, *Records of the General Eyre*, 12–34.

like an affidavit or sworn statement in answer to specific questions). The judges of the eyre did not have to accept the *veredictum* any more than they had to accept the coroners' report. But having got thus far it appears they usually did. Perhaps this was in tacit acknowledgement that, what with the time-lag between death and record and the discretion allowed them as visiting grandees, the eyre judges' version might be weaker on sheer fact than those of the coroners. At all events, the eyre clerks entered just the bare essentials of the case, factual and financial, onto another prepared sheepskin. The entries this time, also in Latin, were commonly as short as two or three lines. That allowed twenty or more such entries on one side of the skin though these quantities vary. Whether or not they are traps for the unwary, the eyre rolls remain an uncommonly rich source of legal and social history: 272 cases in our suicide dossier come from them.

This is how the records, at least the bulk of the English group to be used here, were made. It must now be asked why some survived and others did not.

THE SURVIVAL OF ROLLS

After an eyre roll had been made the preliminary documentation would normally be discarded.[19] As the coroner had usually thrown away his own notes, so the eyre clerks usually threw away the coroners' rolls prepared from them. Coroners' rolls are mentioned from 1201 onwards but none survive until those of 1238. From then until the end of the eyres we possess only thirty-four coroners' rolls. If these seem few for over a century, it is because most were automatically thrown away. The few that survive do so for some reason peculiar to themselves, usually because the copying-out into the eyre roll got interrupted. (Nearly all surviving coroners' rolls of this period are cancelled with one or more lines, which show that the copying had begun.) Similar exceptional circumstances explain the survival of fifty-three eyre *veredicta*, from the many thousands that must have been made.

Meanwhile the eyre rolls based on these longer documents had a better chance. The judges in eyre would take their own rolls back to to Westminster to supply the Exchequer with the necessary data. At first the Exchequer, too, washed its hands of the constituent record once it had copied the necessary figures, and then allowed each judge to take his own rolls away with him unless there was some special reason to the contrary. That is why, though we know eyre rolls were made from 1176, none survives until 1194 (it being a roll from that year that mentions the new coroner). But in 1257

---

[19] Hunnisett, 'Reliability'; Crook, *Records of the General Eyre*, 34–6.

in magnā uolupcace. Iste g̅ n̅ qdem fr̅icida. ƒ peior suicida. stoic̅ pfessione. epicur̅ morte. putas̅ ne cū nerone. socce. � catone suicidis. recep̅s̅ sit celo. Crede m̅ meli̅ illi erat. si nat̅ n̅ fuillet hō. m allec̅p semp luxuriar̅ in balneo. Dec decreat d̅ ier̅

1. The first appearance of the word 'suicide'. 'Iste igitur non quidem fraticida set peior suicida, stoicus professione, epicurus morte; putasne cum Nerone et Socrate et Catone suicidis receptus sit celo?' (Walter of St Victor, *De Quatuor labyrinthos Franciae, c.*1178). See p. 38.

2. The death of Henry of Hohenstaufen, King of the Romans (1242). An illustration, in a fifteenth-century Flemish manuscript, of the suicidal version of Henry's death retold in Boccaccio's *De casibus virorum illustrium* (*c.*1357). Here the work is in French translation. See pp. 50–3.

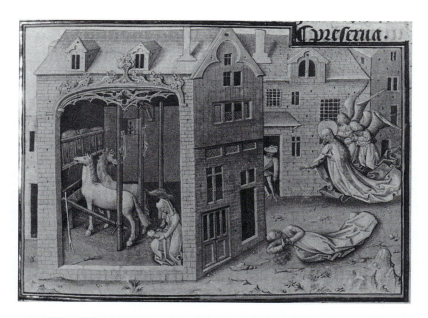

3. The woman infanticide.

a) A Marian miracle (see pp. 264–71) retold in Jean Miélot's *Les Miracles de Notre Dame* (*c.*1455) and imagined here in a town in the Burgundian Netherlands. The woman kills her baby on the left and attempts suicide on the right.

b) A second miniaturist, of about the same date (1460), has given testimony to public familiarity with the story by employing the technique, designed to lend variety to a well-known picture, of reversing it by means of a mirror.

4. The jealous wife of Rocamadour. An ill-founded doubt of her husband's fidelity leads a lady to stab herself, in an old miracle retold in *Cantigas de Santa Maria* by Alfonso X of Castile (1252–80). See pp. 272–4.

5. St James's pilgrim. Another old story retold, in *Les Miracles de Nostre Dame* by Gautier de Coincy (*c*.1177–1236), as illustrated in a manuscript made between 1320 and 1350. The miniaturist has sought to render the suicide heroic rather than depict it as in the text. See pp. 277–86.

judges were ordered to deposit all their rolls, so the series swells in the late thirteenth century, while remaining far from complete.[20] After 1294 eyre rolls grow fewer because eyres grow fewer, though there are still some from church 'immunities', where the crown was anxious to assert jurisdiction during episcopal vacancies and therefore kept the eyre going. The last eyre roll is dated 1348. The total of surviving eyre rolls, from beginning to end, is nearly 1100.

In the matter of survival, the rolls of the coroner came into their own *after* the eyre which created him. Well over 400 medieval coroners' rolls survive from the middle of the fourteenth century onwards. Their better survival is due partly to the growing judicial respect for all records and partly to the combined effect of that and of the growing stratification of courts. This latter meant a well-written coroner's report was potentially too useful, to too many courts, to be thrown away.

One class of record remains whose survival calls for less explanation. These were the records made at Westminster. We shall occasionally meet cases from the King's Bench, whose duties included that of supervising lower courts, so that criminal cases of all kinds could finish up there, and which kept good records. More often, we shall meet special enquiries, *inquisitiones*, about the deaths of persons to whose succession the Crown could lay claim, either on grounds of felony (when lower courts had failed to find it) or because the dead man was claimed as a tenant-in-chief of the Crown. The suicide of a wealthy person provided a positive invitation for conscientious Crown officials to hold such an *inquisitio post mortem*. No fewer than twenty-four suicides in our dossier come from this source.

The subsequent history of the survival of these records is largely that of the Public Record Office, most of whose enormous holdings can be consulted only in the fragile original rolls. About thirty eyre rolls and about ten coroners' have been published or calendared (or summarized entry by entry in English). Many more of both types of roll have been used and quoted by legal historians, in printed books and typewritten theses. Calendars have been made, and are being made, of special inquisitions and of the Letters Patent and Close related to them.

How all these records affect the study of medieval suicide can be told from the relevant section of the Register on pages 432 to 455, which is culled from them, and from Chapters 7 and 8 below. The search behind these results has been most thorough in respect of the eyre rolls and the printed inquisitions. Coroners' rolls have been systematically searched for certain counties but not all. Those of King's Bench have only been sampled. As

---

[20] Crook, *Records of the General Eyre*, 12–13.

explained earlier, the build-up of this dossier has been the work of more than one scholar and there is every hope that yet others will augment and improve it.

ECCLESIASTICAL COURTS

Finally, among English legal sources, some reference must be made to judgements by bishops. In the terminology of canon law bishops were usually called 'ordinaries', that is, holders of ordinary jurisdiction as distinct from appellate. The ordinary's task was to judge cases on ecclesiastical matters and persons. At the bishop's level these would not normally include suicide. In so far as the matter was left to the church at all, the question of the burial or non-burial of a suicide in a consecrated graveyard lay within the competence of a parish priest, whose decisions were not regularly recorded. So the appearance of suicide in bishops' registers is accidental, and comes largely in what lawyers call rescripts, that is, written answers to questions posed from outside. Thus a bishop might occasionally have to judge a disputed question concerning burial, or the consecration or reconsecration of buildings. Other suicide entries in episcopal registers concern either a bishop's licensed exercise of quasi-royal jurisdiction over suicides by his own clerics,[21] or, much more often, disputes with royal jurisdiction in the same connection, especially with regard to the suicide-clerk's inheritance. The boundary between episcopal and royal jurisdictions was a matter of chronic uncertainty, kept at bay mainly by convention punctuated by dispute; and it is this latter, dispute, that gives the historian his documentation, since all parties took pains to record the material details.

Episcopal records on suicide therefore have their own chronological profile and their own perspective.[22] The secretariats of English bishops began producing registers in the fourteenth century to preserve copies of bishops' official correspondance. With them are the rescripts and disputes that sometimes tell of a suicide. Their references have a pattern of emphasis all their own, and unlike that of all secular court records, making the bishops' registers all the more useful as 'controls' for other sources.

To read through the history of all these medieval courts, secular and ecclesiastical, is to enter a world in constant evolution, a fact easy to miss if they are studied only for one time. The names of offices can remain the same while the offices change in response to shifting conditions (the sheriff

---

[21] It is a case in the diocese of Exeter in 1329 that lies behind this assertion. F. C. Hingeston-Randolph, ed., *The Register of John de Grandisson, bishop of Exeter (1327–69)*, pt 1 (London and Exeter, 1894), 529.

[22] A full bibliography on English bishops' registers will be found in C. Gross and E. B. Graves, *A Bibliography of English History to 1485* (Oxford, 1975), 755–92.

being the classic example). The relationships between these changing offices were themselves evolving in response. And the essence of an old office can thus also reappear under a new name, as the eyre essentially reappeared in the King's Bench on circuit. All this change, and change within change, affects the records, which are themselves evolving *qua* records, in ways distinct from the evolution of the institutions that produced them. Nuances in the history of these institutions and records are thus irrecoverable in any short introduction, and the present sketch has had only the limited aim of indicating the genesis of the records we are about to read. It will enable us, in doing so, to form our own judgement of the tensions and anomalies found there.

   The judicial institutions of France, as I said earlier, were rather different.

French Registers

In the recording of suicide the English judicial records are recommended by the qualities of their creator, the Plantagenet Crown. These qualities were precocity, wide national extent, and a matter-of-fact preoccupation with money. The character of the French records reflects a different legal development, and one to whose differences the suicide evidence is peculiarly sensitive.[23]

SEIGNEURIAL JUSTICE

In the late tenth century, as Charlemagne's public authority disintegrated, jurisdiction over life and death, alias High Justice, had passed to a thousand

---

[23] In addition to the works by Esmein, Lot and Fawtier (above, p. 120 n. 1), and to edited sources listed in the relevant section of the Bibliography (pp. 472–3 below), my authorities behind the following sketch of French justice are: (for Parlement) A. Vuitry, *Études sur le régime financier de la France avant la Révolution de 1789* (Paris, 1878–83), vol. 3 (= nouvelle série: Philippe le Bel et ses trois fils; les trois premiers Valois, vol. 2 (Paris 1883)); (for a summary of Letters of Justice in general) F. Olivier-Martin, *Histoire du droit français des origines à la Révolution* (Montdirestien, 1948), 524–5; and especially, for the idea of grace and its expression in Letters of Remission, P. Duparc, *Origines de la grâce dans le droit pénale romain et français du Bas Empire à la Renaissance*. Thèse [droit] (Paris, 1942). References to ordinances (between 1318 and 1366) are to the standard edition: *Ordonnances des roys de France*, ed. M. de Laurière and others, vols 1 to 4 (Paris, 1723–34). The expansionist and royalist character of the Paris *prévôté* can be learned from Arsène Perier, *Hugues Aubriot, prévôt de Paris*. Mémoires de la Société bourguignonne de géographie et d'histoire, 24. (Dijon 1908); though his old misunderstanding about the origin of the office is corrected in the authoritative chapter on the subject by Lot and Fawtier (bk 4, ch. 6: 'Le Chatelet'). Princely centralization, modelled on royal, is described by J. Le Patourel, 'King and princes in fourteenth-century France', in J. Hale, R. Highfield, and B. Smalley, eds., *Europe in the Later Middle Ages* (London, 1965), 155–83.

seigneuries. Each seigneur was a miniature Charlemagne, and they arranged themselves according to the skill and luck of each generation into interlocking pyramids of homage and land tenure, topped, finally, by some two dozen conspicuously successful dynasts, mostly vaunting the title of duke or count. From 987 the Capetian king was one of these, and at first not much more.

From this epoch until the late fifteenth century the French legal system would be distinguished by two characteristics, mutually complementary. The first was the stubborn survival of its atomized jurisdictional structure. The main single cause for this was mentioned earlier, namely that from 1066 one of the king's vassals was simultaneously king of England. But it is its main single result that now concerns us. I refer to conservatism. Those petty Charlemagnes tended to cling not only to their old jurisdictions but to old procedures. These did not include written records. For the study of suicide what all this means is that whoever did commit suicide in France in these centuries is overwhelmingly likely to have done it in a seigneurial jurisdiction and that therefore, even if his act did come to a lord's attention, it would not have been recorded. We are gazing over the edge of another black hole.

As before, we can learn something of the black hole by looking carefully at the edge, where visibility ends. There are occasional exceptions, a glint here and there, as when a case from a lord's court gets re-heard on appeal in the Paris Parlement. Then we learn about the traditional procedures employed before it got there. An alleged suicide of *c.*1366 from near Beauvais, for instance, belongs to this category, and will be considered in Chapter 10. But as guides to seigneurial procedure these exceptions are few and far between. Another kind of exception is more systematic. It is best exemplified in the practice of a small group of old abbeys near Paris. Like many bishoprics and abbeys these had inherited, from long before Capetian times, seigneurial jurisdictions exercised through the abbey's 'Official', jurisdictions which included High Justice, and were essentially the same as those of other seigneurs. Like these, the abbeys' Official used conservative, unwritten procedures. But there were two differences, whose combination it is that gives the historian his chance. Being abbeys, these particular seigneurial judges had easy access to scribes and records. Although the procedures were unwritten, writing could be resorted to if special circumstance prompted. And special circumstance did prompt. Nearby was Paris, home of the expanding criminal jurisdiction of its powerful royal Prévôt. In the thirteenth century the abbeys near Paris suddenly found it important to have down in writing exactly what criminal judgements their courts *had* made, in case their powerful royal neighbour challenged the abbeys' right to make them. Thus these few abbeys near Paris, all founded in Merovingian times, have left registers of verdicts by their own courts' High Justice from about 1250. They include some twelve suicides, shining a rare light into the black hole of French seigneurial jurisdiction.

Other records of seigneurial sentences, where they exist at all, are more fragmentary. Not entirely by accident, the nearest surviving rival to the abbey registers is a fragment from that same royal Prévôt of Paris. He too exercised a kind of seigneurial jurisdiction, though of a unique kind. A Prévôt was traditionally a seigneur's general manager. The Prévôt of Paris was different because his seigneur, the Count of Paris, had become king. As Paris grew its Prévôt modernized his court, and the modernization included the keeping of a register. A fragment survives from 1389–92, recording criminal sentences passed at the Châtelet, and with a whisper of suicide to be heard in its place.

From French jurisdictions of first instance two further kinds of record survive. Books of 'Very Ancient Customs', of this or that French province, began appearing at the same time as the abbey registers and for the same reason, to protect customary rights. Because their evidence is generic it only rarely, and by the way, records particular suicides. Last but not least are the 'seigneuries collectives' towns. I shall take soundings from two towns, one northern and one southern, samples which choose themselves by the chance survival of their criminal records.

Atomized, conservative seigneurial jurisdiction, then, was one main characteristic of medieval French justice. The second was the opposite, which might at first glance seem to cancel out the first. It is royal jurisdiction on appeal. Rather than cancel out seigneurial courts, in fact, royal appellate jurisdiction formed with them a dialectic that runs the entire length of the medieval period. It was one exceptionally complicated in its results, but at the same time fruitful for the student of medieval suicide, since it produced for him, at one extreme, the longest and most detailed of all European judicial records on the subject. How this came about can be explained, I hope, without too much labour.

APPEAL: THE *BAILLIS*

In principle no one could appeal from a seigneur's sentence because it was a divinely sanctioned 'ordeal', a 'judgement' (essentially the German *Urteil*: judgement). All a man could do if he did not like a judgement was to accuse his human judge of judging falsely and challenge him to battle. On this stem a kind of seigneurial appeal did develop in the twelfth century (its origin preserved in a symbolic blow on the shoulder given by appellant to his judge of first instance).[24] But proper judicial appeal implies, not 'falsehood', but intellectual human error inviting discussion by a higher court. As a royal bridgehead into seigneurial justice, appeal became established in France in the thirteenth century for two distinct reasons. In combination, their bearing on records of suicide can be seen graphically in the second line of Figure 2 (p. 127).

The first of the two reasons was Roman law. Roman law had allowed appeal, as in Acts 25:11 when St Paul 'appealed to Caesar'. Traces of this Roman appeal had survived in canon law, in some early Germanic codes, and even in French royal practice. But for its full revival the Roman model had to wait until the Crown was for other reasons ready to use it. That was after it had got its hands back on the Plantagenet heartlands in 1204. Bologna had just then begun to produce a stream of Roman law graduates. This timing, bringing civilian lawyers on the heels of military success, explains big differences in the criminal systems, and therefore records, of the two main monarchies to produce evidence of suicides. The English kings had centralized just too early to employ those Bologna graduates even if they had wished. So they built their system with local material, firmly enough for the system to resist Roman influence when it came. Hence the improvisations of the eyres and coroners. The French kings, because their building work was delayed (largely by the English), became ready for Roman influence at just the moment it became easily available. So they took from Roman law those concepts they found useful, and developed them, making up for lost time.[25] Appeal was one. Another was the writing down of evidence: the *inquisitio*, the standard Roman procedure for a prosecution conducted by the state, involved a verbatim record of witnesses' statements made by notaries publicly sworn for the purpose. Appeal and writing came at the same time and combined their effects.

This Roman contribution to the growth of appeal in France was more effective because joined by a second: a long-standing association of the Capetian dynasty with the church. Its own incidental High Justice apart, the role of canon law in secular justice had traditionally been to soften the latter's rigours. The Capetians' sacral aura therefore put them in a position opposite to that of the Plantagenets towards the criminal law of their land. The French kings kept a power, claimed by Carolingians when the Franks had recently been converted to Christianity, to dispense from barbaric laws as 'too cruel for Christians'. The ecclesiastical side of Capetian authority thus made a firm foundation for the appellate powers built on it by St Louis's

---

[24] Lot and Fawtier, bk 4, chs. 2 and 3 (vol. 2, pp. 301–31).
[25] The feudalization of Roman law, ibid., 334.

Roman lawyers.[26] The building was again all the firmer because of its relative lateness. The king of England, by thrusting his way early into the day-to-day business of crime and punishment, had got blood on his hands. That was why it was left to the Crown's martyred victim Becket, critic of its criminal justice, to win popular affection. By contrast, the French Crown had been excluded from most criminal justice, so it had kept a kind of innocence. This was a boast of no small value in a century when French cultural development was anyway outgrowing the barbarities of seigneurial justice. The crown's early ostracism from justice thus became its best recommendation, placing it ideally for the interventionist role it came to play in Saint Louis's time. 'Saint' Louis: it was now the supreme judge of appeal, not (as in Becket's case) the judge's victim, who became the saint.

The significance of this evolution for the student of suicide will become clear gradually. France will emerge as a land of contrasts. In the penal treatment of suicides' bodies and property, French law, being mainly seigneurial, can be shown to have been the most severe of any.[27] On the other hand, our 'portraits' will shortly be testifying to an opposite current in French medieval justice, one shown in decisions exceptionally sympathetic to suicides and their families.[28] That contrast is not capricious, but reflects the peculiar, dialectical evolution of French law.

The establishment of royal appellate jurisdiction in France was fed, then, by two traditions, Roman law and the church. It also appeared on two levels, regional and national. Its regional expression was in the royal officials invented after the crown's conquests from Bad King John in 1204, the *baillis*, or in the south, *seneschaux*. The *baillis* were partly modelled on the English eyre judges but with a difference which again reflected the later cultural climate. The *baillis*' ideal was to increase the king's land, and hence effective power, without trespassing on anyone else's rights.[29] To do this in the face of entrenched noble jurisdictions required that the *bailli* offer a service conspicuous for quality and availing itself of the latest sophistications, including written procedures. They were used not, now, mainly for accounting purposes, but for judicial ones. This was the procedure of which the jealous old jurisdictions had reason to be afraid, and which on different levels they copied. But the appellate justice was essentially royal and it was this that led the way in making records. Only fragments survive of the *baillis*' own criminal registers. But a selection survives, made in Paris for a

[26] Duparc, *Origines de la grâce*, 24–59; cf. Powell, *Kingship, Law and Society*, 82–5.
[27] To be demonstrated in *The Curse on Self-Murder*, chs. 1 and 2.
[28] See Chs. 9 and 10.
[29] Philippe de Beaumanoir, *Coutumes de Beauvaisis*, § 20, (ed. A. Salmon (Paris, 1899), vol. 1, p. 25): 'cil est bons baillis en qui main la terre son seigneur croist sans fere tort a autrui.'

special purpose, of various *baillis'* verdicts passed between the years 1248 and 1318, a selection known as *Olim* from the first word of the first volume. In view of the harshness of seigneurial 'punishments' for suicide, we should expect the *baillis* to have heard a few appeals. And there they are, in the *Olim* registers, which contain four suicides, fragmentary pointers to another, smaller but this time more tantalizing, hole in the evidence.

From the middle years of the thirteenth century, then, the French *bailli* and his officers listened for reports of ill-explained deaths as opportunity arose, inspected the corpses, and kept records of the results. If the appeals to the *baillis* still mostly fail us, it is because the records have vanished. On a higher appellate level, by contrast, records were even better made and, this time, carefully preserved.

APPEAL: PARLEMENT AND ITS LETTERS OF REMISSION

The office of *bailli* was scarcely there before it was subject to appeals in its turn, and it was to consider these that there grew up in Paris a more authoritative court of appeal, Parlement.[30] It is no accident that this French 'Talking' should have grown into a law-court which fortified royal power, while its English equivalent, its name originally identical (*parlemenz*), became an assembly to limit it. The difference echoes the legal evolution of the two monarchies. The French Parlement emerged in the second half of the thirteenth century to give effect to the lawyers' idea that the king was the righter of wrongs. According to one story, professional judges had sat in Louis IX's presence under an oak tree at Vincennes to hear private petitions, and *parlement* had grown from then. Whatever its origin, by 1303 the court was quasi-permanent. It was indeed several courts, the main ones meeting in allotted parts of the Palais Royal on the Île de la Cité in Paris—opposite today's Cité Métro station. The Palais Royal thus became the scene of many anguished appeals from verdicts of suicide. The judges of Parlement, some of whom heard the appeals, were by that date a permanent corps serving for life and drawn, deliberately in equal proportions, from laity and clergy.

The most informative of the French portraits of suicide will come from one subdivision of Parlement, the 'Court of Requests'. The number of its judges fluctuated around eight, again half-and-half clergy and laity and all

---

[30] Vuitry, 401–7; Lot and Fawtier, 332–54. No appeal against Parlement: Lot and Fawtier, 324. The oak: Joinville, *Vie de S. Louis*, ch. 12, § 59, ed. N. de Wailly (Paris, 1906), 25–6: 'Maintes foiz avint que en estoit il se aloit seoir ou bois de Vinciennes après sa messe, et se acostoient à un chesne, et nous fesoit seoir entour. Et tuit cil qui avoient afaire venoient parler à li, sanz destourbier de huissier ne d'autre.'

distinguished as judges (some reappear as Presidents of Parlement). These Judges of Request were, of all Parlement judges, those who remained closest to the king's ear, since their office had grown out of the *poursuivants* who had 'pursued' the king wherever he went (even into Mass in chapel).[31] Once these 'pursuers' had become a sedentary institution and changed their name, their court sat in shifts of two men each on a bench in one corner of the Palais Royal, with their clerks on a bench in front. They examined all petitions that came to the king and sent most of them on to the appropriate section of Parlement, like a mail-sorting office, to act as which they had to sit near the door, so that one folk-name for them became 'Judges of the Door'.

One kind of petition, the Judges of the Door kept to themselves. It was the kind that produced the reports on suicide.[32] These were petitions that invoked the king's grace. This quality lay in the king's person and hence had to be exercised, at least until *c*.1500, only by judges with easy physical access to him. The idea of grace again had a Roman-law background. It is put in Latin (as *gratia*) even in documents otherwise in French.[33] But historically it owed more to the king's special Christian status. Although grace was not the same as appellate jurisdiction, their procedures could look alike and the growth of one strengthened the other. Parlement nourished both, and from the viewpoint of suicide the most significant distinguishing feature of royal grace, fruit partly of its Christian ancestry, was its emphasis on equity towards 'povres et miserable personnes', that is, the extremely poor.[34]

For our present subject this downward-looking feature in royal grace has this material consequence, that because normal French justice was so unusually severe on a suicide's family the latter became 'povres et miserables personnes' *par excellence*. And this put suicide, if qualified in other respects, squarely into the province of the Court of Requests. There was a more technical reason for it to go there. Royal grace had a special association with homicide as such. This was because all old Germanic law, French seigneurial law included, set little store by a homicide's intention. A corpse was a corpse. The person who had made it a corpse must pay even if the death

---

[31] Lot and Fawtier, vol. 2, 82–4; Vuitry, 401–2; *Ordonnances*, vol. 1, pp. 669–70, 733: an *ordonnance* of 16 Nov. 1318, reinforced by one of 1320, forbids 'que nuls deputez à penre, ou oir Requestes, ne soit en nostre Chapelle, tant comme nostre Messe se dira' (669).

[32] Vuitry, 401; evolution of Maîtres de Requêtes, ibid., 404–6. Where they sat, ibid., 405 and *Ordonnances*, I, 731 [Dec. 1320, 4]. Letters of Remission, Lot and Fawtier, vol. 2, 75–84; Duparc, *Origines de la grace*, 90–145, and more especially on the writing and registration of Letters of Remission, ibid., 131–45. Cf. the briefer description in Olivier and Martin, *Hist. du droit français*, 525–6.

[33] Duparc, *Origines de la grâce*, 60.

[34] e.g., Duparc, *Origines de la grace*, 93, 98–100, and the ordinances referred to in n. 37 below.

were an accident. Historically, this principle was not modified in the substance of the law but by the use, as if from a *deus ex machina*, of a royal power to dispense defendants from its associated penalties. Such dispensation was thought to fall directly into the remit of royal grace and therefore of the Court of Requests. One result is that the latter's proceedings concentrate to a peculiar degree, in respect of all kinds of homicide and including suicide, on the question of intention. I said earlier that the different kinds of source complement each other. Decisions from the French Court of Requests, by thus concentrating on intention, dovetail to perfection with records from the English rolls. These are psychological examinations, albeit couched in a literary rhetoric designed, in the petitions that succeeded, to exculpate the prisoner.[35] We shall see how often English rolls were content to summarize the outcome of a palpably subjective judgement on a suicide's state of mind.[36] In France, doubt on this score qualified the case for appeal. There, in the few lucky cases that got through to a document, the symptoms and circumstances of suicide were narrated *in extenso*, and indeed almost in the style of a novel. The one class of case on which English rolls tell us least, in other words, formed in France the object of painstaking description.

The description came in what the lawyers called a Letter of Remission, and our last task is to see how this kind of document came to exist. An appellant—in the present case the threatened family of an alleged suicide— would normally come in person to the Court of Requests and put the case. Because *povres et miserables personnes* were often involved, Parlement allowed for free legal counsel and other help.[37] On hearing the petitioner's account, the Judges of Requests would check it carefully, sometimes sending emissaries to the place where the request had originated even if that were far away, or even riding off there themselves (expenses being allowed for up to three horses). If the request was approved, a written instruction would be sent to the *bailli* or other legal officer concerned, telling him *not* to enforce the sentence. This instruction was the Letter of Remission.

We shall be looking at a total of thirteen of these. Guaranteed by royal seal, like all acts of the Parlement, the Letter of Remission had two further warrants of authenticity. Its 'short story' would underline the motives of the

---

[35] N. Z. Davis, *Fiction in the Archives* (1987). This richly documented book confirms the interest and credit of the Letters of Remission at a slightly later period. 'Fiction', the author points out (p. 3) is from *fingere*, and means 'shaped' rather than 'feigned'. The author identifies ways the stories of witnesses could and can be checked (esp. pp. 17–24) and in one instance (p. 59) is able to compare and contrast the account of an incident in a Letter of Remission with that in a *Nouvelle* of Marguerite of Navarre.

[36] In Ch. 8.

[37] *Ordonnances*, vol. 4, 508 [Nov. 1364, no. 7]; cf. ibid., vol. 1, 733 [Dec. 1320, no. 2].

Remission, based on a narrative compounded by the court from the testimony of all witnesses. Secondly, it would be registered within Parlement as verification in case the original was challenged. For that, it needed only to be kept for a few years. In the event, thanks initially to a particular Chancellor around 1380, and subsequently to their lucky escape from the various hazards that have thinned out many French public records, most Parlement registers are there to consult.[38] As evidence of suicide, these Letters of Remission might in theory invite an objection that their subject-matter must by definition not be suicide, since remission would not have been granted if it had been. I shall come back to that, and it will be found that the objection is easily met in most cases we have to consider.

ECCLESIASTICAL COURTS

It remains to mention, in France as in England, the ecclesiastical courts. Two kinds are at issue. Like the English, the French diocesan 'ordinaries' had canonical jurisdiction of ecclesiastical persons and causes. This, let it be repeated, was distinct from any secular, seigneurial jurisdiction some of the larger churches still kept—and of course kept longer in conservative France than in centralized England—from the early Middle Ages. Where the relationship of suicide to criminal jurisdiction is essential (since suicide is homicide), to canonical jurisdiction on this level it is accidental. That is to say, there was no reason for bishops as such regularly to consider suicide: they only had to solve questions which had baffled the judgement or custom of parish authorities. One case that illustrates this is from around 1200, and raised the question whether a certain alleged suicide should have Christian burial. The question went step-by-step up the hierarchy all the way to the pope, and made canon law. Such questions were usually settled at ground level without bishops, and never got recorded. This is illustrated, if not proven, by the earliest of surviving French bishops' registers, that of Archbishop Odo Rigord of Rouen, made between 1248 and 1269. Its 700 printed pages tell of madness, epilepsy, heresy, apostasy, drunkenness, fornication, and innumerable other failings and vices among clergy, and among laity too. But there is no mention of suicide.[39]

The second kind of ecclesiastical court at issue was the special

---

[38] The history of the archive, and of its debt to the chancellor Gérard of Montaigu, is told in J. Favier, ed., *Les Archives Nationales: État générale des fonds*, vol. 1 (Paris, 1978), 212.

[39] T. Bonnin, ed., *Regestrum visitationum archiepiscopi Rothomagensis* (Rouen, 1852). Cases of madness (p. 307) and epilepsy (168), condemnations for heresy (160) and relapse into Judaism (541), together with the record of innumerable monastic and clerical offences, confirm the Register's capacity to record personal *accidentia*. The case of *c*.1200, an appeal from Tours, will be found in the Register below, on p. 460.

commission for the detection of heresy, set up by Gregory IX in 1231 to conduct *inquisitiones* into heresy, and since the 1530s monopolist in the title 'inquisition'. Like all inquisitions, that for heresy left peculiarly careful records. Indeed, it did so more than other inquisitions because its officers were all clerks, and the matter subtle. Suicide was not a heresy, though views on it could be. But heresy suspects were sometimes suicidal. This fact, like everything else, would be put in the inquisitor's records and earn these, duly, a small place in our dossier.[40]

Even this quick history will, I hope, explain the bigger asymmetries in the distribution of sources charted in Figures 1 and 2 (pp. 126–7). But its aim has been more than that. The aim has been to allow us to interpret correctly the descriptions that follow, descriptions which will in turn illustrate and extend the foregoing lessons. I have spoken here only of the monarchies that produced most judicial records of suicides. There is no reason at all to think Italy or Germany lacked suicides in the same years. But there is, as we shall see in Chapter 14, reason to think that conditions for recording them were different, and a consideration of these conditions will duly be left until later.

These, then, are the media: few, fragmentary, of diverse origin, and such as they are, created for their own purposes. The purposes were quite other, let it not be forgotten, than to reveal anything to us, hundreds of years later, less still to transmit to us living portraits of people once as much alive as we are now, so long ago. But then, which of us knows what purposes *our* documents will serve, many centuries hence, if fire or commotion has not destroyed them in the meantime?

[40] Generally on the heresy inquisition, see W. Ullmann's introduction to his abbreviated re-edition of H. C. Lea, *The Inquisition of the Middle Ages* [1st edn., New York, 1888] (London, 1963); B. Hamilton, *The Medieval Inquisition* (London, 1981), esp. 40–59.

7

Portraits from English Courts I
Criminals, Debtors, and the Sick

AFTER chronicles, then, judicial records form a second potential tool for a historian's necromancy, and it is time to start using it. The choice of English records as a point of departure is not just a question of starting from home. In approaching any subject it is usually best to start with a general view and focus on the detail later, and English judicial records allow us to do this. This is because of numbers. Nearly 400 cases of medieval suicide survive in English court records, far more than from the French or any other monarchy. Their ensemble offers, besides any snatched portraits of this or that individual *iam morientis nondum viventis*,[1] a synoptic panorama of the fields in which suicide could occur.

The price is paid by brevity. Most entries in courts' rolls will just record the name and fact of the suicide; who first found the body and is, or is not, suspected of homicide; often the place; usually the method; and nearly always the verdict and the value of the chattels. An adverb like *gratis* or *sponte sua* ('of his/her own free will') is sometimes added to the record of the act to emphasize its deliberate character. The strict verdict of suicide was *felonia de se* (abbreviated in the margins of rolls as *felo de se*), though we shall see variants. A final note usually says who is to be answerable for handing over to the Crown the money value of the chattels, together with a record of anyone inviting 'amercement' for judicial irregularity.

A sample of entries will illustrate the concision:[2]

Ailwin de Tachebroc killed himself. No one else is suspected. Felony of himself. He had chattels worth 28 shillings, the sheriff to answer. [Warwickshire, 1232]

---

[1] 'Still in the act of dying, not fully alive'. Cf. p. 6 above.
[2] To avoid overburdening this and the next chapter with references, I shall merely include in each case enough identification to allow its source to be found through the relevant section of the Register, on pp. 425–75.

Richard le Webbe killed himself in Fynchingfeld vill. The first finder and four neighbours appear and are not suspected nor is anyone else. [Felony of himself. He had chattels worth 9 pence, the sheriff to answer. [Essex, 1285]

John le Mascun spontaneously killed himself in Wallingford vill. The first finder comes and is not suspected, nor is anyone else. Felony of himself. He had chattels worth 22 shillings and 4 pence, the sheriff to answer. [Berkshire, 1284]

Although most entries in the Eyre roll are terse, few go as far as these. Most add at least the method of death, thus:

Robert Brat hanged himself. Noone else is suspected. Felony of himself. He had no chattels. [Somerset, 1243]

Robert son of Galfrid of Tratreston hanged himself of his own free will. Noone else is suspected. . . . etc. [Northumberland, 1279]

A handful, even beyond certain special categories I shall come to, add macabre details, as when

Simon of Cheldrincton struck himself in the stomach, tore out his intestines with his own hands and tore himself apart and speedily died. No one is suspected . . . etc. [Wiltshire, 1249]

As well as the method, most entries mention also the place. Thus

Geoffrey a la Broke hanged himself in his home in Leamington vill . . . etc. [Warwickshire, 1262]

or

Henry of Onibury [near Ludlow] went to the Onibury pond and drowned himself . . . etc. [Shropshire, 1256]

or (in combination with the method)

Alice daughter of Hugh spontaneously set fire to her home in Meopham burgh [near Gravesend] and burnt herself in it so that she died at once . . . etc. [Kent, 1293]

The Essex Eyres of 1272 and 1285, remarkably, mention no fewer than three cases of suicidal drowning in marl ponds.

All these elements at once, with further details and the conditions of discovery, are present in certain exceptional circumstances. One is when the scribe of an Eyre roll forgets he was meant to abbreviate his jury's evidence. Thus an Eyre roll from Kent in 1313–14, after exceptionally recording the year of a suicide (1300–1) describes how a man in Chevening near Sevenoaks

when he had breakfasted and sent his whole household to work, at around the third hour went to his room and shut two doors after him, and having taken with him a rope which he had previously procured from under his carter's bed, climbed to a beam in the room and, with the rope, spontaneously hanged himself.

The repeated emphasis on privacy, in this and other reports, may have reflected the facts. But that is not why it is there. Jurors wished to make sure no one else was involved.

Occasionally the Eyre jury's evidence itself survives, in a *veredictum*. One such is from the Devon Eyre of 1281–2, about a suicide that had occurred five years earlier, some ten miles north-west of Crediton:

On Tuesday the Feast of St Michael 4 Edward I [29 September 1276] Alexander Barganel of Coldridge tithing was alone in his house at Coldridge around the hour of terce and he took a bowstring and climbed on to an oven in the house, and hanged himself with the cord from a beam, and so died by hanging. Christina his wife, returning home, found him dead around the hour of none and raised the hue, to which the country came.

Coroners' rolls, of their essence, were more expansive. One from Leicestershire in 1378, for instance, describes how a porrson at Garthorpe, near Melton Mowbray, rose

in the middle of the night ... at the temptation of the Devil, in the chamber in which he normally slept, and went and took a cart cord worth 1d and a ladder worth 1d, and on the same ladder [tied it] to a beam in that chamber, knotted the other end of the cord [in a] *ridknot* round his neck, and with his feet pushed the ladder away and so ... hanged himself with that cord so that he died at once.

A striking feature of even the shortest entries is the frequency with which they mention the instrument of death. When the case is one of drowning this detail is subsumed in the place, as in the last cases quoted. But when the place is not specified the kind of water is: 'in a ditch', 'in a well', or 'in a pond' are common. When the case is one of self-stabbing the record usually says what the stabbing was with: most commonly a *cultellum* (knife), but sometimes a razor, chisel, or axe. A gratuitous character is added to this detail when it is prefixed with *quadam* or *quodam*, 'with a certain' (knife, razor, and so on), as if the court had not seen it but still wished to include it in the record. Since hanging was the commonest method of suicide, it is in connection with hanging that the feature is most noticeable, as in the *veredictum* just quoted, with its mention of a bowstring. Other examples include:

Dulcia, the wife of Llewelyn, hanged herself with her wimple in her house at Kempton. [Shropshire, 1256; Kempton is near Craven Arms. A wimple was a woman's head-dress, of a kind that survives today in the dress of some nuns]

William Wulmaare hanged himself with a noose in his house in the vill of Shepreth. [Cambridgeshire, 1260; Shepreth is just south of Cambridge]

Humphrey le Leper was found hanged by a linen sheet . . . [Bucks, 1241]

A veil, a belt, a tether, or, more usually, simply a cord or rope, are among articles thus specified. Occasionally the stationary element will be mentioned, as 'from a beam', 'on an oak', 'on a certain apple tree (*quodam pomerio*)', 'on a cart', and so on.

This specification of the instrument reflected a regular consequence of felony. The weapon of a felony was forfeit to the crown. If one man stabbed another the knife went to the king, and the same rule applied in *felonia de se*. This interpretation is born out by a look at suicide entries in the coroners' rolls. In these it is not a matter of their mentioning the instrument occasionally, or even often: they *always* do, together with its value in money for commutation. Thus a coroner's record will end, to a modern eye incongruously, with a phrase like: 'the beam was appraised at 3 pence and the cord at 2 pence';[3] or 'the aforesaid beam and cord at a farthing'.[4] One Shropshire coroner, in 1394, even values the water in which someone has drowned himself: 'the water is worth 6d yearly so it is ordered that the water be seized into the king's hand and the said four vills are charged with the value of the water, that is, for 6d.' These values are sometimes merged, to modern minds absurdly, into the narrative, so that a man can be 'found hanging by a rope worth a halfpenny'.[5]

This financial fact might be thought enough to explain the emphasis, even in Eyre records which did not have to mention it, on the instrument of suicide. Another explanation could be that the Eyre wished to supply the kind of detail to corroborate its bare record: the latter would look more plausible if the instrument was named. But since the Eyre records, unlike the coroner's, name it frequently but not always, and in other respects aim at brevity, the importance attached to the instrument is also evidence for the court's psychology. The instrument, it seems, commanded a measure of fascination in the minds of onlookers to the extent that it became integrated with the act of suicide. This circumstance will play its part, in an appropriate context, in explaining the psychology of certain public attitudes to suicide.[6]

But it is the psychology of the suicides, not of the courts, that primarily concerns us if we are to raise them from the dead. On the minds and motives of those who died the rolls have so far told us little, scarcely breaching the

[3] Bedfordshire, 1273.   [4] London, 1321.   [5] Norfolk, 1378.
[6] Attitudes I plan to discuss in *The Curse on Self-Murder*, ch. 13, in relation to the concept of suicide as a source of social pollution.

reticence of other categories of document. One instance of their own reticence concerns the suicide's religious condition when he died. Only seven out of the nearly 400 reports (if we except two surviving only in a treatise by the Tudor jurist, Sir Anthony Fitzherbert), tell us about his religious state of mind at the point of death.[7] The seven are all coroners' rolls. One from Yorkshire, in 1368, tells of a man who, 'voluntarily struck himself to the heart with a knife so that he died at once, unconfessed'. Another, from Northamptonshire in 1317, tells of a thief who stabbed himself but 'was confessed and received the sacrament and died two days later'; while a third, in Norfolk in 1365, spells out that a certain woman 'repented after that deed, confessed and, contrite, took the last rites, and then died'. A Wiltshire coroner appears to have been especially interested in this detail, for two Wiltshire entries of 1344 speak respectively of a woman and a chaplain, both allegedly deranged, who stabbed themselves and then 'had her/his ecclesiastical rights (*habuit jura sua ecclesiastica*)', while another, of 1347, of a woman who had 'the church's mercy'. The most graphic example concerns that Leicestershire parson (see p. 151) who hanged himself in 1378 and who was found 'with both hands raised by [God's?] mercy to the salvation of Christ, and they say that otherwise he did not have ecclesiastical rights.'[8] Five further coroners' entries—and again this occurs only in coroners' reports—say the suicide or attempt was at the devil's instigation: *per instigacionem diaboli*, to borrow the expression used in 1366 about a Norfolk woman (who has also expressly been said to be 'of sound mind [*sane memorie*]'). Another such expression was *per tentationem diaboli*, as a Yorkshire coroner said of a man's self-drowning in 1355: and another, of Shropshire in 1394, of a woman who tried to drown herself in the Severn.

If we are looking for accounts of the psychology rather than the bare facts of English suicides, these stray references are a meagre harvest. They are scarcely augmented by the rare allusions to suicide in episcopal registers, whose reference to the person and act of the suicide can be even briefer. An example is the order for an inquisition by a bishop of Exeter in 1329, on the death of 'Richard of Wydecombe, former vicar of the church of Tunstall' who 'is said to have brought death on himself by voluntarily drowning himself in water'. To the meagreness of the royal rolls in this regard, however, two categories of account form exceptions, and deserve review.

---

[7] For the status of the 'nearly 400' as a basis for counting, see the introduction to the Register, referring to the counting of cases on p. 425. Except for suicides mentioned in the present paragraph, all others in this and the next chapter are from the smaller total of 343.

[8] JUST 2/58 m8d: 'mīa ambabus manibus suis motis ad salvationem Christi levantibus'. I have preferred the harder reading for the puzzling *mīa* ['mercy']. Dr Summerson sensibly suggests it may be an error for *miraculose*. The same case forms one of the five that follow, of suicide *per tentationem diaboli*.

The sources to be explored are vast, the reports usually brief. So the review will necessarily, at times, read like the cast-list of a play, with its name and vestigial *curriculum vitae* of each character. As model I can again only appeal to our Tuscan guide, with his *lunga tratta di gente: si lunga*—'such a long succession of people, undone by death.' As we move past them I hope the reader, like Dante, will both discern recognizable faces and, as the parade goes on, rhyme and reason in their ensemble.

Criminals and Debtors

Among recorded suicides in English judicial records the first big category to show any psychological dimension is that of people who killed themselves under criminal suspicion or accusation. Their motive for suicide is often implied by the circumstances. A total of twenty cases in the Eyre rolls fall in this class. Two were murderers. One, William Lanval, is mentioned in the Hampshire Eyre of 1249 as having stabbed a man to death near Christchurch and fled by boat, 'wanting to cross the sea'—whether to France or the Isle of Wight is not said—but 'seeing that he could not escape he got out of the boat, and of his own accord drowned himself in the sea.' The other, John Ban, is described in the Eyre of 1280–1 in the same county as having killed a man and fled to a wood, where 'before he could be captured, he killed himself with his knife.'

The remaining nineteen suicides in this group were thieves, over two-thirds of them having stolen, or allegedly stolen, booty expressly identified. The identification of booty begs similar reflections to those just made on the naming of instruments of suicide. No fewer than six had stolen sheep; three, horses; one each an ox and a pig; two, corn, and one—only one—money. This money-thief—or rather would-be thief, for he got no further in his break-in to a Cistercian grange in Berkshire—was pursued to his home by people who had witnessed the break-in. But

as soon as he had entered his courtyard [the Berkshire Eyre roll of 1261 says] Robert struck himself in the stomach, and he was arrested immediately afterwards and taken to Faringdon to the Abbot of Beaulieu's prison [the grange belonged to Beaulieu] and imprisoned there, and died of the wound three days later.

The dramatic quality of that account is equalled in other accounts of runaways. The case most inviting the epithet 'dramatic' is that of Sir Thomas of Hopton (possibly Hopton Wafers near Ludlow, now just in Shropshire) recorded in the Worcestershire Eyre of 1275. Sir Thomas, his esquire, and some mounted companions including three Welshmen 'were found by the coroners' rolls to have been outlawed in this county on the accusation of a certain William, son of William the Poor' (probably a gentleman, not poor at all), for unspecified robbery. The party were pursued twenty miles to an inn in Dudley, whose owner and his family are all identified. Next morning it was found that Sir Thomas had 'got up from his bed at night and wounded himself with his knife in his chest, so that he died of it next day'—to be duly condemned as *felo de se* by the Worcestershire Eyre of 1275.[9]

Other scuffles with justice present problems of interpretation. Late in November 1317, six pigs were reported stolen from woodland round Benefield, near Oundle in Northamptonshire. The rascally reputation of a certain local family drew accusing fingers towards it, and the constable had the family arrested; all, that is, except the most suspect. He was Robert Aunfley, who according to the coroner's roll was 'in the fields of Benefield, tending cattle.' So

the constable and tithingman went to him wishing to arrest him. And Robert, seeing them come, fled, carrying in his hand an axe with which he struck himself twice on the head, and then drew his knife and struck himself in the stomach so that he died.

Before dying, Robert had time to confess and receive the Eucharist. (He was one of those seven suicides whose religious condition is specified.) Robert's body, with its two axe-wounds on the head and another 'in the stomach under the navel in his bowels from a knife', was inspected by a coroner in the abbot of Peterborough's courtyard at Oundle. Too late? For could the coroner *really* have known that the suspect had not died in a scuffle with his pursuers, and that this unlikely story—why does it make him use the axe before the knife?—was not his captors' invention?

The next chapter will reflect on possible 'convenience' verdicts of this kind. Meanwhile we have some less problematic accounts of victims of justice. Two in this group killed themselves in or near sanctuary. Sanctuary (usually in a church) was not a criminal's passport to go scot-free, but rather a judicial device, tolerated on different excuses by all parties to get a fugitive's case reconsidered, especially by the local community. The upshot for the criminal might well, despite the delay, still be the gallows or at least exile.[10] This reading of sanctuary helps explain the fatal anxieties of John Maheu, who according to the Northamptonshire Eyre of 1329–30, stole four lambs from Duns Tew in Oxfordshire. He was pursued by their owner, Robert Jacques, as far as King's Sutton inside the Northamptonshire

[9] Cf. R. H. Hilton, *A Medieval Society. The West Midlands at the end of the thirteenth century* (London, 1966, reprint, Cambridge, 1983), 254.
[10] G. Rosser, 'Sanctuary and Social Negotiation in Medieval England', in J. Blair and B. Golding, eds., *The Cloister and the World. Essays for Barbara Harvey* (Oxford, 1995), 57–79.

boundary. Robert there raised the hue and cry, so that Maheu abandoned the animals and sought sanctuary. The villagers rallied and blocked the church door so that he could not get in. The community had already made its judgement. It did not like sheep thieves. So John took out a knife and killed himself. The owner of the sheep, the breathless Robert, had to content himself with this revenge for, thanks to the suicide, he did not get his sheep back. They went to the king, for a technical reason. The judges, brought up on the tradition enshrined in Henry II's famous Assize of Novel Disseisin, saw their remit as confined to questions only of possession and not of ownership. The stolen lambs had been the 'possession' of the thief Maheu. But Maheu was a felon, and that meant, in turn, that they were forfeit to the king. It may have been this feature among others which earned the case inclusion in the Tudor jurist Fitzherbert's *La Graunde Abridgement*.

The other sanctuary case is less spectacular. It appears in the Yorkshire Eyre roll for 1268. A horse-thief killed himself in a church, St Nicholas's in Thirsk, where he 'shut the chapel door so that [the pursuer] could not enter, took out a knife and killed himself'. He, too, apparently had a low view of his chances with the local community. Horses were too easy to steal. A third case concerns a man who had been in sanctuary and had been exiled. It occurs in the Northumberland Eyre for 1293, when a destitute scavenger successfully gained sanctuary in the church of Ulgham, near Morpeth. The authorities only released him after he had taken an oath before the coroner to leave the kingdom, exile being a not uncommon option in such circumstances. *En route* to his exile, perhaps to Scotland, the penniless man hanged himself.

No fewer than four other thieves in the Eyre rolls escaped from their captors by drowning in rivers: one before imminent arrest; two after it and *en route* to prison; and a fourth after escaping from prison. Perhaps this last one was a bit like that destitute Northumbrian, and felt the future bleak for all his freedom. The prison he had escaped from was in Bristol, the river the Frome, and the case is recorded in a *Communia* roll of 1297.[11]

Finally, six of the suicide-thieves committed the act when already fast held in prison or the stocks. In Stoke, near Rochester, a prisoner for 'divers robberies' struck himself in the stomach with a knife and died four days later,

[11] The others referred to, in order, were the Wiltshire Avon, the Severn near Gloucester and, probably, the Dove on the Staffordshire border, where a general-purpose thief called Thomas of Sheen, mentioned in the Eyre in that county in 1293, struggled free of his guard 'and spontaneously fell from a bridge into the water and drowned himself'. In addition to the cases mentioned here, and outside the count, the 'latecomers' to the Register include an escaping burglar in the Kent Eyre of 1313–14.

according to the Kent Eyre of 1313–14. Another, named in the Berkshire Eyre of 1261, slashed himself in the stomach with a razor and died at once. Then there were the stocks. Prisoners in the stocks were not as a general rule expected to commit suicide. Otherwise their knives would regularly have been confiscated. Since two of four thieves who killed themselves did so with a knife (according to the Eyres of Northamptonshire of 1285 and Kent in 1313–14) we can assume this precaution was not regular. But I said 'as a general rule'. The danger of suicide cannot have been unknown to the wise, for one suicide in the stocks had to hide his weapon, and kill himself 'with a razor he had in his shoe'. Another, William de Bonheg, used a means against which no precaution was proof. According to the Dorset Eyre of 1288, William had stolen one-and-a-half bushels of corn from a houseowner in Blandford. But

the watchmen of the vill arrested him and put him in the stocks at Bryanston and guarded him there for eight days. And William meanwhile would not eat or drink so that after eight days he died there. The jurors, asked if William died by any torture or ill-treatment inflicted on him while he was in custody, say no.

Torture or ill-treatment in the stocks remained, probably, the greater danger, and the one subject to more regular official precaution. Of course we do not always have to believe all these stories. That a man had starved to death in the stocks would not reflect well on the local population. But once he was dead, who was going to gainsay a version which said his death was all his own fault? We have to judge each account as it comes, and some of them, at least, carry their own warrant of authenticity: too many witnesses are involved, with rival interests, to suggest they are all telling lies.

Here, then, at last, are descriptions which, albeit brief and occasionally unreliable, amount nearly to 'portraits', the motive of suicide being implicit in its circumstances. Just occasionally the motive is explicit. The Northamptonshire Eyre of 1285 has two examples, one of which concerns another of those prisoners in the stocks. William Bercarius had been found at night driving four sheep, arrested on suspicion and put in the stocks in the lord's courtyard at Faxton (a village near Kettering now deserted),

and as he sat by himself at night he took a knife and struck himself in the stomach as he did not want to be hanged, so that he died.

In a second case in the same roll a gaoler, after the escape of a prisoner 'for fear of that escape spontaneously hanged himself in prison with his belt'. The Eyres venture thus far, but in this category not beyond, into explicit psychology. Only a special criminal inquisition, of a kind ordered directly from Westminster to deal with difficult cases, would be likely to venture further.[12]

Criminals, suspected or convicted, belonged to a category broadly definable as 'enemies of society'. Their common factor was that they had made their fellow-men turn against them. English court records mention only a handful of these 'enemies of society', other than criminals. But the handful is significant. Their motives, with different degrees of certainty, were economic. A strict analysis of cases by economic category must wait for the moment when all legal sources, from England, France, and elsewhere, can be treated together. When they are, it will be seen that many suicides, especially in the surviving coroners' rolls, were poor, and even destitute; while many others, especially in the Westminster rolls, were rich, and even very rich; and that there were many in between, mainly (it follows) in the Eyres. So generalization by inference from small samples calls for caution, beyond an assurance that from top to bottom of the wealth range we do find suicides apparently precipitated, from the highest to the lowest levels of wealth, by economic shock or despair.

At the top, first of all, is Robert Olyver, a self-made shipowner of Newcastle who drowned himself in 1393, probably in the Tyne. Robert had been Mayor of Newcastle and was one of the two members it sent to the Parliament of October 1383. He was rich, and apparently remained so. The motive for his suicide is not spelt out in the Patent roll which is the principal witness to it, even though the inquest it records was made by commissioners expressly with the object of its discovery. What they did discover was a massive debt. The drowned magnate had owed 500 marks (£333) to the Earl of Northumberland; and it was almost certainly this debt, greater in value than the capital value of some noble honours, which drove Robert to his death. It was also the occasion for the surviving record, since the earl had a brief tug-of-war with the crown before recovering his money from the suicide's estate.[13]

Suicides with an economic motive were not, however, a prerogative of the super-rich, but extended to lower ranges of wealth. In the Huntingdonshire Eyre of 1286 we read of a Richard 'le Vicarre' who drowned himself at Tose-

---

[12] Thus an inquisition in Shropshire in 1309 acquitted two men thought to have killed a thief whom they were marching away under custody. The thief, a shepherd who had stolen thirty-six sheep, was found to have jumped voluntarily from a bridge while being led away, 'fearing death for that theft'. C 144/3, no. 3. (This case is another of those supplied to me by Dr Summerson after completion of the statistical exercise summarized in chapters 15 and 16, so it is excluded from the 'count' in those chapters.)

[13] C. H. Hunter Blair, 'Members of Parliament for Northumberland', *Archaeologia Aeliana*, 4th series, 14 (1937), 22–66; 28–9; *Calendar of Patent Rolls: Richard II, 1391–6*, 239, 266, 290.

land near St Neots. Richard had been a reeve or farm manager, a post which commonly implied serfdom albeit of a superior and often prosperous sort. (His surname may possibly reflect that function.) The Eyre says his master, John de Offord, had been amerced on a charge of taking the suicide's chattels without warrant. John de Offord indignantly explained his action to the Eyre and got a local jury to back him. He insisted that he had taken the chattels before the suicide as settlement for arrears; and indeed it was this loss of his chattels that had driven Richard to his death. 'He drowned himself [the Eyre spells out] out of grief at his chattels being thus taken.' The story certainly served the interests of John de Offord, who kept hold of the chattels. But it does not have to be untrue; and, if true, suggests another suicide from economic shock. Yet another man who may have expected such a shock, if no worse, was an exceptionally wealthy chaplain whose suicide by hanging dates just a fortnight after the outbreak of the Peasants' Revolt.[14]

Since a man's economic level was far from being a question only of money (a truth reflected, incidentally, by the solitude of that money-thief on our list just now of eighteen thieves) these victims of economic collapse merge with those whose social status was damaged. An Essex coroner's roll of 1389 mentions an 'illegitimate' man who hanged himself on a maple tree.[15] Another man whose social status was under threat was Adam le Yep. Adam's motive for drowning himself in the river Severn came out clearly at a *post mortem* inquisition in 1293, and contributed to his condemnation as a suicide. The Earl of Gloucester, it was said, had alleged that Adam held his tenement from the earl on villein tenure and was therefore of unfree status. According to the testimomy of his wife and neighbours, Adam had said repeatedly that if reduced to villein status he would drown himself. He did. So he was adjudged *felo de se* on the evidence of his threats.[16]

Among the very poor it remains for the most part a matter of guesswork whether destitution, on its own, ever sufficed as a motive for suicide. One Eyre alone, in the Channel Islands in 1309, spells it out, whether or not on good authority then at least in accordance with general belief. A Geoffrey 'le Cu', says the Eyre roll, had 'hanged himself long ago, out of poverty and grief.'

In respect of the suicides' mental condition these are at best bare sketches,

[14] E159/159, Easter *Recorda*, rotulets 11, 11d. The suicide was William of Hoby, in Leicestershire.
[15] JUST 2/33a m 15 d § 14: 'illeg'. The entry is faint and I may have misread this.
[16] J. W. Willis Bund, ed., *The Inquisitions Post Mortem for the County of Worcester*. Worcester Historical Society, 12, pt 1 (Oxford, 1894), 47–8. Adam le Yep's case was discovered and discussed by R. H. Hilton, 'Peasant Movements in England before 1381', *Economic History Review*, 2nd series, 2 (1949), 117–36, on p. 135.

scarcely portraits. But the sketches, where they rise to that, build on the strength of this type of document, realism. Most appear to be sketches from life.

The Sick

English court rolls venture further into states of mind in respect of a third category of suicide, that of the sick. In the Register at the end of this volume the number of sick suicides is about the same as that of the criminals, that is, about twenty. In these, even those accounts not anxious to excuse a suicide suggest that sickness was a main motive. 'Henry, son of Richard, being seriously ill, rose from his bed, went to the river Avon and drowned himself in it' records the Warwickshire Eyre of 1262. Its very next entry tells a similar story about a young woman near Leamington who 'being seriously ill, rose and went to the river Leam and drowned herself'. An Assize at Wark in 1279 (part of a Northumberland Eyre in that year) meanwhile records the suicide of a pregnant woman 'in her chamber with a razor'. In only one case of this category, of a man 'gripped by disease' who drowned himself at Reigate in Surrey, was the verdict softened to *infortunium*. The Oxford coroners' rolls include comparable verdicts. One refers to a sick Oxford don 'in St Edward's Hall',[17] by name Master John Forest. On 23 December 1387 the Oxford coroners (in the plural, since Oxford was a burgh and had two coroners) heard how Master John Forest had been lying ill three weeks before

and around cockcrow he rose naked from his bed and struck himself in the chest with a small knife or awl. He survived this wound until the said Monday. The jurors say that meanwhile he recovered strength and received pardon from the Church.

Pardon from the Church (Forest's case is another of the seven which attend to this matter) did not entail pardon from the Crown. The verdict was *felonia de se*, and the chattels saved from the Crown only by university privilege.

A commoner class of entries say the sickness had damaged the patient's reason. In Lichfield, Henry de Barton 'in the grip of fever in the house of Agnes Lotrix de Lythe, left Agnes's home and drowned himself in a ditch,' according to the Staffordshire Eyre of 1293; while that of Herefordshire, in the previous year, describes how the burgess William le Enveyse was 'suffering severe pain so that his mind was affected', and 'rose by night' and

---

[17] For the Hall, see J. I. Catto and T. A. R. Evans, eds., *The History of the University of Oxford*, vol. 2: *Late Medieval Oxford* (Oxford, 1992), map 2, nos 41 and 83.

threw himself into a local river. A reference of this sort usually anticipates an acquittal. Asked if Henry de Barton 'did this out of felony', the jurors said 'no, but by madness and misadventure'; and William le Enveyse's jurors, challenged with the same question, said his act was not felonious 'but because of the severity of his disease only'. Both verdicts were duly recorded as *infortunium*.

Although this was not universal, Eyres tended to acquit the sick who could also be described as having lost their reason. The same was true of coroners, whose fuller descriptions threw more light on the thinking behind such verdicts. Thus the Bedfordshire coroner in May 1273, called to see a body at Thurleigh just north of Bedford, recorded how

Geoffrey le Wodeward, who had been ill for nine days with the hot sickness, rose from his bed in Thurleigh, as well as he could, went from the house into the court-yard in a frenzy, stood by a well and through the sickness and by misadventure he fell in and drowned.

The words 'frenzy' and 'misadventure' anticipate the verdict: *infortunium*. It was the same when the Oxford coroners came to view the body of John Finke in 1348. The dead man was said to have been

lying sick in bed, when about midnight he rose, as if he were as it were mad, and for want of guarding he went forth from the house and fell in the cesspit and was drowned.

And they, too, allowed a verdict of misadventure. A Norfolk coroner, in 1369, likewise acquitted a 24-year-old wife at Edgefield near Cromer, who

worn out by severe illness so that she became of unsound mind [*fatigata magna infirmitate per quod devenit extra sanam memoriam*], went to the the pond of Sir John de Willoughby's watermill, and being of unsound mind, drowned herself there, without there being any other cause of her death.

In reading that last coroner's report we notice that the expression 'unsound mind' comes twice and anticipates an acquittal. Two years before, the same coroners had shown similar clemency at Thursford near Walsing-ham for a suicide who was again said to be 24. He too was a man 'of unsound mind, and suffering from the falling sickness'. In this condition he 'ran from his bed in Thursford to the common of Little Snoring, and was drowned in a well there while of unsound mind, there being no other cause of his death'. The repetition of the phrase 'unsound mind' is again notice-able and again prefaces an acquittal. The coroner in the Little Snoring case ordered that the well be stopped up as if the well were to blame. But at least the man was not. No verdict is recorded.

Descriptions which include both elements, sickness and insanity, more often than not ended in acquittal. This rule holds even for cases which reached Westminster, to judge from the two in the Register (respectively from 1277 and 1297). Where there were exceptions, and the suicide is judged a felon, the 'insanity' receives palpably lighter emphasis. One such is the case of Humphrey 'the leper', who was found hanged by a linen sheet in a house in Taplow and duly set down by the 1241 Eyre for Buckinghamshire.

The twelve jurors say he had lain sick in the home of one Levyna de Holmed and that out of madness caused by that illness he hanged himself.

The word 'madness' is not repeated. The verdict is felony. The same severity was shown by the Oxford coroners to the suicide, in March 1343, of Henry de Bordesle. The jurors had sworn that

Henry had long been sick with divers diseases, and on the Saturday before the said Monday he took a knife and stabbed himself in the belly, as if he were as it were mad; and afterwards he lived until the Sunday and then died of that wound.

Henry was again only once 'mad'; and only 'as it were'. This again proved too weak an assertion to avert a guilty verdict. The man was a *felo de se*.

I come finally to the large category of those said to be insane but not physically sick. In these, the proportion of verdicts is the opposite to that found with the sick and insane. Most of the merely 'insane' were condemned as felonious. This is surprising, but a look at the verdicts will go some way to explain it.

The Insane

We can begin with a hard fact about insanity, namely that it is chronically hard to define. Medieval doctors themselves found it hard.[18] Judicial verdicts, while borrowing their basic terminology from the doctors, did not share the doctors' hesitation in applying it: to judges, a defendant was either mad or not. What madness implied, for judges as for doctors, was a disease that struck at its victim from the outside independently of his will. In the rolls, the commonest term for the disease is *frenesie* or a Latin equivalent. The meaning of the word can be told from the reports. A Premonstratensian canon of Sulby, mentioned in the Northamptonshire Eyre of 1285, had stabbed himself to death when *detentus frenetica infirmitate*: 'gripped by the sickness of frenzy'. Isabella de Pampesworth, in a London coroners' roll for 1321, had likewise 'for the last two years and more suffered from a

---

[18] e.g. Ishâq ibn 'Imran and Constantinus Africanus, *De melancholia*, ed. K. Garbers (Hamburg, 1977), p. 111.

disease called *frenesie'*. The concept of an attack by frenzy introduces some of the most vivid of the suicide reports. One such concerns Emma le Bere of Yielden, on the Bedfordshire–Northamptonshire border, who 'suffered from an illness called *frenesye'*, according to a coroner's roll for the former county in 1316. Having lain for some time in her bed with that 'illness', on 15 June of that year Emma

rose from her bed, took an instrument called a pole-axe and cut the throats of John, Helen, Felise, and Maud, the sons and daughters of [her husband] John le Bere. Thereupon she immediately hanged herself, on a beam in her house, with two hempen cords. Nicholas, [another] son of John le Bere, first found them and raised the hue.

The view of frenzy as a specific complaint, with symptoms of its own, is betrayed in a judge's summary of the case of Asselot Eliot, of Wothorpe near Stamford in 1307. It is quoted in Sir Anthony Fitzherbert's *Graunde Abridgement*:

a woman had spontaneously drowned herself while in frenzy [*en frenesie*]. The jury was asked if her malady [*maladie*] had got worse day by day, or came in fits [*par fethes*]. They said 'by fits', so her chattels were forfeit.

What the court probably meant was that Asselot had stabbed herself in a lucid interval, and was guilty for that reason. Whatever the logic of that verdict, frenzy was again seen as an involuntary state. Some expressions in the rolls are less specifically medical but even they see *frenesie* as an intruder, attacking its victim from outside. Thus Thomas le Clerck, in a Westminster Inquisition of 1282, was 'afflicted with frenzy'. A similar Inquisition a century later, in 1381, spoke of William Sprat as having 'happened to fall into a frenzy'. The chattels of both men were forfeit, for all that.

One last example of such external 'affliction' comes from the roll of the same, apparently humane, Norfolk coroner who reported on the young bride from Edgefield. It comes nearer than any other of the English judicial portraits to depicting its subject sympathetically. The coroner records that at Necton, between Norwich and King's Lynn, in 1365, Leticia Grundlok had been

afflicted [*tacta*] by excessive sorrow so that her reason was diminished [*dolore nimia per quod caruit bona memoria*], and in this state she went to Necton wood and there struck herself in the stomach with a knife so that her intestines came out. She repented of what she had done, confessed, and took the last rites in a state of contrition.

As in the Thursford case, no verdict is recorded. That almost certainly means the case was waived as another *infortunium*.

Conceptually, the difference between acts committed by a sane and by an insane person was clear-cut. One was criminal, one not: it depended on whether an act of conscious will was involved. Not only would this be stated in law-books, it is the presupposition behind many verdicts. A typical one of this kind is that on Thomas Robekin recorded in the Norfolk Eyre of 1286: 'he did this out of frenzy and not felony.' His case was therefore put down to misadventure. But the application of the distinction in general practice is not an easy matter today, nor was it then. The very terms for 'diminished responsibility', as modern courts call it, were vague, so it is unsurprising that their results were inconsistent. As shown by the cases of Asselot Eliot, Thomas le Clerck, and William Sprat in the last paragraph, the chattels of those who had killed themselves while *non compos mentis*, or 'under the influence of frenzy', were far from protected by these clauses. There are plenty more instances. Walter, son of Fulk, and Robert Hardwine, both mentioned in the Cambridge Eyre of 1260, were adjudged *felones de se* for having killed themselves when 'led by madness'. William le Marchant of Weston (near Newbury) was similarly 'mad' when he stabbed himself to death. But the Berkshire Eyre of 1261 took his chattels just the same. So did the Essex Eyre of 1285 those of Robert de Porta, of Eastwood near Southend, who had cut his throat when 'moved by insanity'. Fitzherbert himself, in his *Graunde Abridgement*, reports without comment, a few pages apart, two judgements in direct mutual contradiction, from 1349 and 1315 respectively:

A certain lunatic [*lunaticus*] struck himself with a knife and later recuperated from his infirmity, received the rites of the church, and died by reason of his wound, and his chattels were not forfeit.[19]

and

A certain lunatic struck himself with a knife and later recovered from his infirmity and had the rites of the church, and died by reason of his wound, and his chattels were confiscated etc.[20]

It would be easy to go on reciting such inconsistencies.

In the logic and procedure of courts mental incapacity was a weak element. It was intrinsically hard to judge yet was crucial to the question of guilt. Here was a contradiction. An unanswerable question had to be answered. Put another way, objective truth alone could not give a verdict, since no one could tell for sure what the truth was. Yet there had to be a verdict. In the presence of this sort of impasse, other criteria than truth are

[19] Edition of 1577, fol. 217r (Plea 244).
[20] Ibid., fol. 220v (Plea 412).

brought to bear on a decision, criteria drawn from its political context but kept incognito to preserve legal appearances. At these points the historian must tread with special care; the surface of the records is treacherous. But let us be bold, put on soft shoes, and tread it.

8

Portraits from English Courts II

'Insanity' and Some Optical Illusions

HISTORICAL evidence calls for reading in two ways: directly, for what it says, and indirectly, for what it reveals without saying. Of silent modes of revelation none is more fruitful than anomaly. That is why Jacques Le Goff, the French social and intellectual historian, has taught us the principle 'recherchez l'anomalie.' For anomalies usually reveal influences at work behind the writer's shoulder and of which he is unaware, influences urging him to say or imply contradictions.

At the end of the last chapter we saw Fitzherbert's *Abridgement* quoting two contradictory judgements almost side by side, without comment or reconciliation. Both suicides were insane. The circumstances appear identical, but one lost his chattels and the other did not. This pair of cases forms an appropriate point of departure for a study of those judicial records in which influences behind the compiler, not openly acknowledged by him, have unmistakably shaped his description of the death. This chapter will accordingly study three types of account: one in which the 'insanity' of a suicide is in question; a second in which a court gave a verdict of *felonia de se* when there was probably no suicide, or vice versa; and a third in which a family has tried to conceal the felony.

'Insanity' as an Arbitrary Element in Judgement

I begin with 'insanity'. Let it be repeated that insanity is not easy to determine. It is difficult to define and, when defined, difficult to attribute to a particular case. This is true now and was then. But if a verdict of felony, with its awful consequences, rested on this intrinsically uncertain foundation it is surely here that the structure of the law, theoretically impartial, was at its most vulnerable. It was here, that is to say, that the non-judicial factors, which necessarily jostle round any legal decision—fear, favour, greed, pity, and so on—could impinge on the verdict. The French Parlement will show us many examples of this mechanism, but it had its English manifestations too. It may be said that in looking at this factor we study portraits not of suicides but of courts, whose attitudes are not in issue at this point. But it closely touches the present question of 'portraits' of individual suicides, for two reasons. One is that 'insanity' is so common a concept in suicide reports that their correct reading depends on our understanding of its limits and peculiarities. The second is that, because the concept often formed the 'waxen nose' in a judgement—the bit that could be bent this way and that—it often occasioned dispute, and dispute has, for the historian in this field, the lucky result of creating fuller documentation. In England this effect yields less spectacular profit than in France, but it does so for an earlier timespan and for more cases.

English judicial records, at all levels, often mention that a person who killed himself was insane, but rarely mention specific evidence for the insanity other than the act of suicide. They identify the method and instrument of suicide and itemize the perpetrator's wealth, but on the critical question, on which the man's guilt or innocence depended, they rarely say anything. This contrast suggests conspiratorial convention not to expand on the suicide's state of mind: it was just too hard to judge. The exceptions I have found are all in Westminster inquisitions, in some of which the general speech and conduct of an alleged suicide appears to have been investigated as a guide to his state of mind.

Westminster recognized this as the key question. Rich suicides aroused its interest not just because the Crown wanted to get its hands on property by maximizing the number of suicides. Property was what much of the law was about; any dispute about a lot of it called for adjudication, and this, in a suicide case, meant an investigation of sanity conducted locally. A writ to the sheriff of Hereford in 1278 suggests the central judges understood all this better than all the local officers. A Hereford citizen, Robert of Dekaston, had drowned himself in a ditch outside the city. The coroner had seized the man's smallholding and chattels, the latter worth 20 marks. But the dead man's daughter Agnes appealed. She said her father's mind had been disturbed by illness and he should have been guarded. The writ tells the sheriff to investigate precisely this question of the man's moral responsibility, and seems to lean to the daughter's side. Agnes had shown, it says, that her father had only drowned himself 'during an acute fever from which he suffered, when left unguarded', that he had been 'led by a spirit of madness through the excessive anguish of heart by which he was oppressed'. The letter spells out that 'the actions of persons thus suffering from fever and madness are wont to be adjudged in such cases for mischance and not for felony, as it is said.' The sheriff is to acquit Robert if he finds that he 'was not of sound mind but mad, and that he drowned himself by reason of the anguish and through lack of guard, and not in any other way'. The sheriff, as well as the coroner, needed teaching.

That was only one of several such instructions. Another is addressed to the sheriff of Carlisle and concerns Ralph le Deblet. Le Deblet had died in Carlisle on the evening of 1 November 1285. A report reached Westminster that he had committed suicide, possibly while drunk. So a writ to the sheriff ordered an enquiry whether he had 'killed himself *furore ductus* [led on by fury]' and produced this account:

Ralph le Deblet [on 1 November 1285] by evening was so drunk that he did not know what he was doing [*nichil scivit de seipso*], and went by night to the house of Thomas the Taylor of Carlisle, walked up the stairs of a solar [an upper floor], and fell upon Thomas as he lay asleep in bed. Thomas woke up crying out and asking what had fallen on him, and Ralph, going down the stairs in his drunkenness, fell upon a cartload of wood and was wounded in the head even to the brain, and died of it. Misadventure.

It actually turned out that the Westminster lawyers had got it wrong. In 1292 or 1293 an Eyre came to Carlisle and learned that the suicide story had been a fake in the first place, designed to get Thomas le Taylor off a charge of killing Ralph by a blow on the head. So the Eyre dismissed the suicide story and had Thomas hanged.[1]

Other verdicts in this category were usually less complicated. Thus at another post-mortem inquisition in 1283, in Yorkshire, the York sheriff and coroners were told to enquire whether John of Balnea, in Mickefield, had hanged himself *furore ductus*. After due enquiry they replied *inter alia* that John 'took off his clothes and fled to the park of Kypaske and there hanged himself as one frenzied [*frenseticus*] by a cord from a hazel tree'. A comparable detail, this time about the duration of the fit of madness, likewise established beyond doubt that one William Sprot was mad, when in 1381 the sheriff of Berkshire found that William

happened to fall into a frenzy about Epiphany [6 January] and thereby immediately became mad and so remained until [22 May], when he threw himself in his madness from Hurley into the river Thames.

Even here, we notice, it is as much on repeated assertion as on circumstance that the report relies. It does not *prove* he was mad, but only says so again and again. This assertive repetition recurs at all levels of record.

---

[1] JUST/1/137 m 25.

To see how the question of insanity admitted non-judicial influence let us first recall that coroners, being local, were likely to be biased towards the excusing of suicides. At once, when this is understood, coroners' allegations of insanity appear in a new light, in that they seem to have been giving a suicide the benefit of the doubt. Thus in the handful of split decisions, where coroner and Eyre judges have given opposite verdicts, it is more often than not the coroner who gives the milder one. Again, in those rare instances for which a coroner's description of a suicide survives, the concept of insanity often plays a part in the acquittal. An example will illustrate this from that same London coroner's roll of 1321. In it, jurors accounted for the death of one Isabella de Pampesworth as a victim of medical insanity. They offer no corroborating fact other than the bare suicide. To read the account is to be left, as the coroner was, with no choice but to believe the jurors' assertion, which here too is repeated. They say that Isabella had 'for the last two years and more suffered from a disease called *frenesie*', and go on:

on the preceding Sunday at the hour of Prime [Isabella] was alone in her chamber whilst Christiana de Iseldone, servant to John de Pampesworth [Isabella's husband], went to the kitchen to get her some food, and she hanged herself with a cord from a small beam in the gallery when nobody was present, whilst suffering from the aforesaid disease. The said Christiana when she entered the room raised the cry, so that a certain William Scott ran thither and cut the cord with his knife, and Isabella fell to the ground alive, and so lingered for the space of quarter of an hour . . . and then died from weakness of the said disease and the hanging.

The expression 'the said disease' comes three times, and was enough to persuade the coroner to release her chattels to the family.

Such bald accounts in coroners' rolls may explain the anomaly I began with, namely the apparent inconsistency in Eyres, which seem alternately to condemn and excuse allegedly insane suicides, with no open logic. Whatever logic the Eyres possessed may have been latent in the accompanying coroners' rolls, now lost. Some of their attempts to clear suicides doubtless sounded more convincing than others, for an Eyre was in general more likely to judge suicide harshly. In the last chapter we often saw them condemn as felons suicides allegedly 'insane', and amerce coroners for leniency, and it is only occasionally that we find an Eyre decide the other way. Thus a London Eyre of 1321 reversed the condemnation of an allegedly 'mad' suicide by a sheriff's court. It did so precisely by re-examining the relevant coroner's roll and, no doubt to corroborate the insanity, re-hearing the original witnesses who had appeared before the coroner. The roll of 1321 duly records that it was found by the coroner's roll that a certain J [oan] went mad [*fut arage*] and ran in her madness to the Thames and drowned herself and her chattels were taken, at 3 shillings, for which the sheriff of that time was to answer. But the [Eyre] court sees by inspection of the coroner's roll and also by the jurors who witnessed to it that she was in such condition [*de tel estat*] that she could not forfeit those chattels, because of her bad health [*pur la noun saunte*]. It therefore orders the sheriff that those chattels be given as alms for the soul of the said Joan and that the king has no more claim on them.

Occasionally, but only occasionally, we find things the other way round: that it is a coroner who judges the question of a suicide's insanity the more harshly. Rather than make havoc of the principle that coroners tended to respect feelings among local families, this exception just shows how effective were those frequent amercements of coroners. They learned to fear the Eyre judges, knowing that excessive leniency might be punished. This, at least, would explain the case in a Surrey Eyre of 1263, where Gilbert de la Mare had fallen into the river Mole at Esher. The coroner said Gilbert had drowned himself 'in a fit of madness', but took his chattels all the same. The Eyre re-examined the question of the suicide's state of mind by re-hearing the original witnesses, confirmed the 'madness' and consequently reclassified Gilbert's death as 'misadventure'.

At a low or medium social level, a plea of insanity might soften the results of suicide for a local family. At a higher level a different consideration was at work. The judicial system is rare which always treats great and small identically, so it is no irreverence to Plantagenet justice to suggest that extra-judicial considerations may have swayed some judgements on suicide. There is a distinct ambience of landownership, for instance, about a 'Richard, son of Reginald de Upton' who was acquitted of felonious suicide after having 'struck himself in the stomach with his knife'. He was buried, when he died three days later, without a coroner's seeing the body: Richard was *freneticus*, no questions asked. But for a 'son of Reginald de Upton' we do not have to believe that this was the only reason for his acquittal, since dynastic influence was possibly at work. A more spectacular case still was that of Edmund Mordant of Turvey, between Bedford and Northampton, which can be followed through several Westminster rolls. The kernel, as told in a Close Roll for 1373, was that

the said Edmund being mad, on the Sunday before Saints Simon and Jude last [namely, on 23 October], in his madness slew Ellen his wife, and the same day being in his madness, in a pond on the manor of Turvey, drowned himself.

In as many lines, again, Edmund was three times 'mad'. It was as well that he should be, for he belonged to a family of local distinction of which the coroner himself (William Mordaunt, author of a coroner's roll still extant in the Public Record Office)[2] was probably a member. Edmund had held half the manor of Turvey on feudal tenure, with military obligation of a quarter of a knight's fee. He and his ill-fated wife had left a healthy son and heir, whose inheritance to his father's property may have been thought conducive to stability in regional patterns of landholding. There were good reasons for not making his father a felon.

Uncertain Verdicts: Pretended Suicides

'Insanity', then, formed the first flexible element in otherwise rigid principles of judgement. The second was sheer uncertainty about the facts, in that not every court could be sure how someone had died. The conceptual frontiers between a coroner's three options—*felonia de se*, homicide, and misadventure—might be clear, but in practice a case could find its way across them. The rolls thus include verdicts of suicide which may, in reality, have been homicides or misadventures, and vice versa. These vagrants are the historian's friend, for the same reason as those debates about insanity. Uncertain verdicts tended to evoke special interest, so they leave more documentation.

Let us look first at deaths which may not have been suicide but which jurors swore were so. Why should they swear it? The commonest reason was that their oath shielded a murderer. Mysterious cases of this kind can appear in Westminster Inquisitions. In the courtyard of the Hospitallers at Melchbourne, ten miles north of Bedford, on the night of 1 October 1291 a well-to-do peasant called Benedict le Vilor was wounded, carried in a wheelbarrow by the Hospitallers' domestics as far as the stocks outside the courtyard, and left there. At dawn next morning he was found dead. The dead man had been a visitor from Boarstall in Buckinghamshire, where he had farmed a fair-sized holding. He had come to Melchbourne with a servant, Thomas of Cockermouth. Thomas was arrested and charged with the 'premeditated murder' of his master. Thomas denied everything and said that his master had killed himself. While Thomas was detained in Bedford gaol his allegation of Benedict's suicide was reported to the sheriff of Buckingham, who duly prepared to distrain on Benedict's property. Someone, probably the landlord of his farm, then appealed to Westminster. On 2 December an order went out for an *Inquisitio post mortem*. This inquest met on 15 February 1292, cleared Benedict of suicide, and said he had been killed by

[2] London, PRO, JUST 2/6.

persons unknown. Nothing was said of Thomas. But Thomas was meanwhile actually languishing in Bedford gaol, waiting for the next visit of the
justices. When they finally came, on 19 May, seven-and-a-half months after
his master's death, Thomas got a jury to confirm the story of the suicide
and was let out. Neither acquittal mentions the other, and it seems the real
murderer got away, as most did. But can we be certain? The story of Benedict's suicide might, by a stretch of imagination, have been true. Only one
alternative remains: that Thomas was saved from hanging by twelve per-
jurers, and unanimous ones at that.

The murderers were unluckier in the case of Thomas de Cherleton (or
Cherlinton) of Haseley, three miles north-west of Warwick. It is recorded
in three Westminster rolls, two of them from the Exchequer (because this
Thomas was rich). Thomas of Cherleton's servants had apparently strangled him and thrown the body into his own fishpond. The servants prevailed
on friends in a neighbouring hundred, not his own, to attest the case as one
of suicide, so Thomas's chattels were confiscated. But this anomaly too
attracted interest, for it was noticed that the fishpond was in the wrong
hundred. So the case was re-heard in the right hundred, and the murderers
hanged. The Exchequer was told to repay the value of Thomas's chattels to
his heirs and kinsmen 'to bestow in alms and to distribute for the soul of
the deceased' (*ad erogandum et distribuendum pro anima dicti defuncti*).

The Eyre rolls contain several similar cases of murderers who sought to
evade justice by this means. One can be reconstructed from an entry in the
Devon Eyre of 1281–2. On Sunday, 27 March 1278, a young peasant called
William le King was found by his mother dead beside the river Taw near
Burrington. She raised the hue, the coroner came, a jury of locals was
empanelled and declared

that on the previous Saturday William le King was harrowing on the land of
William, son of William Baghel on the marsh beside the Taw with Osbert Hure-
ward, and he became mad and took his own knife and killed himself with his knife
in his heart, dying instantly.

The roll goes on to repeat another version, with no attempt to bring concord
to the discordant stories:

but the twelve jurors say that the rumour is that William son of William Baghel
killed him with his knife.

Three years later the Eyre investigated the rumour. It ignored the allegation
of suicide and just declared that William le King had been murdered, the
knife in his heart having been put there by William Baghel junior. The killer
may have abandoned his first defence more easily because he had found

another. He pleaded 'clergy', so was passed on to the milder care of a church court.

Once more, the hardest cases in this category, like the one at Melchbourne, were brawls. Whose knife struck whom? We cannot answer this question any better than the court could, but we can, at least, sometimes doubt whether the court was on sure ground. It may have been letting a doubtful case go through to save the surviving brawler from hanging. France, again, will prove this with its fuller reports. But at least two cases from English Eyres suggest this may have been the case here too. One is that of Walter, a groom to the Earl of Warwick. Walter's death at Brailes, near Shipston on Stour, is mentioned in the Warwickshire Eyre of 1285. He had quarrelled with one 'Hugh of Shrewsbury', from the sound of him a military man. The record says Walter attacked Hugh with a knife, but that the knife 'turned' and struck Walter himself in the stomach so that he died at once. That may, of course, have been true, but these things are hard to prove, unless the twelve jurors were all watching and waiting for a homicide to happen. Approximately equal conviction, or lack of it, is carried by an account of the death of Clement Hund in Beccles in Suffolk, probably in 1278, though the case was not heard until the Eyre of 1286. Clement had quarrelled with one Robert le Denys. Robert had struck him on or near the fork of his body (*renes*) with a stick, so hard, one account said, that Clement died a month later. That account, left like that, would have sufficed to hang Robert. Robert's friends must therefore have rallied jurors with a different story. Clement, they said, went home after the fight and deliberately wounded his own arm with a chisel, was 'sick of that wound for a month' and then died of it. The motive for this unusual form of suicide, they said, was to get Robert hanged for his murder. Which story was true, or what combination? French registers, again, will offer similar testimonies to village solidarity.

The shelter of murderers, then, may be suggested as one reason for the invention of an occasional suicide story. An incident from a time long after the epoch of the Eyres will echo this principle, for a brutal burlesque of the same story would be enacted in 1455 during a chaotic phase of Henry VI's reign, by the murderers of Nicholas Radford. Radford, a famous Justice of the Peace, lived at Upcott near Tiverton. He was widely respected for fairness, but fairness cut no ice with the lawless Earl of Devon and his henchmen. Radford had given legal advice to a baron they regarded as their enemy. So they murdered the famous magistrate, held a mock inquest in Upcott chapel over his body—one henchman acting as coroner and the others as jurors with assumed names—and passed a verdict of *felonia de se*. Radford's servants were then forced to carry the corpse and tip it naked into an empty grave in the churchyard. Radford had stored some stones in the church to make his own tomb, so his murderers took the stones and heaped them on the 'suicide's' makeshift grave.

The supposed 'suicide' verdict in that story would not be sheltering murderers, but merely expressing contempt. In the period of the Eyres this motive is once detectable as having pushed an inquest towards a suicide verdict when the death was almost certainly misadventure. In 1248 or a little earlier, according to the Sussex Eyre of that year, an Eastbourne man called Gilbert atte Welle found a body on the seashore which was soon identified as that of one Remigius of Esthalle. An inquest was held and the jury of neighbours said Remigius had committed suicide by drowning. But the records are in doubt, for the coroner, on viewing the body, had seen 'no signs indicating that he had drowned'. The Eyre roll then adds:

it is testified that the men of Eastbourne greatly hated Remigius and hardly let him be buried in the cemetery.

The Eyre summoned the first finder, Gilbert atte Welle

and as he vacillates in his presentment it is ordered that he be taken into custody.

Testimony was given that Remigius had fallen into the sea from his horse, and the Eyre finishes: 'Eastbourne hundred is in mercy [that is, was amerced] for presenting the case falsely to the County Court.' In other words, Gilbert had been Eastbourne's *bête noir* and the townsmen had falsely made him a 'suicide' from contempt.

It would be easy to go on listing dubious suicide verdicts from the English rolls. The obscurity of the reasoning behind some of them is a positive challenge. Thus the 1272 Essex Eyre passed a verdict on a man found dead at Woodford 'as if by starvation [*quasi inedia extinctus*]' and put him down as *felo de se*. We do not have to search for the anomaly there: it cries out from the record, though there is no way of knowing what lay behind it; and other such puzzling cases could be added, each a witness, in its own way, to the non-judicial forces at work behind apparently candid judgements.

Our investigation began with the recognition that suicide was intrinsically secret and that even when it did, for particular reasons, get into surviving records, it leaves signs that it was trying to escape. The English rolls, with their suicide-hunting judges, may have seemed an exception to these rules. But in fact they go a long way to prove them, for the motives that made a royal judge hunt down suicides worked also in the opposite direction, adding to the motives the suicide's family and friends already had to conceal the suicide from him. Who knows what success the latter may have had, and how big the resulting black hole is in our records? Fortunately a few records do survive of suicide in the act of trying to escape: that is, of attempts made by family and friends to cheat the law and its rolls. Reading them, we may have a better chance of guessing how often such attempts may have succeeded.

Hidden Suicides

If a member of your family committed suicide it was strongly in your interest to hide it. At least four unsuccessful attempts to do so are recorded in the Eyre rolls. The first comes in an Assize (part of an Eyre) for Northumberland in 1256. The events probably happened a year or two before the Eyre but we do not know just when, only where. At the village of Lucker, near Bamburgh in Northumberland, a young man called William, son of Henry le Muir, came into the house one day to find his mother hanging by her wimple and already dead. He must have seen at once it was suicide, and must have known, too, it was his duty to report the death publicly to the village. Instead,

the jurors attest that [William did not report the death] when he found his mother hanging, but cut the wimple and took her down, took her to a bed, gave his neighbours to understand that she had died a natural death and had her buried in the cemetery.

It was all very well to pin blame on the young man, as these jurors did. But the dead woman's husband too must have colluded; and it is likely, at least, that a neighbour saw the body and, whether through neighbourly tact or for lack of close inspection, took the two bereaved men at their word, with the result that no one interfered when the body was buried in the churchyard. The story might have ended there. But other neighbours, or even *one* other neighbour, must have turned 'king's evidence', with the upshot that twelve jurors were empanelled to tell all they knew. William and Henry were both arrested for concealing a felony, and the village as a whole fined, for failing to give full assistance to the enquiry.

Two comparable but more elaborate attempts at concealment are recorded in a roll for the Devon Eyre of 1281–2. A beadle—again the death must have been a year or two earlier—had hanged himself in his house in Ottery St Mary. A jury later betrayed to the Eyre that

Henry's wife Raghanilda and Thomas Henry at once took Henry [the Beadle]'s body and put it in a bed and covered it. Later they sent for one Henry de

Cornubia, a chaplain, and gave him 30 shillings to conceal this felony. They executed Henry's will and later buried the body in Ottery St Mary cemetery, without a coroner's view.

The chattels of the deceased were worth 60 shillings. So the payment to the chaplain can be seen as a 50 per cent commission on the expected profits. Anyway, on hearing this story from their jury the judges sent constables to arrest the widow and her accomplice, who were clearly suspected of murder. This they denied, getting a local jury to swear to their innocence, so that they were let off with a fine of 6s 8d for burying the corpse without a coroner's inspection. Perhaps the court forbore to press further charges against a widow who must have been near ruin, for her husband's 60 shillings-worth of chattels had vanished, and so had that bribe of 30 shillings, to the chaplain, who is unmentioned in the arraignment. What with that 6s 8d fine, on top of those other losses, the widow had lost a total of £4 17s 2d. Living beadles were notorious for their exactions. Dead, this one had ruined his widow.

The same roll tells of another attempt at concealment, complicated, and from our point of view enriched, by the entry of a new type of interested party: a lord, jealous of his villein's chattels. Henry le Rede had been a well-to-do villein, living in a village near Bideford in Devon. His chattels were worth well over half those of the beadle just mentioned. At some unknown date before the Eyre of 1281–2—the coroner's roll which might have told us is again lost—Henry had hanged himself in his own barn. The bailiff and his constables were not summoned to cut down the body and must later have said as much. But if they had not cut the body down, who had? Again we have two stories, unreconciled. One said it was Henry's wife Agnes who had cut the body down, and thrown it in a river. The Eyre judges duly had her arrested. But she came and again denied 'the death and everything', demanding an inquest of local jurors, who said she had neither killed Henry nor moved the body. Only at this point did someone on the Eyre staff look in the relevant coroner's roll (the entry just says: 'Later it was discovered from the coroner's roll . . .'). There it was recorded that the body had been hidden by one Richard de Prendiswurthe, a lord whose villein Henry had been, and who would in normal circumstances have been heir to his chattels. The coroner's roll said that Lord Richard had swept the body away to save these chattels, worth 38s 2d, from going to the king. Once again men were sent out to arrest the accused, and the same scene followed. Lord Richard denied moving the body and demanded an inquest with its own jurors, who again supported him. Had neither Agnes nor Richard moved the body then, as local jurors swore? Or had both done so, in collusive combination? And had the parish scandal, now a year or two old, been rendered impregnable to royal justice by local solidarity? All that interests us now is that a suicide had nearly been hidden. We catch it in the act of 'fleeing from the camera', and almost succeeding.

A fourth and last case came nearer still to success. It is from the Cambridgeshire Eyre of 1299, and concerns the death of Gillian Newton. At some date in the 1290s Gillian was drowned in a ditch near the house where she and her husband lived, at Witchford near Ely. About a week later, the coroner recorded that she had fallen accidentally while trying to cross the ditch by a 'beam'. This story, which reads like scores of others in the Eyre rolls, had the unanimous backing of a jury of twelve from villages nearby, including the son of a chaplain. The verdict *infortunium* was duly entered on the coroner's roll. Unfortunately for all of them, especially for the coroner, someone had kept the copy of a report he had made at another, earlier inquest, one made within hours of Gillian's death and in the presence of the body and neighbours. In this first inquest the coroner had been content to conclude Gillian had drowned herself deliberately, and set about, as usual, valuing the chattels left in the house of her husband, Reginald. But Reginald clearly had local friends. They sympathized with his misfortune and persuaded the coroner to have second thoughts, so he held a new inquest with twelve of them as witnesses. But when the Eyre of 1299 came round it somehow—it only takes one traitor to ruin a plot of this kind—got its hands on both the records, and wasted no time in reaching a conclusion. The Eyre knew which way deception was likely to go, and the first decision had been made in the presence of the corpse; so the judges preferred the first version, imposed amercements all round, and especially on the soft-hearted coroner.[3]

Four cases have been rehearsed as examples. In each a bereaved relation, with the connivance of one or more neighbours—in one with the connivance also of a lord, in another also that of a coroner—tried to hide the fact of suicide. Whether or not the attempt succeeded depended on two factors: on one hand, on the resolution of the Eyre judges, and on the other, on the degree of solidarity a neighbourhood could muster to keep a friend out of trouble, at a distance of years, it might be, from the tragedy. In another context I propose to consider 'breakers and benders of the law' across a wider, European field,[4] and will enquire then why such attempts at

---

[3] JUST 1/96 m 71d. I have guessed time intervals, the identity of the coroner in both hearings, and that he was punished more severely: the report ends, after saying the twelve jurors are 'in mercy', 'and judgement on the coroner'. The coroner's two rolls were available to the Eyre of 1299 but had served their purpose and do not survive.

[4] In *The Curse on Self-Murder*, ch. 13.

concealment were often betrayed to the law, as the above four necessarily were. It is enough now to know from the English rolls that such attempts were certainly made, and with substantial backing.

Among other fruits of that knowledge is our capacity to read less explicit records in the light of those four examples. For instance, another case in that Devon Eyre of 1281–2 left this puzzling report:

Robert le Pestur, wishing to bathe in the river Exe, was accidentally drowned. Sabina his wife, who first found him, has died. Later it was established that he voluntarily drowned himself. *Felo de se*. He had no chattels.

The record is again self-contradictory, perhaps for the same reason as before, namely the apparent nonchalance of the court about which account was true, for the dead man had no chattels. Courts would care more, as Westminster rolls show, when the suicide was rich. So we can only offer our own possible explanation of the drowning in the Exe: that the penniless widow had found that her husband had drowned himself and, with the connivance of neighbours, concealed the fact, burying him normally without a coroner's view. When she was dead, the story came out, and got endorsement by the Eyre.

Short, ambiguous reports of this kind lead us finally to that open frontier of all suicide history, the 'death by misadventure', with no breath about suicide but which may nevertheless conceal it. Guessing how many 'deaths by misadventure' may conceal suicides is an occupation potentially endless, for the medieval as for any other period. The concealers of suicide succeeded there, at least, in keeping survivors guessing. But to assure ourselves that all this applies to medieval English rolls we need only remember that usage I mentioned in Chapter 2, of *infortunium* as a euphemistic synonym for suicide (as used, for instance, by the thirteenth-century English law book *Fleta*, to head a chapter all about suicide).[5]

How many 'misfortune' cases in the rolls invite a reading of suicide is a matter of judgement. In *The Medieval Coroner* Dr Roy Hunnissett forebore to quote more than a handful of possible examples, and that was from coroners' rolls alone.[6] The Eyres and *veredicta* would yield more. But a long review of doubtful cases would lead to no solid conclusion except that specialist students of suicide are afflicted by a temptation to see it everywhere. How far I have fallen victim to that temptation can be judged in the context of the statistical exercise in Chapter 15. For now, rather than lose our way across this frontier, it may be instructive to gauge just how open the frontier may be by reflecting on a single final example, which survives in just enough detail to feed speculation on this point.

[5] *Fleta*, bk 1, ch. 34. See p. 37 above.
[6] *The Medieval Coroner*, 20, n. 2.

It occurs in a coroner's roll for London in 1322. Around noon on Sunday, 20 June in that year, a boatman navigating the Thames near Greenhithe found a corpse afloat in the water, dragged it to the water's edge and 'raised the cry'. Residents of the ward came and looked at the body, which was recognized as that of Robert, 'son of Ralph of Leyre in Essex'. Robert's friends got the body out of the water and took it to a local shop, where the coroner came and inspected it. He empanelled a local jury of twelve men, who swore that:

on the Friday before, Robert went to the wharf called 'le Fishwharf' and entered the river to bathe, no one being present. He was by accident drowned and so remained in the water until the following Saturday, when, about noon, a certain John Curteys, a boatman, found him drowned and raised the cry, so that the country came; that at the request of Robert's friends his corpse was taken out of the water and placed in the said shop, for better inspection. They suspect no one of the death, but only the mischance aforesaid.

The report is remarkable for its gaps. It contains no sign of any of Robert's kindred except that father of his away in Essex. Nobody, it appears, went looking for Robert when he was late back from bathing on the Friday evening, though if his friends were really his friends perhaps they tried and failed. In that case, was that because 'le Fishwharf' was not his regular bathing place? We cannot know just how Robert died. But nor could the jurors, 'no one else being present'. Yet here were twelve men, swearing to a man, to circumstances they could not possibly have known as eye-witnesses, and they were believed. Robert had no property so it was in no one's interest to challenge the story. Perhaps it is not in ours. But the certainties, set beside that big uncertainty, generate a picture as we reflect on them: a destitute immigrant to Edward II's London, probably young, effectively kinless and possibly friendless except for acquaintances who hardly noticed he was gone, was found dead in the river more than twelve hours after he had last been seen or heard of.

Because suicide was elusive, and seen partially and usually obliquely, when seen at all, and often in the act of running away, we resolved at the outset to build up a picture of it from as wide a range of documents as possible; or rather to build up several pictures, each from its own category of document and reflecting its idiosyncrasies, the pictures to be combined afterwards. True to this plan we turn next to a category both similar and different, in its portrayals of suicide, from that employed in these last two chapters, namely to the judicial records of France.

9

Portraits from French Courts

FRENCH legal structures, as well as English ones, left records of suicide. But the French structures were more complicated and so left them in a different pattern.[1] Political decentralization had allowed a mass of local jurisdictions to survive, and these mostly kept old procedures which used no records. So in France the black hole is vast, its character only to be inferred, once more, from occasional points on the perimeter where more literate jurisdictions tried to draw cases in. These were of two main categories. A few jurisdictions originally seigneurial, or quasi-seigneurial, did come to make registers for special reasons, and in imitation of procedures seen elsewhere. More important, from the thirteenth century, royal justice was increasingly on the watch for dubious verdicts in the old courts, to be re-heard. When this happened, especially when verdicts reached one of the courts of Parlement, records could be excellent.

Our search for portraits of suicide will begin with the fragments that survive from the seigneurial end.

Abbeys

The most instructive of these fragments are the criminal registers of some half a dozen abbeys in the Île de France, near Paris (and today more or less in it). As I explained earlier, their criminal jurisdictions were 'dinosaurs' enduring from Merovingian or Carolingian times, when the only way to establish a monastery was to give it a panoply of seigneurial lands and rights, including High Justice. By the thirteenth century, new approaches to crime were beginning to render all such seigneurial courts anachronistic. But it was only a beginning, and for a long time the balance between new and old was fine enough to create lasting rivalries. The main rival to the abbeys

---

[1] The reasons are set out in Ch. 6 above, pp. 139–48.

was the Prévôt of Paris. His court at the Châtelet was itself seigneurial in origin, but it had become powerful with the growth of Paris, and partly modernized by its nearness to the king. In the face of the Prévôt, the old abbeys near Paris kept having to prove their traditional right of judging crime in their lands, so from the early thirteenth century some of them began to keep criminal registers.

Here, duly, we find suicides recorded. Persons who killed themselves were sentenced, as homicides, to have their bodies 'dragged' and to lose their property to the holder of the jurisdiction. The registers are consequently interested in the bare fact of the suicide, where it happened, and who punished it, and not for its own sake, in the motive or character of the perpetrator. The bare fact is barest of all in the case of strangers. Thus the register of St Maur-des-Fossés mentions 'a certain woman from elsewhere [*extranea*]' who 'threw herself into a certain well and was drowned there' (who inexplicably was not punished).[2] At Epinay-sur-Orge, similarly, it was just 'a man' who was 'found drowned in the river under Epinay and in the land, seigneurie and justice of Epinay, [who] was said to have drowned himself'.[3] Local suicides, by contrast, are likely to get a name. Thus the Ste Geneviève register recorded a 'Robert de Jedin who had murdered himself [*s'estoit murtri*]',[4] and that of St Maur, that 'Ysabeleta committed murder of herself by hanging herself at night.'[5]

That Epinay case has a date attached, 1257. The date of the others has to be guessed by its place in the register. The common datelessness is reminiscent of the English Eyre, which gathered up business from the previous septennium but remained vague. A case from St Germain, of a 'Jean Carbonnier, barber, resident of [St Germain]' who hanged himself there, is dated '14 . . .', as if the scribe was conscientious but did not know, for he says it happened 'in the time of Brother William Tubeuf',[6] relying on community memory. Other suicides are assigned to a year, much more rarely to a month or day. As for place, the interest of the registrar is in establishing the suicide was on abbey lands. He only occasionally adds a corroborative topographic detail, as if to lend verisimilitude. Thus at Epinay, in 1238, a woman called 'Melissent' hanged herself in her grange at Borest;[7] and again, in 1266, 'there hanged herself in her house at Borest a woman called Mehant du Molin.'[8]

The registers therefore still leave us short on motive. Just occasionally it is implied, as in the case of a prisoner in St Maur in 1274, when one

[2] L. Tanon, *Histoire des justices des anciennes églises et communautés monastiques de Paris* (Paris, 1883), 334.
[3] Tanon, *Justices*, 398–9.   [4] Ibid., 359.   [5] Ibid., 335.
[6] Ibid., 430.   [7] Ibid., 400.   [8] Ibid., 400.

Pierre, called Crochet, of Boissiac, was captured on suspicion of the murder of Pierre, called Bardos, by the wood at Boissiac. He was brought to Boissiac and imprisoned there, and while he was in prison he did murder on himself [*murtrum de se ipso*] by hanging.[9]

Rather than condemn the abbey justiciars for sloth in not recording more details, we should wonder at their courage in the face of difficulties. With no coroner and no jury, how could they know the truth? That drowned man at Epinay 'was said' to have drowned himself. In a phrase like that the absence of juries is palpable. It is not as if the abbey justiciars did not try to find out. Take those of St Martin-des-Champs, who were positively conscientious. Thus for 10 December 1317 their register records

a man who had been found dead and who had hanged himself, as people said, in Hauvervillier, in a stable. He was called Geoffrey Goule. The body . . . shall remain as a prisoner until the procurator and baillif have enquired how he died.[10]

St Martin's was scrupulous also in taking no more than its due. In 1317, it records,

Belon, daughter of the late Birart Feret, hanged herself at Noisy, according to the accusation, for she was found dead in her house. Officers of St Martin's took the body and took it to St Martin's manor in Beauvoir where it remained two or three days. It could not be proved that she had done herself any harm. St Martin's officers delivered the body to her friends and it was put in holy ground.[11]

Again, St Martin's might exonerate a suicide as insane, like

a furrier of St Martin, found hanged in a house in the rue Quincampoux, [who] was returned to his friends because the mayor's enquiry showed he had long been mad and out of his wits [*tout fol . . . hors du sens*].[12]

One entry shows the St Martin's baillifs at work, judging accidental deaths this way and that, by rule of thumb:

Item, many men have often been found drowned in the river Marne. St Martin's baillifs [*genz*] have pulled them out of the water and buried them in St Martin's land. Often they have kept the property and effects of these dead men, like their clothes, and other things they had with them, but often, too, they have released these personal effects to their friends.[13]

The judgement whether a death was suicide or not clearly invited a measure of improvisation. That is the way legal institutions develop. The registers themselves, after all, were a kind of improvisation.

[9] Tanon, *Justices*, 332–3.
[10] L. Tanon, ed., *Registre criminel de . . . S. Martin des Champs* (Paris, 1877), 223.
[11] Tanon, *S. Martin*, 228.
[12] Tanon, *Justices*, 37, n. 26.   [13] Tanon, *S. Martin*, 229.

Towns

The Île-de-France abbeys were an exception in seigneurial justice because of their records. Towns, with their own laws, were an exception for another reason. In northern France their jurisdictions had been established as deliberate parentheses in the seigneurial network, and partly on those grounds shared some of its idiom. We shall see this more clearly in Germany, whose towns took on much of the public peace-keeping that fell to the king in France. But it was still true in a measure in France. This had its effect on our evidence for suicides, for some of the French towns with High Justice also kept registers, and where they did, suicides are there.

An example from northern France is Abbeville, whose criminal register, the 'Red Book', survives and has been well exploited by the town's historians. The format of reports in the Red Book is curt, like the abbeys', but more regular and more generous with names and dates. Thus the Red Book tells in 1305 of 'Fremin Ibisnat, a clerk and merchant, [who] went off to Amiens and when he got there he despaired and hanged himself'.[14] In 1336 there is a 'Jacques Aude, who had hanged himself at S. Riquier through despair round Pentecost last'.[15] In 1349 a suicide is recorded, exceptionally, without name or sex.[16] But in 1364 it was the turn of 'Maroie Parvaise, wife of Watier Cosse', who, 'living in the burg of Wimeu [a quarter of Abbeville] despaired and hanged herself [*se désespéra et pendi*] in her house and was found in this state'.[17] When it comes to prisoners, this urban precision brings us close enough to recontruct a suicide's motives. The Red Book records that in 1382 'on Sunday, 18 May, it happened that in the house of Sandre was found an Englishman called Henry, who was said to be Sandre's prisoner held for ransom, and who had hanged himself';[18] a soldier of small estate, perhaps, of whom we know of many during the Hundred Years' War, whose captors had named a ruinous ransom. Two years later, again, on 23 July 1384, a man with an illegible name 'born at Doswerke in the Beoulenois, hanged himself and died in the house of Martin d'Oysencourt, and for this was hanged and dragged'.[19] Two fifteenth-century suicides by hanging, of men of whose lives we know nothing more, end the medieval series from the Red Book.[20]

[14] J. Boca, *La justice criminelle de l'échevinage d'Abbeville au moyen âge, 1184–1516* (Lille, 1930), 80.

[15] Boca, *Justice criminelle*, 80–1.

[16] F. C. Louandre, *Histoire d'Abbeville et du comté de Ponthieu*, vol. 2 (Paris, 1845), 264.

[17] A. Thierry, ed., *Recueil des monuments inédits de l'histoire du Tiers état*, 1re série; *Chartes, etc., Région du Nord*; vol. 4 (Paris, 1870), p. 200 (no. 11); cf. Boca, 81.

[18] Boca, *Justice criminelle*, 81. The dating is still imperfect. In 1382 the 18 May fell on a Monday.

[19] E. Prarond, *Les Lois et les moeurs d'Abbeville, 1184–1789* (Paris, 1906), 163.

[20] Boca, *Justice criminelle*, 82 (whose date I follow in preference to '1403' in the older

Southern French towns had different legal traditions. But in the right rare circumstances these were no less capable of leaving records of suicide. The circumstances obtained at Manosque, a town in the Provençal Alpine foothills forty miles north-east of Marseilles. Manosque had grown up under an old-fashioned count, who in the late twelfth century had granted to its consuls—the southern, Roman-law influenced equivalent of the Abbeville échevins—their own criminal jurisdiction; but he had been replaced by an ambitious religious order, the Knights Hospitaller, and their shifting rivalries for jurisdiction had the result that both sides took more care over procedure and records, of which a big archive is extant.[21] A mere sounding among its published fragments confirms that in Manosque, too, suicide could occur and be recorded. The tenor of a report of 1318 reveals the care taken by judges and notaries, as southern counterparts in this to the coroner, to ascertain the cause of death, at least when murder might have been suspected. One 'Hugh', had been charged with theft.

And while Hugh was being held in the court's prison on account of his theft, soon after noon today, 25 November [1318], he was found dead in prison, hanged by a thong taken from his breeches. He was discovered by Lord Brother Hugh of Les Tours, *bayle* and warden of the court, and by numerous other trustworthy men whose names are written below.[22]

Nine names are here recorded. They

said they found the said Hugh dead [hanged] by a noose, as it seemed to them, and on inspection of the body they found nothing that might have caused his death other than his being strangled by the noose.[23]

Finally comes a medical opinion:

On the same day Master Antony Imbert, a surgeon, said and deposed on oath after inspection of Hugh's body, that he found him dead by hanging from a noose, which noose he had round his neck, and so far as appeared from the medically recognized symptoms apparent on the dead man's lips and tongue, the dead man did not die otherwise, as it seemed to him.[24]

Louandre, vol. 2, 264–5); Boca, 81–2 (Louandre, vol. 2, 265; Prarond, 239–40. The entry is printed in A. Thierry, ed., *Recueil des monuments inédits*, 282–3. In addition to some of the cases cited by Boca, Louandre (p. 264) mentions a woman who killed herself at Montrueil, whose body was brought to the échevinage of Abbeville, shown to the public, and burned.

[21] F. Reynaud, *La commanderie de l'hôpital de St Jean de Jerusalem de Rhodes et Malte, Manosque (xiie siècle–1789)*. Société d'études des Hautes Alpes (Gap, 1981), 7–11, summarizes the history.

[22] The document is printed by J. Schatzmiller, *Médicine et justice en Provence médiévale. Documents de Manosque, 1262–1348* (Aix, 1989), no. 39, p. 138. I have read 'cordule braerii' as 'cordule bracerii'.   [23] Ibid.

[24] Ibid.: 'et prout apparebat signis apparentibus in labiis et lingua, que signa sunt in arte sua cognita, et aliter non est mortuus ut ei apparet.'

In its medical examination of a newly dead corpse Manosque may have been a pioneer: evidence of its doing so survives from 1280, eight years before similar evidence in Bologna, otherwise first in that field.[25]

Prisons

Seigneurs with High Justice normally had prisons. Prisoners to be put to death, with or without previous torture, might be kept there, and chroniclers have told us of a number of prisoners who killed themselves to avoid this fate. Did this happen in the world of French seigneurial justice? It is an elusive world. Occasionally a chronicler gives a glimpse of this effect, as when Orderic Vitalis told how Luke de la Barre reacted to his prospect of blinding, killing himself by banging his head against a wall, or as in the tradition, echoed by Dante, which said the same of Pier della Vigna. To expect evidence of such suicide from French courts of first instance is ambitious. Whatever other testimony drifts up from that world, and it is little, is not likely to include suicides *à la* Luke de la Barre. There are, nevertheless, roundabout ways of confirming from this angle too that others may have died as he did.

Two courts with prisons did keep records. The prospects of their inmates were comparable to those attaching to the hundreds of prisons elsewhere in France but with this difference, that memoranda were kept of important events in prison life. They were the prison of the Paris Châtelet, and that, or those, of the heresy inquisition. The Châtelet belonged to the Prévôt of Paris, his jurisdiction not so much a dinosaur, like that of the abbeys, as a hybrid monster. Part of its genetic descent was as seigneurial as anything in France, and that was why the Châtelet had a prison, bigger if no better than others. But, being in the busy, academic capital, and near the king, the Châtelet had updated its methods on the model of the Roman *inquisitio*. That meant it wrote down interrogatories and kept them in registers. Of its medieval registers only one volume survives, covering from late 1389 to early 1392.[26] Its entries are on quite a different scale from those of the registers of abbeys and towns, having been made by trained notaries. Since that

---

[25] Schatzmiller, *Médecine et Justice en Provence*, 39–40. In M. Hébert, ed., *Vie privée et ordre public à la fin du moyen âge. Études sur Manoque, la Provence et le Piémont (1250–1450)* (Aix, 1987), also based on this archive, I find no mention of suicide, only abundant murder.

[26] Ed. J. Duplès-Agier, *Régistre criminel du Châtelet de Paris du 6 sep 1389 au 18 mai 1392*. 2 vols. (Paris, 1861–4). The documentary context is described by Y. Lanhers, 'Les régistres du Châtelet', in C. Braibant, *Guide de Recherches dans les fonds judiciaires de l'ancien régime* (Paris, 1958), 207; the legal context by Lot and Fawtier, *Histoire des institutions françaises*, vol. 2, 372–85.

Roman procedure of *inquisitio*, besides recording witnesses' answers, also approved judicial torture, and since Paris custom comprised horrible punishments, the Châtelet registers make grim reading.

The corresponding experiences must have been grimmer. So should we not expect suicides? For all its expansiveness on other matters, the surviving register records none, so we are entitled to wonder, why not? It could reflect mere lack of desire; or it could show the authorities took effective precautions; or, finally, it could be that suicides occurred but eluded the register, and that here is another black hole. To learn about black holes earlier in this book we have relied on the partial exceptions, the evidence caught vanishing. Fortunately, an exception is to hand, which proves a prisoner might wish to commit suicide, that the authorities expected it, and, in exceptional cases, for special reasons, took energetic precautions to prevent it.

Let us come at the matter through the eyes of the Châtelet authorities. The suicide of most prisoners merely saved the prison staff the trouble of killing them. But a small minority were better kept alive. Top of the list of these were spies, or suspected spies, for the suicide of a spy involved loss of his secrets, and so was worth the trouble of prevention. Thus arose the exception in the surviving Châtelet register. A man called Pierre Fournet 'le Breton' was charged with spying, and his story preserved in an interrogatory of September and October, 1390.[27] He had been in the corps of King's Mounted Messengers, and in late August or early September of that year he had gone with secret letters from the king to the duke of Berry and the duke's chancellor. The letters never arrived. Fournet's story was that he and a companion had been attacked in a forest *en route*, had dismounted to fight the attackers, lost their horses and found, when all was quiet again, that the letter-case had gone. The Crown officers did not believe it. They thought Fournet had been bribed to divert the letter and was lying, so he was locked in a cell in the Châtelet and given reason to expect a stretching on the rack. Fournet made no secret of his fear, for he had watched a prisoner suffer this torture, and die from it. Perhaps he had let slip to someone he might commit suicide to escape the torture, for the authorities clearly thought this a possibility and feared he would die with his secrets. So they moved another prisoner to his cell, telling him to keep Fournet from doing himself harm,[28] and at the same time to report on his conversation. Later, the same companion was removed and was asked *inter alia* whether Fournet had made any suicidal remarks. Had he said he would kill himself? Yes, said the witness firmly. Fournet, he went on, had often said he would rather be put to death

---

[27] *Registre criminel du Châtelet*, vol. 1, 516–56; cf. Schmitt, 'Le suicide au moyen âge,' 24, n. 37.

[28] Ibid., 545–6. 'Ne se deseseprast ne aussy se feist aucun mal'.

than put on the rack, that he 'would accept death with a good grace, and, and on his soul, if he was made to die would take death with good grace.'[29] In other words, no, for the witness had clearly tried to tell the authorities what they wanted to hear: it paid to do so in the Châtelet. But the best the companion could do, the quoted remark, was not suicidal, so the episode only shows the warders thought suicide likely and, in this one instance and for a special reason, took cumbersome measures to prevent it. That suggests there were others, unrecorded. In the event Fournet was tortured but not killed, and sentenced to be branded and 'wear papers' (that is, carry notices, in front and behind, publicly identifying his offence).

Fournet's experiences in the Châtelet are suggestive. So are those of prisoners of another court which used inquisitorial procedure. The church's heresy inquisition had grown *pari passu* with the advance of the royal *bailli*, but with a different geographical centre of gravity. The original heresy inquisition was designed both for a special purpose and a special area. This was south-western France, where both royal and episcopal justice were weak and whose seigneurs, for their part, had been disgraced by their support for the Albigensian heresy. So in 1233 the learned friars, principally the Dominicans, were told to purge the area of the heretical ringleaders, and to use the *inquisitio* procedure to discover who these were. In the narrow sense of efficiency, that of the resulting procedure exceeded the efficiency of all other contemporary courts. If its ultimate purpose was imperfectly conceived, to say the least, that fact only increased the court's severity and the terror it inspired. For the same reason as at the Châtelet, then, we should expect prisoners' suicides.

Under appropriate circumstances, the inquisition judges also expected them. Records of the Languedoc inquisition note an occasional suicidal act by a prisoner, and the judges' awareness of this danger. Here is an entry of 1273 about a suspected Cathar 'Perfect'. (*Perfecti* were the Cathar élite, rather like priests or friars but with appropriately different theology). He was called Bernard of Rivoli:

Bernard of Rivoli, after long confinement in prison, in leg-irons, because he was found not to have confessed [his heresy] fully, was discovered with a head-wound. I, Atto the notary, had gone to the prison to see him and to find out if he was prepared to confess more, and he admitted to me that he had struck himself and wounded his head in an attempt to kill himself, because he wished to die.[30]

---

[29] Ibid., foot of p. 545 and lines 1–3 of p. 546.

[30] Paris, Bibl. Nat., MS Doat 25, fol. 14v: 'Anno quo supra [1273] . . . Bernardus de Rivoli praedictus diu detentus, et ad huc existens in carcere compeditus, pro eo quod reperiebatur minus plene confessus repertus est in capite vulneratus, et recognovit coram me Athone notario supradicto, qui veneram ad carcerem visurus eundem Bernardum et auditurus si plura

The notary adds a list of witnesses. There is reason to believe that Bernard of Rivoli had been subjected to torture, a weapon added to the armoury of the heresy inquisition in 1252.[31] If so, his motive for suicide was similar to that of Pierre Fournet.

But occasionally the heresy inquisition would use its ultimate sanction, which it called euphemistically 'relaxation to the secular arm', which meant burning alive. It is dangerous to assume, on the basis of possible modern reactions to the prospect of a death of this kind, that a prisoner would necessarily have seen suicide as preferable. But with or without assumptions we know this could happen. In 1329 a heresy inquisition in Béziers was prosecuting extreme Franciscan 'Spirituals', and had in its prison a Brother Pierre de Julien. The court had agreed on part of its sentence. The friar, it had decided, should be degraded from clerical status and imprisoned. A bare majority was prepared to go further and sentence Brother Pierre to be 'relaxed to the secular arm'. For either alternative, the help of the local bishop was needed, to degrade Brother Pierre from clerical status before his other punishments could begin. When this obstacle was pointed out, the rigorist majority suggested the sentence be announced at once but its execution delayed until the bishop came. The others, more experienced, then raised this objection:

If the verdict is passed and announced today or tomorrow, unless the degradation and execution follow at once, there is a danger that Brother Pierre de Julien, seeing he is to be degraded and handed over to the secular arm, may possibly despair and, in despair, perhaps suffocate himself or kill himself some other way.[32]

confiteri vellet, quod ipsemet se percusserat, et vulneraverat in capite, mori desiderans, et se volens interficere. Horum testes sunt Bernardus Boneti, Sicardus Lunelli, Jacquetus Carcerarius, et ego praedictus Atho de Sancto Victore publicus inquisitionis notarius qui haec scripsi.'

[31] Paris, fol. 11v: 'diu detentus in carcere *correxit se* et dixit quod . . .' Bernard then confessed to having participated in Cathar ritual and gave away names. On the probable significance of the words I have italicized see G. Lizérand, *Le dossier de l'affaire des Templiers* (Paris, 1964), 42–3 and n. 1.

[32] Paris, Bibl. Nat., MS Doat, 27, fol. 162r–v: 'si dicta sententia modo vel die crastina ferretur et promulgaretur, et nisi dicta degradatio protinus et continuo executionis [?] debite demandetur periculum immineret pro eo videlicet quia si dictus frater Petrus Juliani videret et perciperet se degradendum et Seculari Curiae relinquendum forsitan desperabit et per desperationem se posset forsitan suffocare vel alias morti tradere et etiam dicto per aliquos ex eis quod multa alia pericula imminebant: tandem conclusum fuit per omnes uno excepto quod dixit licere et non expedire quod expediebat dictam sententiam differe usque ad diem magis propinquam et accomodam qua et quantocius dicti domini [fol. 162v] Episcopi vel alterius Episcopi praesentia poterit haberi, ita quod tunc dicta sententia proferatur et dicta degradatio actualiter exequatur'. For the general experience of inquisitors in this matter see Eymerich, *Manuel*, 178. While judicial records usually had reason to pass over the extreme consequence of the legal process, cruel execution, its very extremity gave it a natural home among miracle stories (when victims were saved from it). We shall duly find more suicidal prisoners there among miracle stories (in Ch. 13). This is a point at which our pictures from the two types of document converge closely.

The argument went on so long that feelings cooled and allowed the humanitarians to get Brother Pierre let off with degradation and prison.

Readers familiar with the history of medieval heresy may have noticed a peculiarity about the attempted suicide of the suspected Cathar *perfectus*, Bernard of Rivoli. His method had been to knock his head against a wall. But there was another recommended way for Cathar *perfecti* to kill themselves. They are supposed to have starved themselves to death by a procedure known in Provençal as *endura*. The feature which made the *endura* central to the concerns of the inquisition makes it peripheral to ours. It was institutionalized suicide, binding its subject more closely to his group rather than separating him from it, like the 'ordinary' suicide which this book is about. This is not the place to discuss the *endura* at length, but two facts about it do concern us, and need briefly stating.

First, the *endura* is not a 'myth'. It has been dismissed as that,[33] but that is an over-reaction, by twelfth-century historiography, to a claim by pioneers in the study of Catharism, who assumed it never changed and therefore read back, to the origins of the movement, testimony from the late thirteenth and early fourteenth centuries.[34] That late evidence is unequivocal, especially that of inquisitorial records which tell of individual cases of self-starvation. The way the records use the term *endura* is indeed itself an additional kind of evidence. They sometimes do, and sometimes do not, use it when describing a ritual self-starvation; and when they do, it often comes embedded in a Provençal phrase, like *en la endura*, intruded into an otherwise Latin record.[35] It is all as if the term was an established one for a known practice. The earliest inquisition record of such a death dates from just before 1274, near Pisa,[36] and there are several more from just after 1300.[37]

---

[33] By R. I. Moore, *Origins of the European Dissent* (Oxford, 1985), 224.
[34] As explained by Y. Dossat, 'L'évolution des rituel cathars', *Revue de synthèse*, 64, new series, 23 (1948), 27–30.
[35] e.g. in J. Duvernoy, ed., *Le régistre d'inquisition de Jacques Fournier (1318–25)*, 3 vols, (Toulouse, 1965), vol. 1, p. 462; vol. 2, p. 414. (My references to this edition take account of the *Corrections* issued by the same author and publisher in 1972.)
[36] Paris, Bibl. Nat., MS Doat 25, fol. 175v: 'praedicta Domina juxta postquam fuit haereticata per quindecim dies vel circa nihil comedens nec bibens [fol. 176r] non [= nisi?] aquam, et ipsa testis survivit, et continuo usque ad obitum sciens eam haereticatam.' Dossat, *art. cit.*, 30, cites fol. 300, and makes the case occur in Paris in 1275. The evidence I have quoted was heard in 1274, the heretic a (noble) woman, the place apparently Palaia near San Miniato.
[37] The considerable bibliography on this subject can be entered through a note by J. Duvernoy to his edition of the Fournier register, vol. 1, p. 235, n. 93. That register itself contains several cases, unindexed in Duvernoy's edition but traceable through E. Le Roy Ladurie, *Montaillou* (Paris, 1975; itself unindexed), on pp. 271, 314, 326, 332, 335, 337, 339–40, 343, 543 (to which should be added Fournier, *Reg.*, vol. 2, p. 414). Other cases appear in P. A. Limborch, ed., *Liber sententiarum inquisitionis Tholosanae. 1307–1322*, published with that scholar's *Historia Inquisitionis* (Amsterdam, 1692), and referred to and discussed, with other evidence on the subject, by A. Borst, *Die Katharer* (Stuttgart, 1953), 197; G. Koch,

The second fact that concerns us is about the nature of the *endura*. In what sense was it suicide? From one point of view it hardly counts as that, for it was normally conceived as something for very sick or old people, due to die anyway, after full reception into the sect. From cases we know of its true character could usually be said to lie in strict dietary abstinence, excluding everything except cold water, so that death was a mere secondary consequence.[38] Indeed, according to one Italian manual, dating *c.*1250 and written by a convert who knew Catharism at first hand, the essence of the dying Cathar's self-starvation lay not even in the abstinence, but in the patient's physical incapacity to say the Lord's Prayer before eating: as if to eat without a prior *Paternoster* was irreverent, and if someone was too weak to say it he must starve.[39]

So a case could be made, for some forms of Cathar *endura* at least, that it was hardly suicide at all. But that was not how contemporary critics saw it, whether in or out of the sect. To them, the *endura* meant taking one's own life, which was a task for God, not for man (to quote one rebellious Cathar).[40] It was this common-sense approach that makes the *endura* our present business, for the term could occasionally be extended to suicide *tout court*. That it was is clear in a case recorded by the Toulouse inquisition in 1309. A woman was said by two witnesses to have 'put herself to the *endura* so that she should die in it'; and they then identified her methods and motive, in ways which give no hint of the strict Cathar meaning of the term. The woman had thought of being bled in a hot bath and then lying in the cold straight afterwards; of taking poison and adding broken glass to it for speedier effect; and of piercing her heart with a tailor's awl. In the end, the witnesses said, the woman had killed herself by a combination of the poison and the bath. As for motive, it was simple: to escape the inquisition, so that if its police came for her, she would stab or poison herself.[41]

Frauenfrage und Ketzertum im Mittelalter (East Berlin, 1962), 85–8; R. Manselli, *L'eresia del male* (Naples, 1963), 239–40 (referring to earlier works by the same author, whose defence of a twelfth-century dating is nevertheless refuted by Duvernoy in the note cited above); Y. Dossat, 'Les cathares d'après l'inquisition', *Cahiers de Fanjeaux*, 3 (1968), 85–7; and J. Duvernoy, *Histoire des Cathares* (Toulouse, 1989), 330–1.

[38] The view of Duvernoy, in the note referred at the beginning of the last footnote *supra*.

[39] Rainerius Sacconi, *Summa de Catharis*, ch. 7 (easily accessible in the translation of W. E. Wakefield and A. Evans, *Heresies of the High Middle Ages* (New York and London, 1965), 334; cf. 303, and the editors' (excessive) doubts on p. 743 n. 15.

[40] Fournier, *Reg.*, vol. 2, p. 484; Le Roy Ladurie, *Montaillou* (Paris, 1975), 332.

[41] Limborch, *Liber sententiarum cit.*, 70–1: 'Item ipsa vidit et scivit quod dicta Guilelma posuit se in endura ut moraretur in ea, et balneabat se, et dicto balneo fecit sibi minui', et ipsa Alasaytz adduxit barbitonsorem ad eam, et post recessum barbitonsoris dicta Guilielma diligavit brachium in ipso balneo ut sanguis exiret, et sic debilitaretur et [*sic*] cicius moraretur, quia timebat capi per inquisitores . . . [etc.].' The second witness's evidence is on p. 76. The evidence is compromised by both the variety of methods envisaged and the interest of the

This broad usage, accepted without demur by an experienced inquisitorial court, suggests that the Cathar *endura* may sometimes have included ordinary suicides. In this, its use adds to the testimony, from our various legal records, of suicide by a prisoner or other 'enemy of society', committed simply to escape cruel punishment.

Baillis

The foregoing examples and analogues have sought to probe the great darkness of ordinary French justice, the same area covered in England by the coroner and Eyre. But analogues apart, French judicial records start improving when the Crown challenges a case and summons it to a royal court. The improvement arises partly because Crown lawyers were more literate, but it also arises because cases called into a higher court were by definition knotty. These were the ones that required careful debate. The paradox here, in fact, will be found in a disjunction between an improvement in records, on one hand, and on the other, their concentration on cases where facts or jurisdictions are in doubt. Historians cannot have everything. The more we know about a case, the more problematic the case tends to be.

Baillis were meant to intervene in their district on the king's behalf if they saw reason to. *Baillis'* working memoranda do not survive directly, in respect of suicide or of anything else. But we can divine them indirectly, from dealings they had with other authorities, especially Parlement. So I start with an example from a Parlement letter to the *bailli* of Vermandois, dated 15 July 1326, telling of a suicide in Rheims.[42] The dead woman was a female burgher of Rheims, a 'woman of good reputation', Emelina la Baronne. She had been seriously ill and 'fell' into a well in her courtyard. Rescued half-dead, she lived long enough to repent of her act and receive the sacraments before she died. The Parlement letter generously describes her as having fallen into the well 'by chance [*casualiter*]'. A local teller of tales had nevertheless persuaded the archbishop of Rheims' official that Emelina had

---

main witness. She had married Guilielma's husband, allegedly on the dying woman's request, and therefore had reason to value an inquisitorial endorsement that the death was suicide. (Duvernoy, in the note cited in n. 37 above.) But not only does the second witness confirm the first story. What matters now is what the court accepted. Borst, *Die Katharer*, 197, disagrees with the court in calling this suicide an *endura*, but which has the authority? Borst observes that the methods envisaged by Guilielma echo those in Tacitus, *Annales*, bk 15, chs. 64 and 69.

[42] The letter, in the name of Charles IV, is P. Varin, *Archives administratifs de la ville de Reims* (Paris, 1843), 420–33, no. 328. Cf. Schmitt, 'Suicide', 87 n. 82.

thrown herself into the well deliberately. What with her repentance and the sacraments we might imagine an archbishop would have let the case go. But this was another conservative jurisdiction. Not despite, but because of, the repentence, the archbishop's official claimed Emelina's goods. For her repentance showed she had been *compos mentis*. So Parlement told the *bailli* to investigate the facts. No doubt they expected him to use the detective methods laid down by Philippe de Beaumanoir a generation earlier. If the fall was deliberate, the letter said, Emelina's goods were forfeit, if not, not. If they were, they were anyway to go to the Rheims muncipality and not the archbishop.

It is often said that difficult cases make bad law. In Emelina's case we learn that they can make good history; indeed, in this regard, the only history. Similar suicidal anomalies make their way into all the higher layers of legal document, reflecting cases the *baillis* have called in at some point. A few such are mentioned in jurists' case-law, to become the stock-in-trade of law schools, attention going, in such cases, less to the suicide (which is quoted merely as bare fact) than to the argument it supports. Thus a late thirteenth-century French jurist will set a long international learned debate in train about 'a certain widow who hanged herself', under such-and-such circumstances, a widow of whom we know nothing else from the records,[43] and the much-read late fourteenth-century French jurist, Boutellier, let all lawyers know about 'a woman imprisoned in Tournay for theft, who hanged herself in despair', with such-and-such consequences, of whom, again, no breath survives in court registers.[44] Even an advocate in court can adduce suicide case-law to illustrate a point, as in a reference to the case of a suicidal 'man of Malyneul' in Paris in 1460. Yet again that brings to light a real suicide of a kind otherwise lost forever in the black hole.[45]

Until 1303, when Parlement was more strictly regulated as a court of appeal, *baillis* still frequently sat on it, absenting themselves only when their own cases were heard. So *baillis* might themselves toss suicide cases to Parlement, appeal or no appeal, if they felt them too hard to handle. The *Olim* books, selected from the earliest Parlement registers, thus also reflect the *baillis'* experience of suicide. At least, that is true if we define as a kind of *bailli* the hybrid Prévôt of Paris. Thus in one *Olim* book we hear that 'a member of the cathedral chapter of Soissons hanged himself at Mesnil . . . and the *bailli* of Vermandois demands jurisdiction over him' against the

---

[43] Quoted from Peter of Belleperche in Cinus Pistoiensis *In Codicem* 6, 22 ad 7 (edition of Frankfurt, 1578, fol. 364rb).

[44] Jean Boutellier, *Somme rurale* (edition of Paris, 1538, fol. 84r). Cf. Bourquelot, pt 2, 262.

[45] 'L'omme de Malyneul' is mentioned *en passant* in the case of Philippe Braque. See below, p. 198.

Soissons Dean and Chapter;[46] in another, that jurisdiction over 'a certain woman who hanged herself in Auxis' had been claimed against the abbey of Fleury by the *bailli* of Sens.[47] We learn similarly of two self-drownings in 1254 and 1257. In the first, a woman had thrown herself in the Oise near Chauny. The seigneur claimed suicide, the family appealed to the *bailli* on the grounds that she had been insane, and the *bailli* sent the case to Parlement, which accepted the family's plea.[48] A second such case went the other way, and perhaps would not have got into the record otherwise. For the officer who drew the case to Parlement's attention was here the Paris Prévôt, acting *à la bailli* in calling a case in from the seigneur of Beaumonten-Gâtinais. A man in Beaumont had thrown himself in a river. His family, too, claimed his mind was unsound, so confiscation and disgrace could not follow. The problem here was that the man had been pulled out alive and lived long enough to have shown 'signs of repentance'. That showed his mind had been 'sound', as it had for Emelina la Baronne. So his soul was saved, while his family lost the inheritance because he had died as the result of a deliberate homicidal act. The goods went in theory to the Crown, but in fact they went to the Prévôt, whose eagerness to prosecute the case would have lost nothing from the circumstance that his office was at that time privatized or 'in farm'. Perhaps it was the disembodied spirit of that suicide from Beaumont, from his vantage point in Heaven, which persuaded the Crown to *de*-privatize the post again eight years later and make it a salaried office.[49]

The *baillis'* records have all but vanished. Once, in our dossier, we see them doing so. The case is one luckily preserved in a Parlement register. Denis de Blanchy, a villager of Étouy, near Clermont-en-Beauvaisis, had been found drowned at a date probably in the early 1360s.[50] When the village seigneur, Ansault de Ronquerolles, heard the news he summarily[51] had the body hung up on the gallows as that of a suicide, and claimed the man's effects. What was so exceptional? Only that the seigneur was found out. We might not know the details but for the seizure of the château of Clermonten-Beauvaisis by *routiers* while the case was being heard there by the *bailli*.

---

[46] Beugnot, *Olim*, vol. 1, 517 (ix). The 'Mesnil' was apparently Mesnil St Laurent near St Quentin.

[47] Ibid., vol. 2, 135.

[48] Beugnot, vol. 1, 431 (xxv); calendared in E. Boutaric, *Actes du Parlement de Paris*, 1re série, 1254–1358. 2 vols. (Paris, 1863), vol. 1, p. 3.

[49] Beugnot, *Olim*, 442 (vi); Boutaric, vol. 1, 14 no. 158. The contrasting fortunes of soul and chattels are noticed by Schmitt, 27, n. 82. On the farming of the Prévôté, see Lot and Fawtier, vol. 2, 373.

[50] Paris, Archives Nationales, X[1a] 19, fols. 184v–185a, no. 308. I deduce he was a villager since there is never any doubt about his identity.

[51] 'Nemine prosequente'.

All his documents were destroyed,[52] but since the case went to Parlement we know some of the story from its summary. The seigneur had been in chronic friction both with the *bailli* and with another villager of Étouy, called Philip- pot, whom Ansault's men had more than once manhandled, so it is a fair guess that Philippot was the *bailli*'s 'mole', and shopped the seigneur for irregular procedure.

The local director of public prosecutions at Clermont duly summoned the provocative seigneur to the *bailli*'s court. Ansault prevaricated and alleged the summons came too late, and that local custom did not recog- nize a summons after such delay. The *procureur* and *bailli* held their ground until interrupted by the soldiers. Ansault doubtless rejoiced at the château's seizure, but it did not affect the royal justices, so he played one last card and appealed to Parlement. History is unkind to old-fashioned landlords because records come from the learned rivals who replaced them. Ansault lost and had to pay costs. That included a charge for having the Parlement report written out. So we should be grateful; grateful enough, at least, to think it possible that Ansault was right about one thing, namely that Denis de Blanchy's death was a suicide. For the Parlement register says Denis 'a casu inventus fuerat submersus'. The 'by chance' could there apply to the finding or the drowning, that is, the phrase could mean that Denis fell in the water by chance or was found by chance. It seems deliberately ambigu- ous, as if Ansault's critics were unsure of the facts. Then why did they pursue him? It was a matter of procedure. It was the seigneur's summary justice *nemine prosequente*, in the context of an adversarial procedure, that the Crown lawyers pounced on. They surely did not mind too much about the facts. Ansault, patriot of local custom, was no lawyer, and may have missed the point and seen things the other way round, sticking to his story because he knew it was true, procedure or no procedure. Villagers, after all, often do know what is true down the road, with or without formal investigation. Would all those local juries, after all, have made any sense otherwise?

Other Appellate Courts outside Parlement

Any scholar acquainted with the medieval French legal system will know that my scheme of seigneurs, *baillis*, and Parlement is a massive oversim-

---

[52] 'Actaque et processus predicte instancie in captione castri Claromontensis facta per inimicos Regni amissa fuerant et combusta'. I have indiscriminately ascribed the damage to *routiers*, notorious in northern France between 1360 and 1365, without debating whether the troops of Charles the Bad of Navarre deserved that name. They were at work in the same years and especially in 1364.

plification. French legal structures were baffling even to those who worked in them, and among modern scholars their complexity is proverbial.[53] So I shall say nothing on the royal appellate jurisdiction other than *baillis*, and outside Paris, except that it, too, occasioned records good enough to let us glimpse cases of suicide rising from the murk of seigneurial justice.

An example here is the Norman Exchequer, cousin to the English, which remained in action after the Capetian reconquest of Normandy in 1202. In 1342 the Norman Exchequer disputed the facts of a suicide on the king's behalf against a bishop. A 'Guillaume le Pelletier' had been caught thieving and escaped the gallows by drowning himself in a pond, or so the Exchequer said. The bishop's official, who would otherwise have got the chattels as those of an intestate, insisted Guillaume le Pelletier had died by accident, falling in the pond while searching for lost sheep. This time it is the very Englishness of the Exchequer's inquest that lends authenticity to the record. The jurors swore to the suicidal version of the incident and gave the dead man's effects to the Exchequer.[54] It is in the context of the same Exchequer, too, that we hear of three suicides by Norman peasants (respectively in 1394, 1401, and 1413) recorded in inventories of their livestock and other goods. In Normandy, inventories were made after criminal executions or suicides to facilitate the sale of the dead criminal's goods in the local market, the profit going to the Paris Chambre des Comptes, by then ultimate beneficiary of confiscations to the Norman Exchequer.[55]

Another such case to survive in a register is that of Pierre le Drapier, who may or may not have attempted suicide in late March 1351 in St Quentin in the Vermandois. The anomaly here derived from a double doubt, about the man's status and about his intention. From our view-point the case has this extra peculiarity, that it relates to attempted suicide. Attempts were normally beneath the notice of the kind of French court that kept documents. The account comes in a *vidimus*, that is, a confirmation by Parlement of a decision by a delegated Crown jurisdiction, this one in the name of the king's sister Blanche, Queen of Navarre.[56] It says Pierre le Drapier was a burgher of St Quentin and a 'notoriously married clerk'. A clerk who lived like a layman was in danger of judgement by a lay court rather than an

[53] Cf. Lot and Fawtier, vol. 2, 321: 'La complication du régime des fiefs avait sa répercussion fatale sur l'organisation de la justice.'

[54] Floquet, *Histoire du Parlement de Normandie* (Rouen, 1840), vol. 1, p. 166.

[55] Guy Bois, *Crise du féodalisme* (Paris, 1976), 164–6 (English edition, *The Crisis of Feudalism* (Cambridge and Paris, 1976), 180–2). Bois assesses the peasants' economic status but deliberately (p. 215) ignores details of the legal structures behind the inventories, of which twenty-six survive in the Bibliothèque Nationale in Paris (distributed between the years 1375 and 1471, pressmarked variously from MS Fs. 26012 to 26074). I have assumed these confiscations belonged to the Norman Exchequer on principles analogous to those used by the English Eyre.

[56] Paris, Arch. Nat., JJ 81, fol. 13rv, no. 26.

ecclesiastical one. Of this Pierre was painfully reminded when, around March 1351, after being ill for some time, he acquired a gash in his throat. Word got to the *jurés* who governed the town that the 'notoriously married clerk' had attempted suicide, an offence which then and there would almost certainly have attracted a substantial fine.[57] So communal police were sent to arrest him. Under arrest, Pierre found strength to remember that an ecclesiastical court would treat him more leniently than a lay one, and to appeal to the official of the Dean and Chapter. The communal police duly handed him over to the official under arrest, charging that

under direction from a malign spirit, not having God before his eyes and forgetful of his salvation, [Pierre] struck himself savagely in the throat with a knife, giving himself what seemed a mortal wound apparently with the intention of killing himself.

The official could not just let the clerk off, so he put him in prison to be nursed, and organized an English-type jury inquest 'especially from those who had looked after and nursed Pierre in his infirmity and who were best placed to know the truth', to discover if he had really gashed his own throat. They swore to a man (or woman) that it was accidental. What sort of accident had gashed his throat they left suspiciously undefined. The simple 'not guilty' charge was duly put in the official's report of 28 March.

Pierre was still alive at that date. By 13 May he was dead.[58] Perhaps a wound big enough to evoke a police charge was big enough to kill a sick man, or perhaps he was so sick that he would have died anyway. On his death the local *gardien* of royal rights thought the former. He scorned the official's inquest and seized Pierre's possessions. But the official had meanwhile handed over the body to Pierre's next of kin, who appealed against the *gardien* to the next layer of royal justice upwards, held then by the king's sister Blanche. Her judges endorsed the ecclesiastical official's inquest. Pierre was declared not a suicide and the goods returned to the family, the whole procedure then being approved by Parlement's *vidimus*.

What busybody, we may ask, had told the St Quentin *jurés* about Pierre's wound in the neck and said it was self-inflicted? It was not the nurses, whoever they were, for they swore otherwise at the official's inquest. But nurses are tender by reason of their function. Laws were harsh by reason of

---

[57] G. Espinas, *La Vie Urbaine de Dovai au moyen âge.* 3 vols (Paris, 1913), vol. 3, p. 327, no. 427; cf. ibid., vol. 1, p. 782.

[58] He is nowhere qualified as deceased in the document of 28 March but is *feu* by 13 May.

theirs. Such a concourse of harsh and tender can give birth to economies with the truth, and may have done so here. We shall see more of this in Letters of Remission in the following chapter. Here, as there, a Parlement document tells a vivid story but leaves the historian guessing.

The Prévôt of Paris as *Bailli*

THE MYSTERIOUS DEATH OF PHILIPPE BRAQUE

The Prévôt of Paris's jurisdiction and procedure give his Châtelet court a special place in this history of suicides; the suicides not, now, of prisoners he kept locked up as might any seigneur, but of those within the Prévôt's delegated role as justiciar of Paris. In the quality of its records as an ordinary criminal court the Châtelet was comparable only to the Inquisition. Records of two of its suicide enquiries were preserved with the Parlement registers. Again both involve doubt. The first might or might not have been an accident. The second might or might not have reflected insanity. At this level of record, doubt is inevitable. That was why the cases got there. But what the documents do give us, now, is the wherewithal to judge for ourselves.

I shall try to reconstruct each case as far as the record allows, and start with that of counsellor Philippe Braque, who died in 1460.[59] At the beginning of that year Braque was about 50 years old, and a lay counsellor of Parlement. Of good family,[60] Braque had belonged to the Châtelet Council in 1438 and to Parlement itself in 1441.[61] By 1460, as a member of the Parlement's Court of Sessions, Braque could be publicly referred to as a man of outstanding reputation, an exemplary Catholic and faithful family man.[62]

But his character had another dark side. Acquaintances recalled disquieting remarks. One said Braque had told him it would be better dead than

---

[59] Paris, Arch. Nat., X^{1a} 8306, fols. 219r–221v, recording an appeal by Braque's widow. I found this document exceptionally difficult to read and would have failed to make any sense of it without the expert help of Mr P. S. Lewis. At the risk of insulting the palaeographical skills of scholars who follow the case up I shall help them to trace the lines quoted by giving the line-number as well as the folio of passages, and shall quote more liberally than I would for an easier document. 'Fol. 219r.5' refers to line 5 on that folio. I have also simplified the case, especially omitting elements I still do not understand, including the exact legal structures that relate the Prévôt to the Procureur du Roi (who plays a bigger part than my résumé allows), and the apparent hovering rivalry between the widow's family and Braque's own.

[60] Fol. 219r.12: 'noble homs'.

[61] Schmitt, 22, n. 25, acknowledging the researches of Mme Françoise Autrand.

[62] Fol. 219r.12–13.

alive.[63] Another had heard a remark suggestive of the insanity we know to have put one of Braque's nieces into wardship,[64] namely that he would kill his wife and children.[65] But Braque's public image was untarnished when, after feeling 'feeble' during the day, he died of a 'fall' just after Vespers on Easter Tuesday, 15 April 1460. He had a Catholic funeral and the Prévôt himself led the mourners.[66]

How sincere his grief was may be doubted. The Prévôt had not known the Parlement counsellor well,[67] and a certain chronic, latent tension underlay relations between the rough, no-nonsense Châtelet court and the learned Parlement it was meant to respect.[68] But to Braque the citizen, the Prévôt was chief of police; and the funeral was barely over when a Paris doctor arrived at the Châtelet and asked to speak to the Prévôt or his lieutenant, privately giving them his opinion that Braque had hanged himself.[69] The doctor had been one of those called to inspect Braque's dead body, and had found damage to the neck vertebrae, consistent with hanging, and not with a natural fall.[70] The doctor had bided his time before telling the story. Perhaps he had not wanted to shock the crowd of domestics and neighbours at the death, less still to interrupt the funeral with scandal. Other informants had meanwhile noticed a second suspicious circumstance. Two hours after Braque's death his widow had had the bulk of Braque's movable fortune removed from the house, in the form of a quantity of plate and jewels.[71]

The Prévôt and his lieutenant checked these stories with a group of

---

[63] Fol. 221r.8–11: 'A ce qu'en l'omme de Malynaul [?] fut confisqué etc., dit [it is the widow's counsel who speaks] que le le cas n'est pas pareil, et a veu aucunefois le dit Braque qu'il sembloit mieulx mort que vif et aveques ne s'estoit voulu autrefois precipiter.' This apparently means that the confiscation occasioned by the death of 'the man of Malynaul' on the grounds of some suicidal remark does not stand as a precedent for Braque, who despite gloomy moods in the past, had never attempted suicide.

[64] Schmitt, 'Suicide,' 23 n. 31, referring to Paris, Bibl. Nat., Clair, 763, p. 340, no. 12, dated 23 Jan 1455, and p. 388, no. 1, 23 July 1463.

[65] Fol. 220v.24–6: 'A ce que il y a tesmoin qui dit que Braque avoit dit qu'il tueroit [?] sa femme et enfans etc., dit que se il estoit insanité [*insanus*?] pour tant n'y auroit confiscacion.'

[66] Fol. 219r.15–16.

[67] Implied by the Prévôt's lieutenant's ignorance that Braque had belonged to the *cours de céans*, fol. 220r.24–5.

[68] Lot and Fawtier, *Hist. des inst.*, vol. 2, 382.

[69] That the Prévôt's suspicions began around Friday, 18 April, is implied by fol. 220r.3–4: 'et vint a la notice du prevost qui avoit attendu a y proceder bien x jours.' For the probable informant compare the Prévôt's description of his witnesses as 'de cirurgiens et d'autres' of fol. 219v.16–17, with the 'cirurgiens et medicins' called in by the widow on fol. 221r.18.

[70] Fol. 220v.20: 'blesseure au col et espondilles du col'. We must still assume it was the same doctor, with or without a colleague with the same experience.

[71] Fol. 221r.24–5: 'Dit que incontinent les biens *scilicet* la vaisselle et joyaulx furent transportez bien deux heures apres le trespas.'

hastily assembled witnesses,[72] their number not including the domestics and others who had come first to the death scene.[73] The news sped fast within the discreet walls of the Châtelet,[74] some of its counsellors recommending nothing be done until the Court of Sessions itself had been consulted. But as effective *bailli* of Paris the Prévôt knew custom entitled him, on the king's behalf, to take the chattels of suicides. For this purpose a Crown prosecutor had a right to seal Braque's house preparatory to an investigation.[75] The Prévôt meanwhile sent a commissioner to make an inventory of Braque's possessions.

The widow had little reason to think her husband's death would be taken as anything but natural. The staff and neighbours who had rushed into the room, at her scream on seeing the corpse, had not suspected anything. Some of them were prepared to swear Braque had died a natural death.[76] The funeral had gone off publicly and without breath of suspicion. But something must have been on her mind. There was the affair of the plate and jewellery. Her counsel, Poupaincourt, claimed the plate had left the house the day before Braque's death as a loan to a friend giving an important dinner party.[77] But the Prévôt's side dismissed the dinner party as fiction and said the plate had been moved *after* the death.[78] Perhaps equally tell-tale, when the Prévôt's commissioners turned up at the house to make their inventory on 24 April, the widow's lawyer was already there, as if trouble was expected.[79]

The widow was clearly a fighter. She is described as 'fort passionnée'.[80] Her lawyer, Poupaincourt, was equally combative. And Poupaincourt knew

[72] Fol. 219v.16: 'Dit que ceulx du Châtelet ont fait grant informacion de cirurgiens et d'autres.'

[73] Fol. 221r.16–17: 'et au cry vindrent aucunes gens qu'ilz n'ont fait examiner en leur informacion'; cf. fol. 220v.26–7: 'par quoy n'en devroient faire autre informacion, se ilz en avoient assez?'

[74] Discretion: fol. 219v.19: 'On leur respondy que ilz y procederoient le plus doucement qu'ilz pourroient'; fols. 219.29–220r.1: '[Symon] a dit aux parens de Braque qu'ilz n'avoit point intention que la matiere feust divulguée.'

[75] Fol. 220r.21–3: 'et est tout cler que biens de ceulx qui se precipitent appartiennent au hault justicier, et pour savoir se il y avoit precipitation ou non le procureur du roy avoit cause de faire seeler.'

[76] Or Poupaincourt, the widow's counsel, would not have wished to have them interrogated, fol. 221r.16–18: 'Dit que le premier qui le trouva ce fut sa femme, qui s'escria et au cry vindrent aucunes genz qu'ilz n'ont fut examiner en leur informacion, et se il se s'est precipité . . . n'eussent envoié querir les cirgiens et medecins'.

[77] Fol. 221r.2–6: 'A ce qu'on print la vaisselle chex Braque et transportee etc., dit que voirement le jour avant le trespas maistre Philippe Le Begue donnoit a disner au contrreroleur a Apcher [?] et autres, et emprunta de la vaisselle chex Braque et chex lui [= Poupaincourt?]'.

[78] Fol. 221r.24–6. See n. 71 above: '. . . bien deux heures aprés le trespas et ne l'emporta l'en pour le souper d'Apcher [?] ne d'autres.'

[79] Fol. 219v.1–2: 'jeudi derr. passé . . . Poupaincourt y fut.'

[80] Fol. 220r.18.

his procedure, or rather, procedure*s*, for there were several, and Poupaincourt used them all, consistently or otherwise. His one aim was to protect the chattels. His discourse never raises any question of possible shame or disinterment. Poupaincourt had challenged the commissioners as they entered the house and made them return to the Châtelet for a warrant. When they did, bringing with them a member of the Châtelet's unsqueamish corps of *sergents*, Poupaincourt lodged an appeal on the widow's behalf, insisting the whole case be heard thoroughly and properly by Parlement's Court of Sessions. At no point, at the house or in court, did Poupaincourt allege any personal grudge in the Prévôt or corruption of his witnesses, but threw most of his weight into attacking their irregular procedure, as 'badly deliberated and badly pursued and justifying an appeal'.[81] He rejected the Prévôt's arguments one by one. The Prévôt alleged custom. But, said Poupaincourt, custom had no place *in criminalibus*.[82] That Braque had lived and died a good Catholic and been properly buried, Poupaincourt argued, should protect him from foul accusation, an accusation of a foulness, he added, Braque had never had to endure in his lifetime.[83] Suppose, Poupaincourt went on, that Braque had merely attempted to kill himself and failed, would the Prévôt be claiming his property then? No. In that case, what business had the Prévôt to claim it now?[84] There was no question but that the case should go to the Court of Sessions. Poupaincourt mentioned in passing Braque's former membership of that court but laid no emphasis on it. He may have trusted Braque's friends there to judge the case favourably.

If so, he would have trusted correctly. To the intense displeasure of the Prévôt the case went to the Court of Sessions, and no further court register or chronicle breathes a word of Braque's suicide. So we must ask ourselves, had it happened? Here was another split tradition about a great man. We have learned enough of the magnetic fields from which such evidence emerged to warrant our re-examination of the case. The Prévôt's charge of suicide had a lot wrong with it. It was raised several days too late, after the funeral, and relied on a mere handful of witnesses. Confiscations went to his court, so he had an interest in conviction. Prévôts, furthermore, were in general resentful of educated grandees like Parlement counsellors. On the other side of the balance should be weighed the quantity and quality of people who wished *not* to believe Braque had killed himself. The Prévôt would not have acted without any grounds at all. His medical witnesses said Braque's neck vertebrae were damaged. Poupaincourt's reply was that

---

[81] Fol. 119v.22.3.   [82] Fol. 220v.13.   [83] Fol. 219v.23–4; fol. 220v.11.
[84] Fol. 220v.9–11: 'et se le dit Braque vivoit et qu'il feust accusé de se vouloir precipit[er] si ne seroit il dessaisy ne desappoinctié de ses biens.'

hanging would damage the front of a man's neck, not the back, and that Braque could anyway have hurt his neck on a cask that Poupaincourt 'well believes' stood near Braque when he fell. But these are hardly the words of an expert, convinced of what he said.[85] There are other loose ends in Poupaincourt's version. He says at the start that 'a female relation' of Braque's had died two days before him,[86] and that on the day of Braque's own death 'a feebleness' had taken hold of Braque, so that he fell.[87] The name or kind of relation is left blank. It may have been his or his wife's aunt, because the subject on which the Prévôt's commissioners wished to interrogate the widow was not just her husband's death but his (or her) aunt's, too.[88] Had the aunt also committed suicide? Or had Braque killed her and been attacked by his 'feublesse' as a result, that is, killed himself for fear of the investigation which he knew must be on its way? Some speculation, in this direction if not as far, has to explain why the police wished to investigate the aunt's death in the context of that of Braque.

In the creation of judicial records we have seen that it is the hard cases that make the better history, because it is the hard cases that rise to the higher courts. A corresponding paradox lies in the records' interpretation. The stronger case then appears the weaker now. In *l'affaire* Braque, the stronger case at the time was Poupaincourt's. The Court of Sessions was his natural ally, and the preliminary hearing in our register was part of Poupaincourt's strategy for reaching that Court. Within the hearing the balance of legal skill was on Poupaincourt's side. He accumulates argument upon argument in the style of a professional lawyer. He says Braque did not kill himself; that the procedure of those who say he did is wrong; that the Prévôt has no right anyway to the property of suicides; that Braque's decent burial pre-empts further investigation; and that attempted suicide is not punished by confiscation, so why should the act be? The Prévôt's party, finally, have suggested Braque may have been insane. Rather than deny it, Poupaincourt fastens on the idea as yet another escape route from confiscation. He knows who the widow's friends are and wants them to handle the case: the domestics with their evidence, Parlement with its sophisticated jurists, half of them (unlike any of the Châtelet court) clerical.

---

[85] Fol. 220v.21–3: 'car ung homme qui se pend [?] ne se bleçe derriere mais seroit plustost bleiçé devant, mais croit bien que quant feu Braque cheut yl y avoit ung poinçon aupres et se peut bien bleçier.' I take it that *poinçon* can mean either a cask or a chisel. Either would fit. But my reading of the word (it might be *poinçé*) is anyway too uncertain to give Schmitt, 22, n. 25, conviction in placing Braque's death in the wine-cellar.

[86] Fol. 219r.16: 'Dit que sa parente de [blank] trespassa la vieille de Pasques.'

[87] Fol. 219r.17–18.

[88] Fol. 219v.5–6: 'respondirent que avoient charge de interroguer la vesve du deces de son mary et de sa tante'.

The opposing advocate, whom the record calls Symon, is by contrast bluff and dismissive. His allegations contain precise detail. He scarcely quotes a word of Latin, relying for his procedure on custom, remembered case-law, and on an '*arrêt* he has read' allowing one of those Paris-area abbots, of St Germain, the property of suicides on his lands.[89] There is a rough assurance in the Prévôt's case, contrasting with the erudite, manoeuvring ingenuity in Poupaincourt's. No wonder Prévôts disliked academics. So the winner then may, as often, be the loser in the court of history. At least, Poupaincourt's looks the weaker case in respect of the story he was sustaining. In other words, the chances are that Braque's death *was* a suicide, and his advocate managed to conceal it. But let us not forget his purpose: kindness to the widow and to his friend's memory. It was a *pia fraus*.

THE SUICIDE OF PHILIPPE TESTARD

Braque's suicide was relatively private, and doubt lingered about what had happened. But the fact of suicide was sometimes known to too many people to admit doubt. Doubt, once jurisdiction was settled, could then only attach to the question of responsibility, that is, whether the self-killer was mad. It was this question that brought the case of Philippe Testard into historical record. He had died in Paris in March 1278 after falling from a window overlooking Les Halles. As a possible case of self-homicide the incident came naturally to the Châtelet, and it is from the resulting interrogatories, recording verbatim evidence from nearly a dozen witnesses, that we can piece together the last years of Testard's long life.[90]

Since he is described variously as 'well over ninety' and 'nearly a hundred' years old, Philippe Testard must have been born in the 1180s, and almost certainly in the small town of St Julien du Sauz where he spent most of the later part of his life. St Julien lay seventy-five miles south-east of Paris on the Yonne and under the secular jurisdiction of the archbishop of Sens. Philippe Testard earned his living as a travelling merchant and had some standing in the town. He had for a short time been appointed as one of the archbishop's two prévôts.

The reason why he held office only for a short time was some people doubted his sanity. The commune had had him dismissed prematurely as

---

[89] Fol. 221r.27–221v.1: 'A ce que touchant la confiscacion n'y a coustume etc . . . dit que s'y a, et sur ce a leu ung arrest donné / en pareil cas et a l'abbé de Saint Germain confiscacion en sa terre.'

[90] E. Boutaric, *Actes du Parlement de Paris*, première séries, 1254–1358, vol. 1 (Paris, 1863), 198–200. Cf. Schmitt, 22 n. 27 and 23 n. 33; Signori, 9–15. The investigation was made, not by Parlement (Signori, 9), but by 'Master Ralph, Clerk of Guy of Meso, Prévôt of Paris' according to a Latin endorsement on the roll; though it was published by Boutaric in his *Actes du Parlement*, an unwitting source of confusion on this point.

unfit to act, and around the same time the archbishop himself declared Philippe's testimony invalid. In another context we might suspect these charges as inventions with political motives. But the Châtelet enquiry gives an unusually sharp picture of Philippe's condition, which almost certainly involved hereditary illness. Philippe had had an aunt, dead long before, but whose story was remembered by the younger generation; she had for the last three years of her life been 'bound as a madwoman [*liée comme fole*]'. While nothing of the sort was said of Philippe's own parents or brother, Philippe's fraternal niece had been similarly 'bound as mad' since infancy and was still, at the time of the enquiry, alive and in an institution. Philippe's own dubious reputation went back a long way though no one could agree how long. At the enquiry, some swore he had been perfectly sane and sensible until about a year before his death. Others, including one whose memories of Philippe went back to his own infancy around 1240, swore with equal assurance that Philippe had always been looked at askance as being 'feeble in the head' (*foibles de la teste*). Many of these said the man's more obvious bouts came when the moon was crescent: he was literally a 'lunatic'.

Where no one disagreed was that the old man's eccentricities had recently grown worse. Some said the deterioration had begun five years ago, some only a year, and several thought in between. It is tempting, from the stories, to see a sort of method in Philippe's madness. It is as if he had been wearied by a lifetime of accounting. While walking on a road he would recite out loud what others owed to him and he owed to others. Once during Mass at St Julien, when the priest came to the solemn elevation of the Host, Philippe raised his joined hands and said audibly 'twenty-seven livres, *maugre Deu* [God be cursed]!', whatever that may have meant.

In the weeks before his death the witnesses were unanimous that the eccentricities had become insupportable. Philippe had come to Paris from St Julien just over a week before he died. On 17 March, a Thursday, he had been *en route* and had joined another group of traders in an inn at Ponz, a few miles south-east of their destination. As often happened on such occasions, the traders agreed to travel together. While going through the forest of Sénart (on the road now called the N6, south of Orly airport) Philippe had suddenly emptied all the money he had from his purse onto the ground. (A companion, who later gave evidence, had picked it up and, he swore, carefully conserved it.) Meanwhile Philippe would hurl insults and rude words at his companions, spit in their food and drink, and in their faces, eat and drink like a pig (*glotement*), and refuse to pay his share of the bill. One witness—one only, young, and at first disbelieved—said he had seen Philippe tear at his hair and face like a madman.

Whatever the truth of that detail, the final scene came in a Paris house near Les Halles. The place was a favourite for St Julien traders and Philippe had been coming there for some ten years. According to another St Julien lodger there who had come with his own father, both having been acquainted with Philippe for some years, Philippe must have got his money back by now for he started throwing it round again and refusing to count it. It was the landlady, this time, who took responsibility, and had always regarded Philippe Testard as mad, and was now vindicated by seeing him appear stark naked in front of her and the other residents, 'like one completely out of his wits'.

Every particular of Philippe's last acts was coaxed by the Châtelet court from the two or three witnesses closest to it. By compounding the three sets of evidence we get the following picture. On Monday morning, 20 March, Philippe had left the lodgings with the avowed intention of returning home to St Julien. But that evening he had come back, without explanation for his change of plan, got very drunk at supper, and then gone to bed as usual in the loft of the lodgings. A total of four beds in the loft were occupied, all by lodgers from St Julien. In the early morning of Tuesday, 21 March, one of the others, an Étienne Fuse who knew Philippe well from their home town, woke early and got up to relieve himself out of a window (the account speaks of this as the most natural thing in the world) overlooking Les Halles. Before closing the window Étienne called to Philippe: did he wish to go and do the same? The old man, who may or may not have been woken by the suggestion, retorted 'Mind your own business!' ('*De quoi vous meslez vous?*'). Étienne closed the window and went back to his own bed. He had barely settled to sleep again when he heard Philippe's voice: 'I'm away, I'm away!' ('*ge m'an vois, ge m'an vois*'). Remaining 'asleep', as he later put it, Étienne took no notice.

We must believe Étienne's word. If the court had done otherwise he might have faced a charge of murder, so he had to stress how little he had had to do with Philippe's death. But his account, on which we must rely for the next few minutes, ties in with the others and excels them in the kind of detail it would have been hard to invent. After being thus 'asleep' for a minute or two, Étienne thought he had better get up and see how the old man was. So he went over to Philippe's bed, and found it empty. The window was now open again but Philippe was not at it. (The report says '*une* fenestre': whether it was the same or a different window makes no material difference.) Étienne rushed to the window and looked out. There was Philippe's body lying on the ground below. He roused his two companions, the father and son, and rushed downstairs with them to the rescue. On the stairs they were met by the night watch coming up (probably in the form of two men), carrying Philippe, who was badly hurt by his fall but not dead. Together they all put him back in his bed, and since he might be dying they sent for a priest. The priest arrived at once, and now offered the dying man confession and communion. Philippe replied 'Do whatever you will [*Fètes ce que vous vourroiez*].' The priest, as he was bound to do by canon law in the face of such an equivocal answer, then questioned Philippe about his faith. Did he believe that the Host being offered to him was his Saviour? Philippe said 'I shall believe whatever you like [*Ge croira ce que vous voudroiz*].' The priest urged him further. Philippe gave inconsistent replies. Once he said 'I believe.' Straight afterwards he would say he did not believe. The priest went on until he said again that he did believe, and then thought it prudent to drop the questioning, and gave him communion.

The three companions had done their duty by Philippe. But they had their livings to earn and had now to leave the house, Philippe lying, confessed and dying, in the loft. The companions were away for what must have been at least an hour. On their return they found the sick man recovered sufficiently to be playing a sort of 'game'. It was a dangerous one, using a knife. Philippe was pointing it at his own stomach and stabbing at it ('*un coutel, ansinc contourneé et s'an piquoit an la pance*'). His stomach was already bleeding.

'What are you doing?' they asked him.
'Playing with a knife.'

Étienne took the knife away and, judging the wounds bad enough for medical attention, sent for a doctor. One came, tended the wounds, and said afterwards to Étienne, who had not watched, that the wounds alone were in the doctor's opinion bad enough to kill the old man even without a fall. Étienne then left the house again, doubtless on business. Part of the way through the morning (at tierce) he heard that Philippe had died.

The Prévôt would no doubt have liked, in principle, to have clung to the dead merchant's chattels. But with all these witnesses and evidence there was no doubt about the case. With a pedantry forced on the judges by the laws they operated they must decide just what had killed Testard. Was it the drink he had had the night before? Was it the fall? Was it the self-stabbing in the stomach? In the end most witnesses, and the court, agreed to put the blame on the fall and to attribute that, in turn, to Philippe's double madness. He had been for a long time *forson*, had got worse recently by reason of age, and, the crucial fact, was at the time of his act completely out of his wits. So he was recorded as a *furiosus*.[91] The convergence of witnesses'

---

[91] In reconstructing the same case, Signori ingeniously contrasts the statements of different witnesses and observes that Testard's symptoms are exclusively antisocial or blasphemous. So she treats the madness as unproven. I shall incline here to the judgement of the court but would not make an issue of it.

stories here leaves the historian, like the Prévôt, with no room for doubt. If sanity has a border Philippe had crossed it.

The evidence offered in this chapter has climbed a ladder. At the bottom, where most discovered suicides were judged, the courts left next to almost no evidence, and when exceptional circumstances urged them to do so the evidence was summary. As the evidence climbed the ladder two qualities changed. It became fuller, and concentrated more on doubtful cases. The doubt generated detail, but made the record harder to interpret. At the top was Parlement. Several of the cases just examined, from various *bailliages* in the *Olim* registers, from St Quentin, and the two just rehearsed from Paris, were considered in Parlement and preserved among its records. But there can be a top of a top. At the top of Parlement was the court closest to the king, at the slender pinnacle of the judicial structure. The rule still holds. The records there are the most complete, and simultaneously most prone to anomaly: that is why they exist. Our aim must be to discover whether the one quality outweighs the other, whether, that is, from their wealth of information a portrait can be reconstructed of the real, sane suicide, *iam morientis*.

IO

Portraits from Letters of Remission

THE study of French medieval suicide through Letters of Remission faces a logical obstacle. A Letter of Remission, by definition, declared its beneficiary not guilty. Issued on a suicide's behalf it must prove he was not a suicide. So these letters should, in principle, be no exception to the obscurity intrinsic to suicide in French legal documents. That they are is due to acknowledged peculiarities in the milieu which gave them birth. They were issued by the Court of Requests, the organ of Parlement nearest to the king, source of both the law and the grace which could suspend it. While it would go too far to say the Masters of Requests were arbitrary in granting remission, they were in principle above the law. Lucky for beneficiaries then, lucky for historians now; for, contrary to the ostensible logic of their existence, some letters do record real, deliberate suicides.

Since this chapter will be devoted to reviewing them I shall begin with two letters which illustrate this last point to assure us, right at the start, that the letters are not all they were supposed to be.

The Fox-Keeper's Unhappy Wife and a Jacquerie Bandit

The first of the pair is dated April 1352, and concerns the death of Isabel Tronart, wife of a *vulperarius* (a sort of Master of Fox Hounds), in the huge forest of St Germain.[1] We learn that at the time of her death, at some date in that month, Isabel had long been discontented with her husband, Robert, and he with her. According to the words of our document her discontent had found expression in 'immorality of life [*vitae inhonestas*]', sufficiently notorious, some eighteen months or more earlier, for Robert to have got licence to lock his wife in the house when he thought appropriate. One day Robert returned home from the forest to find Isabel hanged. Since the house

---

[1] Paris, Arch. Nat., JJ 81, fol. 179v, no. 363.

was locked and undisturbed by intruders, no one else was suspected. The suicide was duly reported to the local prévôt, and officers came to remove the woman's corpse and movable goods. To all appearances the immoral wife had had the last word.

She would but for one circumstance. Robert was not just any *vulperarius* but the king's. It had been from the king that Robert had got licence to lock his wife up in the first place. It was now duly to the royal Masters of Requests that Robert looked to relieve the scandal. He petitioned to have his wife's goods and body returned. The resulting letter, proof of his success, is remarkable for its silences. It says not a word to mitigate Isabel's suicide. It does not say she was insane, or sick, or irresponsible, or provoked, nor is any doubt raised about the fact of it. She had been locked in the house and no one else could have killed her. Isabel's role, as unexcused villain of the story, is all the stronger because her confinement is blamed expressly on her own misconduct.

Although purportedly about Isabel, the document is in fact made exclusively for Robert. It remits him from 'any stain of infamy' he may have incurred as 'attaching to such a disordered life': a phrase meaning, in so far as it is spelt out, that Robert is not to be blamed for the immorality of his wife, or for having driven his wife to suicide by locking her up. That the law might tacitly have implied such guilt itself deserves notice. Some contemporary German custom attached guilt to a suicide's negligent friends and relations.[2] But this suicide was all Isabel's fault. Robert had treated her justly and by royal licence, so he can have the chattels back. More still, he can have the body so that 'he can give it ecclesiastical burial as shall seem appropriate in his eyes for the salvation of the said Isabel's soul.' That provision, too, is a document. It reflects both the court's ecclesiastical line of descent and a tendency, witnessed earlier in England,[3] for secular courts to say whether a suicide went into the churchyard.

The second letter of the pair is dated in late July 1358, and was issued by the dauphin Charles, the future Charles V, while his father the king was a prisoner in England. Defeat at Poitiers had made France ungovernable, and at the time of the letter the dauphin and his chancery were outside Paris, trying to fight their way in. Meanwhile the popular revolt known as the Jacquerie was coming to its brutal end. The Jacquerie might have gone on longer but for a particular act of treachery by two of the rebels, Jacquet de Fransures and Jean Petit Cardaine. To judge by their crimes, and by the existence of the Letter of Remission, they may have been runaway soldiers in

---

[2] *Wendisch-Rügianische Landgebrauch*, titulus 247, § 3; ed. T. H. Gadebusch (Stralsund and Leipzig, 1777), p. 320.

[3] Above, p. 153. For the ecclesiastical roots of royal grace, see above, pp. 142–7.

the service of the lords of Coucy. But in early July 1358 they were among an army of peasants who raged through Picardy, destroying castles. On arriving before that at Lignières (between Amiens and Rouen) the peasants were met by a force of 120 professional soldiers, commanded by the seigneur, Guillaume de Picquigny. A parley was agreed and the seigneur rode forward alone to discuss terms. Treacherously, Jean Petit killed him. The waiting soldiers then charged, cutting down large numbers of peasants. The letter gives the number as 2000.

They did not include Jacquet and Jean Petit, for the pair of them fled and made for the castle of another seigneur, Contre-en-Beauvaisis, which they found well defended. Worse, its High Justiciar, Colart d'Estrées, sent a force to hunt them down. Jean Petit escaped into a forest. Jacquet de Fransures was taken, put in prison, and lashed to a stout post with a rope round his shoulders. While men from the castle were searching the forest for his companion, he worked the rope loose and hanged himself.

Whose offence, it may be asked, was this letter remitting? Certainly not that of the suicide. The answer is, of course, the most apparently innocent person in it, the High Justiciar Colart d'Estrées. However delinquent, the bandits were men in the service of the Sire de Coucy. In semi-anarchic conditions, where one lord might seek occasion for war against another, the Sire made the death of one of his men, in prison, a charge against Colart d'Estrées. When news of the accusation arrived Colart was conveniently serving in the regent's army before Paris, so he got his remission. Simeon Luce, the nineteenth-century historian of the revolt, saw the whole episode as 'mortel pour la Jacquerie'. For the victim of the original murder had links with the Capetian Wounded Tiger, Charles the Bad of Navarre, and it was soon after his protégé's treacherous murder that Charles finally opted to side against the peasants, with his brutal army, and end the revolt.[4]

The idiosyncrasies of these two letters, then, give cause for hope. The first shows how a grant of remission, at this level, was subject to pressures peculiar to the Court of Requests, pressures which could cause it to defy its own logic by presenting and excusing a real suicide, as here, without a breath of pretence that it was anything else, or vice versa. The second shows how, under near-anarchy, a letter could record a suicide occurring, to all appearances, in the course of a normal criminal process.

The next series of examples has a different character, reversing that of Isabel's case and extending that of the case of Jacquet de Fransures. The purpose of each letter now is to excuse homicide, so the victim must be

---

[4] S. Luce, *Histoire de la Jacquerie d'après les documents inédits* (Paris, 1895), 80–4 (the suicide is on p. 83). Cf. Schmitt, 24, n. 37. Luce gives a puzzling reference to Paris Arch. Nat. JJ 86, p. 165, but I have not been able to trace this letter among the folios of that volume.

demonstrated as having killed *himself*. We saw this, too, in England, at the lower judicial level of the Eyre. There, equity-conscious juries interpreted confused events in such a way as to save a man they thought did not deserve hanging. In France, the events behind this group of letters are equally confused. They say a lot of motive and state of mind, but present the alleged suicide in less convincing terms than those employed in either of the two previous examples. Testimony to the fact of suicide is vague. More to the point, the whole narrative is manifestly slanted, by general collusion, to save a survivor's neck.

This is again best shown by a case of an unhappy wife.

A Drunken Wife Drops Dead

Her name was Marguine la Faucharde.[5] Marguine was married to a man described by the court as 'pauper et miserabilis', Martin de Pontchavel. By the time of her death, in September 1354, they had been married some years and had an able-bodied daughter, Marion. All three lived in a house of at least two storeys, with a garden, in the village of Lesches near Meaux. According to the Letter of Remission, drawn up after Marguine's death, Marguine and Martin quarrelled. It describes Martin as having borne her insults and foul language 'patiently', though even the letter admits that he was 'angry' with her on what proved the last day of her life. This was Monday, 15 September 1354. Before then, according to Marion and other witnesses, Marguine had 'on many occasions said injurious and rude things to her husband without any reasonable cause'. When interrogated, the witnesses defined what some of these *injurias et verba turpia* were. She had called her husband depraved, a crook, a libertine, a thief, and a murderer, and had gone as far as to say

that she would not mind in the least if he killed her. Then he would be hanged for it or die by some other bad death [*mala morte*]. And several times it had happened that Martin would be sawing down trees in his garden and Marguine was told that it was dangerous and she should mind out. And she refused, saying she would *not* mind out, she would be only too happy if the branches fell on her and killed her so that Martin would be hanged.

'Martin bore all these insults patiently, to avoid the danger of worse,' the report goes on; and it describes Marguine's attempts at suicide: 'several times [the report says] Marguine jumped from the windows of their house to the ground so that she should die and perish.'

[5] Paris, Arch. Nat., Reg. JJ 82, fol. 395r–v, no. 620.

So the death of such a woman was not lightly to be attributed to murder. Nor, in the event, would the charge have been justified by the circumstances. On the fatal day Martin and Marguine had gone with a group of villagers to drink at Latigny-sur-Aire, another village some two miles away. On the way back Marguine, drunk, had returned to her bad language. Martin was *iratus*, and on returning home went straight off to lie down on his bed. There he allegedly fell asleep, but not so his wife. 'Very drunk', she left the house again and stood in the street shouting quarrelsome remarks on her own even though there was no one to quarrel with, and reeling off foul expressions.[6] Two or three times she fell to the ground and picked herself up again. On hearing her mother in the street Marguine's daughter, Marion, had rushed out to try to coax her back in again, supporting her mother's weight as the latter staggered. Marion got her mother as far as the door. Then, suddenly, Marguine dropped, dead as a stone. Already exhausted, Marion the daughter was dumbfounded. She started to weep, then raised her voice and shouted for help. Her shouts woke her slumbering father indoors, who at once came down. It was now Martin's turn for a shock as he saw his wife lying there dead. He was giving way to his grief when his neighbours, already gathering round, warned him to escape since if he did not he would at once be arrested and interrogated under torture. On their advice, 'fearing excessive rigour of justice', Martin fled the district, and in due course heard that the High Justice of Lesches, then in the hands of 'the Lady of Lesches', had summoned him to answer for his wife's death. He was in hiding for about a month. His daughter and friends started at once to try to clear his name. They soon prevailed upon the Lady of Lesches, but although she wished to pardon him, hers was a small jurisdiction and she did not dare decide the issue on her own, so the case was taken to the safer authority of the Court of Requests. The testimony of a handful of bibulous peasants might, perhaps, not on its own have persuaded the Court. But it had come with the endorsement of their immediate judge. This clinched the matter and the bereaved father and daughter were allowed home in safety. As far as the Court was concerned Marguine had killed herself.

Before dismissing the above account as pure fiction we should remember that many deaths do admit a suicidal interpretation. Those of alcoholics are only one case in point, matched by those attached to various kinds of dangerous living. Even the deaths of perfectly ordinary sick and wounded people sometimes follow their 'giving up the struggle' to live. So perhaps all deaths are suicide. But even without stretching language, some deaths, while

---

[6] 'Sibimet rixando et plura verba turpia dicendo'.

falling short of the formal suicide—with the overdose and the note—could be described so by a stretch of the imagination. How big the stretch, in any one instance, can depend on what is at stake. For Marguine's husband his neck was at stake. So all witnesses stretched their imaginations at once, and the goal was achieved.

A comparable mechanism can be seen at work in respect of village brawlers, of whom legal records suggest there were many: those packed communities were not all harmony. Though it takes two to brawl, one side can still be more the aggressor than the other, and who can judge which? Only, surely, a community which knows both well. Students of medieval legal institutions keep noticing how certain chronic inadequacies in law were supplied by conventions about its application. We saw this in respect of the English medieval jury. It is equally true of sanctuary. In medieval France the king's grace was the perfect stock on which to graft a convention of this kind. Thus there grew up a practice of using royal remission to ensure that a notorious bully, who died as a result of his own provocations, should not occasion a death penalty for his killer. So he must somehow be made a suicide.

This did not, let it be repeated, make the story an invention. All concerned were bound by oath to speak the truth or undergo dreadful sanctions. But there is more than one way of relating any series of events, and the witnesses chose the 'suicidal' one, often with the result of giving us, to adapt the words of W. S. Gilbert's Pooh-Bah, 'corroborative detail designed to lend verisimilitude to an otherwise bald and unconvincing narrative'.[7] The reconstruction of four case histories, all from 'JJ' registers, will illustrate this.

Four Brawlers

Laurent Tellier

The most palpable example is the supposed suicide of Laurent Tellier, reported in a letter of 1354.[8] We hear of it through the testimony of his surviving enemy, Jean Bourrelier, endorsed by the *bailli* of Vermandois and the Masters of Requests. Bourrelier and Tellier lived in the same unidentified

---

[7] Some secondary authorities for all these remarks will be found above on pp. 122 n. 4 and 155 n. 10. Judicial insistence on truth from witnesses in the sixteenth century is documented by N. Z. Davis, *Fiction in the Archive* (Stanford, Calif., 1987), 17–18, 22; a defence for homicide in contention that the victim ignored medical care, ibid., 41; Pooh-Bah's rule in sixteenth-century letters, without the attribution, ibid., 45.

[8] Paris, Arch. Nat., JJ 82, fol. 306v, no. 438.

village in the *prévôté* of Laon. According to our source, Tellier was a bully.
One day he was 'hitting and beating' Bourrelier's boy brother 'without reasonable cause'. Bourrelier asked Tellier to leave his brother alone and Tellier
responded, first, by hitting the brother harder,[9] and then by setting on Jean
himself with 'a certain thick stick'. Jean, *iratus* and 'moved by heat', 'with
a certain sword he was carrying on him' struck Tellier 'a single blow on the
head'. Tellier was an invalid for eight days and then died, to all appearances
and by general report, from nothing but the sword-blow.

Jean Bourrelier was duly summoned to appear before the prévôt of
Laon. He knew nothing more of Tellier's death than was generally reported.
But he knew that if the general report was believed he faced 'dragging
and hanging', so he did not appear. After an interval he heard he had been
'banished from the kingdom' for contumacy. Again the record does not
say where or how long Jean was in hiding, but while he hid, more was
learned, and no doubt recorded carefully by the boy who had occasioned
the whole incident. In the eight days between the fight and his death Tellier
had said—all courts were satisfied by the witnesses on this score—'that
he would eat no more, so that he would die and the aforesaid Jean
Bourrelier would be hanged'. If he really did say those words he may have
enjoyed the sweetness of anticipated revenge, but the words deprived
him of its fruit. Together with the dead man's allegedly bad reputation
and Bourrelier's allegedly good one, those few words from Tellier sufficed
to exculpate his enemy. Tellier had by now almost certainly been buried
in the churchyard. There is no sign or suggestion that he be dug up and
posthumously 'executed'. But it is unlikely that the Court of Requests
would concern itself with such details at a distance of years, and as far as
survivors were concerned, his death was suicide. No one need be hanged
for it.

GOBILLARD LE MUNIER

A similar but more vivid portrait of an allegedly suicidal brawler is that
given of Gobillard le Munier, in a Letter of January 1355.[10] Once more the
case came to the Court of Requests from the region of Laon. Perhaps the
incident belonged to Laon itself, for both parties were under the High
Justice of its archbishop, and the supplicant was a clerk. The scene, if not
the exact stage, is by now familiar. Once more the supplicant was a man
drawn into the quarrel of a relation, this time his cousin. Gobillard le
Munier had had a quarrel with the cousin and had threatened to kill him.

[9] 'Magis attrociter percussit'.
[10] Paris, Arch. Nat., JJ 82, fol. 387v–388r, no. 607.

Soon after this the supplicant, Arduoin, was allegedly standing in the public street, talking with the said cousin about something quite different, when Gobillard approached them and said to Ardouin: 'Within eight days I shall kill Guillaume Raynemard [the cousin] and you too if you interfere.' Arduoin replied, according to his later testimony, that Gobillard had better not try and that he, Arduoin, would not just stand idle if he did. Gobillard replied with more contumely and threats. 'And thus fighting with words,' the letter continues, 'they walked on together and had got as far as the alley called Esdigues. There, proceeding from words to blows [*de verbis ad verbera*] they had exchanged fisticuffs when, finally, Gobillard was hit and wounded in the shoulder and shin.' Gobillard was taken to bed and died fifteen days later.

Gobillard's death was notified to the criminal authorities of the arch-bishopric of Laon, who summoned Pierre Arduoin to appear. He failed to come and was duly banished from the kingdom. Again, while he was in hiding—this time we know his banishment lasted for about a year—facts were usefully discovered which encouraged his friends to suggest an appeal. It was said that

when Gobillard was lying in bed and was visited by surgeons he did not wish to accept their visits or remedies, but asserted often and publicly that he wished to die, and that against the surgeons' advice he would lie on his face, in order to die sooner, so that by occasion of his death Pierre Arduoin should be executed.

Here was another Ezzelino da Romano, but with malice aforethought. Once more all the courts accepted the testimony to these remarks, and none of Gobillard's family or friends appeared to contest them. The judges allowed that it was a possibility, and no more, that Gobillard might have lived if he had attended to 'the doctors' and surgeons' advice'. But that—together with the familiar contrasting reputations of the dead man and of his virtuous killer—was enough to place Gobillard's death firmly in the category of suicide. There is again no mention of his being disinterred or posthumously 'punished'. But Pierre Arduoin got his remission, and we, thereby, our only knowledge of the episode.

GUILLAUME RAUCHART

In the introduction of his treatise *On Anger* Seneca said

anger is entirely violent . . . Its violence will not stop short of self-injury so long as it can harm another. It will even rush on to the point of a weapon, eager to wreak revenge on another, be it at the cost of sharing his fate.[11]

---

[11] Bk 1, ch. 1.

Illustration for Seneca's view can be found in a Letter of Remission of May
1352, describing the death of Guillaume de Rauchart.[12] Guillaume had lived
in Henin, north-east of Arras, in the midst of his family: a wife, a father,
and two brothers are mentioned as near kin. Also at Henin lived a clerk of
the archdiocese of Arras, a Jean Fourment, 'alias Durant'. In the first week
of May 1352, Fourment organized a gang of partisans to attack Guillaume
at night. They did so and left him so wounded that he died soon afterwards.
At least, that was the version that spread among responsible neighbours
in the village. Their clamour beat on the ears of Fourment's ecclesiastical
superiors, 'not once but often'. He received an indignant summons to the
archbishop's court, but Fourment had another version and produced witnesses to prove it, swearing he had acted in self-defence. But for this nocturnal foray, he said, he would have stood in the gravest danger (*discrimen*)
himself. And in fact, Fourment added, the wound that had caused Guillaume's death had not been inflicted by himself or his henchmen but by an
angry and vengeful Guillaume himself. Yes, Guillaume had fallen on his own
sword.[13]

Let us run through the circumstances in which this allegation was
accepted by the court. The Rauchart family had been summoned to court
to give witness on their own part. They may have mistrusted the impartiality of an ecclesiastical court in judging a clerk, but in any event, they failed
to appear and were judged contumacious. Their case went by default, if,
that is, they had one. The proceedings of the archbishop's court were
checked over by two royal tribunals in turn, those of the *bailli* of Amiens
and the Paris Parlement, and the archbishop's version was endorsed as
'clearer than light'. Guillaume de Rauchart, they all agreed, had fallen on
his own weapon.

Because Guillaume's case hung on events remembered from an instant in
battle, remembered only by enemies whose necks were at risk with no corroborative details and by apparently merciful courts, we read it with caution.

JEAN RAOUL LE BRETON

I come finally, among allegedly suicidal brawlers, to the death of Jean Raoul
'le Breton'. At the time of his death, probably in 1344, Jean Raoul was the
procurator or chief financial official of a church court, whose area covered
the village of Mandres, twenty miles south-east of Paris.[14] He had a name

---

[12] Paris, Arch. Nat., JJ 81, fol. 300r, no. 583.
[13] 'Qui se ultroneus et quasi furibundus super gladium se impixit'.
[14] Paris, Arch. Nat., JJ 832, fol. 138v, no. 205. My identification of the present Mandres-
les-Roses depends on its proximity to the only Corbeil where a royal prévôt might have sat
with a corresponding jurisdiction, namely Corbeil-Essones.

for bullying. His 'vexations and molestations' in and out of court had made him, through the 'troubles and expenses' incurred, a thorn in the side especially of a certain Tuilier, probably himself resident in Mandres. The record does not give this Tuilier any more of a name, since the record was made ten years later and the matter was no longer important. And we only know his surname because it was through the fortunes of the man's brother, Jean Tuilier, that Jean Raoul's misdeeds got out. One evening in 1344 Jean Tuilier was drinking at the same inn in the village as the procurator, Jean Raoul. While they drank, the latter's molestations of Jean Tuilier's brother sparked a quarrel. No sooner had they left the inn and got to open country than Jean Raoul (according to his enemy) bared his sword and attacked Jean Tuilier. Tuilier 'happened to be holding a staff' and, to defend himself 'and meet force with force', Tuilier began with his stick to thrash at the inexpert swordsman. The battle was effectively ended when a strong blow from Tuilier's stick landed on Raoul's leg and broke his shinbone. Right or wrong, Tuilier had won, and the procurator had to drag himself from the field or be dragged by friends, and put to bed. There, a 'certain woman' looked after him. A doctor was sent for, pronounced the leg broken, and said Raoul should not walk on it. The objection that, as a court official, Raoul earned his living by going on his rounds did not impress the doctor, who said he must not walk. Raoul apparently saw himself as checkmated. When the doctor was gone he asked the woman who looked after him to bring his knife. She left the room soon afterwards, and by the time she came back he had stabbed himself to death.

This, at least, is the story in the Letter of Remission. It is a pity that the 'certain woman' was not available to the Court of Requests when the case came up, ten years after it had happened, for she was the only witness to a story that saved the life of Jean Tuilier. At the time, the district and the authorities were allowed to believe that Raoul had been killed by the latter in a fight. So Jean Raoul, being an ecclesiastical procurator, doubtless got an ecclesiastical burial. Meanwhile Tuilier was arrested and locked up by officers of the holder of High Justice, the faraway monastery of Maroilles (another Merovingian foundation that had hung on to its jurisdictions). It is unlikely that Jean Tuilier himself knew any better than anyone else exactly how Raoul had died. What he did know is that, if convicted of homicide, the best he could expect from the seigneurial court was a long prison sentence, and the worst, to be dragged alive to the gallows and hanged.

But if the seigneurial justice of Maroilles was old-fashioned, so was its prison. Tuilier escaped and fled the district. The escape was publicized, and both the Maroilles authorities and the Crown's local representative (eight miles to the south, the prévôt of Corbeil) summoned Jean Tuilier to reap-

pear. When he did not, the prévôt formally banished him from the kingdom.
Where he hid is never revealed, but his own later story suggests he could
easily have found a haven for anonymous survival in France, with its feeble
gaols and atomized jurisdictions. But his life remained unsafe. Eventually,
after ten years, Tuilier arranged through discreet friends to have his cause
reheard. Parlement delegated the enquiry to the prévôt of Corbeil, who
called in whatever witnesses he could find. Besides details of the quarrel and
of Raoul's deathbed episode, the prévôt asked them about the reputations
of the two parties. He was persuaded that the dead man had been a 'mo-
lester of good folk, a debauchee, a rascal, an ill-living lout from the dregs
of society', whereas Tuilier had at all times been 'a peaceable man of good
life and reputation, honest in his ways and industrious in earning his living'.
The Court of Requests had little choice but to accept the prévôt of Corbeil's
account, and Jean Tuilier was pardoned.

   According to the anonymous nurse's story, then, Jean Raoul had died
after the fray. Whatever we think of the reliability of her version she cannot
herself have been ignorant of the truth, for Raoul had been lying there
disabled and in bed. It is wounds inflicted in the heat of battle that usually
muddle memories afterwards. Where did this or that blow come from?
Who held the sword? Was Jean Raoul's death an illustration of Seneca's
self-destructive anger? Or only near enough to it for a court to pretend it
was?

Six Close-up Suicides

A Letter of Remission, then, provides a kind of portraiture. It is portraiture
of a group of leading actors and supporting casts, caught in a particular
crisis. The Letters' descriptions of individual suicides are misread away from
that context. That lesson, learned from the letters so far, will help interpret
those that follow, for we are now to look at letters issued to save, not a
suspect from hanging, but a guiltless family from ruin. There was only one
way a court could do this. It had to show a suicide was not a suicide. That
was the dilemma—the 'Catch 22'—that began this chapter, but now it has
shed its terrors. The cause of someone's death, whether it is 'suicide' or not,
may be a moot point, but it is scarcely more moot than whether someone
is mad or not. Perhaps everyone is a bit mad. But if that, again, is to stretch
the meaning of language, it is less of a stretch to say that suicides are 'mad'
or, at the very least, that many suicides are. And then, by a stretch of the
imagination, where the motive is strong. . . . We have learned, not that
Letters of Remission may be read between the lines, but that they *must* be,

and that if they are, then there is no reason at all they should not include real suicides.

We saw in the case of Robert and Isabel Tronart that the letters can mention real suicide without any interpretation at all when it is incidental to another case. The allusion is then as brief as anything in an abbey register. Since examples were given from the abbey registers I give two more here to confirm this comparison. A Letter of Remission of 1341 grants out to a third party property confiscated by 'the wife of Pierre le Sage of Fontenailles, who killed herself as we understand'.[15] Another letter, of 1350, grants a petition from a boy and three girls whose mother has been killed by their father. It allows that the 70-year-old man was mad, 'out of his mind and memory these last three years or thereabouts',[16] part of his madness being that throughout those three years

he would try to throw himself in a well and kill himself and send himself to perdition, and would have done so but for the careful guardianship of Richeu his late wife and of Jençon, Marie, Jehanne, and Ysabeau their children.[17]

The father's attempted suicide is there treated as a means for excusing him from murder, to save further loss and disgrace to the motherless girls. The language of the document is worth noting, since it states the madness three times, and with emphasis, attributing it to physical *goute*, or gout. This repeated emphasis on insanity will be another key to the reading of letters on suicide.

For where the fact of a killing was not in doubt remission depended normally on a plea of insanity. Four of the following six examples make this plea, and to substantiate it give corroborative detail enough both to qualify them as portraits, and to allow us, now we have been tutored by half a dozen examples, to read between the lines of the report.

JEAN MASSETOIER

I start with the case of Jean Massetoier.[18] Massetoier lived in the 1370s and 1380s in the baillage of Senlis, at Coramcourt. He was 'a man of good life

---

[15] Paris, Arch. Nat., JJ 174, fol. 173r, no. 293 [29 Sept. 1341]: 'de la femme Pierre le Saige de Fonteneles la quelle s'est occise si comme nous entendons'. Cf. *Régistre de Philippe VI*, pt 2, p. 288.

[16] Paris, Arch. Nat., JJ 78, fol. 145r, no. 262: 'par l'espace de trois ans ou environ et encore soit hor de son sens et de tout bon memoir . . .'

[17] Ibid.: 'Pour le quel temps il s'est efforcié de se gecter en un puis et de se occire et mettre β perdicion et l'eust fait so ce ne feust la bonne garde et diligence de feu Richeu jadis sa fame, de Jençon, Marie, Jeahanne, Ysabeau leurs enfans. Et le dit Jehan estant hors de son senz et memoire comme dit est et impotent de ses memoires pour cause de maladie de goute . . .' I have assumed Jençon was a boy.

[18] Paris, Arch. Nat., JJ 146, fol. 65r–v. Cf. Schmitt, 'Suicide', 22 n. 29. I have not identified Coramcourt, although the fact that Massetoier's home was on the river Thève places it along

and reputation, physically hardworking, and had always lived peaceably by his labour'. Suddenly he was struck by illness. We are not told his age, or what illness it was, only the date: 2 (or 3) July 1392. Massetoier took to his bed. Within two or three days—it was now Sunday, 5 July—he was so ill that 'the candle was held out to him'[19]—he was thought to be on the point of death. Instead of dying, Massetoier made a slight recovery.[20] What follows I tell in the words of the report. After Jean's slight recovery on the Monday:

through mental melancholy he got up (sick though he still was), dressed, left the house and went straight towards the river Thève, without telling anyone where he was going. However, his wife Jacquetta saw him go, in a state as he was, and went after him asking where he was going. He said he was going to take exercise [*esbastre*] on the river. She was very surprised by this and followed him, never letting him out of her sight. When the two of them got near to the river, Jean began to run ahead, rushing forward towards the river as if he wanted to drown in it. Jacquetta, highly alarmed at the sight and thinking him crazy, put on a spurt and overtook him to try and stop him leaping in the river. Despite her, Jean got to the river and dived in head first, showing he wanted to drown in it, as he confessed later. In the nick of time [*incontinent*] Jacquetta caught him by his gown and clothes and with great effort tried to get him out; but, not being strong enough to succeed she started shouting 'murder!' and 'help!' In no time at all [*tantost*] a man appeared. His name was Perrinot le Cordonnier, and he had a companion, Rogiet le Chantre (both men having been on their way to the Coramcourt meadow towards Moudamville mill). The moment they heard the woman's cry they came and helped her get her husband out of the river. They got him out, took off his clothes and put on new. When Massetoier had recovered somewhat, they asked him why he had jumped into the river. He, full of fatuity—or of the illness he had—said they had done him a great wrong [*pechiez*] to pull him out. They should have let him die. And on this, Jacquetta, with her brother Perrinot Massetoier, who had come to help, led Jean back quietly to his house at Coramcourt, put him in bed and made him tidy.

The report makes no pause between Act One of the drama, and Act Two, which follows *incontinent*:

All in vain, Jean's brother soon disappeared and went off to work. Instead of him, an old woman called Symonnete-aux-Boeufs, came over to visit Jean in his illness. The moment his brother had gone and Symonnete had come, Jean rose from his bed, totally naked in the middle of his room, went to the door of the room and said to Symonnete that he wanted to take a bit of air. This she allowed, but held his arm as he went out. But after a short while he suddenly hit Symonnete in the face with his fist so that she fell to the ground. Thus escaping, Jean rushed off, and before

the course of that river, between Mortefontaine and Royaumont (where the Thève joins the Oise).

[19] 'On lui tinse la chandelle en la main'.
[20] 'Apres ce qu'il se fut un pou revenue'.

anyone could get after him or catch up he threw himself down a deep well in a courtyard nearby, in which there was water. Great madman [*forson*] that he was. He was taken out by some people who had seen him run to the well and seen him in it, and who had gone at once to get him out. But by the time they got him out he was dead. He was pulled out and laid on the ground and there he was arrested [*anesee*] by the local justice until investigation could be made on the case.

The report alludes to Jean Massetoier's illness four times (including the summing-up, which I have omitted), each at a critical point in the story. But does it protest too much? And does it mean the illness was merely physical, or also mental? Jean's first attempt at suicide occurred 'par melancolie de teste . . . combien qu'il feust encor malades'. In confessing his suicidal intention after the rescue Jean was (the report says) 'plain de fatuité ou de maladie qu'il avoit'; and after his successful jump down the well the letter is content to comment 'grant forson si comme il fu'. The interpretation of these terms will be helped by reflection on two further themes in the report: that Massetoier had led a virtuous and industrious past life as a 'homme de bonne vie & renomée laboureux de braz'; and that the punishment of his body and estate could bring shame on his relations and children.[21] Neither theme is relevant to the question of Massetoier's sanity, but the report brings them in for all that. They helped everyone believe that the judgement was according to law.

The same threefold compound—imprecision about symptoms, and references to a virtuous past and to the threat to survivors—reappears, with variations, in the next four cases.

MICHELET LE CAVELIER

One of these, the example chronologically the latest in the portfolio, from a 'JJ' register of 1423, is that of Michelet le Cavelier.[22] Michelet's second name literally means 'the horseman' but was for him almost certainly a surname. He lived in the faction-torn Paris left by the Lancastrian invasion of France in 1415. He followed one of the capital's luxury professions as an embroiderer (*brodeur*), and his wife and he lived with their six small children in a house next to the Halles. (It looked over what was then the Halles des Chaudronniers and is now part of the rue de la Ferronerie.)

Early in May 1423, Michelet fell ill with a malady unspecified even in the

---

[21] 'Redonder en grant opprobre & vitupère desdiz supplians et de son lignage'.

[22] A. Longnon, *Paris sous la domination anglaise, 1420–1436* (Paris, 1878), p. 111 (no. 56), from Arch. Nat. JJ 172, no. 313. Schmitt, 'Suicide', 22, n. 27; Signori, 'Rechtskonstruktionen', 15–16. The disposition of the Halles is reconstructed in J. Favier, *Paris au XVᵉ siècle, 1380–1500* (Paris, 1974), 35.

flawed terminology of the day. He went to bed and suffered for two months 'tres grant paine et douleur'. He was looked after by his wife Opportune and a living-in woman assistant. In principle they could watch over him by night as well as by day. But at dawn on Saturday, 3 July, they were both asleep. Michelet, who cannot have failed to observe this fact, used the occasion to get out of bed, go to the window, and jump out of it. He was killed more or less instantly. Since he had got out of bed too quickly to dress, the body lay naked on the pavement of the Halles, where it was found and in due course removed by the Châtelet police.

Opportune, the widow, with her six small children (and another on the way), may already have thought she had suffered enough on going to bed the night before. She awoke to worse. The pair had always lived 'honest, hard-working lives'[23] had never fallen foul of the law, and were respected in the neighbourhood (the phrase comes again: *de bonne vie, renommée et honneste conversation*). The couple can have had no wealth to spare. Now, besides seeing her husband's body maltreated as that of a homicide, she was likely to lose everything in the house.[24] Could the family survive at all? If ever there was occasion for judicial pity it was now. This, at least, seems to have been the view of the Court of Requests. The threatened measures would be (they are given as the petitioner's words but with implicit approval) *une chose moult piteable, et pourroit estre la destruction d'icelle suppliante et de ses diz enfans*. So the petition was granted on the only grounds open to the court: that the self-homicide 'did not know what he was doing'. Because of his illness, the judges agreed, 'he had entered and did enter[25] into a great frenzy, which likewise gripped him for a long time in great pain and suffering.'

The letter gives no corroborative illustration for this last crucial circumstance, only for the pitiable state of the widow. That is what moved the judges. Once more, therefore, a Letter of Remission bears witness despite itself to a real suicide. 'Despite itself'? One detail proves that the court knew it was bending the law. The widow, it stipulated, could have the body of her husband back and bury it in holy ground. But on a condition: 'provided [the letter finishes] that no solemnity attends the burial'. It is an implicit admission. The judges' 'Remission' was designed for the living. They were uneasy about the dead. I have not found this reservation about burial in other Letters of Remission.

In the case of another Parisian craftsman this peculiarity is replaced by another, also with religious significance.

---

[23] 'Gaignans leur povres vies par la peine de leurs corps'.
[24] 'Tous les biens meubles et heritages qui estoient communs entrée elle et son dit feu mary'.
[25] 'Tant . . . que . . . il feust et soit entré'.

DENISOT SENSIGAUT

The craftsman this time was Denisot Sensigaut.[26] Denisot's case, from a slightly earlier 'JJ' register than Michelet's, was heard in 1421. He was a baker, working and living at St Marcel (then a suburb of Paris) with his wife Jeanette and their 1-year-old daughter. Jeanette was expecting another child. Immediately nearby he had other close relations. One day towards the end of July 1421 the baker was struck by a fever. The report identifies it as *chaleurs* and *fièvre continue*, sicknesses 'which are going around just now [*qui courent a present*]'. Denisot went to bed and was nursed by his wife, with assistance from others. These included Denisot's young nephew from nearby and a certain unnamed woman, a near neighbour. This regime continued for just over a fortnight. No doubt because there was fear for Denisot's life, at some date near the end of the fortnight a priest visited him to hear his confession and give communion. Not long after taking it, Denisot 'fell into a frenzy'. He had been in this state of 'frenzy' for a day or two when the crisis came.

As usual in these reports, the focus grows sharper towards the dramatic climax. From his sickbed, Denisot sent his wife to Paris to take a urine sample to the doctor and get various necessities. Normally he would have been cared for by his nephew and/or the 'woman'. But Denisot then proceeded to send the nephew away too, out into St Marcel to get milk. That left the invalid alone in the house with the 'woman'. In the absence of Denisot's wife Jeanette, one of 'the woman's' tasks was to cook, which she did in her own house nearby. On the critical day she had duly slipped out to get something for the patient to eat, and Denisot, left alone,

got up from his bed, went and shut the front door of his house (some witnesses say), and when he was thus shut in he took a rope, attached the top of it to a screw on the wall outside his chamber, scraping away some plaster from the screw in order to do so and tying the cord also to some wood which was there, and hanged himself.

The letter adds two adverbial clauses one after the other, in contradiction: he hanged himself (it says) 'both through the temptation of the Devil [*Ennemi*], and through the said frenzy and illness'. Which does it mean? The Devil, madness, or illness? The judges' ambiguity is more forgivable because it proves they did not know what had caused the suicide. And if they enlarged their doubt, enough to let the petitioners take the benefit of it, the Letter of Remission reveals their motives. It states the considerations it sees as relevant, one after the other. The deceased had, once more, led a virtu-

---

[26] Longnon, pp. 19–20 (no. 10), from Arch. Nat., JJ 171, no. 429. Schmitt, 'Suicide', 22 n. 27; Signori, 'Rechtskonstruktionen', 18–19.

ous life. He had never come to the notice of courts before. He was on the contrary a man of 'bonne vie, renommée et honneste conversation'. Again, the widow was a young woman with a baby and expecting another. It would be 'tres dure chose' for her to suffer forfeiture, to mention only that. Not only destitution, but also shame, for public execution on the body would bring disgrace to a family, who are 'notables gens et de bonne lignée'. Last but not least: during his illness Denisot had confessed and received communion.

Who really knows, or knew, what state of mind Denisot was in when, according to the witnesses' reconstruction, he so carefully waited until his guardians were away, shut the front door, scraped away at the plaster, and hanged himself on the screw he thus revealed? The court's verdict of 'frenzy' looks like an improvisation for motives foreign to the judgement. So Denisot's name was cleared. So we learn about his suicide.

The religious factor, rendered strong in Denisot's case by his confession and communion, is stronger still in our fifth direct portrait of a medieval suicide. Like those of Isabel Tronart and Marguine la Faucharde, it is the picture of a passionately discontented wife.

JEANETTE MAILLART

Her name was Jeanette [Jehanette] Maillart.[27] She must have been born around 1400. At the time of the reported events, in 1426, she was the respected wife of a rope-maker (*cordier*), Michelet Maillart. They lived in Paris in the rue de la Tonnellerie on the west side of the Halles, with their one son, 5 or 6 years old. From there her husband would go off to work each day at a workshop under the city walls where the other Paris *cordiers* generally practised. The pair were respectable and substantial people[28] and Jeanette, in particular, had the public reputation of being a God-fearing and virtuous woman.[29] But privately her character was not above the criticism of survivors, and her husband testified that, especially after drinking, she would flare up in jealous rages—the jealousy being (he said) quite unfounded.[30] A mood of this sort may have fallen on her on the morning of

[27] Longnon, pp. 208–9 (no. 102), from Arch. Nat. JJ 175, no. 392. Schmitt, 'Suicide', 22, n. 27; Signori, 'Rechtskonstruktionen', 16. The topography is defined by J. Favier, *Paris au XVᵉ siècle*, 34–5, and hours of work by B. Geremek, *Le Salariat dans l'artisanat parisien aux XIIIᵉ–XVᵉ siècles* (Paris and The Hague, 1968), 78–9.
[28] 'Gens de bien et d'honneur'.
[29] 'Bonne catholique et preude femme . . . elle feist bonne vie, renommée et honneste conversation.'
[30] '. . . comme furieuse, tant par trop boire dont elle se sentoit delegier, et par souspeçon de jalousie qu'elle avoit sans cause . . .'

Friday, 5 April 1426. Her husband had gone to work as usual. Soon after his departure—the order of events has to be inferred from what we know of Paris artisans' working hours and a mention of the visit at the trial—Jeanette left the house and went to the local monastery (*moustier* perhaps St Magloire on the rue St Denis) probably (at that hour) to attend Mass. She was seen there and then not again. Or rather, when she was seen again in the marital bedroom at home soon afterwards, at seven or eight o'clock, she was dead, hung by a thin cord.

The 'first finder' is not regularly identified in these French records. The most likely guess here is that the first eyes to see the dead woman were those of her 5-year-old son (on other grounds than that he is said, like his father, to be *tres doulens* at his mother's death). From the boy, if he was indeed the finder, news at once sped to neighbours and from them to the Châtelet police. Officers duly came, cut the body down, and took it back for the attention of the Court of the Prévôt's lieutenant. It can be inferred that Michelet had not been in the house when Jeanette's body was discovered, but he had meanwhile found out; and because the Prévôt was expected to 'execute' the body as that of a self-homicide and confiscate the goods, the new widower quickly rallied a posse of relations and friends to support a joint petition to the Crown.

Their plea was the familiar one. Jeanette was of unsound mind, a *furiosa*. Despite her reputation as a good and virtuous Catholic, they said, she had often been 'diminished in her understanding'[31] and 'in a sense a *furiosa* ['*comme* furieuse': my emphasis]'. The double claim appears twice. The letter protests it. But its supporting evidence, that Jeanette was jealous and got in rages when she had been drinking, are inconclusive. Judging from other pictures surviving of *moeurs* in fifteenth-century Paris, Jeanette's vagaries would have been beneath notice if she had not gone and hung herself. What is, on the other hand, conclusive, in the wording of the Letter of Remission, is the court's emphasis on factors irrelevant to the suicide. It says she was a 'good Catholic' (proven, if need be, by her having been to church on the very morning of her suicide). It says she had an upright reputation. It mentions the grief, shame, and prejudice to the family if full execution for self-homicide went through. And it puts a slight, but just detectable, emphasis on the fact that both the dead woman and her husband were native Parisians. Many, we know, in the war-torn capital were not. A non-Parisian suicide might have found less favour with the Court of Requests. Then we would have been back in the dark. As it is, through the working of compassionate favouritism we inherit a judicial

---

[31] 'Ebetée de son entendement'.

close-up of what appears, once more, to be an ordinary, a deliberate suicide.

In the fifth and sixth of this group of episodes the question of madness did not arise. Corresponding weight is put instead on the subjects' losses by reason of war. In the first of the pair the judges also conjured doubt out of another feature of the case. By doing so, they again shielded a widow and her children, and, as it turned out, left a vivid picture of private suffering.

JEAN LUNNETON AND PERRIN LE VACHIER

A few miles north of Senlis runs a road locally known today as the 'Route des Anglais'. Its sinister past was as a route on which soldiers marched between Flanders and the Île de France during the Hundred Years' War. If the troops were ill-paid or ill-disciplined this could spell trouble to farmers *en route*. Weather conditions were bad in the winter of 1386–7, and one farmer in this position was Jean Lunneton, tenant of the grange of Commelles, a farm on the estate of the monastery of Chaalis.[32] By 4 December 1386 Jean Lunneton and his wife were exhausted. A Letter of Remission of January 1387 says so, and goes on to describe their reaction:

Because the soldiers had done the couple many injuries, both by pillage and in other ways, about three weeks before Christmas, having heard that more soldiers were on their way, Jean had a number of their belongings loaded onto a cart to take them to safety in Senlis. It happened one morning just before daybreak that, on her husband's instructions and for fear of the soldiers, his wife Perotte took their three children, harnessed the cart to the cart-drawer, and went off to Senlis. They arrived there at sunrise. Meanwhile Perotte left her husband in bed, since he had not wished to make the journey with her and the children. She had suggested several times he should come with her but he gave her no answer. (She had also left behind Perrin Cousin, John's nephew, and their girl-servant, both of whom lived with the family at Commelles.) The same day, as soon as she had discharged her belongings and lodged her children, Perotte returned to Commelles with the intention of taking her husband to Senlis. She had heard that men were being beaten up by the soldiers. But when she got up to Commelles she found no sign of him. Both that day, and for several days afterwards, she had enquiries made but, to her great dismay and desolation, she could get no hint of what had become of him. About eight or ten days later Jean was found hanging on a tree in the wood of Chantilly, about half an hour's journey from the steading at Commelles.

Jean's death triggered off the local machinery of High Justice. Officers of the seigneur of Chantilly cut the corpse down, identified it, and handed

---

[32] Paris, Arch. Nat., Reg. JJ 130, fol. 152v, no. 264. Schmitt, 'Suicide', 23, n. 35; Signori, 'Rechtskonstruktionen', 18.

it over to the jurisdiction in which Commelles lay. It was assumed that the death was suicide, which meant the family's entire movable possessions were forfeit to the family's seigneur. Probably on the advice of a Senlis lawyer, the widow petitioned for royal grace. Her success is once again witnessed by the existence of our source. The letter justifies the grant of the petition on the grounds that 'it cannot be known for certain whether the death occurred through her husband's *desperacion* or otherwise.' For certain, we may agree, it cannot, but we may be inclined, on balance, to agree with the seigneur's verdict. The Letter of Remission makes it clear that, in enlarging the loophole of doubt, the court has been moved by considerations foreign to this particular charge. Once again it lists these irrelevant considerations: the couple's good reputation; the pillaging the family as a whole has suffered; the shame for the family if the corpse were 'executed'; in short, and above all, 'pour compassion d'elle et de ses diz enfans'. Like Robert Tronart the fox-keeper, Perotte is allowed to have the possessions back, and, like Robert, to bury her suicide-spouse's body in holy ground. The stipulation imposed on Michelet le Cavalier, that there be no solemnity, is absent.

The last remission in this group is another that falls short of attributing the suicide to 'frenzy'. Instead it puts weight on a wide range of other mitigations: destitution, sickness, and death of children, as well as, again, the likely impact of confiscation on the widow. Perhaps the absence of 'frenzy' explains why the letter only remits confiscation and says nothing of burial. The suicide was Perrin le Vachier, a butcher in Sarcelles, a village just north of St Denys. Perrin's relations and friends asked for remission, and the letter granting it is addressed to the Prévôt of Paris, dated September 1418. It dates the suicide to the morning of the previous Sunday, and explains that

the said Perrin had for some time been and was still gravely sick. He had seen two of his three children die in his presence, and his wife was very sick. He had lost the greater part of his possessions by the fact and occasion of wars, to the extent that he hardly had anything on which to feed his wife and children. Nor was there anyone to comfort or aid them in their sickness. For these reasons or others the deceased, tempted by the enemy, went off to hang himself on a tree, where he died and strangled himself. By occasion of which the king grants grace of the confiscation incurred.[33]

Perrin 'avoit esté et estoit très griefvement malade'. His wife was 'très fort malade'. Neither had any to aid them in 'leur maladie'. The sickness is emphasized but it is all physical. At last the Court of Requests is calling a

---

[33] JJ 170, no. 154, printed in L. Douët d'Arcq, *Choix des pièces inédites relatives au règne de Charles VI*. Société de l'Histoire de France, vol. 2 (Paris, 1863), 176. Schmitt, 'Suicide,' 23–4, n. 36. The suicide is mentioned also by P. S. Lewis, *Later Medieval France* (London, 1968), 287. The day of the suicide could have been 28 August, or 4, 11, 18, or 25 September.

spade a spade and granting its remission only through compassion for the family.

This and the last chapter have shared a purpose. To claim that they have rendered visible the invisible would be to claim too much. The portraits that do survive leave much still to guesswork. They could not have been made if suicides were never, ever, to be caught in surviving records, but that these ones were caught was, it has been clear, due to rare sets of circumstances which folded into each other like Chinese boxes; most immediately, in most of this last series of Letters of Remission, by benign double-thinking on the part of judges.

These, then, are the French judicial records, as far as they tell us of suicide. They remain records written, when they were, for other purposes than for our curious eyes to look at, and have survived, when they have, by rare configurations of lucky escapes. They remain a fragment of a fragment, full of *trompe l'oeil*, jealous even of the glimpses historians can shake out of them; yet once more they allow us to see, for all that, into a world as real, then, as ours is now.

I I

Portraits from Courts in the Empire

THE previous four chapters have rehearsed accounts of suicide culled from the judicial records of England and France. Reflecting the conditions that gave rise to them, the records of each monarchy cast their light in different configurations, the English excelling in quantity, the French, at their best, in vividness. There is no reason to think that the truth behind these records differed generically from one country to another, as the records do; rather the opposite. But it is enough now to recognize that, in examining the two groups of record, we are using two cameras, made by different craftsmen and on different principles, recording comparable scenery.

But this study is one of Latin Christendom. Its aim is to tour as wide a horizon as possible. Of territories contributing to Latin Christendom one group has a claim strong enough to make it a natural companion to England and France. These were the territories designated by western contemporaries from the tenth century onwards as the Empire, more pedantically the Roman Empire, or more pedantically still, after 1157, the Holy Roman Empire. They covered most of what are now called Germany and Italy, together with Austria, Switzerland, and parts of south-eastern France. Although in many ways diverse, these areas shared features in political development which put them on the same footing as suppliers of the judicial secrets we are looking for.

Germany

WHY GERMAN LEGAL RECORDS YIELD FEW PORTRAITS

They are niggardly suppliers. In Germany the shortage of judicial records of suicide came about primarily because the German monarchy developed differently from the English or French. Or rather, it did not develop, and never gave Germany the kind of king whose officers looked out for dead bodies.[1] Many reasons for this have been put forward. No doubt one was that the Germany's rich colonial east dangerously divided the country's centres of gravity, so that Germany was never, even in the Middle Ages, properly unified. Again, the Emperor's universalist claims were probably more a hindrance than a help to the building of strong monarchy, Italy, in particular, proving in the end more trouble than its attempted subjection was worth. But if one German fact of life played the role of the Plantagenets in France, as an unconquerable obstacle to the long-term build-up of a national crown, it was the Rhineland bishops. Ecclesiastical heirs of Roman frontier towns, the big bishoprics of Mainz, Cologne, and Trier had gained by the trade of the Carolingian and Ottonian 'common markets', and were able to maintain in the German constitution an elective principle stifled by the dynasts of France and England. Those three archbishops were electors, with a strategic power they were in no hurry to lose by allowing one dynasty to monopolize the crown. So they fossilized the political configurations of the ninth century, much as the French seigneurs had fossilized those of the eleventh.[2]

On the growth of German criminal law this failure to build a monarchy had a conservative effect, an effect quite as drastic as that exercised by the endurance of seigneurial jurisdictions in France. The old horizontal principle, based on a kindred's revenge, therefore remained stronger in German criminal justice than elsewhere. In the late fifteenth century the most conspicuous of all embodiments of the principle, in Germany or anywhere else in Europe, would be the German *Fehde*, a right to private war even against the king, a practice long outlawed elsewhere. In normal criminal procedure its most lasting vestige was the rule, 'no accuser, no judge.' There was no coroner or *procureur du roi* to hunt out Crown pleas, so that courts had to sit and wait until an accuser came to precipitate a hearing. This legal conservatism had one useful result. A medievalist who looks for evidence in sixteenth-century records of German custom will have one more reason to believe, besides others in the documents, that

---

[1] For the specifically legal history of Germany my main authority has been H. Mitteis, *Deutsche Rechtsgeschichte*, 18th edn ed. H. Lieberich (Munich, 1988). On the early development of royal public criminal justice: Mitteis, 98–100; its febrility in the fifteenth century, as mentioned at the outset of the following paragraph: ibid., 100, 251–2 (absence of effective appellate jurisdiction); 303 (sharing of the king's grace with numerous lower officials, even down to the hangman!). The exceptions, largely for fiscal purposes: ibid., 253.

[2] Early stimuli to the elective principle are identified by Mitteis, 112; the Marches as 'soil' for states, ibid., 109. The late development of a formal electoral college is described by A. Wolf, 'Von den Königswahlen zum Kürfürstenkolleg', in R. Schneider and H. Zimmermann, eds., *Wahlen und Wählen im Mittelalter*, Vorträge und Forschungen, 37 (Sigmaringen 1990), 15–78. On Trier as a prototype for the princely immunity, see K. Zeumer, *Die goldene Bulle* (Weimar, 1908), pt 1, p. 58; pt 2, pp. 22–3, n. 3.

these particular customs are old, since nothing had happened to change them.[3]

In the search for actual suicides, by contrast, the effect of these German peculiarities is negative; so much so, that if the conservativism of German criminal law had suffered no exceptions we would never know, from judicial sources at least, that any medieval German ever took his own life. But there were exceptions, one of which, luckily for historical research, left records of suicide.

The exceptions were of three main kinds. They all reflected the febrility of German state justice, and all shared an *ad hoc*, self-help character. The first, often mentioned in the narrative sources, was the 'Regional Peace' or *Landfried*, a pact between a miscellany of authorities in one region to rouse lower courts to prosecute and generally to 'keep the peace'. If suicide records are not found in the *Landfried*, that is because it was too clumsy a hammer to crack individual homicides. Its shortcomings are confirmed by the second exception. This was the *Vemgericht*, literally 'punishment court', whose sinister workings at Donaueschingen we sampled in Chapter 3. The *Vemgericht* grew directly from the lack of effective criminal law in Westphalia, theoretically under the distant archbishop of Cologne. The Westphalian free peasantry, impatient of lawlessness, picked judicial *vigilantes* to punish crime. The *vigilantes* got royal endorsement, and this, and the swiftness and severity of its punishments, allowed the Westphalian court to advance like an invading army on more conservative jurisdictions, so that by the early fifteenth century its writ ran far outside its homeland. Hence that suicide scene, or pseudo-suicide scene, with the hanged peasant in Swabia. If the *Veme*, too, leaves no suicide records that is largely because it was killed by its own success, its reign of secret terror having made it too unpopular. Perhaps its jurors should have read books and learned a more moderate jurisprudence. Then they would have left us, as historians, something to record. But for all their supposed efficiency the *Veme* jurors clung to old, unwritten procedures, perhaps to their own undoing and certainly to ours. For they did not even leave enough records to give any hint that they were interested in suicide, let alone record any.[4]

---

[3] *Sippenrache*: Mitteis, 38–9, 97–8. *Fehde*: ibid., 193 (the *Fehde* as paralysing the action of other courts); 301–2 and *passim*. 'Wo kein Klüger, da kein Richter': ibid., 45, 110. General petrification of procedure: ibid., 195. Non-learned character of law: ibid., 292. Atomization of jurisdictions: ibid., 290–1. The main modification of the principle that a wronged party must accuse was the *Rügeverfahren*, a procedure comparable to indictment by jury in England: ibid., 110, 254 (used by the Vemgericht), 303–4.

[4] *Inquisitio*: Mitteis, 111, 195, 256 (the latter reference includes the initiatives of Mainz and Trier in 1121). *Landfrieden*, ibid., 192 (as stiffening *Land-* and *Zentgerichte* (the last being equivalent to the English Hundred Court); 193 (as reversing an earlier fiscalizing tendency to commute penalties); 301 (tries to stamp out the *Fehde*). *Vemgericht*: ibid., 254–5. The Donaueschingen case: pp. 104–5 above.

THE FEW: *STADTBÜCHER* AND THREE EXAMPLES FROM CASE LAW

Only one jurisdiction dared resist the *Vemgericht* in its heyday. This was the third exception to the febrility of criminal law in Germany, and it is the first to leave day-to-day records of its sentences of both homicide and suicide. Appropriately, it has supplied no less than forty cases to the present study. I refer to town jurisdictions. We scarcely hear of German merchants before we all hear of a Merchant Law to protect them, guaranteed in theory, like the others, by the king. From this grew a Town Law, or *Stadtrecht*, for individual towns. At first strictly dependent on a Town Lord—a role commonly filled by the bishop if there was one—the Town Council, or *Stadtrat*, grew in autonomy as its knowledge grew more necessary in tax assessment. By the early fourteenth century many Town Councils, each with its own Town Law, had a growing universality of jurisdiction within their own boundaries. Here, at last, was to be found the legal idea of an enduring public Peace to which homicide, including self-homicide, was an offence. The Peace was not periodic like those *Landfrieden*, but permanent. Town officers were therefore appointed to inspect the victims of violence and investigate.[5]

These, then, were the officers who discovered and recorded suicides, among other victims of violence. In comparison with France their role in Germany is in one respect comparable with that of the royal Court of Requests, namely as the main salient exception in a milieu of otherwise conservative and largely unrecorded justice. In character, however, the approach of the German towns to homicide and suicide is more like that of the Plantagenets, with its dogmatic insistence on a perpetual Town Peace, its improvised variety of officers with a duty to investigate, a keen interest in money, and, last but not least, its relative freedom from learned models. For at this stage Roman law, the learned model they later adopted, played a minimal part in the procedure of German town courts. Their partiality for writing, and hence leaving records for the historian, came from different sources, mainly the demands of accounting (again, to be compared with that of the English Exchequer), and the need to defend a jurisdiction against jealous neighbours (like that of the Paris abbeys). So enthusiastic, indeed, were the German town clerks for writing things down, in a legal world where few other people wrote, that not just privileges drawn up by clerical notaries,

---

[5] Officers with a variety of names; at various times Nuremberg (one of the first in the field because it had no bishop), laid this function on the *Schultheiss, Büttel, Marktpfänder* and the *Stadtknechte*: J. Dieselhorst, 'Die Bestrafung der Selbstmörder im Territorium der Stadt Nürnberg', *Mitteilungen des Vereins für Geschichte der Stadt Nürnberg*, 44 (Nürnberg, 1953), 81–3. For *Handelsrecht* and *Bürgerrecht*, see Mitteis, *Deutsche Rechtsgesch.*, 277–9, 294. *Burgfried*, ibid., 278–80; conceived as perpetual, ibid., 280. Strengthening of the *Rat* through the need for tax-assessment, ibid., 281. Urban opposition to *Rügeverfahren* on grounds of social disturbance, ibid., 304. The self-made and local character of town laws: Dieselhorst, 294.

but almost every kind of land register or other archival document found credit in town courts. The promiscuous character of their records helps explain the stylistic similarity, described earlier, between German town chronicles and legal registers.[6]

These conditions also explain why, although the late medieval urban records mention a relatively high number of suicides they yield next to nothing which resembles a 'portrait'. In this, too, they resemble the blunt accounts of the Plantagenet Eyres. Those town chroniclers, for their part, may just rise to portraiture. But court clerks were more interested in what happened to the bodies of suicides, even in the executioner's wages, than in the motives and circumstances that led to anyone's death. So Town Registers, *Stadtbücher*, can play an important part in the study of how suicides' bodies were treated,[7] but a small one in that of the suicidal human beings themselves, of whom the *Stadtbücher* entries give only an occasional glimpse.

How occasional is shown by the paucity of the following group of examples. Those are the only entries, among nearly fifty suicides mentioned in the strictly legal sources of these German towns, to give any personal description at all, beyond the barest word of the person or act of the suicide.[8] Thus in Frankfurt in 1404 there was a man 'who hanged himself in prison in the tower on the bridge'; in Basle, in 1425, a weaver's apprentice who 'hanged himself, but was cut down by passers-by', and revived (these records include attempts: another mark of their pragmatism). In Frankfurt, in 1488, 'the wife of Stroichin the tailor at Schaffhausen hanged herself, while she was out of her reason', while in 1498, 'the mother of Michel of Ezonss the Jew, on Saturday last past, drowned herself in the well in her street.' Another of the few suicides who rises above near-anonymity, in 1486, was Peter of Walustadt, 'a town councillor [of Frankfurt], arrested for embezzlement, who hanged himself in prison'.

In describing the slow evolution of public criminal justice, and hence of its records, I spoke of three exceptions. But at the very end of the Middle Ages there would be a fourth, destined to become after 1500 the most important. This was the princely state. If the great archbishoprics were an obstacle to a German national monarchy, they played the opposite role with that less ambitious political animal, the princely state, to which the bishoprics were a model and source. The bishops' canon law had long been acquainted

---

[6] Writing: Mitteis, 257–8, cf. 296–9. *Rad und Galge*, as power to execute as distinct from sentence and as mark of jurisdiction, and jealousy for the same: ibid., 193. For the town chronicles see Chs 3 and 5 above.

[7] To be the subject of the first chapter of *The Curse on Self-Murder*.

[8] References to sources will be found in the Register (pp. 461–4 below).

with procedures more sophisticated than any found in secular courts, and which influenced the latter. For a time, in the 1220s, the archbishoprics of Mainz and Trier had extended to their secular jurisdictions the procedures of canon law, including *inquisitio*, with its public prosecution of crime. The contemporary popularity of this experiment attests to the vacuum it filled. But the effect was local and temporary. Only in the late fourteenth century, when the Mainz episcopal 'state' became a model for newly self-conscious secular princes, did Roman-style state law begin the advance which would end in its domination in the modern period. The process was too slow, the survival of its records too precarious to have left behind any regular judicial records of homicide, and therefore of suicide, from strictly medieval princely jurisdictions. All it did leave was traces of case-law in law-books, and these, as we should expect (from the French model), very occasionally record flesh-and-blood cases which include suicide.

Let me give a few examples. A collection of decisions from Leipzig, made in the sixteenth century but using fifteenth-century material, mentions very briefly an undatable case of a thief who hanged himself in prison. It says nothing more about him, and derives its historical substance mainly from its resemblance to similar cases we can date.[9] A second example is more forthcoming. It is from the abbey of Echternach in Alsace, where the abbot claimed immemorial high jurisdiction over much of the region. Unlike the abbots of the Île-de-France he was free of any overpowering neighbour, and consequently saw himself as defending numerous communal village jurisdictions, perhaps equally old, against surrounding secular lords. Here too the political geometry round an old abbey could produce the record of a suicide. In 1453 the village of Dreis was defending its right to hang a particular criminal. A lord nearby, who claimed high justice, wanted merely to cut the man's ears off and let him go. But the village spokesman pleaded this precedent:

In the year of Christ 1429 [he said], a woman in Dreis hanged herself in a shed and died. The village officers cut her down and dragged her body to the mountain where the gallows are and buried her there. The lord's commissioners rode over and asked who had given the village permission. They said, no one, because they did not need permission. The jurisdiction, they said, was theirs. They had had it from the monastery of Echternach, and according to what their elders told them had always exercised it. It was still valid.

---

[9] G. Kisch, ed., *Leipziger Schöffenspruchsammlung* (Leipzig, 1919), no. 205 (p. 178). The work was composed in 1523–4. No. 205 is not among the *Sprüche* that go back to the fourteenth century or the first quarter of the fifteenth, but the basis for the whole collection, and hence of this case, could be a collection made *c.*1450, ibid., pp. 72*, 111*. Of similar urban collections (listed by Mitteis, 273) I have searched W. Ebel, ed., *Lübecker Ratsurteile*, vol. 1: AD 1421–1500 (Göttingen, 1955) and found no mention of suicide.

This law report may tell us little directly about the woman's suicide, but it does say something about the village and its law. The spokesman's memory had to go back twenty-four years for his last example of the village's homicide jurisdiction; and for the latter's origin, to word-of-mouth passed down by elders, *alderen*. No wonder our records are so rare.[10]

A third reference from this type of collection is equally informative. The collection this time is from Ingelheim on the Rhine, not ten miles from Mainz and seat of one of the high courts in that most precocious of secular princely states, the Rhine Palatinate. The case comes as close as any of these German judicial accounts to portraiture. The judgement in question is dated 8 February 1415, and settled a dispute about inheritance, passed up to Ingelheim on appeal from a lower court at neighbouring Uffhofen. Like most appeals, the case is complicated. But like most appeals, too, for the same reason, it is historically informative, since it conveys, as did some of those Parlement cases in France, the impact of identical events on two distinct layers of society, represented respectively by the lower and higher courts. So I shall give it *in extenso*.[11]

The events were these. A man 'bought' a woman, and the woman conceived and gave birth to a bastard. The man fell sick and asked the woman (the word is *wib*, which can mean either 'woman' or 'wife') that she make the bastard her heir. She, in turn, consulted her mother, and all three—man, woman, and the woman's mother—went off to the Uffhofen court to declare the child their heir, but on certain conditions. Whichever of the parents died, they agreed, the child should have half of that parent's property, it being understood that the other half, if the woman should die first, should go to her own relations, represented by her mother. This arrangement was duly authorized by the court.

Then the unexpected happened: a suicide. The woman, according to the appeal court's version, was treated so badly by the man that she hanged

---

[10] J. Grimm, *Weisthümer*, vol. 2, co-edited by E. Dronke and H. Beyer (Géttingen, 1840), 335: 'Vortherr Heyntzen Hanss, er sy gewest zu eyner zender des dorffs . . .' The debate with the lord, Nicholas of Esch, follows, and is concluded thus by the village *Zender*: 'In den jaren Christi dusent vierhondert nun and zwentzich hait sych eyn frauwe zu Dreys selber erhangen in eyn schuyr und hat sich verdarfft. Do hayt dye gemein dye frauw abgehauwen und eyn loch under dye swel gemacht, und die frauw darauss und dardorch gezogen byss uff den berg, da dat gericht steht und aldar begraben an das gericht. Do synt die voigthern zugefahren und dye gemeyn gefraigt, warumb sy das gethaen habe, wer inn das erlaufft hab? Antwort dye gemeyn und sprach, sie hetten nyemans orlauff geheischen, das gericht were ir, si hettens von dem gotzhaus zu E. Das hetten sy allwege also gepraucht und van iren alderen gehoret, ess bleyff auch zu der ziit daby.' Cf. Geiger, 'Der Selbstmord im deutschen Recht', 13; Signori, 'Rechtskonstruktionen', 28 (with explanation and bibliography on the legal context). I have slightly shortened and simplified the passage in translation.

[11] Ed. A. Edler, *Die älteren Urteile des Ingelheimer Oberhofes*, 4 vols. (Frankfurt-am-Main, 1952–63), vol. 2, no. 1991, pp. 250–1.

herself.[12] Because of the manner of her death, the man then affected to ignore her declared will, and keep all her property for himself and the bastard son. Protesting at this, the woman's friends would have been glad, they claimed, to let him have half of her share. But the man and his son insisted on all. So the woman's party appealed to the high court at Ingelheim, whose judge agreed to their claim, declaring roundly that 'the hanging does not affect the claim of the woman's relations.'[13]

The Ingelheim judge had been reading Justinian. Only so could he have been so cocksure that suicide did not invalidate a will. But there were clearly powerful, if unlearned, people who thought otherwise, for if there had not been, the contrary claim would never have been sustained firmly enough to force an appeal. Nor, even among learned lawyers, would the judge's decision have been thought worth recording if the issue had been a foregone conclusion. The doubt is informative. It is also, once again, historically fortunate, since it occasioned the appeal and hence the record, to bring us, in this one datable case, as close to a case-history as we are likely to get among the sparse, blunt court records of medieval Germany.

Italy

WHY ITALIAN RECORDS YIELD ALMOST NO PORTRAITS AT ALL

In the other main region of the Empire, Italy, the development of public responsibility for homicide was analogous to that in Germany. That is, there was no strong national monarchy, and legal development in this particular, despite early moves in the Lombard and Frankish periods, remained conservative.[14] But there were two differences. Politically, the role of the Rhineland archbishops was played by the papacy. The popes, unwilling to brook menace to the Petrine lands in central Italy, repeatedly ensured during the medieval centuries that no monarchy covered the whole peninsular. The popes' task was made no easier by the presence in the south, in Sicily, of Byzantine state traditions which, at the very moment the papacy was resisting them, were serving as inspiration to the inventors of non-ecclesiastical national states further north. But in Italy the popes won. Sicily

---

[12] The maltreatment of the wife is described only briefly: 'nu tedt der man der frauwen solich liden, daz sie sich irhing.'

[13] The final *sententia* ends: 'und schadit der frauwen erben ane iren rechten daz irhangen nit'. Let me add that the character of the testimony is not entirely clear. I have chosen the only interpretation of the case that seems to make sense of it.

[14] A. Pertile, *Storia del diritto italiano*, vol. 6 (2) (Turin, 1902), 1–29; and more cursorily, C. Calisse, *A History of Italian Law*, trans. L. B. Register (London, 1928), 178–9.

and its Neapolitan offshoot remained marginal. That left the creation of effective public legal authority not to a monarchy, from north or south, but to the same *tertius gaudens* we have just met in Germany, the independent towns.

Besides their earlier development and greater vigour, the legal history of Italian towns embodied a second difference from its German equivalent. They were closer to Roman law. The continuity of medieval with classical towns in Italy was more pretence than reality, but even the pretence was a kind of reality; and it gave the townsmen, especially when in rivalry with ecclesiastical authority, an eagerness to feed on Roman law when drafting their own town statutes. This feature tended to moderate, without destroying, the Germanic adversarial principle of homicide actions, and allowed the Roman law model of *inquisitio*, joined by corresponding canon-law influences from the new Rome of the popes, to play a part in the towns' crime-prevention measures, pragmatic though these were. Thus by the early fourteenth century the more successful Italian communes had procedural means available for the *ex officio* public prosecution of homicide. The upshot was, as in England with its coroner, an official 'Criminal Investigation Department'. Some communes came to require doctors to examine all corpses and report on the causes of death, suicide along with the rest.[15]

Italian town justice thus moved earlier than German towards public criminal prosecution. Since it was also precociously literate and created judicial archives, some of which have survived despite the heavy ravages of war (notable ones, for instance, in Florence and Perugia), we might think it reasonable to expect from Italian towns abundant records of suicide, rich where others are niggardly.

So it is surprising, and hence instructive, that this hope is disappointed. Until the very end of the Middle Ages, and in an exceptional area, suicides in medieval Italy are unrecorded. From surviving Italian civic criminal archives no scholar has so far brought to public attention any direct reference to completed suicide from the medieval period. Nor do the indications available at present promise that any will.[16]

---

[15] Modification of the adversarial principle is described by Pertile, ibid., 3–6; effect of canon law: ibid., 6–8. Doctors' inspection of dead bodies *c.*1300: N. Siraisi, *Taddeo Alderotti* (Princeton, 1981), 36, 47 f.

[16] This negative assertion rests on standard secondary studies on Florence, Padua, Venice, and other cities, whose authors make use of criminal archives, and on a sounding made specifically for the purpose among the criminal registers of Perugia. I looked especially, in the Perugia archive, at the registers of the Podestà and Capitano del Popolo, which extend to many hundreds of volumes. Cf. also Simonetta Scioppa, *Il 'Fondo Giudiziario' del Comune di Perugia dal 1258–1280*, Tesi di Laurea, Università degli Studi di Perugia, Facoltà di Lettere e Filosfia, 1977; and the same scholar's 'Le fonti giudiziarie per una ricerca sulla criminalità a Perugia nel duecento', *Ricerche su Perugia tra due e quattrocento* (Perugia, 1982), 59–144. I have also

Mention is made of the occasional attempt, but that is a different matter.[17]

Since we know for certain that people did commit suicide in Italian cities, and, as it happens, with a frequency notorious in the city with the most comprehensive surviving archive,[18] Florence, the silence of urban judicial records needs explaining. The immediate explanation is that Italian urban law did not treat suicide as a crime, as did the northern monarchies. Civic statutes do not mention suicide as culpable at all, on its own or in combination.[19] But that only moves the question one step further away. Why did Italian cities, alone, avoid penalties for suicide? One explanation may lie in the influence of Roman law, whose insistence on the intrinsic innocence of suicide I have already referred to, and whose evaluation by the communes' legislators was one more facet of their pride in being latter-day Romans. But Roman law cannot be the only answer. The communes, after all, did not follow it more slavishly than any other medieval jurisdictions. Roman law could subsist in late medieval France together with severe penalties for suicide. Nor did Italians necessarily think suicide innocent as early Roman jurisprudence did, to judge, at least, from their treatment of attempted suicide. Dante and his first readers had no reason to place the souls of suicides otherwise than in Hell. So Roman law cannot be all the answer. The rest may lie in the field of penalties, for a completed suicide could only be

gained from the experience of scholars with more experience than mine. Dr Jean-Claude Maire-Vigueur, of the École Française de Rome, who first guided me to the Perugia criminal registers, confessed that in his own reading of them he had noted no mention of suicide, while acknowledging that this might have been because he had not looked for it. He expressed to me optimism that this 'océan de documents qui n'a jamais été systématiquement exploité', and which largely escapes inventory, might yield cases of suicide if at the cost of 'un travail évidemment trés fastidieux' (Letter to the author, 5 July 1984). But when Dr Attilio Bartoli Langeli of the University of Perugia kindly agreed to take on the fastidious *travail* of an independent 'sondaggio' of his own, he reported in a communication to me of 20 October 1984: 'il risultato però è stato nullo', and that 'sul suicidio, la nostra documentazione è silenziosa, o talmente reticente da essere inutilizzabile.' Dr Philip Jones, Dr John Henderson, and others have conveyed similar impressions from the archives in Florence. Most notably, Dr Francis William Kent, in conversation during his visit to Oxford in early 1991, told me he could not recall a single case of suicide in his own exploration of the Florentine communal archive. The fact that he remembered later, and kindly communicated to me (in a letter of 3 January 1992) a possible reference to suicide in 1454, from a notary's diary rather than from a judicial document, only underlines the value of his negative impression from the wider field. The diary entry records the fall of the notary's own father from a roof two days after having been diagnosed as having cancer of the throat, and immediately after making confession and receiving communion: (Acquisti e Doni, 11 (inserto i), fol. 3r).

[17] R. Davidsohn, *Geschichte von Florenz*, vol. 4, pt 1 (Berlin, 1922), 312. G. Dahm, *Das Strafrecht Italiens im ausgehenden Mittelalter* (Berlin and Leipzig, 1931), 348–9.

[18] For the Florentines' reputation for suicide see pp. 85–92 above and p. 368 below.

[19] J. Kohler, *Das Strafrecht der italienischen Statuten vom 12–16 Jahrhundert* (Mannheim, 1897), 320–9, rehearses the statutes' provisions on homicide, with no hint, in any commune, of penalties for suicide.

punished by ill-treatment of the corpse or confiscation of the property. The latter penalty was in certain cases allowed by Roman law, but was by contrast deeply unpopular in city law, because it made havoc of the principle on which the balance of urban life depended, namely property.

These factors must form valuable accessories to any enquiry into attitudes to suicide,[20] but in the search for individual cases they serve only to demarcate another black hole, all but co-extensive with Italian judicial records. We know there was suicide there, from Dante and his admirers and by occasional witnesses, but the judicial documents do not usually report it.

I say 'not usually' because medievalists do not despair. And there are, in fact, two kinds of exception. Each was created by legal conditions exclusive to itself and both, together, show what suicides may have been happening in the dark, outside these narrow bands of legal documentation. The first is ducal Milan, in the late fifteenth century.

THE FIRST EXCEPTION: LATE-FIFTEENTH-CENTURY MILAN

Alone among major north Italian communes, Milan had for a long time not swallowed its bishopric. Its bishop was just too strong, almost a pope (indeed almost an emperor too) for Lombardy. But the bishopric of Milan had another fate. Early in the fourteenth century, almost overnight, an astute nobleman, who happened also to be archbishop of Milan, dismantled its economic foundations in favour of a young kinsman of his own; and when Europe woke up next morning it saw, where the archbishop had been, the first secular Renaissance despotism, that of the Visconti. By the middle of the fifteenth century, partly by its bribery of a feeble German Emperor, the despotism had become a hereditary duchy, its territory stretching from north of the Matterhorn to south of Bologna. All these lands lay under a duke who, in theory, had quasi-regal power.

The duke of Milan's lawyers therefore had different ways of reading Roman law from those of the republican communes. Their duke was the keeper of law and order. His government agents did not fail to inspect dead bodies and kept a record of their findings, while as a despot he was less fastidious than plain, equal citizens about confiscation as a punishment. Suddenly, therefore, in Milan around 1460, Italian judicial records of suicides suddenly start appearing. They are still not many. A great Italian antiquary, Emilio Motta, who spent much of his life in Milanese archives in the late nineteenth century and was sharply on the look-out for suicides, was struck

---

[20] They will do so in chapters 2, 5, and 8 of *The Curse on Self-Murder*.

at how few there were.[21] But he found half a dozen. They are both an epitome and a variant of what has been learned from our other sources, so let us look at his findings.

Three of Motta's little dossier come from the Milanese mortuary registers, the records of corpses for which the city government was responsible. These registers cover a bigger social range than more casual sources on the subject, and it is significant that all the three suicides were of persons of low social consequence. This fact suggests, as do the English coroners' rolls, that the rarity of very poor suicides in our records reflects only the rarity of sources that record them. Two of Motta's three were young women, both of whom had had committed suicide by poison on different dates in 1480. One, 21 years old, resident outside the Porta Ticinese in the parish of San Lorenzo, had 'of her own volition, her soul incited by passion', taken the poison and died of it, in the verdict of two doctors. The other, Giovannina, the 18-year-old 'famula [servant]' to an upper-class family in the parish of San Michele al Gallo, 'half out of her mind and not entirely in control of herself [*semi fatua nec ex toto sui juris*] of her own volition poisoned herself with arsenic'. This latter one, Giovannina, survived long enough to tell her parish priest what she had done and complete her confession and penance before dying. She was an Emelina la Baronne, but in Milan, and under a non-confiscating regime. These formalities over, Giovannina died in the presence of two nurses and two licensed apothecaries, no doubt called in to search for an antidote.

The third suicide from the Milan mortuary registers is that of a 30-year-old male prisoner. He had hanged himself in the city's main criminal prison, on 9 September 1488. His name, Giorgio di Piacenza, suggests an immigrant from one of Milan's subjected towns, Piacenza being forty miles from Milan and by then part of the Milanese state. Nor is there any sign in the record of Giorgio's family, personal connections, or property. The uninquisitive official who recorded the death merely commented tautologically that Giorgio had hanged himself 'ex melanconia'.

Motta found three of his six cases in mortuary registers. The three others come in miscellaneous communications between agents of ducal government. The cases would not have attracted Motta's notice unless the suicides had been persons of consequence, and all three are. One is that of the commandant of the ducal guard at Lodi (on the Po thirty miles from Milan and then under its domination). The commandant, Danino dell'Acqua, had

---

[21] 'Pochissimi': E. Motta, 'Suicidi nel quattrocento e nel cinquecento', *Archivio storico lombardo*, 15 (1888), 96–100: see also his 'Suicidio d'un abbadessa nel 1463?', *Bollettino storico della Svizzera italiana*, 2 (1886), 234–5; 'Un suicidio in Lodi nel 1468', *Archivio storico lodigiano*, 2 (1882), 3 pp. (separately printed).

hanged himself in his house in Lodi in June 1468, 'induced', the record again tautologically states, 'by some kind of desperation [*inducto de qualque desperatione*]'. As usual, we hear of this case because of a dispute. The official of the bishop of Lodi, whose jurisdiction included suspected witchcraft (*maleficium*), had gone with other officials to the spot and confirmed that the man 'had hanged himself of his own accord'. The source for all this, a letter to the duke from his commissary in Lodi, resembles an English legal account in that it dwells on the dead man's property, the real bone of contention. The property had been taken by the bishop, but was claimed also by the duke, and by the dead man's relations. It was a three-cornered tug of war. Who would win? The writer of the letter does not know. But his stake is apparently on the duke, for he conveys a request from the bishop that the confiscated goods be returned to the bishop, not as of right, but as a gift. The bishop's plea—a plea, not a claim—is that a ceremonial canopy had been spoiled when used at the duke's triumphal entry to the town two years earlier, and the bishop would like to use the windfall of the suicide's property to replace the canopy. (Neither duke nor bishop, it is clear, whatever may have been their other debts to Roman law, paid any attention to the Roman rule that suicide did not entail confiscation.)

A dispute about property was the occasion for that record. As in the English rolls and on the same grounds, the writer was uninterested in the motive and circumstances of Dannino dell'Acqua's death. A second letter, a year later, is more informative, hinting indirectly at a motive.[22] It is dated in 1469, in the reign of Duke Galeazzo Maria Sforza. The letter is from one of the duke's most confidential counsellors, and concerns an attempted suicide by a man in prison, called Piattino. We know nothing more of Piattino than the letter reveals, that is, that he was the duke's enemy. For at 10.00 on the evening of 29 May 1469, Piattino had tried to hang himself in his cell. The duke's confidant sends thanks to the prison governor for informing him of the attempted suicide. Then he reveals, indirectly, why the man might have wished to die. On the duke's behalf, the writer expresses his government's *deepest disappointment* that the attempt did not succeed, and adds the ducal instruction that if Piattino should try again to kill himself, he should be given every assistance. We do not know if Piattino did try again, but we can guess his motive the first time. Life under such a tyrant must for him have been unbearable, and it is hardly a surprise that the duke's own death, when it came, seven years later, was by assassination. Nor would the conjunction of suicide and despotism have surprised Durkheim.[23]

[22] E. Motta, 'Un mancato suicidio nel 1469 e lo strano gusto del duca di Milano', *Bollettino storico della Suizzera italiana*, 1 (1884), 239–41.

[23] *Suicide*, 346–60, 370–90.

There is one more case in Motta's Milanese dossier. Its date is earlier than the others', probably 1463, and the source a letter by the same duke of Milan, Galeazzo Maria Sforza. This one concerns the suicide of an abbess at Lomello, thirty miles south-west of Milan. The abbess had been found drowned in her own conventual fishpond, the morning after being discovered in bed with a man. The man is called 'fra Nigro' so he must have been a friar. A bishop had tried to protect him from secular justice, which for the friar would probably have meant prison rather than decapitation. But the Lomello town governor had arrested fra Nigro, so the bishops had excommunicated him, the governor. The duke now writes to clear the matter up and tells the bishop:

Since it seems that this is an episode it would be wrong to ignore, it would appear to us that Your Reverence should send an armed guard to put fra Nigro in custody and to hold him there until you decide whatever you think opportune in his regard. And if the governor of Lomello has fallen under any excommunication, for having arrested the friar, you will be pleased to absolve him.

In a postscript, the duke recommends an appropriately aristocratic candidate as the abbess's successor. The letter is a model of legal correctness. It allows that the friar is under the bishop's jurisdiction, but implies that it remains the duke who has the strong arm, and will use it if necessary.

Milan, then, is the first exception to the rule that Italian judicial sources never record suicides. Perhaps it is a partial exception only, since only the mortuary registers are strictly of a legal character. But in a despotism, political correspondence comes near to that character, and we must be grateful for what we get.

The second exception has been left until last. Although it is earlier in date than any of those Milanese cases, it is recorded with a degree of eye-witness detail unique, certainly, in Italy, and in some respects in Europe as a whole. So unique is it that we can profitably reflect on why it should be so. The explanation, yet again, lies in the nature of the legal institutions that produced the records. Careful examination of Italian urban judicial sources reveals another black hole. This one covers now not only suicide, but all crime outside the perimeter of communal jurisdictions. There, in the vast *contrada*, we notice in the day-to-day records of communal courts the signs of older, non-urban jurisdictions akin to those widespread in Germany, and of whose judgements record was not made or kept.[24] In other words, if we

---

[24] For instance, Archivio di Stato Perugia, Regist. Podestà, No. 8 (25 June to 31 Oct 1301), fols 21v–24v, where the communal forces, presumably because they are the only ones strong enough to deal with the case, capture and unpleasantly hang a notorious robber, in a manner not prescribed in any of the contemporary Perugia communal statutes (namely, of 1279 or 1342) and indeed disapproved of by the podestà's recording notary (fol. 24v).

could only find some judicial 'camera', free from whatever inhibition it was that barred suicide from the cognizance of urban rural counterparts and able to penetrate this rural outback, we might have a chance of catching Italian suicides, after all.

To find such an instrument we need to reflect for a moment on Italian legal history. Urban jurisdictions, in Italy more than elsewhere, had extended at the expense of rural seigneurs. But the losers had also been the old-style lordly Italian bishops, most of whom (not Milan or Rome) were in retreat before their communes by 1200. Characteristically, the church made up for its retreat on one level by advancing on a higher one. Roman law, by way of canon, had given the church the *inquisitio*, the sophisticated legal procedure with interrogatories and records, some of whose results we studied in France. Churchmen had known this procedure long before it was recruited for heresy in the 1230s. But inquisitorial procedure was expanded then both for heresy and for other concerns, and many of its interrogatories survive. The reader of Emmanuel Le Roy Ladurie's *Montaillou*[25] needs no telling how well they can document daily life and belief, often in areas untouched at the the time by records from any secular tribunal. Suicide was, of course, included.

Again we shall not see these interrogatories in Italy, or not on the same scale. There could be no Italian *Montaillou*. Why not is that, because most communes had overpowered their bishops, the areas of Italy whose heresy might have provoked an inquisition would not have tolerated its sessions. The communes were too strong, and supported the inquisition only, in the main, against rebels agreed to be such, for their own purposes.[26] We do indeed catch the occasional heretic suicide in Italy. Thus a Cathar drowned himself in the Tiber in 1237, possibly in disappointment at having failed to get papal absolution. But that case, an isolated one, was significantly not in communal Italy, nor in the direct purlieus of the inquisition, and was recorded only in a foreign chronicle.[27] Further north in Italy the inquisition on its own was just not strong enough. The church's loss of judicial authority on this level was nevertheless, here again, made up for on a higher one. Look at it from the church's point of view. Its function lay in defining not only those too bad for membership, namely heretics, but also, at the top

---

[25] (Paris, 1975).

[26] This sentence resumes an argument of my 'The Inquisition: an instrument of secular politics?', *Peritia*, 5 (1987), 161–200, esp. 180–92.

[27] Y. Dossat, *Les crises de l'inquisition toulousaine au xiie siècle (1233–1273)* (Bordeaux, 1959), 126, from Guillaume Pelhisson, *Chronique* (ed. C. Douais in *Les sources de l'histoire de l'Inquisition dans le Midi de la France* (Paris, 1881), 95–6). The motive is a surmise by Dossat, expressed orally to E. Dupré Theseider: cf. the latters 'Le catharisme languedocien en Italie', *Cahiers de Fanjeaux*, 3 (Toulouse, 1968), 316, n. 46.

end of the range, the paragons of Christian virtue whom all the faithful had to follow, namely saints. Canonization procedure forms a celestial mirror image of that for prosecuting heretics, and the evolution of one was reflected by that of the other. Competition among devotees of candidates for canonization had grown palpably since the eleventh century and engendered ever stricter rules. The same century, the thirteenth, which saw the church adopt and perfect the inquisitorial procedure to investigate heresy, saw roughly the same procedures applied for testing sainthood. The court personnel were broadly the same. Both types of tribunal, that for heresy and that for canonization, invoked the service of the devout, skilful, mendicant friars, who acquired the associated expertise in questioning and recording.[28]

In the nature of things, then, we should expect the canonization process to provide the missing legal source for Italy, shorn of others, in the present regard, by the dominance of urban communes judicially indifferent to suicide. So now we know where to look. Let us look there. At once a planet spins into sight. The principal case in question is from the Papal States, an area already, by the fourteenth century, becoming the Promised Land for canonized saints and at the same time a relative rural outback where, modernizing mendicants apart, conservative judicial procedures were most likely to endure.[29] The Papal States are thus ideal territory for a sounding. By chance the process I refer to includes a suicide. The record gives a level of descriptive detail equal to, or greater than, that provided at the same date, on comparable but different subjects, by the register of Jacques Fournier, inquisitor of Montaillou.

Some will say the alleged suicide here is only an attempt. The man in question, supposedly dead, was brought back to life by a miracle. It is sometimes hard now, and could be all but impossible then, to tell if a person nearly dead was actually so.[30] That modicum of reasonable doubt sufficed to reconcile, in the minds of judges and witnesses, a zeal for factual truth with a belief some might today reject as imaginary. The combination, at all events, gives us the one suicidal incident to emerge with any detail from Italian judicial records. The event is of a kind so rarely described, and is plotted with such verisimilitude and attention to detail, confirmed by

[28] The process: A. Vauchez, *La sainteté en occident aux derniers siècles du moyen âge*. Bibliothèque des écoles françaises d'Athènes et de Rome, fasc. 241 (Rome, 1981), esp. 39–120.

[29] On Italy as Promised Land for saints: D. Weinstein and R. M. Bell, *Saints and Society* (Chicago and London, 1982), 167, where a table of countries in which saints were born yields an Italian proportion rising as follows: saints dying in the twelfth century, 23%; in the thirteenth, 50%; in the fourteenth, 69%. The Papal States play a conspicuous part in this conquest.

[30] A point made, with illustration, by R. C. Finucane, *Miracles and Pilgrims* (London, 1977), 73–4.

disciplined examination of more than one witness, that it is worth careful reconstruction.

The record concerns a peasant called Giacommuccio Fatteboni. Giacomuccio was a villager of Belforte, a small community perched over the river Chienti, four miles south-west of Tolentino and now in the province of Macerata. Belforte was then in the Papal States and gazed up, from the east, towards the same Appenines that Assisi, thirty miles away over the peaks, looked at from the west. In 1320 Assisi had had its saint for a century. Pressure was mounting on this side of the Appenines for a saint for Tolentino too. The most likely candidate had died in 1305. He was Nicholas, an Austin friar of the Tolentino priory and a man much valued *inter alia* as a confessor to the laity round about. In the summer of 1325 the convent finally sent one of its theologians to join forces with a lawyer, appointed by the town, to hear witnesses to Nicholas's posthumous miracles and press for his canonization. Hundreds of witnesses came, and among them were four from Belforte. It is from their testimony, teased out by an expert tribunal, in the same late summer months in which Jacques Fournier's inquisition was closing its enquiries into Montaillou, that the story of Giacommuccio can be put back together.[31]

Giacomuccio was 55 years old. He had just married again. Two sons by his first marriage, Piero and Vanne, were old enough for field-work and a daughter, Planucia, was 25. The family was apparently not native to Belforte-sul-Chienti but had moved there three years before, perhaps on the death of the mother. Giacomuccio had remarried a local woman, a well-to-do villager and probably young. She was called Bionda, and had some land which was worked by her brothers and one or two labourers. They all lived close together in or near Bionda's house in a main street, next to the fortress. On remarriage, a mere two months before the incident, the bridegroom had moved in, adding six young pairs of hands including his daughter's (who

---

[31] In *Il processo di canonizzazione di S. Nicolo da Tolentino*. Edizione critica da Nichola Occhioni, O.S.A. [1970]. Prefazione da André Vauchez. Collection de l'école Française de Rome, 74 (Rome, 1984), 278–86. The hearing: pp. xi–xii; the witnesses: xcvi–xcix. Topography: Carta d'Italia [Istituto geografico militare] 1:25,000: sheet 124 II N.O. The hills are today covered by vineyards but in the testimony the general use of ovens, and the vowing to the saint of a sack of grain, point to an economy dominated in 1320 by cereals. Cf. P. Jones, in *The Cambridge Economic History of Europe*, ed. M. M. Postan, vol. 1, 2nd edn (Cambridge, 1966), 384–5, 391–2. Since making this reconstruction I have been pleased to find the case appreciated also by Professor Michael Goodich (*Violence and Miracle* (Chicago and London, 1995), 81–3). Minor discrepancies between his and my readings will, I hope, draw the curious back to the document itself.

lived nearby) to the family's workforce. In no time Giacomuccio became a familiar figure to the neighbours.[32]

Of these, the most observant may have thought the new husband a trifle sickly and strange. His grown-up daughter knew he talked and behaved a little oddly from time to time. But she did not make this public and had no reason to guess anything was seriously wrong. Everyone, therefore, was struck as if by lightning when disaster happened, on a dry afternoon in April 1320. It was a Thursday. One witness recalled it as the Eve of St Mark, so the precise date must have been 24 April. Why everyone remembered the day was that on Thursdays the communal oven at Tolentino was available for Belforte villagers, and Bionda had been away using it. She arrived home about two or three o'clock. Her husband was on his own, Planucia (who lived in another part of the village) having just left. Nothing seemed to be amiss. Giacomuccio told his wife that his two sons would need something to eat when they came back from work that evening, and that she should go to the smaller village oven up the street ('about six houses away') and bake a pie for them. So while he sat at home 'on a certain bench', off Bionda went along the street, put her pie in the oven, and walked back home. A watchful neighbour saw her both going and returning, and again, nothing seemed wrong.[33]

That is, until Bionda got back to her own front door. Entering, she saw her husband hanging from a beam, his feet a yard or so clear of the ground, his face swollen and black, his tongue black and forced between his teeth. Bionda shrieked at the top of her voice. She at once dragged a chest under the body, climbed up onto it, and tried to tear loose the slip-knot round her husband's throat. His weight was too much, and on her own she would have managed nothing. But her shriek had brought her next-door neighbour round, and another woman from the street, and these two, Margarita and

---

[32] I have ignored, in testimony to the ages of Giacomuccio and Planucia, the 'et plus' added in both cases, a mark of the lack, and excess, of fastidiousness usual respectively to witnesses and courts. The second marriage: Margarita, the next-door neighbour, had known Giacomuccio 'forsitan duobus mensibus antequam accideret dictus casus, quia erat tunc temporis nupta in illa contrata' (280.82–4); while Mathiola de Andrea de Campolarzo (wife of Georgio Bartolomeo di Alessandro) had known Giacomuccio 'VIII annis et ultra, quia erat et est vicina eius' (283.91–2)—a difference suggesting, unless I misinterpret the tenses, that the two had become neighbours three years before the incident. The sons work: 286.76–7. Their names: 278.17. Non-family workers: 'et filios et alios de domo Iacobucii supradicti' (282.50–1). The same, and Bionda's brothers: 'pre dictis filiis suis et alie familie et fratribus dicte domine' (284.28–9). Bionda as *noverca* to Planucia: 285.54, 64. (Planucia is called Plana at 280.46.) Giacomuccio's house is 'iuxta cassarum dicti castri [Belfortis]' (285.73–4), and in 'contrata Cassari dicti castri' (278.23).

[33] Giacomuccio's earlier condition may be surmised from Margarita's informed view that he had been 'homo melioris conditionis et vite quam fuerit ante' (281.85–7). Planucia's experience, perhaps exaggerated to excuse the act, was that her father 'erat aliquando fatuus et fantasticus et non boni sensus' (286.92–4). Cf. n. 37 below.

Piana, held Giacomuccio's heavy body up while Bionda loosened the knot. Together, the three of them dragged the body across the floor to a bed and laid the body on it. The whole of Giacomuccio's body was swollen and black, the black tongue distended and sticking out. He looked 'just as dead people look when they have been hanged'.[34]

The news had meanwhile travelled. Away out of earshot Giacomuccio's daughter Planucia, having left her father in apparent good health and spirits just before, was quietly at home when a neighbour rushed in and said: 'What now, Planucia, with your father dead?' It was the first Planucia had heard. 'Dead? How so,' she demanded, 'when I left him in perfectly good health only a moment ago? Who has killed him?' 'He has hanged himself,' Rosa replied. Planucia rushed back to her father's house and found it true.

The house was now full of neighbours of both sexes, who looked with horror at the darkened body on the bed. According to Planucia it was 'stinking'. (While there is no reason to doubt that, it must be remembered that by the time of the hearing all the witnesses were trying to prove a miracle.) In the midst of it all, Giacomuccio's young wife Bionda was distraught, weeping and tearing at her hair and clothes. At some point, early on, someone present had suggested that Bionda pray to the late friar Nicholas. She caught at the idea (she said at the hearing) and began praying aloud. Her words were remembered thus by Margarita, her next-door neighbour:

O blessed Nicholas [Bionda prayed], pray to God that Giacomuccio should not die so shamefully, that he should not lose his soul, and that neither he, nor I, nor his sons should be thus disgraced. Let him be revived at least enough to do penance, through your prayers and merits.

The other woman-witness, who had arrived later, recorded the same prayer but in indirect speech and added (after the mention of 'disgrace'), 'for he would have to be taken to the town ditch [*fossum*] for burial'. One witness, Planucia, said her young step-mother finally offered to present a sack of grain at Nicholas's tomb if her prayer was granted.[35]

If the story had not ended happily we would not, of course, have heard it. Bionda's offer was taken up. Around four o'clock the villagers had started to drift off in the unanimous conviction that their neighbour was now a widow. Not long before sundown Bionda and her step-daughter, left on their own, nevertheless thought they noticed movement in Giacomuccio's body. He began to move his eyes, then his hands and feet, and to touch himself.

---

[34] 'Ut sunt suspensi mortui' (279.35); cf. 279.33–5, 282.37–40, 285.44–9.
[35] The prayer (according to Margarita): 280.57–61, cf. 282.41–4 (Mathiola) and 285.58–9 (Planucia).

Mathiola (the one who had helped take the body down but who had gone home) now returned and saw the encouraging signs for herself. Giacomuccio was clearly alive. Any doubt about his condition vanished next morning when he got up and walked around, perfectly well. According to his own testimony later he had forgotten everything, and had to hear the story from everyone else. But he was well enough to fulfil his wife's vow to carry a sack of grain to St Nicholas's tomb, though he may not have felt up to carrying weights, for the record says he took his two sons with him. The whole party of them were seen going off to Tolentino with a saddle-bag full of grain to present to the holy man's tomb as a thank-offering. The next-door neighbour, Margarita, was prepared to say, as if to underline the miracle, that since the incident five years before Giacommuccio had actually seemed healthier, as well as saner, than before.[36]

We have no means of guessing what moved Giacomuccio to suicide. The incident was one embarrassing to recall in front of arbitrators, both ecclesiastical and lay. It was this, no doubt, which led to the witnesses' oblivion and confusion on this question. Planucia said her father was 'sometimes *fatuus* and *fantasticus* and lost his good sense [*non boni sensus*]'. Margarita, the next-door neighbour, said Giacomuccio had been 'sick and apparently not in his right mind, so that, provoked by some evil spirit, or for some reason or other, he hanged himself.' The other neighbour, Mathiola, pressed on the same point, said 'she did not know, unless, as she believes, it was because he was out of his mind [*fantasticus*]'. The judges gently urged Giacomuccio for his own recollection on whether he 'had some melancholy or sickness or deception of the Devil,' as a cause for his act. But Giacomuccio had conveniently forgotten. No one present pressed the issue further. It was all long ago, and the common mind of the village had long associated their elderly neighbour not with a diabolic but with a saintly event.

We are free of their constraints; free to observe, for instance, that Giacomuccio's two sons were not among witnesses to the miracle worked for him. Nor were his brothers-in-law. Nor, most notably, was his wife. There is no hint that she had died in the five years between the incident and the trial, nor that she was present but barred from giving evidence beside that of her husband. She has just vanished from the scene. It is therefore possible, from the slender evidence we have, that we are witnesses of yet another episode brought on by an unhappy marriage: unhappy for Giaco-

---

[36] Mathiola's departure (which I have treated also as a sign for that of others): 'per unam horam' (282.45); '. . . quia parum stetit in domo domini Iacobucii, quod redivit ad domum suam propriam' (282.46–7); 'per parvam horam' (283.93–4). Margarita's view of the patient's improvement is quoted in n. 33 above. For parallels to Giacomuccio's amnesia after the event, see pp. 325, 328, 330–1, 337 below.

muccio, with his new bride, and, after the incident, unhappy enough for her to have left him.[37]

The evidence of Giacomuccio is distinguished by the clarity of its focus, a clarity extending to all details of the episode except the one question—marginal to us though crucial to the witnesses—whether Giacomuccio had really died. This clarity makes the evidence exceptional, to a degree reflecting the same judicial conditions that gave the evidence birth. Whether the event it described was also exceptional is another question. The Giacomuccio dossier goes only as far as to show it was not unique: for Bionda is represented as praying that her husband's body would not be thrown into a ditch for burial, an allusion which lets us know, as no other testimony does, not only that that was how a suicide's body might be disposed of in rural Italy, but also, and at this point more significantly, that she, Bionda, knew this fact perfectly well. An ordinary Macerata peasant, that is to say, was sufficiently aware of the existence of suicide to need no tutorial as to what might be done to the corpse.[38]

Giacomuccio's attempted suicide, then, cannot have been unparalleled even in an Italy poor in records of suicide. We shall have a chance of confirming this surmise through some of the free-standing miracles, told independently of any canonization tribunal, of Italian saints. But because one such miracle is contemporary with the Tolentino process and relates—with appropriately greater concision—much the same kind of incident, it may give useful reassurance on this point to consider it now, as a postscript to Giacomuccio's new tragedy. It is a miracle of St Peter Martyr, a Dominican preacher and latterly inquisitor for Lombardy, who was assassinated in 1252 and canonized the next year. His miracles were still being collected in the early fourteenth century, and one, from Genoa, begins like this:

A certain woman in Genoa, at the Devil's instigation and on account of some despair or other, shut the door on herself, hanged herself in her own house and with her own hands. She hung as dead from the beam for over an hour.[39] A group of

---

[37] The principles for interpreting court evidence on this point are examined on pp. 166–71 above. Margarita's view was that he was 'infirmus et videbatur quasi mente captus ita quod nescit quo malo spiritu ductus vel qua de causa . . . suspendit se' (279.15–17). Mathiola: 'se nescire, nisi quod credit pro eo quod erat fantasticus' (283.99–100). For Planucia, see n. 33. Giacomuccio's amnesia: when asked 'si habuit aliquam malanconiam vel infirmitatem vel deceptionem dyaboli propter quam ipsemet se suspendisset, dixit se non recordari' (278.8–10); and again: 'si tentatione dyaboli vel alio modo fuit, dixit se non recordari' (278.13–14).

[38] 'De vituperio quod erat sibi et filiis suis: quia debebat portari ad fossum ad sepeliendum' (282.42–4).

[39] The phrase used is 'per magnam horam'. It echoes 'per parvam horma' in Mathiola's evidence in the Tolentino dossier (*loc. cit.*, 283.94). The expression was about to receive its death-sentence in the late 1320s with the spread of mechanical clocks, when hours became equal.

neighbours looked for her and banged on the door, but got no answer. So they peered through cracks in the door, and saw her, hanging on a beam. They broke in, cut the rope and found her quite dead.[40]

A senior female devotee of the Martyr had kept a scrap of his cloak, and suggested its application to the dead woman's throat to revive her. It worked. In bare essentials the incident seems a replica of the one at Belforte.

Lewis Carroll's Alice passed unconsciously through the looking-glass as she talked, and once through, was startled to find herself in a world with new rules and coordinates. We have done the same. Moving from traditional courts to inquisitions, from inquisitions to the canonization processes, we have slipped finally from there to the 'miracle', as read from pulpits and office-books. A frontier has been passed between two great categories of medieval record. How could we make this transition, when the demarcation was so clear at the start? The ingredients of an answer are all in our possession and, when made up, will make a useful guide for what lies ahead.

The law-courts in their own way, with their own configuration of priorities and procedures, sought to establish one kind of historical truth. It was the truth courts needed to uphold their idea of justice, giving each his due. The miracle writers did the same. But they did so within *their* configuration of priorities and procedures, and on another register of justice. At bottom, for all the differences of idiom and context, the authors of both narrative genres—for both were that, the 'one-liner' of the English eyre rolls no less than the tellers of religious tales—understood themselves as historical. Both affected to tell objective truths about the past. While that claim aspires to strength it also carries an obligation. Someone who pretends to speak the truth about the past must be ready for challenge, and fight it off by appeal to the evidence he shares with his attackers. The minds that shaped both legal and religious records faced the challenge. On the forensic side, the retreat of ordeal before juries and inquisitions, and the burgeoning of appeal systems in all courts, were developments mirrored, in the alternative world of religion, by a growing fastidiousness, born of competition and a desire for order, in the recognition of saints and the critique of their miracles. So while each genre, legal and religious, remains distinct, and while the pattern of impulses behind each obeyed its own geometry, some of their deepest assumptions were shared. As the Tolentino hearing

---

[40] *Mirac. s. Petri Martyris*, § 74; *Acta sanctorum*, April 3 (1675), 709A: 'Mulier quaedam apud Genuam, instigante diabolo, prae desperatione quadam, in domo proprio, clauso ostio, manibus propriis se suspendit, et per magnam horam ut mortua ad trabem pependit. Dum autem a quibusdam a vicinis quaereretur, et ad ostium pulsantibus, nullum daretur responsum; per rimiculas respicientes, viderunt eam in trabe suspensam. Per violentiam igitur irrumpentes, fune abscisso eam omnino mortuam repererunt.' Cf. Trier, Stadtbibl., MS 1168/470, fol. 149r ('desperatione *die* quadam'). Goodich, 81, dates the event to 1317.

demonstrated, the procedures they used for working out those assumptions could at certain points be indistinguishable.

That is the lesson of the last two examples, a lesson incidental to what they have revealed about suicide in Italy. It is a lesson to keep in mind as we move more completely into the looking-glass world, leaving in the clouded distance the one we have come from. That is what we now do, as our search for fugitives turns away from court records to explore a third large sector of the written legacy, miracles.

12

Man, Woman, and Child

> This little ship, my spirit, hoists its sail
> To run through kindlier waters now; my ship,
> Which leaves that harsh sea in its trail.
>
> Dante, *Purgatorio*, 1: 1–3.[1]

PASSING from Hell to Purgatory, our guide, Dante, knew he had much pain still to witness, but it was pain transformed by hope.

Medieval chronicles only mentioned suicide, exceptional circumstances apart, in proportion as the chronicle lost its character, and took on that of two other types of historical source, respectively legal and religious. Legal sources formed the next category after chronicles to be combed for traces of suicide. It is now time to turn to the third. I called this one 'religious' sources, and it consists mainly of stories with a miraculous element. The reader can share Dante's relief. As a rule, judicial records were about dead people, miraculous literature about living. Miracles told, in general, of people who had had grim experiences but had survived, and whose exploits were publicized so that others could be saved that way too. So stories with unhappy endings are now the exception. There are still a few, but death and disaster are not the focus of this literature. They form instead distinct zones round its edge, so that their victims, while serving as warnings, are denied the kind of psychological elaboration which, applied to the survivors, is the primary contribution of the genre. The next three chapters, but for that exception, will therefore be happier than the last, the waters still rough and with a few casualties, but the sea less cruel.

Miracle Stories as a Literary Genre

A word more is due, first, about miraculous writing as a genre. Of the two broad traditions into which it divides the first is associated with the saint's *Life*. This was a literary form related distantly to classical biography and

---

[1] 'Per correr miglior acque alza le vele / omai la navicella del mio ingegno, / che lascia dietro a sé mar sì crudele.'

immediately to the needs of the Christian liturgy. In the early Middle Ages, at a time when Latin Europe had almost no other literature, monastic calendars would mark the day dedicated to this or that saint as it came round, year after year; and as appendices—sometimes in the form of marginalia, but increasingly as separate documents—there grew a body of writing to explain who each saint was and what he had done. The literature thus formed came to be used especially for reading aloud during monastic devotions, notably at the night office: they were 'fit to be read', in Latin, the gerundive *legenda*. That was not the only way the genre was nourished but it was an important one, and thus guaranteed its existence. The genre got a momentum which took it far from anything we would call historical. Those well-known stories of St Laurence's gridiron, for instance, and of St Catherine's wheel or St Sebastian's arrows, are most unlikely to have been historically true. Hagiographers (*hagios*: saint; *graphia*: writing) gave themselves the kind of licence claimed today by novelists. If the character was right, well, all sanctity came from Jesus anyway, so why should any saint's life differ much from that ideal? And there were, of course, plenty of miracles to show that holiness was effective, miracles mostly of healing, but a few of other kinds too.[2]

For all its autonomous momentum, and like all literary forms, hagiography responded to the influences of each age it passed through. Sometimes, and always more in some circles than in others, the dominant factor in shaping a *Life* was the Ideal Type. When it is, the historian can use the result rather as he might use imaginative literature, keeping his eye more on the author than on what he is talking about. Other milieux were more interested in observed reality. Then, the *Vita* had to come to terms with people's actual memories of a saint's activities, or of events they assigned to his influence after his death. This sort of realism obtained briefly in the ninth century, and more consistently in and after the late twelfth when, for various institutional reasons, standards of verification tightened up. The historian can then profitably search a story for its historical substratum. How much of that there is, in proportion to how much embellishment or hyperbole, will depend on judgement in each case. Specialists can dispute finer boundaries. The important fact remains that we do not have to believe all the miracles, or indeed any of them, to put them to use as ways in to the

---

[2] The best introduction remains R. Aigran, *L'hagiographie. Ses sources, ses méthodes, son histoire* (Paris, 1953). Legendary tendencies, gridirons, etc., are the subject of H. Delehaye, *Les légendes hagiographiques* (Brussels, 1927). Relation to folklore: H. Günter, *Die christliche Legende des Abendlandes* (Heidelberg, 1910). Recent literature: G. Philippart, *Les légendiers latins et autres manuscrits hagiographiques*. Typologie des Sources du Moyen Âge Occidental, Fasc. 24–5 (Turnhout, 1977; Mise à Jour, 1985); and J. Dubois and J.-L. Lemaître, *Sources et méthodes de l'hagiographie médiévale* (Paris, 1993).

world they were set in, a day-to-day world to which entrances are all the more welcome because it is largely closed to other kinds of document.

The story of Giacomuccio Fattaboni, told in the last chapter, illustrates this. It was not part of a *Life,* but it was material collected towards the writing of a *Life*, material of a type well-represented from the thirteenth century onwards. Giaccomuccio's story itself encapsulates many of the features common to hagiographers, all the more clearly because its link with canonization is so overt, for pressures were put on the whole genre by competition to get saints into the liturgy. That was what canonization was essentially about. These pressures fostered, in writers, a creative tension between ideal and actual, and spurred them to productivity. This was considerable. Altogether, over 28,000 saints' *Lives* survive, not all yet printed. Among their paramount advantages, for present purposes, is that they stretch from one end to the other of the Middle Ages. Like those French seigneurs and German archbishops, miracle stories help define the medieval period. The genre gathered strength as the Roman Empire declined, and was still flourishing, in new circumstances, in the fifteenth century. Then it more or less stopped. Luther said *legendae* were really *lügende* (liars). In the face of this challenge, the Counter-Reformation became less eager to continue the genre than to do a huge stocktaking of the *corpus* it had so far produced, much of it suddenly an embarrassment. One result, due especially to a group of historically minded Jesuits known thenceforth as the Bollandists (after Jean Bollande, one of them), was the preparation of critical editions of the mass of *Lives*. Only in the last thirty years of the present century, at last, have the postures of Reformation and Counter-Reformation relaxed enough for academic historians to recognize this evidence for the thesaurus it is, especially for social historians and their kindred. The late Frantiçek Graus, in Prague; Jacques Le Goff, Jean-Claude Schmitt, and their school in Paris; and others in England, America, and elsewhere, have begun putting this mass of material to good account.[3]

But I said there were two traditions in miracle literature. The second centres less on the saint's *Life* than on the *exemplum*. The *exemplum* is the invisible medieval ghost present when we write 'e.g.': '*exempli gratia*: for the sake of example'. It is a ghost mainly, this time, of the later Middle Ages, from the thirteenth century on, and in particular of literature generated to help preachers. The *exemplum* was a story told to illustrate a moral point.

---

[3] F. Graus, *Volk, Herrscher und Heiliger im Reich der Merowinger* (Prague, 1965); P. Assion, 'Die Mirakel Literatur als Forschungsgegenstand', *Zeitschrift fur Kulturgeschichte*, 50 (1968), 172–80. Le Goff and Schmitt: see next note. A recent contribution, with a guide to the growing bibliography, is T. Head, *Hagiography and the Cult of Saints. The Diocese of Orleans, 800–1200* (Cambridge, 1990).

Strictly, this meant it was the only 'story' that could with propriety be told, at least in writing. Mere anecdote, after all, belongs to tittle-tattle of the wicked world. It is immoral. But such is the human urge to tell stories, with or without moral, that the *exemplum* became the vehicle for much contemporary narrative which would otherwise have been judged not worth recording.[4] Here, the rules for miracles were less strict than in the saint's *Life*. Many *exempla* do happen to contain miracles. At times they overlap in character with those collections of a saint's posthumous miracles, which formed Book III of a *Life*, and were told one by one. Collections of *exempla* can indeed have the word 'miracles' in the title. But that was partly to win readers. *Exempla* are wider-ranging than *miracula*, and the boundaries of the genre can indeed be bafflingly vague, some stories being borrowed from classical or Arabic sources, or both, and some belonging to the world of fable or even folklore, then being barely disguised illustrations of values different, or indeed opposite, to those of Christian theology. The bulk of *exempla* are nevertheless of a broadly similar character, which can be called moral-historical. 'I heard recently of a woman who . . .'; 'In France not long ago there was a man who . . .'; 'In the time of King Phillip it was said that . . .', a narrator will begin. Whatever the historical basis of each *exemplum*, it is more or less embellished and given a moral point. In some, hyperbole gives the account a miraculous character. The death of Giacomuccio was again an example (if, that is, we think his attempted suicide never actually succeeded). In others, elements in the account are shifted to make it a 'better story'. A study of these elements will help us judge the story's historical value. In general, in doing that, I shall hold a principle to be justified as we go along: 'good story: bad history' and 'bad story: good history'.

These two categories, hagiography and *exempla*, have been grouped together here as 'religious sources'. They obeyed, or were meant to obey, narrative criteria set by Christian doctrine, and most have a miraculous element. The adjective 'religious' is deliberately loose because the category was loose. We first glimpsed it, in fact, from over the uncertain frontier it shared with chronicles. A few of the seventy-odd 'religious' stories to be told here could equally well, by contrast, have been included as 'chronicles'. Meanwhile the Giacomuccio story marked the boundary *miracula* shared with court records. All categorization creates these problems. Lack of precise definition is one too small to mar the utility of making the distinction I have proposed here.

---

[4] In general: J. T. Welter, *L'Exemplum dans la littérature religieuse et didactique du moyen âge* (Paris, 1927). Recent literature: C. Bremond, J. Le Goff, and J.-C. Schmitt, *L' "exemplum"*. Typologie des Sources du Moyen Âge Occidental, Fasc. 40 (Turnhout, 1982); and J. Berlioz and M.-A. Polo de Beaulieu, eds., *Les 'Exempla' médiévaux* (Carcassonne, 1992).

Even from what has been said so far, it will be clear that these religious sources approach suicide from a perspective of their own, complementary to that of legal. We saw some of it at the start of Chapter 3. Legal sources characteristically began with a dead body; religious, with a survivor. So legal sources beheld the suicidal act from the outside; religious, from the inside. Legal sources, for the same reason, were mostly about completed suicides; religious, about attempts and thoughts. Legal sources were particular about dates, places, names, and monetary wealth; religious sources about motive and personal circumstance. Compiled by different sorts of writer, for different purposes, the two types of evidence stood, finally, in different relationships to historical reality. Legal documents were written to convince officials of the facts of one case, religious narrative to give plausibility to a moral principle. Legal documents were distorted, when they were distorted, by pressures from a coercive governmental system; religious, by infection from folklore and other narrative traditions. The two types of document, in consequence, have had opposite fortunes from recent critical scholarship. Judicial records, despite flaunted precision, have been found to hide make-believe; miracle stories, despite apparent fantasy, to include probable fact. These differences are what offer the historian his opportunity. He can combine information from the two sides. Because the two genres have different perspectives and chronological profiles, the historian can add their lessons together and then, adding both, jointly, to those learned from the chronicles, build a more reliable picture of suicide than he could have had from any one type of source alone. Implicit in the next three chapters, this advantage will come into the open in Chapters 15 and 16.

We turn, then, to look at medieval suicides through a new kind of optical glass. Mindful of the evidence taken earlier from law courts, I shall present the following *miracula* thematically. They will come in three main groups according to the main apparent motive for the suicide or suicide attempt. First, in this chapter, will come those arising from dislocation in family or erotic relationships. These will be followed in Chapter 13 by the suicidal crises of persons who have become acutely poor, or have made themselves in some other way 'marked men'. Third, in Chapter 14, I shall consider suicidal acts triggered off by illness or pure melancholy. If the present chapter is much the biggest of the three (indeed the biggest in the book) that fact alone says something of the interest listeners had in the relationships which it will illustrate. Within the chapter that lesson will be underlined by special studies of three 'best-seller' stories, each within this triangle of relationships, and all destined to be among the most widely known of any in the last two or three medieval centuries.

Before approaching the first 'best-seller' let us look at some humbler *miracula* on related themes.

Mothers and Newly Born Children

The first group of these concerns the bond of mother and child. The bond may be the strongest of all human bonds, and if it is, it follows that its disturbance can be traumatic to either party and in extremes drive either to suicide. In surviving documents it is the mother's problem we are more likely to read of and it is duly there, in a small cluster of *miracula*. My first example illustrates the problem known to modern doctors as 'post-natal depression'. Suicidal acts with this origin are all but absent from medieval *miracula*. But that they could have happened, and might in different literary conditions have beaten their way into the genre, is suggested by the one exception I know of. Let us hear the story first, and then discover what is exceptional about it, and what it teaches.

The miracle comes in a collection begun in 1482 at the monastery of St Gall, now in Switzerland, and twice revised from a written memorandum during the next three decades. The record names both the mother, 'Anna Zipperlin', and a number of relations and others whom locals could have identified. Soon after Anna had given birth, the writer says, her family and her midwife became anxious for Anna's mental stability, and resolved that a watch be kept in her room. So her husband and the midwife established themselves there to be ready for any emergency. In the depths of the night the husband was woken by a noise from the mother's and child's bed. He thought the mother might have hurt the child and rushed towards the bed in the blackness. His groping hands found the baby safe, but the mother not: she had hanged herself, his hands told him, from the superstructure of the bed, and with a sash. The husband tore the sash away and took his wife's body down, still alive. Then he and the midwife, by now wide awake, made the distraught mother eat something while they tried to calm her down. As they talked the mother hid a knife under her clothes, so that the husband had to intervene again to make her give the weapon up. After more discussion, all three got down on their knees and offered prayers and a vow to the Virgin Mary 'at St Gall'. The woman at once grew calmer, and days afterwards, the husband went to St Gall with an offering and the sash, and gave the story to the abbey's registrar of miracles. The page on which the registrar took it down was fastened to a pillar near the shrine, whence it passed, via revisions, into the abbey's permanent repertoire.[5]

Could this sort of thing—a suicide attempt during post-natal depres-

---

[5] Signori, 'Aggression und Selbstzerstörung', 117–23. Prof. Signori prints the text from the MSS in Stiftsarchiv St. Gallen, Bände 388b (no. 428) and C 389 (no. 238, 182 f) (pp. 117–18 and 123 n. 28), credibly reconciles the three versions, and assesses the evidence from a medical angle.

sion—have happened earlier in the Middle Ages and not been caught up in a miracle story? It is easy to suggest a reason why the record, not the event, may have been the exception. Right at the end of the Middle Ages, in southern Germany, conditions were edging *miracula* ever further into the verisimilitude we saw at Tolentino but with one fruitful difference. In a canonization process, miracle-smiths had to meet the tight critical standards of a quasi-inquisitorial court. Those of the abbeys, by contrast—ancient abbeys besieged, like those we met in the Île de France two centuries earlier, by thrusting towns, and resorting for defence to *miracula* as their tried cultural resource—did their own quality control. Yes, the abbeys had to convince a possibly sceptical public. But their procedures were less formal, so there was less red tape, so more miracles got in. The miracles ranged, as a consequence, more widely across the spectrum of domestic incidents. In a word, there might have *been* earlier suicidal acts prompted by post-natal depression, but ones never thus recorded.

A second theme touching mothers and the newly born is meanwhile commoner. It is that of the dead child, especially the overlain baby. Unlike the last, this theme enjoys examples over a wide chronological range. There is a hint of it in the late ninth-century Franconian *Life of St Walpurga*, where a woman sees three of her young children successively carried off by disease, and 'for grief she turned her wild eyes upon herself, calling repeatedly for the same death that had borne away her dear ones, to come to her, too.' Before she can harm herself she is alerted to the miraculous powers of St Walpurga.[6]

A more explicitly suicidal story is one told in the eleventh century of St Melanius of Rennes, in Brittany. This early bishop of Rennes had died around the year 530, but survived in the memory of the Rennes abbey of St Melaine. At a date probably just after the millennium a monk of that monastery updated an account of the saint's miracles and added one of his own, told to him, his claim ran, by monks of his own monastery, allegedly present.[7]

[6] *Mir. s. Waldburgis Monheimensis*, ed. A. Bauch, *Ein bayerisches Mirakelbuch aus der Karolingerzeit* (Regensburg, 1979), bk 2, ch. 4, p. 216. 12–14: 'Pro dolor, tum mater torvis luminibus semetipsam aspiciens et eandem, quae cara pignora tulerant, mortem sibi saepius imprecans . . .' That overlying was a current problem is clear from the humane penitential recommendations of Ratramnus of Corbie: G. Schmitz, 'Schuld und Strafe. Eine unbekannte Stellungnahme des Ratramnus von Corbie zur Kindertötung', *Deutsches Archiv*, 38 (1982), 363–87, esp. 386–7.
[7] The miracle is printed as *Aliud miraculum auctore Anonymo monacho* appended to the *Vita sancti Melanii* in *Acta sanctorum*, Jan. 1 (1643), 328–34, on p. 334. I have accepted the Bollandists' attribution to a monk of S. Melaine. Other texts relating to St Melanius: J.-C. Poulin, 'Sources hagiographiques de la Gaule' (= SHG) Part 3: 'Les dossiers des saints Mélaine, Conwoion et Mervé (Province de Bretagne)', in M. Heinzelman, ed., *Manuscrits hagiographiques et travail des hagiographes*. Beihefte der *Francia*, 24 (Sigmaringen, 1992),

Here it is. One Saturday a citizen of Rennes had taken his son to bathe in the river Vilaine. On hearing the bell of S. Melaine sound for church, the father had left the boy playing and gone to church. Afterwards the boy was missed, and his mother launched a search. The boy was found drowned; as his body was drawn from the water the mother's grief rose to such a pitch that she fainted. She recovered from her fit, but that night,

as her servants [*famuli*] kept the customary vigil by the body, the mother, overcome by the weight of her grief, and as if impelled by the furies of malign spirits, stole away from the throng and ran towards the river Vilaine not far away, to throw herself in as if she did not wish to survive her dead son.

She was followed, stopped, led back home by prudent neighbours, and guarded by her own family until next day. This was Sunday. As the abbey bell of S. Melaine sounded again for Sunday Mass (where 'abbot Triscandus was to celebrate Mass as usual'), the mother 'came to herself'. Persuading the servants to let her take the boy's body to S. Melaine and lay it before the altar, she knelt next to the body, and besought the saint to restore him to life. The saint did so.

The same pattern of events recurs in miracles from both the following two centuries. In the *Life* of St Antelm, bishop of Bellay (†1178), a mother lost a baby and likewise 'wished to kill herself', until the child was revived by a posthumous miracle of the saint.[8] More dramatic descriptions of the motif occur in the posthumous miracles of St Edmund Rich of Abingdon, Oxford scholar and archbishop of Canterbury.[9] The collection was made soon after Edmund's death in 1240, and its anonymous author gives special attention to incidents at or near the saint's tomb at Pontigny, the Cistercian abbey near Auxerre. He represents all the miracles as recent. Two miracles concern overlain children. In one, a mother is named as 'Ersandis', wife of David of Aureoles, a nearby village. While nursing her 1-year-old daughter Bertula, Ersandis fell asleep and lay on the child. The alarm was raised by the child's grandmother (Ersandis's own mother), who had been elsewhere in the house and was puzzled that the child had stopped crying, and went

119–60. In my attempt to date 'Aliud miraculum' I have been guided by Poulin's dating of the *Vita interpolata*, (pp. 147–8). An early ninth-century *Life* of St Melanius includes his resuscitation of a child who has hanged himself (*Vita Prima S. Melanii*, ch. 16), thought, however, by Poulin (p. 133) and others to be a direct borrowing from Sulpicius Severus' *Vita Martini*, ch. 8.

[8]   *Vita beati Antelmi*, § 48 (ed. J. Picard (Bellay, 1978), 37.17): 'et seipsam necare volens'.

[9]   *Vita et miracula s. Eadmundi cantuarensis archiepiscopi*, in MS Oxford, Bodleian, Fell 2, pp. 1–44. Context: C. H. Lawrence, *St Edmund of Abingdon* (London, 1960), 1–105. Cf. R. C. Finucane, *Miracles and Pilgrims* (London, 1977), 93, 137–9, 242. Vauchez, *Sainteté*, 550, 553, finds a multiplication after 1300 of miracles concerning overlaying, but I have met no more which involve the threat of suicide.

to look. She woke Ersandis, who looked down, too late, to see her baby dead. Ersandis tried to revive it but eventually laid the dead baby down in despair and,

gulping down her tears in the violence of her grief, she ran this way and that, shrieking and crying out that she was the most wretched and unlucky of women.

After more barren efforts Ersandis burst out: 'O unhappy woman that I am! What a curse and disgrace have fallen upon me!' And the account goes on:

She tried to speak further and recover her courage. But at the instigation of the Enemy of the Human Race, and because of her extreme misery, she fell into the pit of despair. Adding sins to sins she resolved to drown herself, and so to end her shame, making her last deeds worse than her first. So she tried to fulfil this terrible resolve. But her mother held her back, saying 'O how unhappy I am, my daughter. What are you planning to do? If you go ahead, then let me warn that I shall die with you. Then—think of that—you will make yourself guilty of matricide.'

As the speaker, we might add, of blackmail. Luckily, in the midst of this chorus a thought came 'by divine will' into the grandmother's head, that the dead child should be dedicated to St Edmund. So she and her daughter went back to the corpse, fell to the ground beside it, and in tears begged St Edmund to resuscitate the child. They added 'if you do not call the girl back to life we shall kill ourselves.' This line of threat appears to have been a family characteristic. Despite it, the saint did what he was asked and the two women promptly took the child to the tomb at Pontigny to show recognition.[10]

---

[10] MS Fell 2, pp. 28a–29a: 'Christi bonus odor in omni loco beatus Eadmundus novis atque mundo insolitis coruscat miraculis vitalium mellifluis, prout in Bertula unius anni puella sequentia declarabunt. Nam cum mater eius Ersandis nomine uxor David de Aureoles, quadam nocte filiam suam ante lectum suum in cuius vagientem lactaret, dormitando expansis brachiis super lactantem toto atque corpore inclinato in profundum sompnum relapsa obdormitavit atque sic accumbens super faciem filie sue oppressit. Cumque mater opprimentis Ysabella nomine intelligeret atque videret filiam suam negligenter agere, non modicum admiratur eo quod vagitus infantis nec vocem lactantis, prout consueverat audire, non audiret. Unde timens atque tremens extensis auribus ascultavit si vox vel sonus evigilantis, vel perpendiculum dormientis mulieris insonuisset. Et cum diutissime more dispendio summum silentium tenerent omnia in domo, eadem Ysabella, inmenso horrore arrepta, suspicabatur atque merito timuit per negligentiam filie sue aliquid novi atque insoliti accidisse. Propter quod de lecto consurgens sed / [col. b] attonita, filiam suam Ersandis invenit accumbantem, super puellulam iam oppressam. Quam voce clamosa excitavit atque ingemiscens ait illi: 'Surge, surge, filia, ecce filiam tuam oppressisti'. Ipsa vero a sompno excitata repperit filiam suam mole corporis sui oppressam. Que cum conspiceret corpus exanime extunc anima eius in amaritudine constituitur. Palpatoque vultum puelle invenit eam absque flatu vitali atque oculos signa mortue praeferentes. Tunc ambe mulieres ammotis panniculis, quibus dum oppressa est erat involuta, eam sollerter intuentes atque studiose contractantes, reperiunt corpus frigidum, menbra rigida, nervos poplitum contractos, atque utpote in mortuo rigidos, obduratos, et, ut brevius dicam, totum sine spiraculo vite. Mater vero arripiens corpus exanime in ulnas, satagit sedulitate materna corpus alere atque casso conatu corpus mortuum

The same collection tells a comparable story of the death of an older child, also near Pontigny. An unnamed mother and daughter went to drink at a well. The mother left the daughter beside the well while she herself went to fetch a vessel to drink from. In her absence the daughter fell into the well, and returning to discover the accident the mother shrieked 'and as if possessed by fury tried to throw herself into the well so that she might die with her daughter. But other women successfully restrained her.' A strong youth arrived on the scene and offered to help, lending persuasive asymmetry to the story because, unlike the heroines, he is named (as 'Theobald'), and also because we are told he had been at a tavern, and went about his task clumsily. That detail adds nothing to the force of the narrative. It therefore invokes the rule 'bad story: good history'. By the use of ropes, Theobald eventually raised the girl to ground level, apparently dead, but a prayer to St Edmund brought her back to life.

At the beginning of this section I said that when the mother–child relationship was badly disturbed it was the mother's woe we were likely to hear about. Yet psychologists might say it is the child who is the more vulnerable, even though—doubtless partly because—its troubles are less likely to be noticed. Our handful of cases bears this out. Of suicidal episodes involving a mother–child crisis, in only one is it a child who despairs, but here the child goes through with it, and kills himself. There is no miracle.

The incident occurs in the Life of St Margaret of Cortona. Margaret died in 1297, after twenty-five years as a Franciscan 'penitent'. She lived in Cortona, thirteen miles south of Arezzo, and worked miracles, assiduously collected by the Franciscans who had known her, especially when, in 1308,

ad vitam revocare. Cumque conperisset se inutiliter laborasse, proiecit parvam atque doloris vehementia lacrimas absorbente huc illucque discurrit eiulans, seque miseram atque infelicem vociferans. Sicque secundo atque tercio hoc idem cura corpus, absque profectum studiosius egit. Sciens demum atque certior effecta, quia humana sedulitas sitie sue non nullo ullatenus posset subvenire, decidit a sua spe, unde in talia verba prorumpit dicens: 'Heu me miseram, quomodo data sum hodie inproperium atque obprobrium.' Cumque hoc dixisset voluit adicere amplius ut resurgeret, set instigante humani generis inimico lapsa est in foveam desperationis pre dolore atque tristicia que enim peccata peccatis adiciendo voluit se submergere, atque sic / [p. 29a] suo opprobrio finem inponere, atque novissima sua facere peiora prioribus. Que statim arrepto itinere, voluit illud nefandissimum quod conceperat perpetrare. Set mater sua illam detinuit, dixit atque ei: 'O me miseram, filia mea, quid est quod vis agere? Scias si hoc egeris ego tecum moriar, atque sic eris matricidali polluti contagio.' Ipsis vero simul contristantibus, atque inter se talia conferentibus, venit nutu divino matris in mentem, ut santo Eadmundi de Pontiniaco infantem voveret. Dixit atque filie sue. 'Adhuc nobis superest unicum remedium but videlicet puellam sancto Eadmundo commendamus quo puella per merita ipsius vite redimata, a tantis miseriis atque angustiis liberemur.' Revertentes itaque ad puellam corruerunt in terram iuxta corpus flentes atque dicentes, sancte Eadmunde ne permittas nos hodie perire. Nam si puellam istam ad vitam non revocaveris, nos ipsas interficiemus. Cumque ita clamassent misertus earum sanctus infantem vite restituit.' The story told in the following paragraph here will be found in the same manuscript, pp. 35b–36a, the suicidal episode on p. 35b: 'et tanquam furore arepta, voluit se in puteum proicere, ubi una cum filia sua moraretur. Set mulieribus renitentibus non ita factum est . . .'

Cortona began a successful campaign to get a bishopric of its own. One miracle, long displayed on the wall of the town's main church, showed Margaret rescuing a suicide, and we shall consider it in Chapter 14. But a citizen who had *read* the Life of Margaret—as distinct from looking at the public-relations version on the church walls—would have seen that her dealings with suicide were far from exhausted by that edifying miracle.

Margaret's own son had killed himself. She had not always been a saint. Born near Arezzo, she had become at the age of sixteen the mistress of a local nobleman and had born him a son. After nine years the nobleman had died, and Margaret had undergone what her biographer presents as a religious conversion, moving to Cortona to live near the Franciscan convent there. That was in 1272. Margaret was about 25. On settling in Cortona she made arrangements for her son—who cannot have been more than nine— to be schooled in Arezzo, and make the thirteen-mile journey to lodge and eat with his mother. This arrangement may itself have been a challenge to the boy, but it was not his main problem. Margaret's confessor-biographer not only says she left the boy in 'extreme poverty', but that her death-to-the world had caused her 'to put off her maternal affections, and be as if she had never had a son.' Her 'withdrawal of maternal care' (to use yet another of the biographer's expressions) thus left her son effectively an orphan. One day someone in his Arezzo school noticed he was not there, and a search was made in the school, and in other Arezzo schools. Then a messenger was sent to his mother to see if he had gone home to her, but he had not. Finally the boy was found drowned in a well, with every sign that he had thrown himself in 'through an excess of grief'.

We saw in Chapter 4 that Arezzans had a reputation for choosing wells as their method of suicide. The verisimilitude of the account is further enhanced by what it says of Margaret's reaction to the news, which was announced to Margaret by her son's discontented schoolmaster, who had come for his pay. He chose a moment when some Franciscans were in earshot, whose embarrassing presence he might well have spared her. But on hearing of her son's death Margaret said nothing. The schoolmaster could get no response at all. Gradually he grew abusive, not without gentle remonstrance from the Franciscans. Later, when it was a question of getting Margaret canonized, her biographer, who had been present, would represent Margaret's silence on that occasion as a virtue, in that it showed Margaret's 'constancy' that she would not reply to men, only to God. Neither Margaret nor, apparently, her biographer showed further interest in the boy's fate, a fate itself easier for modern minds to understand in the light of these reactions. It is fair to add that this all happened just after the 25-year-old Margaret's 'conversion', and the death of her lover. By the time of her own death, another 25 years later, everyone agreed Margaret had become a model of penance, for personal sins she saw as innumerable and immeasurable; and perhaps that of having been an appalling mother was among them.[11]

Family Murder

The three miracles just told concern the suicidal impulses of mothers suddenly robbed of their children. A further pair of *exempla* belong beside them only on the grounds that in each a parent's suicide, this time completed, follows at once on the death of the offspring. That the suicide is now accomplished is enough to show we are looking at a different kind of *exemplum*. It is one showing providential punishment. Nor is the parent here merely bereaved, since it is the parent who has done the killing, murdering the children before his or her own suicide.

Both *exempla* may refer to a historical incident. In the first, in a late thirteenth-century English collection, a certain woman was lying sleepless in bed beside her husband. He asked what anxiety it was that kept her awake. She said she had been accessory to the murder of her own mother, and had never been able to bring herself to reveal this in confession, so dreadful was the crime. 'But you have had so many good priests in this diocese, why could you not have confessed to one of them?' asked her husband. 'How could I confess such a dreadful thing to people I saw every day?' she replied, expressing a reservation commonly felt at that date. Her husband suggested an equally common remedy: 'you could confess to the friars.' She went on resisting her husband's advice, and one day in Lent, having arranged for her husband to go off to their fields to inspect the sheep, she took a razor, cut the throats of her three young daughters, the youngest still in the cradle, and then cut her own. Her husband came back to see the bloodbath 'which is still spoken of in that neighbourhood'.[12]

This last remark raises the question of historicity. The source of the *exem-*

[11] *Vita b. Margaritae de Cortona*, auct. F. Iuncta Bevagnate, ch. 2, § 26; *Acta sanctorum*, Feb. III (Antwerp, 1658), 300–57, on pp. 304–5, the suicide on pp. 304E–F: 'narratum est quod filius eius ab ea in extrema paupertate relictus, cui maternas subtraxerat manus, se in quemdam puteum Aretinum prae nimietate tristi-/[F] tiae suffocaret.' On the legend and murals: J. Cannon 'Marguérite et les Cortonais: iconographie d'un "culte civique" au xive siècle' in A. Vauchez, ed., *La religion civique à l'époque médiévale et moderne (Chrétienté et Islam)* (Rome, 1995), 403–13.

[12] *Speculum laicorum*, § 134; ed. J. Welter (Paris, 1914), p. 30. In one fifteenth-century version the woman kills both her parents. For this and other traditions: J. A. Herbert, *Catalogue of Romances in the Department of MSS in the British Museum*, 3 (1910), pp. 381 no. 134, and 681 no. 59. F. C. Tubach, *Index exemplorum* (Helsinki, 1969), no. 1192. That the story ends 'usque hodie in partibus illis permanet publicatum' is one of the considerations suggesting it must have been conceived as occurring a few years before the time of writing.

plum is the *Speculum laicorum*, an English collection destined for sermons to the laity. The compiler deliberately hid his identity, but the prominence of stories about Franciscans, stories largely coming from eastern England, especially Kent, lifts his disguise, and he has generally been identified as John of Hoveden. The mention of Pecham as archbishop of Canterbury also gives a date-bracket to the compilation, of 1279 to 1292.[13] The *exemplum* just quoted was one of many circulating at that time on the subject of confession, and was destined to be copied in later medieval collections, with or without the addition of narrative polish. Even in its primitive form, as a horror story, it lacks the kind of narrative protuberance which I have suggested as one sign of historicity. But it has other marks. Its earliest form is consistent with an oral source, as if told to a priest by the husband of the main character. It is carefully placed 'in the vicinity of Bury St Edmund's' and its approximate dating, to the late 1240s or 1250s, rests both on the date and phraseology of the text, and on a mention of mendicant friars at Bury. As a criminal 'horror' it is not unlike some we have already seen in court records, and is of a kind that would have got into them if records were complete. It happens that Eyres did reach that part of Suffolk at more than one appropriate date between 1240 and 1268, and it might be asked why their surviving records contain no mention of this crime. There are two answers. These records are very fragmentary, only one roll (that of the 1251 eyre) being both complete and containing the Crown pleas which would have covered such a multiple murder and suicide. Second, if the case occurred within the liberty of St Edmund's abbey, as much suggests it did, it would have escaped Crown records altogether. On balance, therefore, there is no reason why the narrator's pretence of historicity should not be taken at face value.[14]

The second *exemplum* on this theme comes in the same collection. This time it gives no hint of its date or place, though another *exemplum* near it is put in 'Kent in the time of Henry III'. So the same time-bracket, and a geographical origin somewhere in eastern England, could equally well apply. The moral here is about not confession but drunkenness.

A certain man [the *exemplum* runs] went home from a tavern very drunk, and found his wife and two young boys sitting by the fireside. But he thought he saw four boys and asked his wife who, or whose, the two were who were not his own. She said

---

[13] J. Welter, *L'Exemplum* (Paris-Toulouse, 1927), pp. vii–viii, xx.

[14] Eyres: D. Crook, *Records of the General Eyre* (London, 1982), index of places, under 'Cattishall'. Eyres were held in Cambridgeshire in 1240, 1245, 1251, 1257, 1261, and 1268, though Bury St Edmund's had immunity from them. Dr Summerson has sent me the transcript of a further copy of the story from British Library, MS Royal 7 D 1, fol. 70r, saying he had failed to find any trace of it in the rolls. Cf. p. 434 (first two entries) below.

there were only two there, and both his. He replied 'you are lying, they are children of your adultery.' So he began to beat her, and he beat her to death. When she was dead he also killed the boys whom he thought were not his own. Afterwards, when he had digested his drink somewhat, he came back to his senses and, seeing his wife and children dead, fell into despair and took a rope and hanged himself.[15]

There are of course many cases of male suicide in our legal dossier, originating in eyres in eastern England in Henry III's reign. But none of them do, and none of them would, give details allowing the identification of this particular tragedy. So we are left, again, with the possibility that the *exemplum* represents a real incident whose circumstances survived only in anecdote, repeated among the friars who heard confessions.

These two accounts have been put here with the other four because they concerned a bereaved parent. But their narrative form has its own peculiarities, attaching to a different literary habitat, as moral *exempla* rather than a saint's miracles. So they are more likely to end badly. They also introduce, implicitly, a psychological factor important enough in this context to demand treatment on its own. It is the concept of suicide as the product of inexorable fate, which I plan to return to in my third volume.[16] The woman in the first *exemplum* had failed to confess an earlier sin: *this*—murder and suicide—was the fate that awaited her. The second links the tragedy similarly with drunkenness. In both, free will has been lost or weakened.

Meanwhile we turn to another category of family problem, a potential occasion for self-destruction. 'Family problem' may be putting it mildly, beside post-natal depression and overlaying. Medieval listeners rated these offences seriously, and as actually occurring. I refer to incest, abortion, and infanticide. It might be thought that the three do not go necessarily together, but they do in one suicide miracle. It is the first of what I called earlier the three 'best-seller' stories of this chapter, whose fortunes attest how widely the human situation concerned was recognized. It is the miracle of the woman infanticide. Like the last two it probably came from confession, or at least the culture of confessors, so it is time I said an explanatory word about that.

The Combined Dangers of Incest, Abortion, and Infanticide

Confession as a historical source had only become available in the thirteenth century. In theory, confession had been developing for centuries, and in some

[15] *Speculum laicorum*, ed. Welter, § 204 (chap. 29), p. 44.
[16] *The Mapping of Mental Desolation*, ch. 8.

areas had been actively practised during the twelfth. But an effective bid to make it universal had been growing only since *c*.1200. In 1215 the Fourth Lateran Council had cemented matters by declaring that everyone, male or female, had to make confession annually. The Council said that it was to one's own parish priest, not any priest at all, that confession should be made. But in practice the system could only be made to work when Dominican and Franciscan friars came to the priests' aid, soon after the Council. By the late 1220s the friars, with a reputation for confidentiality, theological knowledge, and high personal standards, were already popular as confessors.

Confession was meant to be secret. But active pastors who heard confessions also attended people in their crises and learned a lot about their emotional lives. It was in everyone's interest that they should, and that they share this knowledge with their colleagues. Friars had plenty of occasion for this sharing, since they walked rather than rode, and spent a long time travelling, between cities or to general chapters hundreds of miles apart, travelling in pairs with no rule of silence. One result was that they fed on a collective pastoral experience and recorded some of it, thinly disguised, in *exempla* and *miracula*. Miracle stories with this origin thus render accessible areas of emotional life otherwise elusive.[17]

It is thus no accident that it should be from the thirteenth century, not before, that we first get close-up pictures of a particular kind of female predicament: parentage of a baby that constitutes evidence of prohibited intercourse, of which the most severely prohibited was incest. Incest and suicide come together in the first of our 'best-seller' stories, a miracle attributed to the Virgin. It is illustrated in Plate 3, from Jean Miélot's *Miracles de Notre Dame*. That book was compiled around 1455, and I shall start by summarizing *its* version of the miracle. Miélot tells how a woman of noble birth, in Germany, had three children in succession by her uncle. Each time she went to a stable to give birth, and at once strangled the child and threw it in the privy. Gripped by melancholy, she swallowed three spiders, to kill herself (it was believed then that spiders were poisonous). Then she stabbed her chest with a knife. Feeling herself to be dying, she called on the Virgin, who appeared, made the woman make confession, and guided her into a Cistercian convent.

The wide circulation of that miracle, in other collections as well as Miélot's, has a historical lesson I have already drawn. But we are concerned here with the possible historicity of its central elements. As it stands, the miracle just told is remarkable for, on one hand, narrative polish, with its *three* illegitimate children in series; and on the other, anomaly, since there

---

[17] My 'Confession before 1215' and 'Confession as a historical source', esp. 289–94, argue these points more fully.

are two methods of attempting suicide, methods improbable as a pair. The first makes it too good a story. The second suggests it combines at least two others. Let us take a look at the possible incidents that may have lain behind it.

The first should be dated between the early 1220s and 1236, for the friar-confessor from whom the account came is said to be Brother Jordan of Saxony, pastorally active from about the former date and dead at the latter. Our earliest record of it was nevertheless written in 1260 or 1261, by Brother Gerard of Frachet. His *The Lives of the Brethren* is an approximate Dominican equivalent to the foundation histories of conventional monasteries. Since the Order of Preachers was anxious that the sanctity of its pioneers did not go unrecognized, Brother Gerard was given all the help he needed, so he could call on a big treasury of memories, his colleagues' as well as his own, to take him back to the early days of the Order.

The result was the following. It constitutes one chapter of the *Lives of the Brethren*:

A noble, and very beautiful, young lady was left by her father in the wardship of her maternal uncle. But she received corruption instead of instruction. Twice she was got with child, and on the uncle's persuasion procured an abortion [*procuravit aborsum*]. It happened a third time and, unable to resist her uncle, she fell into the pit of despair, not daring to reveal her crime to anyone. So she got a knife and stabbed herself, so hard as to rip open her stomach. Although in agony from her dreadful wound, she was visited by God's mercy and felt wholehearted compunction for her sin. Turning in tears to the Mother of Mercy, she begged that her customary pity might grant help, at least saving the young woman's soul from perishing with her body. The Virgin appeared at once, healed her wound, and told her to submit herself totally to the counsel of Master Jordan, who would shortly be coming that way. With the utmost devotion she did so. Subsequently she entered the Cistercian order, and persevered in it.[18]

That is fairly near the 'best-seller' version as told by Miélot. It lacks only the infanticide—abortion is not infanticide—and the spider. The spider is easy to find, for it comes in a second miracle in the same *Vitas fratrum*, nine chapters later. This one is about a recidivist, that is, one who sins repeatedly. Brother Gerard writes:

Constant recidivism, into grave sin, drove a certain woman downwards into despair, to the point of trying to kill herself by swallowing a poisonous spider. As death approached she felt compunction and began with tears to invoke the Mother of Mercy. Then she heard a voice telling her: 'Brother Jordan, Master of the Order of

---

[18] *Vitas Fratrum*, pt 3, ch. 26, ed. B. M. Reichert. Monumenta ordinis fratrum praedicatorum, 1 (Rome, 1897), 121–2.

Preachers, is on his way and indeed is here. So call on him, and say it was I who sent you. Confess to him and you will be saved.' The holy man came, the sinful woman made her confession, and vomited up, with her sins, both spider and poison together.[19]

It should be noted that this second story from *The Lives of the Brethren* divides its miraculous content into two parts. On one hand, the Virgin comes when called and gives prescient advice. On the other, the sacramental confession precipitates the spitting up of the poison. Confessional stories, especially from Dominican circles, often underlined the efficacy of the sacrament in this way, showing by an analogous 'miracle' the sacrament's cathartic, purgative quality. Here the feature may be read as a mark of possible historical authenticity, for it indicates that the account emerged from circles who heard confessions, and might thus have learned about this kind of experience.

Confession, then, left its stamp on these two *miracula*. How much so is shown when the stamp begins to erode, in versions further from the source. At about the time that Gerard wrote, a poetic version of both stories appeared in north-eastern France, in a collection with the potentially misleading title *Les Vies des Pères*. Its treatment of the events marks a first stage in the miracle's journey to the 'best-seller' version. The French poet merges the two stories and adjusts their emphasis. First, the recidivist in Gerard's Story 2 is identified with the incestuous niece in Story 1. This composite personage, after burying her third infant, attempts to poison herself with a spider, or rather with *three* spiders. She briefly thinks of hanging herself. But then, like the original niece, she also stabs herself in the stomach, the poet having to invent details which explain the two-stage attempt. At the point of death, the poet's heroine calls on the Virgin, who gives copious advice on the wrongness of despair. She then says Brother Jordan will soon be passing that way—proof that the source is still Dominican. The heroine is cured and, as in Gerard's Story 1, enters a Cistercian monastery.

This poetic version takes no fewer than 540 lines and adds numerous details, other than the two extra spiders. Among them we notice a shift of emphasis away from sacramental confession and towards the Virgin, and a monastery as source for the dying girl's cure. The Virgin does indeed recommend confession;[20] and the poet has the penitent tell Brother Jordan her

---

[19] Ibid., pt 1, ch. 37, ed. Reichert, 109.
[20] Paris, Bibl. Nat., MS fr. 1546, fol. 138ra: 'Tu ten iras ma douce amie / Tantost et te confesseras / Et le siecle deguerpiras / Et seras en religion / Pour avoir merci et pardon.' On the MS: J. C. Payen, *Le motif du repentir dans la littérature française du moyen âge, des origines à 1230*. Publications romanes et françaises, 18 (Paris, 1967), 519. Since I am concerned here

life-story *à la* confession, 'all in order, how she had murdered her three babies, how she had them of her uncle . . .' and so on.[21] But there is no hint of a sacrament with a miraculous cure attached. By contrast, it is explicitly the girl's entry into a religious order that constitutes the substantive agent of her cure.[22] The poetic version has thus jettisoned its direct Dominican imprint, and with it that warrant of authenticity which the imprint had given it. It has already become a 'good story'.

The first of even Gerard's two miracles may, in fact, have been part-way to becoming a 'good story' by the time he wrote it, for the woman had had three bastard babies. That number, as with the spiders in the poetic improvement, already smacks of improvement. So, while it is possible for a woman to have had three babies by incest, and to have aborted them all, it is rather *more* possible that narrative imagination had been at work in the forty years between the event (the 1220s or early 1230s: Brother Jordan's active dates) and the first prose record; and that the poet, by combining the niece and the recidivist and by removing the Dominican hallmark, has only taken matters further.

Let it be added, also by turning the *abortion* into *infanticide*, for in the poem the infanticide has already arrived. Since it would endure in the final version let us now look and see if it too may have had a historical origin. There can be no doubt about the place to look, for the poet has the composite event happen 'As I hear tell, in the country of Almaine, a land not far away, and in our own time'.[23] Brother Gerard's original does not say it happened in Germany, only that Brother Jordan of Saxony played a part in it; but we know that Brother Jordan's career was partly passed in Germany. So Germany it is. It happens that another *exemplum* about an incestuous, suicidal mother does involve infanticide, and does come from Germany, and does come, like the other two, adorned with marks of a friar-confessor as its source. This time it is also furnished with an approximate date: *c*.1258. The written source is an *exemplum* in Thomas of Chantimpré's *The Uni-*

---

only with the origins of the story I ignore later versions, notably a didactic French poem written in the second quarter of the fourteenth century by the *Jongleur* John of St Quentin. It is printed with commentary by J. Morawski, 'Mélanges de littérature pieuse, II: Les miracles en quatrains alexandrins monorimes', *Romania*, 65 (1939), 327–58; text on pp. 352–6; later and related versions, pp. 347–8. John of St Quentin expunges Brother Jordan altogether, perhaps more through oblivion than design (cf. Morawski, 337–8). The Cistercian role is maintained, that of the Devil much magnified.

[21] MS fr. 1546, fol. 138rb; 'tout en ordre li descouvri / Comment ses iii enfans murtri / Coment de son oncle les ot / Et coment bien celer les sot / Et comment elle satourna / Des praingnes quelle menga . . .'

[22] MS fr. 1546, fol. 138ra, as above: 'Et seras en religion / Pour avoir merci et pardon.'

[23] Bibl. Nat. MS fr. 1546, fol. 136va; 'Il avint si con i oi dire / En la contree dalemaigne / Qui nest mie terre lointeigne / A nos tens fu que ce avint.'

versal Good Concerning Bees. This collection was presented as an elaborate moralization on the life and habits of bees. Written between 1256 and
*c.*1260 by a Dominican with over twenty years' experience as a confessor,
its material was drawn especially from an area north and west of Cologne,
and augmented by conversation with many fellow-Dominicans and other
churchmen. Thomas's wealth of pastoral knowledge was probably the main
motive for the compilation of his long book.[24]

One *exemplum* concerns a woman called Agnes. It starts at an unidenti-
fiable convent of nuns near Cologne, perhaps one of those which Caesarius
had written of thirty years earlier. The 1250s had witnessed an interregnum
in Germany, and the outback of archiepiscopal Cologne was especially
exposed to lawlessness. In the *exemplum*, war so disturbed the convent that
it dissolved, and the nuns were sent back to their families. Agnes was one
of the nuns, and went back to the house of her father, a knight or *miles*.
There her more serious troubles began. Her father raped her and made her
pregnant, and when the time came to give birth, Thomas relates, she
secluded herself, confiding her agony only in a cousin, himself a monk. Or
rather, Thomas says, he was a monk only in appearance and really the Devil
in disguise. By the time the baby was born, Agnes's grief had driven her
'nearly to despair'. The Devil-cousin pointed out that the unsympathetic
relations she lived with would be bound to get to know of the birth sooner
or later. He advised drowning the child. The mother, 'worn out by the dreadful burden of her struggle, at length, after tears and grief, and filled with
shame, overcame her maternal feelings'. She threw the baby into a pond.
Then, in Thomas's words:

No sooner had she done this than the Devil said to her, utterly crushed as she was
by her misery: 'O most wretched of all women! What can you now expect? Only
scandal for your family and yourself! Only the peril of death! [Women infanticides,
we know from elsewhere, could then be burned alive.] It would surely be better
to throw yourself into the water after your son.' At these words the woman
shrieked with horror, and cried out to her who helps us against the Devil, the
glorious Virgin Mother of Christ. The Demon vanished and the woman at once felt
comforted.[25]

The Devil, habitué of law courts, had envisaged Agnes's death as looking
like an *infortunium*. But the Virgin had prevented it and the Devil had vanished, as he must do, on the mention of her name. Perhaps it is a pity that
the Virgin did not resuscitate the baby. But historians must not ask

---

[24] Thomas of Chantimpré, *Bonum universale de apibus*, bk 2, ch. 29, § 21; ed. G. Colvenerius (Douai, 1627), pp. 300–3. On Thomas: A. Kaufman, *Thomas von Chantimpré*
(Cologne 1899), 8–15, and my 'Confession as a historical source', 286–313.
[25] *De apibus*, 300.

everything of a miracle, not, at least, if they want it to keep some credit as a historical document.

Before drawing a conclusion from that part of the account, let us see what happened next. Rejecting suicide, Agnes resolved not to go back to her relations, and walked instead to the next town. There she found a lodging with an 'honest matron', who soon procured for the good-looking, clearly well-born stranger a position in the town as a nanny. Her charge was to be the young son of a wealthy Jewish family. Living with the family, Agnes nursed her secret grief, fasting twice a week on bread and water. 'Hardly anyone ever saw her smile.' After five years as a nanny Agnes went and confessed her story to a priest. We are again given his name: 'Brother Conrad'. He recognized Agnes's sin as one of the 'reserved' category: that is, absolution for it was not normally in his power. So he sent Agnes to the pope, who gave her absolution.

We might think that would be enough to point a moral. But Agnes's troubles were not over. During the five years with the Jewish family, she had naturally often conversed with her mistress. The conversations had swayed the Jewish woman in favour of Christianity. This maddened the Jewish husband. For him, Agnes's return from Rome was a last straw. She was sleeping off the journey in her room when the master attacked her with a knife, gave her three wounds 'in or near' the heart, and left her for dead. Again she survived, and at dawn next day was able to escape and, this time, find safe lodging—perhaps through the good offices of the archbishop of Cologne. Agnes lived for two more years, and died *in maxima penitentia*. She was able, before she died, to bequeath one last index of her and her narrator's temperament. The Jewish mistress, learning that her husband had killed Agnes but that Agnes had escaped, could only say Agnes had been revived by a 'miracle of the Virgin'. The husband's violence thus ended with an effect opposite to that he had intended, and the wife became a Christian. Months later, Agnes met her mistress again, heard this miraculous account of her escape, and insisted that no miracle was involved. She had only been wounded and 'I only *seemed* to be killed,' she said.[26]

That last detail is one of many features in the *exemplum* to 'ruin' what might otherwise have been a good story. No wonder it never got into any collection of *Miracles of the Virgin*. It is not even a good *exemplum*. It illustrates too much and explains too little. Why should the converter of a Jewess have to do so much penance, even after absolution by the pope himself? It does not even sit properly in Thomas's collection, ostensibly ordered as this was according to moral subject-matter. For Agnes's saga should have come

---

[26] *De apibus*, 301–3.

under one of his other moral headings like Chastity, or the Virgin, or Temptation. Actually it comes in a group of stories about Jews. It blunders in with a 'since I speak of Jews . . .' As a miracle it ends feebly. As an *exemplum* it scarcely begins. If it remains 'impossible to put down', it is surely because it reads as if true. Brother Conrad had been walking and talking. Thomas, here as often elsewhere, has picked up a set of experiences basically historical. His time indications, accordingly, are relatively precise, as befitted a learned friar, and justify a dating of the near-suicide to around 1258.[27]

There is no reason, then, why Agnes's crisis, told in German Dominican circles, should not have added the third element, the infanticide, to the composite version of Brother Jordan's two recollections. What we know for sure is that the threefold compound was told as having occurred 'in the country of Almaine, not far away, and in our own time', from a time when both Brother Jordan and Brother Thomas were active confessors. The compound version was to become well-known in Latin, vernacular, and even oriental languages. Because we are dealing here with historical suicides or would-be suicides, not with what people thought about them, the late medieval literary history of that version of the story cannot be our business now.[28] All that is, is the probability, from features within the *exempla* and from all we know of how they came into circulation, that these particular personal crises actually happened.

A Woman Loses a Man

If a woman's relationship with her child could lead to calamity, so could that to the child's father or potential father. A woman could lose her man. Imaginative literature would have no image more poignant or enduring than that of Dido, driven to suicide by the loss of Aeneas. This theme, or something approaching it, is the subject of a second 'best-seller', as well as of two or three miracles marginally less well-known.

[27] Conrad of Hochstaden, who saw Agnes's wounds, was archbishop of Cologne from 1238 to 1261. The Jewish wife was alive when Thomas wrote, *c*.1267. 'Brothers Conrad' occur in the following *exempla* of De apibus: bk 2, ch. 1, § 22 (p. 121); bk 2, ch. 57, § 23 (pp. 553–5) (two, one of them Conrad of Marburg); bk 2, ch. 2, § 12 (p. 116). Cf. 'Confession as a historical source', 289–90.
[28] Cf. below, p. 278; also A. Poncelet, 'Index miraculorum beatae Mariae Virginis quae latine sunt conscripta', *Analecta Bollandiana*, 21 (1902), 241–360, §§ 538, 1134, 1177, 1270, 1271, 1302, 1550, 1756. For versions in oriental languages, and bibliography: E. Cerulli, '"Il suicidio della peccatrice" nelle versioni araba e etiopica del Libro di Maria', *Annali dell' Istituto Orientale di Napoli*, ns 19 (vol. 29), fasc. 2 (1969), 147–79. Signori, 49–50, for further bibliography.

The 'best-seller' is a miracle of Our Lady of Rocamadour. Its popularity would again render it, by the end of the Middle Ages, indistinguishable from imaginative literature. But there is no reason to think this of its earliest version. This comes in a collection called *The Miracles of Our Lady of Rocamadour*, gathered around 1140 at the monastery of Rocamadour on the southern slopes of the Dordogne valley. The collection includes material going back at least to the early eleventh century. Again, *if* a real-life incident lay behind the miracle, it could have happened within that bracket, probably nearer the end than the beginning.[29]

The miracle concerns a knight (*miles*) of the Rocamadour region, and his wife 'whom he loved very much'. During a light-hearted talk the wife, 'honest and chaste woman as she was', asked her husband if he was loyal to their marriage or whether he preferred 'the love of some mistress'. He replied teasingly: 'do you suppose I am content with you alone and that I do not have girl-friends?' The wife 'happened to be holding a knife', and putting it to her breast said she would kill herself if she had reason to believe what he had said. The threat had the more force because she was carrying their first child. But the knight stuck to his game and added 'you will find I am telling the truth.'

The woman could bear the shame no longer. She lost her self-restraint and, forgetting her sex, stabbed the knife into her own entrails.

In the earliest recension of the miracle we are given to understand that the woman was at this point dead, though the narrator never goes so far as to say so in so many words. The knight, for his part, only complains that it is his child who has died by the pregnant woman's suicidal stab. The rest is marginally less definite, except that the knight behaves, and even speaks, as if the wife *were* dead: laying his grief before the Virgin ('of Rocamadour') he protests he had never ever in his whole life been unfaithful to his wife, but was suffering as if he had. Now it was his turn to wish for death:

'I cannot live, now that our first-born is dead. O my beloved wife,' he groaned, 'who will vouchsafe to me to share your lot and die for you? [This is the nearest we get to an explicit death certificate.] I live, yet do not live. For, living in perpetual woe my body wastes away. O that my spirit might waste with it!'

At length the knight promised the Virgin a waxen image, of a weight equivalent to his wife, if the Virgin would resuscitate her. This worked. The knight pulled the knife from his wife's body, the knife which no one till then had touched through fear 'that by removing it they would also draw out her life spirit'. That phrase implies that the wife was in fact still alive, though

[29] E. Albe, ed., *Les miracles de Notre-Dame de Roc-Amadour* (Paris, 1907), no. 7, pp. 83–7.

on the danger list. But the miracle has to happen, so that the wife 'who had
been incurable by medicine, was cured by the Virgin Mary and restored to
her previous health'.

That first version of the Rocamadour miracle is consistent with attempted
suicide and with nothing else. It is moderately embellished, with a lot of
speech-making and talk of death, but will not take the step into the truly
miraculous. These limitations are again set in relief by later versions which
eroded them. Among these is one datable only to between 1140 and the
middle of the fourteenth century. It is redolent of romance, starting with
the knight's building an altar to the Virgin. Each night, when he thinks
his wife asleep, he goes off to pray at it. The wife becomes suspicious and
challenges him. 'O yes,' he replies, 'I do love a woman fairer than you.' The
narrator has introduced the dramatist's familiar conjuring trick whereby the
audience knows the one vital fact denied to the heroine: *we* know whom
the knight is praying to, *she* does not. Tragedy follows. It is real tragedy
this time. The ensuing suicide is explicitly complete, the wife definitely
dead. The unborn child inside her has also, incidentally, become a pair of
twins.

There were other improved versions. Alfonso X of Castile took the material for one of his *Canticles of Saint Mary*, a 96-line poem. In it, the woman
takes a knife and stabs herself dramatically, *à la* Lucretia, the loss of blood
bringing her a death quick enough to be decisive while not so quick as to
prevent a substantial pious exclamation.[30] Plate 4 illustrates this version,
from an illustrated manuscript of the work in the monastery of El Escoriál
near Madrid.[31] Again, a late fifteenth-century recension, taking matters even
further, has the knight convicted of murdering his wife, and her resuscitation comes just in time to save him from the gallows.[32] Each literary

---

[30] No. 84 (1257–83); in *Cantigas de Santa Maria de don Alfonso el Sabio, las publica la
Real Academia Española* (Madrid, 1889), vol. 2, pp. 133–5. Verse 9 (p. 134) relates the suicide:
'E tomou log' un coitello / con que tallavan o pan, / e deu-se con él nu peito / hũa ferida atan
/ grande, que sen outra cousa / morreu logo manaman. / Diss'enton o cavaleiro: / —Ay Deus,
qué máa vijon!'

[31] Ed. J. Guerrero Lovillo (Madrid, 1949), p. 395 (Lamina 93).

[32] Albe, as n. 29, pp. 87–8 (n. 2) prints the 14th-century French adaptation. To reconstruct
the original version Albe used one 12th-century MS and two 13th-century (pp. 6–7), all copies,
of three different (p. 8) originals, each a collection of Marian miracles not exclusively about
Rocamadour. Alfonso X, *Cantiga* no. 84 (ed. J. Guerrero Lovillo (Madrid 1949), p. 395
(Lamina 93), date: 1257–1283) tells a death and resuscitation version. (Cf. Schmitt, 'Le
suicide', 26, n. 68) Two further versions in British Library MSS are calendared by Herbert,
Catalogue of Romances, 3. (1) MS Arundel 506 (first half of 14th century, formerly the property of St Michael's monastery near Mainz), no. 98 (p. 547), fol. 20b: a knight daily adores
an image of the Virgin he has carved on a tree in his orchard; the Devil, disguised as an old
woman, persuades his wife that he goes to the orchard to meet his mistress; she kills herself
but is revived by the Virgin, in response to the knight's prayers. (2) MS Additional 2391 (about
1500, northern? English), fol. 234b (no. 9) (Herbert, p. 709 cf. 333): the Devil, disguised as an

reworking showed how indifferent a structure the first version had had. It was a 'bad story', and the less historically improbable for that.

THREE MIRACLES FROM CAESARIUS OF HEISTERBACH

The Rocamadour miracle concerned the jealousy of a married woman. In the present suicide dossier it is the only miracle to do so, a fact which may, in fact, help explain its relatively wide and long-lasting circulation. It monopolized a niche and became in that measure public property. The other three miracles about a woman who loses her man have a different literary history. Since the work they appear in became the best-known medieval *exempla* collection—and, incidentally has the biggest single tally of suicide *exempla*—I shall choose this moment to say a few words about it.

The work is Caesarius of Heisterbach's *Dialogus miraculorum*. This book was already in the late Middle Ages, and remains today, one of the richest, perhaps the richest, single source of medieval moral anecdote.[33] Heisterbach was a Cistercian monastery forty miles upstream on the Rhine from Cologne. Internal evidence shows that Caesarius, its novice-master, wrote his twelve books of 'Dialogue' between the years 1219 and 1223. The title can mislead and was probably meant to. Not only does the 'dialogue' turn out to be an unequal match between teacher and pupil, a loquacious 'Monk' and a taciturn 'Novice'; the word 'miracle' in the title overstates. Some of the book does consist of miracles of a kind that would have fitted a saint's *Vita*. Several have physical wonders in, albeit wonders often more akin to those of non-Christian fable than to *miracula*. But the great majority of Caesarius' so-called *miracula* are mere anecdotes. They are told with an eye more or less strict on the moral subject to which each of the twelve 'distinctions' is dedicated (the Eucharist, Contrition, the Devil, and so on), and given a more or less supernatural twist, especially in that many stories concern the physical appearance of demons. Most of Caesarius' stories are presented, like those of Thomas, as true accounts of a recent past in or near the region of Heisterbach. Because Caesarius was a novice-master he would,

---

old woman, is again the instigator; the wife is carrying unborn twins; and the knight is convicted for her murder. The wife and her twins revive as he is led to the gallows.

[33] Ed. J. Strange (Cologne, 1851). Cf. K. Langosch, in *Die deutsche Literatur des Mittelalters. Verfasserlexikon*, 2nd edn, ed. K. Ruh and others, vol. 1 (Berlin and New York, 1978), cols. 1152–68. The best-illustrated characterization remains that of A. E. Schönbach, 'Die Wundererzählungen des Caesarius von Heisterbach', in three parts, being parts 4, 7, and 8 of that author's 'Studien zur Erzählungsliteratur des Mittelalters', respectively in three numbers of *Sitzungsberichte der kaiserlich-königliche Gesellschaft zu Wissenschaften in Wien*, Phil.-hist. Klasse, 144 (1902), Heft 9 (= pt 1, 93 pp.); 159 (1908), Heft 4 [= pt 2, 51 pp.]; 163 (1909), Heft 1 (90 pp.).

like Thomas later, have heard confessions and taken a broad interest in the moral lives around him. Nor did the fact that he belonged to the Cistercians, an order theoretically silent and enclosed, rob his book of an interest going well outside his monastery walls and into layers of social life not ostensibly ecclesiastical. If there had been a Dominican order when Caesarius was a young man he might have joined it. His facility in preaching, interest in moral theology, and capacity to illustrate lessons with 'scenes from everyday life' make his *Dialogue* only slightly distinguishable, in literary and historical flavour, from Dominican *exempla* collections.

Of Caesarius' seven suicide stories, three concern women. Of the three, two appear in the book of the *Dialogue* devoted to 'Temptation'. Here, as elsewhere, Caesarius' manner is occasional rather than systematic. He has told one incident, and that reminds him of others. He relates these suicide stories without moral, stated or implied, and whether or not there was a moral he might have wished to draw. In that respect they are like Thomas' 'bad stories', and it should not be too surprising that they were not among Caesarius' *miracula* to be much copied or developed in later collections.

The first of the group was told to Caesarius by a nun. She said it had happened in a convent of her own order, the year before Caesarius wrote the story down. That would date any incident behind it to around 1221. The sufferer was a young nun in the convent. A man 'religious in garb but not in mind' won the nun's affection by the use of magic and she 'became so demented that she could not endure the temptations he had engendered in her'. Telling no one of her passion, she put in a request to leave the convent because 'I regret having joined.' Afterwards, one or two of the sisters remembered that the girl had given urgency to her request by adding that, if she was not allowed to leave, she would 'drown herself in the well'. This was remembered when, after the request had been refused, the girl was missed and searched for everywhere. The remark was recalled, the searchers looked in the well, and found her dead body. 'Driven by her grief' (*tristitia urgente*) the girl had kept her word.[34]

The next miracle—next here as well as in the *Dialogue*—is equally bare of adornment. Caesarius tells it this time from his own experience. Thirteen years before the time of writing—that is, about 1209—Caesarius and some fellow-monks from Heisterbach had been sailing up the Rhine and put ashore at a village near Cologne called Rotenkirch. There they were shown the body, 'still lying on the ground', of a girl who had in that very hour (*in ipsa hora*) 'ended her life'. Caesarius does not state the method. The monks were told

---

[34] *Dialogus miraculorum*, distinctio. 4, ch. 42 (p. 211).

that she had borne a child to a certain man, and because she was repudiated by him had been led by the vehemence of her grief [*ex vehementia tristitiae*] to inflict this death on herself.[35]

Caesarius records the bare fact. There is no miracle. In that time and place there is no chance of checking this death against a judicial record. But there is no need, either. From both a literary and a moral angle the story is manifestly 'bad'.

Book IV of Caesarius' *Dialogue*, where these two incidents occur, bore the heading 'Of Temptation'. Book V was called 'Of Demons'. A call to tell miracles about demons gave rein to the author's penchant for the mere accumulation of amazing incidents. One moved him on to the theme of heretics, and in the course of retelling what he knew on this theme he recalled an incident told by 'those who were present'. A reference to Archbishop Reynald of Cologne, and independent testimony to the episode, dates it to 1163, some sixty years before Caesarius wrote. So we can do our own arithmetic. Caesarius' informants, if the story is true, must have been old, he young. Caesarius' account is consistent with other accounts of heresy in the Rhineland, which heresy historians commonly take as the cradle of European Catharism.[36]

A group of heretics were being burned alive outside the walls of Cologne. The heresiarch, *magister* of the sect, was one 'Arnold'. In the flames he comforted his fellow-victims, laying his hand on their heads, 'half-burned', and exorting them to courage. His followers included a young woman, 'beautiful,' says Caesarius, 'but heretical'. Rescued by 'the compassion of certain people' she had been consigned instead to a choice between marriage and a convent. As the flames raged round her companions' corpses she said to her captors: 'tell me, which one is the arch-seducer?' They indicated the body of Arnold. At this she slipped from their hands, 'covered her face with her garment' and leapt onto his body, as Caesarius says 'to burn with him in Hell for ever'.

A tendency for a suicide, especially a woman, to cover her face before the act is known from post-medieval sources. That adds verisimilitude to Caesarius' story because he is unlikely to have known of it. What he relates is both less and more than 'suttee': less, since there is no suggestion of an

---

[35] *Dial mirac.*, dist. 4, ch. 43 (vol. 1, pp. 211–12). Cf. Tubach, *Index exemplorum*, no. 4666.
[36] *Dial. mirac.*, dist. 5, ch. 19 (vol. 1, pp. 298–9). Cf. W. L. Wakefield and A. P. Evans, *Heresies of the High Middle Ages* (New York-London, 1969), 244, and 723 n. 9; R. I. Moore, *The Origins of European Dissent* (Oxford-New York, 1985²), 175–82; and G. Koch, *Frauenfrage und Ketzertum im Mittelalter. Forschungen zur mittelalterlichen Geschichte*, 9 ([East] Berlin, 1962), 42–3.

erotic relationship between Arnold and his female disciple (and biased contemporaries would have been quick to make one if there had been); more,
because the type of suicide in which a sectary, usually male, leaps into the
flames, was not uncommon in accounts of executions of heretics. The young
woman was one of a class.

The foregoing group of *exempla* suggests that the genre tells more often
of female than of male agonies. That is the case. But it is only a matter of
degree. These four stories about female suicides are matched by only one
on the male side. But it is the third and biggest of our 'best-sellers': the
miracle of St James and the suicide pilgrim, and its literary career would be
the most prodigious of any connected with our theme.

A Man Loses a Woman

Chapter 1 of this book told the tragedy of Henry, prior of the Augustinian
house of Le Dale in Derbyshire, as related a generation later in the history
of the foundation of that priory. Worn out by the poverty of his poor house,
it will be recalled, Henry had taken to false coining and to cohabiting with
a local woman. Forcibly removed, he had killed himself. The 'miracle' there
was confined to the narrator's moralizing slant: he painted Henry as a reprobate, who appropriately died like Judas. It was not an edifying tale and that,
doubtless, was among reasons why it remained locked in a house chronicle.
The opposite fortune attended the episode we now come to. In it, according to the most widely received versions, a young man had had a brief affair
with a girl, parted from her, and became suicidal. But this time the man's
adventure *was* edifying, and the whole world got to know.

It should be clear from the *exempla* told so far that every story has its
own history, its 'story of a story'. The miracle of the Santiago suicide
pilgrim has a history as revealing as its content. The miracle would become
a favourite partly because it brought in not one, but two saints, the Virgin
and James the Apostle, so it got into the specialist collections of both, the
more easily for the harmonious hierarchy it established between them. But
that can be only part of the reason. The other part was that it concerned
a subject widely recognized and feared, suicide; and gave it a benign
interpretation.

What matters here is that the story was told, from the start, with marks
of verisimilitude, and in particular, in nearly all recensions, was ascribed to
St Hugh, abbot of Cluny, well known as a teller of contemporary anecdotes.
Hugh was better known for that, indeed, than for miracles of his own. Since

he was an indubitably historical person, likely to know, and grave enough for his stories to be believed, they were.[37]

But should they have been? In particular, should we believe this one? So far in this chapter I have told the miracle first and then examined its credentials. The complications of this one dictate that the order be reversed. I want to tell it at length in the earliest recorded version, and the question which the earliest version is therefore to be tackled first, so only an outline of the content is now needed. It is that a pilgrim to Santiago was deceived by the Devil in disguise into committing suicide; had a supernatural experience in which he was saved from damnation; and was then restored to life. Those are the bare bones. Could any of them have been historical?

The suicide miracle is one of a cluster of Santiago miracles whose birth can be reconstructed, and partly has been.[38] By comparing the recollections and itineraries of a group of Hugh of Cluny's acquaintances, R. W. Southern once worked out how this series of stories found its way into the main European miracle collections. In 1104, he shows, Abbot Hugh recounted them to the exiled Anselm of Canterbury during the latter's visit to Cluny. Their long conversations in Latin were overheard by a witness:

I was often present [the witness remembered], and heard among other things, much about St James the apostle, brother of John the Evangelist.[39]

From Anselm and his companions the suicide miracle got to the so-called *Dicta Anselmi*, written before 1114, and thence, almost certainly, to the English *Miracles of the Virgin*. Further oral tradition from the same conversations lodged it in *The Book of St James*, compiled in Lyons at roughly the same time, and destined to become the standard Santiago collection.

[37] The most reliable standard version of the miracle is in *Liber sancti Jacobi*, bk 2, ch. 17; transcribed by W. M. Whitehill, in *Codex calixtinus*, 3 vols. (Santiago, 1944), vol. 1, pp. 278–82. French recension: M. L. Berkey, Jr., 'The *Liber S. Jacobi*: the French adaptation by Pierre de Beauvais', *Romania*, 86 (1965), 77–103. Marian versions: Gautier de Coincy (1236), *Miracles de Nostre Dame* [in verse], bk 1, miracle 25 (208 lines) [ed. V. F. Koenig, vol. 2 (Geneva-Paris, 1961), 237–45]; A. de Laborde, *Les miracles de Notre Dame compilés par Jean Miélot* (Paris, 1929), vol. 1, no. 16 (= Miracle no. 9), p. 87. Further MSS: A. Poncelet, 'Index miraculorum b. Virginis Mariae, § 30 [p. 247]; augmented by Herbert, *Catalogue of Romances*, vol. 2, p. 606, no. 14 etc. Cf. Schmitt, 25, n. 64; G. Signori, 'Rechtskonstruktionen und religiöse Fiktionen', 41–8. Signori accepts the common but erroneous claim that the English version, made soon after 1100, is the earliest, and this eases her characterization of the miracle as a 'religious fiction'. In what follows I make the opposite assumption.

[38] For what follows: R. W. Southern, *The Making of the Middle Ages* (London, 1953), 252–3; *Saint Anselm and his Biographer* (Cambridge, 1963), 218, 260; and (especially) 'The English Origin of the "Miracles of the Virgin"', *Medieval and Renaissance Studies*, 4 (1958), 176–216, esp. 188–90 (Anselm's travels), 207 (relationship with *Codex calixtinus*), 208–13 (text). The *Dicta Anselmi* with their appendix of miracles are published by R. W. Southern and F. S. Schmitt, O.S.A., *Memorials of St. Anselm. Auctores Britannici medii aevi*, 1 (Oxford, 1969). The suicide miracle is on pp. 200–7.

[39] *Dicta Anselmi*, ch. 21; p. 196. 10–15.

These facts, as set forth by Southern, have become familiar to historians of the period and subject. But Southern was looking for the passing on of a story, not for any incident that may have lain behind it. We are looking for an incident, so let us try harder, and start with the question of chronology. When could the supposed incident have happened? Hugh was abbot of Cluny from 1049 to 1109. He says the pilgrim-hero came to him at Cluny soon after his adventure, and showed him the scars from the attempted suicide. So the supposed incident must be dated with a time-bracket from 1049 to 1104; that is, from Hugh's accession as abbot, to the time of his conversations with Anselm. The very size of the bracket has probably dulled the focus of the historicity question. If an imagined incident cannot be dated more accurately, why try?

We can reduce the bracket radically. First, the *terminus a quo*, 1049, can be brought forward by some years. This can be done with the help of a version itself relatively late. Some time in the 1120s, the Paris theologian, Hugh of St Victor, was at work on his book *On Sacraments*, and came to the question where mortals go when they die, together with the accessory question what, if anything, anyone living is in a position to say on the matter. Hugh of St Victor refers generally to reports by those who claim to have died and come back to life, and he pauses at length, and in particular, on the experiences of the Santiago suicide-pilgrim, allegedly brought back to life after being 'out of body'. Now I said a moment ago that nearly all versions of this miracle attribute it to Hugh of Cluny, or someone who must have had it from him. This is *not* true of Hugh of St Victor's version. His is the only exception, and it deserves a closer look. This is what Hugh of St Victor says:

I should not pass by in silence [he begins, having spoken generically of extra-corporeal experiences] what I have myself learned in this regard. A certain brother, whose word can be relied on, told me he had heard the account from his abbot, who had affirmed it to be true. The abbot had once had occasion to make a visitation of certain brethren who had been placed under his authority. As is normal, the abbot had stopped off somewhere *en route* at a hostelry. There he heard that the episode had occurred a few days before. By the time he arrived it was the talk of the whole locality.[40]

This chain of witnesses could, of course, be mere narrator's invention. It is usually hard to tell whether it is or not. It was often meant to be

---

[40] *De sacramentis*, pt 16, ch. 2; *Pat. lat.* 176, 583 AB: 'Ego quidem quod de hac re audivi tacere non debeo. Quidam probati testimonii frater narravit mihi se a suo abbate veraciter hoc affirmante audisse, quod cum aliquando ille ad quosdam fratres eminus constitutos visitandos pergeret, in itinere, ut solet, quodam loco hospitium accepit. Ubi factum tunc apud omnes ejusdem loci habitatores celebre paucis ante diebus contigisse didicit.'

hard to tell. But let us remember the serious, investigative tone of *De sacramentis*, whose author was an intellectual, writing for intellectuals, and was trying to prove something. Can we not take his chain of witnesses at face value? In the Cluniac account it was the pilgrim who went to Cluny, and showed his scar to the abbot. In Hugh of St Victor's account, an unnamed abbot is himself on the move, and learns the episode from the villagers.

How does Hugh of St Victor's account change the miracle's time-bracket? It is a question of arithmetic. Suppose the two intermediaries, the 'brother' and the unnamed abbot, each had some thirty years of active monastic profession in which to hear and remember anecdotes. Hugh of St Victor wrote the account within a few years of 1125, and is unlikely to have heard it before 1121 (when he came to France from his native Germany). So a maximum allowance for delay to both intermediaries would yield a *terminus a quo* of *c*.1125 *minus* sixty (30 + 30), and suggest a date *c*.1065. The hypothetical incident, that is, could have happened at any time after *c*.1065. Incidentally, a date then or later would also fit easily with an internal feature of the story: in the Cluniac versions (not this one) the pilgrim earns a professional living as leather-worker or shoemaker in Lyons. Along the valley of the Rhône and Saône, specialists have identified a marked rise in monetary circulation in the 1070s.[41] None of this is binding; but it is suggestive of a *terminus a quo* around the 1060s.

We now turn more boldly to the *terminus ad quem*. This, too, can be shifted: backwards, by about twenty-one years. For we left the elderly Abbot Hugh, most authoritative source for the miracle, talking to St Anselm in 1104. But in 1083 a younger Abbot Hugh had been on his travels, and had passed through Italy.[42] The suicide episode must already have been in his repertoire, since it was recorded in a private, Monte Cassino version that never gave rise to a tradition.[43] A reason for its privacy was that, though written in Latin, it was in the local Beneventan script, read only in southern Italy. Its recorder was a monk, Guaferius, who must have been sufficiently impressed by this episode, among others he heard from Hugh and other visitors to the monastery, to choose the suicide miracle as subject of one of only two big narrative poems from his pen (the other being about the conversion of a Jewish family in Salerno). Guaferius' other writings show a special interest in the destiny of dead souls, a key point of the suicide

---

[41] *Ars pelletaria: Dicta Anselmi*, ch. 22, ed. Southern and Schmitt, p. 200, II, line 4 (etc.); *ars sutoria*, *Pat. Lat.* 147.1288A (see below). G. Duby, *La société aux xie et xiie siècles dans la région mâconnaise* (Paris, 1953), 332–6 (new edn (Paris, 1971), 263–6).

[42] H. E. J. Cowdrey, *The Age of Abbot Desiderius* (Oxford, 1983), 34.

[43] Printed in *Pat. lat.*, 147.1285D–88A.

miracle,[44] and suicide may anyway have interested him as a subject. For one of his fellow-monks was writing a book on 'Melancholy' at about the same time: he was Constantine the African, an immigrant convert from Islam, and Constantine's preface to the book says melancholy 'abounds especially in this part of the world', meaning Italy or the Christian West. Since melancholy was the recognized antecedent to suicide, the monks must have known suicides happened.[45] Guaferius was interested in the soul, and the two subjects, soul and suicide, may have come together to spur him to record the episode. But it was left in his esoteric script and few people noticed it.

But it is the original incident, if there was one, that is our quarry, and Guaferius' version is the closest to it. Perhaps it is even as close as a year or two. So in telling the miracle *in extenso*, as it is now time to do, I shall follow Guaferius, and remark afterwards on differences that appeared in later decades. After a long preface, about Christ's redemptive power and the need for repentance, Guaferius tells how a group of 'Franks' were travelling together to Santiago de Compostela 'to unburden themselves of their sins'.[46] One of the party was 'by nature especially simple and puerile, easy to influence this way or that'. One evening the group lodged in an inn and the simple young man went off for a walk on his own. During the walk he met a handsome stranger whom Guaferius at once identifies as the Devil in disguise. The Devil easily gets the young pilgrim into conversation, asking, in a polite and reassuring manner 'which might have deceived much wiser men' where the young man is going, and why. The youth reveals he is going to Santiago. The Devil says that he, the Devil, knows a quicker and easier way for the youth to get what he wants. 'Do you know who I am?' he asks. The simple boy answers as a simpleton, *simplex simpliciter*, that he does not. 'I am the very Apostle to whom you are journeying.' The youth falls flat on his face and begs for help, and in particular for 'relief for his sins'. I continue in the words of the poem, translated line for line:

> Death's author thereupon, for blackest death
> Gave counsel, yet exacting ere he counselled
> Blind obedience. Obedience sworn, he spoke
> 'If, with your hand, you do not separate

---

[44] On Guaferius: F. J. E. Raby, *A History of Christian Latin Poetry* (Oxford, 1953), 240–1. H. E. J. Cowdrey, *The Age of Abbot Desiderius* (Oxford, 1983), 23–4 (as 'Waiferius'). As for the date of Guaferius's death, he had time to appear in a posthumous vision to his friend Alberic, who died in 1088: *Pat. lat.*, 173.1032B, quoting Peter the Deacon, *De just. Casin.*, ch. 48. My remarks on Guaferius' character are based on his writings and on Peter the Deacon's portrait in *De viris illustribus casinensibus*, ch. 29 (where he is also called 'Benedictus'), *Pat. lat.*, 173.1037A–38A.

[45] Constantinus Africanus, *De melancholia*, ed. K. Garbers (Hamburg, 1977), 84.

[46] *Pat. lat.*, 147, 1286B.

Your soul and body, you aspire in vain
To lasting bliss. You seek eternal life?
Cast off its transient counterfeit in time!'
Horror arrests the youth. To hear such crime
Suggested makes him bold to say 'this act
Impugns our faith.' But devilish words persuade.
The act agreed, he only asks the means.
'Go to your tavern. Dine. Disguise your troubled
Purpose with fair words. Then, all asleep
But you, pierce with your sword your inmost throat.
Then slit your paunch. To finish all, impale
Yourself upon the selfsame blade.' The Fiend
Speaks as he lists. The youth departs. He dines.
His comrades yawn, and sleep. Alone, he stabs
His throat and veins, and slashes every sinew,
Piercing at last his entrails. Then the pain
Of dying, and the crime, goad him to cry:
'Ah me! Ah wretch! By my own hand to die!'
Then down he falls, lifeless.[47]

I have spoiled the story for the reader by revealing that a miracle is at hand. But before it happens let me point out a feature of this particular Devil. He faintly resembles other unauthorized spirits we know to have haunted the same Santiago route in better-documented times, spirits we briefly met in Chapter 9 and more briefly already in this chapter: the Cathar or Albigensian *perfecti*. A century later the Cathars too would denigrate sacramental penance and pilgrimage, be severe to sin, impose on simple minds, and recommend suicide as a way to eternal life. Evidence for that type of heretical dualism in the eleventh century is thin[48] and the similarity may be accidental. But the place is right, and the coincidence worth remembering.

To return to hard facts. The next the poem tells of are supernatural, and will have to wait for a context not devoted, as this is, to an attempt at the recovery of earthly history. Their upshot is, St James and the Virgin secure the return of the boy's soul to his body. The sequel is earthly enough. The corpse comes back to life:

It yawns. It rises, speaks and walks around
That has been dead. The comrades, who had seen
Him die, behold the proof of miracle
And seek no other. For the rest, the scar

---

[47] *Pat. lat.*, 147, 1286C–7B.
[48] A. Borst, *Die Katharer* (Stuttgart, 1953), 71–80.

> Alone remains, from either wound, lest men
> Should doubt his homecoming from very death.[49]

Resuscitated, the young man goes to Cluny and tells Abbot Hugh of his experiences, asking for admission as a monk. Hugh asks him about his age and background. Finding he has been trained as a tailor and supports both himself and his mother by this trade, Hugh tells him to return to it, and allow his adventures to serve himself and others as a warning.

This last wish was fulfilled. The pilgrim's adventure was recounted to more people than Hugh could have guessed. Guaferius's poem may not have been read outside the little world of Monte Cassino. But Hugh himself was not to die until 1109, and had plenty of time to tell other people, Anselm included, each with his own circles of friends, and with good memories. So the miracle of the suicide pilgrim got out and, with flexible details, came to rest in the regular St James repertoire, including versions in French and Spanish. In the thirteenth century, when 'Sant Jago' had lost some of his glamour in northern Europe, more weight came to be put on the Virgin's role. The miracle would then be better known from books with the title *Miracles of the Virgin*, like the famous *Miracles de Nostre Dame* by Gautier de Coincy (†1236), monk of St Médard in Soissons. Gautier put the story into French verse. An illustration from an early fourteenth-century manuscript of it is shown in Plate 5(a). Another was again the well-illustrated version made in French prose in 1456 by Jean Miélot. One Miélot manuscript of it has a miniature of the story which retains, despite the text, a reminiscence of the original predominance of St James, and is shown in Plate 5(b).

After Guaferius' time, I said the details of the story had become flexible. As in the other *miracula* we have looked at, the emendations tended to make it a 'better story', and once more, the ways in which they do so emphasize how *bad* a story it was in Guaferius. Look, for instance, at Guaferius's last four lines.[50] They abruptly introduce the mother of the pilgrim as a new character and tell us the youth was a tailor. Both of these facts we should have learned either at the beginning or not at all. *The Book of Saint James* duly removes this untidiness and improves the literary effect. Take another passage, Hugh's rejection of the postulant. It erodes the moral impact of the whole story. It is the opposite of what was to happen with the woman infanticide. The Marian revisions duly correct this, and have the repentant pilgrim become a monk in a conventional 'happy ending'. From *The Book*

---

[49] *Pat. lat.*, 147, 1287D.
[50] *Pat. lat.*, 147. 1288A: 'Contentum reperit quibus ars sutoria sese / Foverat et matrem, quam ne sinat imperat. Ergo / Ad matrem redit.'

of St James onwards, again, most repetitions give the pilgrim a name, 'Gerard', a city, 'Lyons', and make him a furrier rather than a weaver.[51] Northern professionals had been at work. The recounting of true facts was clearly thought too important a matter to be left to those who had the most direct knowledge of them. To reach a big public, truth needs a certain amount of editing.

Its narrative shortcomings, early date, and direct access to the most probable source for the anecdote thus recommend the Monte Cassino version as the nearest to an original incident if there was one. Gauferius himself may nevertheless have edited it, by bowdlerization, for what the writer of *The Book of St James* had learned from St Anselm, who had in turn learned it from Hugh, was the nature of the sin the pilgrim had to repent of: lust. The youth had 'lain with a woman'. His self-stabbing is preceded in this version by self-castration, recommended by the Devil as a specific penance for a specific sin. This feature is emphasized even further in the one early version not attributed to Hugh directly, but to someone who must have got it from Hugh. This is the version by Guibert of Nogent, recorded in 1115, when Guibert was about 60, with the claim that he got it from an older monk called Godfrey (Joffredus), born a Burgundian nobleman, 'lord of Semur and other Burgundian castles', and for this and other reasons (he says) trustworthy. Godfrey, for his part, had claimed to have heard it from a person senior to him, who had seen the ex-pilgrim with his own eyes and could describe the scars. Why Guibert does not mention Abbot Hugh is a puzzle, since that description would fit him perfectly, Hugh having died, aged 85, in 1109. Hugh of Cluny's own father had furthermore been lord of Sémur, and the town was in easy travelling distance of Cluny. So Guibert's version must again be on the Cluniac template.

Now Guibert of Nogent's autobiography reveals that his own early monastic years had been troubled by sexual temptation. It may have been this that made Guibert a good listener to Godfrey for the theme to which he now gave emphasis—if he did not invent it, for Guibert 'improves' the story in his own way. First, he misses out the other improvements. In Guibert's version St James's pilgrim has no name, trade, or mother, and like Guaferius, thirty years earlier, Guibert says nothing of Lyons, placing the pilgrim's origin only 'in the higher parts of the lands adjoining' those of Godfrey/Joffredus. What Guibert does supply, as compensation for all those omissions, is two extra features. One is a motive for the pilgrimage. It was to finish with, and atone for, a long-standing cohabition with a woman: 'he was coupled to her not in lawful, matrimonial love, but with unlawful, and

---

[51] Signori, 44–7.

as it were usurious love.' This is linked to the suicide. At the pilgrim's meeting with the Devil, the Devil challenges the pilgrim about a girdle he wore. It was a gift from his girl-friend, the youth confesses. The Devil upbraids him:

You have lain hitherto in the slough of fornication. Now you wish to seem penitent. You offer, as an earnest of repentance, a brave start, saying you propose to visit me. Yet you still wear the loose woman's girdle.[52]

Ashamed, the pilgrim asks for advice:

If you wish to do fruitful penance for the revolting things you have done you must, for loyalty to me and to God, cut off the member with which you have sinned, namely your penis, and after that, by cutting your throat, end the life which you have abused.

When the youth's comrades are asleep he acts, first cutting off his *mentulam* ('drain'), then 'sinks his knife in his throat'. As in Guaferius, so in Guibert, the other pilgrims are woken by 'the cry of the dying man and the sound of gushing blood'. They bring a light, see a gashed corpse, and suppose their comrade murdered. 'They knew nothing of the Devil's counselling.' This introduces the second of Guibert's peculiarities. The comrades go ahead and say a funeral Mass for their dead friend. God accepts the Mass, and is 'pleased to heal the throat-wound, and resuscitate the dead man through his Apostle'. The revived pilgrim then tells of the Devil's false appearance and of the favourable judgement he had had from the Virgin.

This last feature of Guibert's account deserves a moment's notice. Guibert is a punctilious theologian and canon lawyer, and observes that a funeral Mass should not have been said for a suicide. The pilgrims are excused, Guibert says, only by their ignorance of the circumstances. They knew nothing of the Devil and the suicide. But the reader does, and is entitled to interject that God, who knows everything, was not so excused. So Guibert's God is not a good canon lawyer, and his indulgence to the suicide is an anomaly. It makes the miracle a 'bad story', rendered a slightly better one only by Guibert's supply of a motive for the young man's despair. The motive was certainly plausible in the age for which he wrote it, but scarcely less so for the age when the pilgrim may have performed his suicidal act, in the 1060s. So, we may imagine, would it remain, as the miracle was heard and remembered in the remaining four medieval centuries.[53]

While the early history of this miracle is fresh in our minds I would like to remark on a feature which I shall have occasion to notice much later. The

[52] *De vita sua*, bk 3, ch. 19; ed. E.-R. Labande (Paris 1981), 442–8.
[53] See above, p. 278, n. 37. Bibliography: Signori, 41–8.

miracle of the suicide pilgrim was 'born', that is, put in writing, in a milieu of serious, saintly, ascetic monasticism. That is, those who nourished and recorded it were exceptionally pious, devoted men of prayer, not any old monks, abbots, or bishops. We do not know who the abbot was who first learned and recalled the story to his juniors, and whose story got into the pages of Hugh of St Victor. But he was one of a big congregation that needed visitations, that is, a 'reforming' congregation.[54] Meanwhile the fullest memory of the incident was preserved and spread by St Hugh of Cluny, perhaps the most admired monastic reformer in Christendom. It was celebrated by Guaferius, whom Peter the Deacon, chronicler of Monte Cassino's 'golden age', did not hesitate to describe as 'conspicuous in sanctity and religion'.[55] It was cherished and repeated by St Anselm of Canterbury. Nor has the seriousness of the monastic spirituality of Guibert of Nogent, who told his own version of the miracle, ever been in doubt. These were no run-of-the-mill chroniclers. The four or five men who conspicuously launched this optimistic story, and without whom it never would have appeared in writing, were all at the saintly end of the monastic spectrum.

A woman infanticide, then; a jealous wife; a remorseful pilgrim. That is the end of our three 'best-seller' *miracula*, on relationships within the triangle of man, woman, and child. I finish by looking at two less prominent themes, embodied in texts with a less spectacular literary history.

Other Themes of Suicide and Love

INOPPORTUNE LOVE: REMORSE AND REPUGNANCE

A breach in the relationship of man and woman could occasion suicide, and I have rehearsed half a dozen cases, 'best-sellers' and others, to illustrate this. It would be tempting to conclude that a broken heart, *à la* Dido, was the classic occasion for suicide in this domestic area, but that would be to ignore the variety of circumstances illustrated: the misplaced nun; the forlorn heretic; the pilgrim tortured by remorse; the demoralized prior. None of these is a stereotype, and their variety forbids their being read as such. To do so would be to surrender, if unconsciously, to the influence of purely imaginative literature, and it is important not to confuse this with the few traces that survive of flesh-and-blood history. For the influences which pass both ways between literature and history are themselves part of

---

[54] *Pat. lat.*, 176. 583A. See n. 40 above.
[55] *Liber de viris illustribus cassinensibus*, ch. 29; *Pat. lat.*, 173, 1037A.

history, and to decipher them we must know just where, on the scale between reality and imagination, each *miraculum* lies.

There are also, as it happens, almost as many stories of an opposite kind to which the same warning applies. That is, there are stories about, not the inopportune separation of man and woman, but their inopportune coming together. In literature, the classic example would be Lucretia, who killed herself after rape. Both in fact and in literature there were some early Christian imitators.[56] But after the early fifth century every serious theologian knew that the pagan Lucretia's suicide, if nothing else, ruled her out as a model. None of our medieval stories parallels Lucretia's suicide. The late thirteenth-century French poet, the voluble and salacious Jean de Meung, actually regretted (disingenuously) that there were no imitators of the chaste Lucretia in his own day.[57] And the *miracula* bear him out. They do occasionally tell of a woman's opting for suicide to protect her virginity. Thus Caesarius' *Eight Books of Miracles*—a fragmentary work distinct from the *Dialogue*—has the story of a girl who jumps from a tower to preserve hers.[58] Thomas of Chantimpré, similarly, tells of an Apuleian noblewoman who escaped a forced marriage by jumping from a high rock into the sea, and survived (whether she deserved to or not) to end as a hermit in male dress, in the Peloponnese.[59] But there are no Lucretia-like suicides after rape. Giordano of Rivalto, the famous Dominican preacher in Tuscany, whose sermons abounded in real-life recollections, told a Florentine audience in 1304 of a girl who had 'thought the sin would be enjoyable and wanted to try it out, and did. When she discovered she had lost her virginity and could not get it back she killed herself with a knife.'[60] But that girl was scarcely a Lucretia, since her loss was deliberate.

This last theme, of suicidal regret at deliberately lost virginity, is nevertheless more frequent. And sometimes, as in Giordano's story, it bears marks of having happened. Thus the Dominican Stephen of Bourbon gives an anonymous and undated account—conceivably from a confession he had

---

[56] Lucretia's medieval literary fortunes will be chronicled in *The Mapping of Desolation*, ch. 3.

[57] *Le roman de la rose*, line 8621 (ed. F. Lecoy (Paris, 1968), vol. 2, p. 13).

[58] Bk 3, ch. 7; ed. A. Meister, 'Die Fragmente der Libri VIII miraculorum des Caesarius von Heisterbach', *Römische Quartalschrift für christliche Altertumskunde und für Kirchengeschichte*, 13, Suppl. Heft (Rome, 1901). Tubach, *Index exemplorum*, no. 4933.

[59] *De apibus*, bk 2, ch. 29, § 38 [p. 316], conceived as occurring between 1186 and 1204.

[60] C. Delcorno, *Giordano da Pisa e l'antica predicazione volgare* (Florence, 1975), 247: *Incipit* 'L'una vergine pensava essere beata cosa quel diletto, vòllelo provare e provollo . . .', with summary. The text is in E. Narducci, ed., *Prediche inedite del beato Giordano da Rivalto*, O. P. (Bologna, 1867), 357. Delcorno gives analogues on pp. 247–8, the only one of which to augment our historical dossier is in the Tuscan-Venetian *Fiore di Virtù*, where a woman called Jaciva/Jacinta hangs herself after losing her virginity.

himself heard—of a 'certain virgin' who had placed high hopes in sexual pleasure and 'suffered herself to be corrupted'. She did so only to find, as the friar puts it, that the pleasure was vile and brief, and had (for some unexplained reason) proved financially expensive. So she tried to kill herself (*adeo doluit, quod se occidere voluit*).[61] Thomas of Chantimpré relates a more circumstantial incident of this kind from his own experience. A virtuous theology student in Thomas's diocese, Cambrai, was advanced to a rich canonry but renounced it through a desire to serve in a parish. For seven years he served as priest, winning souls by preaching and by the example of a pure life. But by doing so the priest made himself a 'target of the Devil'. His hair-shirt was washed by an unmarried woman of 60, whose employment as his laundress entailed her regular entry into his bedroom. *Quid plura?* 'What more need I say?' Thomas asks wearily. Both priest and laundress lost their long-guarded innocence. The priest, 'having experimented in that which was previously unknown to him, still persists, I believe, in a life of lust'. And the laundress? 'Through an excess of remorse she accelerated her death in lamentation [*prae nimia amaritudine mortem acceleraret in planctu*].' Once more the prose turns suddenly vague when it comes to a death which may have been suicide, and which therefore, since this trait is common in Thomas, probably was.[62]

Giordano, Stephen, and Thomas were Friars Preacher. They related those incidents as cogent *exempla* against non-marital sexual relations. But we have learned from law courts, as well as from miracles earlier in this chapter, that real life was not so clear-cut. A marriage ceremony did not invariably inoculate against suicide. It may even, indeed, have failed to do so against this particular *genus* of suicide, that is, one occasioned by one party's reservations about sexual relations. Another late German case may help here. It comes from Eberhardsklausen, a monastery near Trier, and dates from around 1492. As at St Gall, in the example quoted earlier of post-natal depression, the Reformation tide was rising round Eberhardsklausen and its miracle-smith knew his stories had to withstand local scepticism. So he tried to get the details right and gives us a corresponding assurance that his story reflects a real incident. It happened at Kaimt on the Moselle, between Trier and Coblenz. A man whom the discreet writer does not name but describes just as 'newly married' (*novicius in matrimonio*) threw himself from the bedroom window soon after getting into bed with a wife who loved him 'as a mistress her lover' (*quasi amica post amicam*). These are the writer's words:

---

[61] *Anecdotes historiques* (Paris, 1877), § 448, pp. 385–6.
[62] *De apibus*, bk 2, ch. 30, § 47 (p. 353).

The man was newly married. One night he had just got into the bed in which his wife was already lying and soon afterwards suddenly got up and jumped from the window, which was pretty high above the ground.[63]

The window cannot have been of a height necessarily fatal, for the distraught wife followed her husband out 'to see what had happened to him'. But that the man's intention was suicidal is strongly suggested by what the wife found. Her husband was unconscious, blood gushing from his ear while he 'writhed with inhuman movements'. When daylight came she saw his face was horribly deformed, and she felt a physical repulsion for the man 'for whom she had previously had a strong conjugal love'.[64] She nevertheless did all the right things, praying at once to the Virgin and taking the invalid husband to Eberhardsklausen for a cure. It took three visits and busy help from her father, but in the end her husband got better and lost his facial distortion: 'and the love which the woman had lost for her husband returned in its entirety.'[65]

The author attributes the whole episode to witchcraft. But whether that played a part or not the erotic nuances are unmistakable. The man may have felt overwhelmed by his wife's sexuality. If that is correct, the Kaimt story is to be added to those which show, collectively, how wide a variety of erotic situations could occasion suicide. Which did so more frequently is impossible to tell: whether the broken heart, on one hand, or sexual remorse or repugnance on the other, that is to say, it is impossible to tell from the literature because both sorts of author, the more romantic and the more homiletic, had their axes to grind. We must be content to know that both sorts, from inopportune separation and from inopportune coming together, were the subject of stories whose core was probably historical.

Within the triangle of man, woman, and child, the mutual traffic between literature and life is more visible in a second area: suicide as an idea in what can be called 'lovers' rhetoric'.

---

[63] Wilhelm von Bernkastel [†1536], *Die Mirakelbücher des Klosters Eberhardsklausen*, ed. P. Hoffmann and P. Dohms. Publikationen der Gesellschaft für rheinische Geschichtskunst, 64 (Düsseldorf, 1988), 78–9, § 122; 'Nam quadam nocte: cum se in lectum colocasset, ubi et coniunx sua iacebat, non diu post insperato surgit / et de fenestra saltavit, cuius altitudo satis longe distabat a terra; fecit autem hoc versus in amencia nesciens, quod fecit.' The author and his works: ibid., xii–xiii. Signori, 'Agression und Selbstzerstörung', 139, gives a sensitive reconstruction and an assessment, as sceptical as mine, of the 'insanity' to which the discreet Wilhelm von Bernkastel attributes the act. Bibliography: ibid., n. 88.

[64] Wilhelm von Bernkastel, ibid., 79: 'iacentem mutum sine sensu cum moribus inhumanis ... amisitque mulier affectum coniugalem et amore ad virum, quem prius satis magnum habebat.'

[65] Ibid.: 'et affectus, quem mulier erga virum perdiderat, totus reversus est.'

Inopportune Love: the Importunate Hussy

Suicide and lovers' rhetoric go well together. Together they constitute an important theme in poetry. But to indicate the varieties such rhetoric could take in real life let me start by quoting an *exemplum* of Giordano of Pisa, preaching in Florence in 1303. He refers to a Florentine youth who

> went to a young lady and said 'what do you want me to do?' She said 'jump in the Arno.' And he went and jumped in the Arno.[66]

Giordano says he was a fool and that he was lucky to be fished out with some life left in him. The intention is not clearly suicidal. It may have been. Giordano is indifferent to the question anyway. But as an hors d'oeuvre to this little category, the gesture was a *kind* of rhetoric.

A more regular kind comes in the motif, often repeated, of the importunate hussy. The motif was attached to more than one saintly figure, but its most confident association is with a priest called Dominic: contemporary, compatriot, and colleague of his canonized homonym, founder of the Dominican order. To avoid confusion with *Saint* Dominic [†1221] I shall call this one 'young' or 'brother' Dominic. Young Dominic, the story eventually went, served at the court of a princely magnate. He denounced the courtiers for lechery and a plot was hatched to ensnare him. A loose woman of well-proven appeal was to approach young Dominic under the pretext of wishing to confess her sins. When alone with him she should declare a carnal passion for his own person, threatening suicide if he denied her. To that point the plot prospered. But the priest, thus cornered, appealed to miracle. He had dry sticks and straw hidden under the bed and set alight as he lay on it, and then invited the woman to join him. While *he* was miraculously preserved, *she* shrank away in horror, and publicly confessed her duplicity. Brother Dominic was publicly vindicated, the courtiers duly converted.[67]

The miracle as just told I have in fact pieced together from three thirteenth-century sources. Following the tactic in this chapter of trying to pursue 'good stories' to a possibly historical origin, let us look at the three. The earliest was Caesarius' *Dialogue*. He tells the miracle as having occurred 'very recently', and claims he had it from Gerungus, cathedral schoolmaster of Bonn, Gerungus at the time having just returned from a stay in Paris.

---

[66] D. Moreni, ed., *Prediche del beato fra Giordano da Rivalto, O.P., recitate in Firenze dal 1303 al 1306*, 2 vols (Florence, 1831), vol. 1, p. 302: 'ci l'ebbe tale in questa città, ch'andò alla donna, et dissele: che vou' tu ch'io faccia? quella disse, che tu ti gitti in Arno; quelli andò, e gittavavisi, e fu pressochè morto, se non che fu campato.'

[67] Gerard of Frachet, O.P., *Vitas fratrum*, pt 4, ch. 4, § 2; ed. B. M. Reichert, 159–60, with an editor's note listing other versions. The theme in literature: J. Coppin, *Amour et mariage dans la littérature française du moyen âge* (Paris, 1961), 17 (Lutisse).

Caesarius does not name the hero but makes him the chaplain at the court of a high French nobleman, and adds that he, the hero, entered the Dominican Order soon after the miracle and in gratitude for it. Since that Order was effectively founded in 1215 and the tenth 'Distinction' of the *Dialogue of Miracles* written in 1222, Caesarius clearly conceived the incident as having actually happened between 1215 and 1222. That date would fit an association with an actual 'Brother Dominic' whom we know from a Dominican source to have died in 1230.[68]

The next teller of the story was Gerard of Frachet, Dominican author of *Lives of the Brethren* or *Vitas fratrum*. This was the collection of biographical anecdotes about early Dominicans we met earlier, written between 1256 and c.1260. Gerard actually names the hero as the Dominican 'brother Dominic' and identifies the court as that of a king of Spain. That reference, if it refers to a particular king, must refer to Alfonso VIII of Castile, who ruled from 1198 to 1214. In Gerard's version it is nobles round the king who put the woman up to her attempt at seduction; and Gerard makes Brother Dominic protest, as an excuse for putting fire to his bed, that age had cooled his passions.[69]

The third narrator is Thomas of Chantimpré, writing c.1265. Thomas writes without any apparent reference to Gerard's *Lives*, and claims that he heard the tale nearly forty years before, 'at the very beginning of the order', that is, at about the time Caesarius was writing it into the *Dialogue*. Like Caesarius, though unlike Gerard, Thomas ascribes the initiative in the plot wholly to the woman, and Thomas finds her motive in a mixture of lust and bravado, not (as in Gerard) revenge for her victim's puritanical influence. The king, in Thomas's story, is hostile to the whole experiment and threatens the woman, if her experiment fails, with death by burning. In the event she is saved from this fate only by the holy man's intercession.[70]

The threat of suicide occurs explicitly only in Caesarius' version. Gerard makes the woman solicit the priest 'both instantly and ardently'. Thomas, a writer who often comes nearly to the point of talking about suicide but never quite, makes her beg the priest's favours 'before I die'. Only the ever frank Caesarius makes the hussy say explicitly: 'I will kill myself unless you do as I ask'; and the priest, 'terrified', suggest a rendezvous 'so long as you do not kill yourself'.

[68] *Dial. mirac.*, dist. 10, ch. 34 (vol. 2, pp. 241–2). Caesarius, ibid.: 'nisi mihi consentiendo ignem a vobis succensum extinguatis, vivero non potero'. 'Si non feceritis quod postulo, ecce me ipsam interficiam.' For Caesarius' frankness on suicide see p. 275 above. For the date of dist. 10 see E. Langosch in *Verfasserlexikon*, 1, col. 1157.

[69] As in n. 67.

[70] *De apibus*, bk 2, ch. 30, § 45 (pp. 349–51), in which the king seems, here too, to have been Alfonso VIII. Cf. Kaufmann [as in n. 24 above], 55–6 for yet other versions.

I have told the story about Brother Dominic, at a date between 1215 and 1222, because three writers do so, writers all of whom, as a general rule, mix reliable history in their *miracula*; and because one of them, known anyway to be egregiously frank on the subject, includes a threat of suicide in the woman's strategy. But the story should be seen in the context of analogues before and after that date. The burning bed features *without* a threat of suicide in the *Life of Saint William of Vercelli*, who died in 1142 as leader of an eremetical community near Salerno.[71] After Brother Dominic's time, the burning bed *with* an apparent threat of suicide would be linked to another Dominican, St Peter Gonzalez. Knowing what we do of euphemism in this regard, we are entitled to read as a suicide threat the woman's warning to St Peter Gonzalez that, if she does not have her way 'she will not live a moment longer.' St Peter Gonzalez died in 1246. Since the *Life* was not written down until the beginning of the sixteenth century, we have no means of knowing whether the story became attached to his name in his lifetime, in reference to some incident in his experience, or whether it was added centuries later as a stock embellishment.[72]

All we do know is that thirteenth-century Dominicans did hear confessions, including those from attractive women, and that the temptations to which they were thus exposed, with or without miraculous beds to help fight them, made a constant headache for the authorities of the Order,[73] and not only to them. If this kind of anecdote, with its underlying suggestion of the perils to which the order was exposed, became attached to Dominicans, that is partly because they spoke to each other of their experiences and wrote them down. But the same could happen to a secular priest, who had no religious order round him and may have been subject to even stronger temptations. He might, like the notorious Pierre Clergue of Le Roy Ladurie's *Montaillou*, avoid this particular temptation by indulging it; and it is certain that many priests got 'married'. But not all; and it cannot be mere chance that when we do hear of one who was not, and who suffered similar temptations from a suicidal woman, we do so because the priest in question *became* a Dominican, partly as a result of his experience. That is, it is again

---

[71] *Vita s. Guilelmi Vercellensis, Acta sanctorum*, June 5 (1709), 127.

[72] *Vita s. Petri Gonzales* [*c.*1190–1246], by Stephan de San Pelayo, ch. 2, §§ 10–14; *Acta sanctorum*, April 2 (1675), 393D–394D; esp. § 12 [394AB]: 'quod nisi meo acquiescas desiderio, minime ultra superfutura sim. His et aliis similibus verbis, tamquam melle lito gladio, venenosa haec peccati filia, sanctum et honestum Dei famulum Dominum Petrum, transfodere cogitavit. . . ."Non", inquit, "filia, Deus permittat, ut ego tuae repentinae mortis causa existam aut fiam."'

[73] H. Grundmann, *Religiöse Bewegungen im Mittelalter*, 2nd edn (Hildesheim, 1961), 199–318.

the Dominican network that got the story preserved. I will finish this chapter with it.

The importunate hussy in question had one important difference from the others—besides her having targeted a secular priest rather than a prior. She did commit suicide. So rhetoric may be the wrong context for it, for we are not told whether she did or did not threaten to do so first. But in so far as a historical incident may have lain behind the miracle, it was certainly of the kind the amorous rhetoricians had in mind, or at least on their tongues. The case comes to light in a miracle of St Bridget of Sweden (†1373). It was put in her canonization process in 1379, and constitutes one of those late medieval *miracula* whose writers, conscious of the need for quasi-legal authentification, gives the historian a glimpse of what may otherwise have happened in the black hole. The witness in this case was a Swedish Dominican prior, and he spoke of the central figure of the story, his fellow friar John, as dead by 1379. As a secular priest, the prior recounted, John had once found himself 'burning with carnal temptation as from a fire', in respect of a particular woman parishioner. The priest, as perhaps also the parishioner, was much troubled by erotic thoughts and found it hard to pray. He claimed he had preserved lifelong priestly continence up to that time and did not wish to throw it away. So John went to St Bridget and asked for her counsel and prayers. Bridget judged the amorous woman to be unbelieving, stubborn, and lustful, and strengthened John's resolve to have nothing more to do with her. The upshot was, three nights later, that the amorous woman bit off her tongue and plunged a knife into her private parts, bleeding to death with dreadful shouts and imprecations, heard by many. This is told as a 'miracle' of St Bridget. It is a pity she could not have purified the woman too. But then historians, as we have learned, cannot have everything. John the priest, sobered by the shock, at once joined the Dominican Order and observed its rule until his death.[74]

I have rehearsed stories of suicide, or threats of suicide, arising from relationships between the sexes, as displayed in just over a dozen stories. Eleven

---

[74] I. Collijn, ed., *Acta et processus canonizacionis beate Birgitte*. Samlinger utgivna av Svenska Fornskrifts ällskadpet, Andra Serien, Latinska Skrifta, vol. 1 (Uppsala, 1924–31), 513: 'dominus Johannes . . . fascinatus erat taliter quod ardebat temptacione carnali quasi ignis, ita quod nihil cogitare poterat nisi sordidas cogitaciones carnales nec orare poterat more solito. Qui cum iam quasi extra sensum nolens perdere longam continenciam et castitatem, quam servaverat . . .' The consultation with Bridget follows, then 'ut asseruit ipse testis loquens, tercia nocte illa . . . facta est furiosa mordens irriguam suam et arrepto cultro lesit se in inguine et clamans cunctis audientibus . . . sic cum tam horribili clamore miserabiliter vitam suam finivit.' I have omitted those elements which attach to the charge that the woman had employed diabolic enchantment on the priest. They can be read in Goodich, *Violence and Miracle*, 64–5.

of them concern women. The suicidal crises of the two males, furthermore, namely Henry of Le Dale and the Santiago pilgrim, are presented as deriving as much from some religious tension (obedience to an abbot for Henry, penance for the pilgrim) as from mere *chagrin d'amour*. This qualification is applicable, among the female suicides, only to Caesarius' bewitched nun. Other female cases reflect the natural hazards of emotional life. This imbalance is not out of harmony with what we know of the different positions of the sexes in the church itself. The imbalance suggests here that tensions with a strong religious element, bearable or unbearable, were more likely to strike men than women, other things being equal, and therefore leave women more exclusively exposed to the dangers of inter-human emotions. A dozen cases form a slender sample and the imbalance in question may be meaningless. We shall have to interpret it afresh in looking at further statistical comparisons. But if, at this stage and in this context, the imbalance has any significance, this is it. The conclusion draws strength from another circumstance. When we turn to consider the suicide stories relating to troubled relationships between, not one family member and another or between man and woman, but between the individual on one side and social institutions on the other, we find that all the stories refer to men. This will be one lesson of the next chapter.

13

The Enemy of Society

THE miracles told so far have been about close personal bonds within the family or potential family. A further group touch on disturbances of a more social character: quarrels with the law, with a lord or master, or with a community or its spokesman. Of course the groups are interconnected. A suicide does not stop to makes his motives fit straight lines. But let the category be taken broadly, as that of suicides who had become, or thought they had become, enemies of society.

Society's most obvious enemies are victims of the law. Suicides have already been met in judicial records among persons accused, arrested, or hunted for crime. Court records were naturally interested in criminals and it is fair to ask whether, being forensic, they give this type of suicide a false prominence. The answer must be, not entirely, for an association of suicide with crime is confirmed by *miracula*. A few of these have already been told. Agnes's family tragedy, after all, made her also a criminal. We know her motives because the Devil numbers them off (perhaps, as I suggested, because the woman herself had confessed them to a Dominican friar from whom the details had leaked through to the narrator). And among these motives, together with Agnes's private feeling of wretchedness and her shame in the face of her relations, was fear of execution. She was an infanticide, exposed to burning alive. The same must have been true of another of those family tragedies, that of the matricide of Bury St Edmund's. That one had no Devil to itemize her motives. We are only told her crime, and that she would not confess to a priest. We might have known her thoughts if she had. But it would be surprising, especially in the light of Agnes's example, if one factor in the matricide's desperation had not been fear of execution. Those two family stories, in other words, give us an idea of what to look for among enemies of the law.

Murderers

The most serious class of enemies of the law is that of murderer. The suicidal propensities of a murderer duly appear in one of the earliest of all our medieval suicide *miracula* to have survived, and from a century otherwise unrepresented. It is in a *Life* written about 894 by Wolfhard of Herrieden, a monastery near Ansbach in Franconia, about St Walpurga, the English-born abbess (popularly celebrated on Walpurgisnacht) who had died around 779. Wolfhard speaks of witnesses to his miracle story as still alive. But since that sounds like part of an inventor's literary equipment, there is no way of telling if it is meant to be literally true; only that, if an event did lie behind the story, it is conceived as occurring in Wolfhard's time, that is, around 870–890.[1]

There was a severe famine in Franconia. Two travellers, so weakened by starvation that they could hardly walk, met a third, who claimed to be on a pilgrimage to the shrine of St Walpurga. The third traveller had food, and although he was ready to share it, the other two agreed to kill him and take it all away. They did so. But they then faced the problem of how to dispose of the body. The companion who had *not* struck the fatal blow heaved the corpse on to his back. Then came the miracle. The body stuck to him and he could not get it off. It made no difference that his guiltier companion meanwhile repented and made a vow, to be fulfilled later, to go and seek pardon from St Walpurga. The bearer of the corpse could not get rid of it, try as he might. In his wanderings he came with his accomplice to the Rhine, where:

overwhelmed by shame and by his burden he preferred to plunge into the peril of death rather than drag out any longer the unheard-of disgrace of his hateful life. Opting therefore for an unprofitable course he entered the rough waters of the river, there to give deep burial to the long-dead body on his back, and at the same time to discover in its waves, by taking his own woeful life to the same swirling flood, the same burial for himself.[2]

He was now thwarted by a second miracle.

But the moment the marble-cool flow of water touched the wicked murderer it knew he did not belong to it and spewed him forth like filth on to the river bank.[3]

The murderer had clearly reckoned without the intrinsic innocence of water, premiss of the contemporary ordeal by water. This setback, at all events,

---

[1] *Miracula s. Waldburgis Monheimensis*, ed. A. Bauch, *Ein bayerisches Mirakelbuch aus der Karolingerzeit* (Regensburg, 1979), bk 2, ch. 6, pp. 222–32. This book also contains the miracle of the possibly suicidal mother, told on p. 257 above.

[2] *Mir. s. Waldburgis*, pp. 230.21–6.   [3] Ibid., lines 26–9.

proved the last straw for the hitherto loyal accomplice, the murderer who had actually struck the blow. He now went off on his own to the monastery of St Walpurga, completed his repentance, and made a satisfactory confession. His burdened companion remained. He tried to follow but was mysteriously prevented from approaching the monastery. We are given to understand that he was never freed. He has been seen, Wolfhard asserts, by persons still living, still with the corpse clinging to his back.

This story attracted a comment from the distinguished authority on early legend, Heinrich Günther: 'rarely,' he wrote, 'has a bad conscience been more vividly portrayed.'[4] No doubt. But a bad conscience could still have been portrayed more consistently. The man who struck the fatal blow wins pardon while, for reasons unexplained, his companion is punished, and that despite his repeated, praiseworthy attempts to reach the shrine of St Walpurga. The story is supernatural enough. In that sense it qualifies as miraculous. But of the three supernatural wonders it relates, only one is at ease with Christian doctrine, namely the adhesive corpse. For both the fastidious river and the unapproachable monastery are moral anomalies, of the kind I meant when I said hagiography could be alloyed by folklore. The anomalies may or may not make Wolfhard's account a bad enough story to claim a historical kernel. But at least we can be sure that, in late ninth-century Franconia, no apology was needed for the idea that a guilt-ridden murderer might try to escape by killing himself. No apology, and not even —*nota bene*—the statutory Devil, regular instigator of suicide. The same remained true in a late eleventh-century version, where the story of the guilt-ridden murderer was to be repeated with the suicidal element enhanced. Around 1070, Bishop Adalbold of Utrecht wrote his own *Life of St Walpurga* and included this miracle with, among other variations in wording, a phrase to emphasize the murderer's suicidal intention. In place of 'he entered the river [*introivit fluviam*]' Adalbold, as if to underline the wish for self-destruction, puts 'he threw himself into the whirling abyss with all his force.' But there was still no Devil. Perhaps a murderer was not thought to need him.[5]

The would-be suicide in the Walpurga legend makes the only certainly suicidal miracle story I have found that can be dated definitely between the sixth and the late tenth century. One story is nearly an exception but not quite, and is worth a moment's attention. The Merovingian King Dagobert II is said to have been murdered in 679, and one account says his murderer hanged himself. But a close look at the account throws a rare light on the character of this literature as a lamination of fact and fiction. For a *Life* of

---

[4] *Christliche Legende des Abendlandes* (Heidelberg, 1910), 128–9.
[5] Adalbold, *Vita S. Walpurgis*, ch. 3, § 19; *Acta sanctorum*, Feb. 3 (1658), 546C.

Dagobert's contemporary St Wilfred of Hexham, written soon after Wilfred's death in 709, mentions Dagobert's murder but says no more of the murderer, or what became of him, than that the Frankish bishops had connived at the killing on the grounds that the king was a sinner. The murderer's suicide only makes its appearance in a second tradition, which has Dagobert as a saint, not a sinner, and his killer therefore a wicked traitor. This second tradition betrays its lateness by giving the assassin-traitor a name, 'John', a name shared with no other known character in Merovingian circles, but which was common in late Carolingian times. The earliest *Life* of Dagobert, which includes the suicide, therefore cannot, by general agreement, be dated earlier than the tenth century, since it is a patchwork of common hagiographical motifs of which no trace appears in corresponding accounts nearer to Dagobert's time. The 'Judas' suicide of Dagobert's betrayer thus loses all authority for the seventh century.[6]

A story like that miracle of St Walpurga both is, and is not, complementary to murderers' suicides in judicial sources. It is complementary because, from its own independent viewpoint, it makes the same association of the two sorts of homicide, of oneself and of someone else. It is not, because this particular kind of miracle belongs to a different period, and necessarily so. For this was the dark age of public prosecution of crime. Between the collapse of the Carolingian Empire until the late eleventh century was consequently a golden age for miracles of this type, a 'police' miracle in which a crime, theoretically indictable by public authority, is left to supernatural forces. But supernatural forces cannot have been as effective as desired, for more earthly forms of justice were soon brought to their aid. As they came, police miracles tended to drop away from hagiography.[7]

Among the small class of miracle stories which do mention suicide the only exception to this rule is of the kind which proves it. One of Thomas of Chantimpré's *exempla* would tell of a group of murderers who killed themselves. But this, we must remember, was an *exemplum*, which had freer rules than a miracle; and the suicide occurs in the context of a Crown prosecution. The *exemplum* tells how, around 1200, some Augustinian canons of Blois had been sent a new-broom abbot, a graduate from the University of Paris. They resisted his reforms and hired assassins to kill him. A splinter group betrayed the plot and got the entire convent of canons detained on suspicion. Some confessed and were sentenced to life imprisonment, while

[6] F. Graus, *Volk, Herrscher und Heiliger im Reich der Merowinger* (Prague, 1965), 403–6.

[7] B. de Gaiffier, 'Les revendications de biens dans quelques documents hagiograpiques du xie siècle', *Analecta Bollandiana*, 50 (1932), 123–38.

others were stripped of their orders and put to death. Of these, sixteen—who were believed to be the most closely implicated in the crime—laid homicidal hands on themselves in prison, and killed themselves by hanging or in other ways.

This report came from one of the splinter group, 'Robert', who later left the Augustinians and became a Dominican friar; whence, indirectly, Thomas learned of the incident.[8] It is a rare intrusion by an *exemplum* into a purely judicial province, where the incident appears in no surviving records.

Thieves

That was murder, or planned murder. Of criminal acts murder is the gravest but not the commonest. Among the commonest is theft, and the economic changes of the eleventh century, which put more money into circulation, made it commoner. Three miracle stories, all from after the millennium, duly make theft the occasion for suicidal behaviour.

One was written at a monastery in Verdun at the very end of the eleventh century, in a collection of miracles attributed to the monastery's patron, the early seventh-century bishop, St Paul of Verdun.[9] One of its miracles concerns an ex-slave in Verdun called John, whose adventures the writer claims to be relating from his own experience. John must have been the slave's baptismal name, imposed, from what we know of slavery in Verdun at the time, on a man of Slav origin. Doubtless expecting to enjoy the intense personal loyalty for which Slavs were noted, the master made John chief manager of his business affairs. One day, as John was duly giving orders to the other *servi*, he suddenly fell to the ground, groaning, and biting himself. Perhaps it was epilepsy. The affliction, at all events, brought John to the attention of the monastery whose patron, St Paul of Verdun, had a reputation locally for curing demonic attacks. So the slave John was taken there, exorcised, and sent back to his master. The same happened again. Again he was returned to the monastery for a cure. It all happened a third time. The attacks, and subsequent cure at the monastery, became so regular that the master 'after consultation with his wife' finally decided to make the monastery a present of his slave.

---

[8] Thomas of Chantimpré, *De apibus*, bk 1, ch. 16, § 2 (pp. 54–7; the suicide is on p. 56). Louis, Count of Blois, who imprisoned the canons, held office 1191–1205.

[9] *Miracula s. Pauli Verdunensis*, § 8; ed. J. van der Straeten, S. J., *Les manuscrits hagiographiques de Charleville, Verdun et St-Mihiel*. Subsidia Hagiographica, 56 (Brussels, 1974), 136–49; at § 8 on pp. 143–4. Date: p. 133 and cf. 5 (p. 141): 'ad ea que vidi veniam', and the appearance of Thiery II, duke of Upper Lorraine (1070–1115) in § 9 (p. 144). Slaves: C. Verlinden, *L'esclavage dans l'Europe médiévale*, I (Bruges 1955); at Verdun in particular, 222–5.

John's gift to the monastery opened a new and eventually calamitous phase in his career. He served peaceably for a year but gradually became 'insolent'. John started to spend his money—this being one of very few texts of the period to reveal that slaves could have money—on loose women and on drink, the latter, we know from elsewhere, another notorious forte of Slavonic slaves. The miracle writer thinks John's problem stemmed from the excessive leniency of his new employers: the monks had taken special care not to be harsh with John after his fits. Whatever the reasons, John ran short of money and borrowed. Unable to repay, he began to steal small articles from fellow-slaves to sell for cash in the market. The objects were missed, and although, at first, no one knew who the thief was, security was tightened. So John turned to different and bigger booty, and, during the monks' lunch-break broke into the monastery church, stealing the silver cross and silver-studded Gospel book.

John's luck now turned. 'By chance [*casu*]' the custodian of the church was passing, saw the door open, looked in, saw the cross and the Gospel missing. He raised the alarm. The other monks, rushing in at another door, almost collided with John as he was leaving with the booty. John was expelled, for ever. Since he had no means of livelihood he went back to his former master, with what sort of reception we are not told. For the narrator speeds straight to the end:

Not long afterwards the Devil took control of him and threw him into a nearby river, thus battering and bruising him until he had finally shaken out the poor wretch's life.

Now the *antiquus possessor* who threw John into the river was the same Devil who had been mentioned as author of the original fits (*diabolo se invadente*). The circumlocution here may be a reference back. But the phrase is ambiguous. The tendency of a narrator deliberately to choose ambiguous expressions in this connection is something we have met before, as we have the role of the Devil in them. The ambiguity of the narrator's account therefore leaves open a suicidal, as distinct from a merely epileptic, interpretation.[10]

A second story of a suicidal thief is free of this ambiguity. It appears in *The Miracles of St Mary of Laon*, compiled by Hermann, a canon of Laon, around 1118.[11] In 1112 the cathedral in Laon had been burned in a riot, and

---

[10] *Mir. s. Pauli Verd.* § 8, p. 144: 'sed mox antiquus possessor eum invadit et in flumen, quod erat proximum, proiecit, ubi tamdiu vexatum attrivit quousque spiritum miserabiliter excuteret infelici.'

[11] *Mir. s. Mariae Laudunensis*, bk 2, ch. 20; *Pat. lat.*, 156.985.

to collect money for its restoration a posse of canons had taken on tour the cathedral's most treasured possession, the relics of the Virgin. The aim was that the relics should procure miracles and thus precipitate gifts. Having toured northern France with modest success, the canons came to England, where they travelled from Canterbury as far west as Totnes in Devon. There their enterprise was subject to derision by three youths from a well-to-do local family, who claimed that the alleged 'miracles' were in fact magic, performed by the canons out of greed. One of the youths went further, suggesting to his two companions that the three together should steal offerings from the altar where the relics were, the plot being that the three should pretend to kiss the relics, but meanwhile secrete coins in their mouths. The plan proved too much for the two cousins, who declined to participate. So the inventor of the plan fulfilled it on his own. Having completed his theft he returned to his cousins, and invited them to drink the proceeds in a tavern. Again they declined. So the thief drank on his own, from his ill-gotten gains. Then he rode off on horseback to a wood half a mile away, and 'there tied a flaxen rope round his neck and hanged himself on the branch of a tree'.

The riderless horse ran back to the village, where its appearance, and the line of hoofprints behind it, led the two cousins to their kinsman's body, already dead. They took him down and, finding in his purse some coins still wet with his saliva, they returned the coins to the reliquary. Those inhabitants of Totnes who had witnessed the incident were dumbfounded, both by the sacrilege and the swiftness of the nemesis it had provoked. At least, they were according to *The Miracles of St Mary of Laon*. As for the author himself, he saw the story as 'a terrible miracle . . . whose occurrence is rarely to be read of since the time of Judas'. Guibert of Nogent, giving excerpts from the itinerant Laon canons' miracle stories in his own autobiography around 1121, included a rubbed-down version of the same suicide.[12]

To the Totnes thief, suicide was a punishment. So the act was completed. In the third of this trio of thief stories, suicide is presented in the form more normal to *miracula*, namely as a diabolical temptation frustrated by a saint's intervention. Because the attempt was here unsuccessful, and because it was recorded at a time when storytellers put a premium on psychology, its description of the mind of a would-be suicide is more careful than the other two. The miracle in question was performed posthumously by St Thomas Becket, and comes in both the two principal collections of Becket miracles,

---

[12] *De vita sua*, pt 3, ch. 13, ed. E. R. Labande (Paris, 1981), p. 392. My reasons for treating Book I of the *Mir. S. Maria Laudun.* as following a model completed before 1121 are explained in *Trans. Royal Hist. Soc.*, 6th ser., 3 (1993), 67 n. 70.

respectively by Benedict and William, monks of Canterbury.[13] William's account is longer and more circumstantial, but both relate essentially the same story. If, again, the story reflects a real incident, the incident should be dated between about 1171 and about 1177. It is placed at Ifield in Kent, then a village (now on the southern outskirts of Gravesend).

The beneficiary of the miracle was the 13-year-old daughter of a well-to-do Ifield villager, Thomas. The daughter, Salerna, was the younger of two sisters, and during an absence of her mother she let herself be persuaded by servants to steal a cheese from her mother's larder. When the mother returned and found the cheese missing she suspected Salerna, threatened her, beat her, and (according to Benedict's account at least) undertook next day, unless Salerna confessed to the crime, to 'beat the life out of her'.

Salerna passed a sleepless night, and when her mother was away at church next morning, went to a remote room of the house on the pretence that she was tending her infant brother. What she was in fact doing was climbing out of a window into the orchard behind the house. There

she walked this way and that, horrified at the crime she was proposing. On one side, fear of death held her back. On the other, the Enemy of the human race, in the form of a servant woman, urged her on.[14]

After a spell of this uncertainty Salerna leapt over a wall, reached the well which supplied the house with water, took off its cover, and got as far as putting her legs in and hanging by her arms. At this point she was seen by a ploughman. He could tell even at a distance that something was wrong. Aware that she had been spotted, Salerna acted quickly, Benedict saying she was 'urged downwards by the promptings of Him who is below', William, merely that she dropped into the well.

Both authors agree that, as Salerna fell, she called on St Thomas Becket. So we know the outcome. The vigilant ploughman rushed over. He woke a farmhand who, providentially, had returned early from the mill and was asleep in a nearby granary. The farmhand undressed and tried to climb into the well. He could not. So he changed his mind, found a horse, and rode off to tell the girl's mother at the church. The mother, now bemoaning her own harshness to the child, recruited, with help from neighbours, a certain Ralph, a local man renowned for his strength and ingenuity who, again providentially, happened to be nearby. Ralph lost no time in lowering himself on a rope into the well, and after divers setbacks, recounted at length by

[13] *Miracula s. Thomae auctore Willelmo Cantuariensi*, bk 3, ch. 3; J. C. Robinson, *Materials for the History of Thomas Becket*, vol. 1. Rolls Series, vol. 67a (1895), 248–61. *Mir. s. Thomae anct. Benedicto*, bk 6, ch. 2; ed. J. C. Robinson, Ibid., vol. 67b (1876), 263–6.
[14] William, *loc. cit.*, 258.

Benedict, discovered the girl standing on a joist near the bottom of the well. He managed to hoist both her and himself to safety. The girl was cold but uninjured. Both authors introduce the invisible saint's help at various junctures. They point out, for instance, how unlikely it would otherwise have been for a girl to fall into a fifty-foot well (William makes it a *one-hundred-and-*fifty-foot well) without being killed. In both accounts, as Salerna is extracted, she asks to be 'measured' for St Thomas: that is (as in the miracle of Rocamadour in the last chapter) to have a candle as long as herself presented to his shrine.[15]

Salerna of Ifield was one of many thieves to enjoy domestic protection. Severe her mother may have been. But if Salerna had stolen outside the family she might have got harsher treatment, and at the right period (which this was not) reached our judicial records. Her adventure is in one respect another 'family' case. The penalty she feared was the displeasure of a domestic authority. This feature is shared by a fourth miracle, which I append for this reason to the three stories of thieves we have just heard.

This fourth miracle concerns a woman called Eve, guardian and governess to the adolescent Andreas of Fleury.[16] Andreas became a monk, and in due time, in the early 1140s, author of several books of miracles worked by St Benedict, in and around Fleury-sur-Loire. While most of Andreas's miracles come from other people, one is a recollection from his own childhood. Its date we can very roughly determine as between 1010 and 1030, knowing only that Andreas would at the time have been about 15.

Andreas's governess, Eve, also acted as maid of all work for his father. One Feast Day the family was leaving the church at Fleury. It was about eleven o'clock, and the two great monastic bells were ringing as the crowds dispersed to get some food ('we did not eat before Mass in those days').[17] One of a group of local nobles approached Andreas's mother, to ask if her family would like to come to his house for a meal. The mother accepted, and asked Eve to pass her her (the mother's) gown. Eve could not find it, searched up and down for a long time, and finally gave up hope. In recounting the story, decades later, Andreas says nothing on Eve's state of mind at this point. The fast, and the presence of local nobles, might have heightened

---

[15] William, *loc. cit.*, 260; Benedict, *loc. cit.*, 265. 'Measuring': R. C. Finucane, *Miracles and Pilgrims* (London, 1977), 95.

[16] *Mir. s. Benedicti*, bk 7, ch. 9; ed. E. de Certain (Paris, 1858), 265–6. This part is by Andreas of Fleury. A. Vidier, *L'Historiographie à Saint-Benôit-sur-Loire et les Miracles de Saint Benôit* (Paris 1965), 202. Andreas collected his miracles from 1041 and wrote them down after 1043.

[17] Cf. P. Browe, 'Die Kommunionvorbereitung im Mittelalter', *Zeitschrift für katholische Theologie*, 56 (1931), 375–415 at 408–9; frequency of communion: P. Browe, *Die häufige Kommunion im Mittelalter* (Münster, 1938), 20–1, 65–7.

any shame induced by her negligence. Or was it more than negligence? In the early eleventh century a noblewoman's robe was a valuable article, of a kind often mentioned among robbers' booty. Is it conceivable that Eve was suspected of conniving at its theft? Her reaction must otherwise seem an over-reaction, for Andreas's recollection goes on:

through excessive grief at this mishap her thoughts were suddenly turned by the Old Enemy. She happened to be holding a knife at the time and was so rash as to take her life with it.

In her madness (*vesania*) Eve had hardly stabbed herself when she was grabbed by bystanders and, under the direction of Andreas's family, taken back into the monastery. There she was laid in the crypt under the eye of a priest ('a spiritual doctor'). She at once fell asleep and woke at three in the afternoon, perfectly healed. 'For Satan's wiles could not prevail against the merits of St Benedict.'

A Prisoner under Torture

With the exception of the plotters of Le Mans, the half-dozen killers or thieves rehearsed so far had in common that their guilt did not involve the law. In this they illustrate the broadly inverse relationship, noticed a moment ago, between miracles as 'police' and the effectiveness of legal institutions. Where a criminal was swiftly arrested and punished by human agency there was less need for supernatural policing. This may explain the relative silence of miracles and *exempla* on a kind of suicide relatively common in both legal records and in those chronicles nearest them in genre. I refer to that of the apprehended criminal, escaping the law's punishment. The rescue of such suicides is very rare in *miracula*. This should not be a surprise. A considerable number of *miracula* were concerned to modify the cruellest punishments, not least by freeing lucky or meritorious victims from the gallows. But it could not be the job of miracles altogether to dissolve the criminal law by favouring its suicidal culprits. Miracles were more often, as in the examples just quoted, the law's supplement and precursor.

An extension of this rule applies to victims of torture. Torture was something even legal records did not like to talk about. As canon law, even at its most severe, sent convicted heretics to certain death under the euphemism of 'relaxation to the secular arm', so criminal law, for its part, from the middle of the thirteenth century and with comparable euphemism, called judicial torture the 'question', and normally forbore to volunteer in its records the cruelties the term was meant to hide. Suicide to avoid the cruelties may have escaped for the same reason. If so, it is a point of silence matched in religious sources. I have found almost no miracles telling of a prisoner under torture killing himself, or trying to do so, and being rescued by a saint. Perhaps the moral message of such a story would have been too confused for a pulpit. Both the being in prison and the suicidal intention would combine to stamp the hero with too compromised a character to invite an overlay of redeemability. If such suicides happened, this suggests, in those grim medieval dungeons, they happened in a black hole in a cognitive as well as an architectural sense.

This is a hypothesis, based on external considerations about the black hole. But it may be another rule confirmed by its exception, which comes from south-eastern France. If a miracle was, despite those disincentives, going to shine its light into a torturer's dungeon, no region would have been more appropriate than this. South-eastern France was governed, in so far as so far-flung a province of the French monarchy was likely to be governed at all, by a chessboard pattern of families disposed either against or towards the church. The former provided the dungeons, the latter a human soil receptive to miracle. It is from this region, consequently, that we might expect the exception to come. It does, and in a context equally favourable to this type of miracle: a context in which literary criteria, like the disincentives mentioned in the last paragraph, would have had least opportunity to reshape an original incident. It was a context where miracle and legal records came closest, namely a canonization process. One of the leading pro-ecclesiastical families of south-eastern France from the late thirteenth century was that of the Grimoards, who lived and ruled out of Grisac, in the hills of the Gévaudan, sixty miles north-west of Avignon. The most famous of the family's churchmen died in 1370 as Pope Urban V, and at once miracles began to occur all over the area, in proof of his sanctity. The miracles were collected at the monastery of which he had been abbot, St Victor of Marseilles, and one of them concerns a man suicidal under torture.

This victim too was exceptional. Not only, that is, was he in the right geographical area for his plight to be recorded, and the context the most promising. He was the right sort of man: he was innocent of crime or blame, a victim of arbitrary accusation and imprisonment by an unsupervised castellan. On top of that, he was a Santiago pilgrim, of a kind noted for the hair's-breadth escapes that fed the best-known miracle collections of the late Middle Ages. Yet none of these collections adopted this particular miracle, of a man suicidal under torture, a fact which only underlines the literary disincentives attached to this type of incident.

Here is the miracle. A man called John de Mondeuil, of Chateauneuf near

Sarlat on the Dordogne, had made two pilgrimages, one to Santiago, the other to St Antoine on the Isère above Valence. He was returning from the latter, on the road that runs along the course of the Isère, when he was arrested as a spy and put in the dungeon of St Nazaire-en-Royans. The nervous castellan was convinced John was in a plot to take and betray the castle, and kept him

imprisoned for five weeks in the most wretched conditions. He would be brought and interrogated by the castellan's legal officers. He confessed nothing because he had no idea what they were talking about. So then he was lifted on the rack four times, and by dint of the sheer force he confessed what they asked. Back in prison, he was attacked by many diabolical temptations to kill himself, since he was of the view that he would never escape death. But after a while, by God's grace, he regretted having had such an evil thought and called to mind Pope Urban V of holy memory. He recommended himself to Urban devoutly and asked him to intercede with God for him, so that he should not fall into desperation and lose his soul. If Urban could procure his release, he promised to visit the pope's tomb and make an offering.[18]

The *Deus ex machina* came at once, in the form of a suggestion by two other prisoners that the three of them escape by capturing the guard, and fastening sheets together which would let them down from a window. John insisted that the guard should not be killed, and his accomplices agreed. This restraint cost John some pain, for as the guard entered, rather than kill him, John put a firm hand over the man's mouth, and got his thumb bitten (the scar still showing at the time of the hearing). After more hide-and-seek the guard, one against three, found John again and knocked him to the ground, leaving him there, however, to look for the others, for long enough for John to scramble to his feet and evade the bemused, puffing guard once more. So John escaped to tell his tale. The other two were recaptured and returned to prison. It is to be presumed that they had failed to make vows to St Urban V.

The critical principles appropriate to a proper reading of this account are similar to those we would apply to the advertisement of an insurance company. We have to weigh up for ourselves how typical the case is. But it

---

[18] J. H. Albanès, ed., *Actes anciens et documents concernant le bienheureux Urbain V, pape*, vol. 1 (Paris-Marseilles, 1897), 458–9, no. 51. The suicidal passages run 'redditus in carcere (p. 459) habuit multas diabolicas temptaciones ut se interficeret, quia credebat quod non posset a morte evadere; tandem Dei gratia dolens de hujusmodi mala cogitatione, evenit sibi in memoria dominus Urbanus . . . rogavit eum ut pro ipso intercederet apud Deum, ne veniret in desperationem et perderet animam suam.' My translation introduces the ideas of 'attack' and 'view' to represent respectively the perfect and imperfect tenses in the original: John's temptation, it suggests, was acute rather than chronic. For the miracle in the context of other canonization miracles, cf. Goodich, *Miracle and Violence*, 56–7.

is only a matter of similarity. While an insurance company seeks out all sorts
of customers, the beneficiary of a miracle was not just anyone. Virtue, as
well as God's power, came into it, so that a recorder of miracles had to be
selective. The recorder of this one carefully sets down John's stipulation (a
costly one) that the guard be not murdered. And this need for virtue in a
beneficiary mattered all the more if the miracle occurred in circumstances
as compromising as a justiciar's dungeon. The high moral score of this
particular pilgrim, rare witness to a tortured prisoner's temptation to
suicide, distinguished him from the desperadoes who probably made up the
majority of the dungeon population, and whose sufferings and suicides
would have had correspondingly less claim on a narrator. The plight of
Urban V's protégé, John of Mondeuil, that consideration suggests, may be
like that of Pierre Fournet le Breton in the Châtelet register: one of a class,
rare only in respect of the string of chances that got it into a historical
document.[19]

Economic Loss

Whether through murder or theft, crime isolated the perpetrator, making
his fellow-men into active foes. Similar social dislocation, leading at its
extreme to suicide, could follow economic loss. How often? Court records,
whether English, French, or German, identify between them only a small
handful of suicides provoked expressly by debt. But then courts rarely noted
down motives, and the fact that lawyers, if not court scribes, were aware of
debt as one motive for suicide is shown by the jurists' endorsement of 'debt
[*aes aliena*]' in this regard, notably in reference to the Florentine suicide epidemic *c.*1300. At first glance the miracle dossier is no more forthcoming.
With a big exception I shall come to, it says next to nothing of debt or economic loss as occasions for suicidal impulses. But here again there is reason
to doubt the impression given by this silence. Miracles hoped to point a
moral. The 'moral' of a debt was more likely to fault a creditor than a
debtor, a plunderer than one plundered. It was the oppressive landlord and
his like who needed the warning of a miracle, not his victim. Suppose a man
were in heavy debt to a Jew, after all. Why should a writer waste his miracle

---

[19] Goodich *Miracle and Violence*, 56–7, quotes a miracle from the same collection in which
a farm-worker falsely accused of murder is similarly tortured, and 'his body's strength all but
totally exhausted, he wished at that point to die rather than live' (Albanès, *Actes . . . Urbain
V*, 242–3, § 173: 'septimo quadam die volebatur suspendi in eculeo, et ipse esset corporis sui
quasi totaliter viribus destitutus, cupiens eotunc potius mori quam vivere.') But the suicidal
implication is too weak, lacking as it does its tell-tale identification as a 'diabolical temptation', to make that case another exception to the rule.

in saving a debtor from suicide when it might be better employed in punishing the Jew?

Here again the rule may be proved by the exceptions to it, exceptions, that is, created by untypical circumstances. One such exception is from another of those late fifteenth-century German miracle books. It was made at Altötting, a monastery in Bavaria a few miles from the Austrian frontier. On Trinity Sunday, 1497, a respectable artisan from the Austrian side came to thank the Virgin Mary at Altötting for her help. He had been threatened with eviction because of arrears in rent and been driven to contemplate suicide, but before he got to that point the Virgin had revealed to him a hidden treasure which paid off his rent and other debts. The man came to Mary's shrine at Altötting and his story was duly recorded by the miracle registrar. The circumstances of this miracle are unusual for two reasons. The economy of Bavaria and Austria was by *c.*1500 exceptionally monetarized, so monetary debts were commoner, and hence more likely to force their way even into an inimical genre. Second, we learn that the artisan's debt was almost certainly to another monastery. For all its rivalry with Altötting, another monastery would have been less appropriate than a Jew, or a robber baron, as the target of a punishment miracle. Here, at last, nothing stopped a miracle writer from recording the despair of a morally qualified debtor.[20]

The second exception concerns a suicidal impulse provoked by war. Among French legal documents we saw such a person in the widow whose husband had lost everything in war, Jean Lunneton. That kind of despair, too, is generally absent from religious narrative. Again this must be because its moral was too confusing. It is hard, after all, to make an elegant moral *exemplum* even from the ups and downs inherent in business life, and how much more from an individual's losses in war where, for the most part, they have no obvious rationale.

The exception here comes from a genre of miracle we have already shown to have followed rules of its own, canonization processes. Miracles for these were gathered by an even sweep over contemporary experience, whatever that was. They were less morally selective. The incident only had to illustrate a saint's power. A case which does so comes in the canonization process held in 1219–20 for Hugh, Bishop of Lincoln, who had died in 1200. Among *viva voce* witnesses to Hugh's posthumous miracles was a John of Ancaster. Before being healed by contact with St Hugh's tomb at Lincoln, John had

---

[20] R. Bauer, ed., 'Das Büchlein der Zuflucht zu Maria. Altöttinger Mirakelberichte von Jacobus Issickemer', *Ostbairische Grenzmarken*. Passauer Jahrbuch für Geschichte, Kunst und Volkskunde, ed. J. Oswald. Institut für ostbairische Heimatforschung, vol. 7 (Passau, 1964–5), § 67, p. 225. Cf. Signori, 'Aggression und Selbstzerstörung', 140.

spent a month with his limbs 'bound' at the behest of his father and others, on grounds that he had been *furiosus*. Lucid and unbound, John of Ancaster told the commissioners a reason for his former 'fury' which suggests he had been tied up to stop him killing himself. This evil (*malum*) had happened to him, he said, through excessive sorrow at his despoilment in war of all he possessed (the 'war' in question being the notorious depredations of the mercenaries who served King John).[21] In other words, here was a Jean Lunneton before his time.

But I said there was a big exception. This was where economic loss *did* point a moral. It did so among those who had only themselves to thank for their disasters, because they had been foolish and greedy; in a word, among gamblers. The gambling could be through business speculation or at the gaming table. In this group of *exempla*, all economic suicides fall into one of these two categories. Thus Jacques de Vitry, preaching around the year 1230, told his large and enraptured audiences a moral tale of speculators in the sensitive area of grain. They bought grain cheap and waited for the price to rise, he said, preferring to let the grain rot than put it on the market at a low price. And he told, with unsuppressed approval, of what happened when things went wrong:

I heard of a man who accumulated grain to sell it when the price went up, and waited years for this to happen. But God sent good weather, year after year, so the wretch was cheated of his hope and ended by hanging himself in his own grainstore.[22]

The body, no doubt, was taken down and *justicié* by some seigneurial court.

But there were purer gambling games than grain and the weather. Hazard was of their very essence. Caesarius of Heisterbach includes in his clutch of suicide stories one of an *adolescens* in Cologne, some ten years earlier (that

[21] D. H. Farmer, ed., *The Canonization of St. Hugh of Lincoln. Lincolnshire Architectural and Archaeological Society. Reports and Papers*, N.S. 6, pt 2 (1956), 102: '[xviii] Iohannes de Aneschaster et pater eius et quidam alius iurati dixerunt quod idem Iohannes fuit furiosus per mensem, quem pater eius duxit ad tumbam memorati episcopi ligatum, et post paucos dies reduxit eum sanum factum. Addidit et idem Iohannes pre nimietate doloris hoc malum ei accidisse quia omnibus bonis spoliatus fuit in guerra.'

[22] I quote from London, British Library, MS Harley 463, fol. 15r: 'Quidam avaricie labe infectus frumenta congregant et abscondunt ut carum tempus adducant et aliquando tantum servant quod efficitur putridum et nulli usui aptum et malunt sibi servando ammittere quam bonum fori facere vel pauperibus erogare. Audivi de quodam qui multum de blado congregavit et per multos annos ut carius venderet expectavit. Deus autem semper bonum tempus dabat. Unde miser ille spe sua fraudatus, tandem prae tristicia super granum suum seipsum suspendit. Nec mirum, quia erat de illis de quibus dicitur in parabolis, maledicti qui frumenta abscondunt in populis.' Another text from Paris, Bibl. Nat., MS lat. 17509, fol. 116v is printed in T. F. Crane, ed., *The Exempla of Jacques de Vitry* (London, 1890), 71. A. Lecoy de la Marche, *La chaire française au moyen âge* (Paris 1886²), 409, understands such suicide *accapareurs* as plural but neither MS of this particular story supports that reading.

is, *c.*1212), who had 'gambled away [*deluserat*] his clothes', and the misfortune rendered this youth, too, so melancholy [*tristis*] that he climbed to the balcony of his house and ended his life with a noose.[23] If a cautionary tale like that could be put in a book for monastic novices, how much more did it fall to popular preachers to tell them. In surviving thirteenth-century popular sermons we hear warnings against gambling which include references to the 'despair' of the unlucky ones. A study of the uses of that word strongly suggests that, in that context, it meant suicide. Thus our Dominican informant Thomas of Chantimpré said the habit of dicing, by robbing the poor man of his clothes and the nobleman of his standing, made men *desperatissimi*. In Thomas especially, there is reason to think he had suicide in mind.[24] For an *exemplum* explicit on the subject we nevertheless have to wait for 1424, when the Franciscan St Bernardino of Siena was preaching in Florence. We know, from many other accounts as well as his, that gambling was endemic in that city.[25] Like the sermon cycle it adorned, this *exemplum* is known to us because a listener took down Bernardino's Italian in shorthand.[26] Bernardino was dilating on the 'sin of gaming' and itemized the constituent sins within it with *exempla* to display the drawbacks of each. The eleventh of these was *la disperazione*, and one field came at once to mind as offering the best illustrations.

How many people fall into despair [Bernardino said] by reason of the cursed habit of gambling! Such people hang themselves by the neck when they have lost their clothes.[27]

To this generalized reminiscence Bernardino added particular 'miracles', as he called them. One he recalls as having occurred 'not long ago', when

a gambler hanged himself three times, from desperation. The first time he failed to kill himself. Only on the third occasion did he drop effectively, and die. And thus the Devil had his soul.[28]

Tuscan suicides denied to us by court records are thus supplied liberally by the preacher.

---

[23] *Dial. mirac.*, dist. 4, ch. 44 (p. 212).
[24] *De apibus*, pt 2, ch. 49, § 11 (pp. 450–1). For his euphemisms, see above, pp. 35–6.
[25] I. Origo, *The World of San Bernardino* (London, 1965), 147–50.
[26] Ibid., 12.
[27] C. Cannarozzi, ed., *Le prediche volgari di San Bernardino da Siena* (Pistoia, 1934–58), vol. 1 (Pistoia, 1934), 425–43, for the whole sermon 'del giuoco', and on p. 431: 'Quanti ne vengono in disperazione per cagione del maladetto giuoco, e tali che s'impiccono per la gola, quando ànno perduto la roba, e per disperazione ne vanno a casa maladetta.'
[28] Ibid.: 'Non è molto tempo ch'uno giucatore tre volte s'impiccò per la gola per disperazione. La prima e la seconda non gli venne fatto; alla terza pure s'abbattè e morì. Così impiccato el diavolo ne portò l'anima sua.'

In the same sermon Bernardino tells a second gambling 'miracle'. It is more complicated and ends less drastically. Another man, he says,

after gambling, fell into such despair and blindness that on returning home he decided to kill not only himself, but his wife and children at the same time. So when the rest of his family were in bed he set fire to the house. The blaze was well alight, and he was waiting for the moment when it would be fierce enough for him to throw himself in, when by chance a friend passed by and, seeing the fire, began to shout 'fire! fire!' so that people arrived and put it out. Later the friend sought out the house-owner and asked how the fire started. It was then that the man confessed that, through despair, he had tried by this means to kill himself, and take his wife and children with him.[29]

A caso: the man's life was saved by chance, not God. Once more a narrator buys credit for his *exemplum* by walking carelessly past the only opening it gave him to make it supernatural. Bernardino could well have heard it among the chatty friar-confessors of Florence's Santa Croce, where he stayed during his visits to the city.

Opponents of Saints

The law, prosecuting murder or theft; nemesis of financial ruin: either, in *miracula* and *exempla*, could render a man defenceless before a hostile world. As occasions of suicide none is unfamiliar, and the religious stories only add depth and colour to kinds of suicide we would be aware of from other sources. But one further kind is peculiarly at home in this literature. Glimpses have already been seen of it in chronicles, in those frontier zones where chronicles most resembled hagiography, and it is in hagiography especially that it strikes root. I refer to the 'Judas' miracle. With or without the Gospel reference, a stubborn opponent of the holy man ends by committing suicide for no other apparent motive than a bad conscience. It is the hagiographer's equivalent of political assassination.

Of seven or eight possible examples of this theme only four have express references to suicide. The first occurs in the *Miracles of Saint Foy*, the long miracle collection of Conques, a monastery set in the Lot valley forty miles south-east of Rocamadour. The miracle comes in a part of the collection

---

[29] Ibid., continuing: 'Un altro fu che, avendo giucato, venne in tanta disperazione e cecità che, tornato a casa, diliberò di morire egli, la moglie e figliuoli. E andato a letto la moglie e figliuoli, misse fuoco nella casa, e ardendo aspettava el fuoco fosse grande per gettarvisi drento. E, a caso, vi s'abbattè un suo amico, e veggendo el fuoco cominciò a gridare: "al fuoco, al fuoco . . . !" E fu soccorso e spento. Trovato el buono uomo el domandò del caso. Confessò, per disperazione, voleva uccidere, per quel modo, sè, la moglie, e figliuoli.'

that was compiled around the year 1020.[30] Bernard of Poitiers, the author, had carefully explored the recent history of the monastery, and his stories abound in circumstantial detail. In one he speaks of a prior of Conques, in office around the year 1000, who was peculiarly bellicose in word and deed. The prior's official tasks included that of guarding the sanctuary which held the precious relics of the monastery's martyred patroness. If anyone attacked the relics, or the monks who served them, Prior Gimo would reach for his weapons or, if that seemed tactically unwise, would attack them with a compound of prayer and insult unique to himself. Bernard justifies this two-pronged strategy both by biblical example and because it worked. 'For,' Bernard goes on,

many of the malefactors of that time are said to have come to various fatal ends. Some threw themselves from high rocks, some choked themselves on food, others put themselves to death by their own hand.[31]

The three phrases used here are *de summis saxis se precipitantes; cibo se strangulantes;* and *alii propria manu sibi mortem inferentes.* Of these the third certainly means suicide, *propria manu sibi mortem inferre* being one classical Latin expression for suicide in general (by hand or otherwise). To understand it here as meaning strictly 'by hand' is to remove the only objection to a suicidal reading also of the first: *se praecipitare* is another classical term for suicide. Bernard adds nothing about the motive of any of these ill-advised violaters of St Foy's sanctuary. It was enough that they were her enemies, punished by a prior's curses.

Two comparable passages occur in the miracle books respectively from Fleury-sur-Loire and from Egmond in Holland. In the *Miracles of St Benedict* it is Andreas of Fleury again who makes the records, in the long middle section of the collection, and once more he refers to a period probably around 1020. The *miraculum* here concerns a Breton lady called Rojantric. She had just lost her husband. Thus defenceless, she was approached by a certain lecherous man of knightly class. To protect her honour she took a vow of continence and put herself under the protection of a local church, St Salvator, and expressed her new status by a change of clothing. St Salvator's power should have been enough to protect her, but in the event St Salvator's intervention was limited to vengeance. For Rojantric's besieger gathered a posse of accomplices, broke into the church and 'prostituted' Rojantric and her one daughter. This was sacrilege as well as rape, and the intruders were duly punished, since all died soon afterwards. Andreas records the fates of the ringleaders, first of them a man who

---

[30] *Liber miraculorum s. Fidis*, ed. A. Bouillet (Paris, 1897), Introd., x–xiii.
[31] Ibid., bk 1, ch. 26 (p. 69).

snatched by a demon, sat on his horse, stuck his sword in the ground and then, holding the point of his lance to his chest, spurred the horse into a charge so that he fell dead to the ground as the lance's head went through him.[32]

It is St Salvator, not Andreas's own St Benedict, who thus vindicates his injured client. In its context it is for that reason a 'bad story', with a consequence now familiar.

The case from Egmond, in northern Holland, occurs in a twelfth-century miracle book, and tells how the Egmond monks had built a dam to prevent sea-flooding. A group of local magnates, led by a family of six brothers, smashed the dam on grounds that it diverted floodwater to their own lands. The monks had been abused and injured, and had no source of protection other than the relics of their patron, St Adalbert. St Adalbert's revenge was severe. One of the offending brothers killed another. A third, 'Walbrand, killed himself by falling on his sword. He left behind a fearful example, for none rises with impunity against God and his saints.' Further members of the delinquent family went mad or fell into unspeakable poverty. Suicide was again one 'bad end' among others.[33]

The monastery of Lobbes, in Flanders, still enjoyed in the late eleventh century the miraculous protection of St Ursmar, who had died in the eighth. He, too, may occasionally have inflicted suicide as a measure of revenge. The *Miracles of St Ursmar*, written in the 1090s, tell of an incident apparently envisaged as having happened around 1070.[34] A riot was caused near the monastery by visitors from two neighbouring villages. Those of one, Thuin, were the smaller party, and took sanctuary behind the strong doors of St Ursmar's church. Among visitors from the other village was a baker who had come to the monastery to collect kitchen waste. But once the riot had begun he joined in it, and was in pursuit of a man from Thuin when the latter shut the door behind him. The baker snatched a bow and arrow and fired in the fugitives' direction. The arrow struck the monastery door. This 'rashly offended St Ursmar'. The story of the riot stops there and the narrative switches to the fate of the sacrilegious baker. When next day's baking was done he died by being burned in his own furnace. How he got there is masked by a certain linguistic obscurity. I give one possible translation of the relevant passage:

[32] *Mir. s. Benedicti*, bk 7, ch. 7 (pp. 259–64; suicide on p. 260): 'lanceae aciem pectori applicans, impulso in se viriliter cornipede, trajectus acinace exspirans delabitur terrae'. For date see n. 16 above.
[33] *Vita s. Adalberti Egmundani: Alia miracula*, ch. 1, § 6. *Acta sanctorum*, June 5 (1709), 105D.
[34] *Vita et miracula s. Ursmari*, ch. 6, § 27; *Acta sanctorum*, April 2 (1675), 557–78; at 572F. Date of the miracle: the previous story refers to Abbot Adelard (1053–76) and the next to Count Baldwin VI (1069–71).

When his bread was made the wretched man heated the oven hotter than usual, and when the whole furnace was raging at its maximum he 'turned bloody steel against himself' and, his hands clasped behind his back, fell at the Devil's instigation into the midst of the blaze.[35]

Sanguineam volvens aciem, revinctis manibus a tergo . . . diabolo instigante. What could the Devil have been instigating, then, other than the baker's own will? No one else is mentioned as present.

An account one degree more explicit appears in the *Life of St Stephan of Obazine*.[36] Obazine (the place now spelt Aubazine) was a monastery in the western Massif Central near Brive, which after the time of the story would become part of the Cistercian Order. Stephan had died in 1159. The relevant part of his *Life* was written around 1180, its chapters rich in local colour and detail. The story in question introduces the abbot of a neighbouring monastery, St Martin of Tulle, which belonged to the longer established, less austere 'black' monasticism against which the zeal of the Cistercians and their allies was a reaction. The abbot of St Martin was Ebulus of Turenne, brother of the count of Tulle. We know from sources other than the *Life* that Abbot Ebulus died in 1152, but only the *Life* says how. Ebulus and St Stephan were together in Limoges, and quarrelled. Ebulus' angry words to the saint included threats about his future. Stephan answered with soft words, the *Life* insists, and sagely reminded Ebulus that the latter could not know what the future held. That very night Limoges was woken by a public commotion.

As all the bells rang out it was noised that Abbot Ebulus had suddenly died. And although it seemed that it was his own fatal act which had killed him, through the drinking of poison, nevertheless it astonished all who had witnessed the two abbots' dispute that St Stephan's utterance had been so soon fulfilled.[37]

Quamquam veneni haustu propria morte videretur extinctus. Once more the Latin is not transparent. It could, with ingenuity, be translated other-

---

[35] *Vita et miracula s. Ursmari*, p. 572F: 'ille miser, confectis panibus, clibanum solito amplius succendit: cumque per concavum loci illius totis viribus dominaretur incendium, sanguineam volvens aciem, revinctis manibus a tergo, in medio flammarum, diabolo instigante, precipitatur.' I have treated *sanguineam aciem volvere* and *manu propria sibi mortem inferre* as among metaphorical substitutes for suicide. As for *revinctis manibus*, did someone *else* tie the baker's hands and throw him in the oven? In that case, why had the baker himself heated the oven hotter than usual? Again, I treat the passive mood *precipitatur* as euphemism, reading *diabolo instigante* as the decisive factor. The meaning of the passage is certainly obscure, and that fact alone is a kind of evidence.

[36] *Vie de Saint Étienne d'Obazine*, ed. M. Aubrun (Clermont-Ferrand, 1970). Date: p. 6.

[37] Ibid., pp. 156.14–20: 'sequenti nocte, clamor in civitate cum ululatu exortus est, in quo predictus abbas repente mortuus signis undique concrepantibus ferebatur et quamquam veneni haustu propria morte videretur extinctus omnes tamen qui predicte contentioni interfuerant mirabantur quod sermo viri Dei, quamvis illo multum dolente, tam velociter fuisset impletus ipseque de illa injuria celeriter vindicatus.'

wise, but still with anomalies; and between two anomalous versions, we have learned, the more probable choice is that whose ambiguity can be explained by an author's wish to hide something.

My last example in this group concerns a critic, not of one holy man but of the entire Christian religion, namely a Jew. Perhaps because the villain of the piece is thus doubly vulnerable, the narrator can for once drop all inhibition and describe a suicide in detail. The incident is one of *The Miracles of Saint Frideswide*. St Frideswide had died, in Oxford, in 735; her relics were given solemn Translation in 1180 and her miracles, mostly in and near Oxford, written up at the same time. The Jew's suicide is told as if it had happened in the previous year.[38] The story involves a Jew by the name of Moses of Wallingford. Moses had a reputation in Christian Oxford of being less detestable than other Jews, but this praise did not extend to his corpulent son, who habitually mocked and mimicked St Frideswide's cures. The fat youth pretended, for instance, to limp, and then to recover his normal gait, to suffer paralysis of the hand, and then open it out normally, as if miraculously cured, and boasting that he was himself quite as worthy of offerings as St Frideswide. Although his father often rebuked the youth's blasphemies, it was without effect until one day, at the family table, the father went so far as to place a curse on him. The curse was specific:

At table the young Jew's mockery of St Frideswide had been more persistent than usual. Roused, the father with the utmost indignation put this curse on him, that whatever was to be his destiny at the end of his life might happen at once.

The curse was fulfilled as follows. I leave in Latin two expressions for kinds of melancholy:

On hearing these words the blasphemous youth became a little quieter. Not long afterwards he fell into *accidia*, and as it were went out of his mind and suffered total psychological collapse. For God's Providence procured this effect, that a man who had used his mind shamefully should be handed over to the agents of Satan. The young man was invited to dinner by his father, and refused, being afflicted by *taedium vitae* and thinking how he might accelerate his own death.[39]

His opportunity came in the depths of the following night.

When the nocturnal tranquillity of night succeeded to the day's toil, at the dead of night when all was quiet, the unhappy youth rose from his bed and went to his

---

[38] *Acta Sanctorum*, Oct. 8 (1853), 576–7. Cf. A. Neubauer, *Notes on the Jews in Oxford*. Oxford Historical Society, 16. Collectanea, 2nd ser., pt 4 (Oxford, 1890), 277–318, on pp. 282–4.

[39] *Acta Sanctorum*, Oct. 8, 576F: 'in accidiam delapsus, tamquam mente alienatus totus animo consternatus est: id nimirum agente Dei providentia, ut qui in reprobum sensum datus fuerat, Sathane satellitibus traderetur. Invitatus ad coenam a patre, respuit, vivendi taedio affectus, et circa suae mortis accelerationem solicitus.'

father's kitchen. He sealed the inside of the door with wax, so that nothing should interrupt the dreadful design his spirit had conceived. For a noose, he used the girdle he wore round his waist. Casting it round both a beam and his neck, he ended his own unhappy life, in this like the traitor Judas.

Even in the mechanics of the Jew's death the author finds a trace of the miraculous:

And indeed it is a sign worthy of wonder that a thin cord should have suspended a heavy body for so long a time. For morning has broken when the father misses his son. Looking for him high and low without success, he finally breaks down the kitchen door and finds him hanged.

Shocked, the father tries to hush up the tragedy:

Deeply shaken by what he has seen, he calls his colleagues together secretly, urging them not to let this occurrence become public and least of all to allow the Christians to know it. And so, just as their forefathers sought in vain to suppress the glorious news of Our Lord's resurrection, so that impious race tried to conceal that stroke of divine retribution, in vain: for human wit cannot conceal those things that make manifest God's wisdom and power.

Despite Moses of Wallingford's efforts, the news raced through Oxford, bringing joy to the faithful and confusion to the infidels. St Frideswide's just punishment even extended to her mocker's last journey. For as the Jews were conveying his body to London for burial the body fell off the cart, breaking its neck. It was the very neck through which the blasphemies, conceived within the fat boy's body, passed through to the thoughts of his heart, had been emitted. Serve him right.

Hagiography exalted a saint; *exempla*, morals. High among moral principles was obedience to church authorities whose refusal incurred excommunication. So it should be no surprise to read in *exempla* of suicidal disasters that befell excommunicates. Our only surprise, once more, must be that they are so few. Their paucity is testimony, with much else, to the declining force of this sanction in the thirteenth century, the century when *exempla* effectively began, and helped to fill the space left precisely by the waning fear of excommunication. Thus only one *exemplum* I know of makes suicide a sanction for the defying of excommunication. It is told by Stephen of Bourbon, who claimed he had heard it from the archpriest of Marcigny (between Avallon and Dijon), an ecclesiastical lawyer of just the sort who would treasure up cautionary tales about delinquents. Stephen, who was not such a lawyer, merely tells it as an instance of sudden death. Five people, he says, were crossing the Loire in a ferry. Two had been excommunicated for contumacy. The Loire was in flood, and the ship in danger of wreck on the pile of a bridge. The two excommunicates were elderly and weak, and were put out for their own safety onto one of the big timbers of the bridge. The others crossed safely, and roused the men on shore to rescue the two castaways. But as the rescuers climbed down to reach them the two excommunicates said: '"Why bother yourselves? It is better that we die here." And so saying, they dived into the water and died.'[40] That is all. Here, again, it is hardly a 'good story', so it probably happened, at some date in the 1240s or 1250s.

This chapter has rehearsed a total of some nineteen religious stories. Eleven are from *Miracula* collections associated with a particular saint after his or her death, two of these being from a canonization process; two more are from the actual *Lives* of saints, while six or so are *exempla* from sermons or related literature. With the exception of the murderer's suicide in the late *Life of Dagobert* (a motif best interpreted in terms of purely literary history), all the accounts are from sources written within a generation or two of the incidents they purport to describe. All, with that exception (and perhaps that of St Walpurga) give details consistent, in varying degrees, with the historicity of their main suicidal incident.

Together, they are just enough, in quantity and quality, to give a glimpse into an aspect of our subject which might otherwise be pure conjecture. In each, a suicide, or suicidal thought or act, follows an event of social dislocation, whether from crime, disgrace, or financial ruin. I shall have occasion to return to some of them again, in another volume, in the context of social reactions to suicide. For now, we must follow our map. There is still one stage to go. The next chapter, the last in the group, will make a journey not, like the one just ended, outwards from the family, but inwards, to the suicidal act with no obvious occasion at all outside the mind or body of the person committing it.

[40] *Anecdotes historiques*, § 313; ed. A. Lecoy de la Marche (Paris, 1877), p. 263.

14

The Sick and Melancholy

MAN being a social animal, it follows that a shock to his domestic or social existence will cause emotional shock, which when severe can trigger suicidal feelings. But the immediate occasion of suicide does not have to be external. The social animal is also a microcosm, a world in himself, full of hopes and memories. This fact is reflected in the deposit of *miracula* about suicide. A whole category of them, quite as circumstantial as the others, concerns suicidal impulses due directly to a person's own private condition, physical or spiritual.

The Physically Sick and Wounded

The first group are about the physically infirm. The Conques miracle book, *The Miracles of St Foy*, has several examples. Its ninety stories, picturing life in a small area of south-western France around and just after the millennium, include no fewer than six about someone so sick or wounded that he longs to die. Some of these did no more than long. A *miles*, or knight, of the nearby Auvergne suddenly lost all his hair, withdrew from society, lived at home at his mother's expense 'like a boy', and failed to protect his lands against acquisitive neighbours; and as a consequence became 'so tormented by *acedia*, which we call a detour of the mind [*quod devium mentis vocamus*]', that 'he thought death preferable to life' until St Foy, on his request, restored the hair.[1] The low spirits of a second sick knight led him further than longing, to desperate action which would have endangered his life. The disease was in the genitals. It wore him down with pain, so much that he often prayed for death as an escape from the pain. So he approached a blacksmith to put his genitals on the anvil and hit them with his hammer. The blacksmith recoiled, saying 'these are not words of healing but of jest.

[1] *Mir. s. Fidis*, bk 3, ch. 7, ed. A. Bouillet (Paris, 1897), pp. 138–41, esp. 139.

If you pursue this idea you will be guilty of your own death.' (Apart from any question of principle, the blacksmith said he was afraid of revenge by the sick man's kindred if he thus connived at his death.) But the knight insisted. As the hammer was about to fall, he shrank in horror, and was cured of his pain by St Foy instead.[2]

A further four *milites* in the Conques miracle book had suffered wounds in battle. One had a paralysed arm which induced such grief in him that 'he wished rather to suffer the extremity of death than drag out the tedium of his useless life, with a body so dishonoured.'[3] He was cured by a miracle without further danger. To another knight, whose face was cut down the middle so that he could not eat, his hateful life lingered on and on (*odibilis vite mora diu protractus*) until, like the others, he was cured by St Foy.[4]

Of none of the four sufferers does the writer say he tried to kill himself, only that he was sick of life and in one case driven to initiate an act reasonably seen by a blacksmith as fatal. A fifth case brings in the tell-tale word 'despair'. A knight was wounded by an arrow. He tried to heal the wound himself. But after a day 'all his hope suddenly collapsed, and was replaced in him by hateful despair, than which nothing is more harmful [*desperatio qua nihil est infelicius ei invisa subinfertur*].'[5] And in one last case the suicidal intention is stated openly. A knight, 'Gerbert', had been blinded by an enemy and became dejected to the point of wanting to die. He had learned from medical folklore that anyone who drank goat's milk soon after being wounded would die of it. So he went to ask a peasant for goat's milk. It was refused. So he asked another, then another, and always it was refused, for the same reason as that for which he was making his request. The peasants knew he was asking for poison. So the knight tried to starve himself to death instead. After persevering for eight days he was put on the road to recovery by a vision of a noble, chaste young woman, who proved to be St Foy.[6]

The idea that someone could be so sick as to be weary of life is well-represented in the Conques miracles. But it is far from peculiar to that collection. The only question, usually, is whether weariness of life always implies suicide. As the Conques writer showed, allusions to a patient's despair, *taedium vitae*, desire for death, and so on, are intrinsically ambiguous. A patient's feelings on the matter, after all, may themselves be ambiguous; and when they are not, a discreet writer will supply the ambiguity in

[2] *Mir. s. Fidis*, bk 4, ch. 23, pp. 217–18.
[3] *Mir. s. Fidis*, bk 4, ch. 10, p. 194.
[4] *Mir. s. Fidis*, bk 2, ch. 7, pp. 112–13.
[5] *Mir. s. Fidis*, Appendix 2, ch. 3, p. 235.
[6] *Mir. s. Fidis*, bk 1, ch. 2, pp. 16–21, esp. 18.

his description. It is only when ambiguities sink towards zero that science is possible and that is not often. An ambiguity short of absolute zero, for example, is one in a *Life* of St Anselm of Lucca, who died in 1086, by a near-contemporary. In the *Life*, a Mantuan patient suffers such chronic pain that 'he said the only medicine that would cure him would be if he could cut away his clothes and then was allowed to use the same knife to cut open his chest.' The biographer goes on that 'since he had got to the point where nothing filled his mind but the expectation of death' the miraculous cure was applied.[7] Here is the Latin: *dicebat se hac sola posse sanari medicina, si vestibus conscissis, permitteretur cultro fundere et pectus. Cum autem iam de sola mortis expectatione cogitaret* . . . No number of Latin dictionaries will reveal beyond all doubt what the sufferer was proposing to do. The capacity to hide things, as well as reveal them, is a positive practical recommendation in a language. Latin has it, and writers were grateful for this fact when confronted, as from time to time they were, by a spade they had reasons for not calling by that name. For statisticians this is a quicksand.

Explicit attempts at suicide are another matter, but these are not so common. Two incidents to be considered in a moment include sickness as one among a range of motives for suicide. But on its own, sickness is rarer than we might expect, not least in view of its prominence in legal records and despite the bias in many of these for including it. A similar bias might well be expected in *miracula*. Helpess infirmity, after all, made a fitting 'extremity' to highlight a saint's power of rescue. Most of the thousands of miracles in hagiography are about this kind of infirmity, healed by a saint. If they do not often bring in suicide, one reason may be that suicide complicates an issue otherwise simple, compromising a patient's trust in a saint's power to help, rather as we saw, or I suggested we saw, in respect of victims of torture.[8] Another could be that it makes bizarre reading, like the Conques stories of the blacksmith and of the goat's milk. For infirmity actually makes suicide difficult to commit. A sick man may lack the strength or means to kill himself.

If we doubt this, we can banish doubt by a look at the only other circumstantial account I am aware of, of a suicidal act prompted mainly by sickness. It comes from Villers, a Cistercian monastery fourteen miles southwest of Brussels. If the story is historically true, as it gives every appearance of being, it can be dated approximately to 1300. It was written down about

---

[7] *Vita s. Anselmi episcopi Lucensis, auctore Bardone presbytero*, ch. 71. *Mon. Germ. Hist, Scriptores*, vol. 12, p. 32.23–29.

[8] Above, p. 305.

a generation later in the monastery's *History of the Foundation.*[9] A *conversus*, or lay-brother, was struck by leprosy and was put on his own. The demoralizing effect of ostracization, to which lepers were regularly exposed, is a well-known feature of medieval documentation on the subject. The leper at Villers was not exempt:

Separated from the community, living on his own, he found the weight and persistence of his sufferings too much to bear, and began to lose heart. What followed was due partly to the boredom of solitude, partly to the disgusting nature of his disease, and partly to the promptings of the Enemy whose attack on him never relaxed. He resolved to go secretly, at night, and throw himself into the nearby pond, there to put an end to his misfortunes. Only one obstacle caused him apprehension. Dogs ran loose around the abbey at night, and would upset his plan. As Christmas approached, he devised a way round this. On Christmas night the monks would all be at night Office, and the dogs tied up. What more need I say? Christmas came. The brother whose job it was to serve the leper left him alone, to go to church with the others. When the leper saw his custodian gone he rose from his bed. But his legs, weakened by leprosy, would not support him. He tried to walk, but fell, and lay there in agony, unable to return to his bed.

So there is no miracle. The story is all too natural. Nor must we forget that none of this would be known to us unless the story had a happy ending. One of the monks in church at the time was a notably devout man called John, aged 80. While physically in church, he said later, John had visited the leper 'in the spirit' and witnessed his unsuccessful sortie from his sickbed. The leper, for his part, at the same time confirmed that he had indeed received this spiritual visit, as one of four: respectively by the Virgin Mary, St Catherine, St Agnes, and his holy fellow-monk John. The four gently persuaded him to accept the scourges sent by God, and see them as a sign of God's fatherly love. As a result the leper lived thenceforward as a model of holy patience, and died in peace not long afterwards.

The predicament of the leper at Villers is another reminder of, among other things, the two extensions physical illness enjoys beyond its attack on the body. It affects a man's social relations and his mood. The Villers leper

---

[9] *Historia monasterii Villariensis in Brabantia, ordinis Cisterciensis*, bk 3, ch. 8; in E. Martène and U. Durand, *Thesaurus novus anecdotorum*, 3 (Paris, 1717), 1368C–1369B. Cf. Bourquelot, pt 2, pp. 250–1 and n. 3. On the monastery: L. H. Cottineau, *Répertoire topo-bibliographique des abbés et prieurés*, 2 (Mâcon, 1937), 3395–7. I have omitted as doubtful the case of William de Ferrers in the infirmary at Pontigny, mentioned in the *Miracles of St Edmund of Canterbury*, but he may have been in a similar condition. As this deteriorated he prayed he should not die without confession and communion but 'became mad', was bound and guarded, escaped, and threw himself down a latrine. He was saved from drowning, madness, and his sickness by St Edmund. Oxford, Bodleian, MS Fell 2, p. 26; on the collection, cf. above, pp. 258–60.

was wearied *tum taedio solitudinis, tum foeditate morbi*: 'as much by the tedium caused by ostracism as by the revolting nature of his disease'. Disability isolated him, rendering his private disease in this degree a public matter, not to be treated as different in kind, as occasion of suicide, to the kind of social accident reviewed in the last two chapters. As a general principle the same is true in the other direction. Physical disease is a psychological matter, too. It is therefore linked in the same way to the internal, mental states next to be explored.

The Mad

By contrast to the physically sick, the person mentally deranged is positively common in suicidal miracles. The terms used for such a person are usually from the range *amens* ('out of his mind'), *freneticus* (from *frenesis*, the term we encountered in legal records), *subactus vesaniae*, and *demoniacus*. The 'demoniac' had been an *habitué* in this literature from patristic times onwards, and self-threatening behaviour had long been one of his common hallmarks. Here is a problem, which we met before in law-courts. If suicidal behaviour was a madman's only distinguishing feature, how can we trust that the man was indeed mad, rather than the beneficiary of some writer's merciful intepretation? To illustrate the problem I take first, as a mere sample of a big genre, six suicidal descriptions whose details do suggest serious mental illness.

Of the six, the first five are short, and are typical, in this and other respects, of many more. The big eleventh-century miracle books from Conques and Fleury contain a few cases which will serve to illustrate others. The Conques book has two side by side. A peasant, whose name the author says he has forgotten (because of the huge quantity of miracles he has had to remember), began raving 'and endangering his life by running around on steep rocks' and jumping off rocks into torrents. Manacled once, he was released, but 'plunged at once into the whirlpools of the Dordogne'. Saved again, he was healed of his malady by St Foy.[10] The very next miracle concerns a girl who would 'afflict herself with countless torments' and, like the peasant in the earlier story, run around on high, dangerous rocks as well as threatening violence on her keeper.[11] The Fleury miracle book, in a part written around 1100, tells of the madness of one Raculf, a count of Tonnerre just over a century earlier, who had been driven mad by his own moral depravity. Raculf's condition became so grave that 'he tried to attack both

---

[10] *Mir. s. Fidis*, Appendix 2, ch. 1; pp. 230–1.
[11] Ibid., ch. 2; pp. 231–2.

himself and people round him with a sword or with cudgels, or with whatever missile came to hand.' He was cured by St Benedict.[12] This type of sufferer would make regular appearances in miracle collections. To take an example almost at random, a collection made in honour of the Blessed Humiliana de' Cerchi of Florence tells, as an incident datable to 1248, of a demoniac girl called Mingarda, who lived at home with her father Guido near the Florentine church of San Piero Maggiore. Mingarda was 'vexed by demons' who, besides using her mouth to utter foul language, would drive her to jump into the Arno so that 'she might be killed'. She was cured when taken to Humiliana's tomb.[13] Another example of the genre appears in the *Life of the Blessed Robert of Saleto* (near Lecce), who died in 1341. A woman called Hilaria had been 'vexed' by demons for twenty years. She would roam the woods and wilderness, howling like a dog. Her demon 'threw her into fire and water, and was very frequently trying to kill her by hanging'. Hilaria, too, was healed by a visit to the saint's tomb.[14]

It asks too much of a modern reader to judge cases so briefly described. The detail, for one thing, is suspiciously close to a 'type'. My sixth and last example is chosen to meet this objection. Its unusual character and vividness suggest that a real incident lay behind the story and that the main symptoms may have been something like those described. The case is among the posthumous miracles of St Virgil of Salzburg,[15] a dark-age Irish missionary who became bishop of Salzburg and died there in 784. In 1181, work began on the rebuilding of the main Salzburg monastery, belonging to the canons of St Rupert. St Virgil's relics were allegedly found, and soon after 1183 an anonymous canon started writing down miraculous cures they had worked. Most of the cures are described briefly. Thus a woman had difficulty in giving birth, and did so easily after she had given a candle to St Virgil's tomb; a blind five-week-old baby was brought to the tomb and was cured; and so on. One cure is described at great length. Its beneficiary was a young canon of the house itself, and his affliction lay precisely in his refusal to believe any of the miracles. The canon's office, as deacon, put him in contact with public visitors to the church. That made things worse, since his public contempt for the cult compromised the monastery. His colleagues warned him, but in vain.

Crisis point was eventually reached one evening, at a date which cannot have been far from 1182. A woman had come to pray before St Virgil's tomb.

---

[12] *Mir. s. Benedicti*, bk 1, ch. 32; ed. E. de Certain, pp. 69–70.
[13] *Miracula b. Humilianae de Cerchis*, § 30; *Acta sanctorum*, May 4 (1685), 406C.
[14] *Vita b. Roberti Salentini*, ch. 7, § 77; *Acta sanctorum*, July 4 (1725), 509C.
[15] *Vitae et miracula sanctorum iuvavensium Virgilii, Hartwici, Eberhardi*, ed. G. H. Pertz in *Mon. Germ. Hist., Scriptores*, vol. 11, pp. 88–90. 'Iuvavia' was Latin for Salzburg.

The young deacon, alone with her in the church, told her to leave, and pooh-poohed the relics and their alleged power. Suddenly he was struck, and became possessed as by a demon. A priest in the sacristy nearby was the first to notice the deacon's condition. The priest had been working at an inventory there, when suddenly the deacon burst in and attacked him, boxing his ears and scratching at him with his nails. Hearing the disturbance, a passing housekeeper rushed in to the sacristy and rescued the priest from his attacker. The two fled to an adjoining cubicle, shut the door, and looked through the keyhole in terror. They saw the madman snatch a knife (kept in the sacristy for trimming priests' beards), remove his thick monastic habit, and start stabbing the knife into his own chest. The two observers were too scared to risk coming out to stop him, and in due course saw the deacon, covered in blood though still only wounded skin-deep, fall to the ground and begin stabbing at his neck and throat. At last the priest and his rescuer took heart, rushed out, and overpowered the deacon, forcing the knife from his hand.

By this time half the monastery—canons, boy pupils, and servants—had come running to see what was wrong. The wounded deacon saw he was on the point of arrest. Knifeless, still covered in blood, he slipped from his custodians' grip and sprinted into the darkened church. From there he ran to the steps to the tower, and the next thing those on the ground knew was that the demoniac was roaming around in the dark belfry. His mad purpose became clear. Two of the nimbler boys had sprinted after him into the church, raced up the dark steps after him, and after a minute or two of groping in the belfry, reached forward and felt with their hands the deacon's body, hanging by the bell-rope. Though almost lifeless the deacon was still breathing. The boys quickly untied him, carried him down the steps, and took him through a crowd of bystanders towards the tomb of St Virgil.

The demon inside the deacon now unleashed his full fury against the saint he had wronged. As the deacon's limp, half-dead body was carried towards the saint's tomb, the demon inside it writhed and spat, shielding its eyes from the holy sight of the tomb. So the sick deacon was carried back to the sacristy. The allergy got no better there. The priests of the monastery agreed to form relays, to say continuous prayers over their afflicted colleague. They would concentrate on exorcisms and litanies. Even then, the man's form would writhe and groan furiously at the very utterance of St Virgil's name.

Meanwhile the monastery bells had been ringing and a crowd of Salzburg citizens had come to the scene, women prominent among them, loudly horrified by the madman's outrages. But at length the priests' prayers and exorcisms, and the lighting of candles and torches, seemed to be having an improving effect, and after one last, heartfelt, prayer by all present, bystanders thought they heard the crackle and hiss which marked a demon's departure. The deacon was given the Eucharist and carried to bed, still half-dead but now more peaceful.

For three days the sick deacon could not speak. He communicated by signs and by writing. It was enough to indicate that his religious views on St Virgil's relics had not changed. He was stubborn even when mute, nay, the author says, he was mute because stubborn, for this was St Virgil's revenge. Only when the weakened body seemed at the point of death, and a priest was administering the last sacrament with a suitable admonition, did the deacon acknowledge his mistake, and he at once received his speech back.

For some days now the former demoniac appeared fully repentant. He started going about his religious duties again, with apparent contrition for earlier misdeeds. But he was not, deep down, any better, for his earlier contempt for the relics remained, and even remained public. So he suffered new attacks. In one of them, again suicidal, he announced that he would set fire to the buildings and himself die in the fire. This time he was put under close arrest. After a long time, apparently weeks or even months (*diu*), he recovered, finally abandoned his view of the relics, and revealed publicly 'that which he had concealed earlier'. This was that his trouble had begun, at the moment of his high-handed treatment of the devout woman, when an evil spirit entered his mouth, with a rush of wind, in the form of a bat. And his trouble had ended, he said, when St Nicholas—to whom he had a particular devotion—had joined St Virgil himself in making intercession. In the end the saintly pair, Nicholas and Virgil, had jointly drawn the wicked spirit out of him in the form of a long, filthy, black length of cloth (*velum*).

The deacon's weeks-long speechlessness, after injuries sustained during a suicide attempt, is a feature we shall meet again in this chapter, and one said by modern medicine to follow certain kinds of brain damage. The degree of detail which reveals this is a quality we owe here to the victim's membership of a religious order. It was the same with the Villers *conversus*. I shall touch on this literary bias again at the end of the chapter. Meanwhile, a comparison between the place of 'madness' in religious and in legal sources suggests one striking similarity. In both categories of source the *really* mad and the doubtfully 'mad' are in approximate balance. Credible cases of madness, that is to say, are about equal in number, in *miracula* as in judicial records, to those where the 'madness' seems to amount to little more than a suicidal disposition.

The Mad or Melancholy

I shall offer five cases to which this last description applies. The first is from the *Life of St John Gualbert* by his disciple, Atto of Pistoia. The miracle allegedly occurred while the Tuscan reformer was still alive, and presiding over his monasteries of Vallombrosa and Passignano, both within a fifteen-mile radius of Florence and with the Arno running between them. If the incident occurred at all it is datable to around 1060 or 1070. A certain man 'full of madness [*plenus insania*]' was sent from Vallombrosa to Passignano to be cured by the saint, staying in the latter monastery. While crossing the river Arno by boat, in mid-river, the man threw himself into the water 'driven to do so by his madness'. As he fell, the man had the presence of mind to cry out: 'now we shall see what sort of man John is.' He was duly borne up by the waves and swept safely to the further shore 'by the merits of the holy man'. Atto, the author, stops there.[16] He does not speak of any cure specifically for the madness. It appears, as in a merciful court, to have been introduced for no other purpose than to accommodate the attempted suicide.

Almost the same can be said of a story in the *Life of St Honoratus of Amiens*. This bishop lived in the seventh century but his *Life* was written in the late eleventh, and a miracle close to the one in question is dated 'about 1060'. The miracle runs as follows:

A certain shepherd was tending his flocks in the fields when he was seized by a demon and tried to throw himself into the river Somme. He was rescued and held by the other shepherds. But when he got home he attacked bystanders with his teeth and was found to be mad. He was bound and brought by his parents to Amiens cathedral, where they called on the name of St Honoratus, and by the saint's merits he was freed from the demon, came to his senses, and gave thanks to God.[17]

That the man was 'found to be mad [*compertus insaniae*]' may be thought persuasive. Biting may show madness, or it may show mere rage. There is little else to establish insanity beyond what was implied by the attempted suicide.

My third example is of a noblewoman who tried to hang herself in the convent of St Amand in Rouen, in 1107. She may belong in the category of a wronged wife, like the knight's wife at Rocamadour, rather than that of

---

[16] *S. Joannis Gualberti vita, auctore Attone*, ch. 34; *Pat. lat.*, 146.667–706, at cols 682D–683A.

[17] *Vita s. Honorati Ambianensis*, ch. 10, *Acta sanctorum*, May 3 (1680), 614E: 'correptus a daemonio, se in fluvium Sommonae praecipitare tendebat: sed a pastoribus prohibitus est et detentus. Qui domum reversus, morsuque obvios impetens, compertus est insanire. Quem parentes ejus vinclis correptum in Ambianensem ducentes ecclesiam, pro ipso beati Honorati nomen inclamant: per cuius merita . . . [etc.]'

the demonically possessed, but it was as a demoniac that her contemporaries treated her. This was partly because St Amand (a seventh-century bishop) was noted for his power with demons. The abbess of St Amand's convent in Rouen recorded this example of the saint's power in a letter to the abbot of the male brother-house, St Amand in Flanders. She asked him to include it in the collection of St Amand's miracles he was editing. That he did not, and that the miracle survives only in a letter, may be another witness to writers' reticence. If so, it was a male reticence, for the abbess shrank from no clinical detail, and if this was too much for the abbot it makes her letter all the rarer as a document.[18]

As often, the suicide's identity is discreetly concealed. She is an 'illustrious woman from near Lisieux'. The abbess, Marsilia, thinks the illustrious woman's crisis was not so much her own fault as an instance of the Devil's rage, divinely permitted to let God's glory shine more clearly through St Amand. The trouble had begun when a female gossip of the illustrious woman's acquaintance had persuaded her, falsely in the writer's view, and with the guile once exercised by the Serpent on Eve, that her husband was having an affair with someone else. Whatever the truth of the story the illustrious woman fell into the 'sadness [*tristitia*] that worketh death'. Her mind became 'agitated by various malign fantasies', until finally, 'losing her natural reason, she thought of nothing but how she could escape human company and stab herself to death, or kill herself by hanging or drowning or in some other way.' By diabolical cunning she would have succeeded had not her husband often stood in her path as she tried to dash off. When her husband sought to persuade her from her 'devilish madness' she answered 'in wretched desperation' that he should let her 'go to Hell with the Devil, to whom I am predestined and dedicated'.[19]

The woman's family and friends at last decided to bring her to the church of St Amand. There, they suggested she make the sign of the Cross. But she would not listen. A posse of senior, learned monks came to talk to her privately. But she replied, her voice perfectly composed, that she was destined for 'infernal flames and sulphurous pains'; that she already felt a portion of these flames and pains in this world; and that of what remained she expected to have acquaintance in a short time. The wiser heads among the nuns

---

[18] Henri Platelle, 'Les relations entre l'abbaye Saint-Amand de Rouen et l'abbaye Saint-Amand d'Elone', in *La Normandie bénédictine au temps de Guillaume le Conquérant (XIe siècle)*. (Lille, 1967), 104–6, printing Valenciennes, Bibl. Mun. MSS 500, 502. *Bibliotheca hagiographica latina*, vol. 1, p. 57, no. 16. Cf. Schmitt, 'Suicide,' 22 n. 30. For an interpretation of the story in the light of questions relating to the position of women in the church: Penelope D. Johnson, *Equal in Monastic Profession: Religious Women in Medieval France* (Chicago and London, 1991), 239–41.

[19] Platelle, 105: 'sinite me ire in Infernum cum Diabolo, cui predestinata et data sum.'

discussed an appropriate cure and decided that a jar of water be blessed and, next morning, poured on the troubled woman, together with a prayer that Jesus' power should heal her.

The woman listened to all this without further reaction than sullen, agitated sighing. 'But the madness of the Enemy raged within.' Put under twenty-four-hour guard for a whole week, she appeared to grow calmer, and one evening she persuaded her guards that she, and they, were all too tired to stay awake. She got her own bed ready and lay down as if to sleep. Then, around midnight, she rose and

looking round to see that no one was there, dressed only in her chemise, she secretly climbed a high-looking wall, and, taking the shawl from her head, tied one end of the shawl to the top of the column of the wall, ingeniously forming the other end into a noose which she put round her own neck. She then jumped, with a shock that bent her neck so that blood came out of her mouth and stained the wall opposite.[20]

Just after midnight one of the guards woke and saw the woman's bed was empty. He looked round the church without result. Finally he saw her hanging, her body stiff and obviously dead. He at once raised the alarm. The nuns, woken by the shouting, came running in horror from various parts of the convent, calling tearfully on St Amand to help and 'not to let his dignity perish'. Candles were lit. The dead woman's neck was untied from the noose and her corpse thrown on to the floor of the church.[21] Three stout-hearted and capable[22] sisters went off into the dark to tell the archdeacon of Rouen—the local chief of ecclesiastical police—to ask what to do. He said the body should be removed from the church before dawn and thrown into 'some ditch', and then he followed the nuns back to the scene.

While the three messenger nuns had been away, others had stayed near the body. One, with an ear to the chest,[23] sensed there was still breath in it. Then she noticed a touch of colour returning to the cheeks. The eyes began to open a little and a deep sigh came from the woman's chest. The bystanders watched this keenly and began to beat their own chests, praying loud and earnestly for St Amand's help. As they did so the dead woman gradually came back to life. Like the deacon of Salzburg, and doubtless for the same physiological reasons, she was dumb for all that day and the following night. But in the thirty hours after her hanging she recovered so much strength that, at the end of them, four men could scarcely hold her.

---

[20] Platelle, 105: 'in quem collum injiciens et cum impetu prosiliens, cum tanta vi collum flexit ut radius sanguinis e gutture exiens parietis obstantis partem maculasset.'

[21] Ibid., 106: 'super templi pavimentum dejicitur.'

[22] Ibid.: 'que audaciore vel prudentiores esse videbantur.'

[23] I have surmised this detail. The phrase (Platelle, 106) is: 'palpitantem in pectore spiritum sensit redivivum.'

Finally, at dawn on the day following that which she had begun with her attempted suicide, the woman spoke. Her religious rectitude was fully recovered. Her first words were 'Holy Lady, holy Mary, Mother of God, help me!' and she proceeded vociferously to praise and thank God the Father, his Son Jesus, and Jesus' Confessor St Amand. A priest was sent for and the woman made full confession and received absolution, with all due humility. With yet more thanks to Jesus and St Amand for having 'saved me from the most pernicious Enemy and from the throat of Hell' she finished, according to Abbess Marsilia's letter, with a repetition of the Christian's baptismal promises.

Among peculiarities of this miracle is its theological idiom. The illustrious woman suffers the '*tristitia* that worketh death', and the loss of her 'natural reason', both concepts from the ABC of contemporary moral theology. She ends with confession, absolution, and the repetition of her baptismal promises. This was all in an idiom appropriate to a neighbour of Bec, with its famous school, and of the not so distant Laon, whose masters were pioneering theology in 1107, still untroubled by the riots that would kill the school, and diffusing its message through the lively, reformist Norman church of Henry I's time. Slothful 'illustrious' women cared nothing for its message. On-the-spot ones, like the Abbess Marsilia, did, and got it right.[24]

I add two further miracles of this kind, one short and one long. The short one is from the *Miracles of St Edmund of Abingdon* and refers, like the other two from this collection quoted in Chapter 12, to a period just after the saint's death in 1240. A married woman called Regine lived near the monastery of Vauluisant, not far from Sens. She had been 'mad for five days [*insaniavit per quindenam*]', and was 'brought to such a peak of madness [*in tantam insaniam ferebatur*]' that she threw herself into a well, ten fathoms deep. Pulled out, she gave thanks at St Edmund's tomb in nearby Pontigny, and returned to her husband, cured. That is all.[25] The story again suggests no symptom of madness other than suicidal feelings.

The last miracle of my five is again the most circumstantial, and may help

[24] Cf. *The Life of Christina of Markyate*, ed. C. H. Talbot (Oxford, 1959), 84, and my comments on it in 'Confession before 1215', 75.

[25] Oxford, Bodleian, MS Fell 2, p. 34r: 'insaniavit per quindenam mulier Regina nomine de villa nova divitum Homeri iuxta vallem lucentem que in tantam insaniam ferebatur quod se ipsam in puteum proiecit, cuius profunditas decem teisias habuit, set nutu divino viva inde extrahitur et ad pontiniacum adducitur. Ipsa vero ibidem cum magna difficultate cibum sumpsit et pauca verba edidit. Que cum in porta abbatie aliquandiu commoraretur meritis sancti restituitur marito suo qui eam adduxerat fide non ficta pro ea interpellante.' The Villeneuve 'aux-Riches-Hommes' in question appears to be the modern Villeneuve l' Archevêque, standing a mile and a half south of Vauluisant, some twelve miles east of Sens on the road to Auxerre. It lay twenty-seven miles NNW of Pontigny. A *teisia* (or *toise*) was a fathom.

us judge the others. It is from the *Miracles of St Frideswide*, and is to be dated to the same year as the story of the blasphemous young Jew, that is, to 1179, in this case to late September or early October.[26] The miracle concerns a 'girl [*puella*] of adult age'. That expression would make her at least 16. Called Emmelina, she lived in the village of Eddington near (now in) Hungerford. In the autumn of 1179 Emmelina

was afflicted by the loss of her wits [*mentis alienatione*] and sank to such depths of madness [*amentiam*] that she tried to take her life with her own hands as the final remedy for all troubles. So one night she left her mother's house secretly, and although the course she was embarking on was a deadly one [*funestum propositum*] she armed herself with the sign of the cross and then hastened to the nearby river, called the Kennet, and stood on the river bank. Despite the fact that she was preparing to plunge in and end her unhappy life, through the seductive and depraved suggestion of the Devil, she nevertheless said out loud, as she had learned them, the words of salutation said by the angel to the Blessed and Glorious Virgin Mother of God, 'Hail, Mary, full of grace.' Then, once more fortifying her brow with the sign of the cross, she dived head-first into the river.

Again we would know none of this if that had been an end of the story. But it was not.

Now there was a mill-wheel nearby, turning as it worked the mill. The current swept the girl under it. Yet no drop of water, as Emmelina insisted afterwards, got into her mouth or ears. It swept her back to land on a slight prominence in the river's course. Meanwhile the miller, whose name was Alfred, was asleep at home a short way from the mill. In his sleep he was warned that he should hurry to the mill and lose no time in removing from the water what he found there. He awoke at once, rushed to the place, and to his amazement found a girl. He took her from the water, unwilling though she was, and returned her to her mother, who had been in a tearful state looking for the daughter who preferred to die than to live.

Emmelina did not recover at once. Instead she fell prey to the condition we observed in both the deacon at Salzburg and the illustrious woman from Lisieux. Her speech began to fail. By Christmas, three months later, she had stopped speaking at all. She remained in this state of mental alienation (*mentis alienatione*) until May. Emmelina's mother and brother then hit on the idea of taking her to sleep at St Frideswide's shrine. In sleep she was instructed to reconcile herself to the Virgin Mary by saying the 'Ave Maria'. For four or five days nothing happened, and Emmelina's mother, regarding the experiment as a failure, dragged her unwilling daughter back from the shrine. It was *en route* for home that the miracle happened. Emmelina fell, and in doing so suddenly (like Proust on the loose paving-stone) discovered

---

[26] *Miracula s. Frideswidae*, § 31, *Acta sanctorum*, Oct. 8 (1853), 574D–5755A.

her voice. She began to speak again, badly at first, then fully. Having entirely recovered her mental composure as well as her speech, she expressed her thanks to St Frideswide by becoming a 'bondwoman' of her church. Soon after her recovery she recited the entire adventure before the bishop of Norwich. It was probably from notes taken at this recitation that the author of the *Miracles* got his information. She would not have related her escapade before a bishop without dissociating herself from the heinous act she had committed. 'Alienation of mind' was for her, and her listeners, an appropriate apologetic device.

'The miller, whose name was Alfred': as well as its clear depiction of this type of aphasia, Emmelina's miracle reminds us, among other things, of the parallels to be discovered between our religious and judicial sources. Certain parallels were noticed already, in Chapter 11, in connection with an Italian canonization process. Both kinds of document had to identify sources. From the time canonization rules began to be tightened up in the eleventh century, a miracle too needed its witnesses, complete with their corroborative details: 'the miller's name was Alfred.' The need to tell the right sort of story, and make it sound true, was as much a factor in the written result here as it was in the coroner's court, or in the Paris Court of Requests. That we get vivid accounts out of both is due to this similarity in their conditions of origin. They are conditions which, in *miracula* as in court records, make the historian 'sing for his supper' by applying rules of interpretation, appropriate to each category, to the exciting stories he reads.

Physical infirmity, then; madness or 'possession'; the same, but attributed possibly to mere depression: all three conditions are represented in *miracula* as antecedents to suicide. None of the categories is exclusive. The first, we acknowledged, merges with the one before it. The last, as we shall now see, likewise merges with the next after it. I am referring to the category of sheer, undisguised melancholy.

Religious Melancholiacs: Attempts

The cases to be rehearsed are of 'religious' melancholy, and an ambiguity must first be cleared up. 'Religious' can denote a preoccupation with God and his ways. But here I mean a status, that of someone under vows and in an order, like a monk, nun, or friar. Only two stories in this chapter so far, and only two in the two previous chapters, have been primarily about 'religious' in that sense. Nearly all those that follow will be, whence the adjective. That does not rule out its psychological sense. While melancholy as such does not have to be of a religious kind, it must be so for anyone who even tries to be a Christian believer. 'God does not love me,' he will think; or 'God is asleep, and plays no part in the world'; or even 'there is no God.' The melancholy Christian is necessarily bound to think this because if he really trusted in God, however gloomy the world seemed, he would not have to be gloomy. As it is, these religious misgivings depress him, and all the more, the more he has 'stood up to be counted' as a believer. A priest or monk who stops believing in God, for instance, is in terrible straits. He has given up everything for God. Now God seems to have vanished.

To commit suicide from religious melancholy, as from any other sort, is to do so without any palpable, external motive. The fact that nearly all examples of this type of suicide are from people in orders must raise a question. Is it the case that medieval lay people committed suicide only with such a motive—like imprisonment or the loss of a spouse or child—while people in religious orders did it by merely being alone with their own thoughts? Prima facie it must seem so. The distribution of extant cases suggests it. There may even be some truth in the suggestion. Just how much, I shall discuss later.[27] But before we pre-empt that discussion by accepting this apparently reasonable hypothesis as fact, we should reflect for a moment about the nature of the 'religious sources' in which these stories appear. The 'religiousness' of these sources too can be understood in more than one sense. Nearly all of them, whether they were about people in religious orders or not, were written by people themselves in such orders.[28] That had an important consequence for their use as a historical source.

The consequence relates to the type of story they record. In particular, it relates to whether the theme of a narrative was psychological or practical, that is, more about thoughts or more about acts. Let me for the present purpose distinguish these two types of narrative as 'thought-heavy' and 'act-heavy'. In reaching our religious sources the two types of story were like physical bodies with different mass:volume ratios as they travel through a medium. Consider how persons in religious orders got their news from the lay world. Pastoral orders like the friars learned a lot about laity. From the middle of the thirteenth century, as we have seen, they learned a great deal from confessions; and although they forgot most of that (it was weary work), and were forbidden to reveal the rest, there was still a residuum of generalized, anonymous knowledge friars got from this function, and above all from its periphery, say, at a deathbed or in solving a domestic problem. Being of value to other pastors, this information would pass back and forth among confessors. Some of it went into our *exempla* collections. Without

---

[27] Cf. pp. 391–5 below.

[28] I say 'nearly' because Hugo of Trimberg will be an exception; see below, pp. 345–6.

these we would know much, much less than we do about the realities of moral life among the laity.

In reaching the written page such stories had nevertheless passed through a medium. A priest first had to learn of it, remember it, and repeat it; and the story might go through this process several times before being written down. The 'thought-heavy' story travelled less well through this medium than the more factual sort. Most of the reason for this was given a classic exposition by C. S. Lewis when, in *The Allegory of Love*,[29] he explained why allegory came into being, with its personifications of mental dispositions like Wrath and Perseverance. It was, he explained, precisely because those personifications made the dispositions easier to grasp, and hence made better narrative. The demons and angels of our miracle stories served the same function. It is as if my rule of thumb for evaluating miracle stories was here inverted. So far the rule has been 'good story; bad history'. But in the present context it should read: 'good story: good traveller'. And the converse of that, in face of this particular question, is 'thought-heavy' story: 'bad traveller'. The report of a dramatic gambling loss, arrest, or abandonment by a lover, travelled like a cricket-ball. It was spectacular, easy to grasp. So it completed the journey from the lay world to the monastic. Stories about mere thoughts and feelings, from the same milieu, travelled more like a balloon. There were fewer of them, and these were lucky to arrive at all.

Meanwhile, within the cloister and within a religious order, this whole scheme of things worked back to front. Here balloons travelled easily. For thought-heavy stories, whether or not fleshed out with demons and angels, were the very stuff of professional monastic literature. Monks and nuns, after all, suffered a lot of trials and difficulties inside their heads. Think of all the trials entailed by the preservation of obedience or celibacy. The whole idea of a religious order, as distinct from a scattering of hermits, was that they should support each other. So stories about psychological experience, and how it was best tackled, passed easily and often, both orally and on the page. They were part of the monks' professional equipment. The conclusion of all this is plain. A story of mere melancholy was 'thought-heavy'. While unlikely to travel well from the lay world to a monastic scriptorium it was, by contrast, positively likely to do so within the orders. When both sides of the matter are thus considered simultaneously we should not be surprised that, in respect of seriously suicidal melancholy, surviving stories are all about people in religious orders. That does not prove the monks and nuns did not, in fact, suffer from such melancholy more than anyone else.

---

[29] (Oxford, 1936), pp. 322–4.

That question can remain open, at least at this point. What it proves is that that particular conclusion cannot be reached solely from the uneven distribution of the stories. The distribution is better explained by the circumstances of their origin.

That done, it is time to return to the portraits. The present category divides into two groups, of attempts, and of completed suicides. For a reason now familiar—namely that the 'hero' survived and could relate his experiences—we know more of the motives of the first than the second group, so I start with those.

I said 'nearly' all examples are of religious melancholy, in the sense that they affected someone in a religious order as well as being religious in character. The one exception relates to a scholar. One might expect more from this quarter. Too much ratiocination, after all, has in most ages been a recognized cause of melancholy, and may have contributed to at least one suicide in the coroners' records of Oxford—the only university city where such are available. Academic melancholy may be hidden in some of the religious suicides that follow now. But I have come across only one medieval suicide miracle about a person distinguished *only* by learning. It was ascribed to that unmarried mother Margaret of Cortona as another of those recorded by the eighteenth-century Franciscan, Pelago, when collecting documents on her cult. St Margaret's miracle merely tells how 'a certain learned man' (as usual anonymous) fell into despair and tried to hang himself. Like the old monk John, at Villers, St Margaret, while at prayer alone in her cell, had a vision of what the would-be suicide was doing. Together with her companions she ran, found him hanging and on the point of death, and saved him. A fresco once in the Cortona city church (Plate 6) depicted the man in his scholar's gown, hanging from a beam, a devil hovering in attendance. St Margaret, having apparently broken down the door of his house and run up to his study window, is leaning out and cutting the rope. Two of her companions support the weight of the body as it is released. The man's gown suggests he was a canon lawyer.[30]

That was a suicidal scholar, of a type rare in *miracula* though not unknown, as we have seen, in chronicles or judicial records. In turning now to review examples of religious melancholy in the more technical sense— that of melancholy *religiosi*—it will be useful to identify one last factor in their re-telling, as accessory to the stories' interpretation. It is our old friend tabu. It may seem surprising, after all that has been said about balloons and

---

[30] A book on the cult of St Margaret of Cortona is being prepared jointly by Professor André Vauchez and Dr Joanna Cannon. My introduction to this miracle is one of many debts this book owes to the generosity of Professor Vauchez. I learn the original colour of the man's gown (blue, suggesting canon law) from the paper cited on p. xx.

6 St Margaret of Cortona saves a professor. Warned in a vision, St Margaret (†1297), leads companions to save a professor from suicide, in her haste tearing a door from its hinges, while the demon of despair vanishes top left. See p. 334.

thought-heavy stories and of their easy passage within monastic orders, that a tabu could still attach to the suicidal element of a reported episode. But it did so for the same reason that those psychological accounts otherwise moved easily. A religious community, let me repeat, existed for mutual support, hence its interest in stories with a psychological content. But in a tight community, with a network of exchanges of this kind, viruses can also spread quickly, and the mere mention of suicide was such a virus. This applied as much to a pastoral order, like the Dominican, as to an enclosed one, like the Cistercian. Thus Thomas of Chantimpré, the Dominican, despite his indiscretions about the laity, is high on the list of suspects as euphemistic about suicide. By contrast, the most candid of all narrators of *miracula* on the subject was Caesarius of Heisterbach, a Cistercian; and Caesarius, for his part, knew that in relating these incidents he crossed a barrier. 'I fear it may not be prudent for weaker brethren to hear or read these things,' his revelations about suicide began.[31] His subsequent garrulity on the subject only emphasizes the solidity of the barrier, for it exemplifies

---

[31] *Dial. mirac.*, dist. 4, ch. 40 (vol. 1, p. 210): 'sed timeo quod infirmis non expediat talia legere vel audire.' Cf. his hastiness in dist. 3, ch. 13 (vol. 1, p. 125).

that human tendency which, on breaching a taboo, thinks 'better be hung for a sheep than for a lamb.' In this, Caesarius provides yet another example of the 'oscillation'—the being black or white, never grey—which we have found, and shall find again, as characteristic of suicide as a subject of thought.

Before sampling more of Caesarius' 'free flow' let us look at another of these exceptions that prove the rule, in this case the rule that most monks tended to reticence. The exception is a Cistercian *exemplum* in an anonymous collection, dating probably from the late thirteenth century. It is about a monk who tried to hang himself. Or rather, the monk *did* hang himself, on the Devil's instigation, and was resuscitated by the Virgin.[32] For the story is definitely a miracle. The rule about all stories holds also about miracles: 'good miracle: bad history'. The kernel of this one is a 'good miracle'. It could indeed have been borrowed *en bloc* from a similar one, centuries old, in *Lives of the Fathers*, where the similar resuscitation of a monk-suicide was attributed to the Apostle Paul. The historical pretensions of the present Cistercian story are nevertheless saved by two details. Although the monastery is not named it is ascribed to the family of Clairvaux; and that, together with the Cistercian provenance of the manuscript, strongly suggests that the material, fictional or otherwise, is in-house Cistercian. If it does stem from an incident, the latter is datable to some date in the 130 years after 1120. The second corroborative detail is that the Devil comes back a second time to repeat his mischief, but this time the Virgin anticipates him and puts him to flight. That is an asymmetry. A single diabolic visit would have made the point. It does in other analogues. These details are just enough to suggest the story might have had a historical germ; just enough, and no more. For otherwise the history is as vague as can be. It gives no name, even of the house; no time, no motive, no other characters or circumstantial details. It is a vagueness altogether appropriate, in other words, for a topic it was not right even to mention.

This then, was the background of Caesarius' sudden burst of eloquence. We can now approach his two stories of attempted suicide. Both are apparent descriptions of an event, with no or little 'type', and much topical detail. The first he relates in *c.*1222 as recent. A nobleman, Baldwin, *advocatus*, or noble patron, of the city of Brunswick, was 'moved by God' to abandon the world and enter the Cistercian order, and did so at the house of Rittershausen near Brunswick. Unlike some other religious melancholiacs, Baldwin had thus not grown old in a lifetime of external monastic perfection. He was a convert, in a strict, personal sense, and had

---

[32] Ward, *Cat. Rom.*, vol. 2, p. 666, no. 5. The MS is Egerton 1117, fol. 117 vb.

appropriate zeal. Already as a novice, Baldwin had attracted reproof for excessive zeal.

He was so strict with himself that, throughout his probationary year, his abbot and his *magister* often reproved him about it. When he became a full monk, he was not content with the common monastic obligations but added a lot of special ones of his own, like working while others rested, and staying awake while they slept.[33]

Baldwin's career reads strangely like that of the early careers of some medieval monastic reformers, restless as they were in monasteries of lax observance. Caesarius does not say enough to reveal where the difference lay, except that Baldwin's fervour destroyed his balance of mind.

At length, as a result of excessive vigils and labour, (Baldwin's) brain dried up [*exsiccato . . . cerebro*]. It became thereupon so enfeebled that one night, before the community had risen for mattins, he went to the church, climbed onto the novices' bench, tied the bell-rope round his neck, and jumped off. The weight of his body had the effect of making the bell ring. The monk whose job it was to oversee the church heard the sound and was terrified. But he was even more terrified when he came and saw a monk hanging there. He ran up, cut the rope, and laid out the man's body, almost strangled but with the heart still beating, and succeeded in reviving him.[34]

It is that bell-rope again. The revived Baldwin, like the revived Salzburg deacon, was found to be another man after his hanging. His former character (*sensum pristinum*) had gone. From then on, Baldwin cared nothing for what or when he ate, or how long he slept. Caesarius believes Baldwin was still alive at the time of writing, in this sad condition; an example, he concludes, of how *acedia* can result from 'indiscreet fervour'.

Of Caesarius' two stories on this theme I put second the one which, in the *Dialogue of Miracles*, begins the whole series of seven *miracula* on suicide. I mention this because I shall suggest, apropos of the completed suicide that directly follows it in the *Dialogue*, that it was this recent incident, a mere attempt, that broke Caesarius' reservations and got him reminiscing on even graver incidents. The setting of the story in question was a convent of nuns under the authority of a male prior, described as 'above the river Mosel'. (A female dependency of the Cistercian house of Himmerode in the Eifel would fit this description best.) Caesarius dates the incident a few months before he wrote, that is, probably in 1221–2. His memory was fresh.

A few months ago [he writes] a certain nun, of great age and with a reputation for special holiness, was so severely afflicted with the vice of melancholy, together with

---

[33] *Dial. mirac.*, dist. 4, ch. 45 (vol. 1, pp. 212–13).   [34] Ibid. (p. 213).

onslaughts from the spirit of blasphemy, doubt and disbelief, that she fell into despair. She started having the gravest doubts about all she had believed since infancy, and was bound to believe. Nor could anyone prevail on her to take the divine sacraments. The other nuns, not excluding her own niece, asked her why she had grown so obdurate. She just answered, 'I am one of the reprobate, one of those, that is, destined for damnation.'[35]

One feature of religious melancholy—'religious' in the psychological sense —is its exposure to logical contradiction. Not unlike the 'illustrious woman' of Lisieux, Caesarius' nun had lost her belief yet believed she was damned. If Caesarius had heard the story right, she sinned against faith and hope at once, in two dispositions distinct, though commonly found in compound.

One day [Caesarius continues] the prior was moved to warn her. 'Sister,' he said, 'if you do not cast off this unbelief and come to your senses, I shall provide that you are buried [when the times comes] in the open fields.' The nun heard and remembered his words but kept quiet at the time. Then, one day, some of the sisters had to take a journey somewhere. The nun I speak of followed them secretly to the bank of the Mosel below the monastery. When the boat carrying the sisters had got under way she jumped from the bank into the river. Those in the boat heard the splash and, looking back, saw her body but thought it was a dog. But by God's wish a man on the shore decided to ascertain what it was, ran up, and, seeing a human body, got into the river and dragged it out. Everyone now realized it was the nun we have spoken of, and that she was almost drowned. Shocked, they gathered round to revive her. As soon as she was able to speak, having vomited some water, they asked her, 'Sister, why did you act so cruelly [*crudeliter*]?' Pointing to the prior with her finger she said 'he threatened to have me buried in the open fields when I die. So I chose rather to plunge and be swept away by this river than be buried like an animal in the fields.' The others took her back to the monastery and kept a close watch on her.[36]

In the *Dialogue* the Novice-Master adds a pedagogic comment:

Behold [he says] what malice is born from melancholy. The woman had been reared in the monastery since childhood. She was chaste, a virgin, devout, strict and religious; and I was told by the Mistress of Novices [*Magistra*] in a neighbouring convent that all the girls reared under the tutelage of this particular nun were better disciplined, and more devout, than other young women.[37]

And the Novice-Master ends by hoping that

God, who is very merciful, who tempts his elect in many ways and who mercifully rescued her from the river, will bear in mind her earlier labours and not allow her to perish finally.

---

[35] *Dial. mirac.*, dist. 4, ch. 40 (vol. 1, pp. 209–10).
[36] Ibid.   [37] Ibid. (pp. 209–10).

The Novice of the *Dialogue* replies:

I suppose that, since God does nothing without a motive, the reason God permits such things is to prevent anyone, however perfect, from becoming presumptuous about his own virtues or virtuous works, as distinct from attributing all things to God.[38]

His senior agrees. He would. Caesarius was himself the abbey's novice-master.

Age; exemplary monastic observance; wavering faith; despair: we have met each of these elements in other combinations. Three of them, all but the wavering faith, reappear in the story which follows this one in the *Dialogue of Miracles*. There, however, the combination was fatal. It is with four fatal episodes of this kind that I shall end.

Religious Melancholiacs: Suicides

Beside the account of the amorous nun recounted in Chapter 12, three careful, circumstantial stories (*exempla*) certainly relate the suicide of a religious, and one more probably does. But I shall deal first with two briefer references to the suicides of religious. They are both about friars. The friars in question were apostates in that they broke their vows and left the order. The Franciscan one, John of Capella, is mentioned in two sources: the *Fioretti*—the collection of stories and *miracula* about St Francis collected in the early fourteenth century—and Bartholomew of Pisa's study of St Francis's life, the *De Conformitate*, written between 1385 and 1399.[39] As a youth of Assisi, John of Capella had in 1209 become an early companion of St Francis. Later, for undisclosed reasons, he abandoned the saint, contracted leprosy, and hanged himself 'through impatience'. He is portrayed as a 'Judas'. None of the sources attempts to give him a 'fair trial', so we know no more about him. The Dominican apostate, whose death must have occurred a decade or two later (in the 1240s or 1250s), was luckier in his historian. Thomas of Chantimpré had known him, thought he had been harshly treated, and picked on his case as an *exemplum* of what happens if priors are too strict. He had been a 'learned and great man', Thomas says,

---

[38] Ibid. (p. 210).

[39] *Fioretti*, chs 1 and 31; ed. P. Sabatier, ('Actus b. Francisci et sociorum eius') in *Collection d'Études et de Documents*, 4 (Paris, 1902), 2 and 120. Bartholomew of Pisa, *De conformitate vitae b. Francisci ad vitam Domini Jesu nostri Redemptoris*, ch. 8, § 2, *Analecta Franciscana*, 4 (Quaracchi, 1906), 178.13–18. Bartholomew, lines 16–17: 'ob impatientiam se / suspendit'. *The Legend of the Three Companions*, ch. 35, and the *Chronicon XXIV Generalium*, p. 4 speak of John of Capella but not of his suicide. Salimbene's Chronicle, ed. O. Holder-Egger, *Mon. Germ. Hist. Scriptores* (Hanover, 1905–13), vol. 32, p. 225c (= ed. G. Scalia, (Bari, 1966), pp. 60–1) mentions a different early Franciscan suicide. See pp. 118–19 above.

who left the order and later asked to be received back. The prior refused. The petitioner thereupon 'with the utmost impatience fell into despair and died [*impatientissime desperatus, mortuus est*]'.[40] Once more Thomas is opaque at the critical point, and I have applied the usual rule for this author: if it *could* mean the man killed himself, it probably does. Since the Dominican, like the leper John of Capella, had already fallen ill and may have been homeless as well, his death must have reflected more than just religious disillusion. But with an apostate friar some measure of this must have come into it.

Four monastic suicides, certain or very probable, are more fully described. Chronologically the earliest is the probable case of Wolo of St Gall, the large Benedictine monastery above Lake Constance (then in Bavaria). The only surviving account of Wolo's death is both more and less historical than the common run of miracles. It is more so because it concerns known historical figures, and because the death itself is independently mentioned in an Annal; and less so, because the author of the account, writing *c.*1035 about an event a century-and-a-half earlier, has laid himself open to the accusation of intruding events from his own time back into an earlier century. Whether the accusation holds is another matter, and it is wiser, in my view, to give the St Gall author the benefit of the debate. He was Ekkehard IV, and the work, begun in the 1030s, was *Casus sancti Galli*: 'Things That Have Happened (or Cases) at Saint Gall'; this being an anecdotal history of the monastery from the late ninth century to *c.*973. Its unusual title reflects the author's belief, inspired by Boethius, that much that happens in the world is a more or less inexplicable accident of Fortune.[41]

The *casus* of Wolo is an illustration. It is related in a group of chapters devoted to one of Ekkehard's heroes, Notker Balbulus. Notker had been doyen of St Gall's famous scriptorium, a poet and biographer of Charlemagne, and had died as abbot of the monastery in 912, in his early sixties. The incident involving Wolo can be dated by an entry in the *St Gall Annals*, from the same scriptorium, which reads:

976. Louis, the devout king of Germany, died. Wolo fell. The Emperor Charles the Second [the Bald] began to reign.[42]

---

[40] Thomas of Chantimpré, *De apibus*, bk 2, ch. 51, § 9 (pp. 475–6).
[41] Chs 43–4, in H. F. Haefele, ed., *Ekkehard IV: Casus sancti Galli. St Galler Klostergeschichten* (Darmstadt, 1980), 96–100. History of monastery, pp. 1–7. Cf. H. W. Haefele, '*Wolo cecidit*. Zur Deutung einer Ekkehard-Erzählung', *Deutsches Archiv*, 35 (1979), 17–32. Dr Haefele reads Wolo's restless anxiety as characteristic of the eleventh century, not of the ninth, but on inadequate grounds. We know far too little of 'anxiety' in either century to redate events on this ground alone.
[42] *Annales sangallenses maiores*, ed. C. Henking. Mitteilungen zur vaterländischen Geschichte, 19 (St Gallen, 1884) 275.

Wolo cecidit. In Chapter 3 we learned that chroniclers and annalists often drew a veil over suicide. This Annalist's reference to Wolo's 'fall' may be another instance. The reason for thinking so is in chapter 43 of the *Casus sancti Galli*. The chapter begins with this 'case':

There was at that time in our monastery a young monk called Wolo. He was well educated, and the son of a count [of the Kyburger dynasty, according to a modern suggestion]; but his character was restless and unstable. Neither the deacon, nor Abbot Notker, nor anyone else, could bring his stubborn spirit to heel despite frequent verbal reprimands and discipline with the cane. Nothing helped. The whole community was sorry to see such a well-endowed man in this condition, for St Gall only accepted monks of noble birth. Yet the stubborn truth is that some of the more noble did misconduct themselves in this way. Wolo's parents were concerned for him, visited the monastery, and added their own reproaches. That did a little good. But once they had gone home he went back to his former ways.[43]

On the day in question, the account goes on, Abbot Notker received a supernatural warning. A demon told him privately that he and his brethren would have a 'bad night'. Notker thought nothing of it but for safety's sake passed the warning on to his monks. When the message got round to Wolo he characteristically waved it away as an 'old man's dream'. (Notker was less than 40 at the time.)

That day the monks had been confined to the cloister, so they were variously engaged indoors. Wolo was in the scriptorium, copying. The work he was copying was St John's Gospel, and he had reached the passage in it (John 4: 47) where 'a certain nobleman' has asked Jesus to cure his dying son.

He reached the phrase in the Gospel 'he was at the point of death.' On finding these words Wolo suddenly jumped up and, ignoring those near him who shouted 'where are you going, Wolo?' rushed for the steps leading to the bell-tower. His purpose was to soothe his restless soul through his eyes by gazing round at the mountains and fields, since he was not allowed to go out physically.[44]

It is worth pausing to ask ourselves what details the narrator might and might not have known. The copyist's stopping-point would have been obvious with or without Wolo's testimony, from the incomplete manuscript found afterwards. His romantic motive for climbing the tower is more conjectural.

---

[43] *Casus s. Galli*, ch. 43 (ed. Haefele, pp. 96–8).

[44] Ibid. (p. 98). That the studious should seek refreshment in the sight of mountains and fields should not be thought anachronistic: cf. Bartholomeus Anglicus, *De proprietatibus rerum*, bk 15, ch. 57; edn of Frankfurt, 1601, p. 654.

In his climb he reached a place right above the Altar of the Virgins, and there fell from a beam, pushed as we believe by Satan, and broke his neck.[45]

The word for 'beam' there (*laqueare*) could mean 'wooden roof'.[46] But whatever it means, it represents details the narrator must have known because the monks would have gone to inspect. Yet the word remains a small island in a sea of vagueness. Nowhere does the writer say why 'Wolo fell'.

A death-scene nevertheless follows, and occupies the rest of the chapter. Hearing the crash, the monks rushed to the church and found Wolo still conscious on the pavement in front of the altar of the Virgins. The monks' first concern was to give their dying companion the *viaticum*, or portable Eucharist. So he was confessed and then received communion.[47] The monks then wanted to carry him to the infirmary. But the dying Wolo stopped them. 'Let me first pray to the Holy Virgins,' he groaned; 'for they know that, though a wicked sinner in other ways, I have never touched a woman.' Someone had meanwhile gone to fetch the abbot, and the monks who were gathered round the dying man stood back so that Notker could reach him. Notker was aghast and tearful. At once he fell onto his knees beside the dying monk who, seeing it was the abbot, said in a broken voice: 'to you, my Lord, and to the Holy Virgins, I commend my sinful soul.' Notker could hardly speak for grief. But he managed to pray: 'O you Holy Virgins, I trust in you, and commend both this man and myself to your care, and take to myself this man's sins.' A group of monks, standing and kneeling beside Wolo, lifted his damaged body and began to carry him slowly towards the infirmary. When they got in front of the church door they laid him down on the pavement and rested. There, as he lay on the pavement, Wolo clutched Abbot Notker's hand tightly, and expired.

That is all Ekkehard says of how Wolo died. But he adds another chapter on what Abbot Notker did afterwards. During the funeral ceremonial it was Notker who washed the body, laid it in its coffin, and supervised the burial from beginning to end. After the burial, Notker went on praying and saying Masses for Wolo. Within seven days later he learned supernaturally, and with tearful joy, that 'Many sins have been forgiven him, for he loved much' (cf. Luke 7: 47).[48] For the rest of his life thereafter Notker did penances for two monks, himself and Wolo.

Why, we may ask, this unique degree of concern? Disobedient young

---

[45] *Casus s. Galli*: 'Ascendens vero cum super altare virginum venisset, impulsu, ut creditur, satanę per laquear cecidit collumque confregit.'

[46] *Laqueare* as beam (against Haefele's *Holzdecke*): Latham, *Medieval Latin Word-List* (Oxford, 1965), 269.

[47] Ibid., 'confessione dicta communicavit'.

[48] *Casus s. Galli*, ch. 44 (p. 100).

monks like Wolo abound in monastic literature. Wolo was in many ways *less* delinquent than others. Whatever he had done, he had confessed his sins and been absolved before he died: otherwise he would not have had the *viaticum*. Yet one serious sin, fornication, we are told he had never committed in the first place.[49] Why, then, this special anxiety? The answer, surely, can only be that Wolo's last 'sin', despite his confession and absolution after committing it, struck such awe into his saintly friends that they took every extra precaution for his salvation. In a word, he had not fallen. He had jumped.

Of our four completed monastic suicides the second has features in common with the first. It is in Gilo's *Life of St Hugh of Cluny*, written around 1112, and relates to an incident attributed, without further precision, to some time in Hugh's long tenure of the abbacy from 1049 to 1109. Here the fact of suicide is expressly stated, while other details are fewer. All Gilo says is that in Souvigny (*Silviniaco*), a Cluniac house seventy miles away above the river Allier,

a certain brother called Stephan was tripped by the snares of the Old Enemy into seeking a martyr's crown before the proper time. He turned his hand against himself and killed himself in a certain wood. He was however full of anger at the time, and perhaps it was this mood which roused the Tempter to conquer him.[50]

A faint trace of circumlocution lingers in three features of this account: the mention of a martyr's crown; silence on the method; and the use of the classical expression *manus sibi ingerens* for suicide. Stephan's character also remains vague, the allusion to 'stolen' martyrdom being itself too like a stereotype to reveal a motive. Even Gilo, with his 'perhaps' (*forte*) can only speculate, sure merely of the monk's 'anger', which may have given the Devil his occasion: *erat tamen iracundiae gravis, qua ejus complexione tentator excitatus, forte praevaluit.*

In Gilo's narrative Stephan stood to Hugh as Wolo to Notker. For it was Hugh who worried about Stephan's salvation as laboriously, for the same reason. And here too the saintly abbot's prayers prevailed. At first, Gilo's account continues, one of the monks at Cluny got a supernatural message in choir. It told him that the suicide Stephan had not been received into the Cluniac congregation in Heaven, because of the manner of his death. So Stephan was not buried in the abbey cemetery. Then St Hugh prayed, said Masses, and gave alms; and in due course the monk who got messages in choir—the 'radio operator', as it were—said he had seen Stephan's soul

---

[49] *Casus s. Galli*, ch. 43 (p. 98): '"quamvis alias nefandissimus, mulierem tamen non novi"'.
[50] Gilo, *Vita s. Hugonis Cluniacensis*, ch. 7; *Pat. lat.*, 159.913D–14B.

appropriately clothed in a glorious habit. So Stephan's body was moved, and put in the abbey cemetery. The *Life*, let us remember, was written to exalt Hugh's sanctity. Ekkehard's book, in large measure, was likewise written to exalt that of Notker. But Hugh has gone one better. For the suicide Stephan had not even confessed and been absolved. He was a straight, angry suicide, apparently unrepentant, and was simply *prayed* into Heaven by a saint.

In Caesarius of Heisterbach's series of seven suicidal *miracula*, the first place was held by that account of a nun, nearly drowned, from a convent fifty miles away. Yet when Caesarius began to write it down he already knew of a real suicide nearer home, by a monk of his own personal acquaintance. Why had he not put it first? I have suggested it was because the first story had a happy ending, and broke this particular bit of ice. Then, once Caesarius had touched the dreadful theme anyway, memories began to tumble forth. The very next miracle, second in the series, concerns the completed suicide of a monk of Caesarius' own order.

The Cistercian suicide here was not a choir monk, but a *conversus* like the leper at Villers. Caesarius and his community had known the man personally, and his death must have been a traumatic memory. For the *conversus* had

lived among the brethren laudably and peaceably from his youth upwards until old age. Indeed it seemed that no one excelled him in the strictness of his observance or in virtue. But it came about—I know not by what judgement of God—that he grew melancholy and faint-hearted [*pusillanimis*]. His anxiety about his sins grew so great that he lost all hope of winning eternal life. It was not doubts about faith that were his trouble. It was just that he despaired of salvation. Passages of biblical authority were of no avail to set him straight. Nor could *exempla* revive his hope of God's pardon. He is believed to have committed some minor sin. The brethren would ask him, 'what is it that makes you so worried and despairing?' He would reply 'I cannot say my prayers as I used to, so I am afraid of Hell.' His condition got worse and he was put in the infirmary. There, one morning, prepared for death, he said to the monk in charge of him, 'I cannot fight any longer against God.' The other man took the words lightly. But the *conversus* went off to a pond near the monastery, threw himself in to it and drowned.[51]

For a completed suicide the motives of this one are carefully described, and could be, because the community had known the man. In announcing the incident Caesarius can thus employ confidently the terminology of scholastic psychology. His story is announced as that of a man 'who ran miserably into final desperation through an excess of melancholy'. Half-way

---

[51] *Dial. mirac.*, dist. 4, ch. 41 (vol. 1, pp. 210–11). The miracle is retold by, among others, Johannes Herolt, *Sermones discipuli . . . Promptuarium*, under *Desperatio*, § 6 (edition of Mainz, 1612, p. 338).

through he resumes this language, saying the *conversus* 'laboured under the vice of melancholy, was for that reason full of *acedia*, and from this pair *desperatio* was born in his heart'. This was a fair diagnosis but still a shade too theological and schematic. For it does not, in fact, explain everything in the circumstantial narrative, as Caesarius himself admits: 'I know not by what judgement of God [he] grew melancholy and faint-hearted [*nescio quo Dei iudicio ita tristis et pusillanimis effectus est*].' Age, monastic excellence, and *desperatio* remain clear features in this case, as they were in the story of the nun who jumped into the Mosel. Here, physical infirmity is added; and that last affliction, *desperatio*, is embellished by two vivid details, one of which the *conversus* shared with the nun. The *conversus* could not say his prayers, just as the nun had given up the sacraments. Finally, the *conversus*' last recorded words were: 'I cannot fight any longer against God.' They suggest fatalism. The *conversus* felt his will was no longer free.

At the end of volume 3, *The Mapping of Mental Desolation*, I mean to return to the question of temptations to suicide, among both laity and monks; temptations, that is, felt by their victims as chronic states rather than acute attacks. There will be time, then, to look more carefully at psychological peculiarities already in evidence in the present more dramatic episodes. In particular, space will be given there to other instances of this quasi-deterministic experience, of a temptation felt to be irresistible, as if coming from a will far outside one's own control: 'I cannot fight any longer against God.'

Meanwhile we have a fourth monastic suicide to consider. It includes, among other peculiarities, that of being recorded by a layman, who knew of the case only indirectly. Hugo of Trimberg taught at the abbey school of St Gangolf in Teuerstadt, near Bamberg. When he died around 1311, he left to posterity several works in Latin and German, of which latter category only one has survived until today. It is a 24,000-word poem, finished around 1300, called *Der Renner* ('The Runner', a title probably given by an early admirer because of the work's excellent 'run', witnessed by nearly seventy manuscripts). *Der Renner* is a sermon in verse, its main moral burden being the need for moderation, in German, *mâze*. *Mâze* applied also to religious exercises. The schoolmaster's views in this field had been confirmed by a lifetime's experience. In particular, Hugo taught, excessive religious devotion invited the Devil to confuse people's minds. So much did it do so, he says, that 'they hang or drown themselves', or so do themselves such harm that they forfeit any reward from God.[52]

---

[52] *Der Renner*, lines 3830–1; ed. G. Ehrismann, 4 vols (Tübingen, 1908–11), vol. 1, p. 157; with added material by G. Schweikle (Berlin, 1970). On the author: Schweikle, vol. 4, pp. 316–20. Date and MSS: ibid., 305–6. The title: ibid., 4. Cf. Knapp, *Selbstmord*, 81–2.

Now Hugo of Trimberg had almost certainly read Caesarius' *Dialogue of Miracles*. Many had. So that confident plural, 'they hang or drown themselves', may tell us no more than we know already. Again, if it does, the reference may include laity, for forty professional years as a schoolteacher had given Hugo wide knowledge of lay society as well as monastic. But one likely reading of this phrase is that it uses the 'diplomatic' plural, the one we commonly use today to blunt an accusation, and that Hugo had, in fact, a particular suicide in mind. If so, it must have been one he tells us he had learned about from his own son. For Hugo's son was a monk in one of the several monasteries in or near Bamberg which would fit the report. The son told Hugo how one of the novices who had entered at the same time had never been happy in the order, and after five years killed himself.

Not long after generalizing so boldly that 'they hang or drown themselves,' Hugo cites this novice as an example. It occupies fourteen of *Der Renner*'s 12,000 dry, Middle High German couplets, of which I reproduce the relevant ones without (this time) attempting to match their jingling rhyme. The novice, the poem says,

Lived five years [there] such	3835
That his heart was never happy.	
No one ever saw him laugh.	
He spent most of his time	
In fasting, prayer, and vigil.	
The Devil counselled him to take a rope	3840
And go with it to a granary	
And hang himself on a beam.	
As he turned this way and that,	
The rope broke; and forthwith	
He went to a fish-pond and drowned.	3845
That his good deeds earned so little thanks	
From God, that pains me	
But God's secrets are unfathomable.[53]	

Then Hugo, in his turn, speculates on the fate of the young man's soul and concludes that God alone can judge. But he says no more of the novice's life and death, still less (as usual) of his identity.

The long, ghostly parade is over. Each ghost in this volume has been conjured up, whether from chronicle, court record, or miracle, as the spirit of a person once alive. The conjuring has inevitably been imperfect. Mistakes may have entered. Legal scribes may have tricked us into treating as suicides

---

[53] *Der Renner*, 3835–3848; ed. Ehrismann, vol. 1, p. 158.

those who were not, and narrators may have made us believe invention as history. But these deceptions, or fake readings, must remain exceptions. The majority, perhaps the overwhelming majority and just conceivably all, of the phantoms paraded in these twelve chapters were those of real suicides. They fled from all human company, and as far as they knew or cared at the time, may have been fleeing divine company too. Now the human company they fled from certainly included ourselves. They did not expect to be remembered by posterity. Indeed the last thing any of them could have imagined was that *we* would be speculating about their deaths, many centuries later. Life is full of surprises, and this would have surprised them. Perhaps the surprise has been on both sides (like that of Tamino and Monostatos in *The Magic Flute*). The reader may have been thinking, like Dante, as the ghostly parade has gone past:

> There trod so great a throng
> That I, I could not have believed
> Death had undone so many.[54]

Each of these suicides died as an individual, a closed universe on his own. My hope has been to intrude on their privacy and in some sense restore them to human company, which is why these chapters have sought to rescue the suicides we could reach, through three different categories of surviving document. There were certainly many others. But the visible must represent the invisible. These visible, the few, have returned as isolated spirits, fresh from their voyage back across the river Styx, their faces 'still pale and stiff, their eyes wondering at the world's return'. Now we have got them in front of us in this astonished and astonishing condition, our next task must be to introduce them to each other and to make them into a single assembly, so that we can talk with them *en bloc*. Perhaps they will reply. Perhaps they will tell us more of their condition collectively than they have done individually. Perhaps even, dare we think it, they may tell us something of ours. The language they will speak in, at all events, to those of us who can strain to hear its whispers, will be that of statistics.

[54] *Inferno*, 3: 55–7.

15

Absolute Numbers

THE concepts of suicide and statistics are from one angle as remote as two concepts can be. One embodies subjectivity, saying 'that is what *I* think of the world'; the other, objectivity, saying 'that is how the world *is*.' Yet in the last century, academically, the two have become all but inseparable. Three reasons suggest themselves. One is self-defence. Statistics anaesthetize. A subject intrinsically unapproachable becomes, once the victim is part of a percentage, not merely accessible but intellectually bracing, a positive pastime. Read suicide statistics all day, and we must pinch ourselves to remember that each item reflects a tragedy literally immeasurable, a universe perishing in unspeakable, unapproachable agony.

There is a second, more positive reason for the statistics. Like many extremes, suicide offers a visible, tangible indication of that of which it is an extreme instance. For each person driven to suicide by loneliness in old age, for example, there may be fifty more who suffer the same species of loneliness but less severely. So, just as physical medicine now employs statistics to reveal things about our own internal bodily organs which we cannot see, and which even microscopes cannot reveal under autopsy, in the same way, suicide statistics can uncover trends and nuances in our own emotional lives, which we feel dimly and suffer from, but which may not be strong enough to identify. They are a kind of emotional scanner.

The third reason is historical. The history is briefly told. It began when, in June 1886, a young teacher in a French provincial school committed suicide by jumping from a balcony. His name was Victor Hommay, and he had recently graduated from the École Normale Supérieure in Paris. Like most suicides he must have thought there was an end to the matter, that he had finished with the world and vice versa. But, again as with most suicides, his death actually sent a shock wave through the lives of his friends and associates. Some of these, not surprisingly, were at the École Normale Supérieure. Just at that period the École Normale was the powerhouse of a tradition, going back to the Enlightenment, of self-consciously philosophical speculation about human moral affairs, a tradition with the zeal of theology but staunchly independent of it. Indeed the two were usually in opposition. The tradition was well represented by one of Hommay's friends at the school, a young lecturer who had taught him. This lecturer, who took his pupil's suicide particularly hard, thought of himself as a rationalist. No doubt he was, if he thought so. But self-knowledge is usually only partial, especially in the young, and, looking back, we are bound to notice that the young rationalist was the scion of a long line of rabbis, whose moral zeal it may have been that fired his researches. The zeal attached, in particular, to a moral intuition abroad in the contemporary French intelligentsia—still readable, in code, in the landscapes of Corot and Camille Pissaro—that France's old, integrated rural society was breaking up and dragging with it the emotional balance of individuals. It was breaking *people* up. The villains of the piece were industry and cities. They were growing fast. If Hommay had lived his lifetime would have seen country-dwellers across the channel in England, for instance, drop from nearly a half to a tenth of the population. France was changing less hectically, but not by much.[1]

It looked to some of his friends, then, as if Hommay had died as a victim of this change. But only to some. For France was also the home, especially since Louis XIV, of another tradition, namely a fairly rigid Catholicism. Other of Hommay's acquaintances took a strictly moral view of his suicide. He had committed a very heinous act. The rationalistic Jewish tutor thought passionately, *com*passionately, otherwise. There may be dangers in compassion as a fuel for the study of history, but it is hard to think of one more fruitful. At all events, the lecturer began collecting statistical data to prove his point and, thirteen years later, in 1897, published, a long, cogent, lucid, unobtrusively tender sermon on the subject. Where one of the traditional kind would have used scriptural texts, this one used statistics.[2]

If the study of suicide had its own era it would divide into two ages, before and after that book. The lecturer was Émile Durkheim, his book, *Le Suicide*. It was not actually the first book to use suicide statistics for social and moral speculation. We saw in the Introduction how Guerry, another latter-day *philosophe*, had preceded him in 1834, and in the same half-century Morselli in Italy and Ogle in Britain were engaged in comparable statistical enterprises.[3] But the range and intellectual cohesion of Durkheim's book put it in a class of its own. It deserved to, and did, become

---

[1] English rural population 1860–1930: Halbwachs, *The Causes of Suicide* (London, 1978), 35; French: T. Zeldin, *France, 1848–1945*, 2 vols (Oxford, 1973–7), vol. 1, 105–7; further estimates and comparisons: D. Grigg, *Population Growth and Agrarian Change. An historical perspective* (Cambridge, 1980), table 24 (p. 169) and table 40 (p. 203).

[2] S. Lukes, *Émile Durkheim* (London, 1973), esp. 1–85, 191–225.

[3] See pp. 14–16 above.

the starting-point for subsequent study, not only of suicide but of much else in the study of social behaviour.

The status of Durkheim's *Suicide* had a double effect. It anchored future writing on the subject firmly into the statistical method. And it brought keener standards to bear on the figures he had used. In this, too, like a preacher's scriptural quotations, statistics have 'a waxen nose' and can serve different interpretations. In social statistics, standards of criticism since 1897 have grown ever keener. In the case of suicide, at least, this has had the paradoxical result, not unlike that in physics, of producing an uncertainty principle. Students of the subject generally agree that Durkheim was over-confident in his figures, drawn though they were—directly or indirectly—from medical and police reports. But agreement still escapes when it is asked how, in that case, really reliable suicide statistics can be gathered, if they can be at all. Here, as in other fields, there are agnostics, believers, and hybrids in between. All they concur on is to allow to modern suicide the same essential elusiveness we have ourselves found in medieval. It has taken the doughtiest of Durkheim's followers, notably his pupil Maurice Halbwachs (whose *The Causes of Suicide* came out in 1930) to salvage a sensible, common-sense principle out of it all: the principle, namely, that if we believe absolutely nothing we get absolutely nowhere. In other words, for all their traps and fallibility, figures do tell us a few things otherwise unknowable.[4]

Whatever the problems are for statisticians of nineteenth- and twentieth-century society, the problems naturally get bigger the further we go back. In the Middle Ages, for most times and places, they are so big as almost to block the way to statistics at all. Hence the qualified title of the present chapters. 'Quantification from medieval sources,' writes a medievalist who knows, 'is never less than difficult and seldom less than futile.'[5] There we have an unbeliever, or almost. The exercise that follows will proceed in an awareness that a little knowledge (which is all we have) is a dangerous thing, but that, like some other dangerous things, it is better than nothing. This is a medieval version of the faith of Durkheim according to the gospel of Halbwachs. It seeks no more than to identify the dangers as we come to them, and make due allowance.

'Due' allowance. The notion of something's being 'due' is as much an

---

[4] Guerry's *Statistique morale*: Jack D. Douglas, *The Social Meanings of Suicide* (Princeton, 1963), 7–12. Critique, and qualified rehabilitation, of government statistics: Halbwachs, *Causes*, 14–43. Survival of agnosticism: Douglas, 163–231; and of qualified belief: B. Barraclough and J. Hughes, *Suicide. Clinical and Epidemiological Studies* (London, 1987), 94–6.

[5] J. B. Post, 'Criminals and the Law in the Reign of Richard II'. D.Phil. thesis (Oxford, 1976), 319.

enemy to excess as it is to deficiency. In respect of an excess of statistical caution I will start by identifying one big danger. It is theoretical. Some readers may be alarmed in what follows by the smallness of my samples. They may be surprised I have thought it worthwhile to publish them and that they are of no value. It would be no answer to say 'these are all we have.' However true in themselves, if data are insignificant they cannot contribute to knowledge. So let us pause for an instant to digest a fact essentially simple. The cognitive value of a sample does not derive ultimately from its size, but rather from the twin probabilities that the sample is typical, and that, if not, errors will be small. Size can achieve this. But much more important is random selection. If a sample of seven, for instance, is chosen from a million inhabitants, each of which million has the same chance of being selected, then it is more probable than not that the sample will be representative. For instance, if a seventh of a given population cannot read, then it is probable that one (no more or less) of our seven will not be able to read. Of course it is also probable (though not *as* probable) that we may miss the solitary illiterate among the seven, and could make the error of thinking there were none in the population. Size could lower that risk. But size could also run the risk of making it worse. If random selectivity were lost, for instance, by the use of a written questionnaire, that would show everyone was literate, which would be a radical mistake. This is why, condemned to small samples, I shall constantly be breaking them up into even smaller ones according to their means of selection. However small—and hence however dangerous—not even the smallest sample can be denied significance. If two-thirds of a school are boys, for instance, and one-third girls, the chances are that if I pick even *one*, at random, he will be a boy.[6]

That done, let me now say how the estimates that follow were arrived at. Their basis is the Register printed at the end of this volume. The aim of the Register was to list every medieval suicide I could find recorded, in any source, printed or unprinted. From what I have called 'Religious Sources', with their bias against completed suicides, the list also includes 37 'suicidal incidents' (23 such being full-scale attempts). But these will affect the arithmetic only on a narrow front, mainly in respect of motive. Completeness was only an aim, assuredly a distant one. Since it is in the nature of such a cumulative operation never to be finished, I had to close the gates at some

[6] M. Stone, 'Statistical Reasoning', in A. and J. Kuper, *The Social Science Encyclopedia* (London, 1985), 822–5. Although this article cannot be held responsible for any of the above formulation, it elaborates the basic principles with appropriate precision. Medieval examples of the fallacy 'large sample: good sample' are exposed by Dr Edward Powell in his critical article 'Social Research and the Use of Medieval Criminal Records', *Michigan Law Review*, 79 (1981), 967–78.

point to create a stable sample. It was closed when the total was 560. The following quasi-statistical exercises are based on this sample. Items which kept coming after that have been distinguished by different type and prefixed with an asterisk (*). They are there, but were not counted in the calculations. Experts with computers will say this apartheid was unnecessary. But 560 items seemed too few to justify the use of computer, which might have saved me, among other things, what I hope have been merely ephemeral errors. But one effect of a face-to-face, non-computerized treatment of figures of this kind has been the preservation of nuance. That effect can be tested by any reader who has the patience, by inspection of the nine columns of symbols by which cases have been classified—by type, wealth, status, motive, and so on, according to the features volunteered by this or that type of record. Some columns were easy to fill, like those denoting the gender of the suicide and, slightly less easy, the very fact of it. Others presented different degrees of obstruction, since either there was no information or it was hard to classify. Rough justice is unavoidable. One example: a male suicide has been counted 'probably young', with the symbol 'Y?', because his body was first discovered by his mother; and with a further and more hazardous liberty has been counted as 'young', without the question-mark, in the totals. The Register abounds in cases where judgement has had to be thus used, with little more guidance than a sense of fair play. So while the knowledge here remains little and dangerous it is not, I believe, for all that, so insignificant as to deserve throwing away.

Chronology

The chronological spread of recorded cases was already considered in Chapter 6. Figures 1–5 there showed how the 560 cases lie unevenly across the medieval centuries, displaying graphically what centuries are in question in the categories of source. The main asymmetries in this graph were related to the different national histories of appropriate legal institutions. It is worth saying a word more here about how the elements were arrived at. Of 354 suicides in English judicial records, 89, nearly all in coroners' or Westminster rolls, can be dated with confidence to a year. Most others are in the records of Eyres which, in theory, reviewed cases every seven years though the period was usually longer. These have been brutally assigned to the quinquennium before the eyre, so that here the shape of individual quinquennia is less reliable than that of groups of two or more. Cases not datable even so approximately have been omitted. French, German, and Flemish cases have been similarly treated, the main challenge here being the criminal registers of French abbeys, which can include undated suicides, among entries several decades apart. Again I have included only those to which a quinquennium can be approximately assigned. Of literary sources the 'Religious' predictably present the main obstacle. But where a *miraculum* purports, with any show of verisimilitude, to reflect a historical incident, a corroborative detail—like the mention of a king and/or bishop in office at the time—will place it on the scale. The pattern of these graphs, let it be emphasized, is unlikely to represent more than the presence or absence of sources. It does not by itself say anything directly about the frequency of suicide.

Suicide Rates

This last matter, the frequency of suicide, is central to any enquiry such as ours. Was suicide in the Middle Ages frequent or infrequent in comparison with the rates of later centuries? In what regions and periods were rates highest? Under what stimuli did they rise or fall? Unfortunately these questions cannot be answered with anything more than the merest suggestion. For precision there would be two desiderata, and both are lacking. We would have to know the total of suicides in a given place and period; as it is, hardly any of the records underlying the Register even purports to mention *all* the suicides in its remit. Second, if a trustworthy total of suicides were, by good fortune, available, a population estimate for the same time and area would have to be equally reliable to produce a 'rate'. And even that would still apply only to one time and area.

But medievalists have the least excuse of anyone for despair. Courage is our métier. So, while no promise can be given to answer the main question, three ways can be suggested for approaching it.

THE ABSOLUTE RATE

The main modern way of measuring suicide rates is as a figure per million living. In the context of smaller populations the conventional yardstick is a tenth of that, a hundred thousand, and this will be used here. Just now I said hardly any source purports to mention all suicides in its remit. A few exceptions are found among English rolls, and one deserves special attention. It is an Eyre roll from Essex. As Figures 1–5 made clear, the decade 1280–90, which records suicides from as far back as *c*.1270, marks an apex in the number of recorded suicides. Half of these, as it happens, are accounted for by two Eyres alone, those of Devon in 1281–2 and Essex in

1285. Between them these record 22 and 16 suicides respectively. Now Essex, to a markedly greater extent than Devon, is also well furnished with other types of record. Its population can be roughly estimated. More specifically, estimates are made by calculating backwards from a population figure for 1377, in turn based on returns for the Poll Tax decreed in that year. That is the Poll Tax whose thoroughness occasioned the Peasants' Revolt. (I say it is based on the tax return, because not everyone was even meant to be in it. The considerable skills of historical demographers are employed to produce reasoned estimates for shortfalls, from size of household, extent of privileged exclusion, and so on.) After these adjustments, those best-equipped to offer an opinion on the subject have suggested a population for the county in 1377 as in the very approximate bracket of 64,000 to 70,000. That is for 1377. The calculation then has to go backwards. Data from a few Essex villages, apparently both reliable and typical, suggests the Essex population had fallen in the previous century from about double its 1377 figure (actually from 203 per cent but I am rounding all figures). On that assumption the county population in *c*.1277 would have been in the order of 130,000 to 140,000. All these are assumptions, based on other assumptions. But none of the assumptions is plucked from the air. All relate to some compelling portion of the evidence.[7]

We now turn back to those 16 suicides in the 1285 Essex Eyre roll. Since the previous Eyre was in 1272 the 16 should in principle represent thirteen years. Sixteen divided by thirteen makes 1.23, an annual 'rate' for the whole population. If the Essex population was 140,000 that makes an annual rate per 100,000 of just under one, that is, 0.88 (1.23 divided by 1.4 = 0.88). Before following these siren figures any further it will be useful to see what comparative magnitudes emerge from modern societies, where rates are less conjectural. Table 1 shows a selection, all rounded and approximate, and selected here to include figures both typical and extreme.[8]

By comparison with modern analogues, that '0.88' for Essex in the 1270s and 1280s is therefore lower than the low. What can be done with it to make it more respectable? We have to answer several questions, of which the most important concerns coverage. The 1285 Eyre roll should in principle

[7] L. R. Poos, 'The rural population of Essex in the later middle ages', *Econ. Hist. Rev.*, 2nd ser., 38 (1985), 515–30; and the same author's *A Rural Society after the Black Death: Essex, 1350–1525* (Cambridge, 1991), 32–5, 106–10. I thank Dr Poos for showing me how to approach these calculations and accept his warning that the result must still allow for a large margin of error.

[8] References for the figures from medieval Essex and Devon can be found through the Register and bibliography, and for France and its regions in 1872–6 in Halbwachs, *Causes*, 78–9. Cf. Durkheim, *Suicide*, 303, 350, 394; and D. and M. Frémy, eds., *Quid, 1991* (Paris, 1990), 170.

TABLE 1. Suicide rates.

	DATE	PER 100,000
England and Wales	1872–6	15–20
England and Wales	1980	11
France	1872–6	15
[Paris (highest region)		26]
[Languedoc (lowest region)		8]
France	1980	19
United States	1981–4	10
Switzerland	1985	25
Ireland	1981–4	3
Mexico	1981–4	2

cover both the whole thirteen years since the previous Eyre, and the whole inhabited surface of Essex. But that assumes total efficiency in the Eyre. While we know that assumption to be wrong, we do not know how wrong. A very rough estimate of the efficiency of a well-recorded Eyre would not be intrinsically impossible. But it would require a study which has not, to my knowledge, yet been done. So I must limit myself here to saying how it might be done and in what direction the results would be likely to lie if it were.

The task is eased by a study of the same subject in the mid-Tudor period, covering eight south-eastern counties, brought out in 1987 by Dr Simon Stevenson.[9] Although the shape of legal records changed between the thirteenth century and Tudor times, and the material became much more ample, the essential method of investigation is appropriate to both. Dr Stevenson begins by distinguishing the stages—in his case, nine—in the process by which an account of a death found its way from 'first finder' to the King's Bench record. For our present question the most important stage is the third (after the community has found the body and summoned the coroner) namely the coroner's inquest. It was the only source for either King's Bench or Eyre. Did coroners, Dr Stevenson asks, investigate every death in their allotted district? (The fact that from 1487, coroners were offered a fee of 13s 4d per homicide inquest, and that JPs were told to punish slackness, suggests coroners before then had commonly been slack.) Dr Stevenson tested his larger quantities of cases and found signs of two regular variations, respectively of time and place. Of time, first: coroners were expected

---

[9] 'The rise of suicide verdicts in south-east England, 1530–1590: the legal process', *Continuity and Change*, 2 (Cambridge, 1987), 37–76; and 'Social and economic contributions to the pattern of "suicide" in south-east England, 1530–1590', ibid., 225–62.

to report on 'return days', and these were concentrated in February, April, July, and October. The chronological distribution of cases suggests that coroners may have raised their efficiency in those months, because they knew they had to submit returns then, and picked up a fee for each case. In respect of space, secondly, a map of all mid-Tudor homicides subject to coroners' inquests in the region shows a tendency to cluster round main roads. This tendency was especially strong in the eight 'slack' months (that is, months without 'return days' and in which, therefore, coroners were not expecting sticks or carrots to make them perform). This suggested that coroners tended not to pursue enquiries too far off main roads unless goaded or enticed.

Dr Stevenson's study tested many other variables, including the speed at which coroners cleared up after a death, and the relation of this to other factors in the efficiency of a coroner. The Tudor material is more plenteous than ours. Its analysis allowed Dr Stevenson to suggest numerical factors with which to qualify *prima facie* numbers in the records. The thirteenth-century material is much leaner, and different in form. But Edward I's coroners should not, in the end, escape similar appraisal. For instance, a map of the recorded suicides from the Essex Eyres of 1272 and 1285 (opposite) suggests that they, too, derived from inquests grouped near main roads.

Until such a study is done, for Essex or some county with comparable records, even the present tentative estimates are impossible. That figure of 0.88 per annum, per 100,000 Essex inhabitants, is based on a record which purports to be complete, in a period and region exceptionally well-furnished with recorded suicides. But we can be sure it was not complete, so the suicide figure is certainly too low. By what factor should it be raised? Doubled, it would still be lower than all figures from other comparable societies. Trebled? It is easy to be hypnotized by a number, especially one with a decimal point. Readers need no help in calculating other possibilities offered by this one. One possibility, but no more, admitted by the record, is that Essex in the 1280s may, whatever its suicide rate, have had an exceptionally high one for medieval England, or indeed anywhere else.

SUICIDES IN PROPORTION TO HOMICIDES

The judicial sources are more helpful on a second question, subsidiary to the first but a possible guide to its answer. In what ratios did suicide stand to other forms of investigated death, and in particular to homicide? For some investigators this ratio has an intrinsic interest. In modern times, when statistics are available, ratios between suicide and homicide vary in complex counterpoint. Thus it was once thought that murder and suicide were

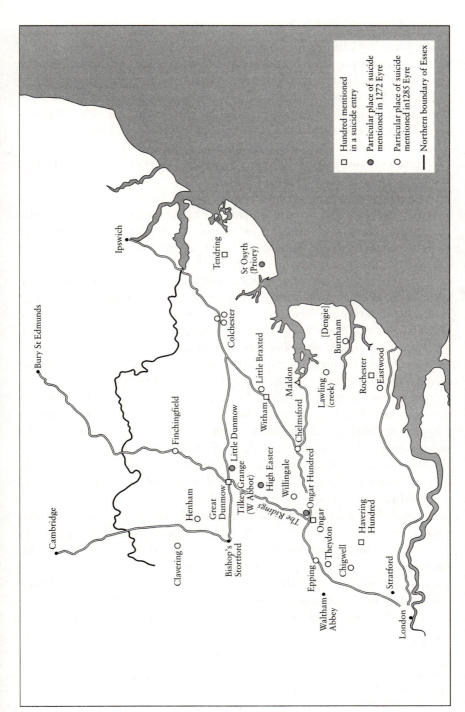

Suicides recorded in the Essex Eyres of 1272 and 1285 (JUST 2/238 and 244) to show their proximity to roads

inversely proportional, as if people who let off their steam by killing other people were less inclined to turn on themselves. That has now been demonstrated as true only in some countries and conditions. The opposite can be true in others, where murders and suicides mysteriously rise and fall together, while in yet a third group no relationship can be established. So in this regard no single modern figure can be used as normal. Thus between 1875 and 1913 the suicide:homicide ratio in Italy switched from three and a half homicides to one suicide, to almost the opposite imbalance, namely two suicides to one homicide. (Supposing always that official figures are near the truth.) In post-unification Italy, then, it is as if the establishment of a unified state made people turn from murder to suicide, as their favourite form of violence. Two late nineteenth-century extremes are even further apart, Corsica in 1891 being marginally more murderous, contemporary Paris being radically more suicidal (with a ratio of 20:1 in favour of suicide).[10]

What do medieval records say about the homicide:suicide ratio? Let me start with France. It should be observed as a preliminary, from one researcher's subjective experience, that suicide seems rare in available criminal records. French suicides in the Register at the end of this book represent gleanings from many volumes, of genres which not only should mention it, but do mention it, and just often enough to show they might have mentioned it more often. An idea of the proportion is given by the subject indexes of nearly a hundred volumes of the 'JJ' series of registers in the National Archive, the series which provided the cases rehearsed in Chapter 10. Within these volumes 'homicide' accounts for more than 600 index entries. That does not include cases which ended in verdicts of death through 'accident' or 'self-defence', or infanticide. Self-homicides number three. If that represented the real incidence of the two kinds of death in late medieval France it would yield a homicide:suicide ratio of 200:1.[11] I have not found this exceptional. The would-be gleaner, rarely helped in this respect by indexes, is often struck by the complete absence of suicide. As we saw from the Paris Châtelet, the register mentions crimes, executions, imprisonments, and other punishments, all garnished with incidental information, but only has one whisper of even a potential suicide. The whisper is enough to show the subject could, in principle, have been mentioned more often if it had been there to mention.[12] Now the Parlement registers in the

[10]   Durkheim, *Suicide*, 349. Halbwachs, *Causes*, ch. 10. K. Levi, 'Homicide and suicide: structure and process', *Deviant Behaviour*, 4 (Washington, 1982), 91–115. Ratios in Italy and the *département* of Seine: Halbwachs, *Causes*, 192, 201.

[11]   The index is that prepared by the Archives Nationales for the *Régistres du Trésor des Chartes*, Part III. For other registers see the Bibliography.

[12]   Above, p. 185.

JJ series, if not the Châtelet register, were drawn from higher levels of justice. So their proportions, like that 200:1, were certainly unrepresentative. Most suicides would not have reached that level. This reasoning is confirmed by the very few registers to survive from the other extreme of the criminal judicial hierarchy, the bottom, more specifically those of the abbeys with High Justice. Here are the figures:

TABLE 2. Ratio of suicides to homicides: criminal registers of French abbeys (*c.*1250–*c.*1400)

A ABBEY	B LENGTH OF PERIOD COVERED (YEARS)	C HOMICIDES	D SELF-HOMICIDES	E RATIO D:C
St Germain	122	16	1	1:16
St Maur	13	22	3	1:7
Ste Geneviève	79	*c.*39	4	1:10
St Martin	36	*c.*80*	4	1:20*
All		*c.*157	12	1:13

* Estimated

This time the ratio of suicides to homicides goes the other way. The average ratio is 1:13. But let us again be cautious. It will be recalled that these registers were drawn up by abbeys to stave off challenges to their jurisdiction. Their cause lay in recording punishments, all the more fastidiously the more public they were, because punishments proved jurisdiction. Thus while fugitive murderers, common in contemporary English rolls, would be under-recorded in the abbey registers, no suicide would ever be left out. This fact accounts for the gulf between the ratio given in the last paragraph and those to be derived from the French abbeys.

It has been worth looking at the apparent diversity of those French records, underestimating at the top, overestimating at the bottom, before looking at the English ones. These are both more forthcoming and more unanimous. Tables 3–5 show the results of three independent series of calculations, all of which point to a suicide:homicide ratio within a fixed range. The first calculation is based on printed proceedings from a selection of thirteenth-century Eyre and coroners' rolls. The 'homicide' figure shows, as far as could be ascertained, the number of persons killed by homicide rather than the number of criminal acts, while the figure for suicide is a simple count-up of verdicts *felo de se*. (Small distortions arising from that procedure can be assessed from the circumstances set out in Chapter 6.)

TABLE 3. Ratio of suicide to homicide: selected (published) Eyre and coroners' rolls.

A ROLL	B TOTAL DEATHS	C HOMICIDES	D SUICIDES	E RATIO D : C
Beds 1227	93	53	1	1:53
Berks 1248	96	54	1	1:54
Kent 1241	13	3	1	1:3
Kent 1255	12	4	1	1:4
Salop 1256	229	183	3	1:61
Surrey 1235	88	21	1	1:21
Wilts 1249	111	53	4	1:13
Yorks 1218–19	346	182	3	1:61
Total Eyres	988	553	15	1:37
Beds Cor 1273	223	102	3	1:34
Oxford Cor	110	56	1	1:56
Total Coroners	333	158	4	1:39

Many coroners' rolls survive from the fourteenth and early fifteenth centuries at a time when the Eyre had all but vanished, so a separate calculation was made with a sample of these. Two counties were chosen with relatively full sets of surviving coroners' rolls, namely Shropshire and Wiltshire. The ten rolls for Shropshire cover various years between 1356 and 1415; the twelve for Wiltshire, years between 1340 and 1384. The counting procedure was made easier by the inclusion, in the 'homicide' figure, of manslaughters adjudged non-culpable; so that figure is slightly swollen. But the results are those shown in Table 4 opposite.

As control to these two sets of findings I include, thirdly, as Table 5, the results of analyses made respectively by Dr Henry Summerson and Professor Hanawalt Westman. Dr Summerson's analysis (unpublished but shown to me in the preparation of this chapter) was of twenty-three unpublished thirteenth-century eyre rolls. That by Professor Hanawalt Westman was of King's Bench rolls, supported by some coroners' rolls, relating to Northamptonshire from 1300 to 1420. It was published in her article 'Violent death in fourteenth- and early fifteenth-century England'.[13] Their results are summarized in the Table on p. 362.

If these figures were to be read at face value, Wiltshire would score, both in the 1249 eyre and the fourteenth-century coroners' rolls, as a county with

[13] *Comparative Studies in Society and History*, 18 (1976), 297–320 on p. 300.

TABLE 4. Ratios of suicide to homicide: the twenty-two surviving coroners' rolls (unprinted) from Shropshire and Wiltshire.*

A ROLLS FOR	B TOTAL DEATHS	C HOMICIDES	D SUICIDES	E RATIO D:C
Salop	463	320	10	1:32
Wilts	574	215	13	1:17
Both counties	1037	535	23	1:23

* The rolls and single totals are as follows (all rolls are in the series JUST/2):

A ROLL JUST/2	B TOTAL DEATHS	C KILLINGS*	D FELONES DE SE	E RATIO D:C 1:	F RATIO D:B 1:
Salop					
142	127	95	4	24	32
143	22	7	0	—	—
144	43	38	0	—	—
145	64	40	2	20	32
146	60	38	1	38	60
147	40	26	1	26	40
148	45	38	1	38	45
149	6	4	0	—	—
150	18	12	0	—	—
151	36	22	(1)	(22)	(36)
All Salop	463	320	9(+1)	32	46
Wilts					
193	32	13	1	13	32
194	141	38	5	8	28
195	175	68	3	23	58
196	4	1	0	—	—
197	11	6	0	—	—
[198 not applicable]					
199	51	35	0	—	—
200	67	25(†)	0	—	—
201	7	2	0	—	—
202	19	5	2	2	9
203	56	20	2	10	28
204	8	2	0	—	—
205	3	0	0	—	—
All Wilts	574	215	13	16.54	44

† This figure includes non-culpable homicide, mostly in 'self-defence', a small category sufficiently doubtful for the historian to mistrust the boundary it represents. (Presumably there would have been a culpable homicide if the act of alleged self-defence had been omitted.)

TABLE 5. Ratios of suicide to homicide: analyses by H. Summerson and B. Hanawalt Westman

A ROLLS FOR	B TOTAL DEATHS	C HOMICIDES	D SUICIDES	E RATIO D : C
23 Eyres 1227–85 King's Bench etc.	4599	2895	107	:127
N'hants 1300–1420	1291*	575	16	:136

* Homicide and misadventure only.

an uncommonly high rate of suicide per homicide. Otherwise the suicide : homicide ratio in these independent calculations is remarkably constant. The six relevant averages (excluding the Wiltshire coroners) lie between 27 and 39. These figures admit of adjustment, reflecting methods of definition, collection, record, and so on. But their relative stability yields a range considerably higher than the main modern bracket mentioned above, and suggests either that English society was then much more violent, or much less suicidal, than our nineteenth-century models; or both. That conclusion is likely on other grounds.

SUBJECTIVE IMPRESSIONS

Was suicide common or uncommon, then, in the Middle Ages? Surviving legal data have been interrogated, for long enough at least to reveal how little they will tell. Even a longer interrogation would not support estimates of comparable precision to that approached for later centuries. Here again, legal records promise precision but fall short. Another kind of evidence promises no precision at all, but again, partly because it affects nothing, it is more helpful. It consists in the subjective impressions of contemporaries. Few such impressions survive, but those that do, far from being deliberate, conscious assessments, were mostly *obiter dicta*, asides allowed to drop casually in the course of some other discussion. Their very innocence of calculation makes them better witnesses.

Most of the *obiter dicta* occurred in the course of some law, or comment, or moral discussion. It will be useful, in the context of the evidence reviewed so far, to assemble the most significant and see if they can at any point be correlated with the legal data, and if not, what this may say about the latter's coverage. This implicit reservation applies especially to the Merovingian and Carolingian periods, when the asides begin. They begin, indeed, in the laws which would become the stock-in-trade for canonists of later centuries, the sixth-century Spanish councils. Thus, the earliest and longest-lasting western canon on suicide, from the council of Braga in 561, refers critically, to the 'many [*multi*]' priests who have been giving full burial rites to suicides.[14] The sixteenth council of Toledo in 693 tackled a different aspect of the question, suicides of prisoners under accusation. But its preamble leaves no doubt that it was the size of the problem that had occasioned the law.[15] The impression given by the Anglo-Saxon and Frankish Penitential Books, in the eighth and ninth centuries, is less explicit. Some do not have suicide clauses at all and some just copy those of their predecessors. But there is enough variety, and verisimilitude, in the half-dozen clauses which do mention suicide, prescribing what funeral rites should or should not be accorded to them, to show that the reality was far from unknown.[16]

This modest conclusion is supported in the ninth century by some more explicit remarks. Hrabanus Maurus, abbot of Fulda from 822 to 847, but with an attachment to the monastery going back to his schooldays there in the 790s, mentioned suicide three times in his writings. Although two of these passages come in the context of biblical commentary, their grammar makes clear, even there, that Hrabanus is aware of actual suicides. On the third of the three occasions, in a homily on the sin of excessive *tristitia*, Hrabanus actually reminisces:

I know of very many [*plures*] who have fallen thus from the right way, both in my own time and in the memory of my predecessors.[17]

That Hrabanus had to declare this, and also to call on his predecessors' memory, may tend to modify that *plures*: he had to insist, as if a reader might not believe him. Meanwhile Hrabanus' near-contemporary Christian

[14] I Braga, ch. 16 (ed. J. Vives, *Concilios visigóticos* (Barcelona, 1963), 74).

[15] XVI Toledo, chap. 4 (ed. Vives, 501).

[16] e.g. *Judicia Theodori*, bk 2, ch. 10; A. W. Hadden and W. Stubbs, eds., Councils and Ecclesiastical Documents Relating to Great Britain and Ireland, 3 vols. (Oxford, 1869–78; reprinted 1965) vol. 3, 197–8. The complex history of this text, and further examples illustrative of the same contention, are accessible through C. Vogel, *Les "Libri Paenitentiales"* (Turnhout, 1978), 68, with an update under the same title by A. J. Frantzen (Turnhout, 1985), 26–7.

[17] *De videndo Deum*, bk 3, ch. 4 (*Pat. lat.* 112.1308A). Cf. Hrabanus' *Comm. in librum regum*, bk 4, ch. 31 (*Pat. lat.* 108.70C); and *Comm. in libr. Macc.*, bk 2, ch. 14 (*Pat. lat.* 109.1254). See also his *De ecclesiastica disciplina*, bk 3, De tristitia (*Pat. lat.* 112.1250CD, 1251A and C).

of Stablo (a monastery between Cologne and Antwerp) gives a similar impression of some, but not much, contemporary suicide. In commenting on St Matthew's account of Judas' suicide, he adds:

It is painful to say this, but even today persons Christian in name do this. This bad practice is the responsibility of bishops, who fail to tell their people that those people who kill themselves do not put an end to their sorrows and unhappiness, but make them worse, since they pass from present troubles to more severe ones.[18]

At a date probably just after 900, not far away at Prüm, the canonist abbot Regino would take up this theme in the tradition of the Penitential Books, by urging his bishop to find out if there were suicides in the diocese, so that episcopal displeasure could be made known, as if the bishop would otherwise be unaware.[19]

These *obiter dicta* from early medieval authorities form a useful prelude to ones from centuries when judicial records exist to compare them with. It will be recalled that Constantine the African, the Arab immigrant who wrote in Monte Cassino in the later eleventh century, thought that the sickness of melancholy 'abounds greatly in these parts'. Although he did not spell out suicide as one manifestation of melancholy, reason has been seen for thinking he had it in mind.[20] In Chapter 13 we heard the narrator of the suicide of a thief who hanged himself, in 1113, describe it as a 'miracle' unheard-of since Judas' time.[21] Yet suicide as such was no unheard-of miracle to St Bernard of Clairvaux, preaching to his monks not longer after then. Pooh-poohing the claim that heretics were martyrs because they seemed ready to die for their belief, Bernard said that a suicidal impulse, like that which the heretics betrayed, was nothing very exceptional. 'We have known many fall into the Devil's power in this regard, drowning or hanging themselves.' Judas' suicide, as distinct from his treachery, was hardly remarkable.[22] From the side of medicine, Constantine the African's successors noticed the same. Around 1160, St Hildegard of Bingen's medical textbook *Causes and Cures* discussed the sickness of melancholy and remarked that 'a diabolic suggestion often coils itself up inside this kind of melan-

---

[18] *Comm. in evang. Matth.*, ch. 43; *Pat. lat.* 106.1416BC: 'Et ecce unus accedens, ait illi . . .'

[19] *De ecclesiastica disciplina*, bk 2, ch. 5, sect. 11; *Pat. lat.* 132.282C.

[20] See p. 281.

[21] See pp. 300–1 above.

[22] *Sermones super cantica*, no. 66, § 13; ed. J. Leclercq, C. H. Talbot, and H. Rochais, *S. Bernardi opera*, vol. 2 (Rome, 1985), 187.8–13: 'Nonne plus est sibimet hominem inicere manus, quam id libenter ab alio sustinere? Hoc autem in multis potuisse diabolum frequenter experti sumus, qui seipsos aut submerserunt, aut suspenderunt. Denique Judas suspendit seipsum, diabolo sine dubio immittente. Ego tamen magis existimo magisque admiror quod potuit immississe in cor eius ut traderet Dominum, quam ut semetipsum suspenderet.'

choly and makes a person depressed and despairing, so that many victims of this kind of desperation suffocate or dash themselves to death.'[23]

Whether or not because all literary references to everyday life multiply in the thirteenth century, it is then, and in the fourteenth, that credible references to actual suicide grow more conspicuous. An English canonist, writing c.1215 on the vice called *tristitia* will say that 'many' kill themselves as a result of it.[24] The same message, in almost the same words, appears in a sermon composed about then or slightly afterwards, by a northern French preacher: '*tristitia* kills many people,' he says.[25] When the Franciscans came on the scene with their compound of high standards and ethical practicality, and consequent aptitude for making confessions, the note both echoes and grows louder. It echoes in Alexander of Hales, c.1240, as he alleges, in the present indicative, 'despair leads a man to kill himself';[26] and again in a German Franciscan novice-master c.1240, when he includes among characteristics of anger that 'It can move people to harm others, or themselves, so that sometimes a man will kill himself.'[27] A Welsh Franciscan professor at Oxford, writing in the 1260s in a tense appropriate to the classical suicide which is his main subject ('Those who killed themselves'), shifts similarly, in the body of his text, briefly into the present, to denounce the 'malice' of 'some [who] flee from life and kill themselves,' in the present.[28] But the note is loudest in the great master of the Franciscan order, St Bonaventura. His commentaries refer more than once to the 'many' who 'kill themselves and hate their lives', or who 'physically kill themselves, from a wish to escape confusion or tribulation'.[29] In another place Bonaventura alludes to a kind

[23] *Causae et Curae*, ed. P. Kaiser. Bibliotheca Teubneriana (Leipzig, 1903), 144.8–11: 'Sed et suggestio diaboli multotiens in hanc melancoliam se intorquet et hominem tristem et desperantem facit, ita quod multi huiusmodi homines in desperatione se suffocant et conterunt, multi autem in hoc malo sibi ita resistunt, quod velut martyres in hac pugna sunt.'

[24] Thomas of Chobham, *Summa confessorum, quaestio* VIIIa, ch. 1; ed. F. Broomfield (Louvain, 1968), 447–9.

[25] Jacques de Vitry, quoted by A. Lecoy de la Marche, *La chaire française au moyen âge* (Paris, 1886), 491, n. 2 (from Paris, Bibl. Nat., MS lat. 17509, fol. 70).

[26] Alexander of Hales, *Summa theologica*, inquisitio 3, tractatus 5, sectio 2, quaestio 4, § 695, *solutio* (edition of Quaracchi, vol. 3 (1930), 682b); '(desperatio) inducit hominem ut se ipsum occidat.' The question of authorship is here irrelevant.

[27] David of Augsburg, *De exterioris et interioris hominis compositione*, bk 2, ch. 39; edition of Quaracchi, 1899, p. 128; *Formula novitiorum*, bk 2, ch. 49, in M. de la Bigne, ed., *Maxima Bibliotheca Veterum Patrum*, vol. 25 (Lyons, 1677), 892G. Cf. Seneca, *De ira*, 1, 1; but David's wording and imagery are his own. (I quote the older and less critical edition because the Arno flood of 1966 rendered that of Quaracchi rare, by destroying much of the stock.)

[28] Johannis Walensis, *De regimine vitae humanae* [= *Communiloquium*], pars 7, distinctio 1, *cap.* 6 (edition of Lyons, 1511, fol. 134r): 'Quod propter maliciam aliqui fugiunt vivere; et interimunt se.' John of Wales is quoting and paraphrasing Aristotle, *Nicomachean Ethics*, bk 9, ch. 4, but with interjections that indicate his endorsement of Aristotle's observations.

[29] *In III Sent.*, distinctio 27, dubium 3 (*Opera omnia*, vol. 6 (Quaracchi, 1887), col. 618a). St Bonaventura is discussing whether a man can fail to love himself and envisages the

of despair which 'very frequently indeed' leads people to put themselves to death.[30]

In the fourteenth century we hear the same note echoed in yet wider circles. Preaching in the 1320s, on St Paul's wish [Philippians 1:23] to 'depart and be with Christ', that scourge of Franciscans, Pope John XXII, explained that this does not mean we should commit suicide on the example of Judas and—the present tense pointing now to his own day—'other examples [*et in aliis patet*]'.[31] Nor were such observations confined to France. In a fourteenth-century vernacular sermon probably from the middle Danube, another preacher on St Paul—this time on the 'sorrow of the world' of 2 Corinthians 7:10—illustrated the extreme form of this sorrow by saying, on behalf of himself and his audience, how 'we have often learned, how a person has hanged or stabbed himself.'[32]

The same awareness of contemporary suicide was meanwhile expressed by poets. That late thirteenth-century French elaboration of the miracle of the infanticide woman, saved by the Virgin, expects his reader to know, as a fact, of contemporary

> *Désespérés*. You will have found
> How some are hanged and some are drowned,
> And women likewise I declare,
> You hear it, it is not so rare
> By their own wimples take their lives
> By hanging, or with sharpened knives
> Their bodies gash and cut to slices:
> All by the Devil's false devices.[33]

objection that 'multi se ipsos interficiunt et vitam suam odiunt.' He later refers more positively to those 'multi' who 'se ipsos odiunt, quia / inordinate se diligendo faciunt sibi ipsis malum et inimicantur, sicut multi, qui volentes fugere confusionem vel tribulationem, se ipsos interficiunt *corporaliter*', ibid. (618ab).

[30] In *In II librum Sententiarum*, dist. 43, articulum 3, quaestio 2, ad 1 (*Opera omnia*, vol. 2, col. 995a) Bonaventura refers to types of despair which have the effect that 'tales desperatissimi frequentissime sibi inferunt mortem.' These passages are quoted by R. Jehl, *Melancholie und Acedia* (Paderborn and Munich, 1984), respectively on pp. 235, 252 and n. 747.

[31] Paris, Bibl. Nat. MS R 25833, fol. 17r: 'aliquando sine affectu gratie et caritatis quis mortem appetit propter timore supplicii vel ad vitandam miserabilem vitam vel propter vanam gloriam et cetera. Exemplum in Juda qui se ipsum occidit non ex caritatis affectu quia dampnatus fuit, et in aliis patet.' The attribution of the text to Hebrews 1 (fol. 16v) is a mistake by the preacher.

[32] Klosterneuburg, MS 902, fol. 37v: 'Auch hab wir das offt vernomen, das sich ainr var laid erhangen hat order erstochen, das haisset der welt traurigkeit'.

[33] Paris, Bibl. Nat., MS fr. 1546, fol. 138vb: 'En veez / De ceuz qui sont desesperez / Perit en est a bien venuz / Li uns noiez lautre pendus / Et des fames autel vous di / Assez souvent avez oui / A leur guinples se sont pendues / Estranglees et deronpues // (fol. 139ra) Et ocises de fres coutiaus / Li anemis li desloiaus / Prent ensi ques les gens au laz.' Cf. p. 267 above.

Again, in a poem set in 1349, we hear another French poet slip into the present tense while expanding on the suicide, this time, of Dido:

> As modern lovers often do
> In counterfeit of lovers true.[34]

These references are both casual and slight. No author is moved to more than half-a-dozen words on the topic. But four fifteenth-century references exceed this limit. One reflects exceptional conditions. It is in a public admonition made in 1405 by Jean Gerson, chancellor of the University of Paris, about the intolerable effects on French society of the royal dukes' civil war. Gerson says they have made 'many people in our time despair and take their lives . . . one by hanging himself, another by drowning, another by stabbing a knife into his breast.'[35] The poets Alain Chartier and François Villon imply the same at about the same time.[36] The French judicial dossier gave us, in Jean Lunneton, a stark portrait of one sufferer from these conditions,[37] and there were clearly many more behind him.

The fact that the other three such references are all from Germany, whose judicial registers confirm the impression from another side, suggests that this relative volubility may reflect a marginally stronger incidence. One is a Carthusian monk in Erfurt, preaching in the 1440s or 1450s on the text 'In those days men shall seek death and shall not find it; and shall desire to die, and death shall flee from them' (Rev. 9:6); and he comments that this desire for death is in itself 'not incredible, since many people kill themselves and throw themselves into water as we often, alas, see done today through *tristitia*.'[38] At around the same time, in a monastery between Cologne and Aachen, another monk was commenting on Boethius' *Consolation of Philosophy* and wrote of 'those who kill themselves to avoid the misfortunes,

---

[34] Guillaume de Machaut, *Le jugement dou roy de Navarre*, ed. E. Hoepffner (Paris, 1908), lines 2109–10: 'Einsi com pluseurs amans font / Qui l'amant loial contrefont.'

[35] *Oeuvres complètes*, ed. P. Glarieux, vol. 7, pt 2 (Paris, 1963), 1171. Cf. Signori, 19–20.

[36] Alain Chartier, *Le livre de l'Espérance*, esp. Prose IV, lines 12–85; ed. F. Rouy (Paris, 1989), pp. 17–20; F. Villon, *Testament*, strophes 44 and 47; ed. V. Dufounnet (Paris, 1992), pp. 120 and 124.

[37] Above, pp. 225–7.

[38] Jacobus de Clusa, *Sermo in dominicam secundam adventus*; in *Sermones* (Speyer, 1472), fol. 6r, col. 1, lines 21–7: 'Apoc. ix: illis diebus quaerent homines mortem et non invenient et desiderabunt mortem et mors fugiet ab eis. Et non est incredibile quia multi seipsos occident aut in aquas precipitabunt sicut hodie heu sepe prae tristicia fieri videmus.' The author: L. Maier, *Die Werke des Kartäusers Jakob von Jüterbog in ihren handschriftlicher Überlieferung*. Beiträge zur Geschichte der Philosophie und Theologie des Mittelalters, ed. A. M. Landgraf, Bd. 37, Heft 5 (Münster-in-Westfalen, 1955), 1–2, 8; and D. Mertens in W. Stammler, ed., *Verfasserlexikon*, vol. 4 (Berlin-New York, 1983), 478–87. The sermon was written at Erfurt no earlier than 1443 and no later than 1455, the death of Pope Nicholas V (1447–55) who authorized the collection. Besides Clusa and Juterbog, Jacobus was also to be known under the surname von Paradies.

weariness and torments of the present life'.[39] In another place the same writer refers to those 'who look for death in the wrong way, as in desperation or a reprehensible weariness with life'[40] and in yet another, again using the present tensive, to the destructive kind of *tristitia* which 'damages the heart and (as has been plain to see) kills many people [*imo (ut patuit) multos occidit*]'.[41] Meanwhile a German Dominican friar, writing *c.*1420 or 1430 on 'despair', in a work destined to be very widely read, makes the point with equal emphasis: how 'such people in the depths of despair frequently kill themselves [*unde tales desperatissimi frequenter sibi inferunt mortem*].'[42]

Whatever differences in nuance lie in these *obiter dicta* their force is surpassed by that of a single cohesive cluster of references from one place and time: late thirteenth- and early fourteenth-century Florence. Fourteenth-century commentators on Dante, and in particular on the anonymous Florentine suicide in the tenth canto of the *Inferno,* were heard *in extenso* in Chapter 4. A glance back at the texts will remove all doubt on this particular. All agreed that 'in those days' many Florentines killed themselves. The impression was independently confirmed by a Pistoian jurist and a Sienese poet.[43] Those witnesses' unanimity suggests that, whatever suicide rates obtained elsewhere, the rate in Florence at that period was higher. There is a further consequence. The fact that Florentine society is commonly considered, in other respects, to have been precociously modern, with its thrusting commerce, vernacular education, and so on, means that in the present respect too it may have been a precocious exception to a medieval rule. That is, that the rate in Florence was thought high because it was not noticeably high elsewhere.

DID SUICIDE RATES INCREASE IN THE SIXTEENTH CENTURY?

Of questions raised by our meagre evidence on suicide rates the most pregnant relates to the end of the Middle Ages. In the early sixteenth century,

---

[39] Denys of Rijkel [Dionysius Cartusianus], *In Boethium. De consolatione philosophiae,* bk 1, *metrum* 1, *art.* 3; in Dionysius' *Opera omnia,* 42 vols. (Montreuil-sur-Mer/Tournai, 1896–1935), vol. 26, p. 27, col. 1C: 'Hic aeternam damnationem merentur qui ut evadant adversa, taedia et tormenta vitae praesentis, occidunt se ipsos. De hoc infra plenius dicam.'

[40] Ibid., bk 4 *metrum* I, *art.* 2 (p. 496, col. 2A): 'Quam (=mortem) aliqui appetunt vitiose, ut ex desperatione, seu pravo taedio vitae.'

[41] Ibid., bk 1, *prosa* 4, *art.* 17 (p. 92, col. 28). Another passage which fulfils Denys' promise (n. 37 above) to 'speak more fully below' of suicide, is his commentary on bk 1, *prosa* 3, *art.* 4 (p. 79, col. 2B–D).

[42] Johannes Nider, *Praeceptorium,* bk 1, ch. 3, para. 7 (edn of Douai, 1612, p. 22); cf. bk 5, ch. 15, para. 7 (pp. 346–7). On the author (1380/90–1438), C. E. Schieler, *Magister Johannes Nider, aus dem orden der Predigenbrüder* (Mainz, 1885). Career: 1–163.

[43] See pp. 85–92.

in more than one country and more than one type of record, suicide rates appear to rise sharply. The question has naturally been raised whether this change in profile reflects a real increase in suicide. The question is far from unimportant for, if the suicide rate did take a leap at the time of the Reformation, it might be argued that the two changes may have been connected, and on more than one level. The dissolution of the old Catholic religious certainties, the hypothesis would run, with their assumption of Christian unity and emphasis on the supernatural, may have caused a corresponding dissolution of the individual psyche. Thus, on this hypothesis, an 'anomy' or 'lawlessness' in the outer dimension engendered an analogous 'anomy' in the inner, a condition potentially suicidal. The theory can be put equally well in the less overtly religious form appropriate to those who see the Reformation as an expression only of social and economic changes. The same changes, they may argue, dissolved a localized, cohesive, face-to-face society characteristically 'medieval', and bore a corresponding harvest of private bewilderment.[44]

Like most questions with a religious dimension, this one evokes enduring historical debate. Its main element invites analysis. The argument is best begun in England, the relative continuity of whose legal records yields both the most tangible data on the subject and the main ground of dispute. It is a fact that in coroners' rolls and sources derived from them, verdicts of *felo de se* increase sharply after 1500 as a proportion of all verdicts. Dr Roy Hunnisett was the first to alert scholarship to this increase. In editing sixteenth-century coroners' rolls from Nottinghamshire, dated between 1485 and 1558, he found an astonishingly high ratio of suicides to homicides, and to other verdicts: a proportion of over 10 per cent of suicide among all kinds of homicide was not unusual.[45] Dr Stevenson's study of mid-Tudor suicide in the eight south-eastern counties, mentioned earlier in this chapter, finds a similar progressive increase. For instance, a count of King's Bench indictments for the south-eastern counties, in a series of years beginning in 1514 and ending in 1565, reveals suicide verdicts as increasing absolutely by a

---

[44] e.g. R. G. Hoskins suggested that in the early sixteenth century the life of family and society were lived 'in a small and personal community' providing 'fundamental compensations' for discomfort, hunger, and frequent death, hence 'suicide was rarely thought of.' Quoted, with views by Durkheim and others, in Stevenson, 'The rise of suicide verdicts', 37, from Hoskins' *The Age of Plunder: King Henry's England, 1500–1547*, 9 (London, 1976), 47–51.

[45] R. F. Hunnisett, *Calendar of Nottinghamshire Coroners' Inquests, 1485–1558*, Thoroton Society, Record Series, 25 (1969), p. 233 for 75 entries representing culpable homicide, including self-defence, and p. 241, for 48 entries under 'Suicide.' Cf. Dr Hunnisett's introduction, esp. p. xviii. My 'over 10 per cent' derives from the 34 inquests of Henry VII's reign sent to King's Bench, ibid. cf. P. E. H. Hair, 'A note on the incidence of Tudor suicide', *Local Population Studies*, 5 (1970), 36–42, at 36–7.

factor of 9.3: that is, there were apparently over nine times as many suicides at the end as at the beginning. A percentage analysis of coroners' verdicts, taken at intervals between 1489 to 1565 from the same counties, shows homicide verdicts as correspondingly declining from 100 per cent of all verdicts (in the small group of surviving rolls from 1489–90) to 7 per cent in 1564–5, while suicide verdicts rose by steps in the same period from nothing to 25 per cent.[46] MacDonald and Murphy's book *Sleepless Souls*, about suicide in early modern England, gives a similar impression. It opens with a graphic representation of the bare numbers of reported suicides as registered in King's Bench and coroners' rolls between 1485 and 1659. From 1485 to 1570 the line rises, in a slightly steepening curve, from around 12 for each ten-year period to nearly a thousand.[47]

These *prima facie* witnesses to a Tudor suicide crisis would be easy to multiply. So sharp is their upward trend that the existence of any doubt may be a surprise. Even allowing for factors of bias, we may be tempted to say, there must be a residuum of objective truth in such emphatic figures. Alas, that is still to tread uncertain ground. Specialist opinion, as expressed by all three authors whose figures I have quoted, is cautious, the caution resting on technicalities whose character we sampled earlier. Those absolute figures, for instance, must be read against a background of a massive increase in all recorded crime. That, in turn, was largely due to government efforts to activate coroners, and the critical question is whether this activation affected suicide out of proportion to other crimes. That is what cannot be easily answered. Besides finding that suicide verdicts rose by a factor of 9.3 between 1514 and 1565, Dr Stevenson measured, in the same body of sources, that verdicts of accidental death had also risen by an even bigger factor, namely 15.[48] Together, that pair of figures could teach one or both of two lessons. It could either mean there really were more suicides, and more accidents, in that period; or that both suicides and accidents lurked in a twilight zone just outside the cognizance of a moderately inefficient coroner, the kind who would notice murders but nothing else, and that accidental deaths and suicides only came into it, and then came tumbling in in abundance, the moment standards of enquiry were improved by tougher government. Meanwhile the rising ratio of suicide verdicts to those of accidental death could signify that all three agents, the coroners, their masters and their juries, were hardening their hearts to suicide and doing away more and more with those euphemistic verdicts of 'misfortune' which, on this interpretation, previously hid many suicides from the record.

[46] Stevenson, 'The rise of suicide . . . the legal process', 39–40 (fig. 1).
[47] M. MacDonald and T. R. Murphy, *Sleepless Souls* (Oxford, 1990), 30, fig. 1.1.
[48] Stevenson, 'The rise of suicide . . . the legal process', 39.

There is room for much subtle judgement here. Some of the factors involved, such as the count-up of *infortunium* verdicts which might have concealed suicide, do admit numerical estimates. Both Dr Stevenson and Professor MacDonald have taken these and the other factors into account. But they have not, for all that partial success, been able to establish whether all, or only part, of the apparent suicide boom is an optical illusion. The debate will certainly continue as specialists well-acquainted with the legal processes and sources, on both sides of 1485, systematically apply these and similar considerations to their material.

Because this debate is still short of a conclusion it is permissible to draw attention to circumstances external to its scope. The first is that prima facie evidence of a suicide boom is not confined to England. Of potential significance to Reformation issues are comparable trends in the German-speaking world. The volume of surviving judicial sources is slighter, their structure different. But such continuous series as do survive can record suicides in numbers increasing in a curve reminiscent, on its smaller and rougher scale, of those in England. One set of such series, of easy access because collected and published by Jörgen Dieselhorst, is that of suicides in late medieval and early modern Nuremberg.[49] A chronological graph of recorded Nuremberg suicides is shown in Figure 5.

A glance at the graph reveals that the half-centuries between 1400 and 1600 score aggregates in the progression: 10, 10, 31, 122, that is, they mark a twelvefold rise during the sixteenth century. Their peak, as in England in general and the south-east in particular, again occurs in the 1570s. A later development of similar shape is that analysed by Markus Schär from Zürich and lands under its jurisdiction. Schär's list begins in 1530 and records only 2 suicides for the first half of the century; 5 for the second half (two of them in the 1570s); then 35 for the first half of the next century, and so on upwards.[50] The beginning of a similar trend—only the beginning since the study stops at 1532—can be seen in suicides mentioned by Rau in his study of criminal law in Frankfurt-am-Main.[51]

There can be not the slightest doubt that some of this apparent trend, in the German world as in England, is due to fuller registration. All German crime, not just suicide, was more fully recorded in the sixteenth century. If the above estimates were set in the context of the criminal records they derive from, the sharp profile of suicide would accordingly be less salient.

[49] J. Dieselhorst, 'Die Bestrafung der Selbstmörder im Territorium der Stadt Nürnberg' (Nuremberg, 1953), 186–9.
[50] Markus Schär, *Seelennöte der Untertanen* (Zürich, 1985). List of cases, pp. 367–76; cf. p. 263 (graph 5).
[51] F. Rau, *Beiträge zum Kriminalrecht der freien Reichsstadt Frankfurt-am-Main im Mittelalter bis 1532*. Diss. Potsdam, 1916, pp. 75, 91, 93; also 66–7.

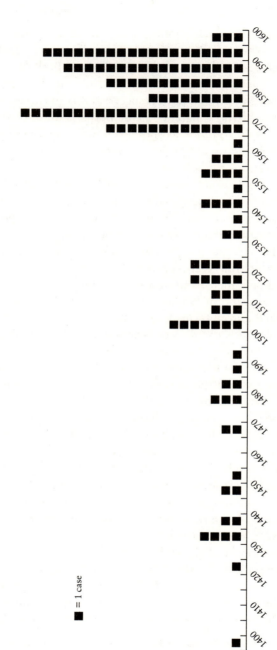

5 Chronological distribution of cases: recorded suicides in Nuremberg, 1396–1600

But that does not mean, any more than in England, that the sharp profile would vanish. Indeed in one set of German records it is easy to show it might not. Schär has himself analysed his Zürich records in respect of both suicide and homicide. As in the English south-eastern counties, but some two generations later, the Zürich suicide and homicide rates gradually change places, making suicide commoner, eventually much commoner, from about 1650.[52]

It is clear that these trends from single German regions are again best analysed by those expert in each particular set of records. Others must be content with a simple observation: that the trend documented in the ample English judicial rolls is one which poses comparable questions in jurisdictions other than that of the English monarchy. That is, broad questions, external to the scrutiny of any one corpus of judicial evidence, may be relevant to the interpretation of each. Before looking at these broader questions, and while still in the presence of strictly judicial documents, one more general consideration bears on them. It is not our business here to review in any detail the punishments inflicted on suicides' dead bodies and memories. But one feature of that review may be relevant to the assessment of suicide rates. There are indications that the indignities heaped on a suicide's body and memory grew more extreme in the early modern period. In Germany we hear for the first time, clearly, of haunting by suicides' ghosts, neutralized only by savage mutilation; in France, we hear of the hanging of suicides' bodies *upside-down*, mentioned by a seventeeth-century legist as a recent innovation; in England, again for the first time, of the extension to suicides of the practice of staking a corpse; while in Italy, no doubt in consummation of a growth in princely authority at the expense of republican, penalties for attempted suicide grew more severe. Popular and judicial attitudes to suicide, in a word, appear to have been sharpening in the very period we are talking about.[53]

This consideration introduces a new principle into the interpretation of our records: namely that the factors shaping evolution in the records may, indirectly, have been helping to determine the actual suicide rate. There are two ways this hypothesis might apply, one political, one religious. Suppose

---

[52] Homicides are also shown in Schär, 263 (graph 5).

[53] e.g. H. Baechtold-Stäobli, *Handwörterbuch des deutschen Aberglaubens*, vol. 7, col. 1632; Pierre Ayrault, *De l'ordre, formalité et instruction judiciaire*, quoted in J. Bregeault, 'Procès contre les cadavres dans l'ancien droit', *Nouvelle revue historique de droit français et étranger*, 3 (1789), 619–44, on p. 624; McDonald and Murphy, *Sleepless Souls*, 19 (but with no awareness that the staking of suicides is not recorded in medieval England); Bertachinus Fermanis, *Repertorium* (1471) (edition of Venice, 1590), vol. 3, fol. 460v; 'occidere volens seipsum capite puniatur'. I propose to elaborate on these and related examples in *The Curse on Self-Murder*, chs. 1, 12, and 13.

the government is pursuing suicides with more vigour because it is hungry for confiscations, and regards suicide as an under-harvested resource. A motive of this kind would help account for several gradients in the profile of recorded suicides, the short ones depicted in Figure 1 (on p. 126) for the reigns of Edward I and Richard II, and the long one under the Tudors. Tough government would thus by itself multiply records of suicide. But would it multiply only these? The impact of tough government need not be confined to records, but may increase, generally, the social tensions which encourage suicide. Durkheim and Halbwachs also found signs that suicide tends to increase under firm and steady government,[54] and one or two recent investigators have gone as far as to relate suicide rates directly to the totalitarian character of a government.[55] A leap in the suicide: homicide ratio after the unification of Italy, mentioned above (on p. 358), tells the same story; nor could the victim of Galeazzo Maria Sforza, identified in a rare letter on this subject in 1469, have offered himself as exception to this law.[56] In other words, while steep rises in recorded suicide may indeed be explained away, that could only be done by reference to factors that might well explain them back again.

The same hypothesis would apply in the moral sphere. Let us suppose that the more eager pursuit of suicide by authorities and by local communities should derive from, not greed, but moral indignation. Would the general community express moral conviction more strongly, or more weakly, let us ask ourselves, if it perceived that suicide was on the increase? The answer is surely, more strongly. If that is correct, then a more vigorous judicial pursuit of suicide—apparent in all four monarchies considered here, in the sixteenth century—would itself indirectly reflect the latter's higher incidence.

So the factors shaping the recording of suicide, and suicide itself, are not as independent as I have tried to treat them so far. That may only be a methodological discovery, not a factual one. But it helps us doubt the doubters. It will help us believe—to put in another way—that the sharp rise in recorded suicide in the sixteenth century, in Germany as well as England, was not all a trick of the light. It may, with various kinds of qualification, represent an actual rise in suicide rates.

We only have to believe this possible to admit yet further considerations, so let me suggest two. One is that we still have, in sources from around and after 1500, some of those contemporary subjective impressions I quoted

---

[54] Durkheim, *Suicide*, 353; Halbwachs, *Causes of Suicide*, 230.

[55] S. Stack, 'Suicide: a decade review of the sociological literature', *Deviant Behaviour*, 4 (1982), 41–66, on p. 58.

[56] Above, p. 240.

earlier, to the effect that there was a lot of suicide around. More emphatically than the medieval ones, they suggest that in the sixteenth-century writer's milieu many people had been killing themselves. The impressions may be few and it might be objected that these, too, are the natural outcome of a growth in the genre of source which contains them, indeed of a greater freedom in speaking of the subject. In other words—the same objection would continue—the greater sharpness of these late fifteenth- and sixteenth-century opinions reflects literary mood rather than rising waves of suicide. This again is a matter of subtle judgement. But our medieval investigation can help here. Let us recall those views on Dante's Florence, as a place with a suicidal reputation in contemporary Italy; and ask whether these, as an exception in the general medieval scene, do not compare more exactly with impressions given, around 1500, by writers from Germany and England.

Let me now rehearse a few of these contemporary impressions, and look, to begin with, at the multiple entries in town chronicles. While earlier medieval French abbeys may have mentioned more than one suicide per page, they were never in the same year; and besides, their registers were expressly devoted to crime. By contrast, in some German town chronicles towards the end of the fifteenth century we find groups of suicides reported in the context of disasters peculiar to the time. Suicide, that is, is recorded as part of a portmanteau of horrors newly-arrived. The best example is that cache of four suicides and two attempts, all in the year 1484, in the anonymous town chronicle of Metz, in Chapter 5: the chronicler there, while not stating expressly that the number of suicides was unprecedented, included them among catastrophes which made 1484 seem so exceptionally bad a year that 'it seemed as if the world were coming to an end.' We hear of comparable armageddons elsewhere in Germany. In 1544 in Nuremberg the mother of a bastard child was said to have killed the child, and then hanged herself when she heard that the priest would not baptize it. Her father then stabbed himself. Finally it was the priest's turn, and he drowned himself.[57] A sense of novelty understandably haunts an acknowledgement by Luther, when writing to a friend in 1544, about the suicide of a young woman whose degree of responsibility Luther discusses in the letter: the reformer acknowleges that he himself has, in his own experience, known of 'many' suicides. Nor was his the only such impression.[58]

[57] Dieselhorst, 'Nürnberg', 63.
[58] Quoted by R. Weichbrodt, *Der Selbstmord* (Basle, 1937), 44–5. Weichbrodt writes of 'eine auffallende Zunahme der Selbstmörde' in Germany *c.*1500 and quotes, as well as Luther, testimony from the superintendent Andreas Celchius on the rise in the number of suicides in the Mark of Brandenburg (ibid., 45). In a copy of the sermons of the Erfurt Carthusian Jacobus de Clusa, composed *c.*1450 and printed in 1472, Jacobus' reference to contemporary

A comparable mood, finally, is present in English reports. Here, from Dr Brigden's *London and the Reformation*, is a part of a letter from the imperial ambassador in London to his master, in 1532:

> On 24 May in the Thames two fishes were caught, each measuring thirty feet in length, ten feet high and eleven feet broad. . . . the people here in general consider this a prodigy foreboding future evil, which they likewise anticipate from the fact that within the last few days fourteen individuals, including men and women, have committed suicide by hanging, or drowned themselves in the Thames.[59]

Most significant of all, surely, as subjective background to our reading of English records, is that it is in the sixteenth century that we first hear a foreign visitor remarking on a high rate of suicide in England. England's exceptionally suicidal reputation is well-documented in France from the time of a letter by Montesquieu in 1696,[60] but it leaves no trace whatever among the abundant French utterances about English character in the Middle Ages. The medieval Englishman's reputation was if anything the opposite.[61] We find the first sign of this reputation in 1562. A young Venetian nobleman then spent two months in London and recorded *notabilia* about the astute, rapacious buying-and-selling class of Londoner. One feature that struck him was that 'many find themselves driven to hang themselves or to throw themselves into a well and drown.'[62] This young man never went near any King's Bench records. But he got the same impression that they give.

The final consideration concerns religion. If suicide really was more frequent in England and Germany in the sixteenth century, one hypothesis for explaining it is that people were unsettled by religious changes. The psychological history of the European Reformation is not to be disposed of with one brief remark. But such a remark is enough to point, at least, to a

---

suicide (as fulfilment of a prophecy in Revelation), has the word 'Nota' written faintly in the margin beside it, by a hand which appears to date from not long after the book was printed. The copy is Oxford, Bodleian Library, Bodl. Auct. 6 Q 5. 10. See p. 367 n. 38 above. Cf. also Kühnel, 485.

[59] S. Brigden, *London and the Reformation* (Oxford, 1989), 208, who kindly communicated to me the longer text from which the quotation was taken, printed in *Calendar of State Papers: Spanish*, vol. 4 (2), no. 773.

[60] J. McManners, *Death and the Enlightenment* (Oxford, 1982), 42–9.

[61] P. Rickard, *Britain in Medieval French Literature, 1100–1500* (Cambridge, 1956), 163–89: esp. 167: 'By far the most constant and oft recurring feature of the Frenchman's conception of the English in the middle ages was intemperance.' For 'variance' or disloyalty, 180, 183–4. There is no mention of melancholy or suicide in Rickard's survey of French views on the English character.

[62] C. Barron, C. Coleman, and C. Gobbi, eds., 'The London Journal of Alessandro Magno, 1562', *London Journal*, 9 (1983), 136–52.

coincidence. Among recorded medieval suicides clerks and religious are prominent. I shall return in the following chapter to the question how far their prominence is due, all or partly, to another trick of the light. But two facts appear certain. Clergy and religious people sometimes *were* suicidal, in thought and very occasionally in deed; and their suicidal feelings, where we know their origin, often reflect no motive more palpable than general mental anxiety, sometimes called *acedia* or *tristitia* in the sources, and often with an explicit element of doubt on religious doctrines. Mental temptations of this kind were not uncommon among monastic novices, and were recognized as belonging to a regular group of difficulties a young convert to asceticism was likely to encounter. If sufferers had all *committed* suicide the history of the orders would have been quite different, or nonexistent. I shall return to this subject at the end of the third volume of the trilogy. For now it is enough to acknowledge that many could feel such anxiety, in mild and ephemeral doses, and this fact gives credence to that handful of sources which say the temptation did, if very rarely, get out of hand and give the Devil a victory.[63]

The significance of this will be clear if we take a step sideways and look at the Reformation from a particular, deliberately chosen angle. Observed from this direction, those trends in late medieval religion which became prominent at the Reformation consist of ideals which had once been confined to religious orders. Now they became generalized among the people. Every believer, for instance, was to be his own priest. Perhaps as important, every believer was also to be his own monk. The hypothesis that suicidal temptation should have been an export from inside to outside monastery walls is one in step with many other, more positive aspects of committed religion. Such religion, like a fast car, could swerve dangerously off the road, especially in times of confessional turmoil. Was it not thought that Cardinal Andreas Zamonetič, the unsuccessful would-be reformer of Sixtus IV's church, had hanged himself?[64] MacDonald and Murphy in England, and Schär and others in Germany, have sketched such sufferings in certain known individuals buffeted by religious change. The most notorious in England would be Sir James Hales, the apostate Protestant courtier who finally went through with his suicide in 1554; while his opposite number in Germany is best found in Heinrich Muelich, whose prominent conversions

---

[63] e.g. David of Augsburg, O. F. M., in *Formula nouitiorum* (c.1250), conveniently available in English translation by D. Devas, *Spiritual Life and Progress*. 2 vols (London, 1937), vol. 2, p. 212. I hope to return to this and similar texts in the last chapter of *The Mapping of Mental Desolation*.

[64] Above, pp. 77–9.

and re-conversions ended in his suicide in 1550.[65] But the portrait gallery is much bigger than these two, and is one already familiar, indeed, to Reformation historians.[66] The medievalist can only add three reflections of his own. First, the form of melancholy attaching to these notorious waverers was one long-established among monks, friars, and nuns. Second, the migration of Christian ideals from religious to laity may have brought this shady stowaway with it, the more dangerously because religious orders had developed, by long-tried and usually effective tradition, prophylactic machinery for containing the danger. Third, last, and most important (if true): this effect may have been large enough to make Hales, Muelich, and the other well-known individual religious waverers only the outward sign of many others, most of them no more than statistics, if that, in the court records.

The word 'statistics' is a signal to return from this detour to our main road. The detour has been justified, I hope, by the vistas it has opened on an important question, insoluble by counting alone. The question is that of sixteenth-century suicide rates and their possible connection with the Reformation. It will not disappear. In so far as real advances are to be made in its investigation they will certainly be made mainly by historians specializing in the sixteenth century. But the medieval dossier is not irrelevant, and has had to be allowed to shed some of its light on subsequent developments. The light it sheds on this one does, I suggest, lend strength to the view, old enough but still unproven, that in Germany and England, at least, medieval suicide rates increased at the time of the Reformation, and perhaps for causes they shared with it.

So much for questions about the absolute suicide rate. We turn next to shorter, better-lit stretches of the road. Who committed suicide? How, where, when, and why?

---

[65] MacDonald and Murphy, *Sleepless Souls* 6–75, on suicides who had been oppressed by sectarian anxieties, esp. 61–3 (Hales). Cf. Schär, *Seelennöte*, 250–94, on sectarian anxieties; and Kühnel, 485, on Muelich.

[66] In London, for instance, religious upheavals were recognized as a dangerously frequent occasion of suicides, Judge Hales's fate being held up as characteristic of apostates and a warning (Brigden, *London and the Reformation*, 560). In Dr Brigden's richly documented pages, notorious suicides arising directly from the religious changes include those of two Eastcheap priests (278, 393), an ex-Town Clerk (217), a City silk-weaver (628, n. 364) and Dr Richard Langrysh, who in 1547, having missed a chance some years earlier to escape to the continent, leapt to his death from the tower of St Magnus' church (427).

16

The Person and the Act

WE turn, then, from counting self-homicides as a proportion of other people, to the internal arithmetic of suicide. That is, suicidal persons and suicidal acts will now be compared with others of the same kind; and let us look first at suicidal persons. Since the records are still highly imperfect it will be best to start in the particular on which data are least equivocal, sex.

The Person

SEX

In the two or three centuries before 1950, in respect of all suicides together and taking statistics at face value, men have committed suicide more than women in a ratio varying between two and three male to one female. Occasionally the ratio has gone as high as over four to one, as in late Habsburg Austria (in the 1870s); but then again it has occasionally dropped towards equality. Two to three represents the normal ratio. In recent decades, the achievement of female equality in civil life has cast a sinister shadow on suicide rates: in respect of suicide, too, the sexes have moved towards equality in advanced western countries.[1]

But medieval women did not usually enjoy modern civic equality, so it should not be surprising that the suicide records in our Register betray an inequality in suicide rates, comparable to those found in subsequent centuries before the twentieth. The English and French legal dossiers (with one

---

[1] R. W. Main, *Pathways to Suicide* (Baltimore and London, 1981), 143 (table 6.2). Women catching up: C. S. Kruit, 'The suicide rate in the western world since World War II', *Netherlands Journal of Sociology*, 13 (1977), 55–64, at 55–6; modified by the subtraction of Americans between 15 and 44 years old, but sustained for eight other industrial countries, by S. Stack, 'Suicide: a decade review of the sociological literature', *Deviant Behaviour*, 4 (1982), 41–66, on p. 44.

exception each: an illegible Eyre entry in Warwickshire and an anonymous
case in Rouen) record the gender of all their suicides; chronicles and religious sources, all of theirs; and German legal records—I shall return to the
possible significance of the shortfall—85 per cent of theirs. 546 suicides
recorded in these show a male predominance of almost exactly 3:1.
(Fig. 6)

But that is not the end of the matter. Medieval inequalities between the
two sexes extended to their access to record, and more will be learned both
about this factor and about the suicides themselves if the fortunes of that
ratio are pursued through the various categories of document. In English
legal records, which account for over 60 per cent of the total, the sex ratio
is normal, as can be seen from Figure 7. However, a breakdown of the
records into three groups shows that the male predominance owes a special
debt to one group. These are the inquisitions and other enquiries organized
at Westminster (Figure 7(c)). Why males should dominate here, at a ratio
of 13:1, will transpire when we come to consider suicides' property later in
this chapter. The suicides of women scarcely justified the elaborate procedure of an inquisition. (Dr Stevenson has found the same factor at work in
the later Star Chamber investigations.)[2] Ratios in the Eyre and coroners'
rolls are meanwhile closer together. In the coroners' rolls the ratio is as low
as 2:1 (Figure 7(a)). A degree of selectivity almost certainly obtained at this
level too, where persons thought to be of no importance or wealth could be
quietly 'dropped' before the eyre.

Similar varieties appear in French legal records, though with a weaker
male dominance. The ratio over all the records is 1.5:1 (Figure 8). But the
French dossier owes nearly half its cases to the Court of Requests in Parlement, and we must remember one main reason cases came there. The
king's grace was doing what it could for families whose breadwinners had
incurred forfeiture, so of course there are more males (Figure 8(c)). Without
the Court of Requests the ratio in French cases sinks to near-equality. Indeed
it sinks to complete equality if 'ecclesiastical' records alone are counted
(Figure 8(a)). These, it should be remembered, are nearly all criminal registers of abbeys. So in one important sense they are not so much ecclesiastical as much as—that rare thing in medieval France—records from a
seigneurial court of first instance. Although the sample is very small, its
peculiarity deserves notice.

Among other categories of source it is only in the religious sources that
an approach to such equality is to be found, with a ratio of just over one-
and-a-half to one for the whole category, sinking to near-equality in hagiog-

---

[2] *Continuity and Change*, 2 (Cambridge, 1987), 234.

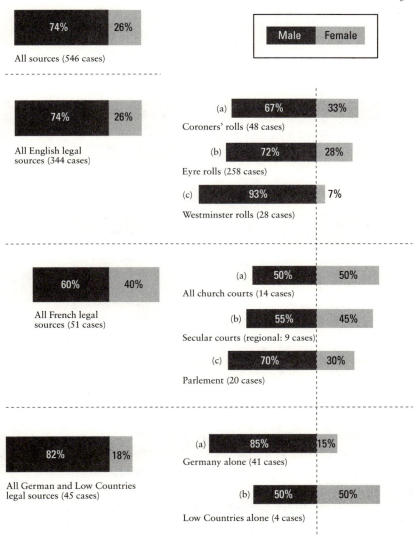

6 Distribution by sex: all sources
7 Distribution by sex: English legal records
8 Distribution by sex: French legal records
9 Distribution by sex: legal records Germany and the Low Countries

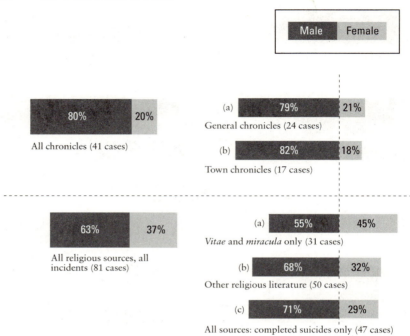

10 Distribution by sex: chronicles
11 Distribution by sex: religious sources

raphy on its own (Figures 11(a) and (b)). But it must be remembered that these religious sources hide suicidal incidents other than full suicide. Take full suicides only, and the male predominance returns at over 2:1 (Figure 11(c)) Meanwhile there are eleven mere temptations, almost all male, as they would tend to be if told by fellow-members of male religious houses. Attempts, on the other hand, together with deeds showing suicidal intention, turn the norm upside down. They give a female preponderance of thirteen to eight (1.6:1). The bulk of this ratio is provided by *Vitae* and *Miracula* alone, not *Exempla* and similar sources. This inversion of the usual ratio may say something of hagiographical literature, home of the otherwise helpless. But we must not rule out an objective foundation. Research in the early decades of the twentieth century, based on big-city populations like those responsible for the usual male preponderance of completed suicides, found that the attempted suicide, treated as an act with its own character, inverts the usual gender proportion. The female preponderance among attempted suicides ranges between 1.4 : 1 and 4 : 1.[3] The ratio yielded by our hagiographical sources is consonant with that. On this point, that is to say, medieval miracle stories do *not* strain credibility; quite the contrary. They correspond to modern findings. This fact, whatever its significance, must modify our reading of the whole sample. This totals 81 cases. Subtract attempts, temptations, and threats (both *threats* of suicide are female, of course—the writers were celibate males), and the sample shrinks to a mere 47. Among these 47, the male:female ratio duly becomes 2.5 : 1, in other words, normal.

German legal records, and chronicles from all countries, mark the opposite bias. They give a higher male ratio than usual (Figure 9). As for general chronicles, their four-to-one male preponderance is well enough explained by the bias of the genre towards persons considered powerful (Figure 10). The bias in German legal sources, which make men more than five times more suicidal than women, cannot be so simply explained. But it is worthy of note that German town chronicles, which make most of the small sample in Figure 10(b), betray a comparable bias. This bias, common to German legal sources and German chronicles, could, of course, mean that there was something about being German that made a woman less suicidal. But other explanations are more likely. The question of property may have come into it, though there is nothing here of the detailed information given in English rolls. Another explanation is more tempting. Alone of our sources, German legal registers frequently (in nearly one in five entries) fail to distinguish the sex of suicides. Those of unrecorded sex total 10. If these were all female the ratio in question would tumble to 2 : 1, a figure of striking normality. To be a suicide, all this would suggest, was shocking enough; to be a *woman* as well made the double horror unmentionable. The same abnormality obtains in both German legal registers and German town chronicles, suggesting the same rule. It is a rule which at least six of its exceptions, across both categories, tend to prove, for three of the said six are women scarcely mentionable anyway (two Jewesses in Frankfurt and a prostitute in Basle); two more were excused by madness (again in Frankfurt and Basle); and the sixth, the hospital bursar of Nuremberg, was so well-known as to preclude silence. This hypothesis may be wrong. But there is certainly an anomaly in these German records. It must have a cause, and this may be it.

---

[3] The pioneering researches of M. Bachi on this subject, in 1924, are assessed and extended by Halbwachs, *Causes*, 44–57, and more decisive modern figures summarized by R. F. W. Diek-stra and W. Gulbinat, 'The epidemiology of suicidal behaviour: a review of three continents', *Rapport trimestriel de statistiques sanitaires mondiales* [= World Health Statistics Quarterly], 46 (Geneva, 1993), 52–68, on p. 54, col. b.

In the records of medieval suicide, then, we have looked at a range of indexes of sex distribution. Apart from one unexplained anomaly, based on a very small sample—the French abbey registers, with equal numbers—the different sources converge, once the special origin of each is taken into account. These sources agree in suggesting that suicide was uneven between the sexes, by an approximate ratio of between two and three males to one female.

Before we leave this matter one more irregularity deserves attention. It concerns English judicial rolls. Among the 316 cases recorded in Eyre and coroners' rolls the phraseology used to describe a suicide is usually formulaic. (Examples can be referred to on page 149–52 above.) Among slight possible variations in the formulae, one serves to emphasize that the act of suicide was conscious and deliberate. An expression is added like *sponte sua* or *gratis*, as if to make doubly clear that the deceased falls clearly under the law's penalties. To describe these phrases I have coined the epithet 'hardening': they 'harden' the verdict. Now if the sex distribution of our sample is extended to include such 'hardening' phrases, we find their male : female ratio slightly greater, in both Eyre and coroners' rolls, than that of the suicides themselves. Ostensibly this should mean that male suicides knew what they were doing better than females. That is what the rolls say. But the courts were not psychologists, and the real significance of this difference—if the lesson of our sample can be taken as such—is that male judges felt marginally more rigorous in judging males to be felons than females. The courts were chivalrous. Their chivalry may be minimal; but that, again, on these data, was what it was. The proportions are shown in Figure 12, where the 'normal' gender distributions, taken from Figure 7, have been indicated to emphasize the judges' relative harshness to male suicides.

The lesson is partially confirmed if approached the other way round. While some formulaic accounts of suicide are thus 'hardened', others are 'softened', in that an adverbial addition shows the suicide was done under some kind of external pressure, like *in infirmitate sua*. Some, but not all, of such qualifications led to the dead person's exculpation, normally as a victim of 'death by misadventure' with no shame or confiscation. Enumeration of such 'softened' accounts (or 'judgements'), and another of verdicts or sentences softened in consequence of them, yields new ratios of sex distribution, as shown in Figures 12–14. They show that, *pro rata*, men were as likely as women to benefit from softened *accounts* of their suicide given in judgements; but that it is the women suicides whose *sentences* were more likely to be modified. Again, that might mean that female suicide was more often attended by extenuating circumstance. What it probably means is that male judges were prepared to say it was. As in Germany, female suicide was

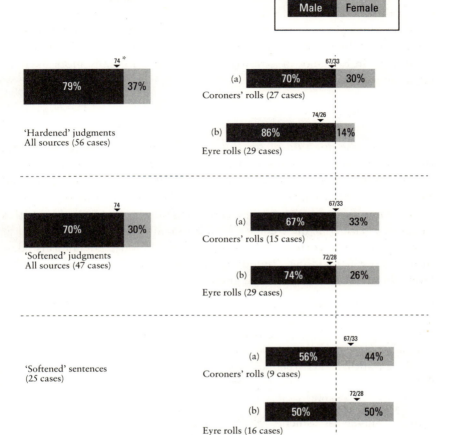

| Male | Female |

'Hardened' judgments
All sources (56 cases)

79%   37%

74 *

(a) 70%   30%
Coroners' rolls (27 cases)

67/33

(b) 86%   14%
Eyre rolls (29 cases)

74/26

'Softened' judgments
All sources (47 cases)

70%   30%

74

(a) 67%   33%
Coroners' rolls (15 cases)

67/33

(b) 74%   26%
Eyre rolls (29 cases)

72/28

'Softened' sentences
(25 cases)

(a) 56%   44%
Coroners' rolls (9 cases)

67/33

(b) 50%   50%
Eyre rolls (16 cases)

72/28

* ▼ The downward arrow indicates the sex distribution of completed suicide in the source (*see fig. 2.1*)

12 Sex distribution of 'hardened' judgements: English legal records
13 Sex distribution of 'softened' judgements: English legal records
14 Sex distribution of 'softened' sentences: English legal records

just too horrible to think about. And that does stand to reason, after all, for if suicide as such was a taboo subject and it was in fact males, by a majority of two or three to one, who made people sometimes think about it, that was enough. Why add horror to horror by gratuitously reflecting on the minority of females?

These irregularities may be slight, and based on a small sample. But they are not quite negligible, and draw a certain force from analogous findings made by students of post-medieval records.[4] If the irregularities do nothing else in this immediate context, they add yet another factor—together with considerations of property, public prominence, and questions of reticence—to factors tending to favour the lower of the two ratios suggested just now as normal. In England, in a word, women were marginally more likely to get away with it.

WEALTH

So much for the question of sex. Our review will best proceed by moving from the precise to the more impressionistic. Next in precision, if only in one group of sources, is the question of a suicide's wealth. English judicial rolls evaluate the movable wealth of the overwhelming majority of convicted felons. Thus our Register provides a counting sample of 277 suicides in this category. I have split the suicide's wealth into six classes, distinguished at arbitrary points to correspond broadly with the following definitions: 'destitute', 'poor', 'middling', 'middling-to-rich', 'rich', and 'very rich'. The levels chosen to distinguish these grades are:

Destitute:	Nothing at all (which may apply to a young dependant or a destitute adult);
Poor:	below 6s 8d (half a 'mark', a common unit of account);
Middling:	6s 8d and over but not over 1;
Middling-to-rich:	over 1 but not over 5;
Rich:	over 5 but not over 10;
Very rich:	over 10.

The 277 suicide assessments fall in these categories according to the distribution depicted in Figure 15. In the graph, the height of a column corresponds to the percentage formed by each category in the totality of 277 cases.

These assessments cover a period of over two centuries. The centuries in question included price inflation: probably of about 50 per cent from 1190 to 1250, and—irregularly—a similar increment from 1250 to 1400.[5] So it may be asked whether the above 'distribution profile' might differ markedly

---

[4] Signori, 'Aggression und Selbstzerstörung', 150, reads a similar conclusion in sixteenth-century German miracle books, and refers (ibid., n. 123) to further secondary literature. Significance surely lies in the fact that my own conclusions were drawn from English medieval records before I knew of any of this literature, or indeed that the matter was one in which historians had shown an interest.

[5] P. D. A. Harvey, 'The English inflation of 1180–1220', *Past and Present*, 61 (1973), 3–30; J. L. Bolton, *The Medieval English Economy, 1150–1500* (London, 1980), 21, 73–88.

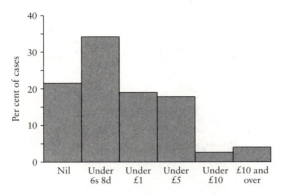

15 Personal wealth of suicides, 1171–1404: all English legal sources (277 cases)

between these periods. The answer is shown by the breakdown of 190 assessments in Figure 16, all from Eyre rolls. The wealth profile of English suicides, this graph suggests, remained approximately constant.

A further breakdown of the figures will be useful, to address the question whether the category of source makes any difference. The following variations in the profile will show that it does, since they indicate that in handling suicides the different levels of court encountered different sectors of the human economic range. Figure 17 shows the same 277 assessments as depicted in Figure 15, but distinguished by category of source.

The direct lesson of these profiles is that over half of the suicides in the records were assessed for chattels worth less than 6s 8d. The poor thus defined form 59 per cent of cases in the Eyre roll and 64 per cent of those in the few surviving coroners' rolls. That they do not feature at all in Westminster inquisitions reflects the latter's admittedly financial function. Westminster was only interested in the rich. A glance back at the chronological profile in Figure 1 (on page 126), will show a special concentration of such inquisition suicides in the reigns of Edward I, Edward III (the last years), and Richard II, all periods when the government is known from other sources to have squeezed its sources of revenue. (The inquisition concerning Richard Holstorne in 1397 tells a story clearly illustrating the effects of strong-arm government pressure.) Such fiscal persecution may, of course, have driven more rich people to suicide than poor, that is, the concentration of rich suicides in these records at these periods may, as I suggested at the end of the last chapter, represent a measure of social fact. More directly and certainly it reflected well-known impulses in the legal mechanism.

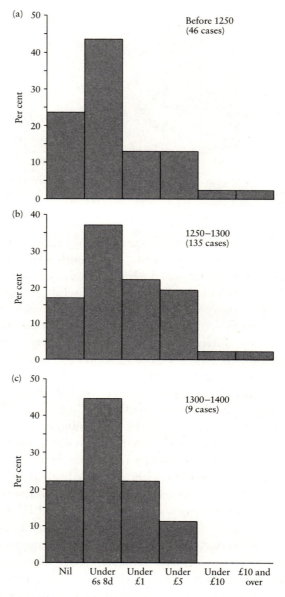

16 Personal wealth of suicides, 1171–1404: percentage distribution of 190 cases from Eyre rolls, distinguished by period

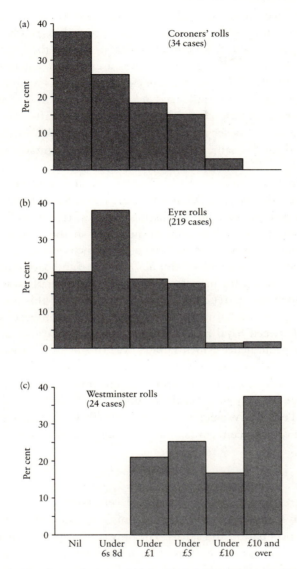

17 Personal wealth of suicides, 1171–1404: English legal sources, distinguished by source

The difference lower down the scale is harder to explain, namely that between the wealth profiles in Eyre and coroners' rolls. Or rather, it is harder to explain it if we believe all coroners' cases came to the Eyre. They were theoretically meant to. But perhaps it was a case, as I suggested earlier in respect of women, of *de minimis non curabat lex*: the law did not concern itself with trifles. An unchallenged *felonia de se* by a very poor person scarcely deserved attention from the Eyre judges, years after the event. *Their* lives were too short, never mind that of the suicide. This would mean that the poor, and for the same reason women, would be under-represented in the Eyre rolls.

Records from monarchies outside England yield next to no precise information on suicides' wealth. What little can be said about their references to it will be said when we come to discuss suicides' trades and statuses. But the French records do offer some comparison in the matter of levels of wealth, in that about half the reports in the French dossier give indications in this respect. Of those which do, about a third indicate that the suicide possessed real estate, for instance, a house. Nearly a half (some the same) say the suicide had chattels. But we know little beyond this for sure, except that the group included some wealthy people, whose property was worth a tug of war between royal and local justiciars, and that one or two of the group had a prominence which implies wealth—as in the case of Philippe Braque—or perhaps former wealth suddenly absent—as in that of the Rouen canon who died in debt and was remembered by Jean Feu. At the other extreme we only need recall the plight of the families of Michelet le Cavalier or Perrin le Vachier to remember, with it, that Letters of Remission, among our scarce records, may have over-represented the poor.

OCCUPATION

The most precise data, then, concerned sex. Next came wealth. In any journey from the precise to the impressionistic the next step must touch on the suicide's occupation and status. The only source to mention occupation, as a matter of course, are Letters of Remission from the French Parlement. Although English inquisitions and some German town registers can run them close, the mass of English rolls, and of other French records, are silent on this particular. The silence is itself evidence. To judge by the details in these undefined cases—like their place of occurrence and the mention of barns and farm animals—the dead person in both France and England was usually an agricultural country-dweller, a peasant. So generally was this understood that courts do not bother to say so unless it helped define the person (like 'the reeve') or unless legal status was at issue, as for that Adam le Yep who died resisting demotion to villein status. Only outside this norm did definition become necessary. Thus, while we know the trades and statuses of about a hundred of the grand total of 546 suicides, most of those hundred references indicate a specialist manufacture or trade rather than direct agriculture. But that has to be 'about' a hundred. For while sources sometimes give an occupation unambiguously they do not always distinguish between the name of an occupation and a family name. The epoch that produced most of our records, the thirteenth and fourteenth centuries, was also that in which surnames were born. But they were born unsteadily. So confusion cannot always be avoided on whether an 'Augustus Smith', for instance (in the 1260 Cambridge assize) was an actual smith or only the descendant of one. The harder cases defy guesswork, though a rule of thumb, fair if not infallible, allows a definite article to distinguish employment from surname, as in 'William le vineter', who thus becomes *a* taverner (with a small 't').

An application of this principle to the Register produces the results set out in Table 6 (pp. 392–4). It represents legal sources and town chronicles, that is, all except general chronicles and religious sources, whose contribution will be drawn on in its place.

Table 6 invites two comments. One is its range. Apart from the paucity of soldiers, whose special position in respect of suicide was discussed in Chapter 3 (pages 61–5) the table does not suggest that any type of occupation was immune. A hard search for absentees might suggest millers, who—we know from other testimony—had a reputation for sanguine temperament. But millers could not have derived their immunity to suicide, if they had one, either from their wealth or from their contact with grain— otherwise a 'baxter' (baker) with both those advantages would not have killed himself, as he did in 1387. The higher and lower ends of the social scale give problems of definition. Suicides at the higher end often had several occupations (like the Newcastle mayor, MP, and shipowner Robert Olyver), and at the lower end, too few. A description like 'beggar' has been put in the table because it is there in the record.

The second comment attaches to the high number of clergy: in England, apparently a third of the entire list. Nor does this particular list owe anything to religious sources, which had their own kind of clerical bias. Does this not prove that clergy and monks were unusually suicidal? It might, but for three qualifications. In the thirteenth and fourteenth centuries clerical status had become entangled with the gradual spread of literacy so that 'clerk' could be said of many people we would today describe as having only

TABLE 6. Occupations of suicides defined in legal records. Square parentheses mean that it is the tradesman's wife or child who has committed suicide. The sign * means that the name may be a surname, not a trade.

	ENGLISH (48)	FRENCH (12)	IMPERIAL (26)	LOW COUNTRIES, OR ITALY (2)
Agrarian	Villeins (2) Shepherds (2) [Shepherd]	[Fox-warden]	Peasants (2)	Peasant
Food	Butcher Bakers (3) Innkeeper	Butcher Baker	Innkeeper	
Clothing	[Weaver] Fuller Burreller [Skinner] [Tanner] Hide-trader Tailor [Seamster*]	Embroiderer Furriers (2)	Weavers (2)	
Other artisans	Smith* [Carpenter] Mason Sawyer Bowyer* Goldsmith 'Workman*'	Barber Rope-maker		

Transport	[Carter] Shipman* Packhorse groom		
Trade	Merchant Chapman Shopowner	Merchants (2)	
Military	Knight Squire		2 compaignons
High officials	Mayor & MP	Counsellor	
Medium officials	Reeve [Reeve]	Procureur	Hospital bursar Straussmeier
Low officials & servants	Gaoler Servants (4) Groom Laundress		Porter
Other	Burgess		Housewives (2) 'Jewesses' (2) 2 Burghers (2)
Criminals/outcasts	Leper Beggar	'Thieves' (2)	Goose-thief (pr) Rapist (pr) Whore

TABLE 6. *Continued*

	ENGLISH (48)	FRENCH (12)	IMPERIAL (26)	LOW COUNTRIES, OR ITALY (2)
Clerical				
Academic/ professional	University master Medicus		Schoolmasters (2)	
Clerical ambience or connections	'Clerk' ['Clerk' (2)] Beadle			
In orders	Regular canon Cistercian monk Cistercian lay brother Parsons (2) Vicars (3) Chaplains (11)	Cathedral canon Prior of S. Croce	Monks (2) Parish priest Bishop (Zamonetič) 'Bishop of Strasbourg'	

the most basic educational qualification, yet whose lives lacked all serious connection with clerical religious discipline. (Secular courts were forever pointing this out when defendants pleaded benefit of clergy. Defendants normally did this if there was a chance of its doing them any good.) So persons called 'le clerc' should probably not be counted as clerical in any strict sense, still less their sons and daughters. (For the same reason I have already put among merchants, not clerks, a suicide at Amiens in 1305 described by a court as *clers et markeans*: 'clerk and merchant'.) The second modification raises the question how likely a clerical suicide was to get into the records. The answer is, 'very likely': because a clerical suicide might engender dispute between ecclesiastical and secular judges about property, and hence enter the records of both. Finally, since clerical status implied subjection to separate jurisdiction, no court could avoid mentioning it if it was there. It was 'over-determined'. It was always mentioned, that is to say, for the same reason, but upside-down, that peasant status never was. So those 19 clergy in the English records (after mere 'clerks' have been banished) should be read as a proportion, not of the 62 defined cases, but of the full relevant dossier of 344. That reduces their proportion to about 6 per cent. Read on its own, that would make them slightly *less* suicidal than the general population. I shall return later to other admissible considerations. But the sample, by itself, proves nothing definite.

AGE AND FAMILY STATUS

Until recently most students of suicide have found that its incidence tends more often than not to rise with age, especially among males;[6] and to sink in the presence of marriage, especially when there are children.[7] These rules invite testing against medieval evidence. How will it respond?

Except in isolated contexts, and late in the Middle Ages, we rarely find ages exactly recorded. Contemporary courts which did ask for it, like the

---

[6] Halbwachs, *Causes*, 60. A. F. Henry and J. F. Short, *Homicide and Suicide* (New York and London, 1954), 135. Sharp rises in adolescent suicide in Britain, France, and some other western countries between 1957 and 1992 have wrought havoc with this rule. See Diekstra and Gulbinat (as in n. 3), 64, Fig. 17. Many of the general writings mentioned in these footnotes offer statistics on age distribution which, like the others, are full of irregularities and puzzles. Among the most illuminating comments on the rough rule that suicide increases with age, and together with striking exceptions to it, are those of O. Anderson, 'Did suicide increase with industrialization in Victorian England', *Past and Present*, 86 (1980), 149–73, on p. 165; in Victorian England, she argues, urban industrialization tended to protect the young whereas in the country, and some towns, older males owned the means of agricultural production or dominated the craft gilds, and killed themselves less.

[7] Halbwachs, *Causes*, 128–56; Henry and Short, 136. cf. Sophocles, *Phaedra*, Fragment 685 Radt; 'ἀλλ' εἰσὶ μητρὶ παῖδες ἄγκυραι βίου [children are a mother's life anchors]'.

heresy inquisition, usually got the answer with a qualification like 'I believe' or 'thereabouts'. Since English Eyre judges were in the habit of sticking to essentials, which in a felon's case (if he was adult) did not include age, none of the suicides in the Eyre rolls give this detail. Indeed in all 357 suicides recorded in the Register from English legal documents a numerical age is given for only 7 suicides: so few, among so many, that on the face of it they seem useless as a sample. They are saved by one circumstance. It is all but certain that they derive from the inquests of a single coroner, and one whose name we happen to know: John Bachelor of Swaffham, in Norfolk. Bachelor appears to have been a man unusually exposed, for a squire, to the arithmetical sensitivities we know from other sources to have been abroad in educated circles in his time (he was a little older than Chaucer). Since he seems to have asked the ages of all his suicides, spread here and there in various parts of Norfolk and over a period of fourteen years, the ages of the seven suicides have a random quality which recommends them for the present survey. They are given in Table 7, together with (for a purpose to transpire in a moment) available details about their family status and chattels. ('No information' is shown by 'x'.)

Most of these are obviously round figures, but though few they are not insignificant. Two facts are worth observing. One is that a random sounding has yielded a wide range, distributed on a discernible bell curve (with the highest near the middle). The other, that the average of the numbers, which are beyond any contriving, comes out near the traditional mid-point of human life (at 36). These accord with the impression gained earlier that suicide could strike anywhere.

The second and third columns in the Table indicate another kind of guess we can make about age. Some incidental details can suggest a suicide was young: a parent as 'first finder'; suicide at the parents' home; identification as 'so-and-so's' son (or daughter); unmarried status; little or no property. While only the first of these details lends the guess any confidence on its own, two or more together, with no detail pointing the other way, can suggest youth. Cases of this sort in the relevant English legal dossier number about 24, or nearly 7 per cent (including John Ricks). 'Young', of course, is understood broadly and cannot include the very young, if only because children under 8 could not be felons. In recent centuries suicide has been uncommon among children even into their early teens,[8] and there is no certain case of such in the English rolls. But let us remember Emmelina of Headington and Salerna of Ifield, those young beneficiaries of the miraculous powers of

---

[8] Halbwachs, *Causes*, 147–8, etc.

TABLE 7. Ages of seven suicides investigated by John Bachelor of Swaffham, coroner (1365–78).

	AGE AS GIVEN IN ROLL	FAMILY POSITION	CHATTELS S.D.
John of Dilham	40 years		12/1
Agnes of Kirton	40 and more	had son	2/0
Leticia Groundlock	26 years	had husband	0
Matilda Hayward	24 years and more	had husband	
Thomas of Wells	60 years	had wife	25/0
John Ricks	24 and more	had father	
John Austin	40 years and more		6/8

Thomas Becket, whose attempts at suicide we witnessed in Chapters 11 and 13: child suicide was possible. Where, in an Eyre roll, a girl without property was 'first found' by her mother—as Emma Widen was, according to the Kent Eyre of 1244—nothing rules out that she was in her teens or even younger.

Those 'first finders' must stay with us. But it will be useful to make a brief excursion into the comparative evidence from France and the Empire. Here too, numerical indications of age are rare, be the account long or short. In the unusually long account of Philippe Testard we heard that the suicide was 100. It has been calculated that Counsellor Braque was about 50. A Letter of Remission meanwhile describes a dead mother as aged 26. These are the only numerical estimates of age available from the French sources, and the rest is a matter of isolated guesses: for instance, that one of the female suicides in the register of St Martin des Champs, who hanged herself at home after her mother's death, may have been young. The situation is similar in imperial records. A Metz innkeeper was said by the town chronicler to be 65. One of the two weavers we met in the last section was in fact a 'Knecht', or apprentice. An Augsburg rapist, who hanged himself in prison, was certainly unmarried and probably young. French and German sources have thus two things in common in this respect: their information is very scarce, and such information as there is, in both countries, confirms the wide range seen in the larger English sample.

The matter of age is naturally linked to that of family position. Does any evidence suggest that marriage and children were a protection, as they would be in the worlds of Durkheim and Halbwachs? The question 'was he or she married?' can be directly answered in the medieval English legal dossier in only 35 per cent of cases. This includes 'probables'; and it includes clergy and religious, who were not married—or not officially. Since clergy and monks admit special treatment they will be excluded for now. Of the non-clerical total the 'knowns' and 'probables' of married status drop to 30 per cent. Of these, the married form about three-quarters. The remainder is divided between those known or surmised to have been, at the time of their suicide, either widowed or unmarried. The proportion of the widowed to the merely unmarried is about one to two, but since the latter include the 'young' there is probably little to distinguish the incidence of suicide between the two types of companionless adult. As for that large majority of married suicides, only 22 per cent of them are expressly said to have had children.

Any force that might be imputed to these figures is reduced by the large spectre, 65 per cent, of suicides inadequately described: the 'unknowns'. We could debate a long time whether marriage was, like clerical status, over-determined, that is, likely to be mentioned if it was there or, like peasant status, more often taken for granted and left unidentified. Rather than enter that debate—although the answer could transform the effect of the sample—let us construct another kind of statistical base. Coroners', Eyre and King's Bench rolls normally refer to the first finder of the corpse, as they were obliged to. Sometimes they actually identify him or her. Often the first finder is a member of the family. Much less often it is an unrelated neighbour. In the 307 cases appearing in such rolls the first finder is identified in 60, and Figure 18 shows their distribution.

Each family relationship *to* the suicide implies at least one other *in* the suicide. One of these, namely sex, can be 'controlled' (because we always know the sex of the suicide). Thus if the above fragment were the only evidence we had, and quantities were multiplied by (say) a thousand, it would suggest a preponderance of male suicides to female, at least among the married, of 1.8 : 1. The relevant rolls (as shown in Figures 7(a) and (b)), offer a ratio of just under 2.5 : 1. Though small, the table is therefore not a freak in the one respect in which we can check it, so the rest of its profile is worth attention. Of 44 suicides 'first found' by a member of the immediate family, 38 (88 per cent) were certainly married, 21 of them (55 per cent of the married) had children, while 6 (14 per cent of all) were unmarried, and young enough to be living in the parental home. The group—by definition limited to those living in families—is over-determined in favour of the married and against (for instance) solitary adults. So it does not prove that marriage and children failed in any measure to protect. What it does show is that the protection was far from absolute and that, once again, the pattern is one of variety.

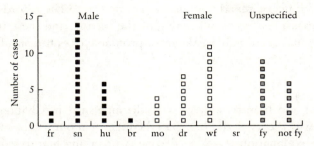

18 English legal sources: relationship of 'first finder' to suicide (60 cases)

The French and German dossiers reflect the same conclusion more weakly. In the French we are told the married status of 11, possibly 12, of the 51 suicides. Of this 11 or 12, 10 were married; and of the 10, 6 had children. But we must not think that marriage in France actually encouraged suicide; on the contrary, it gave privileged access to sources. For we know of those 10 entirely through Letters of Remission, which transmitted royal grace specifically to the helpless and hence, in the case of forfeitures, to the married and the poor. German sources, for their part, reveal the married status of only 9 of their suicides. Seven of these are married—children being in most cases the tell-tale sign—and 2 unmarried (the Augsburg rapist and the weaver's Knecht). As the evidence reaches vanishing point, that is to say, it repeats the familiar lesson.

By mere arithmetic, the dossier has revealed about as much as it will do about the persons of medieval suicides. So let us turn to the other meaning of the word 'suicide', namely the act, and see if arithmetic will throw any light on that.

The Act

If human acts could be thought of as taking no time at all, like a geometrical plane without thickness, then the act of suicide could rightly be treated as distinct from the person. But in fact it is only the critical last phase of a person's other feelings and activities, like the flat end of a piece of Edinburgh rock, which displays on one plane characteristics that run right through the solid stick. So the distinction of person and act is justified chiefly by convenience, and by the records' having mostly made the same distinction. They focused their jet of attention on the short, sharp deed that ended the suicide's life and brought his name into the record. For the historian, the fruits of this attention are mainly three. The records cast light on the motives, methods, and timing of the suicide, and these three facets of the act will accordingly be the most profitable ones to consider now.

MOTIVE

When legal and literary sources were distinguished in Chapter 6, it was explained why the legal said less than the literary about motives for suicide. So further explanation is not needed here for taking literary sources first, with the reminder that they include suicidal acts and temptations which never succeeded. The portraits of individual suicides have said more of their motives than could ever be said by mere counting. No two suicides, in all history, have been the same (since no two snowflakes are: think of those billions of human impulses). But even the portraits were grouped by a rough classification, and a similar classification here will admit numbers which, in turn, will give some idea of the range of circumstances, with the relative importance of each, which drove medieval people to self-destruction.

Of 117 cases in the chronicles and religious sources I have counted 101 which give the reader an idea of the motive. Most of these (three-quarters) are in religious sources. That rough classification of motives has involved two stages. The first produced over twenty categories: those given a symbol in the Register at the end of this book. To make a synopsis these were put into natural clusters. The most capacious was that to do with love and marriage: with 'love', 'jealousy', 'spouse's bereavement', 'suttee', and 'loss of virginity' all put into one cluster. 'Shame' was distinguished from 'disgrace', on grounds that the latter involved objective loss of status; and 'disgrace' was then free to join 'authority' (a term used to signify severe disfavour from authority). So the clusters have formed. They could have been made in other ways, but these suggested themselves. Figure 19, at all events, shows the distribution of 101 such motives from literary sources.

The background and reliability of the general profile (Figure 19) is tested by its being split according to the two types of source ((b) and(c)). The 27 cases from chronicles thus display a different shape to that of the 74 from saints' *Lives*, miracles, and *exempla*. The difference follows a broad rule, determined by the character of the source. It is mainly that of 'outer' to 'inner'. Chronicles, that is to say, tell of adventures of the great, and the rise and fall in their worldly fortunes. So at least 60 per cent of the suicides of these great people, as shown in Figure 19(b), followed physical confinement, defeat, or wounds from battle. These suicides can be characterized as the acts of checkmated extroverts. The world of hagiography and *exempla* (in Figure 19(b)) has the opposite emphasis. More than a quarter of its suicides

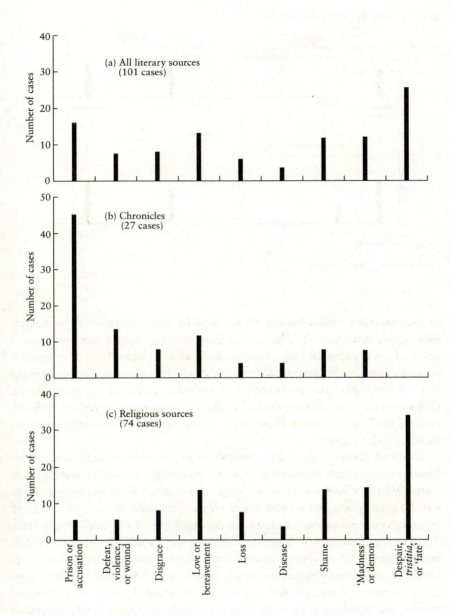

19 Motives: literary sources

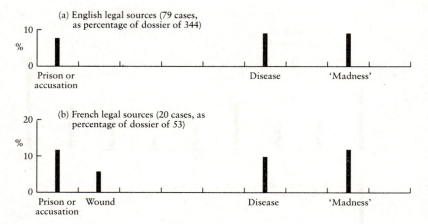

(a) English legal sources (79 cases, as percentage of dossier of 344)

10
%
0

Prison or accusation   Disease   'Madness'

(b) French legal sources (20 cases, as percentage of dossier of 53)

20
%
10
0

Prison or Wound   Disease   'Madness'
accusation

20 Motives: legal sources

or near-suicides—most but not all in religious orders or the clergy—display no tangible motive at all. They suffer from *tristitia, acedia, desperatio*, or a sense of an inexorable fate, pushing them to kill themselves. The genre is correspondingly less interested in the setbacks of extroverts; unless, on the side of *exempla*, the extroverts are unlucky gamblers or speculators. Otherwise the only interest shared by the two categories, with any enthusiasm, is the large group of examples relating to love or marriage, near the middle of the graph.

Which of the two sets of data gives the truer picture of society as a whole? That question is not answerable from the material used so far. But the portraits given in Chapters 12 to 14 suggest one generalization. I hope there will be an opportunity to test it out more fully near the end of the third volume, where attention will focus on the small group who collectively form the odd man out in this context, namely those merely tempted to suicide but who never did anything about it. But since my generalization is one suggested by the present figures let me say what it is at once. It is that laity normally committed suicide for a tangible, external reason, while priests, monks, and nuns were the ones who envisaged, attempted, and committed suicide for invisible motives, motives definable, that is, only in psychological or spiritual terms. This difference is not identical to that shown in the right-hand columns of Figures 19(b) and (c), but it suggests itself, prima facie, as the latter's main single cause.

In previous sections of this chapter we have used literary sources to check legal ones. Can this be done in reverse now? It is difficult, for we run up against the massive silence of legal sources in respect of motive. One case in each of the three main dossiers—England, France, and Germany—mentions circumstances that strongly suggest a suicide had been heavily in debt. Otherwise only three motives are normally indicated. The law had a natural interest in criminals, whether awaiting execution, in prison, under arrest, running from justice, in judicial exile, or even having just committed an act (like a family murder) likely to have judicial consequences. One of these sources' rare excursions into psychology relates to that thief in the stocks who stabbed himself 'because he did not want to be hanged'.[9] With or without such excursions the judicial sources can be assumed to mention criminal status when it was there. The other two circumstances commonly mentioned were sickness and madness, or both at once. For the reasons given in Chapter 8, 'madness' must not be taken at face value, though sickness probably should. When both afflictions are combined I have therefore assigned the case to the 'sick' category, and left that of the 'mad' on its own, at a level almost certainly too high, especially in France with its generous Letters of Remission.

While madness is thus probably exaggerated, and certainly over-determined, there is no reason for radical scepticism about the other two conditions. The records betray no hesitation in mentioning them when they obtained. The reverse is true of all other motives. These are never mentioned, except three 'wounds' in the Letters of Remission, which are doubtful cases anyway. So I have thought it worthwhile to represent these few isolated categories as proportions of the entire national dossier in which they appear, and in a format allowing comparison with Figure 19 and its two satellites. The resulting quantities—in Figures 20(a) and (b)—are different but of the same order. The high rate for illness ('disease'), especially in the more random English dossier, suggests that it was in fact a commoner motive for suicide than chronicles, miracles, or *exempla* would give us reason to believe.

There is plenty more to say about motives for suicide—in law, morals, poetry and elsewhere. But this chapter is devoted only to the interpretation of the few statistics at our disposal, and these remarks must be enough at this point. From motive, then, we proceed to method.

METHOD

Durkheim wrote that 'the relative frequency of different modes of suicide remains invariant for a given society over a very long period.'[10] This had

---

[9] Page 157 above.   [10] Durkheim, 290; cf. Halbwachs, *Causes*, 26.

been noticed before Durkheim. But although many statisticians agreed on it, and even thought it scientifically important in itself (as Durkheim did not) it was Halbwachs, in 1930, who first used this constancy as a means to test other data. First he established certain broad trends in the ratios between different methods of suicide, such as a relative decline in hanging *pari passu* as a society became urban and industrial, and (for different reasons) as the survey moves southwards to the Mediterranean. Beyond these, the stability of the relevant ratios helped, Halbwachs argued, to identify anomalies in less demonstrable areas of the subject, such as those arising, for instance, from extensive concealment of suicide.

The difference between medieval and modern Europe sometimes appears so great that it must come as a surprise to find any reflection of this rule in medieval evidence. But what does that evidence say? In all but a handful of cases the medieval legal records are helpful, since they identify the method. The distribution of their answers, over all the 484 cases in which the information is available, is shown in Figure 21(a). Below it, Figure 21(b) shows in similar format the percentages obtaining in late nineteenth-century Europe. These latter are based on millions of cases, gathered by numerous public authorities and averaged out by Halbwachs. Here, if anywhere, we are surely looking at a *histoire de la longue durée*. Technology, it is true, has laid its subtle hand on the second figure by adding firearms. But if I am right to treat firearms as extending the action formerly confined to swords and knives, then their aggregate contribution is greater, but not much greater, than that of medieval blades. The other main contribution of technology has been poison, the biggest single element among other methods.

The similarity of these two figures does not prove that the medieval data are authentic; but it does supply us with something much needed when investigating our jejune medieval data, namely encouragement. With it, let us look first at the English legal records. The main methods of suicide recorded there are shown as a profile in Figure 22(a). It is by now scarcely rash to dub the profile there 'normal'. But norms admit variation, and variations in this one become apparent quickly when the ingredient data are assessed separately. From Figure 22(b) it is clear that men were readier than women to use a metal blade, and while both sexes were about equal in their recourse to water, women were more likely to hang themselves than were men. These simple gender differences conceal others, revealed when we investigate further the two commonest methods of suicide. Figure 23(a) shows that most of those who hanged themselves did so at home, in their own house (whose open beams would have made the act all too easy). Indeed, if the immediate environs of one's own house, or the inside of

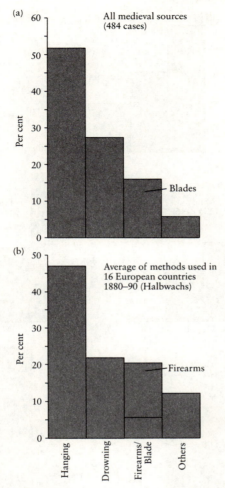

21 Methods of suicide

someone else's house, are included in that majority it rises to 70 per cent of recorded cases. Relatively few went out to the woods to do it. A gender analysis of this figure, as shown in Figure 23(b), shows who these adventurers were: all men. Male monopolies also extended, in these sources, to suicides in prison. Otherwise these more intrepid locales, like isolated trees and agricultural barns, witnessed males as merely predominant, while the women died more often, as they had lived, within the house. This contrast is expressed by diagram in Figures 23(c) and (d).

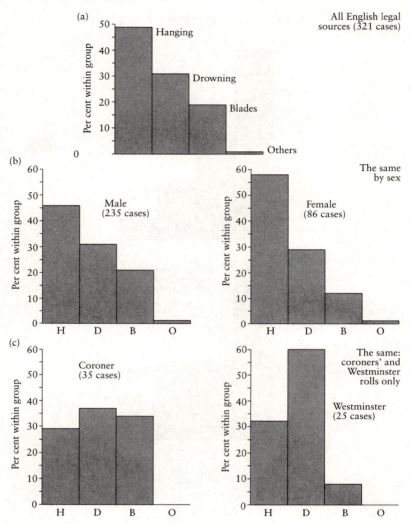

22 Methods of suicide: English legal sources

The analysis of suicides by drowning, a kind traditionally hard to identify, yields weaker patterns. It is shown in Figure 24. The display only emphasizes how much potentially fatal water there was in medieval England, a circumstance which has been used to suggest, plausibly, that drowning accidents were far commoner then than now.[11] There were domes-

[11] P. E. H. Hair, 'Deaths from violence in Britain: a tentative secular survey', *Population Studies*, 25 (1971), 12–15.

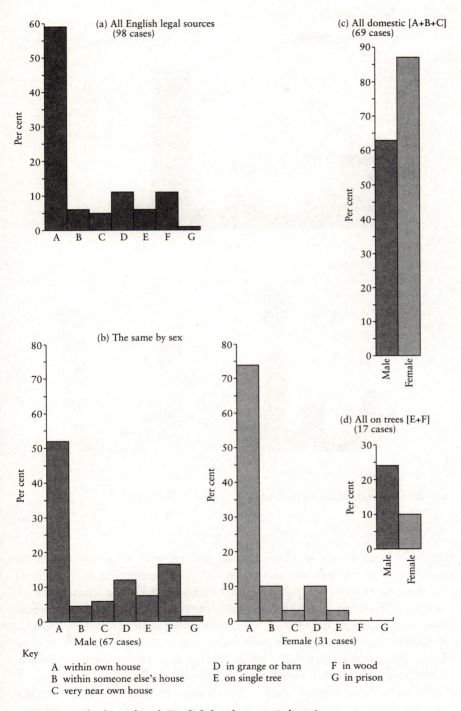

Key

A within own house   D in grange or barn   F in wood
B within someone else's house   E on single tree   G in prison
C very near own house

23 Main methods analysed (English legal sources): hanging

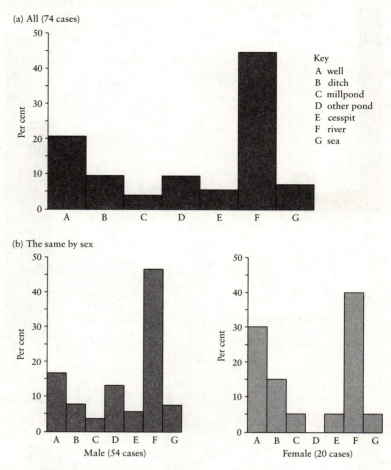

(a) All (74 cases)

Key
A well
B ditch
C millpond
D other pond
E cesspit
F river
G sea

(b) The same by sex

Male (54 cases)

Female (20 cases)

24 Main methods analysed (English legal sources): drowning

tic wells and sewage outflows, ponds natural and artificial (the latter multiplying as water-power was harnessed), not to mention rivers, including those numerous rivers, like London's Fleet, which the modern townsman hears rushing safely under his streets. But the gender difference remains here too, as in Figure 24(b). Women were more likely to drown themselves in a well (often we know, often we must guess, it was the well from which they drew domestic water); men, in rivers and the sea, though their wanderlust is less marked here than in the previous analysis.

Before we leave English legal sources a further analysis may be instructive. It was shown early in this chapter (p. 389, see Figure 17) that different

(a) All (45 cases)

(b) The same by sex

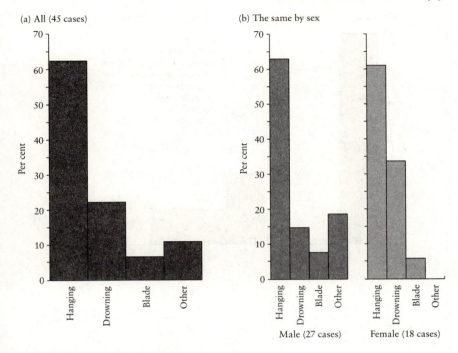

25 Methods of suicide: French legal sources

categories of roll recorded suicides with more or less wealth. Coroners, it seems, dealt with all the population as far down as the destitute; Westminster inquisitions, only with the rich. Did the rich and the poor have their own methods of suicide? It seems prima facie that they did. Profiles based separately on coroners' and Westminster rolls are both abnormal, and Figure 22(c) shows them. Knives, and to some extent the noose, were more an instrument for the poor; drowning, for the rich, unless (the possibility is strong) the high number of rich drownings only reflects doubt attaching to the manner of death and hence an opportunity for government inquisition. The matter would bear further investigation, but the message of the two small samples, as far as they go, is clear.

What of messages from the continental court registers? Forty-five of our French cases give the required information on method, and yield the profile in Figure 25. It is abnormal. But when it, too, is broken down by gender, as in Figure 25(b), its most conspicuous anomaly can be attributed to men; in particular to two men who jumped to death and others who (allegedly) died by self-neglect after fights, swelling the 'other' category against the use of

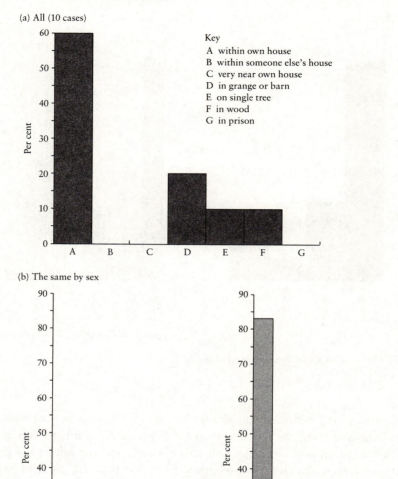

(a) All (10 cases)

Per cent

Key
A within own house
B within someone else's house
C very near own house
D in grange or barn
E on single tree
F in wood
G in prison

(b) The same by sex

Per cent

Male (4 cases)

Per cent

Female (6 cases)

26 Main methods analysed (French legal sources): hanging

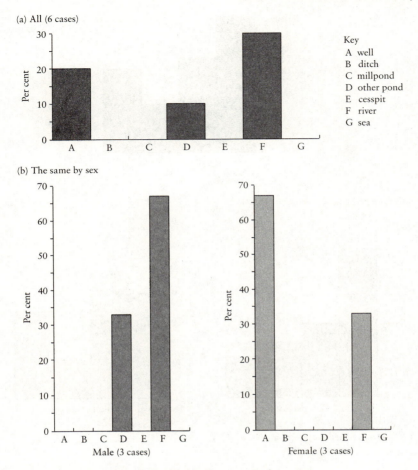

(a) All (6 cases)

Key
A well
B ditch
C millpond
D other pond
E cesspit
F river
G sea

(b) The same by sex

Male (3 cases)

Female (3 cases)

27 Main methods analysed (French legal sources): drowning

blades. Hanging, furthermore, is for once more of a male resort than a female, thanks, again, to those poor bread-earners who figure in Letters of Remission. If we try to analyse the French cases of hanging and drowning by place, as was done to the English, the dossier gives samples of 10 and 6 cases respectively, with the required information on method. The reader may be surprised that I have thought it worthwhile to represent this information in a diagram, but its display in a way identical to that used for the larger English sample has, I hope, a useful purpose. A visual comparison of Figures 26 and 23 (for hanging) and of Figures 27 and 24 (for drownings) reveals how constant these patterns appear to have been, with the women

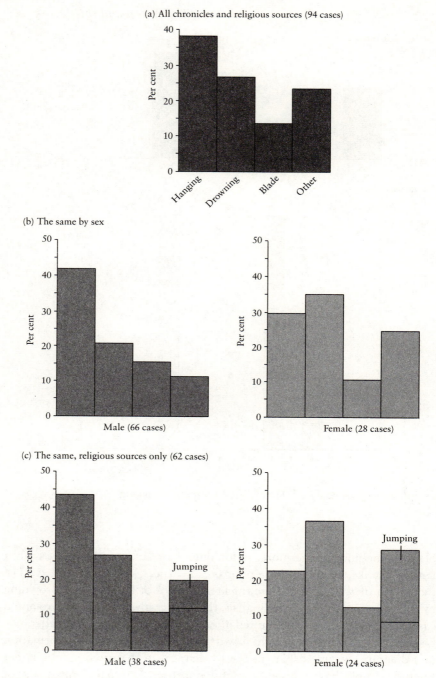

(a) All chronicles and religious sources (94 cases)

(b) The same by sex

Male (66 cases)

Female (28 cases)

(c) The same, religious sources only (62 cases)

Jumping

Male (38 cases)

Jumping

Female (24 cases)

28 Methods of suicide: chronicles and religious sources

hanging themselves at home and drowning themselves in the family well, and the men going further afield for both operations.

The German legal sources describe the methods of only 45 per cent of their cases, and all are cases of hanging. This would in itself produce a freak profile, and our first that cannot be explained away. But a hypothesis that might explain it would be analogous to that earlier for German distinctions of gender: over-determination. That is, if the method was indicated in all suicides by hanging, and not in others, the percentage dying by that method —the only one open to an estimate—would be remarkably normal, at 45 per cent. This is again mere hypothesis, but has that recommendation.

After looking at the various categories of legal document we come lastly to literary descriptions of suicide, and of suicidal thoughts and acts. The methods involved are described in 94 cases. They are shown in Figure 28. Its shape is abnormal. The abnormality is, however, quickly tracked down, if the total is broken by gender, to the female sex. For the men are normal, as shown in Figure 28(b). Do we learn here something about medieval women? More probably we learn something about attempted suicide and about sources. For if the calculation is based on religious sources alone— hagiography, *miracula*, and *exempla*—we find that the swollen categories on the female side were drowning and jumping (Figure 28(c)), and many of these were mere attempts. But then again, these spectacular methods, or non-methods (if they failed), may just reflect literary taste. The stories were told, after all, for edification: there had to be catastrophes, and especially those from which right-minded people were saved; but there were limits, and the thought of a woman's hanging herself was, once more, just too repulsive to contemplate. Such things just did not happen, or not in the thought-world of hagiographers. They departed in this particular, we are now in a position to say, from real life.

The last main set of data, found here and there throughout our sources and inviting quantitative analysis, concern the months, days, and times of suicide. What were the dangerous times?

TIME

Legal records are in this respect the most promising kind of evidence. In fact they differ sharply from category to category, as to the inclusion of dates and times. As a rule it is the courts of first and of last instance that include them, for different reasons. In England that leaves out the Eyre, which normally only allows us to guess the date of suicide within a few years, a fact which gravely reduces the English dossier. Things are no better in France. In the French legal dossier we owe most chronological details to the Parlement registers. So we know the month in 15 cases, the day of the week, and the approximate time, in only 7. The German dossier is even less forthcoming: 6 or 7 of the records give us the month of the suicide, 6 the day, and 4 the approximate time of day.

Month

But the investigation so far has had to be content with little, so it is worth setting out here again what little there is. Of the English dossier from legal records, 67 suicides can be dated to a month. I have omitted from all these figures the suicides of criminals on the run or in prison, on grounds that their suicides are likely to have been precipitated by circumstances peculiar to themselves and less likely to be connected with seasonal or diurnal trends. Among these 67, December, April, and July represent peaks, with at least 9 or 10 suicides each. August, November, and January are meanwhile the safest months, though the progression from January to April is regular. The proportions are shown in Figure 29(a). Its two sequels (Figures 29(b) and (c)) analyse the same proportions according to gender. Women are under-represented, but this is because Westminster inquisitions, which usually recorded dates, play a large part in these data and provide no women. Despite the smallness of the sample certain features leap to the eye. The suicide boom in April, it appears, is largely women's work, as is much of the score for June. Male monopoly comes into its own nevertheless in the peak months of July and December.

Do continental dossiers corroborate these patterns? The 15 French cases and 7 German are set out in Figure 30. (One German case could have been in either December or January, so it is split.) In France, December is again the most dangerous month; and April and July again come immediately behind it. The strength of April in all three charts deserves notice. Since all the German cases here are men, I have divided only the French dossier by sex. The July score is once more a male monopoly, though the December peak is now shared equally between the sexes. None of the three charts, it may be noticed, records a single female suicide for March or October, though March, unlike October, is strongly represented among men. Since the gradient between January and April is clear in the English sources, dis-cernible in the French, and conceivable in the German, it may call for expla-nation, and would find one in the progressive dearth of food common in late winter and early spring.[12] The peak in male suicide in July may, if sig-nificant at all, similarly be explained by the agrarian conditions in that men were subjected to exceptionally long days of work at harvest-time.

[12] Schmitt, 'Le suicide', 9, noticing the same phenomenon in his own sample, attributes the poor diet of these months to ecclesiastical prescriptions for fasting in Lent. But hunger in late winter and early spring pre-dates the church.

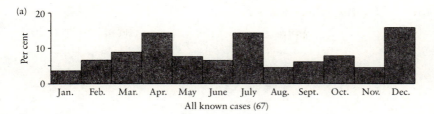

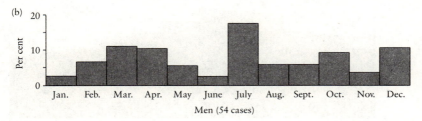

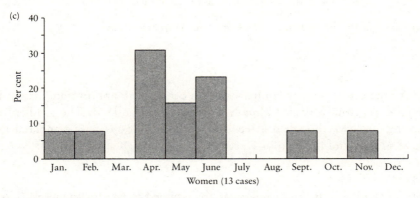

29 Time distribution: months from English legal sources

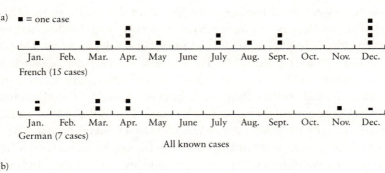

30 Time distribution: months from French and German legal sources

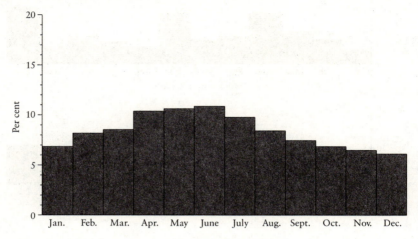

31 Time distribution: France, 1866–70 (after Durkheim, 112)

A nineteenth-century comparison has been put in appropriate format in Figure 31, from a France already drifting from the land. The gradient in spring survives, though nineteenth-century conditions have tempered the heat of July and the cold of December.

Day of the week

Sixty suicides in the English dossier are assigned to days of the week. Their distribution is shown in Figure 32 and broken down by gender in the following two diagrams. (The women are reduced in number by the same circumstance as before.) Monday is the gloomiest day, made so by men. The handful of women appear indifferent between it and Sunday, and indeed between either Monday or Sunday and most other days, except Thursday, a suicidal day off for both genders. The 10 French cases, some of which divide between two possible days, show three similarities (Figure 33). Of the 10, two certainly, and one possibly, can be put on a Monday. The certainties are both men, the possibility a woman, who may—just as if she were an English woman—equally probably have committed her act on a Tuesday. The other gloomy time in France, as in England, was the weekend, with two men on each day—or possibly one on Saturday and three on Sunday. And Sunday, we may note, was a day chosen by at least two of those Germans. Perhaps it was over-determined in that people noticed when suicide happened on a Sunday. But that too is speculation. None of our cases, finally, in any dossier, happened definitely on a Thursday. That fact alone points the contrast with

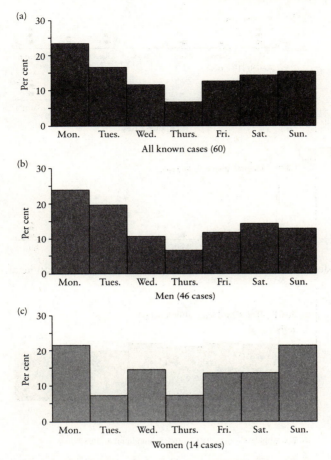

(a)

All known cases (60)

(b)

Men (46 cases)

(c)

Women (14 cases)

32 Time distribution: days of the week from English legal sources

modern findings (Figure 34), because in mid-nineteenth-century France Thursday was the worst day. The gloomy medieval Monday only ran it close. Modern America, for its part, confirms only the grim rise of Thursday.

Time of day

What, finally, of times of day? The 28 indications in English legal sources are set out in Figure 35, with the usual distinction by sex. Time was not given 'o'clock', but by the expressions I have printed on the figure. An arithmetical division of the twenty-fours hours being impossible, the 'scores' of the different times have been counted and given a corresponding position.

(a)

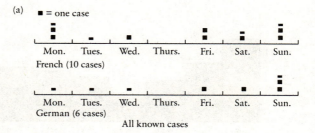

French (10 cases)

German (6 cases)

All known cases

(b)

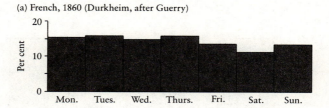

33 Time distribution: days of the week from French and German legal sources

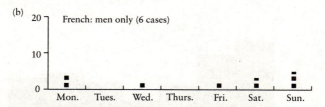

(a) French, 1860 (Durkheim, after Guerry)

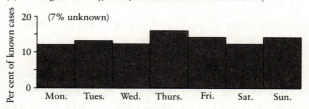

(b) Los Angeles County, 1957 (after Schneidman and Farberow)

34 Comparisons: France, 1860, and Los Angeles County, 1957

Dawn or prime (theoretically at 6.00 a.m.) figures prominently for both sexes; as does night for the men. On this reckoning alone the hours of broad daylight appear marginally safer. That impression is not overturned by the 7 French cases, nor indeed by the 4 German, 3 of which are assigned to prime or dawn. But, as Figure 37 shows, try as we may with nineteenth-century

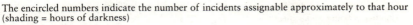

The encircled numbers indicate the number of incidents assignable approximately to that hour (shading = hours of darkness)

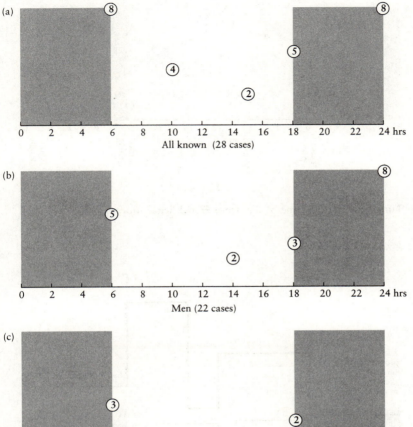

(a) All known (28 cases)

(b) Men (22 cases)

(c) Dawn/prime   Morning   Day/afternoon   Sunset/evening   Night/midnight

Women (5 cases)

35 Time distribution: time of day from English legal sources

figures to achieve a comparable profile, then, at least, the opposite seems to have obtained, in that most nineteenth-century suicide was committed in broad daylight. While that need not affect our reading of medieval data, one way or the other, it remains likely that suicide at 'unsocial' hours was over-determined, since observers were more likely to note the time.

The encircled numbers indicate the number of incidents assignable approximately to that hour (shading = hours of darkness)

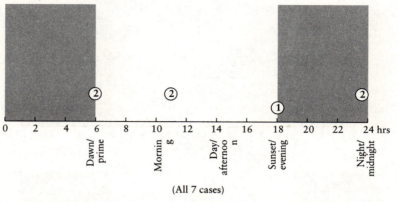

(All 7 cases)

36 Time distribution: time of day from French legal sources

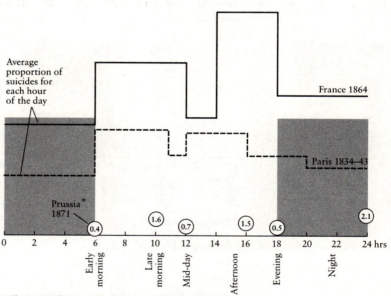

* The Prussian figures, assigned only to a time of day, have been reduced to proportions of 7 to ease comparison with fig. 35.

37 Three nineteenth-century comparisons: France, 1864, Paris, 1834–43, and Prussia, 1871 (after Durkheim, 116–17)

Conclusion

The last two chapters have served a double purpose. By comparing data from different types of document they have tested each type against the others. When all allowance has been made for the peculiar aims of each category, the result has been a degree of mutual confirmation. There was probably no type of source entirely free from bias. The uncertainty principle, native to all such data, means the type and degree of bias will never be known. But the contrary principle is also at work, namely that from the three categories much of the message is shared. No category, whatever can be said of isolated genres within it, was all bias or all fantasy. A central core in the lessons of each is endorsed by evidence from the others, evidence with quite different sources and configurations.

The discovery of this central core has been the second purpose of these concluding chapters. To attempt to summarize would be to threaten its value. The diagrams and conclusions were themselves summaries, and each has enough uncertainty and nuance already to make it dangerous to try any further summary without these vital reservations. But one general observation suggests itself at the end of this long parade. It is that, if the concept of normality is not foreign to this subject, how normal the picture has been. The data behind the portraits are too slender to invite precise comparisons with the suicide patterns of later ages; but if, again, we stick to the core, and to the 'certainty principle' present there, in the medieval as in the modern data, we are surely looking at the same phenomenon, albeit more distantly and albeit, very probably, at much less of it *per capita*.

The suicides, as individuals and collectively, have revealed a little about themselves and their act. They have revealed as much, at least, as they are going to reveal on their own. So far that is how I have treated them: on their own, cut off from all other people. *Divide et impera*. Historians have to cut humanity up into distinguishable lumps, otherwise none of us would ever know anything. But the distinctions usually dissolve if we look at them hard enough, and it is indeed a moot point whether any of the divisions and groupings are really there in reality, and not just constructs of the mental machinery we use to make sense of what our eyes blink at, the software of our cerebral computer. That humanity surprises us alternately by its coherences one day, and by its differences the next. We are forever splitting bits of it up on one criterion and principle and joining bits up on another. 'A man shall leave his father and be joined to his wife.' That does not just happen at weddings but all the time, as it does with clouds which join and separate in a windy sky.

So I make no excuse for having put the suicides all on their own so far. They asked for it. Nor, now, and despite the apparent turnaround, need there be an excuse for setting out another plan, which is to start joining the suicides up again with everyone else and gather the two toothed halves of humanity together again. Were suicides really, after all, a different genus from the people they ran to the granary to get away from and whose cruelty they may have cursed for their despair? Was the bankrupt another species from his creditor, the frustrated wife from her errant husband, the prisoner from the torturer? All these people stayed alive and could not but be affected by the suicide. How they were affected, through how many shades of hostility, bafflement, or pity their emotions passed, makes no small subject: a big enough subject, at least, to bid us bury the wand that has conjured up the ghosts of suicides, abjure this particular necromancy, and give our eyes and thoughts a rest before embarking, after that rest, on the second major aspect of our subject—the reactions of the survivors.

Appendix:
A Register of Recorded Suicidal Incidents

The Purpose of the Register

The Register serves three functions. First, it provides an index to suicidal incidents mentioned in this volume, and simultaneously removes the need for some cumbrously technical footnotes, especially in respect of incidents in English legal sources. (An English case from an Eyre or coroner's related roll can be traced alphabetically through its county, while the relatively few cases from Westminster rolls are ordered by an ad hoc arrangement which explains itself.) Page numbers in bold type are given for those incidents to which precise reference is made in this volume. (The roman numerals 'II' and 'III' apply to incidents to be mentioned in volumes 2 and 3.)

The second function of the Register—a function prior in point of time—was to serve as basis for the statistical exercises in Chapters 15 and 16. After all that was said there (p. 351) about random selection it would have broken the rules to add cases once the counting had begun, so cases omitted from the count have been marked here in distinctive type and with an asterisk. Any small anomalies found in the counting may be due to my use, during the count, of sources and tables too bulky to print, to modify or nuance the summary information given in the Register.

The third function of the Register concerns the future. As explained in the Introduction (p. 18), the discovery of medieval suicides has necessarily been cumulative, the work of many scholars cooperating over two centuries. Short of overburdening the Register I have tried to indicate its main debts to existing published work and I repeat here its debt to the scholars named in the Preface (pp. viii–ix)—a debt especially heavy in respect of English rolls (over half of whose entries are the discoveries of Dr Henry Summerson). A cooperative creation, the Register has also a cooperative purpose in its third function as a work of reference. Like all works of reference it will be subject to additions, and no doubt to correction—not to say elucidation (my efforts to streamline its semiotics risked introducing errors). Despite shortcomings I hope the Register, by its mere existence, will be of use to students in the many related fields.

Key to Symbols

The extreme left-hand column identifies the source in which the incident is recorded. Where explicit mention of the incident occurs in the present volume the page number is given in bold numerals. (The bold roman numerals II and III indicate that mention will be made of the case in *The Curse on Self-Murder* or *The Mapping of Mental Desolation*). Abbreviations for sources are explained in the Bibliographies on pp. 469–80.

The second, 'Name' column identifies the incident. Many of the common words have been shortened (for instance, 'found', 'took', 'bishop', 'abbot' as 'fd', 'tk', 'bp': most are shortened on that principle). The longest section, that taken from English legal sources, has its own scheme of abbreviations, which affect the proper names

Alexander, Geoffrey, John, Henry, Peter, Richard, Robert, Roger, Thomas, and William, while the abbreviations wf/, hu/, dr/, sn/, indicate 'wife (husband, daughter, son) of'. (The oblique stroke / is otherwise used to separate symbols or indicate alternatives), 'Found', 'took', 'house', 'bishop' and 'abbot' are similarly compressed. In the fifth ('Wealth') column 13s 4d is rendered 13^4. In the same section # indicates a serial number, alternatively given as 'No.' ( ) Round brackets containing a place-name indicate the Hundred for which a case is enrolled. When not otherwise stated an unpublished roll is that of an Eyre.

   Symbols used for the numbered columns (1–9) are given in the following tables. Because different categories of source yield different types of information the use of columns is not uniform. Columns 6, 7, and 9 are employed differently in the 'Legal Sources' section than in the other two. Minor changes in the repertoire of symbols also affects columns 1 and 8. These variations in the use of columns have led inevitably to the duplication of symbols (so that a suicide committed under criminal accusation can appear as 'A' in column 1 and—in Section III— as 'ac' in column 6; several more examples will be found). Strict adherence to the key should prevent confusion.

No. of column

1. Kind of Event

Parts I and III: Chronicles and Religious Sources

At	Attempt
D	Suicidal *Deed*(s) falling short of attempt, e.g. fastening a rope round one's neck
S	Completed suicide
[2S	= two suicides; ss = many]
T	Temptation to suicide, suicidal thoughts [tt = many cases referred to]
th	Threat of suicide or strong *thought*
[ ]	Suicidal character of event is conjectural
*	Strong or overwhelmingly fabulous character of incident

Part II: Legal Sources

Completed suicide by a person:

A	under criminal accusation
Ap, As	in prison, in the stocks
F	in a 'frenzy' or 'mad'
m	who has just murdered someone (fy = victim was member of family; ch = victim was child)
re	(signs of) repentance before death
S	expressly said to have acted sponte sua, 'de certain propos', 'of sound mind', etc. (a 'hardened' verdict)
U	Badly sick ('unwell')
W	Wounded
*	Court's verdict has apparently been softened.

*I	The same, specifically from 'suicide' to 'misfortune'.
[ ]	indicates an element of doubt as to the suicidal character of the act
N	indicates an attempted suicide
X	indicates an abortive charge of suicide

2. Method

B	Beating head etc. against wall
D	Drowned c = cesspit* d = ditch r = river w = well (h = at own home) p^d = pond m = millpond s = sea
F	Fire
H	Hanged h = own house* n = near own house o = someone else's house p^r = in prison g = grange or barn w = wood t = tree on its own
hs	Horse
J	Jumping from a height
K	Knife, sword etc. f = in field
P	Poison
S	Self-Starvation
T	Mutual Throttling (= one case in 'Religious Sources')
W	Resisting treatment for Wound

* place-symbols can apply to any method

3. Sex

Male or Female

4. Age and (family) status

Age

Y	Young (translating *iuvenis*, etc.)
O	Old
ch	Child
60 [etc]	The stated age

Family or religious status

ch	has young child or children
xch	has no children
cl	clerk
dr	has one or more daughter
fy	has some kind of near family
Jw	Jew
md	married
mo	is mother (has at least *had* children)
re	religious (monk, friar, or nun)
sn	has one or more son
si	definitely single

| ww | widow |
| * | other noteworthy feature |

5. Wealth

B	Bankrupt (had wealth and lost it)
b	goods (*bona*) are mentioned
D (d)	Destitute (d for a child)
M	Of Middling wealth
N	Noble [I have noticed none other than apparently rich nobles]
kt	Knight [*miles*; a similar remark applies]
O	Same as 'D' (in valuations in English rolls)
P	Poor†
r	real estate mentioned; xr = 'no real estate' (stated)
W	Wealthy†

† In English legal sources which value the suicide's chattels the valuation is given in the form 13^4 for 13s 4d. Where estimates are necessary 6s 8d has been used as the lower limit of the 'Middling' category, £1 as that of the 'Middling to Wealthy', and £5 as that of the 'Wealthy'.

6. Motive or Judicial Circumstances

Parts I and III: Chronicles and Religious Sources. Motive

The motives explored by religious story-tellers hardly submit themselves to summary but I have given them these rough categories, often overlapping:

ac	accused of some wrong (including non-criminal)
am	amorous misadventure
au	disgruntlement with some sort of authority
be	bereavement
dc	demoniac
de	religious *desperatio*
di	disease
df	defeat
dg	disgrace (public)
fa	fate, inexorably driving subject to suicide
je	jealousy
le	leprosy (as motive)
lo	financial loss (cf. 'B' in col. 5)
ma	mad
pr	in prison
r	recklessness in war
sh	shame (private)
su	'suttee': woman following her beloved
tr	*tristitia* or unexplained melancholy
vi	in atmosphere of violence
vy	protection of virginity (à la Lucretia)
wd	wound

Part II: Legal Sources. Judicial Circumstances

a) In English Legal Records: How *found*? These records often record who was the body's 'First Finder', and I have noted these as:

hu	husband
wf	wife
sn	son
dr	daughter
fr	father
mo	mother
br	brother
fy	some undefined member of family
wm	undefined woman
nb	neighbour

Judicial irregularities have also been noted in this column, as:

†	first finder is dead
bu	body buried without the coroner's knowledge
co	body not seen by coroner
di	put in ditch (*fovea*)
fi	('fields') body expressly excluded from churchyard (x = exhumed)
hi	a positive attempt has been made to hide the act
*	other judicial irregularity

b) In Continental Records: **Disposal** (= Dpl): how was the suicide's body (house) disposed of? (French legal records are more informative on this side of the question, less on how the body was found)

B	Burned
D	Dragged
E	'Exposed'
f	buried in fields (aux champs etc, incl.—in Germany—Schindegraben)
H	Hanged
J	justicié (general term for some of the above)
no	positive evidence that body was not 'justicié'
R	Ravaire: the house was destroyed

7. Type or Month

Parts I and III: Chronicles and Religious sources. Literary Type

P	Punished: the suicide is represented, ex- or implicitly, as punishment for opposition to a saint (in the manner of Judas' suicide)
S	Saved: the subject is saved from suicide, or suicidal temptation, or in some cases brought back to life.
S*	A suicide's soul is saved.
T	A strong narrative 'type' (of some other sort) is present.

[Among 'Chronicles' this column can also be used to indicate the month, identified by two letters as below]

Part III: Religious Sources. Month.

Indicated by two letters, as: Jl, De

8. Day/Time

Days of the week are indicated by two letters, as: Th, Sa

Times of day are shown as

pr	At the time of or before Prime (around dawn)
mg	During the morning
dy	Broad daytime in general
nn	Noon
af	afternoon
eg	Evening (at or near Vespers)
su	Around or after sunset
nt	At night
mt	At or around midnight

[In 'Chronicles' and 'Religious Sources' this column is also used, on the rare occasions when the information is known, to indicate the month or season of the incident]

9. Other Feature

*	An irregular feature of a case, eluding category
D	(Mainly in 'Chronicles' and 'Religious Sources', though I have noted the usage elsewhere, with an asterisk, on the rare occasions it is used). The Devil is expressly said to have instigated the suicide.
dl	delay (of a day or two) between act and death
mu	murder suspected at some stage, rightly or wrongly
rr	religious rites administered before death
xrr	religious rites were expressly omitted
we	bad weather superstitiously associated with suicide
th	body expressly removed by hole dug under threshold
cr	body cremated
ri	body thrown in river
br	body expressly put in barrel and then thrown in river
dr	body expressly 'dragged'
hr	body dragged expressly by 'horse'
g	body ends on or near gallows
of	body ends in offal pit
wa	body ends in waste ground
cd	cart used
pu	punishment mentioned (in cases of attempt)
st	split tradition

(*English Legal Sources only*)

*ju	Jurors have lied about the value of a suicide's chattels
co*	An irregularity in the coroner's conduct or report

I. CHRONICLES

The incidents are arranged in approximate chronological order

Page of this book	1 Ev	2 Md	3 Sx	4 A/S	5 Wth	6 Mv	7 Ty/Mth	8 D/T	9 F
*35, 48–9 Edwin, half-brother of Athelstan 933 [William of Malmesbury]	[S]	D	M		N	ac			st
*62 Norsemen in battle 925 [Flodoard]	SS	K	M						
116–7 Demoniac who crit'd Ansfrid c.1000? [Alpert of Metz]	S	H	M	re		sh?	P	nt	
7 n. 12, 80 Heretic Leutard in Champagne 1000 [Radulf Glaber]	S	Dw	M	md	P	ac	(P)		
49–50 King Henry IV 1093 [Bernold]	At		M		N	df			st
72–4 Thomas, skipper of White Ship. Thurs 25 Nov 1120 [Orderic]	S	Ds	M			ac			
117–8 Rich wife crossed ch'yard c.1120? [Simeon of Durham]	S	K	F	md	W	ma	P		
71–2 Lucas de la Barre, arrested 1124 [Orderic]	S	B	M			vi/ac			
*67–8 n. 60 Defeated youth seeks to jump May 1127 [Galbert of Bruges]	At	J	M			vi/ac			
59 Q. Blanche on K's death Sun 8 Nov 1226 or soon afterwards [Mousket]	At		F	ww	N	be			
*62 English soldiers in defeat 1245 [Matthew Paris]	SS	D	M						
80 Ct Regnauld of Boulogne 1227. *Circa Pascha* [Alberic of Trois Fontaines]	[S]		M		N	pr			
*242 n. 27 Raymond of Brouelles of Cahors, in Tiber 1237 [Guilhem Pelhisson]	S	D	M			ac			
50–3 Henry Hohenstaufen Tues 12 Feb 1242	[S]	hs	M		N	ac	Fe	dy	st
118–9 Pisan lay-brother 1243–7 [Salimbene]	S/A	Dw	M	re					
*82–4 Pier della Vigna Chancellor to Frederick II 1249 [Dante]	S	B	M			pr			st
*65–6 Jacques de Castel at Damietta. Feb 1250 [Joinville]	[S]	R	M		N				
53–5 Ezzelino tore bandages off 1257 [Rolandino etc.]	[S]	W	M		N	df/ac			st
*67–8 Manfred of Hohenstaufen at Benevento 25 Feb 1266 [Villani]	[S]	R	M		N				
115 Wife of Benedict Young 1274 [Dunstable Annals]	S	Dw	F	md					*
115 Servant of John Durant 1283 [Dunstable Annals]	S	Dwh	M		P				di*
*68 Lano da Siena at battle of Toppo 1287 [Dante Commentary]	[S]	R	M		B				
*111 Man and wife are tempted. 'Long before' c.1290 [Bury St Edmunds] See Sect. III: Religious Sources									
74–5 Henry de Bray, Escheator 1290 [Bartholomew Cotton]	S	Dr/B	M		B	ac		d	
*84–5 Rucco de' Mozzi Florentine banker Before 1292 [Dante Commentary]	S	Hh	M		[B]	lo			
114 Walter de la Haye, Escheator 1295 [Dunstable Annals]	S		M		[N]	sh?			*
*85 Lotto degli Agli Florentine judge 1291–1300 [Dante Commentary]	S	H[h]	M		N	sh			

Page of this book	1 Ev	2 Md	3 Sx	4 A/S	5 Wth	6 Mv	7 Ty/Mth	8 D/T	9 F
111 A *Straussmair* Mon 25 Apr 1300 [Augsburg]	S	H	M						we
55–6 Corso Donati 1308 [Villani and others]	[S]	hs	M		N	ac			st
*67 n. 60 Raoul de Nesle at Courtrai [Flemish chron]	[S]		M			vi			
*81 Jacques de Lors, aide to Enguerrand de Marigny Early 1315 [St. Denys]	S	Hp^r	M	md		pr			
75–6 Bérengar Cotarel, Marshal of Avignon [*Lives of Benedict XII*] June 1340	S	P	M		N	ac/pr			wa*
112–3 A schoolmaster 1342 [Venice]	S	H	M		P				we
*65 John the Blind of Bohemia [26 Aug 1346]	[S]	R	M		N				
60 Maria Coronel, quasi widow 1353	S		F	(ww)	N	vy			
*81 Pregnant widow of rebel 1382 [Juvenal des Ursins]	S	J	F	ww	P	vi/be			
100–1 A poor sick man 1411 [Regensburg]	S	H	M		P	di			ri
III A priest, cause of bad weather 1417 [Zürich]	S		M	cl					we/ri
*90–1 Saviozzo, Sienese poet 1419 [Gambino of Arrezzo]	S	K	M	60		pr			
100 Bartholomew Sultzer, rapist 1437 [Augsburg]	S	K	M			pr			
111 Woman who *von sinnen kam* 1439 [Basle]	S	J	F			ri			we/ri
*107 A 'pinner', on Palm Sunday 9 Apr 1441. [London chron]	S	H	M				Apr	Su	ca/wa
67 n. 60 Defenders of Constantinople 1453 [Doukas]	SS	J	M			vi			
104–5 Ulrich Huen, greedy peasant Sun 6 Apr 1455 [Easter Day] A *Veme* execution? [Donaueschingen]	[S	Hw	M		M		Apr	Su/dy	*]
*109–10 Anthoine de la Barre Attempt in Chateau-Porcien Late Oct 1461 [Chastellain]	A	K	M	N	R		Oct		
*108–9 A Clogmaker in Valenciennes 1 Nov 1461 [Chastellain]	S	H	M	60/md	M		Nov	Su	
*241 Abbess at Lomello, nr. Milan, after affair with friar. 1463? [Letter]	S	Dp^d	F	re		dg			
*239–40 Dannino dell'Acqua Commander of the Guard at Lodi. June, 1468 [Letter]	S	Hh	M		W		Ju		
101 *Küsterin* at New Hospital Sat 4 Mar 1469 [Nuremberg] Cf. Sect. II (Germany)	S	H	F	re	M	lo		Sa/pr	cr
*240 Piattino, prisoner of Galeazzo Maria Sforza Mon, 29 May 1469, 10.00 p.m. [Letter]	At/Ac	Hp^r	M			pr		Mo/nt	
101 Goose-thief, in prison 1477 [Nuremberg] *Cf.* Sect. II (Germany)	S	Hp^r	M			pr			cr
101 A Nuremberg schoolmaster Sat 17 Feb 1478 'on the Babenberger Weg' 'Not burned'. Payment to bishop [Nuremberg]	S	K	M					Sa	*

Page of this book		1 Ev	2 Md	3 Sx	4 A/S	5 Wth	6 Mv	7 Ty/Mth	8 D/T	9 F
102	'Bishop of Strasbourg' Jan 1484 [Metz]	S	H	M	cl	[N]				br
102	Monk at Sainct Pierremont Jan 1484 [Metz]	S	H	M	re					
***77–9**	Cardinal Andreas Zamonetič 12 Nov 1484. Basle [Glassberger]	[S]	Hp^r	M	cl/re					st/br
102	Jehan Robert, hostellier Thurs 2 Dec 1484 [Metz]	S	Hg	M	65	W	?			th/dr
102	*Ung compaignon*, at dinner. Dec? 1484 [Metz]	S	K	M					ev?	dr
104	Jehan Ruxay, *compaignon* Wed 3 Feb 1485 [Metz]	A	H	M	Y		am			pu
***103**	Godair, notary, rescued June 1485 [Metz]	At	K	M						D
***107**	Roger Shavelok, tailor 1491 [London]	S	K	M		W				
112	A monk of Heilsbrunn 1497 [Nuremberg]	S		M	re				nt	we
	Thomas Southwell, canon of Westminster [London]	[S]		M			pr			
	'Whore [*unrein weib*]' Mon 28 Jun 1509 [Lucerne]	S	H	F		O		Jun	Mo	we

II. LEGAL SOURCES

Source Page of this book	Name	1 Ev	2 Md	3 Sx	4 A/S	5 Wth	6 Fd?	7 Mo	8 D/T?	9 *?

A. ENGLAND

1. Eyre, Assize and Coroner's Rolls (by County, alphabetically)

Source Page of this book	Name	1 Ev	2 Md	3 Sx	4 A/S	5 Wth	6 Fd?	7 Mo	8 D/T?	9 *?
Beds Eyre 1227 [No. 432, p. 162]	Alice, wf/Simon de Cumewith Verdict: *infortunium*	*I	Hg	F	md					
Beds Eyre 1247 [No. 614, p. 155]	Gervasius Duninge		Hh	M	md	18°	sn			
Beds Coroner, 1273 [No. 197, p. 86] 161	Gfy le Wodeward, Thurleigh Fri, 28 Apr 1273. Bedridden.	UF*	Dw	M	Y?	⟨9²⟩	mo	Ap	Fr/pr	
ibid. [No. 277, p. 114] **152, 163**	Emma le Bere, Yelden (Stodden) Tues, 15 Jun 1316. With 'boleax'	Fm/	Hh	F	md		fr	Jn	Tu/fy	
Beds Eyre 1287 JUST 1/12 m24	Wm Godhewen of Barford (Barford)	S	Dp^d	M		4°				
m26	Roger Dolbe of Silsoe 20 Nov 1283–19 Nov 1284 (Flitton)	S	Hh	M	md?	2^6	wm		*ju	
m33d	Richard Oliver (Bedford)	S	Hh	M	si?	£5–10°	nb			
m34	John Peronel of Clophill 20 Nov 1279–19 Nov 1280 (Redbornstoke)	S	Kf	M		20°				

Source Page of this book	Name	1 Ev	2 Md	3 Sx	4 A/S	5 Wth	6 Fd?	7 Mo	8 D/T?	9 *?
m35 **263**	Isabella la Sevene Cf. Sect. I, Chronicles, above, Dunstable Chronicle 1274	S	Dwh	F	[md]	£2–o°		ju*		
m35d **263**	Hny de Letteburne, servant Cf. *supra*. I. Chronicles, Dunstable, 1283	S	D[h]	/M		4°				
*Beds Gaol Delivery, 1292 **171–2**	Benedict le Vilour See CIPM III below									
Berks Eyre 1241 JUST 1/27m32d	Rd de Burton of Schulston (Farringdon)		K	M	md	25°	sn		*ju	
Berks Eyre 1248 [No. 864, p. 343]	Hny Sebarn, South Hinksey Appletree in his garden		Hnt	M	md/ch	£4	dr			
Berks Eyre 1261 JUST 1/40m19	Rd de Nattegrave, in bad fever; Thames (Shrivenham)	UF	Dr	M		o				
m20	Walter de Lambourne, chaplain; 5 days. (Lambourne)		K	M	cl	7⁶				
m23 **164**	Wm le Marchaunt. The parson, a MA, tk (undervalued) chattels Weston (Roeberg)	F	K	M		65⁴				*ju
m23	Rbt, chaplain of Leckhampstead Parson tk chattels. (Roeberg)		h	M	cl	29°				
m27d **157**	Gfy sn/Rbt, suspect thief In bp's prison (Sonning)	A	Kpʳ	M	Y?	o²²				
m28 **154**	Rbt de Burton, cash-thief from a grange of Beaulieu (Farringdon). Died in prison; bailiff dragged him to gallows & was fined.	A	Kg	M		60°	co/ bu			*
m28d	Agnes Potte Geyelhurst (Reading)		Hh	F		16⁸ /r	fy			
m29d	Jn le Reve, in own shop [selda] (Reading burgh)		Hg	M		55°				*
Berks Eyre 1284 JUST 1/48m28d	Alice Parfet, Lambourne (Lambourne)		Hh	F		ro²				
m32	Gfy Ingelram, Hamsteade (Bucklebury)		h	M		o⁵				*ju
m34d	Joan Salomon de Kenyngton, in Cherwell (Hormer)		Dr	F		o	co			*
m41d	Rgr Colsmyth (New Windsor burgh)		Dr	M		o				
m45	Rgr le Whyte de Whytel, Tyelhurst (Reading)		Dr	M		o⁵				

Source / Page of this book	Name	1 Ev	2 Md	3 Sx	4 A/S	5 Wth	6 Fd?	7 Mo	8 D/T?	9 *?
m46d **150**	Jn le Mascun, Wallingford (Wallingford burgh)		Dr	M		22^4				
Bucks Eyre 1232 JUST 1/62ml	Syward le King of Wenge (Cottesloe)		Hh	M		10^5				
m8d	Walter de Hanlegh (Wycombe vill)		Ho	M		o				
Bucks Eyre 1241 JUST 1/55m20 **152, 162**	Humphrey le Leper; linen sheet (Burnham). Fd by forester.	UF	Hw	M		o	co			mu*
m20	Jn, the parson of Hucham; own bed, own belt. Fd by housekeeper? (Burnham)		(Hh)	M	cl	o	(wf?)			mu*
m27d	Jn George (Mulshoe)		K	M		4°				
Bucks Eyre 1247 JUST 1/56m39d	Nigel the shepherd (La Mue)		Hh	M		o^{18}				
m46d	Mary, wf/Osbert le Tanur (Wycombe vill)		Hh	F	md	o	hu			
Bucks Eyre 1262	Matilda, dr/Agnes (Aylesbury)		Hh	F	Y?	o^{12}	mo			
[Bucks Eyre 1272: JUST 1/60. No suicides]										
Bucks Eyre 1286 JUST 1/66m6	Rd del Wylt (La Mue)		K	M		10°	bu			*
m7d	Rd Cres, at Dagenhal (Yardley)		Dhw	M		7°				*
m9d	Agnes, wf/Ptr Sutor (Brill vill)		Kh	F	md	o				(mu)
Cambridge Assize/, Eyre 1260 [p. 2]	Augustus Smith of Whaddon		Hh	M	md	23°r	wf			
ibid. [p. 8] **164**	Walter sn/Fulk	F	K	M		£5–3^3				*
ibid. [p. 24]	Agnes, wf/Rd Gernegem		Hh	F	md	o	dr			
ibid. [p. 30] **164**	Rbt Hardwine of Shepereth	F	Dm	M	md	44^{10}	wf /co		nt	
ibid. [p. 35] **152**	William Wullmare of Shep'th		Hh	M	md	23^8	dr			
ibid. [p. 36]	Agnes of Burton		Dw	F	si?	o^{10}				
Cambridge Eyre 1299 JUST 1/96m71d **177**	Gillian, wf/Reginald de Neweton Witchford. 2nd coroner: *infortunium*	[*I]	Dd	F	md				pr	*co
Cambridge Coroner JUST 2/191m6v [Hu 34]	Johanna Papys Fri, 29 Apr 1345		D?	F		o		Ap	Fr	*
Channel Is. Eyre 1309. JUST 1/1161m18 **159**	Geoffrey le Cu; 'long ago out of poverty & grief'		H	M		o				
Cumberland Eyre 1278 JUST 1/131m6d	Rd Crelbeyn Hutton-in-the-Forest		Hh	M		18°	†			*ju

Source Page of this book	Name	1 Ev	2 Md	3 Sx	4 A/S	5 Wth	6 Fd?	7 Mo	8 D/T?	9 *?
*Derbyshire Eyre 1330–1 JUST 1/166 m2#17	Clemens le Bevver at Staunton [Harold] *gratis ... quodam laqueo*	S	H	M	md?	0^2	wf?			
*m7#8	Thomas of Twyford, at Findern *gratis ... supra quandam trabem*	S	Hg	M		16^6	†			
*m11#12	Margerita, dr/Rbt de Hesley Gratis ... *in quadam fonte* Horsley?	S	D	F	Y?	0	†			
*m14#16	David of Breadsall *gratis ... super ramum cuiusdam quercus.* At Duffield. Oak and noose valued at 6d.	S	Ht	M		0	†			*
*m27#1	Alicia, wf/Wm sn/Hny, gratis Youlgrave. Beam and rope valued at 2d.	S	H	F	md	0				
*m28d#4	Alicia, dr/Wm sn/Elia de Capella *gratis ... cum quodam rasorio.* Boulton. Razor 1d.	S	K	F	Y?	0				
*m28d#13	Margareta dr/Wm Blayn *gratis ... de quodam laqueo* Fairfield	S	H	F	Y	0^4	br†			
*m30d#21	Rd sn/Radulf de Berde *gratis ... cum quodam gladio.* Hayfield.	S	K	M		7^7				
*m36d#23	Wm Barfe, *gratis ... in grangia* Matilde [his wf]. Alfreton.	S	Hg	F	md	0^{15}				
*m39d#7	Jn le Sawer of Breadsall *furore detentus gratis ... infortunium* Derwent	Sl*	Dr	M			†			*
*m40#6	Hny Boost, *gratis,* Derwent	S	Dr	M		0	†			
Devon Eyre 1238 [No. 18, pp. 11–12]	Jn le Heine, in Lupitt (Axminster)		Hh	M	md	o	wf			
[No. 180, p. 36]	Baldwin de Cumbe (Budleigh)		Hh	M		o				
[No. 242, p. 45]	Sara wf/Joel de Paseforde died 8 days after wounding herself (Black Torrington)		K	F	md					dl
[No. 244, p. 45]	Seilda ww/Jordan de Kilward (Werrington Manor)		H	F	ww	14°				
[No. 327, p. 59]	Walter de Dureville, Plympton (Braunton)		H	M	md	£3–8^8				
[No. 346, p. 61]	Ranulf de Allgate		Hh	M		o^5	co			
[No. 383, p. 65]	Hugh le Cat, in Callebrige wood (Witheridge)		Hw	M		2°				
[No. 619, p. 102]	Wm sn/Hny de Breulishille in Breazle wood (Lifton)		Hw	M		37^8				
[No. 762, p. 122] **178**	Rbt le Pestur, Exeter City		Dr	M	md	o	wf/co			

Source Page of this book	Name	1 Ev	2 Md	3 Sx	4 A/S	5 Wth	6 Fd?	7 Mo	8 D/T?	9 *?
Devon Eyre 1244 JUST 1/175m42	Baldwin de Burton, Ermington Hospitallers' land: no *murdrum*	U	Dp[d]	M			†			*
m42	Anon woman fd in Colcis' grange Rd Colci & wf arrested, freed		Hg	F		o	bu			*mu
Devon Eyre 1249 JUST 1/176m37d	Hamelin le Bunehere, Tamerton Attached by x & y who are in mercy		Hh	M		r2°				
m39	Heloise, ww/Nich de Fonte, Sorley		Hh	F	ww					*ju
m40d	Hny le Waleys, Bishopsteignton		Hnt	M		ro[4]				
m41d	Gilbert Duninge, 'in Eggebrien hollow', Wanford		H(w)	M		4°				
m43	Rbt de Castello, 'Whiteley wood', Winkleigh		Hw	M	fy	1°	br			*ju
m44	Clarice de Parkham, in hse of Ralph the cook [= finder], Shebbear		Ho	F		o[8]				
m44	Mariota la Lavendere, in sea nr. Alwinton		Ds	F		2°				
m44d	Gervase de Suhtham, in own cowhouse, Witheridge		Hng	M		50°				*ju
Devon Eyre 1281–2 JUST 1/186m6d	Wm de Lanton, in Winkleigh Vills amerced for 'not coming'		K	M		24°				*

m7;
  [& JUST 1/1569
  = *veredictum*]
  151
	Alexander Bagherel/Barganal, Coldridge [*veredictum*] Tues 29 Sep 1276		Hh	M		o$^{1/2}$	wf	Se	Tu/
									9 mg	

*m7
  [& JUST 1569
  = *veredictum*]
  172–3
	Wm le King, sn/Matilda la Quene 26 Mar 1278. While harrowing nr. R. Taw. Later: clerk convicted of murdering Wm, got benefit of clergy.	X	K	M	Y?		mo	Mr	Sa/
									dy
										*

m7	Walter Ballard, N. Tawton		Hh	M		32[4]				
m8	John Lyllyng, Torrington		Hh	M		3[1]				
m8 **176–7**	Henry le Rede, Priestacott Villein. Lord (& wf?) hid body		Hh	M	md	38[2]	†co			*
m17	Alice, ww of Geoffrey Hellebore Lamerton		?	F	ww	5[3]				
m21d	Hny de la Thorne, unguarded, sick Plympton harbour	U	Ds	M		o[4]				

Source / Page of this book	Name	1 Ev	2 Md	3 Sx	4 A/S	5 Wth	6 Fd?	7 Mo	8 D/T?	9 *?
m23	Rd de Caswell of Kerswill Stanborough		Hn	M		76^{10}				
m23 and m27 [registered twice]	Wm Prophete de Hurbenesford Haberton. Wf 'did not come'		Hh	M	md	6^{7}	wf/co			*
m24	Rbt le Kyng [Roll only records receipt from sheriff]		H	M		0^{12}				
m24d	Wm de la Combe, in R. Dart	S	Dr	M		$21^{9½}$	†			*ju
m25 and m36d [registered twice]	Hamelin de Medenecumbe		Ds	M		$19°$				
m25d	Gfy de la Crusce of Kingswear	S	H	M		14^{1}				
m28d	Imenia, wf/Rd le Palude, de Merlewyll, Ringmore		Hh	F	md	$8°$	hu			
m28d	Joan, dr/Alan de Shofestone Apple-tree in fr's garden		Htn	F	Y	0^{18}	fr			
m29	Rbt Ballard, Fardelwood		Hw	M		$5^{1/2}$				
m33d	Hny Barum, Cotleigh		H	M		8^{8}				
m35	Rbt, servant to the parson, Bradninck; knife in stomach; tk 3 days to die	S	K	M		0^{18}				
m37	Jn Hog, in Otterton field		K	M		0				
m41d	Gunnild, wf/Ptr de Kareswelle, Cliston. R. Clyst. Chattels left 'bec she had a husband'	F	Dr	F	md		(sn)			*
m42 **175–6**	Hny the beadle of Byadetone, Ottery St Mary;		Hh	M	cl/ md	60^{6}	wf&sn co/bu			*ju
Dorset Eyre 1268 JUST 1/202m23	Anon suspect thief, gaoled after arrest by Corfe royal warrener	A	Hp^{r}	M		6^{8}				*co
Dorset Eyre 1280 JUST 1/206m22	Ptr Teste, in 'chamber' of Jn de Vautort (Combs Ditch)	(A?)	KH	M		0^{15}				
m22	Rbt Schurs *furiosus*, Whiteway. Stomach; instant.	F	K	M						
Dorset Eyre 1288 JUST 1/213m29	Jn de Wast de Ramescome Body washed by sea to next hundred	S	Ds	M	md/ fy	12^{6}	sn			*ju
m30d	Wm de Bonhegh, corn-thief Pimperne; starved in stocks	As	S	M						*
m36d **157**	Hny Ideleschethe, ox-thief Brownshall; in stocks, with hidden razor	As	K	M		$4°$				*co

Source / Page of this book	Name	1 Ev	2 Md	3 Sx	4 A/S	5 Wth	6 Fd?	7 Mo	8 D/T?	9 *?
Essex Eyre 1227 JUST 1/229m14d	Mabel, wf/Gfy sn/ Godwin, Nigra Nutelegh (Witham)		Hh	F	md	6°				
m15d	Mabel, wf/Ralph de Stofton (Uttlesford and Freshwell)		Hh	F	md		hu			
m16	Wm the goldsmith of Tucstede (Dunmow)	F	D	M		6°				
m16	Joscelin Prat of Pleshey (Dunmow)		H			o^{20}				
Essex Eyre 1235 JUST 1/230m2	Ptr Kalbe de Widumeford in Stour (Lexden)		Dr	M		o				
m5	Rd le Bret, oak in Taxted park (Dunmow)		Ht	M		o				
m6	Katherine, wf/Hugh de Lacton (Waltham)		K	F	md		hu			
[Essex Eyre 1248. JUST 1/232. No suicides]										
Essex Eyre 1254 JUST 1/235m4	Jn de Fulstrate, Gt Perendon (Harlow).		Ddh	M		13^{4}r				*
m8	Jn Reynald, Dunmow		Hh	M		12^{2}r				*
m9d	Walter Beche of Godchestre, suspect thief. Ongar castle moat? (Ongar)	A	Dd	M		18°				m
m13d	Jn sn/Pain		H	M	Y?	o				*
m23d	Wm Werme, in Walter the chaplain's fishpond (Writtle)		Dp^{d}	M		o^{18}				
Essex Eyre 1272 JUST 1/238m48d	Isabella Alday, in High Estre (Great Easton?) (Dunmow)			F		4°				*
m48d	Rbt le Wode, ditch in Tilkey grange. Abt tk chattels. (Dunmow)		Dd	M		o^{3}				*ju
m49	Ingenulph de Bosco; tether; Little Dunmow (Dunmow)		H	M		16°				
m52	Jn sn/Rgr de Writele found *quasi inedia exstincto* (Beacontree & Havering)	[ ]	S	M	Y?					*co
m52 **174**	Rd le Bedel; tether; Estham (Beacontree & Havering)		H	M		o	†			*co
m54 **150**	Wm sn/Gfy de Donemowe; undressed first (Ongar)		Dc	M	Y?	o^{4}				*ju
m56d	Jn the weaver's sn, St Osyth's (Tendring)		H	M	Y?	3°				*ju
Essex Eyre 1285 JUST 1/244m1d	Those Loucon of Colchester Suthwelde vill (Chafford)		Dp^{d}	M		o				*
m3	Gervase Rose, in bed; Theydon Gernon (Ongar)		Hh	M		o^{12}				
m3d	Margery, wf/Rbt Atteberne; Chigwell. Had hu 'so no chattels'. (Ongar)			F	md	o				

Source / Page of this book	Name	1 Ev	2 Md	3 Sx	4 A/S	5 Wth	6 Fd?	7 Mo	8 D/T?	9 *?
m6d **150**	Matilda la Rede Lawling. (Denlre)		Dc	F	sn	4^6	nb			
m6d **150**	Wm Sweyn de Claketon; Burnham (Dengle)		Dc	M		$4°$				*ju
m10	Cecilia de Manewedene (Clavering)		H	F		o				*
m15d	Jn de la Fonteyne de Henham Sibil (Hinchford)		Hh	M		$2°r$				
m16 **150**	Rd le Webbe, Finchingfeld. (Hinchford)		H	M		o^9				
m21	Elyas, sn/Sarra, Little Braxted (Witham)		H	M	Y?	o				
m24	Margery, dr/Adam Hugheline (East Uttlesford)		Ho	F	Y?	o^{13}	fy?			
m25d	Sarra, dr/Rbt the clerk Willingale (Dunmow)		D	F	Y?	o				
m34	Cristiana, dr/Simon de la Pike Epping vill (Waltham). 'Had no chattels as she had a husband'		K	F	md	o				
m41d	Martin the butcher; knife Colum Conister		Kh	M		$r12°$				
m45d	Matilda, wf/Wtr le Chareter (Colchester)			F	md	o^6				
m48d **164**	Rbt de Porta de Estwode, Eastwood (Rochford)	F	K	M		$16°$				
m49	Rd the chaplain of Chelmeresford		D	M	cl	3^4				
Essex Coroner JUST 2/33a m15d#14 **37, 159**	'Willelmus' [illeg.]. Pleshey. Mon 1 Nov 1389. Maple. Not at own home. *Spontanea voluntate . . . se suspendit cum corda. Infortunium* [only] in margin.	S*/?I	Ht	M		o		No	Mo	
Gloucs Eyre 1221 [No. 22 p. ••] [Maitland 2, 488]	A suicide. *Loquendum* re confiscation.									*
Gloucs Eyre 1287 JUST 1/278m58d **156**	John Ace, horse-thief Severn, en route for Glouc. gaol	A	Dr	M		$10°$				*
Hants Eyre 1236 JUST 1/775m16	Hny le Mire 'because sick'. Had previously bequeathed chattels. Pastrow.	U	Dw	M						
Hants Eyre 1249 JUST 1/776 m25d **154**	Wm Lanval, at sea, after killing Wm Gilberd	Am	Ds	M		o				

Source Page of this book	Name	1 Ev	2 Md	3 Sx	4 A/S	5 Wth	6 Fd?	7 Mo	8 D/T?	9 *?
Hants Eyre 1272 JUST 1/780m24 [cf. Wilts 1280–1, JUST 1/1001m40d]	Wm le Taverner of Merleberge In well in Southampton burgh. [Widow of Wm 'le Vineter', apparently the same, complained in 1280–1 of confiscations]	S	Dw	M		o				*
Hants Eyre 1280–1 JUST 1/786 m20 **154**	Jn Ban, pursued for murder to Sulvermere wood (Shipton Bellinger).	Am	Kw	M		ro[15]				dl
Hants Eyre 1280–1 JUST 1/789 m36	Wm Ruffus, a chaplain, *in church* of Holy Trinity, Southampton		H	M	cl	o	*			
Hants Coroner JUST 2/155 m7#3	Matilda wf/Wm Chaunt[ed] Wed 30 Apr 1382 In Wallop Priorissae	S	Hg	F	md/ dr			dr	Ap	We/su
m20#1 [Post 224]	Alice wf/Jn Bronde/ Brand. R. Test Thurs 11 May 1391	S	Dr	F	md	o				Th/pr
m21#1 [KB 27/529 Fines m10#1] [Post 221f]	Jn Pavy, Woodcote Mon 30 Dec 1387 In 'wood called Prestwode'	F*	K	M		£4				Mo/su
*JUST 2/157 m2#1 [Post 223]	Wm Dene. Set fire to Winchester gaol. Adjudged *felo de se*. Sun 30 Jan 1384									
Hants King's Bench 27/529 Fines m8d#12, 13 [Post 222] 1392–3	Rchd Jay of Christchurch *qui se voluntarie interfecit* Chattels worth £4–10° or £5–11°?	S		M		£4–11°				
Hereford Eyre 1292 JUST 1/303m67 **160–1**	Wm le Enveyse, burgess, Kenford river	U*I	Dr	M					nt	
Hunts Eyre 1286 JUST 1/351A **158–9**	Rd le Vicarre, indebted reeve Husebank (Toseland)		Dr	M		20°				*
Kent Eyre 1244 JUST 1/359 m29#1	Alvreda of Reyherse (Leukfield)		Hh	F	md	4[6]				
m29#12	Agnes wf/Thos Carpenter		Hh	F	md	6°	sn			
m29#15	Aldritha atte Sole (Codsheath)		H	F		6[8]				
m32#26	Emma dr/Widen in Ostdenham		H	F	Y?	o	mo			
Kent Eyre 1255 JUST 1/361 m40#2	Alice Leveney of Northfleet		Hh	F		18[3]	bu			
m43#13	Wm Drippe (East Malling)		Hh	M		35°	bu			
m43#19	Juliana dr/Philip Segar		Hh	F	Y?	3°	bu/co?			
m44#6	Hny Shanke (Haythorne/ Holeborne)		Hw	M		30°				
m55#10	Eglentina, wf/Simon of Luping		Hh	F	md	12[3]				

Source Page of this book	Name	1 Ev	2 Md	3 Sx	4 A/S	5 Wth	6 Fd?	7 Mo	8 D/T?	9 *?
m47#16	Thos de Hedingworth (Street)		Hw	M		43^2	bu			
Kent Eyre 1293 　JUST 1/376 **150**	Alice dr/Hugh In own house, Mepham borgha		Fh	F	si?	$8^{4\frac{1}{2}}$				
m28d	Mabel wf/Theobald atte Nore Medway, Le Deene borgha	F*I	Dr	F	md		hu			
Kent Eyre 1313–14 　JUST 1/383 *m4d	Alice, wf/Gbt Gonne of Wenderton	S	Hh	F	md	0				
m4d 　[*Yr Bks of Ed II*, p. 137]	Agnes, dr/Thomas Rolf of Womenswould		Dw	F	Y?	5^6				
m17 **156–7**	Walter Colehod, robber; Smethe; gaol in Stoke burgh. Stomach, 4 days	Ap	K	M		$0^{9\frac{1}{2}}$				dl
*m17d	Leticia, wf/Jn atte Rode (Calehill)	S	Dc	F	md	0	hu			
m24d	Thos Payn, thief of corn from grange of Christchurch, Cant., at Chart, on imminent arrest	A	K	M		10^{10}			dy	*
*m27d	Alice, mo/Jn le Clerk, Birchilton Alone.	S	Dw	F	sn	0	nb			
*	Jn Sparkeling, alone in bed at home. Beam and ladder. Northburgh St. Peter	S	Hh	M		0	nb			
*m28 **150–1**	Adam de Chenyngdam, 1300–1301 *cum gentari fecisset*, sent hsehld to work, *c.* 3rd hr, shut 2 doors; rope from carter's bed. (Byrchilton)	S	Hh	M	fy	£68–10		mg		
*m39d	Elias Catelote, Cantreworthe Alone	S	Dp^d	M		2°				
*	Alice, dtr/Wm de Suthdich By night	S	Dc	F	si	0		nt		
*	Thos de Oxerode Oak	S	Hwd	M		63^{10}	nb			
*m47	Nich Godinboure By night with knife Coroner tk garment		K	M		32^2		nt	co*	
*m47d	Hota Pynchoun	S	Hg	F		8°				
*m49d	Eldretha le Pot, alone in hse (Faversham)	S		F	si	0^6				
*m50d	Wltr atte Hale, alone in hse Shut door	S	Hh	M	si	5^5				
	Rcd sn/Miles Evelhered, aln in hs	S	K	M		10°				
m51d	Jn Robyn, beggar. Idenne in Northe borgha (Cranbrook)		H?w	M		0^6				
*m54d	Matilda, ww/Jn atte Yeldhalle, alone in chamber	S	Hh	F		31^2				

Source Page of this book	Name	1 Ev	2 Md	3 Sx	4 A/S	5 Wth	6 Fd?	7 Mo	8 D/T?	9 *?
*m58 156	Michael Pecchebroke, burglar on run after break-in	S	D	M						
*m62d	Jn Body, *amens* (Canterbury)		K	M		0				
*m66d	Hny atte Welle, alone in home (Eyhorne)	S	Hh	M		43^3				
*m66d	Ptr le Carpenter of Bromfield	S	Dw	M		$60^{8^{1/2}}$				
*m70d	Rbt sn/Guy de Aldeham	S	Dp^d	M	si					
*m78	Isabella, wf/Matthew de Stokynbery in her bakery	S	Hn	F	md					
*m107d	Joan, ww/Hrofe Gryn, bakery (Ryarsh)	S	Hn	F	ww	$14°$				
Lancs Kings Bench 27/33m5 [Mich 1277]	Margery, wf/Ptr de Brunhill *propria ducta furore*	F	H	F	md	b				*
Lancs Eyres	[No cases in Parker, 1904–5]									
Leics Eyre 1247 JUST 1/455m2d	Wm Enlefenne, in Soar. Buried by parson as pseudo-coroner (amerced)		Dr	M		$100°$				co*
m9	Edith, ww of Roger de Thorp		Hh	F	ww	$12°$	†			
Leics Coroner 1378 JUST 2/58 m8d **151, 153**	[Jn Scot, parson of Garthorp] See CPR, sect. 2 below									
Lincs Assize 1202–9 [No. 918, p. 151] [Warren, 169]	*quidam homo qui se ipsum suspendit* Elloe, Holland Before 1202		H	M						*
London Eyre 1244 [No. 46, p. 16]	Hugo of Essex *le burreler* Sun 27 Dec 1226 [I have taken it as 11th yr *of Hny III*]		K	M		o		De	Su	
[No. 122, p. 49]	*Quidam* Thomas		Dw	M		$2°$				
[No. 141, p. 55] **37**	*Quedam mulier* Matilda *Infortunium de se ipsa*	*I	Hh	F	md	$5°$				
London Eyre 1276 [No. 216, p. 59]	Simon Ferol, in W. Smithfield 'with a rope' Before 27 Oct 1270		H	M		3^1				ju*
[No.. 213, p. 58]	Alxdr Esprigonel, in house of Katherine of Westminster 27 Oct 1270		H	M		17^4				
London Eyre 1321 [I, p. 93] **169–70**	'Jone' ('from cnrs' roll')	F*	Dr	F	si?	$3°$				
London Coroner, [Roll B#4, p. 36] **22–3, 152, 162–3, 169**	Isabella, wf/Robert de Pampesworth 30 Nov 1321	UF*	Hh	F	md	o^9m	fy	No	Su/pr	
ibid. [Roll B#34, p. 60] **22**	John de Irlaunde (Aldresgate) 6 Jul 1322. Fd by neighbours.		Ho	M	si?	o		Jl	Tu/pr	

Source Page of this book	Name	1 Ev	2 Md	3 Sx	4 A/S	5 Wth	6 Fd?	7 Mo	8 D/T?	9 *?
ibid. [Roll H#18, p. 249]	Alice, wf/Henry de Warewyck, 1 Feb 1340 skinner.	F	Dr	F	md			Fe	Fr/ev	
Norfolk Assize, 1198 [II, #10, p. 2]	Agnes, wf/Wm FitzClarice	*I	H	F	md					
ibid. [II, #13, p. 3]	Leviva Tiblot	*I	H	F						
ibid. [*Norfolk 1270	Reginaldus de Puher	*I	Hg	M						
Talbot, *Medicine* 181	Rd Blofot of Cheddestan. Norwich. Tried to drown himself. Killed wf & children, tried to hang himself. Imprisoned. ⟨before 1270)]	Nm	DH	M	mfy/ch					
Norfolk Eyre 1286 JUST 1/579m69d **164**	Thos sn/Hny Robekyn Axe to foot & hand; last rites	F*I	K	M	Y					rr
Norfolk Coroner JUST 2/277m1d	Mazelina Puke de Syreforde Found at Ereford in Toftes vill on 6 May 1284		D	F		o[18]	fy			
Norfolk Coroner JUST/2/104m17 **153**	Agnes de Kirketon, Wiggenhall 4 Jan 1366. Son, no husband.	S	Hh	F	40+/ sn	2°		Ja	Su	D*
m30d **160**	Matilda wf/Jn Heyward de 9 May 1369. Edgefield.	UF*	Dm	F	24+/ md			My	We	
m35	Jn Austin de Suthreye, at 23 May 1370 Bexwell	S	Dp[d]	M	40+	6[8]		My	Th/ su	
m44, m44d **153, 163**	Leticia wf/Smn Grundlok 12 May 1365. *Tacta dolore nimia* Knife in bowels. 3 days. Confessed.	*r	K	F	26/ md	o		My	Mo	rr/ dl
m49 **161**	Jn sn/Ralph Rykkes; of Thursford; 11 Apr 1367 at Little Snoring;	UF*	Dw	M	24			Ap	Su/ nt	*
Norfolk Coroner JUST 2/105m3 15 Jul 1378 **152**	Thomas de Melles de Attilburgh on Mon 12 Jul 1378. Tk 4 days to die. No rites mentioned.		H	M	60/ md	25°	wf?	Jl	Mo	dl xrr?
Northants Eyre 1247 JUST 1/614Bm44d	Jn Torgon, sheep-thief, pursued Culeworth (King's Sutton)	A	K	M		3°				
m49	Jn le Marchaunt de Northampton Staunford (Northampton vill)		K	M		r18°				
Northants Eyre 1253 JUST 1/615m12	Alfred de Stavern, in own garden (no method stated) in Stavern.		?	M		o				
Northants Eyre 1285 JUST 1/623m2d **157**	Rd sn/Emma Talebot, burglar, Huxloe; in stocks; (abt of P'bgh)	As	K	M	Y	o[6]				

Source / Page of this book	Name	1 Ev	2 Md	3 Sx	4 A/S	5 Wth	6 Fd?	7 Mo	8 D/T?	9 *?
m11 **22, 157**	Wm Bercarius, sheep-thief, stocks. Faxton; to avoid hanging	A	K	M		9°			nt	*co
m17 **162**	Rbt de Schaldewell, canon of Sulby. In stomach, tk 8 days	F	K	M	re	o	bu			dl
m25	Rd de Donstable, town gaoler of N'ton, after prisoner escaped		H	M		o				*mu
Northants Eyre 1329–30 [p. 153; =JUST 1/635m3d]	Walter de Oleney, Brackley		K	M		o	†			
[ibid., 183]	*une femme se avoit estrangle*		H	F		b				
[ibid., 188]	*un homme ocist li mesme . . . frenet-ik & de bone memoir par foiz*	[F]	?	M		b				
[ibid., 193; =JUST/••] **155**	Jn Maheu, stole Duns Tew sheep, pursued to King's Sutton church	A	K	M						*
[ibid., 196; =JUST 1/635 m60 =JUST 2/107 m5 =Fitzherbert 324] **163**	Asselot, dr/Wm Eliot *en frenesie . . . par fethes* 11 Jun 1307	F	Dwn	F		7[8]		Ju	Su	*
Northants Coroner JUST 2/106m9 **153, 155**	Robert Aunfley, in family of pig-thieves. Undele, in Abt's courtyard; axe & knife. 21 Nov 1317.	A	K	M	Y			No	Mo /dy	rr
Northumberland Assize 1256 [p. 83] **23, 25**	Rd de Newton, *capellanus, mag. hospitalis S. Marg.* Westgate	U	Hh	M	cl	o	(fy)			
ibid. p. 113	Beatrix de Rodum		H	F		26[5]				
ibid. pp. 121–2 **175**	Eda, wf/Hny le Muer of Luker		Hh	F	md		sn/co/bu			*
Northumberland Eyre 1279 [p. 340]	Stephan le Moner (Corbridge)		H	M		£14-13[6]				
ibid. [p. 348] **150**	Rbt sn/Galfrid de Tratreston	S	H	M	Y?	£3-1[4]1/2				
ibid. [p. 349]	Alicia wf/Ranulph, gratis	S	H	F	md	o[11]				
Northumberland Eyre (Tynedale) 1279–80 JUST 1/649m8 [18 Nov 1279] **160**	Cecilia, wf/Jn Unkutheman, Newburgh. Pregnant; razor; had husband so 'chattels to be discussed'	U	Kh	F	md	17[3]	fy			*co
Northumberland Eyre 1293 JUST 1/653m8	Rd Lewyn le Monner de Chalton (Part beyond Coquet)	S	Dr	M		£11-12[1]				
m11	Thos sn/Huctred de Hanleil	UF	K	M	Y?	101[10]				*co
m20d	Hugh de Craven, lay brother of Newminster (Part this side of Coquet)	S	Hg	M	re	o				

Source Page of this book	Name	1 Ev	2 Md	3 Sx	4 A/S	5 Wth	6 Fd?	7 Mo	8 D/T?	9 *?
m23	Wm de Coquina, exiled after taking sanctuary in Ulgham church as thief.	SA	H	M		o				
m28d	Alxr de Rokesburgh, in R. Tyne (Newcastle).	S	Dr	M		42^8				
m28d	.Roger Tomekrel R. Tyne (Newcastle). Attacher of first-finder dead.	S	Dr	M	sn	o	sn			
m28d	Rd de Beckefeld, fuller Freneticus morbus. Stomach. (Newcastle)	*F	K	M		o^3				
m30d	Emma wf/Wm sn/ Lange, in *vicus* of Pilgrim St or Marketgate (Newcastle). Borough bailiff Jn/Heaton held inquest w.o. coroner. Gaoled, fined.	S	D?w	F	md	o^{12}	co*			
Oxford Coroner, 1322 [Rogers, p. 173]	Walter or Wm of Aslebury	U	K	M	cl	13^4	bu	Fe	Mo/mg	*
1343 JUST 2/2/129 [Salter, p. 26; Hanawalt 9] **162**	Hny de Bordesle Mar 1343	UF	K	M		o		Mr	Sa/	
1348 [p. 37] **161**	Jn Finke of Eton (Osney)	U*I	Dc	M				Jl	Su/mg	
JUST 2/135#15 [Hammer 10 n. 35; Hair 15f] **160, (163)**	Master Jn Forest Sat, 30 Nov 1387	U	Kh	M	cl			De	Tu/pr	
Oxford Eyre 1285 JUST 1/705m5d	Alice Gerland Langtree; beadle ?embezzled chattels		H	F		6^1				*
Rutland Eyre 1286 E 368/61 m21 **23**	Nicholas Horn, *freneticus*, Luffenham, belt	F	H	M		6^8				*j
Salop Eyre, 1256 [No. 487, p. 197] **151**	Dulcia, wf/Llewelyn		Hh	F	md		bu			
ibid. [No. 798, p. 276]	Rd, sn/Reginald de Upton	F*I	K	M			bu			
ibid. [No. 580, p. 393] **150**	Henry de Onyebur'		Dr	M			bu			
Salop Eyre 1272 JUST 1/736 m27	Philip of Northampton, monk, cut throat in Wenlock priory (Found by fellow-monk)		K	M	re		[fy]			*
*m31	Juliana de Stapleton		K	F		0				
*m40d	Edith widow of Ford		H	F	ww	0^{12}				
*m48	Hilde widow of Hny Malede in R. Corve	S	D	F	ww	15^4				

Source / Page of this book	Name	1 Ev	2 Md	3 Sx	4 A/S	5 Wth	6 Fd?	7 Mo	8 D/T?	9 *?
Salop Eyre 1292 *JUST 1/739m83	Jn Heryng (Nordley)	S	Dc			0				
Salop Eyre 1292 *JUST 1/741m1d	Jn Bythebroke, Buledon Cut throat with knife under a fence		K	M		55^8				
*m6d	Rbt Russel of Leegomery		M	K		54^4				co*
m16	Rbt sn of Lawrence de Moklynton, sheep-thief, fell on knife when pursued (Bradford)	[A]	K	M		o				
*m17d	Gonnilda widow of Adam, sn of Wm reeve of Upton		Hg	F	ww/ dr	0	dr			
*m19	Rcd sn/Rd Hervy, Hughly fields (Statterdon)	S	Dc	M	fr	2^6				
*m28	Isolda wf/Everard de Eaton In grange, shut door, beam		Hg	F	md	0	hu			
*m38	Cristiana, ww/Wm Brun of Cruckmeole		Hh	F	ww	0				
*m40d	Thos Pelliparius (Halesowen)	S	H	M		56^4				*
Salop Coroner JUST 2/142 m3#4	Jn sn/Wm le Shepherd Had *bovicola*. Drowned at Hadley [Thur 5 Feb] 1360: 'Thurs after S. Agatha' 34 Ed III. 5 Feb was a Thursday in 1360. (Inquest was on 3 Mar).	S	D	M		2°		Fe		
*m4d#4	Edw Wallicus de Kolsesel (nr. Mkt Drayton) [Sat 1 Oct] 1362	S		M		2^6		Oc		
*m5#4	Rcd of Daunton Fri 23 Jn 1363. In Severn.	S	Dr	M	si?	0		Ju	Fr	
[JUST 2/143	No cases]									
[JUST 2/144	No cases]									
JUST 2/145 m2#1	Jn Aleyn, in pond at Hales Wed 4 Apr 1403	S	Dp^d	M		13^3		Ap	We/pr	
m3#1	Malcolm le Baxter de Salop Sun 21 Apr 1387. Severn. Had grain etc., plus £4–6^8 in silver	S	Dr	M		£8–10°		Ap	Su/nt	
*JUST 2/146 m5d#3 153	Alice wf/Jn sn/Jn of Crenehull Attempt. Sat 24 Apr 1394† *Per tentationem diaboli.* Sutton Maddock, Severn. Inquest is on Alice's dtr who drowned trying to save her mo. No verdict or punishment. [†HS reads 'St. Martin' not 'St. Mark' & makes date 14 Nov]	A	Dr	F	md/ch		Ap	Sa	D*	

Source Page of this book	Name	1 Ev	2 Md	3 Sx	4 A/S	5 Wth	6 Fd?	7 Mo	8 D/T?	9 *?
JUST 2/147 m3#7	Jn Grunge Mon 14 Sep 1394 Water (of 'Blakende') was deodand.	S	D	M				Se	Mo	*
JUST 2/148m4#1 **37**	Isabell Atkys. In Meole, at Monkforest, Shrewsbury. *Per infortunium* Wed 4 May 1401.	S	D	F	md	o	hu			
[JUST 2/149	No cases]									
[JUST 2/150	No cases]									
JUST 2/151m2d#1	Jn Daras of Doddington Gave all his property away by a *carta* on 24 Nov 1407. [Sat 10 Mar 1408]	S?	H	M		o		Mr	Sa	*
*Salop. Crim. Inqn 1308–9, C 144/35 **158**	Wm de la Brokhouse, shepherd, stole sheep. Those who arrested him are tried for homicide. Threw himself from bridge.	A	Dr	M						*
Somerset Eyre 1243 [No. 753, p. 229]	Adam Kade		K	M		46^8	co			*
ibid., [No. 805, p. 240]	Jn Levine of Radeclive		Hh	M	md	2^6	dr			
ibid., [No. 1043, p. 288]	Hny le Clerk of Castle Cary (Catsash)		Hh	M	md/cl	7^7	dr			
ibid., [No, 1235, p. 321] **150**	Rbt Brat		H	M		o				
Somerset Eyre 1280 JUST 1/759m25	Wm de Wedmor, vicar of Chewton		Hh	M	cl/md?	3^{40}	co/sns?			*
Stafford Eyre 1227	Adam de Hethecote, sheep-thief	A	Kp^r	M		$[6^6]$				
Stafford Eyre 1293 JUST 1/806m4d **156**	Thos de Skene, thief, escaped en route from prison	A	Dr	M		$3^{41/2}$			dy	
m22d **160**	Hny de Barton, bedridden chez Agnes Lotrix de Lythe, Lichfield	U*I	Dd	M						
Suffolk Eyre 1286 JUST 1/827m5 **173**	Clement Hund. Revenge after fight Beccles, 1277–8. With chisel.		Kh	M		o^8			(dy)*	
Surrey Eyre 1235 [No. 387, p. 387]	Cristiana, wf/Wm de Langhurst		H	F	md	o				
[Surrey Eyre 1241.	JUST 1/869. No suicides]									
Surrey Eyre 1255 JUST 1/872m32	Felicia de Winton (Farnham)		Dw	F		4^{11}				*ju
m38d	Chelewye de la Crane of Lingfield (Tandridge)		H	F	md	31^6				mu
Surrey Eyre 1263 JUST 1/874A m26	Agnes la Russe, axe, hospital of Thos the Martyr (Southwark burgh)	F	K	F		7^9				*co

Source / Page of this book	Name	1 Ev	2 Md	3 Sx	4 A/S	5 Wth	6 Fd?	7 Mo	8 D/T?	9 *?
m27	Sibyl, dr/Reginald de la Salda Nutfield (Reigate)	F	Ho	F	Y?	o	bu			*
m29 **170**	Gilbert de la Mare of Esher Coroner: suic. Eyre: *infort.* (Elmbridge)	[F*I]	Dr	M						*co
m30d	Andrew the chaplain (Geodley)		Dr	M	cl	3°				
m30d	Rd Heved; chapel of All Saints, Chertsey		H	M		o^{32}				
Surrey Eyre 1279	Jn Staci, a baker, Croydon vill (Wallington)		H	M		8°				
m57 **160**	Rd Payn, diseased, Reigate vill (Reigate burgh)	U*I	Dw	M						*
m58	Alice de Thurne, Dorking vill (Wootton)		H	F	si?	^{12}				
Sussex Eyre 1288 JUST 1/932m8	Wm Potel Hermitage nr. Seaford		H	M		o^8				
m25 **22**	Wm, chaplain of St Olaf's Chichester		H	M	cl	57°				
Warwicks Eyre 1232 **149**	Ailwin de Tachebros (Kineton)		?	M		28°				
[Warwicks Eyre 1247.	JUST 1/952. No suicides]									
Warwicks Eyre 1262 JUST 1/954m52	Anon (illegible) (Hemlingford)	F	D	?		b				
m53	Gunild de Bordesle, with veil in thalamo (Hemlingford)		Hh	F	md?	42°				
m57 **160**	Hny sn/Rd, seriously ill, Avon (Knightlow)	U	Dr	M	Y?	18°				
m57 **160**	Alice dr/Hny de Liltington. (Knightlow)	U	D	F	Y?	2^6				
m57d **150**	Gfy a la Broke, Leamington vill (Knightlow)		Hh	M	md	$r4^6$	sn			
m60	Jn Barngy, Warwick (Warwick burgh)		Hh	M		5^7r				
Warwicks Eyre 1285 JUST 1/956m35	Wm de Wodehay, in mother's home, Berkeswell (Hemlingford)		Ho	M		2^1				
m39d	Jn, vicar of Claverdon (Barlichway)		Hh	M	cl	30^8				*ju
m41 **173**	Walter, earl of Warwick's groom in fight with Hugh de Salopa (Kineton)		K	M		o^6				mu*/ ju
m41d	Rbt de Hayles, own grange (Kineton)		Hg	M		3°				
m45	Jn Tredegold		H	M		33^6				*
Warwicks Crown Pleas 1306										
*JUST 1/966 m3d	Rcd de Belgrave, chaplain Sat 3 Aug 1303	S		M	cl	$5^{2\frac12}$		Au	Sa	

Source / Page of this book	Name	1 Ev	2 Md	3 Sx	4 A/S	5 Wth	6 Fd?	7 Mo	8 D/T?	9 *?
*m5	Rgr de Schulton 1304–5	S		M		18^{11}				
*m5d	Rcd Tredcole of Oulton 1302–33			M		3				
*m6	Rbt the carter 1303–4 of Claverdon, *in quadam infirmitate calidi morbi qua detentus fuit*	U		M		0				
*JUST 2/148m1 Westmorland Eyre 1256	Jn Winson	S	D	M		0		Thr		co*
[JUST 1/979 Westmorland Eyre 1278–9	No cases]									
JUST 1/983 m21	Wm sn/Adam of Colby	S	D	M		33^4				ju*
[m21d	Rd of Kirby, later adjudged accident]	*I	[K]	[M]						*]
m22	Peter de la Rawe	S	H	M		£2–8^3				
m22	Humphrey de Kenger	S	H	M		4^6				
Westmorland Eyre 1292 JUST 1/988 m2d	Ivo del Hil de Wynton 'from a beam ... with a rope'	S	Hh	M		0^6				
m4d	Hny del Wra, in R. Lune	S	D	M	md	0	wf			
m10	Cecilia wf/Walter, Gilbert's man (Appleby)	S	K	F	md	$0^{3^{1/2}}$				co*
Wilts Eyre 1249 [No. 4, p. 153]	Rd le Despenser of Cricklade		K	M		£12–0^7				
ibid., [No. 153, p. 181] **150**	Simon of Cheldrincton		K	M		9^6				*
ibid. [No. 458, p. 239]	Margery la Grasse of Alwarbyrh		Hh	F		3^0				*
ibid. [No. 524, p. 250]	Rbt the Chaplain of Harreham		Hh	M	md/ /cl?	$40^{1/2}$	sn			
Wilts Eyre, Civil Pleas, 1249, [No. 183, p. 72]	Robert Oysel; held virgate worth 5s p.a. from parson		?	M		r				
Wilts Eyre 1280–1 JUST 1/1001m8	Gilbert de Cumbe, *medicus*, on his cart at home (Cawden).	S	Hh	M	*	£14–6^9				*
m10d **156**	John Doget, in Avon, resisting arrest for thefts (Bradford).	SA	Dr	M		0				*
[m40d	Wm le Vineter: see Hants 1272]									
Wilts Coroner JUST 2/193m1d#4	Roger Taillour, in East Street, Malmesbury. *Circa horam nonam* Tues 22 Dec 1338.	S	K	M		0		De	Tu/af	
JUST 2/194m1#1	Axdr Segyn of Fisherton *in gula ... hora matutina* Wed 25 Apr 1341	S	K	M		10^2		Ap	We/mg	
m9	Jn Candel, of Potterne Wick *gulam suam scindit ...* Sat 5 Feb 1346	S	K	M		0^2		Fe	Sa	

Source Page of this book	Name	1 Ev	2 Md	3 Sx	4 A/S	5 Wth	6 Fd?	7 Mo	8 D/T?	9 *?
m11#1	Jn le Somerter, Upton Scudamore. *Puteum* to be blocked. Tues 19 Dec 1346	S	Dwh	M	sn	36°	sn	De	Tu/nt	
m11#2	Rchd le White, Imber Sun 28 Jan 1347	S	Hg	M	fy	10°	fy	Ja	Su/eg	
m11d#2 **153**	Edith atte Valle, Dinys *In ventre sua felonice . . .* Had *misericordiam ecclesiasticam.* Sat 28 Apr 1347 [died Mon 30 Apr]	S	K	F		o		Ap	Sa	rr
JUST 2/195m13d#5 **153**	Alicia Fykays, at Odstock *extra sensum suum proprium cum uno cultello in gurgite se ipsam . . . vulneravit . . . habuit iura sua ecclesiastica.* Sat 25 Sep 1344 [died Sun 26 Sep]	SF	K	F	si?	o		Se	Sa	rr
m14d#4 **153**	Thos Whiteby, *capellanus* from South Perot, Dorset; at Barford St. Martin. *Quadam rabie ipsi Thome superveniente . . . se ipsum in ventre gratis vulneravit . . . et habuit iura sua ecclesiastica.* Mon 17 May 1344 [died Tue 18 May]	SF	K	M	cl	1⁶		My	Mo	rr /dl
m16#3 **450**	Adam Boyer, at Stratford sub Castle, Salisbury; *puteo . . . voluntarie.* Mon 10 Dec 1341	S	Dw	M		o		De	Mo	
[JUST 2/196	No cases]									
[JUST 2/197	No cases]									
[JUST 2/198	No cases]									
[JUST 2/199	No cases]									
[JUST 2/200	No cases]									
[JUST 2/201	No cases]									
JUST 2/202m2#2	Nicholas Workman, at Brixton Deverill. Midnight. *Hospitatus* at house of Thos Henper, who found him. Millpond. Wed 20 Mar 1381	S	Dm	M	si?	o?	nb	Mr	We/mt	
m2d#3 **37**	Rbt Meret. Upton Scudamore. Sat 20 Sep 1382. *De lecto . . . in aurora. Infortunium* in margin, then *felo de se* in new ink.	S	Dr	M			nb	Se	Sa/pr	*
JUST 2/203m3#4	Jn Stephens. Avebury.	S	Hh	M	fy	2°	fy	De	Sa/nt	

Source / Page of this book	Name	1 Ev	2 Md	3 Sx	4 A/S	5 Wth	6 Fd?	7 Mo	8 D/T?	9 *?
m13#1	Jn Pershut. Whetham? Calne hundred. *Pomerium silvestrum in quadam pasture sua.* [Tues 20 Mar 1380] [Doubt bec case is dated by Annunciation, wh was Easter Sunday in 1380. Day and month secure].	S	Ht	M		13°	nf	Mr	Tu	
[JUST 2/204	No cases]									
[JUST 2/205	No cases]									
Worcs Eyre, 1275										
JUST 1/1028 m2#3 [Hilton, *A Medieval Society*, 254] **154**	Sir Thomas of Hopton, knight (and robber). Had *terram liberam* worth 67^7 p.a.	A	K	M		20°r				*
m2#19	Hugh of Colecombe (Pershore)		Hw	M		0^{12}	*co			
m19#12	David, *vicarius de Depnes* (Worcester)		?	M	cl	16^8				
Yorks Eyre 1218-9 [No. 607, p. 237]	Rbt de Tadcaster (R. Wharfe)	*I	Dr	M						
ibid. [No. 672, p. 252]	Claricia de Buggeden	*I	H	F	md		sn			
ibid. [No. 937, p. 341]	Matillis wf/Adam de Thoroldeby	(*I)	?	F	md					
Yorks Eyre 1268 JUST 1/1051m19 **156**	Hugh of Burton, horse-thief, in sanctuary in St Nicholas, Thirsk	A	K	M		8^4				
Yorks Eyre 1279-81 JUST 1/1078m22d	Waldeve, ex-servant of hospital nr. Alverton		H	M		136^4				
m58	Alan the clerk of Thorneton, in parson's courtyard		Hw	M	cl/Y	15^2	mo			*j
m71	Rbt, sn/Gilbert the reeve of Useburn, at Useburn (Boro'bridge)		Hg	M	Y?	68°				*j
m72	Emma Bagge, in new ditch in Scarborough		Dd	F	md	£30	dr			
Yorks Eyre 1305 JUST 1/1108m25	Thomas Gulck of Hunmanby, at Bonyngton (Pickering) on Christmas Day.	S	Hg	M		£7-7^8	De	Sa		
Yorks Coroner										
JUST 2/215 m5#7 [Hunnisett, MC 21] **37, 153**	John Milner (Fishergate, York) Thurs, 23 Jul 1355. *Per tentacionem diaboli submersus per infortunium.* R. Ouse.	*I	Dr	M	si?			Jl	Th	D*
JUST 2/222 m11d **153**	Wm sn/Jn de Sowerby 28 Jul 1368. *Non compos mentis.* Instant. *Unconfessed.*	F	K	M	Y?	2°		Jl	Fr	xrr

Source Page of this book	Name	1 Ev	2 Md	3 Sx	4 A/S	5 Wth	6 Fd?	7 Mo	8 D/T?	9 *?
m14	Amicia wf/Jn Webster de Hornby 11 Sep 1368 Sponte (R. Derwent)	S	H	F	ww?	13°		Sp	Mo	
JUST 2/225 m7	Agnes wf/Rd Noras de Welburn 28 Jun 1372 Sponte	S	Dr	F	md			Jn	Mo	

2. Westminster Records

(a) A Pipe Roll

| 18 Henry II
p. 108, #8 | *mulier qui seipsam suspendit* 1171–2 | | H | F | | 7[1] | | | | |

(b) Inquisitions

(i) Post Mortem Inquisitions

[CIPM I and II	No cases]									
CIPM III [No. 35, p. 31	Benedict [le Vylur]. Bucks coroners to decide if he killed himself. No, murdered, 1291. Cf. Beds Gaoll Delivery, 1292: JUST 3/88 m1d, where Thos de Cokermuth is acquitted of the murder.]									
[CIPM IV–XII	No cases]									
CIPM XIII No. 261	Richard atte Gate of Smethfield, Fri/Sat, 9/10 Dec 1373. Held 8 acres & brewhouse with 3 shops. A bastard.		Hh	M	si	r26[8]			De	Fr/ Sa
Worcs IPM, [No. 34, pp. 47–8; = IPM Edward I, No. 162; Hilton, 'Peasant Movements', 135]. Web 11 Jun 1293. **159**	Adam le Yep, resisting service to Gilbert, Earl of Gloucester, in R. Severn at Clevelode, c.1292–3?		Dr	M						

(ii) Miscellaneous Inquisitions

CIM I No. 561, p. 177	Wm Shypman of St. Edmund's c.25 Oct 1253. Had rents of 9[8] p.a. in Bury St. Edmund's alone.		H	M		rM/W		Oc		
No. 1136, p. 240 **162**	Wm le Stoyl of Gloucester Late 1277	UF	K	M		£4–4[71/2]				
No. 1296, p. 377 **163**	Thos sn/Adam le Clerck 1 Sep 1282. (Claughton) 7 oxen, 15 pigs etc.	F	K	M	Y	£9–9[9]		Se	Tu	

Source / Page of this book	Name	1 Ev	2 Md	3 Sx	4 A/S	5 Wth	6 Fd?	7 Mo	8 D/T?	9 *?
No. 1384, p. 397	Jn le Chapman (Taunton) Dec–early Jan 1286	F	Dr	M	md	M/W		De?		
No. 1411, p. 402	Jn Seman (Berks); trader in hides etc; c. late 1286; Partner's stock valued at £6–15°		?	M		M/W				
No. 1767, p. 490 [cf. CCR p. 152] **162**	Wm ate Children (Borden, Kent) c. Oct 1297	UF	Dwh	M		M/W		Oc?		
[No. 2220, p. 595] [cf. CCR 518, 525] Hurnard, 162.	Hugh de Mysen (Selverton) tried to hang himself, did hang his dr, both in 'frenzy'. Before 14 Sep 1278	NFm								
No. 2261, pp. 604–5 [cf. CCR (1279–88) 218] **168**	Jn de Balnea (Micklefield, Yorks) Thur, 22 Jul 1283. Inquest found him mad and returned goods to heirs.	F	H	M				Jl	Th	
CIM II										
No. 2106, pp. 529f	Hny Pan of Scoter (Lincs) Late Mar/early Apr 1316		Dwh	M				Mr/Ap?		
CIM III										
No. 592, pp. 219f	Jn of Dilham (Norwich) Fri, 25 Mar 1365	S	D	M	40	12^1		Mr	Fr	
No. 609, p. 225 [CPR, p. 282]	Walter Page (Southwark & Surrey) Mon, 1 Jul 1364. Held bonds, farms, treasure.		Dd	M		£409r		Jl	Mo	*
No. 831, p. 314	Wm Baker of Brigge (Kent) Jun–Jul? 1362		Dw?	M		r£10–13^6		Jn/Jl?		
No. 832, p. 315 [CCR, p. 494; and CIPM XIII, No. 270; = C 258/17#26] **170–1**	Edmund Mordaunt, Turvey (Beds) Sun, 24 Oct 1372. Held half a manor.	Fm/fy	D	M	md	N/W		Oc	Su	*
No. 837, p. 316 [CCR, pp. 366f]	Walter atte Boure, Hants early Aug? 1371. Neighbour seized crops, tk down mill.			M		£20		Au		*
CIM IV										
No. 231, p. 130 **168**	Wm Sprot of Hurle, Berks Wed, 22 May 1381	F	Dr	M				My	We	
CIM V										
No. 289, p. 168	Jn Wills of Somerton (?county) Mon, 19 Jul 1389		H	M		6^8		Jl	Mo	
CIM VI										
No. 62, p. 30 [CPR, pp. 350–1]	Robert Brian, Grantham c. end of 1393. Had goods.		Ds	M		M?				

Source Page of this book	Name	1 Ev	2 Md	3 Sx	4 A/S	5 Wth	6 Fd?	7 Mo	8 D/T?	9 *?
No. 153, p. 72 [CPR, p. 184]	John Walyngham, vicar of Barowe, Leics. Wed, 22 Nov 1396		Dr	M	cl	£16–9[11]		No	We	*
No. 202, p. 94	Hugh Cok of Mokleton, Salop c. end of 1397		H	M		20°		De?		
No. 203, p. 94 [CPR, 259]	Wm Edward of Parham, Devon Mon, 13 Aug 1397		H	M		£8	Au	Mo	*	
Same entry [CPR, 259]	Rd Holstorne of Holstorne, Devon Mon, 13 Aug 1397		H	M		£13–4[8]	Au	Mo	*	
CIM VII No. 338, p. 180	Jn, sn/Thos Knight of Biddulph, Staffs. 1st half of 1406			M						

(c) Patent, Close, Memoranda and King's Bench Rolls

Source Page of this book	Name	1 Ev	2 Md	3 Sx	4 A/S	5 Wth	6 Fd?	7 Mo	8 D/T?	9 *?
*CPR 11 Nov 1378 & 27 Nov 1383 **151, 153** [E159/159, Easter *Recorda*, rot. 11, 11d; JUST 2/58 m8d]	Jn Scot, parson of Garthorpe Tue, 12 Oct 1378, c. midnight. Devil's temptation. Hands raised as if in prayer.	re	H	M	cl	£61 –24[10]	nb	Oc	Fr/ mt	D*
CPR, 1391–6, pp. 239, 266, 290 [Hunter Blair] **158**	Robert Olyver, MP (Newcastle) Feb/early Mar 1393. Had ship, big debts; ex-mayor.		D	M		W		Fe/Mr		
*CCR 1272–9 p. 473 **167–8**	Robert de Dekaston 1278. Hereford. 'Anguish'.	FU	D	M	dr	M				
Warwicks. E372/97m7 E159/37m16d 1252 [= CCR 1261–4, 1263, p. 237] **171**	[Thos de Cherlinton/ Cherleton (Knightlow); later found, through 1252 Eyre rolls, to have been murdered & his body thrown in pond at Haseley; chattels of £71.5[4] returned to help as alms for soul]									
Yorks. E159/58m7 *Communia*, Easter 1285	Emma ww/Gfy le Blunt, Scarborough Dead fr's own chattels restored to daughters	S	Dd	F	drs	£29.1[10½]				*
Rutland. E368/61 *Communia* Trinity [16 Jun] 1290	Aubrey de Whitleburgh After dinner; suspected & found by wf & household; wf bought chattels for £300.	S	Dp[d]	M	md	£243	wf		/nt	*
Somerset (Bristol) E159/70 *Communia*, Easter & Trinity 1297 **156**	John Meyon de Breyennole, gaoled in Berton of Bristol for theft, escaped. Had 2 mares & 2 foals. 1294–5	A	Dr	M		100°				*

Source / Page of this book	Name	1 Ev	2 Md	3 Sx	4 A/S	5 Wth	6 Fd?	7 Mo	8 D/T?	9 *?
*E159/159, Easter *Recorda*, rot. 11, 11d. **159**	Wm de Houby, chaplain Melton Mowbray Tue, 18 June 1381 *Cf.* the case of John Scot (Leics)		H	M	cl	£8–13³¹/₂	nb	Jn	Tu	
KB 27/529 Fines m8d#12,#13	Richard Jay	See Hants								
KB 27/33m5	Margery Brunhill	See Lancs								

4. A Treatise: A. Fitzherbert, Le Grand Abridgement (1565)

No. 244, fol. 254v [1577 edn: 217r] **164**	*quidam lunaticus* 1348–9	F*	K	M						rr*
No. 259, fol. 255r [1577 edn: 217r]	*un home* 1348–9		H	M		rW?				*
No. 301, fol. 256r [1577 edn: 218r] [= Eyre, Northants] **163**	*un home* 1329–30. Had chattels.		H	M		b				
[No. 324, fol. 256v [1577 edn: 218v] Eyre, North-ants]	*un feme*] [1329–30] Already registered in Sect. 1									
No. 412, fol. 259r [1577 edn: 220v] **164**	*quidam lunaticus* 1314–5	F	K	M						rr*
No. 414, fol. 259r [1577 edn: 220v]	*quidam non sane mentis* 1314–15	F	D	M						

5. Episcopal Registers

[The date in the left-hand column is that of the letter. Except in the first case the suicidal incident is envisaged as recent.]

Exeter, (1323)	*capellanus qui se suspendit* (in 1234–5 in diocese of Hereford).		H	M	cl	M				
*Exeter (1329) **153**	Rcd de Wydecombe, *nuper vicarius de . . . Tunstal . . . seipsum in aqua sponte submergendo*	S	D	M	cl	M				
Exeter, 30 Jan 1421	Matilda, widow of Jon Hoper of Bideford	F*	H	F		ww				*bu
Lincoln, 22 Aug 1413	Marion Westwood of Haxey		Hg	F						*bu
Lincoln, 14–28 Jun 1417	Clarice w/ Rbt Sprott of Handborough		Hh	F		md				*bu
Winchester, 29 Jan 1285	*sceleratus presbyter* (in Bath and Wells diocese?)		?	M	cl	M?			De/Ja?	

B. FRANCE

1. Abbey registers

[Bibl: see Tanon; *cf. supra* pp. 180–2]

S. Martin [*HJ* 37] **182**	*pelletier*	F	H	M			no			

Source Page of this book	Name	1 Ev	2 Md	3 Sx	4 A/S	5 Wth	6 Disp	7 Mo	8 D/T?	9 *?
S. Genev. [HJ 400] **181**	Melissent 1238		Hg	F		b	fi			
S. Genev. [HJ 399] **181**	*un home noié* 1257		Dr	M		b				
S. Genev. [HJ 400] **181**	Mehant du Molin 1266		Hh	F		br •	fi			
S. Maur [HJ 334] **181**	*quaedam mulier extranea* c.1274–8		Dw			b				
S. Maur [HJ 332–3] **181–2**	Pre Crochet /Boissiac 1274	Apm	H	M		b	DH			
S. Genev. [HJ 359] **181**	Robert de Jeclin Early Feb. 1288?			M			DH			
S. Maur [HJ 335] **181**	Ysabellete la Buffete c.1300?		H	F		rW?	DH		nt	
St. Martin [Reg. SM 223] **182**	Jehannin Charles 13 Sept. 1351	S	K	F			DH	Se	Mo/Tu?	
St. Martin [Reg. SM 228] **182**	Belon, dr/Birart Ferert[t] c. 5 Dec. 1317		Hh	F	Y?		no	De		*
St. Martin [Reg. SM]	Geufroy Goule Haubervilliers. Early Dec. 1317		Hg	M				De		
S. Germain [HJ 430] **181**	Jean Carbonnier, barber Early 1400s		H	M			DH			

2. Town registers

[Cf. supra, pp. 183–5]

Source Page of this book	Name	1 Ev	2 Md	3 Sx	4 A/S	5 Wth	6 Disp	7 Mo	8 D/T?	9 *?
Abbeville [LR, fo. 102r], Boca 80 **183**	Fremin Ibisnart Jan.–Feb. 1305 / merchant		H	M	cl	r	R			*
Abbeville [LR, fo. 84v], Boca 80f **183**	Jake Aude c. 4 June 1335		H	M		r	R	Jn		
Abbeville [LR, fo. 49v], Boca 81 Cf. Louandre 264	Woman 1329		Dr	F			HB			*
Abbeville [LR, fo. 143r/117r], Thierry 197, 200; Boca 81 **183**	Maroie Parvaise [?4–5] Mar. 1364		Hh	F			HB			
Abbeville [= Ltr of Remission] Thierry 746	Anon woman June 1373		H	F			EB			*

Source / Page of this book	Name	1 Ev	2 Md	3 Sx	4 A/S	5 Wth	6 Disp	7 Mo	8 D/T?	9 *?
Abbeville [LR, fo. 144v], Boca 82 **183**	Henri, Engl. prisoner c. Sun 17 May 1382		H	M			DH	My	Sa/Su	
*Abbeville [LR, fo. 148r] Prarond 163 **183**	Man 'né de Dosverke en Boulenois' 23 July 1384		Ho	M						
Abbeville Boca 82 **183**	A bourgeois of Abbeville 1404		H	M			DH?			*
Abbeville, [LR, fo. 256r] Thierry 282f, Boca 281–2. Louandre 265 Prarond 239–40 **183**	Raoullet Gringoire, baker of Tours Sat 28 Apr 1492		Hh	M			DH	Apr	Sa	th
*[Montreuil Louandre 264]	Woman			F						*
*Manosque Schatzmiller, 138 **184**	'Hugo'. Thief in prison, 25 Nov. 1318, p.m. Medical examination.	A	Hp^r	M				Nov	Mo/ af	*

3. Inquisition

Source / Page of this book	Name	1 Ev	2 Md	3 Sx	4 A/S	5 Wth	6 Disp	7 Mo	8 D/T?	9 *?
Limborch 33, 70f; Borst 197 n. 22 **190**	Guillema de Proaudo 'Endwid'	Ac	p	F						
Eymeric 178, 197, 200; Schmitt, 25, n. 57 **188**	Suspect of heresy	Ac		M						
MS Doat 25, fos. 11v–14v **187–8**	Bernard of Rivoli, witness to Toulouse inqn, wounds himself in prison. 1270s	AcN	B	M						
*MS Doat 27, fol. 162r 9/12 **188–9**	Pierre de Julien *may* commit suicide in prison if ...	thpr		M		re				

4. Baillis and other appellate jurisdictions outside Parlement

Source / Page of this book	Name	1 Ev	2 Md	3 Sx	4 A/S	5 Wth	6 Disp	7 Mo	8 D/T?	9 *?
191–2	Emmelina la Baironne Rheims 1326 [June or early July?]	U*	Dnw	F		W				rr*
195	Guillaume le Pelletier, thief, Lisieux 1342	A	Dp	M			DH?			*
*Bayet, 439 HLF 33, 127	Guillaume des Hayes Robert Benart 1397	S	H	M	md	b				

Eschiquier de Rouen

Source / Page of this book	Name	1 Ev	2 Md	3 Sx	4 A/S	5 Wth	6 Disp	7 Mo	8 D/T?	9 *?
*Bayet, 471	Jehan Mignot 1412	S	H	M	cl		fi			

Source / Page of this book	Name	1 Ev	2 Md	3 Sx	4 A/S	5 Wth	6 Disp	7 Mo	8 D/T?	9 *?
*Bayet, 471	Jehan Anbroys Before 1463	S	K	M	cl	b				
Rouen, [*Comptes ... Vicomté*] Floqet 1, 166	Anon. 'carried to fields' 1369 ('others')						fi			
*Bois, 181 **195**	A S. Norman peasant 'in desperation'. 1401 List of livestock sold for benefit of Chambre des Comptes.		H	M		M				
*Bois, 181 **195**	Jehan Fonterel, peasant of Cesseville, nr. Pont de l'Arche. Rich. As last. Mar. 1392			M		W				
*Bois, 182 **195**	Jean Tillart. 'In desperation'. 1413. Belbeuf nr. Rouen. Stock listed as last.		H	M		P				

5. Treatises

Source / Page of this book	Name	1 Ev	2 Md	3 Sx	4 A/S	5 Wth	6 Disp	7 Mo	8 D/T?	9 *?
Beaumanoir 2, 484 §1950f **192**	*une fame* ? c.1279–81	[]	Dw	F		rb				*
192	*quaedam vetula* ante 1313–4 [*ultra montes*]		H	F	O	b				*
192	Woman in gaol for theft c.1370–93 (Tournai)	A	H	F			B			*
Le Coq 287 q. 210	Prior of S. Croce 1373–98 (Paris)	F	Hh	M	cl		no			*
Le Coq 360 f, q. 292	*ung ... noyé*	*	D	M			no			*
Feu fo. 97r, = *Si sibi manus* §§ 54 f	*quidam* possibly as early as 1485		H	M			H			*
Feu fo. 99v, *ibid* § 78	Cathedral canon, in debt possibly as early as 1485 (Rouen; exhumed)		H	M	cl		bu/fix*			*

6. Parlement

(a) *Olim* registers [Beugnot]

Source / Page of this book	Name	1 Ev	2 Md	3 Sx	4 A/S	5 Wth	6 Disp	7 Mo	8 D/T?	9 *?
I, p. 431 **193**	*mulier Calniaci submersa* 1254 (=Chauny)	M*	D	F		br				
I, 442 **193**	*homo qui se voluit submergere* 1257	re	D	M	fy	b			rr? /dl	
I, p. 517 **192–3**	Soissons canon (Mesnil) No date		H	M	cl	b				
II, p. 135 **193**	*quaedam mulier* (Auxis, nr. Sens. No date		H	F						

(b) *Actes du Parlement* [Boutaric]

Source / Page of this book	Name	1 Ev	2 Md	3 Sx	4 A/S	5 Wth	6 Disp	7 Mo	8 D/T?	9 *?
I, 91 [No. 976]	a suicide (disputed, S. Rémi v. abp) No date?			M		b				*
I, 198 [No. 2122D] **202–6**	Philippe Testard 19 Mar 1277 Case heard by Prévôt of Paris, not Parlement	F*	J	M	100	b		Mr	Fr/ nt*	

Source Page of this book	Name	1 Ev	2 Md	3 Sx	4 A/S	5 Wth	6 Disp	7 Mo	8 D/T?	9 *?
I, 356 [No. 368*]	a woman 1279		H	F		b				
II, 249 [No. 5475]	Jean 'Caves' (Saintonge) c.1317			M		W				

(c) *Letters of Remission*

[Arch. nat., Registres du Trésor]

Series X^{la}, 5–8601 (Judgements, letters, decrees).

Source Page of this book	Name	1 Ev	2 Md	3 Sx	4 A/S	5 Wth	6 Disp	7 Mo	8 D/T?	9 *?
193–4	Denys de Blanchi Early 1367 (Ronquerolles)	[]	D	M						
197–202 Schmitt nn. 25, 31	Philippe Braque, parl counsellor 14 Apr. 1460	F*	H	M	md/ ch/50	W?	no?	Ap	Mo/eg	*

Series JJ (Royal chancery registers).

Source Page of this book	Name	1 Ev	2 Md	3 Sx	4 A/S	5 Wth	6 Disp	7 Mo	8 D/T?	9 *?
JJ 74, fo. 173r **218**	Wf/Pierre le Sage 1341			F	md	rM	EB?			
JJ 81, fo. 179v **207–8**	Isabelle Tronart, wf/ *vulperarius* of S. Germain. Apr. 1352	*	Hh	F	md		no	Ap		*
JJ 86, p. 165 **208–9**	Jacquet de Fransures Bandit taken in Jacqueerie, Summer 1358	A	Hp	M						*
*JJ 81 fo. 13rv **195–7**	Pierre le Drapier Married clerk of S. Quentin. Mar. 1381	AU	K	M	cl	b				*
JJ 81, fo. 300rv **214–5**	Guillaume de Raussart, 1352/bully	*	K	M			no			*
JJ 82, fo. 138v **215–7**	Jean Raoul, *procureur c.*1344 (=*c.*10 yrs *ante*)	W*	K	M	cl	M	no			*
JJ 82, fo. 306v **212–3**	Laurent Tellier, bully ?1344–54	W*	S	M	md		no			*
JJ 82, fo. 387vf **213–4**	Gobillard le Munier, bully. c.15 Dec. 1354	W*	W	M	md/ ch		no	De		*
JJ 130, fo. 152v **30, 225–7**	Jehan Lunneton c.4 Dec. 1387	[]	Hw	M	md/ ch	P?	no	De	We?	
JJ 146, fo. 65rv **218–20**	Jehan Massetoier, Mon 6 July 1394	UF*	Drp	M	md	P?	no	Jl	Mo/d	
Douët 2, 176; = JJ 170#154 Schmitt 23–4 n. 36 Lewis 287 **226**	Perrin le Vachier, butcher 4, 11, 18 or 25 Sept. 1418	U*	Ht	M	md/ ch	P	no	Se	Su	
JJ 171 #429 **30, 222–3**	Denisot Sensigaut. Paris baker. Aug. 1421	UF*	Hh	M	md/ ch		no	Au	dy	
JJ 172 #313 **23, 220–1**	Michelet le Cavelier, 4 July 1423 /Paris *brodeur.*	UF	J	M	md/ fy	P	no	Jl	Su/pr	
JJ 175 #392 **30, 223–5**	Jehanette Maillart, wf/ 5 Apr. 1426 /Paris *cordier*	F*	Hh	F	26md /ch		no	Ap	Fr/8 mg	

7. Other

(a) *Codified law*. No identifiable cases

(b) *Bishops' jurisdictions*

Source Page of this book	Name	1 Ev	2 Md	3 Sx	4 A/S	5 Wth	6 Disp	7 Mo	8 D/T?	9 *?
Tours **147**	Gregory IX's, *Decretals* 3, 28, 11. Late 1205/early 1206	*	JDr	F	Y					

Source / Page of this book	Name	1 Ev	2 Md	3 Sx	4 A/S	5 Wth	6 Disp	7 Mo	8 D/T?	9 *?
C. GERMANY (Alphabetically by town)										
Basle										
Hagemann 287 / Kühnel 487 / **232**	A weaving *Knecht* tries to c.s. 1425. Put in neck-iron and expelled.	At	H	M	[Y/si]					*
Hagemann 286	A wool weaver Sat 11 Aug 1498 Family can keep chattels *ausz gnaden.*		H	M	md/ch					* dr/br
Hagemann 286 n. 968 / *Urkundenb.* #16	Anon Sat 24 Jul 1456 Andreas Zamonetič. 1484. See Sect. I, Chronicles.									
Biel										
*Osenbrüggen 339	A resident of Ligerz. 1438. Bern and Biel dispute jurisdiction.		H	M						br
Breslau [=Silesia]										
Schlesische Rechte 150 / **II**	A man at 'Santen' Fri 7 Apr 1385. Churchmen asked how to dispose of body		H	M				Ap	Fr	wi
Dreiss [nr. Echternach]										
Weisthümer 335 / **233–4**	A woman 1429. Village officers cut her down		Hg	F						g
Ingelheim										
Urteile / **234–5**	Ill-treated wife at Fronheim Soon before 8 Feb 1415		H	F	md(ch)br			De/Ja?		*
Frankfurt am Main										
Rau 93 [*RB* 1391, fo. 42v] / Kühnel 480	*der sich gehenget hatte* 1391		H	M						
Rau 93 [*RB* 1391, fo. 76r]	*der sich selb erhengen hatte* 1391		H	M						dr
Rau 66 [*RB* 1404, fo. 34v] / **232**	*der sich in dem sloss erwurget hatte* 1404		⟨H⟩	M						ri
Rau 91 [*RBB* 1414, fo. 11v]	*Eynen der sich selbst erhencket* 1414. /hat	Ac	H	M						hr
*Kühnel 480	Anon 1430		H							
Rau 93 [*RB* 1441, fo. 7r] / Kühnel 480	*der sich auff dem Bruckentorm in gefengnis selber erhengen hatte* 1441.		Hpr	M						hr
Kriegk n. 187 [*BB*, fo. 71]	Anon at Soffenheim. Not *busseling* but must be *forter rechtloiss.* 1447.	At	H	M						pu
*Kühnel 480	Anon 1449. Heirs get goods.		H							th/cr
Rau 93 [*RB* 1450, fo. 54v]										

Source Page of this book	Name	1 Ev	2 Md	3 Sx	4 A/S	5 Wth	6	7 Mo	8 D/T?	9 *?
Rau 91 & 93 [BB 1450, fo. 87v; and RB 1450, fo. 54v] Kühnel 480	*Spielerhennen den alden 1450.*		H	M	[O]					hr
Rau 75 & 93 [RB 1457, fo. 47r], Kühnel 480	*den doden der sich uff dem torn erhanket hatte 1457.* Dragged and burned		Hh	M						hr/cr
Rau 75 [RB 1458, fo. 51r] Kühnel 480	Anon 1458. Man		H	M						cr
Kriegk n. 186. [BB fo. 48]	Man. Heirs *can* inherit. 1458		H?	M		b				cr
Rau 75 [RB 1458, fo. 58v]	Anon *der sich gehangen hait* 1458		H	M						dr/cr
Rau 91 [BB 1458, fo. 59r]	Anon 1458									hr
*Kühnel 480	Anon. 1464.									dr
Rau 75 [RB 1482, fo. 37r] Kühnel 480	Cristian Hennen 1482.		H	M				hr/cr		
Rau 66 [RB 1488, fo. 4r & RB 1488, fo. 69r] 232	*Stroichins hussfrauwe des schroders zu Sassenhausen . . .* 1488. *nit by/vernonfft*		H	F	md					
Rau 75 [BB 1492, fo. 73r] Kühnel 480	Krolle Henne 1492.		Hh	M						dr/cr
Kriegk 549 n. 188 [RB 1486 fol. 45b] 30, 232	Peter Becker 1486	Ac	Hpr	M	sn	W				of
*Kühnel 480 & 488	Krüll, *ein bruckentürmer* 1493	Ac	Hpr							
Rau [RB 1498, fo. 11v] Kühnel 481	*Den armen man . . . wo der nit by vernunfft gewesen were* 1498		H	M		P				dr/of
Kriegk n. 187 [BB, fo. 52]	Man tries; let off with warning *das forter abczustellen* 1498	At	H	M						
Rau 93 [RB 1498, fol. 66v] Kühnel 481	*[Der] schroder der sich selber* 1498 *erhengen hait*		H	M						dr/of
Rau 93 [RB 1498, fo. 105r] Kühnel 481 232	A Juddin, mother of Michel von 1498/ Ezonss. *Sich in dem borne uff irer gassen erdrenckt gehabt hait der Judde nichten.*		H	F	Jw/ mo				⟨Sa⟩	dr/ cr/g
Leipzig *Schöffensprüche* #205 233	A prisoner 15th century?		Hpr	M						

Source Page of this book	Name	1 Ev	2 Md	3 Sx	4 A/S	5 Wth	6 Disp	7 Mo	8 D/T?	9 *?
Nürnberg										
Dieselhorst 186, & Rosenfeld 248	N. Hagenbach 1 Feb. 1396			M						
ibid.	Hans Trager 1422			M						
ibid.	Anon. 1430			M						
ibid.	Georg Schneider 1431			M						
ibid.	Ochs Cuntz Mar. 1433			M						
ibid.	Lorenz Spengler 1434			M						
ibid. Kühnel 487	Polz Dietel 1435	⟨Acpr⟩		M						
Dieselhorst 186 & Rosenfeld 248 *ibid.*	Cuntz Vogler 18 Nov 1439			M						
Rosenfeld 248	Christ Prünsterin 1447 *Gürtlerin*			F						
Dieselhorst 186 & Rosenfeld 248; Kühnel 487	Hans von Teckendorf, thief 1447	⟨Ac⟩		M	⟨H⟩					
Dies & Ros *ibid.*	Agnes Tücher 1453			F						
Dieselhort 186 & Rosenfeld 248 *ibid.*	Anon. 4 Mar. 1469			?						
ibid.	N. Kachelofen Nov. 1469			?						
ibid.	Hermann Beck Jan. 1470			M						
ibid.	Anon. 1477			?						
ibid.	Ot Sülmeister (=Schoolmaster) 1478			M						
ibid.	Paul Ulm Dec. 1478			M						
ibid.	Anon. 26 June 1484			?						
ibid.	Gerlach Duchhester 1484			M						
ibid.	Anon. May 1487			?						
ibid.	N. Endres 1493			?						
*ibid. from Chronicle 310	*Küsterin zum Neŵen* *spital* Sat 4 Mar. 1469 Beguine, lent and lost 200 gilders] See Section I, Chronicles, above.		H	F	rel	lo		Mr	Sa/pr	
*Chronicle 350	*ein gensdiep* *In den gefenknuss.* 1477. See Section I, Chronicles, above		H	M						

Source / Page of this book	Name	1 Ev	2 Md	3 Sx	4 A/S	5 Wth	6 Disp	7 Mo	8 D/T?	9 *?
Zürich										
[*Stadtbücher* 2, 85f], Osenbrüggen 339 Schär 47. **II**	Schennis, a *pfaffen*. 1417. Exhumed because of storms	.		M	cl					*we
Schär, 47	A citizen 1422			?						
Schär, 47	A citizen 1427			?						
D. ITALY										
*Milan mortuary register **239**	Pasola de Trocazano, aged 21 8 Feb. 1480 *anima incitate passione, assumpto veneno argento sublimato*		P	F	21/ si			Fe	Tu	
*Milan mortuary register **239**	Johannina famula Magdalene de Guilis, aged 18, *semi fatua nec ex toto sui juris ... seipam ... arsenicho venenavit ... et yta propro presbitero confessa est penitentiam agens*		P	F	18/ si	P		Jn	Sa	
*Milan mortuary register **239**	Giorgio di Piacenza, aged 30 in prison of Captain of Justice *ex melanconia* 9 Sept 1488	pr		M				Se		
E. LOW COUNTRIES										
Arras										
Comptes du bailli, Espinas 751.	Jehan Prouvost dit Le Loin Just before Thurs 19 Jan 1397		Hh	M			DH	Ja	Tu/We?	
Comptes Maroire urbains, Espinas 751	Blassielle Just before Tues 18 Mar 1399		Hh	F			B	Mr	Su/Mo?	
Brabant										
Comptes des officiers criminels. Poullet 307	Magrieten van Lummen 1428–9		D	F		b	H			
Ghent										
Bouc van Memorien, Cannaert 282–4	Jan van der Stichelen, *poortere* Fri, 6 Apr 1414 (= Good Friday)		H	M	s	w?	H	Ap	Fr/mg	*
Mons										
Rég #308 Cattier 96	Woman On court decision about whether a suicide should be *justiciée* (Cattier refers to several cases from the *Registre aux plaids de la cours de Mons*)	ss		F						

Source Page of this book	Name	1 Ev	2 Md	3 Sx	4 A/S	5 Wth	6 Disp	7 Mo	8 D/T?	9 *?
F. SPAIN										
Barcelona										
*Archivo de la Corona de Aragón, Cancillería 39/166v McVaugh, 233–4	A suicide is declared 'mad' 20 Feb 1277									

III. RELIGIOUS SOURCES

Life or Miracles Page of this book		1 S?	2 Md	3 Sx	4 A/S	5 Wth	6 Mv	7 Ty	8 D/T	9 F
A. Lives and Miracles of Particular Saints										
Adalbert/Egmont 313–4	Rich man offends saint	S		M		W	sh	P		
Amand/Rouen 326–9	Demoniac woman 1107	S	H	F			dc	S	nt	D
*Anselm/Lucca 320	Sick Mantuan thinks of s. c.1090–1100?	T	K	M			di			
Bendct/Fleury 33, 303–4	Andreas' nurse stabs herself 1012–1028	At	K	F	Y	P	dg			D
Bendct/Fleury 312–3	Rapist rides on lance c.1020?	S	K	M		kt?	sh?	P		D
*Bridget/Sweden 293	Woman woos priest c.1360/70?	S	K	F			am	P		
Edmund/Canterbury 258–9	Overlain child (Ersandis) c.1240–50	D	D	F	mc		be	S	p	D
Edmund/Canterbury 258–9	Overlain child (Regina) c.1240–50	S	Dw	F			ma	S		
Edmund/Canterbury 260	Mo of girl who fell in well c.1240–50	T	Dw	F	mc		be	S	d	
Foy/Conques 319	Blinded kt seeks goats milk c.1030?	At	P	M		kt	wd	S	d	
Foy/Conques 322	Mad rustic often jumped etc. c.1030?	At	JD	M		P	ma	S		
Foy/Conques 322	Mad & murderous girl jumps c.1030?	At	J	F	Y	P	ma	S		
Foy/Conques 312	Prior Gimo's foes cmt suic c.1030?	ss	(J?)	M			fa?	P		
Frideswide 25, 330–1	Emmelina of Eddington Autumn 1179	At	D	F	Y		tr?	S	N	
*Frideswide 315–6	Son of Jew, Moses of Wallingford, 1179?		Hh	M	Y		sh?	P	nt	
Giles/Santarem III	Early temptation as novice c.1210?	T		M	re		de			
Honoré/Amiens 326	Shepherd jumps in Somme c.1060s?	At	Dr	M		P	ma	S		
Hugh/Cluny 343–4	Stephan, monk of Sauvigny 1049–1109	S	Hw	M	re		au?	*S		D
Hugh/Grenoble III	Early temptation to despair 1080	T					de			
Humiliana de' Cerchis 323	Mingard jumps in Arno 1248	At	J	F	Y		dc	S		

Life or Miracles / Page of this book		1 S?	2 Md	3 Sx	4 A/S	5 Wth	6 Mv	7 Ty	8 D/T	9 F
James the Apostle 278–86	Pilgrim youth c.1065–1081	S	K	M	Y	P	sh	S	nt	D
John Gualbert 326	Crazed man tries to drown c.1060–1073	At	Dr	M		P?	ma	S		
*Margaret/Cortona 334	Scholar hangs himself Margaret 'sees' it, cuts him down. Early 14th cen	At	H	M			tr			
260–2	Margaret's bastard son throws himself in well through poverty. c.1275	S	Dw	M	c.9	P	tr			
Mary, the Virgin *Vitas fratrum* 266–7	Noble woman left with uncle Before Gerard of Frachet wrote *Vitas, fratrum* 1260–71	At	K	F			de	S		
Vitas fratrum 266	Sinful woman eats spider Same date as last	At	P	F			de	S		
*–/Altötting 308	Man in debt, evicted 1497	T		M			lo			
*–/Eberhards-Klausen 288–9	Bridegroom jumps from window c.1492	A	J	M	md		tr	nt		
–/Laon 300–1	Thief at Totnes 1113	S	Hw	M	Y		sh?	P		
–/Rocamadour 272–4	Teased pregnant wife 12th century	S	K	F	mxc	kt	je	S		
*–/St. Gall 256	Wife with post-natal depression, c.1482	At	Hh	F	mo		tr	nt		
Melanius/Rennes 25, 257–8	Mo of boy drowned in Vilaine After 853; under abt Trisandus	D	Dr	F	mc	W	be	S	d	D
*Nicholas/Tolentino, Can. proc. 244–50	Peasant, resuscitated Thurs 24 Apr. 1320, c.3 p.m.	S	H	M	mc/ 55			S	Th/ d	D
Paul/Verdun 299–300	Dishonest abbey slave c.1090–1100	S	Dr	M	s	lo	au	P		D
Peter Gonzalez 292	Seductress threatens suicide (to St Peter Gonzalez when young. He died in 1246)	th		F			am	*		
*Peter Martyr 248–9	Woman hangs hrslf in Genoa 1316	At	Hh	F	si					
*Philip Benzi III	Woman tempted for 6 years Cured 13 Jun 1317	T	H	F						
Robert/Saleto 323	Mad woman tries to hang hslf	AF	H	F			ma			
Stephen/Obazine 314	Abbot Ebulus de Turenne 1152, Tulle	[S]	P	M	abt	N	sh	P		
Thos. Becket. 24f, 300–2	Salerna of Ifield 1170–80	At	Dw	F	c		au	S	Mo/ mg	D
Thos. Becket. 32	Woman hangs herself, saved 1170–80	At	H	F	m			S		D
*Urban V, Can. proc. 305–6	Prisoner tortured, S. Nazaire	T		M						
Ursmar/Lobbes 313–4	Baker at Lobbes, in oven c.1070	S	KF	M		P?	vi	P		D
Virgil/Salzburg 323–5	Young sceptical deacon Soon after 1181	At	KH	M	Y		dc	PS		D
Walpurgis 296–7	Killer fails to drown late 9th century?	*A	D	M			sh	*		

B. Other Religious Literature

Life or Miracles / Page of this book		1 S?	2 Md	3 Sx	4 A/S	5 Wth	6 Mv	7 Ty	8 D/T	9 F
Adelheid 44–45 III	Peasant tempted for 10 years 1330–1344	T		M	mc	P	tr	S		
Adelheid 45 III	Nuremburger long tempted 1330–1344	T		M	re		tr	S		
Ailred/Rievaulx. III	A. as novice tempted 1134 or soon after	T		M	re		de			
Anon. *Miracula & notabilia,* MS BL Add 18634, fo. 30r III	Peasant who bought clothes from man who resisted suic by daily attendance at Mass. 1274–1322?;	*S		M		P	fa	*		D
Anon. Klapper #151 Tubach 208# III	Recluse misled by Devil Middle of 13th century	*T	Hh	F	re			*		D
Anon. *Miracula undique coll.* BL Add. 15833 fol. 172v Tubach #5282 II	'St' Margaret buried as suicide 13th century									
Anon. *Miracula undique coll. ibid.* III	Merciless man, pen-knife 13th century?	*S	K	M	md	W	sh/fa			
Anon. BL Harley 1288 fo. 44 #24 Tubach #5212 III	Holy water saves Cambs man 1404	T	H	M				S		D
Anon. BL Harley 1288 Tubach #1191 Herbert 681#1 cf. 262	Woman will not confess a sin 14th cen?	S	Hh	F		r	sh?	P		
Bartholomew/Pisa 339	Jn/ Capella, apostate OFM 1210–20?	S	H	M	re		sh/dg			
Bernardino/Siena 36, 309	Gambler on 3rd attempt c.1420	S	H	M		B	lo	P		
Bernardino/Siena 36, 309	Gambler sets fire to home c.1420	At	F	M	mc	B	lo	P		
Caesarius, *DM,* bk 3, ch. 13. 335	Peter, vicar of Bonn c.1200?	S	Hh	M	cl/m		?			
Caesarius, *DM,* bk 3, ch. 14. III	Devil urges suic: unmasked c.1200–1223/4	T	Hh	M	re		tr	nt		D
Caesarius, *DM,* bk 4, ch. 40 24, 33, 337–9	Nun tries to drown herself 1222–4	At	Dr	F	re/O		de	d		
Caesarius *Ibid,* ch. 41 33, 344	Conversus 1220–1	S	Dpd	M	re		tr/fa	mg		
Caesarius *Ibid,* ch. 42 275	Young nun in love 1222–3	S	Dw	F	re/Y		am/au			
Caesarius *Ibid,* ch. 43 275	Abandoned girl in Rotenkirch 1210–1	S		F	Y		am	d		

Life or Miracles / Page of this book		1 S?	2 Md	3 Sx	4 A/S	5 Wth	6 Mv	7 Ty	8 D/T	9 F
Caesarius / Ibid, ch. 44 / **309–10**	Young gambler in Cologne *c.*1200–1210/1	S	Hh	M	A	B	lo			
Caesarius / Ibid, ch. 45 / **24, 336–7**	Baldwin, zealous convert *c.*1200–1223/4?	At	H	M	re	kt	dt		nt	
Caesarius / Ibid, bk 5, ch. 19 / **276**	Girl heretic's 'suttee' 1163, Cologne	S	F	F	Y	P?	su			
*Caesarius, / Ibid, bk 5, ch. 35 / **24**	Man jumps from tower	S	J	M			dc			
Caesarius, *Lib.mir,* / bk 3, ch. 7 / **287**	Girl saves virginity by jump	S	J	F	A		vy	*		
*Ekkehard/St Gall / **36, 340–3**	Wolo [of Kyburg?], restive young monk, jumps Abbot Notker's time (971–5?)	S	J	,	re					Drr
Gerard/Frachet / **290–2**	Seductress threatens suicide (to 'Dominic', 1230–40s?)	th		F			am	*		
Gerard/Frachet	Woman has abortion; woman recidivist. See pt. A.: 'Mary'									
Gervase/Tilbury / III	Tarascon youth dives in Rhône	*S	Dr	M	Y		fa	*		
Hugo/Trimberg / **345–6**	Overzealous monks hang or drown									
Hugo/Trimberg / **345–6**	Monk sad for 5 years End of 13th century	S	Hg/ Dp	M	re		ac			D
Jacques/Vitry / **309**	Bankrupt grain hoarder[s] ?1220s? N France?	ss	H	M		B	lo	P		
Johannes Herolt / III	would-be hermit	T		M	re?		de	S		
Jn/Hoveden, / *Spec. laic.* / **262–3**	Woman matricide kills 3 dtrs *c.*1270? Bury St Edmund's	S	K	F	md/ ch		sh/ vi	P		
Jn/Hoveden, / *Spec. laic* / **263–4**	Drunk kills wf, 2 sons, self	S	Hh	M	md/		sh/	P	nt	
Konrad/Eberbach / III	Young monks nrly 'despair' ?1140s?	tt		M	Y		de			
Le Dale, *Hist.* / *Fundationis* / **1–4, 277**	Austin prior loses *amica* *c.*1180	S	V	M	cl		au			
Odo/Cheriton / III	Man and wife are tempted *c.*1200? cf. Sect I, Chrons, Bury St Edmunds.	2T	Hh	MF	m		de	*		
Peter Damian / III	Clerk drowns in pail	*S	D	M	cl		fa	*		
*Stephen/Bourbon / III	Dominican novice with doubts 1240s or 50s	T		M	re		tr			
*Stephen/Bourbon / III	Noblewoman with doubts 1240s or 50s	T	F	F		N	tr			
*Stephen/Bourbon / **316–7**	Two excommunicates, in Loire 1240s or 50s	2S	Dr	M	0		tr?			
*Stephen/Bourbon / **288**	Woman after loss of virginity 1240s or 50s	At?		F	Y					
Thos/Chantimpré / **36, 298–9**	16 Austin canons of Blois 1191–1205	ss	H	M	cl		ac/pr			
Thos/Chantimpré / **36, 268–71**	Infanticide Agnes *c.*1235?	T	Dp	F		(N)	sh/ac?			

Life or Miracles Page of this book		1 S?	2 Md	3 Sx	4 A/S	5 Wth	6 Mv	7 Ty	8 D/T	9 F
Thos/Chantimpré cf. viii	2 Jews in Pforzheim pogrom 1271	2SS	T		jw		vi			
Thos/Chantimpré 287	Noble virgin jumps from rock	[*S]	J	M	Y	W	vy			
Thos/Chantimpré 36, 288	Laundress loses chastity 1240–56?	[S]		F	60s	P	sh			
*Thos/Chantimpré 36, 310	Dicers 'desperatissimi'	SS		M		D	lo			
Thos/Chantimpré	Rich mad knight rides off [c.1260s]	[*S]		M		N	ma			
Thos/Chantimpré 339–40	Apostate Dominican 1232–c.1256	[S]		M	re		au			
Villers, *Hist. Fundationis* 25f, 321–3	Leprous *conversus* tries 13th century	At	D	M	re		le		nt	

BIBLIOGRAPHY OF LEGAL SOURCES

This bibliography is accessory to the Register and includes only those items mentioned in it, and for which the Register offers no other accessible reference. Abbreviations are included. Sources from England are arranged by category according to the scheme set out under the title. All others are arranged alphabetically.

1. England

(a) Westminster (b) Eyre and Coroners' rolls, by county (c) Episcopal registers (d) Secondary sources

(a) Westminster Records

Pipe rolls, published by the Pipe Roll Society.
Calendars published by the Public Record Office, abbreviated as follows:
CCR Calendar of Close Rolls
CIM Calendar of Inquisitions, Miscellaneous
CIPM Calendar of Inquisitions Post Mortem
CPR Calendar of Patent Rolls
KB King's Bench
Fitzherbert, Sir Anthony, *La Grande Abridgement* (London, 1565), Page references are also given to the edition by Rychard Tottel, Fleet Street, London, 1577.

(b) Eyre and Coroners' Rolls (By County)

Bedfordshire

R. F. Hunnisett, ed., *Bedfordshire Coroners' Rolls*, Bedfordshire Record Society, 41 (1960).
G. Herbert Fowler, ed., *Roll of the Justices of Eyre at Bedford, 1227*, Bedfordshire Record Society, 3 (1916).

Idem., ed., *Calendar of the Roll of the Justices in Eyre, 1247*. Bedfordshire Record Society, 21 (1939).

Berkshire

M. T. Clanchy, ed., *Roll and Writ File of the Berkshire Eyre of 1248*. Selden Society, 90 (1972–3).

Devon

H. Summerson, ed., *Crown Pleas of the Devon Eyre of 1238*. Devon and Cornwall Record Society, N.S., 28 (1985).

Gloucestershire

F. W. Maitland, ed., *Pleas of the Crown for the County of Gloucestershire, 1221*. Selden Society, 59 (1884).

Kent

Year Books of Edward II, 6 and 7: F. W. Maitland and others. eds., *The Eyre of Kent, 6 & 7 Edward II, A. D. 1313–1314*. Selden Society, 1, 2 (1910, 1912).

Lancashire

J. Parker, ed., *A Calendar of the Lancashire Assize Rolls*. Record Society . . . [of] . . . Lancashire and Cheshire, 47, 49 (1904, 1905).

Lincolnshire

D. M. Stenton, ed., *The Earliest Lincolnshire Assize Rolls, AD 1202–1209*. Lincolnshire Record Society, 22 (1926).

London

H. M. Chew and M. Weinbaum, ed., *The London Eyre of 1244*. London Record Society, 6 (1970).

M. Weinbaum, ed., *The London Eyre of 1276*. London Record Society, 12 (1976).

R. R. Sharpe, ed., *Calendar of Coroners' Rolls of the City of London, A.D. 1300–1378* (London, 1913).

H. M. Cam, ed., *The Eyre of London, 14 Edward II, A. D. 1321*. Year-Books of Edward II, vol. 26, part 1. Selden Society, 85 (1968).

Norfolk

D. M. Stenton, ed., *Pleas before the King or his Justices, 1198–1202*. Selden Society, 67, 68, 83, 84 (1953, 1949 [sic], 1966, 1967).

Northamptonshire

D. W. Sutherland, ed., *The Eyre of Northamptonshire 3–4 Edward III, A.D. 1329–30*. Selden Society, 97 and 98 (1981–2).

Northumberland

W. Page, ed., *Three Early Assize Rolls for the County of Northumberland, saeculo XIII* [= 1256, 1269, 1279]. Surtees Society, 88 (1890).

Oxfordshire

H. E. Salter, ed., *Records of Medieval Oxford: Coroners' Inquests, the Walls of Oxford, etc.* (The Oxford Chronicle Company, Oxford, 1912).

J. E. Thorold Rogers, ed., *Oxford City Documents, Financial and Judicial, 1268–1665*. Oxford Historical Society, 18 (1891).

Shropshire

A. Harding, ed., *The Roll of the Shropshire Eyre of 1256*. Selden Society, 96 (1981).

Somerset

C. E. H. Chadwyck-Healey, ed., *Somersetshire Pleas (Civil and Criminal), from the Rolls of the Itinerant Justices (from the close of the twelfth century to 41 Henry III)*. Somerset Record Society, 11 (1897).

Surrey

C. A. F. Meekings and D. Crook, eds., *The 1235 Surrey Eyre*. Surrey Record Society. 2 vols, continuously paginated (1979).

Worcestershire

J. W. Willis Bund, ed., *The Inquisitions Post Mortem for the County of Worcester, pt. 1: From their commencement in 1242 to the end of the thirteenth century*. Worcestershire Historical Society, 12 (Oxford, 1894).

Wiltshire

C. A. F. Meekings, ed., *Crown Pleas of the Wiltshire Eyre, 1249*. Wiltshire Archaeological and Natural History Society, Records Branch, 16 (Devizes, 1960).

M. T. Clanchy, ed., *Civil Pleas of the Wiltshire Eyre. 1249*. Wiltshire A. and N. H. Society, Records Branch, 26 (1970).

Yorkshire

D. M. Stenton, ed., *Rolls of the Justices in Eyre . . . for Yorkshire . . . (1218–1219)*. Selden Society, 56 (1937).

(c) Episcopal Registers (By Diocese)

Canterbury

F. R. H. Du Boulay, ed., *Registrum Thome Bourgchier, Cantuarensis archiepiscopi, A.D. 1454–1486*. Canterbury and York Society, 54 (Oxford, 1957).

Lincoln

R. M. T. Hill, ed., *The Rolls and Register of Bishop Oliver Sutton, 1280–1299*. 7 vols, Lincoln Record Society, 39, 43, 48, 52, 60, 64, 69 (Lincoln, 1948–75).

M. Archer, ed., *The Register of Bishop Repingdon, 1405–1419*. 3 vols (4th in preparation), Lincoln Record Society, 57, 58, 74 (Lincoln, 1962, 1963, 1982).

Exeter

F. C. Hingeston-Randolph, ed., *The Register of Bishop Walter de Stapledon (1307–1326)* (London and Exeter, 1892).

F. C. Hingeston-Randolph, ed., *The Register of John de Grandisson, bishop of Exeter 1327–69*, pt 1 (London, 1894).

G. R. Dunstan, ed., *The Register of Edmund Lacy, Bishop of Exeter, 1420–1455*. Vol. 2, Canterbury and York Society, 129. In conjunction with Devon and Cornwall Record Society (Torquay, 1963).

Winchester

C. Deeds, ed., *Registrum Iohannis de Pontissara, episc. Wyntoniensis, A.D. 1282–1304*, 2 vols. Canterbury and York Society, 19, 30 (London, 1915, 1924).

G. R. Dunstan, ed., *The Register of Edmund Lacy, Bishop of Exeter, 1420–1455.* Vol. 2. Canterbury and York Society, 129. In conjunction with Devon and Cornwall Record Society (Torquay, 1963).

Winchester

C. Deeds, ed., *Registrum Iohannis de Pontissara, episc. Wyntoniensis, A.D. 1282–1304.* 2 vols. Canterbury and York Society, 19, 30 (London, 1915, 1924).

(d) Secondary Sources

Hair, P. E. H., 'Deaths from Violence in Britain: a tentative secular survey', *Population Studies*, 1 25 (1971), 5–24.

Hammer, C. J., 'Patterns of Homicide in the medieval university town: fourteenth-century Oxford', *Past and Present*, 78 (1978), 3–23.

Hanawalt Westman, B., 'The Peasant Family and Crime in Fourteenth-Century England', *Journal of British Studies*, 13 (1974), 1–18.

Hilton, R. H., 'Peasant Movements in England before 1381', *Economic History Review*, 2nd series, 2 (1949), 117–36.

——*A Medieval Society: the West Midlands at the End of the Thirteenth century* (London, 1966; reprint, 1983).

Hunter Blair, C. H., 'M. P.s for Northumberland', pt. 3, *Archaeologia Aeliana*, 4th series, vol. 14 (1937), 22–66.

Hunnisett, R., *The Medieval Coroner* (Cambridge, 1961).

Hurnard, N. N., *The King's Pardon for Homicide, before A. D. 1307* (Oxford, 1969).

Post, J. B., 'Criminals and the Law in the Reign of Richard II, with Special Reference to Hampshire', D.Phil. thesis (Oxford, 1976).

Talbot, C. H., *Medicine in Medieval England* (London, 1967).

Warren, W. L., *The Governance of Norman and Angevin England, 1086–1272* (London, 1987).

2. France

Bayet, A., *Le suicide et la morale* (Paris, 1922).

Beaumanoir, Philippe de, *Coutumes de Beauvaisis*, ed. A. Salmon. Collection de Textes pour servir à l'étude et à l'enseignement de l'histoire, 2 vols. (Paris, 1899).

Beugnot, A. A., *Les 'Olim' ou régistres des arrêts rendus par la cour du roi sous les règnes de S. Louis . . . et de Philippe le Long*, vol. 1: 1254–1273 (Paris, 1839).

Boca, J., *La justice criminelle de l'échevinage d'Abbeville au moyen âge, 1184–1516.* Bibliothèque de la Société d'Histoire du Droit des Pays Flamandes, Picards et Wallons, vol. 4 (Lille, 1930).

Boutaric, E., *Actes du Parlement de Paris*, première série, 1254–1358, vols 1 and 2 (Paris, 1863).

Boutillier, Jean, *Somme rurale* (Paris, 1538).

Bois, G., *Crise du féodalisme* (Paris, 1976).

Borst, A., *Die Katharer.* Schriften der Mon. Germ. Hist., 12 (Stuttgart, 1953).

Cinus of Pistoia, *In Codicem Commentarium* (Frankfurt, 1578).

Doat MS, Bibliothèque Nationale, Paris.

Douët d'Arcq, L., *Choix de pièces inédites relative au règne du Charles VI*, vol. 2. Société de l'Histoire de France (Paris, 1863).

Eymerich, Nicolas, *Le Manuel des Inquisiteurs*, translated into French by L. Sala-Molins. Le savoir historique, 8. (Paris and the Hague, 1973).

Feu, Jean, [= Igneus], *Commentariorum in titulum Sillaniano et Claudiano senatus consulto et quorum testamenta aperiantur, libro Digestorum vigesimonono* (Lyons and Orleans, 1539).

Floquet, A., *Histoire du Parlement de Normandie*, 6 vols (Rouen, 1840), vol. 1.

Gregory IX, *Decretals*, in A. Friedburg, ed., *Corpus Juris Canonici*, 2 vols (Leipzig, 1879–81), vol. 2.

HLF = *Histoire Littéraire de la France* (1753–).

Le Coq, Jean [= Johannes Gallus], *Questiones*, et. M. Boulet. Bibliothèque des Écoles Françaises d'Athènes et de Rome, vol. 156 (Paris, 1944).

Lewis, P. S., *Later Medieval France* (London, 1968).

Limborch, Ph. van, ed., *Liber sententiarum inquisitionis Tolosanae, 1305–1323*, in the same author's *Historia Inquisitionis* (Amsterdam, 1692).

LR = *Livre Rouge* of Abbeville.

Louandre, F. C., *Histoire d'Abbeville et du Comté de Ponthieu*, 2 vols (Paris and Abbeville, 1844–5), vol. 2.

Luce, S., *Histoire de la Jacquérie, d'après les documents inédits* (Paris, 1895).

Prarond, E., *Les Lois et les moeurs d'Abbeville, 1184–1789* (Paris, 1906).

Schatzmiller, J., *Médicine et justice en Provence médiévale. Documents de Manosque, 1262–1348* (Aix, 1989).

Schmitt, J. -C., 'Le suicide au moyen âge', *Annales, E. S. C.*, 31 (1976), 3–28.

Tanon, L., *Régistre criminel de la justice de S. Martin des Champs à Paris au xiv siècle* (Paris, 1883).

Tanon, L., *Histoire des justices des anciennes églises et communautés monastiques de Paris* (Paris, 1883).

Thierry, A., ed., *Recueil des monuments inédits de l'histoire du Tiers État. Première série. Chartes, etc.*, Région du Nord [Collection de Documents Inédits sur l'Histoire de France, Première série: Histoire Politique]. Vol. 4 (Paris, 1870).

Viollet, P., 'Les coutumiers de Normandie.' *Histoire litteraire de la France*, 33 (Paris, 1906), 41–190.

3. Germany

BB = *Bürgermeisterbuch* (of the town in question).

Böhme, J. E., *Diplomatische Beyträge zur Untersuchung der schlesischen Rechte und Geschichte*, vol. 2, pt 2 (Berlin, 1775) [= Part 6 of the whole work (Berlin, 1771–)].

Dieselhorst, J., 'Die Bestrafung der Selbstmörder im Territorium der Stadt Nürnberg', *Mitteilungen des Vereins für Geschichte der Stadt Nürnberg*, 44 [*Festschrift des Vereins für Geschichte der Stadt Nürnberg zur Feier seines 75ten Bestenhens, 1878–1953]* (Nürnberg, 1953).

Edler, A., *Die älteren Urteile des Ingelheimer Oberhofes*, 4 vols (Frankfurt am Main, 1952–63), vol. 2.

Grimm, J., *Weisthümer*, 2ter Theil, ed. E. Dronke & H. Beyer (Göttingen, 1840).

Hagemann, H. R., *Basler Rechtsquellen im Mittelalter* (Basle, 1981).

Kisch, G., *Leipziger SchöffenspruchSammlung* (Leipzig, 1919).

Knapp, H., *Das alter Nürnberger Kriminalrecht* (Berlin, 1896).

Knapp, H., *Alt-Regensburgs Gerichtsverfassung, Strafverfahren und Strafrecht bis zur Karolina* (Berlin, 1914).

Kriegk, G. L., *Deutsches Bürgerthum im Mittelalter . . . mit besonderer Beziehung auf Frankfurt am Main* (Frankfurt am Main, 1868).

Kühnel, H., ' "Da erstach sich mit willn selber . . ." Zum Selbstmord im Spätmittelalter und in der frühen Neuzeit', in K. Hauck and others, eds., *Sprache und Recht: Beiträge zur Kulturgeschichte des Mittelalters. Festschrift für Ruth Schmidt-Wiegand zum 60. Geburtstag.* (Berlin and New York, 1986), vol. 1, pp. 474–489.

Nürnberg, Chronicle of, in C. Hegel, ed., *Die Chroniken der deutchen Städte,* vol. 10 (Leipzig, 1872) [= Nürnberg, vol. 4].

Osenbruggen, E., *Studien zur deutschen und Schweizerischen Rechtsgeschichte* (Schaffhausen, 1868).

Rau, F., *Beiträge zum Kriminalrecht der freien Reichstadt Frankfurt am Main im Mittelalter bis 1532.* Diss. Potsdam (1916).

RB = Rechenbuch.

Rosenfeld, H.-F. and H., *Deutsche Kultur im Spätmittelalter, 1250–1500* (Wiesbaden, 1978).

Schär, M., *Seelennöte der Untertanen* (Zürich, 1985).

Schlesische Rechte. See Böhme.

Schöffensprüchsammlung (Leipzig). See Kisch.

Thommen, R., ed., *Urkundenbuch der Stadt Basel*, herausgegeben von der historischen und antiquarischen Gesellschaft zu Basel, vol. 9 (Basle, 1905).

Urkundenbach der Stadt Basel. See Thommen.

Urteile des Ingelheimer Oberhofes. See Edler.

4. The Low Countries

Cannaert, J. B., *Bydragen tot de kennis van het oude Strafrecht in Vlanderen*, 3rd edn (1835).

Espinas, G., *La vie urbaine de Douai au moyen âge*, 3 vols (Paris, 1913), vol. 1.

Poullet, E., *Histoire du droit pénal dans l'ancien duché de Brabant.* Mémoires couronnées et Mémoires des savants étrangères publiées par l'Académie royale des sciences, des lettres et des beaux-arts de Belgique, vol. 33 (Brussels, 1867), 1–346.

Régistre aux plaids de la cour de Mons (Brussels, 1893).

5. Spain

McVaugh, M. R., *Medicine before the Plague, Practitioners and their patients in the Crown of Aragon, 1285–1345.* Cambridge History of Medicine (Cambridge, 1993).

Addenda

A number of cases mentioned in the text of this book have been accidentally omitted from the Register. They are listed below with page-references: John Beaufort, duke of Somerset (56–8), an abbot according to Walter Map (80), Knights Templar in 1308 (81), Jacques de la Rivière (106), a mother in *Vita s. Walpurgis* (257), a mother in *Vita s. Antelmi* (258), an unchaste girl in a sermon by Giordano of Pisa (287), a man pillaged by soldiers in *Vita s. Hugonis Lincolniensis* (308–9), and a 'mad' woman in *Vita s. Edmundi Cantuariensis* (329).

Source / Page of this book	Name	1 Ev	2 Md	3 Sx	4 A/S	5 Wth	6 Mv	7 Mo	8 D/T?	9 *?
*Walter Map 80	Rapacious abt bit himself to death late 12th century	S	(B)	M	re			P		
*Guillaume/ Plaisians 81	Templars 1308	ss	HKJ	M	(re)	N	pr/ac			
*Paris Journal 106	Jacques de la Rivière. 1413	S	B	M		N	ac			
*Croyland chron. 56–8	Jn Beaufort D of Somerset 27 May 1444	S		M	c.44	N	dg	My	We	st
*Antelm/ Bellay 258	Mother loses baby		th		F		be			
*Edmund /Canterbury 329	A mad woman	At	Dw	F			ma			
*Hugh/ Lincoln 308–9	John of An- caster, pillaged by soldiers ?1215	At		M		B	lo/ma			
*Walpurgis 257	Mother lost 3 children		th	F	md/ch		be			
*Giordano/ Pisa, sermon 287	Unchaste girl	S	K	F	Y/si		sh			
Sussex Eyre 1248 JUST 1/909A m28 174	Remigius de Esthall	[ ]	[Ds]	[M]						

Select Bibliography

The purposes of this bibliography are (i) to help the reader recognize titles abbreviated in the footnotes; and (ii) to document the 'History of a History' in Chapter 1. For legal sources used in the Register see pp. 469–75.

Baechtold-Stäubli, Hanns, *Handwörterbuch des deutschen Aberglaubens*. 10 vols (Berlin and Leipzig, 1922–42).

Bayet, Albert, *Le suicide et la morale* (Paris, 1922).

Berstein, Ossip, *Die Bestrafung des Selbstmords und ihr Ende*. Strafrechtliche Abhandlungen, Heft 78 (Breslau, 1907).

Bourquelot, Felix, 'Recherches sur les opinions et la législation en matière de mort voluntaire pendant le moyen âge', *Bibliothèque de l'École des Chartes*, 3 (1842–4), 539–60; 4 (1844), 242–66; 456–75.

Crook, David, *Records of the General Eyre*. Public Record Office Handbooks, 20. (Her Majesty's Stationery Office. London, 1982).

Dieselhorst, Jürgen, 'Die Bestrafung der Selbstmörder im Territorium der Stadt Nürnberg 44 [= *Festschrift des Vereins für Geschichte der Stadt Nürnberg zur Feier seines 75ten Bestehens, 1878–1953*] (Nürnberg, 1953), pp. 1–115.

Duparc, Pierre, *Origines de la grâce dans le droit pénal romain et français du Bas-Empire à la Renaissance*. Thèse pour le doctorat en droit, 30 mai 1942 (Paris, 1942).

Durkheim, Emile, *Suicide: A Study in Sociology*, trans. J. A. Spaulding and G. Simpson from French edn of 1930 (London, 1979).

Garrisson, Gaston, *Le suicide dans l'antiquité et dans les temps modernes* (Paris, 1885).

Geiger, Karl August, 'Der Selbstmord im französischen Recht', *Archiv für katholisches Kirchenrecht*, vol. 62 (Neue Folge, 56) (Mainz, 1889), 385–99.

——'Der Selbstmord im deutschen Recht', *Archiv für katholisches Kirchenrecht*, vol. 65 (Neue Folge, 59) (Mainz, 1891), 3–36.

——'Kritische Schlussbemerkungen über die Gesetze betreff. den Selbstmord', *Archiv für katholisches Kirchenrecht*, vol. 65 (Neue Folge, 59) (Mainz, 1891), 201–12.

——'Der Selbstmord im Kirchenrecht', *Archiv für katholisches Kirchenrecht*, vol. 61–5 (Neue Folge, 55) (Mainz, 1899), 225–32.

Goodich, Michael E., *Violence and Miracle in the Fourteenth Century. Private Grief and Public Salvation* (Chicago and London, 1995).

Gransden, Antonia, *Historical Writing in England, 1: c.550 to c.1307* (London, 1974); *2: c.1307 to the Early Sixteenth Century* (London and Henley, 1982).

Glorieux, P., 'Le "Contra quatuor labyrinthos Franciae" de Gautier de St.-Victor', *Archives d'histoire doctrinale et litéraire du moyen âge*, 19 (1952), 187–335.

Grimm, Jakob, *Deutsche Rechtsalterthümer*, vierte vermehrte Ausgabe besorgt durch Andreas Heusler und Rudolf Hübner. 2 vols (Leipzig, 1898).

Halbwachs, Maurice, *The Causes of Suicide*, trans. H. Goldblatt from French edn of 1930 (London, 1978).

Herbert, J. A., *Catalogue of Romances in the Department of Manuscripts in the British Museum*, vol. 3 (London, 1910).

Hirzel, Rudolf, 'Der Selbstmord', *Archiv für Religionswissenschaft*, 11 (1908), 75–104, 243–284, 417–76.

Hoof, Anton J. L. van, 'A longer life for "suicide": When was the Latin word for self-murder invented?', *Romanische Forschungen*, 102 (1990), 255–9.

Hunnisett, Roy F., 'The Origin of the Office of Coroner', *Transactions of the Royal Historical Society, 5th series*, 8 (1958), 85–104.

——'Medieval Coroners' Rolls', *American Journal of Legal History*, 3 (1959), 95–124 and 324–359.

——*The Medieval Coroner* (Cambridge, 1961).

——'A Coroners' Roll of the Liberty of Wye, 1299–1314', *Medieval Legal Records . . . in honour of C. A. F. Meekings* (London, 1978), 130–41.

——'The Reliability of Inquisitions as Historical Evidence' in *The Study of Medieval Records: Essays in Honour of Katheleen Major*, ed. D. A. Bullough and R. L. Story (Oxford, 1971), 206–223.

Hurnard, Naomi N., *The King's Pardon for Homicide, before A. D. 1307* (Oxford, 1969).

Inhofer, Matthias, *Der Selbstmord: Historisch-dogmatische Abhandlung* (Augsburg, 1886).

Knapp, Fritz Peter, *Der Selbstmord in der abendländischen Epik des Hochmittelalters*. Germanische Bibliothek. Dritte Reihe: Untersuchungen und Einzeldarstellungen (Heidelberg, 1979).

Kühnel, Harry, ' ". . . da erstach sich mit willn selber . . ." Zum Selbstmord im Spätmittelalter und in der frühen Neuzeit', in K. Hauck and others, eds, *Sprache und Recht: Beiträge zur Kulturgeschichte des Mittelalters. Festschrift für Ruth Schmidt-Weigand zum 60. Geburtstag.* (Berlin and New York, 1986), Vol. 1, pp. 474–89.

Lukes, Steven, *Émile Durkheim. His Life and Work: A Historical and Critical Study* (London, 1973).

Maitland, F. W. (with Sir F. Pollock), *The History of English Law* (1895), new edn ed. S. F. C. Milsom, 2 vols. (Cambridge, 1968).

Masi, Gino, 'Fra savi e mercanti suicidi del tempo di Dante', *Giornale Dantesco*, 39 [new series, 9] (Florence, 1938), 199–238.

Mitteis, Heinrich, *Deutsche Rechtsgeschichte*, 16th edn, ed. Heinz Lieberich (Munich, 1988).

Motta, Emilio, 'Un suicidio in Lodi nel 1468', *Archivio storico lodigiano*, 2 (Lodi, 1882) [Separately printed].

——'Un mancato suicidio nel 1469 e lo strano gusto del duca di Milano', *Bollettino storico della Svizzera italiana*, 1 (Bellinzona, 1884), 239–41.

——'Suicidio d'un' abbadessa nel 1463? . . .', *Bollettino storico della Svizzera italiana*, 2 (Bellinzona, 1886), 234–5.

——'Suicidi nel quattrocento e nel cinquecento', *Archivio storico lombardo*, 15 (1888), 96–100.

——*Bibliografia del suicidio* (Bellinzona, 1890).

Murray, Alexander, 'Confession as a historical source in the thirteenth century', in R. H. C. Davis and J. M. Wallace-Hadrill, eds., *The Writing of History in the Middle Ages: Essays presented to Richard William Southern* (Oxford 1981), 275–322.

——'Confession Before 1215', *Transactions of the Royal Historical Society,* 6th series, 3 (1993), 51–81.

Neri, F., 'Il suicida fiorentino', *Studi medioevali*, new series, 2 (Turin, 1929), 205–7.

Osenbrüggen, Eduard, *Studien zur deutschen und schweizerischen Rechtsgeschichte* (Schaffhausen, 1868).

Poncelet, A., 'Index miraculorum beatae Virginis Mariae quae latine sunt conscripta', *Analecta bollandiana*, 21 (1902), 241–360.

Post, John B., 'Local Jurisdictions and Judgment of Death in Later Medieval England', *Criminal Justice History*, 4 (1983), 1–12.

Rost, H., *Bibliographie des Selbstmords* (Augsburg, 1927).

Schär, Markus, *Seelennöte der Untertanen*. Dissertation in the Philosophical Faculty of Zürich, 1983–4 (Zürich, 1985).

Schioppa, Simonetta, *Il 'Fondo giudiziario' del Comune di Perugia dal 1258 al 1280*. Testi de Laurea, Università degli Studi di Perugia, 1976–1977.

——'Le fonti giudiziarie per una ricerca sulla criminalità a Perugia nel ducento'. *Estratto da Recerche su Perugia tra due e quattrocento* (Università degli Studi di Perugia, 1981), 59–144.

Schmitt, Jean-Claude, 'Le suicide au moyen âge', *Annales. Économies, Sociétés, Civilisations.*, 31 (1976), 3–28.

Scheidman, E. S. and N. L. Farberow (eds), *The Cry for Help* (New York, 1965).

Signori, Gabriela, 'Rechtskonstruktionen und religiöse Fiktionen. Bemerkungen zur Selbstmordfrage im Mittelalter', in Signori, *Trauer. Verzweiflung und Anfechtung*, 9–54.

——'Aggression und Selbstzerstörung. "Geistestörungen" und Selbstmordversuche im Spannungsfeld spätmittelalterlicher Geschlechterstereotypen (15, und beginnendes 16. Jahrhundert)', in Signori, *Trauer. Verzweiflung und Anfechtung*, 113–25.

——ed., *Trauer. Verzweiflung und Anfechtung. Selbstmord und Selbstmordversuche in mittelalterlichen und frühneuzeitlichen Gesellschaften*. Forum Psychohistorie, ed. Hedwig Röckelein, 3 (Tübingen, 1994).

Stevenson, Simon J., 'The rise of suicide verdicts in south-east England, 1530–1590: the legal process', *Continuity and Change*, 2 (1987), 37–76.

——'Social and economic contributions to the pattern of "suicide" in south-east England, 1530–1590', *Continuity and Change*, 2 (1987), 225–262.

Thomas of Chantimpré [Thomas Cantimpratanus], *Bonum universale de apibus*, ed. G. Colvenerius (Douai, 1627).

Thomson, Stith, *Motif-Index of Folk-Literature*. 6 vols (Bloomington. Ind., rev. edn. 1975).

Tubach, Frederic C., *Index exemplorum: A Handbook of Medieval Religious Tales*. Folklore Fellows Communications, No. 204. Akademia Scientiarum Fennica (Helsinki, 1969).

Van Hoof, see Hoof, van.

Vauchez, André, *La sainteté en occident aux derniers siècles du moyen âge, d'après les procès de canonisation et les documents hagiographiques*. Bibliothèque des Écoles Françaises d'Athènes et de Rome, 241 (Rome, 1981).

Villani, Giovanni, *Cronica*, in *Croniche de Giovanni, Matteo e Filippo Villani*, ed. A. Racheli, 2 vols [Biblioteca Classica Italiana, secolo XIV, no. 21] (Trieste, 1857 and 1858), vol. 1.

Vuitry, Adolphe, *Études sur le régime financier de la France avant la Révolution de 1789* (Paris, 1878–83), vol. 3: *Nouvelle Série: Philippe le Bel et ses trois fils: les trois premiers Valois*, vol. 2 (Paris, 1883).

Ward, Harry L. D. *Catalogue of Romances in the Department of Manuscripts in the British Museum*. 2 vols (London, 1883–93).

Index

References to suicidal incidents can mostly be found through the Register and those to main themes through the Contents pages (xiii–xv). The index contains references only to those items difficult of access by these means. The symbol 'R' means '*see also* the Register'. Parentheses ( ) enclose indirect or secondary references.